D0772798

SOUTH AFRICA'S BRAVE NEW WORLD

ALSO BY R. W. JOHNSON

African Perspectives (ed. with Christopher Allen)

How Long will South Africa Survive

The Politics of Recession

The Long March of the French Left

Shootdown: The Verdict on KAL 007

Heroes and Villains: Selected Essays

Launching Democracy in South Africa
(ed. with Lawrence Schlemmer)

Liberalism in Post-Liberation South Africa
(ed. with David Welsh)

South Africa: The First Man, The Last Nation

SOUTH AFRICA'S BRAVE NEW WORLD

The Beloved Country since the End of Apartheid

R. W. JOHNSON

THE OVERLOOK PRESS
NEW YORK

This edition first published in hardcover in the United States in 2010 by

The Overlook Press, Peter Mayer Publishers, Inc.
141 Wooster Street
New York, NY 10012
www.overlookpress.com

Cataloging-in-Publication Data is available from the Library of Congress

Printed in the United States of America
ISBN 978-1-59020-410-8
1 3 5 7 9 10 8 6 4 2

For
Irina, Lawrie, Philippa, Hermann, Anthea and Omry

Contents

List of Illustrations

Abbreviations

Absa	Associated Banks of South Africa
ANC	African National Congress
ARVs	anti-retrovirals (drugs)
Azapo	Azanian People's Organization
BEE	black economic empowerment
CHOGM	Commonwealth Heads of Government Meeting
Cosatu	Congress of South African Trade Unions
DA	Democratic Alliance
DP	Democratic Party
DRC	Democratic Republic of Congo (from 1997)
FDI	foreign direct investment
Gear	Growth, Employment and Redistribution Policy
IFP	Inkatha Freedom Party
MDC	Movement for Democratic Change (Zimbabwe)
MK	Umkhonto we Sizwe
MRC	Medical Research Council
NDR	National Democratic Revolution
NEC	National Executive Committee (of the ANC)
Nepad	New Economic Partnership for African Development
NERSA	National Electricity Regulator of South Africa
NGC	National General Council (of the ANC)
NIA	National Intelligence Agency (formerly NIS, National Intelligence Service)
NNP	New National Party
NP	National Party (also known as the Nats)
NPA	National Prosecuting Authority
NWC	National Working Committee (of the ANC)
OAU	Organization of African Unity; now the African Union (AU)

PAC	Pan Africanist Congress
PIC	Public Investment Commissioners
RDP	Reconstruction and Development Programme
SAA	South African Airways
SAAF	South African Air Force
SABC	South African Broadcasting Corporation
SACC	South African Council of Churches
SACP	South African Communist Party
SADC	South African Development Community
Sanco	South African National Civics Organization
SANDF	South African National Defence Force
SAPS	South African Police Services (formerly SAP – South African Police)
TAC	Treatment Action Campaign
THO	Traditional Healers Organization
TRC	Truth and Reconciliation Commission
UDF	United Democratic Front
Zanu-PF	Zimbabwe African National Union – Patriotic Front

Preface

This book has germinated for many years, starting in the 1980s when I became a regular visitor to the University of Natal at its lovely Durban campus, of which I am a proud alumnus. However, the South African political drama was playing itself out all around me – often only a few hundred metres from the campus in the shape of the bloody war between the United Democratic Front and Inkatha, so I began to write about the situation frequently for *The Times* (London). This placed me in a strange situation at the university, where most of my colleagues were highly partisan UDF supporters and did not welcome press coverage which was less than fully committed to their side. But I had been through all this before, having been a fervent young supporter of the ANC in Durban in the early 1960s, a traumatic period I had shared with the likes of Jacob Zuma and Ronnie Kasrils. I had seen many friends pay a terrible price for their idealism then and later come to realize that they (and I) had behaved naively, even if none of us ever regretted our anti-apartheid passion. In exile in East Berlin, running the ANC magazine, *Sechaba*, my dearest friend and comrade, Barry Higgs, told me that they were instructed to avoid all argument, debate and controversy: the magazine must reflect monolithic unity. 'You realize soon enough that this is exactly wrong, that you should be arguing about everything and all the time,' he told me. With such opinions it was no wonder that Barry didn't stay in East Berlin. He ended up as a bookseller in Devon, and died in his early forties, a fate undoubtedly brought on by the savage torture he had endured from Verwoerd's security police.

Remembering Barry, I could hardly agree to toe the monolithic line again. I was lucky to find a friend in Mervyn Frost, then head of the Politics Department in Durban, who understood. Most didn't. One of my academic colleagues positively clanked with the weaponry he wore about his person for use, he told me, against Inkatha, 'to make sure they don't kill us first'. There was no doubt that he and his colleagues did much preventive and pre-emptive work of that kind. He later died of Aids and was much lamented by many. I learnt from him, as I had from Mervyn and Barry, as also from many others. Some later repented of their earlier passions; some emigrated with their passions intact; while others stayed on, somewhat sadder and wiser. For South Africa is a hard school and it requires, among other things, a sense of humour. The greatest South African social scientist, Lawrence Schlemmer, to whom my debt is incalculable, was wont to say that emigration was a mistake if only because living in South Africa was such a test of character.

From the 1980s on I commuted to South Africa from my post at Magdalen College, Oxford, that most perfect of academic institutions. Magdalen was indulgent of my absences of body and, increasingly, of spirit. Among Magdalen's alumni in South Africa, one may count Sidney Bunting, founder of the Communist Party, Sir De Villiers Graaff, the long-time Opposition leader, my old student, Max Price, now vice-chancellor of the University of Cape Town, and Patrick Cullinan, South Africa's premier poet. I am proud to be one of such a company. But in 1995 I felt I had to choose. Apartheid was gone at last, I wanted to go home and I had to leave Magdalen to do so, becoming instead director of the Helen Suzman Foundation in Johannesburg.

It was, I was told, a mad decision: whites were fleeing South Africa and academics were desperately seeking posts abroad. To give up a secure job in Oxford in order to come out and run a precarious liberal NGO in Jo'burg was quite mad. The ANC was determined to squash such initiatives and both foreign and local donors were scared, so fund-raising would be impossible. This turned out to be exactly right but I never regretted my decision to return. Being at the centre of events in a rapidly changing South Africa was utterly fascinating. It was a bit like being Claude Cockburn back in the 1930s. We weren't respectable but everyone wanted to read what we wrote. Above all, it was enormous fun. We kept this up, against prodigious odds, for six years. The three people whom I associate most with that fine though extremely tough period were Philippa Ingram, Connie Van Hout and Barbara Groeblinghoff. I am deeply grateful to them but also to others from whom I learnt much in that period, including Sibusiso Madlala, Charles Van

Onselen, Anthea Jeffery, Rian Malan, Tony Leon, Costa Gazi, Brian Williams, Graham McIntosh and Ndumisane Mkhize.

By that time I had begun to write for various newspapers. Although many of my former students had become journalists – they have always been particularly numerous on *The Economist* – I had never been a professional journalist and always viewed this as an interesting hobby I had acquired by accident. I have benefited enormously from these journalistic connections, and love nothing better than swapping journo stories with people like Graham Paterson and Jon Swain. Also, I regard Southern Africa as the most beautiful and various part of the world. To be here and to be writing are the two greatest pleasures I know.

Beyond that I realize that many people have helped me, wittingly and unwittingly. Most of them would not like to be mentioned by name. And the person who has helped me most wishes to be anonymous. So my Preface risks becoming a bit like an ode to the unknown soldier. There are many such soldiers in South Africa. When my old friend Harold Strachan became the first anti-apartheid saboteur to go to jail, his wife Maggie decided to pawn their furniture and leave Port Elizabeth where, as his wife, she was such an outcast among the outraged white community. In the end she found a backstreet pawnbroker who said 'Strachan, the saboteur? Jolly good. I'm an Old Menshevik.' He paid her a good price. Similarly, for many years King Zog of Albania lived here, having been kicked out by the Communists in the 1940s. Jo'burg suited him well and he made a good living as an arms dealer. What else, after all? When Communism fell he went back home, claiming his crown and causing no end of trouble. On re-entering Albania, he pointed out, he'd filled in the immigration form; where it asked for his occupation he'd written 'King' and they'd waved him through. So, he argued, they must have known what they were getting. This is an attitude that living in South Africa encourages.

To capture the story of South Africa since the advent of democracy in 1994 is a tall order. For a start, much of what is written is ideological wishfulness or sheer pretence. Secondly, never before has a radical Third World nationalism taken over a sophisticated modern economy on this scale – the journey is unprecedented. Thirdly, it has been a Rabelaisian tale; cynicism, greed, idealism, noble sacrifice and low artifice all compete so richly that sometimes laughter is the only possible response. But hardly a sufficient one, for there are real tragedies here too – mass unemployment, poverty, Aids and the terrible fate of Zimbabwe, which I have followed at first hand. I have tried to be without illusions and to ask what I think are the serious questions. One never quite succeeds in such endeavours but one can only try.

R. W. Johnson

Cape Town,
November 2008

South Africa's Brave New World

I

In the Beginning . . .

It's Spring outside, blossoming trees and sunshine. The world could be beautiful for all men. Such infinite possibilities exist to make them contented and happy. There is so much that could be done – especially here in Africa with its wide-open spaces. Letter to his wife, Lucie-Marie, from General Erwin Rommel, North Africa, March 1943

We wholly conquer only what we assimilate. André Gide

It was 10 May 1994. The whole world had come to Pretoria to see the inauguration of Nelson Mandela as the first democratically elected South African President. It was the greatest assemblage of heads of state since John F. Kennedy's funeral. Mandela spoke in ringing words:

> The moment to bridge the chasm that divides us has come . . . We enter into a covenant that we shall build a society in which all South Africans, both black and white, will be able to walk tall without any fear in their hearts, assured of their inalienable right to human dignity – a rainbow nation which is at last at peace with itself and the world at large . . . We must therefore act together as a united people for national recovery . . . Never, never and never again shall it be that this beautiful land will experience the oppression of one by another.[1]

The march past was led by the army which had played its full part in in trying to prevent the African National Congress from taking power – that is, in trying to avert a day like this. But it was the flight of nine SAAF Mirages overhead, dipping their wings in salute, which brought tears to many eyes. It said so many things: the acceptance of, indeed, the deference to, Mandela by the white establishment, the acknowledgement that he was fully President, able to command all the levers of power – and, for many black people in the crowd, it meant that for the first time the Mirages' awesome power and white pilots were on their side, part of the same nation.

There were other meanings too. The whole white security establishment, despite many fears that it would stage a last-minute revolt against black rule, had acted in exemplary fashion. The Mirages and the resplendent army were also testimony to the fact that the ANC's thirty-year guerrilla war against apartheid had never seriously dented white power. As a result, all the products of that white power, including South Africa's sophisticated economy and infrastructure, were being handed over intact. None of the foreign visitors at the inauguration – they ranged from the leaders of the Western world to Fidel Castro, Yasser Arafat and Muammar Qaddafi – could miss the fact that South Africa was anything but a war-torn country. Many African states let it be known that now would be a good time for South Africa to dispense aid in their direction. Similarly, many foreign activists such as Jesse Jackson wished to claim that they had played a pre-eminent role in ending apartheid and that a good time to have that recognized would be now.

Such doubtful notes were drowned out by the world's elation that the South African problem, so long-standing and apparently so intractable, had been brought to a peaceful conclusion. Indeed, the country was immediately adopted as an international model for problem-solving. The new ANC ruling elite enthusiastically accepted this evaluation, travelling the world endlessly to take a bow as representatives of 'the miracle nation'. But the real miracle lay not in their being willing to enjoy the fruits of victory but in the way that the National Party leader, F. W. De Klerk, had led the white minority to surrender its power peacefully.

There was a great flow of famous visitors to South Africa in the early post-apartheid years. For years boycotts and sanctions had meant that celebrities had had to think twice before visiting the country. Now they flooded in, many wanting to befriend the new regime, or win acclaim as a freedom fighter by posing with Mandela, or simply offer South Africans the celebrities they had long been starved of. The photo opportunity with Mandela was of critical importance to such visitors and many made it plain that their whole visit was dependent on having that moment. The endlessly amiable Mandela was willing to indulge a remarkable number of them, posing with singers, boxers, politicians and rap artists. Later such photo opportunities were frequently linked to large donations.

South Africa's media loved this 'Madiba magic' (Madiba being Mandela's familiar name). This mood – hugely amplified when South Africa won the rugby World Cup in 1995 – led to all manner of unreasonable expectations. South Africa would win the right to stage the Olympics in 2004. South Africa would win a permanent seat on the UN Security Council. South Africa would be asked to use its powers as miracle-arbiter to settle the Irish problem and the Arab–Israeli dispute. South Africa would instruct the rest of the world in how to set up a Truth and Reconciliation Commission. And so on.

This euphoria and ambition was completely overblown and, inevitably, when reality turned out differently the sense of anti-climax was correspondingly deep. (When South Africa failed in its bid to win the 2006 football World Cup President Thabo Mbeki bitterly termed the result 'the globalization of apartheid'.) In 1994 the ANC had swept to power on two slogans – 'A Better Life for All' and 'Jobs, Jobs, Jobs'. The reality was that for many years after 1994 formal-sector jobs shrank at a rate of well over 100,000 a year, with unemployment climbing inexorably as huge cohorts of young job-seekers flooded onto the glutted labour market. By 2001, moreover, 5,000 people a week were dying of Aids, a number which soon increased to 1,000 a day. Life was not only not 'better for all'; for all too many it was both shorter and poorer. Signs of social distress proliferated. The crime rate soared. Begging at traffic lights – by beggars of all races – soon became a general phenomenon. House prices fell steadily in real terms, year after year until 2000, and it became clear that in effect the market was discounting the value of many properties to zero over a fairly short time span, clearly anticipating complete social collapse.

The ANC government had comprehensively lost the confidence of foreign and local investors. Worse, in the country with the world's worst Aids problem, President Mbeki was soon chiefly famous for attempting to deny that HIV causes Aids. The statements of many government ministers evinced a complete disregard for the basic rationale of democratic capitalism. Many of the wealthier and better educated were leaving the country as fast as they could and there were many forced sellers of the rand at almost any rate. By October 2001 the country was reduced to celebrating National Be Positive Day, in itself a testament to how low morale had sunk.

And yet nothing was simple. The temptation was strong to write off South Africa as just another African country ruined by African nationalism. But there were other straws in the wind. South Africa had become a major car-exporter for the first time. The rand dived from R3.50 to the US dollar in 1994 to R10 to the dollar in 2001, but then recovered to R6.40 in 2004. Insatiable Chinese needs pushed up demand for South Africa's bulk minerals, while its strategic minerals, especially platinum, palladium and vanadium, bid fair to make up for its declining gold output. Foreign firms began to locate call centres there. From 2000 on house prices began to soar and by 2004 a full-scale consumer boom was in progress. The index of business confidence compiled by the South African Chamber of Business reached an all-time record level in August 2004.

One visitor who slipped into South Africa in 1991 was the political scientist Francis Fukuyama. He was impressed by the country's advantages over the ex-Communist world, for it 'already possesses three things that the former [is] desperately seeking: a functioning market economy, a democratic tradition (albeit limited to whites and much abused by them in the past), and a civil society, highly developed for the whites but still forming among blacks'. He was, however, worried by the ANC's *étatiste* economic thinking which 'appears to have been placed in a deep freeze for several decades' and its 'instinctive Leninism on economic and political issues'. Not surprisingly, the ANC was preoccupied with redistribution but 'the liberal economic revolution now sweeping Eastern Europe and Latin America, which maintains that wealth must be created before it is redistributed . . . has passed the ANC by'.[2]

Fukuyama wondered if reunified Germany could provide a model for South Africa – 'that is, the developed part of the country will peacefully absorb the less developed part and, while suffering a temporary drop in living standards, will ultimately bring it up to its level'. The other possible models, he thought, were national disintegration along Lebanese lines or a slide towards a Latin American solution.

ANC leaders who cited the German model typically dwelt on the fact that South Africa (like West Germany) was a rich country: its problems could be largely solved if only the whites were willing to share their wealth. Those who criticized the ANC were invariably said to be merely 'protecting white privilege', the assumption being that the task in hand was sharing and that those who dissented simply did not want to share. But Fukuyama pointed out that of these different futures, the one most clearly out of the question is the German model ... It is a widespread misconception, fostered for many years by the apartheid regime but believed by many blacks, that South Africa is a relatively rich First World country that has simply failed to share its wealth adequately with its black population. It is in fact a middle-income developing country with a per capita income on the level of Mexico or Poland ... Clearly, no amount of redistribution away from the country's 5 million whites will be sufficient to bring so large a population up to First World standards, quite apart from the effect that massive redistribution itself and the consequent undermining of property rights would have on the country's ability to create wealth.

Fukuyama thought a Latin American future was the most likely. South Africa could avoid Lebanon's fate but

it is hard to see how it can avoid a long-term economic deterioration. The starting point for this deterioration is the evident need for the redistribution of wealth within the country. To a much greater degree than in other developed countries the rich in South Africa got their wealth at the expense of the poor and it is important to remedy the situation. The problem is that any large-scale attempt to right these wrongs over a short period of time would be self-defeating in that it would wreck the economy, and thereby undermine the basis for wealth creation that is the only hope for black South Africa itself.

Fukuyama was most alarmed by the possibility that the ANC might adopt policies which had the effect of causing whites to emigrate.

While the state can prevent the exodus of capital ... it cannot prevent the exodus of skills. And it is this which presents the greatest dilemma for the ANC ... However unfair the current degree of white property ownership, and however ... injured the black population has been by the apartheid system, the future economic prospects of South Africa will depend to a very large extent on whether the whites can be persuaded to stay on in a nonracial, post-apartheid democracy.

Mass white emigration, Fukuyama warned, was the greatest danger.

It is hard to overstate the potential economic disaster that would await South Africa were this to happen. The rest of sub-Saharan Africa has been moving backward economically at a breathtaking pace ... many parts of Africa are poorer than when they gained independence. Sadly, it would appear that colonialism, far from having been responsible for Africa's poverty, was in fact a major source of skills and infrastructure, and that the region has become worse off economically the further from colonialism it gets. This is not meant to justify either colonialism or apartheid, but only to be realistic about the economic dangers facing this part of Africa.

Fukuyama was much concerned by the ANC's 'socialism', its 'instinctive Leninism' and the fact that 'much of this thinking does not reflect knowledge of economics so much as the moral conviction, quite understandable in South Africa's case, that property is unjustly distributed'. This moralistic Leninism made the ANC 'the main obstacle to black social modernization', for socialism, though always presenting itself as 'progressive', had actually 'been revealed to be an obstacle to social and economic modernization – the hallmark of a certain kind of backwardness ... Let us hope that South Africa, as it makes the necessary transition to democracy, does not move forward into the past.'

Fukuyama's assessment, by far the most far-sighted of the myriad analyses delivered in this period, was completely ignored. For the truth about the new South Africa was monstrously politically incorrect. Any who dared say that something less than a 'miracle nation' was being built immediately attracted abuse as a racist. In effect, Fukuyama had been the little boy who said the emperor had no clothes.

This has always been a necessary role in South Africa. At the age of 14 I got into a furious argument with my schoolboy peers in Durban, one of them later a National Party minister. On the blackboard I attempted to graph the predicted future growth of South Africa's white and black population groups, then reckoned to stand at three million and thirteen million respectively. My contention was that apartheid could not possibly work. Three million whites might hold down thirteen million blacks and, who knows, four million might hold down twenty million, but would five million hold down thirty million – and so on? At some point numbers alone would make majority rule utterly inevitable. So it would be better to prepare for that future. I claim no particular merit for this. The truth, unspeakable in public life, was so simple that any schoolboy could grasp it.

In 1960 I crowded into Durban City Hall to hear Hendrik Verwoerd. He pushed right by me in the throng, and I remember his large bulk, his fixed smile right in my face, his kiss-curl not unlike Bill Haley's. It was like a brush with Goering or Goebbels, a historical monster right up close, at once scary and mundane. He was hailed as Afrikanerdom's supreme intellectual, yet he spoke confident nonsense for hours. Not long afterwards I was one of just three whites (one of whom turned out to be a police spy) in a crowd assembled to hear Nelson Mandela speak, also in Durban. The security police broke up the meeting. I cheered Mandela on, but he too spoke not of realities but in lofty abstractions.

Later I realized this was normal. South Africa was a brutally practical country in which most people lived high on fantasy, often denying what was in front of them. Sometimes they called it religion, sometimes just their principles. There was something about living here amidst Africa's extremities – and at Africa's extremity – which engendered these wilful denials of reality, the somehow safer realm of self-cultivated fantasy. You could see it then in Verwoerd's rhapsodic but irrational affirmation of separate development just as surely as you could descry it in Mbeki's mystical evocation of the African renaissance. Anyone who has lived in South Africa knows that it might take many years and thousands of lives to kill off such phantoms. The simple realities of South Africa might seem enough to deal with. But for those who rule us reality seems never to have been quite enough. We had Cecil Rhodes with his vast imperial dreams, Jan Smuts with his plans to incorporate everything up to Kenya into one vast Southern Africa, Verwoerd and the apartheid nightmare and then Mbeki, with his strange mix of Leninism, paranoia and Aids denialism.

Just outside Luderitz, in southern Namibia, stands the ghost town of Kolmanskop. Once it was the centre of the diamond industry in the whole of South West Africa, a town of fine two-storey houses imported from Wilhelmine Germany. Today no single soul lives there, nor has done for fifty years, and the town stands knee-deep amidst the desert sands but beautifully preserved. You struggle through the sand from the pub and its magnificent bowling alley, the antique machinery for returning the bowls to the bowler still intact, to the old schoolhouse with its photos of smiling teachers and happy children. Not a few of those mustachioed teachers, one realizes, probably died in Flanders while those gleeful, grinning, sunburnt children will often have died while serving the Third Reich in one capacity or another. After all, there is still a Hermann Goering Strasse in Luderitz – commemorating a former governor, not his son, the Luftwaffe boss.

For anyone who lives in southern Africa – not just the members of racial minorities – Kolmanskop asks the unavoidable question: is this our future? We all know the stirring stories of colonial exploration and settlement, how America, Canada and Australia grew from small beginnings to become the world's strongest and most prosperous societies, but colonization did not always work like that. Even in New England there were some settlements that failed, later arrivals scanning the shore in vain for any trace of the pioneers. Thabo Mbeki frequently spoke of the need to 'eradicate the 350-year-long legacy of colonialism and apartheid'[3] as if the eradication of colonialism is unproblematic, an unambiguous good.

Yet South Africa, over the last half-century, has played host to any number of whites fleeing from the disastrous advent of African nationalist rule, from Tanzania, Kenya, Zambia, Mozambique, Angola and Zimbabwe. For the coming of African nationalism (I cheered it on in 1960) has turned out to mean the arrival of a locust plague, of leaders who, in most cases, plundered their countries, abused their people and led their societies backwards, just as Fukuyama says. Generally speaking, the whites fled first but were followed by much greater waves of blacks, which is why, in today's South Africa, Congolese jostle against Nigerians, Mozambicans and Zimbabweans in their millions. All the countries these people fled from were once colonies where order prevailed and where life expectancy and prosperity tended to increase year by year. Look at their condition today and you have to say they were failed colonizations, places where the ethic of order and development failed to 'take'.

Much of Africa south of the Sahara falls under the rubric of 'failed colonization' in this sense. This is not just about white flight. White settlers were not important in Africa's two most successful economies, Mauritius and Botswana. And as one watches, say, Malaysia or India push powerfully ahead no one believes that successful development there has for a long time now depended on white planters or administrators. The fact is that colonialism brought order, unity and modernity to these countries and that these gains have been preserved and built on in the era of independence, whereas in African countries as different as Somalia and the Congo the order, unity and even the modernity of colonial times has been lost. In today's Zimbabwe, once one of Africa's most developed states with its best-educated populace, the question is often asked, 'what did we have before candles?': the answer is, 'electricity'.

In the Congo what were good roads at independence are at best cart-tracks now.

This is what I mean by failed colonization. Some may wish to see this as a justification of colonialism or apartheid or even a nostalgia for them, but that is not what is meant. The question is simply whether the innovative, indeed what Marx rightly saw as the revolutionary spirit of colonialism 'took' or not.[4] Put more crudely, it is simply the difference between going forward and going backwards: the key measures are whether life expectancy and GDP per capita improve, as they did under colonialism and apartheid. These two measures largely define the population's welfare and there cannot be too much argument about them. If these figures improve then speeches about 'a better life for all' and empowerment have some meaning. If these figures decline then such speeches are deceitful nonsense.

Staying with friends in Zimbabwe a few years ago I found myself sleeping in their spare room as they prepared to emigrate. After more than forty years of fighting the good fight against racism they were off to Australia. Lying there amidst the packing cases, the rummage of whole lives, the thought occurred to me: perhaps all whites who stay in Africa long enough will leave as refugees. And black Africans will follow them. In fact, put in racial terms, it is worse than that. Today's black leaders denounce the slave trade which saw ten to twelve million Africans transported against their will to Europe and the Americas, yet the fact is that millions more have, of their own free will, left for those same shores since Africa was independent – and far more would if they could. Whites may flee the locust plague of African nationalism (among whites the old joke is that 'the time to emigrate is after the Jews but before the Asians'), but the larger historical fact is that when whites flee an African country it is a sure sign of a 'failed colonization' in the sense alluded to above. The failure of modernity means that far greater streams of Africans always accompany the whites.

South Africa throughout its modern period was, despite apartheid, not only the most successful African state in developmental terms but was also a multi-racial, multi-cultural rainbow nation. Even apartheid, though it limited its fruitful growth into a truly Creole society, could not entirely stop it. But if this society were to start moving backwards in GDP per capita and in life expectancy, if it were to lose its developmental dynamic, then its already huge losses of the most skilled and educated would accelerate and Fukuyama's worst forebodings would be fulfilled. Moreover, should the minorities flee in sufficient numbers this defining polyglot richness would be lost for ever and with it the country's essential character. Were this to happen nothing is more certain than that more and more Africans would want to flee too and then we would indeed face another failed colonization. Another Kolmanskop. Except that it would not be just 'yet another' example; it would be the last and final case, defining independent Africa as a whole as a colossal human failure. The ANC was bitterly upset when, in May 2000, *The Economist* used the headline: 'Africa: The Hopeless Continent', but the plain fact is that the question of whether the continent as a whole is written off as hopeless sits squarely in the ANC's lap.

These are the highest of high stakes. Should South Africa become another example of failed colonization then the implications for the continent for decades, even centuries ahead would be dire. For Asia and Latin America are developing fast. There would be no Third World community: Africa would stand increasingly alone in its poverty, its failure and its psychological defeat. Mbeki spoke of the twenty-first century being 'the African century'. This is already untrue: the rapid growth of China, India, Korea and Vietnam more or less guarantee that it will be Asia's century. There is no disgrace for Africa in that. But if South Africa fails, and thus Africa fails, long before the end of this century Africa will face a situation infinitely worse than it does now. Such a defeat would doom Africans to an indefinite further period of serving as a source of raw materials – human as well as mineral – for a world leaving it further and further behind, and in which its erstwhile Third World allies would increasingly regard it with scorn or pity. Japan and China have long given aid to Africa and in 2004 their ranks were joined by India. But if Africa ends the century as the only area still begging from all the rest – and that risk clearly exists – this will not only doom all hopes of African self-assertion but render them risible. The damage would inevitably affect relations between black and white around the world. So great is the defensiveness aroused by this question that those who raise it are frequently accused of 'wanting South Africa to fail' but nobody who thinks about it for long can possibly want this to happen.

2
Godfathers and Assassins

The purity of a revolution can last a fortnight. Jean Cocteau

Force and fraud are in war the two cardinal virtues. Thomas Hobbes

The unbanning of the ANC in 1990 and the return of the exiles created enormous hopes. And, as always when all the rules change, it also set off a frantic competition for power and wealth. Much of the public gaze was focused on the heroic figure of Mandela and on Codesa, the negotiations at the Convention for a Democratic South Africa, where a new constitution was hammered out. The oddity was that while white South Africa took it for granted that the ANC would inevitably win a democratic election, many within the ANC found it hard to believe that De Klerk really would hand over power. The ironic result was that the ANC negotiated the sort of liberal constitution they thought would help them in a continuing struggle against white power. Thus the ANC government ended up with a constitution which, with experience of power, it would never have chosen. But the most important deal was on the electoral system: a pure proportional representation list system which gave the party leaders power to choose, expel and switch list members in and out of Parliament at will. Thus South Africa allows neither the representation of constituencies nor independent-minded MPs. Only parties are represented and only party bosses matter.

With ANC victory in the 1994 elections clearly looming,[1] South Africa's social and economic elites moved swiftly to ingratiate themselves with what seemed certain to become the new ruling elite. Clearly, anyone who could achieve influence over members of this successor group might turn it to profitable account. Almost overnight, a whole new class of patrons emerged, anxious to befriend and subsidize ANC leaders. Douw

Steyn, the insurance magnate, made a palatial mansion available for Mandela's use. Sidney Frankel, senior partner of the stockbrokers, Frankel Pollock, adopted the ANC secretary-general, Cyril Ramaphosa, introducing him to trout-fishing and other expensive pastimes. Ramaphosa soon had a child at Michaelhouse, one of the country's most expensive private schools. Sidney Frankel's father, Leslie, had courted the National Party ('Nat') bosses in his day and his office wall bore a large photo of P. W. Botha. He too now courted the ANC for all he was worth.[2] The Indian businessman Schabir Shaik was another who poured money into ANC pockets, particularly those of the country's future Deputy President, Jacob Zuma. Another major patron was Brett Kebble, the mining magnate, who spread his largesse widely, soon owning the entire leadership of the ANC Youth League.

TWO FACES OF CAPITALISM: KERZNER AND GORDON

The hotel magnate Sol Kerzner, who had made a fortune out of the apartheid bantustans, was quick to switch his favours to the ANC elite. It was soon noticeable that despite the still-ongoing anti-apartheid cultural boycott, the ANC cultural desk made special exceptions for whatever entertainments Kerzner put on at Sun City. Kerzner's launch of his crowning extravaganza, the Lost City, an extraordinary architectural monstrosity of Disneyesque bad taste, housing a luxury resort on the edge of the Kalahari desert, triggered off all manner of rent-seeking threats of boycotts, riots and strikes – everyone and his brother wanted to be bought off – but Kerzner used his ANC contacts (particularly Thabo Mbeki) to have these fires put out.

Since both Sun City and the Lost City were located within the Bophuthatswana bantustan, it fell to the local Mafikeng ANC branch to monitor the cultural boycott. Aware that Kerzner had a history of getting bantustan politicians to do his will, the local activists were indignant that he was managing the ANC just as easily and passed a motion criticizing Thabo Mbeki for his 'perceived over-closeness' to Kerzner.[3] Later there was to be controversy over Mbeki's lavish fiftieth birthday party, allegedly paid for by Kerzner, who also financed the honeymoon of Mandela's daughter Zinzi,[4] and made other strategic donations to the ANC elite.

The Liberty Life Foundation, set up by the insurance magnate Donny Gordon, poured money into causes favoured by the ANC, though Gordon, like Kerzner, had taken one look at the ANC and decided to emigrate. But it took time for such would-be émigrés to rearrange their affairs and establish a new base in another country so businessmen who took this route often threw money at the ANC – sometimes even joining the ANC themselves – while businesses were sold and money was moved. South Africa still had exchange controls so this took some doing, but capital flight, like love, always finds a way. Gordon sold his Liberty Life insurance company but Kerzner went one better, earning great public kudos by launching the Lost City, widely celebrated as his greatest achievement, even as he prepared to leave.

The scale and even the nature of this capital and personal flight was largely hidden. No newspaper wrote about it, for it hardly chimed with the compulsory euphoria about the new South Africa. Few noticed that Kerzner had not put a cent of his own into the Lost City; he hardly wanted to invest just as he left. One of South Africa's five richest men, he had quietly disposed of his hotels and casinos, indeed everything except a house in the Cape.[5] Many other businessmen sweated their assets, running their factories into the ground while they extracted the last penny from their operations. Central Johannesburg was plagued for years by landlords who adopted the same attitude to their properties, taking whatever rents they could and, as maintenance problems became overwhelming, simply walked away from them. By the time the municipality wanted to discuss the fact that their buildings were condemned, overcrowded and teeming with rats, the owners had long since settled abroad.

There were a hundred ways of managing such exits. One day a businessman might be happily hobnobbing with the new ANC elite, then suddenly and without fanfare or announcement, the bird had flown. One would hear only months later that he was just not around any more. In many cases such émigrés would keep emitting pro-ANC noises all the way to the airport, though most began to keep their distance from the ANC as soon as their asset transfers had gone through.

Kerzner and Gordon were emblematic figures. Within a few weeks of the 1994 election Kerzner had bought Paradise Island Resorts in the

Bahamas, while also setting up operations in Dubai. He also bought a casino in Atlantic City, New Jersey, and made a fresh fortune by finding a 1,300-strong Indian tribe, the Mohegans in Connecticut, with whom he did a deal similar to those he had done with bantustan chiefs, the result being the Mohegan Sun casino.[6] However, this attracted the hostile attention of the *Boston Globe* and soon of US Federal investigators, who were drawn by allegations that Kerzner had built his South African casino empire by bribing bantustan leaders, for no one with such a record is allowed to enter the US gaming business. By 2000 Kerzner was forced to sell up all his US operations including the famous LA Desert Inn, thus surrendering his long-cherished ambition of breaking into the Las Vegas casino world.[7] In 2002 he was the subject of a major exposé by *Time* magazine.[8] His attempt to get into the UK casino business met with similar obstacles but he continued to prosper in such offshore havens as Mauritius, the Maldives, Mexico, Havana and Marrakesh. By 2003 the wheel had come full circle and Kerzner announced plans for a super-luxury hotel on Cape Town's Waterfront.[9] In 2005 he even helped endow a School of Tourism and Hospitality at the University of Johannesburg.[10]

If Kerzner's case showed the difficulty of shedding an apartheid stigma, Donny Gordon was at the opposite extreme. He moved to the UK, where his Liberty International group rapidly climbed into the FTSE 100 and Gordon himself moved rapidly up the *Sunday Times* Rich List Top 100: by 2005 he was the forty-sixth richest man in the UK, already well ahead of such luminaries as Sir Alan Sugar and Paul McCartney.[11] Gordon quickly became a major philanthropist; indeed his £20 million gift to Welsh National Opera and Covent Garden earned him a knighthood. Although Gordon generously endowed medical facilities and a business school in South Africa, he was now lost to the country – he had gone native to the extent of pondering whether he was perhaps descended from the Scottish Gay Gordons rather than the Lithuanian Jewish Gordons, as he had always previously claimed. It was a major loss, for Gordon was an entrepreneur in the same class as Rhodes and Oppenheimer.[12]

Ironically, Kerzner's influence on South Africa was more lasting. His characteristic blend of nouveau riche kitsch captured something very deep in the South African psyche: all races responded to it and wanted to emulate its luxurious tastelessness. His raffish blend of luxury hotels, casino thrills and superbabe excitement (Kerzner married several such women and was seen with limitless others) also had a distinctly non-racial appeal. The new ANC elite soon showed how deeply it had been impressed by Kerzner. For one of the greatest objects of commercial excitement (and corruption) in the new South Africa was the allocation of casino licences: they were assumed to be a simple licence to print money. By 2005 there was rising public concern about the country's 550,000 compulsive gamblers[13] and the way that many poor people could not resist the casinos' fatal get-rich-quick appeal. For the ANC had interpreted liberation to mean that such casinos, with their inevitable penumbra of crime and prostitution, instead of being confined to a few remote bantustans, could now be based in every major city. The result was that the new South Africa, having abolished all the old bantustans, itself came to exhibit many of the features of a giant bantustan, a likeness which became more disturbing over time.

SEEK YE FIRST THE POLITICAL KINGDOM

Thabo Mbeki was one of the few ANC leaders who attempted to allay business fears in the 1990–94 period. In the giddy atmosphere of the times incipient corruption seemed less significant than 'the choice of society', capitalist or socialist. Corruption also stood in sharp contrast to the overwhelmingly idealist and ideological tenor of the times. The enormous groundswell of black aspirations was quite evident, as was the sincere determination of many ANC leaders to ameliorate the lives of the poor. But such leaders faced severely practical problems about how to make a living in the new situation and ideology and self-interest made not uncomfortable bedfellows. For a new (African) nationalist bourgeoisie was simply replacing an old (Afrikaner) nationalist bourgeoisie at the helm of the state. But the ANC's belief that it held the moral high ground made the situation sensitive – and made the press unwilling to publish the embarrassing facts of the new godfather phenomenon.[14]

Although the situation during the interregnum between the two regimes was chaotic and constantly changing several things were clear.

First, the godfathers were necessary. The ANC, a party of poor people, was hungry for funds which its own members could not supply. Moreover, the ANC leaders lived off per diems, foreign donations and ANC allowances, a situation which reinforced their already profound sense of entitlement. If the Soviet bloc or wealthy Scandinavian governments had been intent on pressing money into your hands as a matter of principle, it was fatally easy to believe you were morally owed a living and, indeed, a lot more than that, and in many cases money that was meant for the movement stuck to private hands. Moreover, many ANC politicians lived chaotic personal and financial lives, had no idea how to manage a middle-class lifestyle, were always broke and needed help.

Secondly, the ANC exiles had long lived in African countries where, after independence, the nationalist elite had quickly become rich and they knew that South Africa was the jewel of the continent, so the pickings here would be much better than elsewhere. They had all assimilated Kwame Nkrumah's dictum of 'seek ye first the political kingdom' and in the phrase which was to become commonplace, they 'didn't join the struggle in order to stay poor'. The sheer sense of excitement, nay anticipation, that there would be a new rich, a new regime, that everything was possible, was palpable. Anyone who lived through it will never forget those heady times. Shortly before the 1994 election I attended a meeting at the Durban Club addressed by Cyril Ramaphosa, who began his talk with the statement: 'On my way here I was wondering whether the ANC, when it comes to power, should nationalize the Durban Club.' Similar jocular but threatening references to expropriation were sprinkled throughout his speech, each eliciting a nervous titter from his wealthy white audience. He was applauded to the rafters and as he sat down he was surrounded by a mêlée of desperate would-be donors, chequebooks eagerly in hand.

Thirdly, many godfathers were Indian or Jewish. Although these groups had prospered through the apartheid years and were South Africa's most talented entrepreneurs, they had been firmly excluded from the commanding heights of public life by the Nats, who were determined to prevent 'yids and coolies' undermining the rule of *die volk*. Now, many members of these groups saw a chance of political influence and rushed forward to take it. They quickly adopted the new political correctness, invited the leading lights of the ANC to their dinner tables and helped them with 'loans'.

This situation had all sorts of knock-on effects. Johnny Copelyn, a white trade union activist and later ANC MP, told me how those who had gone into the unions in the 1970s and 1980s had resigned themselves to a life of poverty.

That was what the struggle was about. You knew everyone you'd been at school with would soon be better off than you and they were. Trade union activists accepted that as a matter of course. But then the ANC exiles arrived back and everyone realized that all these guys were either already rich or intended to be so very soon. You could just see the effect in the unions: these guys were our comrades, after all. People's heads went back and corruption really took off, you couldn't hold it.[15]

Copelyn himself resisted this trend but he soon resigned from Parliament and became a casino and media tycoon, ploughing the profits back into benefits for his union members.

The fact that ANC office was now a path to power sharpened rivalries within the movement. Khalakie Sello, a leading ANC figure in Durban in the 1950s, told me how he had walked through Shell House – typically, Shell had sold the building to the ANC as their headquarters in order to curry favour – and realized that 'I outranked just about everyone there in seniority except for Walter [Sisulu]. I realized that I was therefore a threat. I had no stomach for what that would have meant, so I just walked out again and kept on walking.'[16] But Khalakie belonged to an older generation which had joined the struggle with no thought of preferment. By the 1990s this was already becoming a less common quality.

Later, Allan Boesak, a former leader of the United Democratic Front (the ANC's predecessor and, in part, its internal surrogate in the 1980s), was jailed for having stolen massively from donor funds, including funds from the Paul Simon *Graceland* tour. He always refused to admit his guilt and insisted he would do it all again. Despite this, he received a presidential pardon in 2005, for the whole movement knew that all that was wrong with Boesak was that he had started stealing a bit too soon. A year or too later it would have gone unnoticed in the general Gadarene stampede. After his release Boesak supplemented his earnings as a preacher by using his 'struggle cred' to persuade black and Coloured communities to acquiesce in the building of exclusive golf estates by wealthy white developers. For in the new South Africa 'struggle cred' was a bankable asset and the ANC elite took a keen interest in bankable assets.

As usual, the real casualties were the poor bloody infantry. Most of the old apartheid elite simply went into private life, secured amnesty for themselves or quietly emigrated. Only a handful of torturers and killers were left to face the music. It was the same on the ANC side. No one from Umkhonto we Sizwe (MK) was personally called to account for the torture and murder of ANC dissidents in MK's Angolan prison camps. I remember, at a major Western embassy in Pretoria, finding myself dining with one of the most renowned MK torturers, later a leading figure in the re-formed South African National Defence Force. He was as charming as any torturer would be in a Graham Greene novel but since one of his victims was a friend of mine, I asked my hosts if they knew what they were doing. 'If,' I was told, 'we didn't dine with thugs and crooks, we'd always eat alone.' Meanwhile hundreds of MK soldiers had simply disappeared during the anti-apartheid struggle, presumably killed. No one on the ANC side seems to have been sufficiently keen to learn what happened, so their fate remains unknown. Thousands more MK soldiers became security guards or bank robbers (some even ended up shooting one another), died of Aids (their HIV rate had always been high) or joined the ever-swelling ranks of the unemployed.

THE LEADERSHIP QUESTION

But the biggest question was that of the ANC's leadership in power. Oliver Tambo, the long-time leader in exile, had had a stroke in September 1989. Thabo Mbeki took over many of Tambo's duties and was the de facto ANC leader until Mandela emerged from jail in February 1990. Mandela's re-emergence was a mixed blessing for the exile leadership. His long incarceration had made him a mythical figure and thus the inevitable leader. When Idasa (the Institute for Democratic Alternatives in South Africa) led its famous mission to Dakar to meet the exiled ANC leadership in 1987, at one point some Afrikaners present objected that what they were being told was not what they understood Mandela had intimated. Mbeki exploded, throwing his pencil in the air with irritation: 'Mandela said that! Ha! So God has spoken.'[17] When Mandela did emerge the speech he gave – for which the world was waiting –

was a monumentally tedious ANC monologue, held up for Mandela to read by Cyril Ramaphosa. The cameras of the world's television stations desperately panned around for human interest but the point was clear: for Mandela, the ANC was his life. He would be the loyal servant of the party exiles and would recite the speeches they put in front of him.

Mandela was clearly too old to be more than an interim leader and he had little appetite for power. But the rest of the ANC elite were riveted by the prospect of power. Just ahead lay a division of the spoils on a scale never seen before in Africa. Everything hinged on who won the struggle to succeed Mandela. There were three candidates, Cyril Ramaphosa, Thabo Mbeki and Chris Hani.

Ramaphosa had been leader of the mineworkers' union, a leading figure in the UDF and, inevitably, a Communist Party member – though, like Mbeki, he had 'taken sabbatical' from the SACP in order not to be tarred with its brush in the new environment. Ramaphosa was much fêted by the fashionable left which clustered around the *Weekly Mail*, because he was the man who had led the great miners' strike of 1987 and because he was seen as a master-negotiator, the man in charge of the ANC's negotiation team at the Codesa talks. It was not *bon ton* to point out that the 1987 strike, an essentially political affair ordained by the SACP in Lusaka, had seen Ramaphosa lead his members to the most crushing defeat they ever suffered. The miners did not even contemplate another strike for eighteen years.

It was difficult, too, to judge how good a negotiator he was at Codesa. The dice were loaded the ANC's way there because of De Klerk's urgent need to agree at least an interim constitution in time for the 1994 election. (Worse still, De Klerk had fallen in love with a wealthy Greek woman, much to the distress of his wife, Marike, and was frequently in Greece, lending a classic note of *fin de règne*. Astonishingly, the negotiations on the country's entire future were left in the hands of a junior minister.) Moreover, Ramaphosa's principal interlocuteur, the Nats' Roelf Meyer, took the view that building a relationship with the ANC was more important than sticking to any particular detail, an attitude which made Ramaphosa's job notably easier. Ramaphosa was, though, vastly popular with the old UDF – those who had fought the struggle inside the country – and he easily defeated Alfred Nzo, the long-serving (and utterly ineffectual) ANC secretary-general, at the party's 1992 conference. Ramaphosa thus had the job of organizing the ANC's 1994 election triumph, and he was placed second behind Mandela on the party's list.

Ramaphosa's weak points were that he was a Venda and that he was not an exile. The most powerful group within the ANC were the Nguni – the Xhosa, Zulu and Swazi – and particularly the Xhosa. The Venda were a small and somewhat undervalued group by comparison. The dominance of the exiles was even more overwhelming: they had run the party for thirty years, were far more sophisticated and internationally connected, and they tended to hang together as a group in power struggles, particularly if any 'inxile' (as they were known) was rash enough to challenge them. Hani and Mbeki were both Xhosas, both exiles and both had held senior positions within the SACP.

For years Mbeki was seen as the inevitable next leader; indeed, Tambo had groomed him as such. He was a veritable prince of the movement – his father, Govan Mbeki, had been one of its top leaders – and from childhood on he had enjoyed a privileged education. There had always been foreign funders, grants and scholarships to smooth his way. He was charming, worldly-wise, an experienced diplomat, and within the ANC he was regarded as an intellectual.

Hani had made his name within the ANC's guerrilla wing, MK. Straight-speaking, brave and charismatic, Hani had soared to popularity only in the late 1980s. (Talking to educated ANC supporters in the Eastern Cape during the week that Mandela was released from prison, I found that many already looked to Hani rather than Mandela. Mbeki went unmentioned.) Inevitably, this led to rivalry with Mbeki, who despite twenty-five years near the top of the ANC, was not widely liked or trusted. In particular, the SACP leader, Joe Slovo, distrusted him and went to some lengths in the early 1990s to try to leak to the press a story that he had once had to rush to Moscow to rescue Mbeki from the nearly disastrous consequences of his amorous activities.[18] Though Hani liked to show knowledge of the Latin and Greek he had studied, he was essentially a fighter, whereas Mbeki – physically a very small man – disliked outright confrontation of any kind ('he'd probably faint at the sight of blood', one of his old girlfriends told me). Inevitably, as détente with the Nats neared, Hani urged that the armed struggle be maintained *à outrance*, while Mbeki, who was already involved in secret contacts with Nat emissaries, counselled negotiation. Hani knew Mbeki well – they had been at school at Lovedale together in 1956 – and did not trust him.

De Klerk's security forces saw Hani as their deadly enemy and after the initial return of the exiles in 1990 De Klerk refused to renew Hani's indemnity – making him liable to arrest. Bantu Holomisa, president of the Transkei bantustan, who was close to Mandela, suggested that Hani come and stay in the Transkei. 'I know you don't recognize bantustans but De Klerk has to,' he told Mandela, 'so let them apply for Chris's extradition.'[19] So, to Pretoria's fury, Hani went to train MK activists in the Transkei, where he was greeted as a conquering hero. 'I really liked Chris,' Holomisa told me. 'He was a warm, friendly guy, always very straight and direct.' At the same time, Hani gathered his MK following into a formidable force (I saw him put an impressive contingent through their paces in Mthatha). While Mandela and Slovo bargained for the lifting of his indemnity, Hani's followers pushed him to challenge Mbeki for the ANC's deputy chairmanship. With Tambo as chairman and Mandela as President, this was the highest post up for election. Whoever won it would clearly be the next-generation leader. 'Chris's decision to challenge Mbeki at the Durban conference wasn't really because of great personal ambition,' recalls Holomisa. 'He knew that Tambo and Mbeki had come under huge diplomatic pressure to take the negotiations route. He was suspicious of where that might lead – as was I.'

Hani's MK backing made him a possible Minister of Defence under Mandela – and it was clear that this would be a key position. The long years of sanctions had left South Africa's armed forces with outdated weapons and the big foreign arms manufacturers realized that a lucrative re-equipment deal was in the offing. British arms manufacturers began discreet discussions with one possible Defence Minister, Joe Modise, while their French counterparts wooed another ministerial candidate, Tokyo Sexwale. Indeed, after Sexwale had been wined and dined at the Paris Air Show, the French annoyed the British by boasting that they already had the arms deal sewn up.[20] Given the corruption which legendarily attends international arms deals with developing countries, it was generally understood that the Minister of Defence who signed the deal would doubtless become a very rich man. This was another issue in the background of the ANC's Durban conference.

The conference was a euphoric event, the first real integration of the UDF activists with the ANC exiles. Allan Boesak sat around in the sun wisecracking with the journalists, waiting to be incorporated into the movement's leadership. Mandela even reprimanded some activists for their sloppy dress, insisting that those who wanted to play a role in government start looking the part. The mood was best summed up by the post-conference rally in King's Park stadium, held just after the first Gulf War. As the names of foreign representatives were read out there was a smattering of polite applause, capped by a real ovation for Sweden's representative (acknowledging its generous aid to the ANC), followed by a louder one for Cuba's. But even this was dwarfed when it was announced that Saddam Hussein's Iraq was represented. Indeed, quite a few wore Saddam T-shirts, for he was then seen as the epitome of opposition to Western imperialism. This militant atmosphere was tailor-made for Hani.

Hani's candidacy was a major crisis for Mbeki: suddenly the party leadership which he had so long prepared for might be snatched from him. Worse, he misjudged the conference mood by arguing for the lifting of economic sanctions whose continuation could only hurt a future ANC government. But the ANC rank and file were furious at the leadership's suspension of armed struggle, a decision taken without consultation, while the Soviet Union's collapse threatened to curtail their hopes of socialism. In their eyes, maintaining sanctions was the last radical position left – so Mbeki was booed down. Hani then topped the poll in elections to the national executive, just ahead of Mbeki. Mandela's worry now was that if either Hani or Mbeki won the deputy chairmanship – and thus became heir apparent – the party would be badly split. Accordingly he prevailed upon a reluctant Walter Sisulu to continue as deputy chairman.

The conference had been a disaster for Mbeki. Hani had emerged as the most popular figure and Ramaphosa had been cheered in as secretary-general. The outcome was a nasty shock too for all those – the Pahad brothers, Essop and Aziz, Joe Modise and many more – who had placed all their bets on an Mbeki leadership.

A TRADITION OF ASSASSINATION

It was not entirely surprising that this situation should be 'solved' by Hani's assassination. Assassination was hardly a new feature of South African life. Verwoerd survived one attempt on his life before succumbing to the second. The apartheid security forces had formed hit squads which took out particularly troublesome opponents. Inevitably, many hit men, impressed by the possibilities of their new profession, soon began to carry out other murders, sometimes for personal reasons, more often for money.

Hit men sometimes 'hit' members of their own side, as in 1977 when Dr Robert Smit and his wife, Jeanne-Cora, were murdered in their home. Smit, who had been South Africa's representative at the IMF, was an NP parliamentary candidate at the time of his murder. It seems clear that he was murdered at the behest of the state President, Nico Diederichs, who as Finance Minister had creamed off millions into a Swiss bank account which Smit was about to expose. The Smits were murdered by Tai Minaar, a legendary special forces agent (for years he worked undercover in Cuba for the CIA). Minaar became remorseful about the hit in his later years, saying that his orders had 'come from the very top' but that he now regretted the whole dirty business.[21] Minaar himself was murdered in Pretoria in 2001, as I discovered during research I was then doing into South African biological and chemical weapons. He set up a 'sting' operation, apparently at the CIA's behest, in which Middle Eastern buyers were to be tempted into purchasing these WMD. Some of those threatened by this operation clearly used these weapons on Minaar: within hours of his death his body had swollen to four times normal human size. His death was hushed up.

The ANC was no different. During the years of armed struggle it became normal for those who betrayed the movement – or even just left it, like Tennyson Makiwane – to be murdered. Indeed, when Chris Hani and six of his fellow MK commanders wrote a strongly worded memorandum in 1968, criticizing the corrupt and self-serving MK leadership, the reaction of Joe Modise, the MK commander, was to demand that all seven of them be executed, a fate they narrowly avoided.[22] In the 1970s the ANC, impressed by North Vietnam's victory in the Vietnam War, sent a delegation to Hanoi to study General Giap's 'people's war' doctrine, in which it was standard practice to assassinate chiefs and headmen in order to decapitate the opposition and intimidate the peasantry into accepting Vietminh/Vietcong hegemony. Adopting the same doctrine in South Africa, the ANC used MK hit squads to deadly effect against the Inkatha Freedom Party (IFP) (who, of course, retaliated in kind) and regularly removed township figures who were obstacles to the movement's growth. The Inkatha leader, Chief Mangosuthu Buthelezi, was particularly marked out for assassination, a decision apparently taken at a high level within the ANC since Mbeki himself later apologized to Buthelezi for this.[23]

Hani's assassination occurred in April 1993, in a period of great turmoil and confusion when the hit squads and intelligence services of both the apartheid regime and the ANC were together inside the country. Inevitably, apartheid's hit men and spies had quickly established contact with their ANC opposite numbers when they returned from exile after 1990. In some cases they were already brothers under the skin, for the ANC was riddled with informers working for Pretoria, while some of Pretoria's intelligence operatives now put out feelers about their own possible employment under an ANC government. This strange coming together of spies and assassins required that there be middlemen – and some of these played both sides of the street.

This murky milieu made Hani's murder easier in one sense but it also made it riskier. Assassinating such a charismatic leader as Hani would suit powerful interests on both sides, but it was bound to create a huge, perhaps uncontrollable popular reaction. Moreover, given the effective 'dual power' situation, whether the assassination was carried out by apartheid security operatives or by Hani's enemies within the ANC, it would be almost impossible to mount such an operation without the other side's intelligence apparatus knowing all about it. And given the reaction the Hani killing was bound to provoke, the pressure to expose the culprits – or at least find some fall-guys – would be overwhelming. Thus arranging such an assassination really required that the other side's security operatives agreed to acquiesce in it. This in turn meant a high-level agreement. Lower-level operatives would pick up word of an impending hit and report to their superiors. To let the hit go ahead they would need to know they had cover from above. In other words, Hani's assassination could not go ahead unless it was cleared in advance with at least some of the ANC leadership. After all, Hani was one of the

ANC's top leaders. If he were suddenly assassinated by a white man the rest of the ANC leadership might well panic, decide that the invitation to negotiations was a trap, and revert to the armed struggle. This would be a catastrophe for both sides and could not be risked.

But if the white side – or certain elements in it – got wind of an impending Hani assassination they would be tempted to let it go ahead, for Hani had long been a key target of the old apartheid security apparatus. They would, however, need to find people on the ANC side who also wanted Hani killed, and gain their agreement for the assassination to go ahead. They would need to find someone high up in the ANC and in its security apparatus who would not simply divulge information of an impending assassination to all his colleagues. It should be someone who hated Hani, but also someone with well-established relationships of trust with his opposite numbers on the white side, the perfect person being someone who had actually been their double agent all the time. This is an identikit picture of Joe Modise.

THE WORLD OF JOE MODISE

'During the 1980s in Lusaka there were three recognizable groups in the ANC leadership,' Sibusiso Madlala, a senior MK operative told me.

> One was the Xhosas – Tambo, Mbeki, Nzo and Hani. Tambo was widely blamed for his ethnic favouritism. Luthuli, when ANC leader, had held a balance but under Tambo the Fort Hare Xhosas always had the inside track. Next was the SACP lot – Moses Mabhida, Josiah Jele and Stephen Dlamini, the president of SACTU [the South African Congress of Trade Unions] – all Zulus, plus of course, Slovo and Hani. Finally, there was the Alexandra Township group – Joe Modise, Tom Nkobi, Nzo and Jele. They were loose, shifting groups – Nzo, for example, was a member of all three.[24]

Modise was the central figure, for he commanded the most resources and was the most feared. He was regarded by Mabhida, Hani and Slovo as a mere township thug – for Modise had been a member of the Spoilers, who had contested supremacy within the Alexandra Township of the 1950s with another gang, the Msomis. Modise, a truck-driver, football player and boxer, was physically very strong, well able to look after himself even in the rough world of Alex.

The Spoilers were a cut above the normal township pickpockets and muggers. They aspired to be a criminal elite, dressed stylishly and 'liked to associate with socially acceptable people "such as musicians and politicians"'. As Norris Nkosi, an ex-Spoiler, put it, 'the small-time gangs were not of our class'.[25] They displayed a degree of professionalism in their extensive crime rings and protection rackets, though their elite status could not have been preserved save through exceptional violence. As in all township gangs, the highest status went to those known to have killed with knife or gun and, in an era when blacks were strictly forbidden to own firearms, they 'owned an entire warehouse in which they kept their ammunition'. Like all gangs, the Spoilers had branches inside jail and occasionally carried out horrific ritual killings of rival gang members. Their gentlemanly aspirations did not extend to women – 'their sexual violence and arrogance were in line with the wider sub-culture'.[26]

As a Spoiler, Modise was thus one of the few blacks bold enough to pack a gun in the 1950s. He knew all the shebeen queens and all the rackets. Inevitably, he also knew the police, for there was often a symbiotic relationship between gangsters and police, with the latter taking a cut in return for turning a blind eye. (Only after Modise went into exile in 1962 did the police act to crush the Spoilers and Msomis.) Modise had naturally opposed the apartheid policy of forced population removals from Alexandra and soon found himself swept up into the ANC. He became Mandela's bodyguard and a founder member of MK. By the early 1980s he was its commander, with Hani as commissar and Slovo in third position as chief of staff.[27]

'Bra Joe – that's what everyone called him – was a unique figure among the Lusaka exiles. Although he received military training in Czechoslovakia and the Soviet Union, Modise never became a Communist. Indeed, Hani and Slovo distrusted him and thought he was an informer for the Boers,' said Madlala.

They suspected him partly because they knew that all township gangsters had police links but also because there was a suspicious pattern. Whoever got in Bra Joe's way tended to get caught by the Boers' security police on their next mission. That was why Thami Zulu was poisoned by ANC Security – he was MK commander for Natal, reporting to Modise, and you couldn't but notice that all the Natal MK boys got rounded up by the security police in no time. They could do that to Thami Zulu but not to Bra Joe. Everyone in the ANC was frightened of him. They knew he had killed people himself, that he was completely ruthless and that he had presided over mass torture and executions in the MK punishment camps like Quatro. In any case he was the only one from the Sotho group – actually he was a Tswana – in the whole leadership. That made him sort of untouchable. On top of that he maintained his own gang, so everyone thought that if you crossed him he could easily find a way to make you disappear. Maybe he'd get the Boers to do it, or MK, or his own gang – but one way or another you were a goner.[28]

'People said that Tom Nkobi ran the stolen cars racket for the ANC in Zambia, but really it was far more Modise than him,' Madlala said.

Nkobi [the ANC treasurer] had been in the Spoilers with Joe and they were as thick as thieves – well, they were thieves – with one another and with Alfred Nzo. The ANC needed money and so it encouraged the stolen car racket and bank robberies – we used to call it 'repossessing' the cars or the money – but what it meant was that Bra Joe also had his own gangs doing these things and reporting to him. In addition, as MK commander he had ANC intelligence reporting to him too.

But there was always a deep sense of unease about Modise's position. The investigative journalist Sam Sole quotes one MK member about the repeated allegations that Modise was 'an imperialist agent': 'There was never any real confirmation of these rumours – but they lingered. There was a sense that he was not entirely clean. He lived well and he lived large – even in exile. He was always a man who liked the good life – and there has never been any explanation of how he afforded that.'[29] 'When I met him in Lusaka,' another exile said, 'all he seemed to care about was building his house. He was obsessed with his lawn.' 'I never heard a good word about him,' said another. Others criticized him for his inertia, for his lack of concern for MK troops and for keeping a safe distance from the action.[30]

It was not a pretty picture, but the ANC contained many things: principled heroism, Stalinist apparatchiks and plain thuggery. The poisoning of Thami Zulu was not an isolated incident. He had been detained and tortured for two years by ANC security but at the end of that there was still no evidence that he was the enemy agent they said he was, so he was simply done away with, with no verdict ever declared.

Similarly, when Duma Nokwe's alcoholism led to him being demoted to deputy secretary-general of the ANC, the new secretary-general, Alfred Nzo, felt threatened by the abler and better educated Nokwe. When Nokwe died of poisoning soon after it was believed by many that Nzo had a hand in it. 'They learnt all about poisoning from the KGB,' Madlala told me. Similarly, when Oliver Tambo's long-groomed successor, Tennyson Makiwane, broke away from the ANC over the issue of the inordinate influence of white communists within the movement, it was regarded as normal that he should be murdered by an MK hit squad.[31]

THE FRIENDS OF 'BRA JOE'

The big question about Modise was whether, like so many in the ANC, he was actually a spy for the other side. Or other sides, for once an ANC activist had decided to pass intelligence to 'the Boers', it usually followed that he was ready to make similar deals with the CIA, MI5 etc. (Passing information to the Stasi or KGB was, for most, just a matter of revolutionary duty.) The evidence against Modise is overwhelming. While most of the ANC leadership in Lusaka kept their addresses a close secret for fear of attacks by the apartheid forces, Modise's house in the upper-income suburb of Avondale was no secret and yet he seemed confident that he would not be an assassination target. There were also a large number of other incidents all suggesting that, to put it mildly, Modise's loyalties were complex. He and his henchman Tom Nkobi were so obviously taking their own cut from the stolen cars racket – and driving such beautiful cars themselves – that President Kaunda of Zambia once called Modise in and warned him not to flaunt his wealth so, for even Zambian cabinet ministers could not obtain such cars.[32]

In 1981 Modise was arrested in Botswana for illegal possession of firearms – but reportedly he was also carrying an unexplained stock of diamonds. In 1989–90 he was caught crossing the Kenya–Uganda border with large amounts of foreign exchange which, he claimed, was to buy food for MK guerrillas – though in fact their food came from quite another source. Then in 1985–6 he sold a weapons cache kept near Saurimo (Angola) to a Unita agent acting for Jonas Savimbi, the

ANC's sworn enemy.[33] Everything about their life in exile and Modise's post-1994 career also suggests that Modise and Nkobi were both informants for the apartheid security police. Certainly, when I interviewed operatives of the old apartheid security police (some by then in Mbeki's employ), I found they universally agreed that Modise had been a police informer.

As the MK commander, Modise had also been primarily responsible for the brutal torture inflicted on MK dissidents in camps such as Quatro. The Motsuenyane Commission, one of several bodies to probe these shocking events, heard that Modise held the lives of his MK soldiers so cheap that he would even send them into South Africa on shopping expeditions for himself.[34] In Lusaka Modise had shared a house with a cocaine dealer, known only as Mister Stevens. It was generally assumed that Joe was using his contacts to make money out of the drug trade too: he would, after all, stop at nothing and in any case other high-ranking ANC folk were known to be involved in the drug trade too.[35]

When De Klerk opened the floodgates and Modise returned to South Africa along with the rest of the ANC leadership, Mister Stevens had come winging in on the back of MK to expand several already thriving rackets. Within a year Stevens had several clubs in Hillbrow and Yeoville, all fronts for cocaine dealing and hot liquor which would be 'mis-delivered' by truck-driving comrades in Cosatu. By the end of 1996, however, the Nigerian druglords had moved in and paid the police more, so Stevens found many of his joints closed down. A gang war ensued – it all got very messy, with sex parties for ANC leaders mixed in with a lot of trade in coke and Ecstasy, hand grenades over garden walls, prominent jazz musicians and other celebrities feeding their coke habit while moonlighting ex-MK elements carried out drive-by shootings. No one who witnessed the Johannesburg high life (low life?) of those years will forget the excitement, the crazy contradictions and the sheer violence of it all.

Somewhere en route, Modise discreetly disengaged himself from Mister Stevens, having, after all, bigger fish to fry. In exile he had become a friend and confidant of Solomon Mujuru, the former Zanu guerrilla commander in Zimbabwe, who had parlayed that position into becoming one of the country's largest landowners. Modise, impressed by his example and aware from the Zimbabwean case of just how lucrative the kickbacks from military contracts could be, was determined to become the first ANC Defence Minister, a post he saw as a passport to great wealth. No sooner had he returned from exile than he began to meet with the foreign arms dealers now swarming to the country in search of the inevitable post-sanctions arms deal.

The greatest threat to Modise's position was Chris Hani. After the ill-fated Wankie campaign of 1967 (an attempted MK incursion through Rhodesia) Hani had written a bitter memorandum of complaint to the ANC leadership about the comparison between the hard life of the MK troops and 'the perks and privileges' enjoyed by their leaders, who showed no vigour in prosecuting the war. Hani attacked Modise by name[36] and, as we have seen, Modise responded by attempting to have Hani executed. Hani survived – belatedly, Tambo protected him – but as he rose through the ranks to be Modise's No. 2, the undeniable hero of the MK troops, he became Modise's rival as the real head of MK. Once the exiles returned Hani became an obvious candidate for Minister of Defence. Worse still, after the 1992 ANC conference he seemed likely to overtake Mbeki and win the race to succeed Mandela. Naturally, Modise threw all his weight behind Mbeki, for he simply could not afford to see Hani elevated further.

The resulting alliance between Mbeki and Modise was the pivot on which ANC politics turned. Even those willing to ignore Modise's generally unsavoury reputation often kept their distance because of Modise's responsibility for the torture in the MK camps in Angola, now likely to get a further airing at the Truth and Reconciliation Commission (TRC). But Mbeki seemed oblivious to such concerns and was happy to embrace Modise. This also brought him close to Modise's associate, Mzwandile Piliso, the notorious former head of ANC security who in 1992 had happily admitted to the ANC's Skweyiya Commission that he had personally tortured suspects in the Angolan camps. Piliso was such a byword for brutality that he was shunned by most: indeed, Modise and Mbeki were the only ANC leaders to attend his funeral in 1996.

To the stupefaction of many, Mbeki later had the government's Intelligence Academy in Mafikeng named after Piliso, saying he had 'fought a struggle for democracy'. Similarly, when the TRC Report was issued in October 1998 Mbeki stunned many by opposing its publication because of its condemnation of the human rights atrocities in the MK camps, although, with Mandela happily supporting publication, this left Mbeki part of a losing minority. This was remarkable behaviour. At a moment when many of those involved in MK were keen to distance themselves from the dreadful atrocities in the MK camps, Mbeki, who had never done MK service and was clean on the atrocities issue, was risking his good name by standing up for the likes of Piliso and Modise. There could be no greater testament to just how determined Mbeki was to maintain his alliance with Modise.

THE KILLING OF CHRIS HANI

During the liberation struggle the Soviet bloc had poured arms into MK. With the armed struggle suspended the question was what would happen to all this valuable hardware. Modise knew that the arms would deteriorate if left untouched and he was also both in touch with arms dealers and aware of the caches' market value. According to an affidavit signed by the Mpumalanga ANC youth leader, James Nkambule, Modise sold off one of these caches for $2.5 million in 1993, keeping the matter secret from the ANC leadership and pocketing the money himself.[37] Hani learnt of the deal, confronted Modise, and warned him that if he did not inform the ANC about it then he, Hani, would. Two weeks later Hani was shot dead.

Hani was assassinated by the far right – by Janus Walus, a Polish immigrant, in league with Clive Derby-Lewis, a far-right MP. But there has always been a gap in the official account, causing many to believe that Walus, wittingly or not, must have received help from within the ANC. Hani was gunned down outside his house in Boksburg on a day when his bodyguard had the day off. The far right, it was claimed, were the last people likely to know such crucial details as which was Hani's house, that Hani had spent the night before the murder with a lover at a hotel near Johannesburg airport,[38] and which days his bodyguard was off duty.

Clearly, Modise was a prime suspect for having facilitated the assassination. He had every motive to want Hani dead – and had, indeed, tried to kill him before. As MK commander he was privy to MK intelligence and its contacts. Moreover, like the apartheid security police, the ANC underground had long since become semi-criminalized (more exactly, both had fully criminalized operatives within their ranks) and they shared many of the same contacts. One such contact was Shariff Khan, then Johannesburg's king of Mandrax dealing, who carefully maintained good relations with both sides. His son-in-law Ramon, an ANC double agent, actually warned South Africa's military intelligence of a plot to assassinate Hani just before it occurred.[39] This drugs underworld had no connection with the likes of Walus and Derby-Lewis but it certainly had links with Joe Modise.

The Hani assassination sparked riots around the country but the ANC leadership was determined that it should not derail continued negotiations – a remarkable contrast with their attitude over the Boipatong massacre, when they tried hard to pretend that De Klerk had been behind it and snatched at the opportunity to try to destabilize the government with 'rolling mass action'. Left-wing critics regarded the leadership's attitude with suspicion, wondering if some of them had anticipated, and even welcomed, Hani's death. The ANC set up a committee of six (including Modise) to handle the funeral and other arrangements stemming from the killing, while Mathews Phosa headed an investigatory team.

The Hani assassination remains to this day one of the murkiest and most sensitive areas of South African politics. One investigative journalist who decided to reopen the affair was sent a dead dog, writhing with maggots, as a warning to keep away.[40] He took the hint. The TRC tried – but failed – to find evidence of a wider right-wing conspiracy involving members of the apartheid security services.[41] Given the TRC's political disposition, it was unwilling to look elsewhere. There were press reports – not denied by the SACP – that the ANC and SACP had reached different conclusions about the nature of Hani's murder.[42] Journalists who probed the matter came to believe that there were two separate conspiracies to kill Hani, one by Walus and Derby-Lewis, the other by enemies within the ANC, though details differ. Some believe the latter helped the former, others that the ANC plotters, who were only days away from trying to kill Hani themselves, sighed with relief when they found someone else was planning to do their work for them. Certainly, those familiar with Modise and his methods found it harder to believe that he would not have planned to dispose of Hani than that he had – and it was thought entirely possible that Modise had aided the efforts of Walus and Derby-Lewis without their ever knowing.

The TRC faced a difficult problem with Walus and Derby-Lewis, since its rules said that amnesty should be given to those whose acts of violence had been politically motivated provided they made full disclosure. Walus and Derby-Lewis had certainly been politically motivated – far more so than many who did receive amnesty such as the Pan Africanist Congress (PAC) killers who had charged into St James' church in Cape Town and mowed down eleven worshippers simply because they wanted to kill whites. But the TRC knew that to give amnesty to Hani's killers would enrage the SACP, so the pair were denied amnesty on the grounds that they had not made full disclosure of the wider (right-wing) plot which must have existed. Walus and Derby-Lewis insisted, in vain, that they had worked alone.

I managed to get into Pretoria Central Prison where Walus and Derby-Lewis were held and interview both men.[43] They insisted that they were unaware of any wider conspiracy. Walus said that not only had he not been tipped off about the bodyguard's absence but that even at the time of the assassination he had been concerned about the possibility of another bodyguard somewhere inside Hani's house. The previous day I had met with Janus Walus's elder brother, Witold, who had described the assassination as 'a boy scout conspiracy'. This seemed accurate enough. Janus, for example, had not thrown away the gun he used for the killing because Derby-Lewis had lent it to him, saying it was a favourite gun and that he wanted it back. For this absurd reason Janus was caught in possession of the weapon. Similarly, Janus had carried out the hit in full sight of a white woman, who was able to give a description of him, his red Ford Laser car and its registration number – and yet Janus himself had not seen her.

Witold Walus explained to me that the Walus family had suffered greatly under the Communist regime in Poland – his small businessman father had had eight separate businesses expropriated from him by the authorities – and Janus had decided that if Hani came to power, a similar regime would take power in South Africa. This was such a dreadful prospect that even the most extreme means were warranted to avoid it. Derby-Lewis seemed full of an equally simple-minded anti-communism and, indeed, a sort of schoolboyish right-wingery, an impression confirmed in our prison interview. Witold clearly suspected that his younger brother had in his naivety been made use of by more sophisticated groups which had desired Hani's death. 'Only ten minutes after Janus drove off from the assassination scene his car was stopped and searched by the police and he was arrested. You know how atypical that sort of police efficiency is in South Africa.' It was, he suggested, as if the police had known all about the matter from the outset and had simply waited for Janus to carry out the assassination before arresting him.[44]

Certainly, my prison interview with Walus and Derby-Lewis left me believing that neither man had ever appreciated – and still did not appreciate – just how far out of their depth they had been. The old apartheid security apparatus was regarded as among the most professional outfits of its type in the world, while their ANC opposite numbers had both long experience and, often, training from the Stasi and the KGB. Add together the fact that both outfits were now established and operating inside the same country, trading information with one another, and that splits existed on both sides so that neither security apparatus was necessarily responsive to orders from its political leadership, and you had a surrounding context of treacherous complexity and opacity. Within that context Walus and Derby-Lewis were merely first-time amateurs.

Another version has it that killing Hani was one of a number of secret consensual agreements between leading elements within the apartheid and ANC leaderships, akin to the agreement not to reveal the names of police informers within the ANC. Again, this would place Modise at the centre of events; clearly, he had long worked as an informer within the ANC for the apartheid securocrats, and was thus effectively a figure promising continuity in the realm the securocrats cared most about. Hani, on the other hand, was widely represented in the press as the opposite extreme, an opponent of negotiations, as someone actually raising his own private army in the Transkei, and as an irreconcilable, consorting with the likes of Winnie Mandela. Winnie, for her part, made a speech after the assassination in which she claimed that moderate ANC leaders had 'conspired' to eliminate Hani, passing information about his bodyguard's absence to government security agents who in turn told Walus. Winnie knew that Hani's decision to stand against Mbeki had ruffled many feathers within the ANC, as had his interview with a foreign newspaper in which he had said he was thinking of starting a Communist organization to act as a check on the ANC in government.[45]

Winnie did not support her assertions with any evidence but it is clear that she was only one of a number within the ANC who got wind of such a conspiracy. I later confirmed through quite different ANC sources that there had been an ANC plot to kill Hani some ten days after Walus actually did the deed.[46] The names of various ANC leaders were ascribed to the plot, including that of Modise. This certainly rings true: Modise would hardly have acted alone and to prevent the whole ANC leadership from stampeding in the wake of the assassination there clearly had to be an influential nucleus who were prepared for Hani's death.

Mail and Guardian journalists were able to show that Ramon (aka Mohammed Amin Laher) was quite right in his claim that the National Intelligence Service had had advance warning not only of Hani's assassination and its date but spoke of a 'Polish member of the strike unit'.[47] Documents submitted by Ramon to his NIS handler, Eugene Riley, claimed that members of the ANC's Department of Intelligence and Security (for which Ramon, a double agent, also worked) were involved in the plot.[48] Riley was so sure of Ramon's reliability that he actually told the *Mail and Guardian* journalist Hazel Friedman that Hani would be assassinated a few days before the killing took place and Ramon offered to provide her with documents proving that ANC factions hostile to Hani were involved.[49] Ramon also told the *Mail and Guardian* that not only were 'operatives on both sides of the spectrum' involved in the assassination but so were some ANC leaders.[50] The investigative journalist Stefaans Brummer also interviewed a member of the ANC's own investigation team into the murder who confirmed that they had found evidence of a second group of killers besides Walus. There had been an eyewitness report of a second car besides Walus's, evidence that someone had been hiding behind a wall next door to Hani's house at the time of the assassination, and one of the bullets that killed Hani had been fired by someone other than Walus. Moreover, Hani himself had intelligence that there was a plot against him and had demanded that the ANC step up his security arrangements – but met a stony refusal. The police had proved 'unwilling' to follow up any of these leads.[51] When journalists tried to track down the white woman who had been the crucial eyewitness to the assassination, she had simply vanished – causing some to believe that the whole assassination had been carefully watched and monitored, with the eyewitness part of that exercise.

The documents Ramon submitted to Riley pointed a finger almost directly at Modise, claiming that 'Hani's own agenda has become a big headache for the MK hierarchy' (a phrase which could only mean

Modise) and that members of the ANC's Department of Intelligence and Security had the role of 'facilitating' the Walus/Derby-Lewis hit.[52] But Ramon was extremely nervous about his own role and went to ground when the TRC wanted to interview him and thereafter hid under a variety of aliases. No one ever succeeded in interviewing him again. His nervousness was understandable since the other person who could vouch for the documents, Eugene Riley, was killed by an unknown assassin just eight months after Hani's death.[53] It seemed clear that someone was extremely keen to stamp out this line of enquiry – and with Walus and Derby-Lewis both behind bars the suspicion was that their direct or indirect accomplices were protecting themselves. Riley's girlfriend Julie Wilken confirmed, however, that she had typed out the reports showing advance knowledge of the assassination.[54] Wilken also said that Riley had told her that Walus and Derby-Lewis would be rewarded for their part in the killing by being secretly spirited away to Poland and Australia respectively – an arrangement which also came to the ears of *The Sowetan*.[55] In fact they languished in jail thereafter.

Julie Wilken then vanished into a witness protection programme for more than eight years but I met with her not long after she emerged from it.[56] She confirmed that Riley had had a close relationship with both Shariff Khan and his son-in-law, Ramon (Laher) – who was, she said, an MK colonel – through which he had received information about large-scale drug dealing by a leading ANC figure close to Hani and also tip-offs helpful to Riley's own criminal activities. Two weeks before the Hani assassination Riley had learnt that 'a prominent ANC leader' was to be assassinated and three days beforehand he learnt that this was to be Hani. All this information was known both to the ANC and the NIS. Neither did anything to stop the assassination.

Laher, queried on this point, said that the ANC had decided to give quiet, indeed invisible, assistance to the assassination plot in progress – those leading it (Derby-Lewis and Walus) were too naive even to realize that they were being helped. The reason for the ANC plot against Hani, he said, was that Hani was likely to overthrow Mandela's leadership – he had the support of Winnie Mandela (then a substantial factor) and of the youth in general. And a Hani takeover would constitute a major threat to South Africa's stability and might capsize the ANC itself. The government's NIS was, he said, hardly going to intervene to save Hani, whom they regarded as their most dangerous opponent. But equally, they did not want to be blamed for his murder: they could let the assassination go ahead only because they were assured in advance that this was an outcome desired by powerful elements in the ANC too. And, indeed, despite an initial outburst of popular unrest in response to Hani's murder, the ANC leadership quickly declared that Hani's murder must not be allowed to destabilize the political situation, and did all they could to calm popular anger in the townships.

Clearly, when Laher talked of 'the ANC' he meant only certain elements within it, though elements senior enough in it to represent themselves to him as 'the ANC'. It is impossible that he meant Mandela himself. Mandela would never have countenanced Hani's murder and in any case felt perfectly secure in his own leadership role. Had Hani opposed him, Mandela would easily have faced him down. But the whole idea that Hani might have opposed Mandela is fanciful. Given Mandela's own heroic role, his revered position in the struggle and the overwhelming African respect for age, such a challenge was unthinkable. The real question attached only to the post-Mandela succession. For all these reasons it seems obvious that the ANC leader or leaders Laher was reporting to were a rung below Mandela – and that their explanation of Hani as a threat to Mandela was simply a smokescreen to cloak their own motives.

Everything points to Modise. He alone had both a compelling motive to kill Hani, the seniority as MK commander to represent his decisions as those of 'the ANC', and the necessary access to MK intelligence to play a role from the shadows. He had no need to fear exposure by the NIS for he had been hand in glove with the apartheid security police for years. He was, moreover, a man who had frequently had people killed and who had already once tried to kill Hani. Nonetheless, far more fingers have been pointed at Mbeki as part of the conspiracy that killed Hani, although there is no evidence for this.

We can, though, put together what we now know. It seems beyond dispute that quite early on the Walus/Derby-Lewis conspiracy came to the attention of the intelligence and security apparatus of both sides, though not before a separate ANC conspiracy to assassinate Hani had been set afoot. There seems to have been an agreement between both sides to allow this 'amateur' conspiracy to proceed and even give it invisible help. It is not difficult to imagine the other terms of such an agreement. First, it would be essential to keep knowledge of this situation to as small and confidential a group as possible on either side and, doubtless, to ensure that neither Mandela nor De Klerk was in the know. Secondly, the conspirators from the old apartheid apparatus would have to guarantee that the Hani killing would be an isolated event, not the signal for an all-out assault on the ANC by the forces of the right. For neither side wished the assassination to torpedo the negotiations then in progress; indeed, they probably saw the assassination as a means of ridding themselves of a threat to those negotiations. Thirdly, the conspirators on the ANC side would have to guarantee that they could prevent the ANC leadership from bolting through fear of such an all-out assault. Since Modise alone would not have had the persuasive authority to do that, he would have needed allies within the ANC leadership to help him. And, finally, the actual assassins would have to be promptly apprehended and charged so as to avoid a dangerous hiatus when the finger of suspicion might be pointed at others, or when the tensions within either camp might erupt. That is, Walus and Derby-Lewis would have to be protected and even invisibly helped up to the moment that they killed Hani, but then immediately arrested. This is exactly what happened, so the news of Hani's assassination and the arrest of the assassins were wrapped into a single announcement.

Hani was gunned down by Walus on 10 April 1993. It was a pivotal moment in South African history. His death settled many things. Joe Modise no longer needed to fear exposure for arms dealing. The way was now clear for him to become Minister of Defence, which in turn was good news for the international arms companies backing him: the R60 billion arms deal – Modise's version of it – would go ahead. It was good news, too, for the old regime. They were altogether more comfortable with Thabo Mbeki, who had conducted a long and successful charm offensive in both government and business circles, and it escaped no one's notice that with Hani dead Mbeki was Mandela's likely successor. Hani's death also robbed the SACP and MK of an irreplaceable leader, thus greatly reducing their leverage within the ANC. It may be that Hani's death made South Africa safe for capitalism, for something like the continuation of 'business as usual'. But it also beheaded the revolutionary movement in its hour of triumph, leaving it frustrated, angry – and suspicious.

Mathews Phosa, who led the ANC investigation into the Hani killing, was convinced there had been a wider conspiracy: 'It is very clear that those who aided and abetted Walus *et al.* are now doing everything in their power to further cover their tracks. We, however, remain convinced that the truth will ultimately out.'[57] Phosa's words carried considerable weight. In exile he had been the head of the ANC's legal team and had played a large role in helping to unearth many spies who had infiltrated the ANC.[58] In July 1997 the former KwaZulu-Natal ANC leader, Sifiso Nkabinde, added a new dimension to the affair by suggesting that Leonard Radu, an assistant police commissioner investigating the Hani assassination, had been murdered. Radu, formerly a deputy security chief of the ANC working under Jacob Zuma, the ANC intelligence boss, had been killed in a car accident in early 1997 but Nkabinde claimed that Zuma had been awaiting a call to confirm Radu's death and had received such a call at 11 p.m. on the night of his death. Zuma was by that time already Mbeki's choice as running-mate and the ANC dismissed these accusations out of hand.[59] Nkabinde himself was assassinated soon afterwards, making clarification of his allegations impossible.

DIVIDING THE SPOILS

Mbeki's succession to the leadership was now effectively sealed. Ramaphosa, despite his grass-roots popularity, was not to prove a serious rival. Whereas Mbeki was made First Deputy President in 1994 (De Klerk being Second), Ramaphosa did not enter government and was to grow increasingly frustrated at ANC party headquarters as all real power moved to government and was centralized around Mbeki's office. Mandela favoured Ramaphosa as his successor: always sensitive to ethnic factors he knew how a Tambo–Mandela–Mbeki succession, three Xhosas in a row, would look to others. But the exile bloc behind Mbeki was too strong for Ramaphosa to have much chance. By 1996 he had abandoned his party job for a business career.

With Mbeki's succession certain, Modise was in no doubt that he had been handed the keys of the kingdom and proceeded to take advantage of this in a highly predictable way. He appointed the former MK and South African National Defence Force commander Lambert Moloi (his brother-in-law) to the board of the defence parastatal, Denel, from which position he became a bidder for the third cellphone licence as part of the Cell C consortium, one of the most lucrative deals in the new South Africa. Another crony on the Denel board was Fana Hlongwane, Modise's special adviser, who in turn had a relationship with the daughter of the Minister for Public Enterprises, Stella Sigcau. Unsurprisingly, the daughter soon had a job at Denel and then with British Aerospace (BAE Systems), with whom Modise cultivated a particularly close relationship. Two other Modise clients, Keith Mokoape (a senior MK man) and Diliza Mji, were put on the board of the Armscor parastatal and Mji was later appointed as the non-executive chairman of BAE (Southern Africa).[60]

BAE were determined to land the contract to re-equip the air force, the SAAF. They also bought a stake in Denel Aviation, a shrewd move because with the collapse of South Africa's apartheid-era arms spending the future for both Denel and Armscor looked bleak. By farming out work to Denel, BAE could earn government goodwill and also have a foot inside the door. The pay-off finally came when Modise intervened in the tender process to allocate the contract for jet trainers to BAE's Hawks, despite the SAAF's preference for a cheaper Italian alternative. Mbeki was head of the cabinet committee on the arms deal and doubtless realized that Modise was determined to turn the deal to his private profit. But Mbeki was also aware of how crucial Modise's support for him in the leadership struggle had been, so in effect Modise was allowed to do as he liked. Indeed, later on a letter turned up showing that Mbeki had met with the French arms firm, Thomson-CSF, and had given them help with their part of the deal, a letter which Mbeki refused to discuss despite strong pressure from the Opposition Democratic Alliance.[61] Presumably he had been helping cement one of Modise's deals but this whole area was too sensitive for Mbeki to discuss or, as he claimed, even remember it.

Modise was well rewarded for his partisan attitude towards BAE, but this remained a secret until early 2007 when Britain's Serious Fraud Office (SFO) asked for the help of the South African elite police unit, the Scorpions, in probing the accounts of Modise's adviser, Fana Hlongwane. Already in 2003 *The Guardian* had reported that BAE had paid a commission of £150 million for the deal and that much of this had gone to Modise and Hlongwane. Hlongwane, who refused to comment, had since become chairman of the Ngwane Defence Group, to which he had recruited the former SANDF chief, Siphiwe Nyanda, as chief executive.[62] Mbeki was, however, hyper-sensitive about the issue, perhaps because he feared that revelations in this area would lead to accusations that he had shielded Modise. Three weeks later, before a stunned audience at the World Economic Forum in Davos, Mbeki launched a bitter personal attack on Tony Blair for allowing the SFO probe to go ahead.[63] This was clearly a sign of great personal stress, for Mbeki knew that such attacks ran flat against the Davos culture (Blair refrained from making any reply). But Mbeki was now under serious pressure. As chairman of the cabinet committee on the arms deal he had, at the committee's meeting of 31 August 1998, helped push through the decision to go for the BAE deal even though it cost almost twice as much as the Italian alternative[64] – and the SFO now confirmed that R1 billion had been paid in bribes to eight people for making that decision.

Simultaneously, details emerged in Germany of bribes paid by ThyssenKrupp in return for their securing the frigate and submarine parts of the arms deal. *Der Spiegel* revealed that the German authorities were investigating a series of payments made to people, companies and foundations connected to South Africans involved in the deal. One of these payments alone was for $22 million. Allegedly, one of Joe Modise's chief advisers, Chippy Shaik, had asked for and received a $3 million commission for the deal. The spotlight fell persistently on Tony Georgiadis, an intimate of Mbeki's, who appeared to have brokered the deals.[65] It was peculiar company for Mbeki to keep, for Georgiadis had been a sanctions-buster under apartheid and a close ally of the apartheid government. At the same time Daimler Aerospace made an acknowledgement of guilt for paying bribes, including the provision of luxury vehicles to thirty South Africans, among them Mbeki's (then) close client and ally, Tony Yengeni.[66]

FEEDING AT THE TROUGH: THE ARMS DEAL

Hlongwane and Chippy Shaik were, however, minor players in the arms deal compared to South Africa's new rulers. Under the normal rules of Third World arms deals the defence minister is typically the chief beneficiary of bribes ('commissions'). So one would expect Modise to have had a far greater chance of benefiting than these small fry. Modise was transparently intent on using his tenure at the Ministry of Defence as a springboard to becoming seriously rich, showing almost no interest in doing his ministerial job. He would not even read departmental or cabinet papers, left the job of integrating the old South African Defence Force and MK into the new South African National Defence Force to his deputy, Ronnie Kasrils, and concentrated entirely on the arms deal.[67]

The generals were keen to re-equip the armed forces but such a deal was far from obvious. The ANC had a strong instinctive resistance to building up the security apparatus they had just fought against and both Jay Naidoo, Minister for the RDP, and Trevor Manuel, the Finance Minister, were appalled by the deal's financial implications and the hole it would make in domestic expenditure. The parliamentary defence committee chaired by Tony Yengeni took the view that a new air force design should be resisted until there had been a proper threat assessment and defence review.[68] Parliament accepted this view and called for defence expenditure to be kept down to R10 billion. After all, South Africa faced no international threat of any kind. Accordingly the 1996 Defence White Paper emphasized lower defence spending, arms control and a defensive military posture.

Modise paid no heed whatsoever to this; he did not even read the White Paper.[69] He was already spending much time abroad at air shows, arms exhibitions and the like. He took his proposed arms deal straight to cabinet where it ran into significant opposition. Manuel and Naidoo strongly opposed it, as did the former SACP leader, Joe Slovo ('South Africa's greatest defence will be a satisfied population'), the SACP, Cosatu and the usual panoply of ANC-aligned NGOs.[70] Such a coalition would normally have doomed any proposal, but Modise had one major trump card: Mbeki's support. Mbeki, who was already running the government in every key respect, helped force the deal through, giving Thomson-CSF executives his personal assurance that they would get the contract to supply combat suites for the navy's corvettes.[71] Similarly, Mbeki's was the decisive voice in plumping for the BAE Hawk trainers.

The suggestion that Mbeki supported the deal because of his keenness that South Africa should play an African peacekeeping role[72] makes little sense. Buying submarines and short-range jet fighters made no contribution to such a role, which depended most of all on long-range military transport aircraft – which had to be ordered as a separate addition to the arms deal years later.[73] The only sense one can make of Mbeki's position was that he had to reward Modise for his crucial support in the struggle to succeed Mandela.

Things nearly came apart for Modise in March 1997. Five former security branch policemen, applying to the TRC for amnesty for more than forty murders, claimed that they had the names of former agents and informants now in top government positions. Although the TRC would not allow them to name these agents, a number of names – including that of Modise – leaked into the press. President Mandela immediately demanded that the list of names be exposed. This could have spelt the end for Modise but Mbeki hurriedly got the ANC national working committee to oppose publication, claiming that this 'rumour-mongering' was part of a plot by apartheid-era security policemen to destabilize the ANC. This prevented publication.[74]

Meanwhile, the grotesque deal went through. While no one doubted that the country needed new naval craft to prevent foreign trawlers from poaching its fish, and a case could be made for some limited replacement of obsolete equipment, no case at all could be made for many elements of the deal, such as the purchase of submarines or a whole new generation of fighter aircraft (the Anglo-Swedish Gripen). Not only were the SAAF's Cheetahs (local derivatives of the Mirage) up to any job required – and given South Africa's wholly peaceful environment, no job was required – but there were in any case no pilots left to fly them: affirmative-action pressures had soon led most of the SAAF's highly trained white pilots to quit. The always-remembered fly-past at Mandela's inauguration had in fact been their swansong. They were saluting the new President and, like many other skilled whites, quickly moving on to pastures new, not easily to be replaced.

A key part of the deal had been various offset and counter-trade commitments. Modise had already (in 1997) appointed his daughter, Thereza Magazi, to sit on the board of one of the designated companies for counter-trade agreements, Conlog. He also set up a trust to buy the shares giving her the right to her position at Conlog. On his retirement from government in 1999 Modise took over – though he never actually paid for his shares in Conlog. A variety of financial manoeuvres and asset-stripping saw Conlog (later renamed Logtek) re-emerge as Applied Logistics Engineering, chaired by Keith Mokoape. Various buddies of Modise from the boards of Denel and Armscor served on the board of

Conlog/Logtek: Mji, Zodwa Manase, Ian Deetlefs, and Ron Haywood, with whose wife Modise went into business in another venture. Modise was also close to the head of Eskom, Reuel Khoza – a valuable relationship for Conlog which secured Eskom's order for most of its pre-paid electricity meters. Khoza and Modise also set up a company on their own, Tradescript 30, one of whose directors was Sean McMurray, who had earned notoriety by his attempt to sell off game reserves on the edge of the Kruger Park.[75] It emerged that Modise's Letaba Trust had secretly bought into Conlog even when Modise was Minister – and in time to benefit from the offset deals Modise had negotiated. Similarly, Modise seems to have acquired interests in Labat Africa, another beneficiary of the offset agreements. The usual word to describe this is 'kickbacks'.

JOE MODISE: FATHER OF THE NEW SOUTH AFRICA

The DA leader, Tony Leon, recounted how early on in Modise's reign at the Ministry of Defence he was at a reception thrown by Denel at which a British visitor was expatiating in the manner then fashionable on how generous Africans had been in accepting reconciliation with whites. Modise's approach was more down to earth: 'If you want to see generosity, look at the Nats. We gave them half a dozen seats in cabinet and they gave us the country.'[76]

Certainly, Modise had been given the enrichment opportunity of a lifetime and he intended to take full advantage. There was little trace of the old ANC militant: he fraternized happily with former apartheid generals. He spoke fluent Afrikaans, traded jokes and rugby gossip over a barbecue and made SANDF helicopters available to whisk them all off to game reserves.[77] They were utterly charmed and even accepted his appointment of his wife, Jackie Sedibe (a senior MK commander herself), as South Africa's first woman general. As soon as he left office in 1999 he joined the boards of more than a dozen companies, several of which had benefited from the arms deal. He joined two companies chaired by Mark Voloshin, a controversial Russian businessman with large interests in South Africa. One of these companies, Liselo, supplied solar electricity equipment to Reuel Khoza's Eskom, while the other, the

Marvol Group, negotiated an abortive deal with Denel to provide MiG aero-engines to upgrade the old SAAF Mirages.

Modise's closest intimates all seemed to be men who had profited from the arms deal. Indeed, Modise's will revealed that his associates were 'a band of white arms company executives drawn from the brotherhood of the sanctions-busting era'.[78] L. R. Swan, former CEO of Armscor, witnessed the will. The trustee of Modise's main asset, the Letaba Trust, was John Ellingford, former CEO of the defence company Reunert. Ellingford had had to resign suddenly in 1997 when the CIA informed the Reunert board that Ellingford had an unexplained $2 million in a Swiss bank account. Swan and Ellingford were long-time associates and had both been consultants to the German submarine consortium which had been one of the biggest winners from the arms deal. Another Letaba trustee was Ian Deetlefs, the former chairman of Denel. Deetlefs and the Armscor chairman, Ron Haywood, had both secretly bought into Conlog at the same time as Modise. Naturally, there was no sign of Modise's ill-gotten gains in his will. On his deathbed he was persuaded to put his thumbprint on a new will (he was by then too weak to sign it) placing the Letaba Trust under the direction of his widow, Jackie, Deetlefs and Ellingford, but the copy of this will was (conveniently) lost. Officially, Modise's estate came to almost nothing[79] – which is to say, it was expertly hidden. Modise was known to have secret bank accounts in Malaysia, Lichtenstein and elsewhere, though gossip around the cabinet was that he had tried to get more than one government colleague to make withdrawals from the Malaysian account for him, as if concerned by the security consequences of making withdrawals himself.[80]

Almost immediately after the arms deal was signed there was a hue and cry over alleged corruption, and demands for an independent inquiry. Mbeki resisted this with might and main and insisted that those who demanded such an inquiry were trying to bring down the government. In his determination to prevent an inquiry he used the full weight of the presidential office to force even allegedly independent bodies and institutions into line. The result was to undermine the parliamentary process, the independence of the Speaker, the Public Accounts Committee and much else besides. Andrew Feinstein, the ranking ANC MP on that committee, insisted that if the allegations of corruption were not faced, they would haunt the government for years to come. Feinstein himself was soon forced out but his prediction proved entirely correct.[81] As more details trickled into public view, Mbeki's insistence that there had been no corruption in the arms deal was shown to be completely false. Feinstein, moreover, was told by one ANC leader that considerable sums from the deal had gone to finance the ANC's election campaign in 1999 – that is, Mbeki's first as President.[82]

Although Mandela was the public face of the new South Africa, in some ways Joe Modise was a more representative figure. While Mandela symbolized the way the ANC wanted the world to see it, and wanted to see itself – heroic, principled, a selfless victim – a great deal of the ANC's history was distinctly murky. Corruption and tribalism had often been problems within its ranks, which were always riddled with informers. Quite apart from the atrocities within the MK prison camps, the movement never made any attempt to live up to its own Freedom Charter and, perhaps inevitably, its ways were often ruthless.[83] Modise not only incorporated many traits of this darker side but was also the forerunner of the black economic empowerment phenomenon which saw many others follow his example of leveraging their influence within the ANC for personal gain.

THE GHOST OF HANI WALKS

Naturally, rumour and speculation was rife over Modise's role in Hani's murder and Mbeki's protective attitude towards Modise. Given that Mbeki was the most obvious beneficiary of Hani's death, this led to a good deal of quiet surmise – and quiet allegation, entirely unsupported by evidence. Whenever tensions rose within the tripartite alliance of ANC, SACP and Cosatu, pitting the latter two against Mbeki, they would not only make a very public point of celebrating Hani, the lost leader, but would also issue calls for a fresh investigation into his death, claiming that the full truth had yet to be revealed. It is difficult not to see in this a ritualized form of psychological warfare. Thus, for example, in 2005 in the midst of the bitter Mbeki–Zuma struggle the Young Communist League called for a further inquest into the Hani killing. David Masondo, the League's chairman, said he was sure that Walus and Derby-Lewis had 'collaborated with a number of people. That could point to broader networks.' Asked if he attached significance to rumours that Hani had been the victim of infighting within the ANC, he refused to rule the notion out.[84] When, in 2001, an alleged plot to overthrow President Mbeki was announced, Mathews Phosa was one of the three suspects and it was claimed that he had tried to link Janus Walus with Mbeki and had thus attempted to pin the blame for the murder on Mbeki.[85]

As Modise lay dying of cancer in November 2001 President Mbeki rushed to award him the Order of the Star of South Africa Grand Cross in gold – as Trewhela puts it, 'a suitably Ruritanian finale'.[86] Ronnie Kasrils, his deputy at the Ministry of Defence, published a fulsome obituary which carefully airbrushed away Modise's multitude of contacts with 'the wrong side'. Mbeki's final determination to honour Modise was so peculiar as to arouse critical comment even from so loyal an Mbeki-ite as Mathatha Tsedu, who described the macabre scenes as Mbeki and his entire cabinet rushed to Modise's deathbed in Centurion, a Pretoria suburb, late at night to give him his gold star, narrowly avoiding a posthumous award.

There was, inevitably, some muttering about Modise knowing where all the bodies were buried in both the literal and figurative senses, for as Tsedu pointed out, there was 'no rational explanation' for the way the award was made. Mbeki was keen to dispel any notion that the award was his own idea and 'went to great lengths to explain why and how the honour had been decided upon long before then by former President Mandela' but that it had not been thought appropriate to make the award while Modise was still Defence Minister. Tsedu could not but ask, 'Modise left the government in June 1999, so why wait two years and five months before you race in the dead of night to give [the award] to him barely before he died?'[87] For most Mbeki-watchers such elaborate protestation was the surest sign that the award had been Mbeki's idea. The interesting question was why he was so determined to distance himself from it.

There were doubtless concerns in some quarters that Modise's death would bring to light some of the dirt surrounding the arms deal and the Hani assassination. Perhaps Modise had entrusted information on such matters to his wives, lovers or family, or used it in some way to guarantee that those who had made deals with him kept their side of the bargain? There were many possibilities, but not many would have bet on Modise being singled out to receive the nation's highest honour. Modise was too ill to be shown in pictures of the award ceremony, depicting ministers 'in virtual vigil pose'[88] around the bed of 'Bra Joe' – gangster, killer, car thief, bank robber, drug dealer, arms trader, military commander, police informer, businessman, Defence Minister, decorated national hero and bon viveur.

Mbeki's largesse was to go well beyond the grave. In 2005 the government's decision to join the seven European countries producing the A400M transport – plus its earlier decision to buy Airbuses for SAA – pushed huge offset contracts the way of the state-owned Denel and the private company, Aerosud. This gave the government a dominant influence in Aerosud's BEE deal which followed – indeed, the details were worked out in the presidential office. South Africa's ambassador to the Netherlands, Hlengiwe Mkhize – using unspecified resources – acquired 8 per cent of Aerosud while Phatisma Aviation acquired 20 per cent from the state Industrial Development Corporation (IDC). Phatisma was majority-owned by Herman Mashaba, whose main qualification for making the next generation of large passenger and military aircraft was that he had made money out of his Black Like Me cosmetics firm. He was the best qualified of the lot.

But what really caught the eye was that other Phatisma shareholders included Mbeki's adviser Titus Mafolo and foreign affairs spokesman Ronnie Mamoepa, who had previously worked in the President's office. Most remarkable of all, Jackie Sedibe, Joe's widow, was made non-executive chairperson of Aerosud, although no one pretended she knew anything about aviation. All the participants were tight-lipped about the deal and even though the IDC was a public entity the price which Phatisma paid for its shares was kept secret.[89] Such high-level patronage for the widow of an ANC leader was unprecedented: not even Adelaide Tambo, widow of Mbeki's great mentor, had been shown such favour.

In the week that Jackie Sedibe got her reward and numerous other ANC leaders became instant multi-millionaires as a result of a series of BEE deals, the *Mail and Guardian* led with the headline 'Another Great Week for the Wa-Benzi'. Such cynicism over the construction of a crony capitalist society in the name of the Freedom Charter was now inevitable. Joe Modise may have been the key forerunner but, despite his belated award, his name was mentioned with disgust, if at all.

But Joe Modise was not to sleep easy. The scandal over the arms deal simply refused to die – indeed, the questions about it increased with time. Joe had also simply left his previous wife, Eva Modise, and lived with Jackie Sedibe, his 'customary wife', without ever bothering to regularize matters. Eva fought hard for her full share of his assets and by 2006 had won to the point where she insisted that Modise's remains be disinterred and reburied where she wanted them to be.[90]

As in *Macbeth*, it was neither the assassin's cronies nor the man who had seized the crown who captured the imagination but the ghost of the man murdered to make way for it all. When President De Gaulle was finally disavowed by a referendum on regional reform in 1969 he immediately resigned as President. At his last cabinet meeting passionate younger Gaullists tried to dissuade him but he was having none of it. 'It's true, the French don't want De Gaulle any more. But the myth, you will see the myth grow. [You watch], thirty years from now!'[91] And so it was to be. The same clearly applied to Chris Hani. His myth grew from year to year as the one man who stood by his principles, who, it was assumed, would have thrown the crony capitalists out of the movement like Christ throwing the merchants out of the temple. His myth had a life of its own and that myth was now fused with the sense of the ANC's lost revolutionary purity. It is this which lends such passion to the great annual commemoration of his death on 10 April every year and to the demands for a fresh inquiry into the circumstances of his murder. Sometimes there is an attempt to connect the murder to the CIA or MI5. Few seem willing to look at the far more obvious figure of Joe Modise. But equally the rumours that Mbeki was somehow involved in the plot never cease, though no evidence is ever adduced. The mere mention that such rumours existed caused the banning of an SABC documentary about Mbeki in 2006, while the revelation that Jacob Zuma had visited Clive Derby-Lewis in jail in 2005 to enquire further about the Hani assassination was viewed with rage by Mbeki.

Hani might not have lived up to the myth which now surrounds him. His friend Tokyo Sexwale is a prince of the crony capitalists, after all, and in diamonds, of all things (few industries have attracted worse publicity than the African diamond trade). But it no longer matters how Hani might have turned out. When he was gunned down in a dusty street in Boksburg, Hani's death resembled many another township killing. What matters is that the echo of the shots that downed him has never died away.

3
The Mandela Presidency I: 1994–1996

A party which is not afraid of letting culture, business and welfare go to ruin completely can be omnipotent for a while. Jakob Burckhardt

The ANC's election manifesto in 1994 had consisted essentially of its Reconstruction and Development Programme. The RDP, originally an attempt by Cosatu to give a satisfactorily left-wing slant to the ANC's programme, had been through many drafts and emerged as a vast, unbudgeted wish list. The ANC promised, *inter alia*, to build one million houses in five years, redistribute 30 per cent of the land in the same time, provide ten years of free compulsory education and create between two and five million jobs in ten years. Hence the main campaign poster: 'Vote ANC: Jobs, Jobs, Jobs.' Electorally it was unnecessary – for several years beforehand polls had shown the ANC taking a steady 60–65 per cent of the vote (it got 62.7 per cent).[1] Not a single RDP target was achieved and the programme was ditched two years later. It had by then achieved Holy Grail status, so the pretence was maintained that it somehow continued into the afterlife.

The ANC had been in exile for a generation, endlessly theorizing about 'the seizure of power' and what would follow. In the 1980s and 1990s foreign donors poured money into conferences and seminars about 'post-apartheid South Africa'. There was also much 'scenario planning'. Despite all this, the ANC was completely unprepared for power. Half the movement was still dreaming millenarian dreams about building 'East Germany in Africa'. Even the few ANC sophisticates seemed to have little clue about the country they were about to inherit. Many had been so long in exile that they literally did not know their way round, had not even visited large parts of the country they were about to start governing.

In 1989 I had called at the ANC offices in London and gone to tea with Frene Ginwala, one of the shrewdest brains in the ANC. I put it to her that the ANC would soon find itself in power and that it would then find many continuities with the old white government. It would, for example, be just as keen as the Nats to have a high gold price. 'You're completely wrong,' I was told. 'We've had a party commission on that question and it's been decided that mining will play a much smaller role.' There was no point in arguing. The party commission was more real than the protean realities of South Africa's economic structure. Similarly, during the 1994 election I spoke to Alec Erwin, one of the ANC's key economic thinkers. He was clearly taken by surprise by my suggestion that the ANC would face a sharp devaluation of the rand, which could actually be to its advantage. More remarkable still, it emerged that he did not understand the concept of shareholder equity. He confidently told me that the government would soon construct a large number of state-owned steel mills. This was the shape of things to come. It took no special prescience to realize that mining would be as important as ever and that there would be no state-owned steel mills. But it was a little worrying that even the ANC's best brains were living in wonderland.

So the new ANC government missed many chances because it did not recognize what they were. It came to power at a time when a major assault on the Aids problem would have yielded significant results. Chris Hani alone seems to have understood this. With his death, no attempt was made. Similarly, it was vital to achieve a new trade relationship with the EU, which accounted for two-thirds of South Africa's trade. If the ANC had done its homework, Mandela, enjoying unparalleled international goodwill, would have gone straight from his inauguration to Europe, demanded such a deal and probably got it. But the homework had simply not been done. Instead, one EU leader after another – François Mitterrand of France was the first and most cynical – came out to pose with Mandela and then returned home to block any such trade deal. Mandela and South Africa at large fell for this. Soon any ambitious pop group, let alone political leader, was able to fly out and get their photo opportunity with Mandela. South Africa was still racked by political violence, there was a huge crime wave, a third of the populace was unemployed and a terrifying plague was taking the country by the throat. But the President was busy posing with the Spice Girls or Jesse

Jackson, telling the Irish or the Israelis how they should copy the South African miracle, and helping Bill Clinton get through his Monica Lewinsky moment.

Already, things were in a fair mess. Mandela firmly blocked any proper inquiry into the Shell House shootings, in which Zulu activists had been mown down by gunfire from ANC gunmen. There was no official ANC response to the revelation that six Zulus had been held and tortured in a lift cage inside the ANC headquarters.[2] A leaked ANC report revealed that Winnie Mandela, the President's ex-wife, had stolen large sums from the ANC Social Welfare Department and had taken kickbacks on a farm bought for returning exiles. She refused to attend an inquiry into the matter headed by Oliver Tambo and got clean away with it.[3] Benazir Bhutto, daughter of the executed Pakistani President and a guest at Mandela's inauguration, had also given Winnie $100,000 for the ANC Women's League, which later said it had never received it. (Benazir doubtless understood – she had stolen the money in the first place.) In addition, Mandela tended to make up policy as he went along. He was repeatedly disavowed by the ANC National Executive (NEC) where Thabo Mbeki could generally marshal a majority to overthrow Mandela decisions he did not like.

PUTTING TOGETHER A GOVERNMENT

On election eve, without consulting his colleagues, Mandela announced that if necessary defence spending would be cut to fund the RDP (said by the ANC to cost R39 billion, by Cosatu to cost up to R90 billion). Joe Modise, already deep in discussion with British Aerospace, was visibly upset. But he did not need to worry: Mandela quickly discovered that he lacked power even to pick 'his' government. He offered cabinet posts to the PAC, Azapo and the Freedom Front leader, Constand Viljoen, but all such notions were thrown out by Mbeki and the NEC. Mandela had also promised De Klerk that the Nats would have a security ministry (defence, police or prisons) but this too was thrown out.[4] Mandela appointed his prison companion Ahmed Kathrada to the cabinet – but Mbeki and the NEC objected ('too many Indians'), so the appointment was rescinded.

For the progressives who read the *Mail and Guardian*,[5] the new cabinet was a shock. The leaders of the UDF who had fought the anti-apartheid battle within the country (the so-called 'inxiles') had precious few positions. Jay Naidoo, the former Cosatu leader, was responsible for the RDP – but was only a Minister without Portfolio. Two of the key UDF leaders, Terror Lekota[6] and Popo Molefe, were pushed out into the provinces, becoming premiers of the Free State and the North West respectively. Mandela had said that the choice of the ANC deputy president would be his alone and that five candidates 'stand head and shoulders above everyone else': Mbeki, Ramaphosa, Mohammed Valli Moosa, Mac Maharaj and Slovo.[7] In practice his preferences were swept aside. Slovo was Minister of Housing, but he was dying of cancer. Ramaphosa was not in the cabinet at all. Valli Moosa was only a deputy minister. Maharaj was initially given no post and then only the Ministry of Transport. Mbeki was the only serious candidate.

Room had to be found for some IFP and Nat ministers, for the constitution required that there be a government of national unity for the first five years, but ANC exiles dominated. Several appointments raised eyebrows: Modise at Defence; Alfred Nzo as Foreign Minister, for Nzo had been judged utterly incompetent as ANC secretary-general; Sibusiso Bengu, the disastrous vice-chancellor of Fort Hare University, at Education; Stella Sigcau, an old and very dubious bantustan politician, at Public Enterprises; and, despite Mandela's strong disavowal, Winnie Mandela as deputy Minister for Arts and Culture.

The key was, of course, Mbeki who had backed Modise, Nzo and Winnie. Nzo had never forgiven Ramaphosa for ousting him as secretary-general, nor had Winnie forgiven him for his role on the UDF's Winnie Mandela Crisis Committee after her gang of thugs (the 'football team') had murdered Stompie Sepei. Nzo's incompetence and tendency to sleep on the job appealed to Mbeki, who intended running foreign policy himself via his trusted client, Aziz Pahad, now deputy Minister for Foreign Affairs. To the astonishment of those with cabinet experience, like De Klerk and the IFP leader, Mangosuthu Buthelezi, Mbeki, not Mandela, chaired cabinet meetings and Mandela often left before the end of the meeting. Mbeki was thus the real head of government, though Mandela blithely continued to announce policies of his own. In his 100 Days Plan, announced shortly after his inauguration, Mandela had declared that all children under 6, and their mothers, were to receive free medical care, though there was no advance planning for this and no extra money or even warning was given to clinics and hospitals. The result was chaos, as huge numbers of mothers and children swamped the available facilities. Similarly, Kader Asmal, the Minister for Water Affairs, eager for favourable publicity, had promised clean water for all within three years,[8] an obviously impossible target.

Mandela had appointed Jakes Gerwel, the former head of the University of the Western Cape, as director-general of his office and thus also cabinet secretary and he had insisted on bringing his old Robben Island companion Kathy Kathrada into his office as a political adviser, saying, 'Kathy is the one chap who holds up an honest mirror to me.' So Mbeki tried to control Mandela's office by putting into it Parks Mankahlana as press secretary and his protégé, Joel Netshitenzhe, as Mandela's speechwriter, both of whom reported to Mbeki and largely controlled Mandela's public utterances. Netshitenzhe, though self-effacing, was the real power behind the throne. The long-time editor of the ANC journal, *Mayibuye* (in exile he was known as Peter Mayibuye), he was, like Mbeki, a graduate of the University of Sussex and the Lenin School in Moscow. Mbeki's reliance on him was reflected in the fact that Netshitenzhe was the only member of the eighteen-member inner cabinet, the ANC National Working Party (soon to become the National Working Committee (NWC)), who was neither an MP nor an elected ANC official.[9] Once Mbeki had lit upon Netshitenzhe in exile he had carefully propelled him along the same educational road that he had himself taken, as if consciously building his own understudy.

Mandela was content to sit back and listen in cabinet, allowing Mbeki and De Klerk to chair the important committees. He intervened in discussions only in three areas, national unity, the stability of the state and RDP delivery. This last meant that, to Mbeki's extreme irritation, he was frequently to be found talking to the RDP Minister, Jay Naidoo, who, as a former union leader, was prone both to listen to the grass roots and to adopt a certain independence. Both habits made him unwelcome to Mbeki. From an early stage the press carried inspired reports that Naidoo's days were numbered.[10]

Mbeki's years in exile had taught him that in the ANC one could seldom safely delegate: anything you did not do yourself did not get done. This had turned him into something of a control freak and a micro-manager but he could never be sure that Mandela would not escape from his control. For a start, Mandela's marriage with Winnie had broken down as soon as he was out of jail. The old man was lonely and prone to get up early: one would see him striding along in the early hours near his Johannesburg house. And he loved the telephone. Cabinet ministers became wearily familiar with his 5 a.m. calls. There was no controlling that, nor his frequent telephone calls to foreign dignitaries, nor his ad lib comments, let alone what he might get up to on foreign trips.

There was a striking discordance between what Mandela and Mbeki said. Mandela spoke of how place names should be changed only 'with great care, through consensus' and reminded his voters that he was not just a President of blacks 'but a President of whites as well, and they expect certain standards'. He went out of his way to praise ex-President P. W. Botha, saying that Botha had been the real forerunner of negotiations and they had a warm relationship based on friendly telephone chats. Such sentiments could never be uttered by Mbeki, who was angrily insecure about white talk of slipping standards. Similarly, it was impossible to imagine Mbeki telling Parliament, as Mandela did, that

> Whites in this country have a particular obligation. You have the knowledge, you have skills, you have expertise. We cannot build this country without that knowledge, those skills, that expertise. And we want you to take the leadership in building a new South Africa. We do not regard it as correct that the majority should oppress the minority. Loyal opposition is the essence of democracy ... We are very much alive to the danger of arrogance and being conceited ... I am relieved that the ANC did not reach a two-thirds majority.[11]

Mandela went out of his way to apologize for the government's blunders, something which Mbeki, with the imagined chorus of 'Africans can't govern' always ringing in his ears, was utterly unwilling to do.

THE EMERGENCE OF MBEKI AS RACIAL NATIONALIST

Mbeki's obsession with race and racism had become increasingly obvious. Even as he sat in the multi-racial government of national unity he was busy drafting a five-year strategic plan for the ANC which 'identifies [white] racism as the biggest threat to lasting change' and which suggested that 'counter-revolutionary structures' were intent on placing obstacles in the government's way. It warned that the 'previous regime's counter-insurgency forces still exist, capable of provoking hostile mass action activities, assassinations and disinformation campaigns'. There was, he asserted, a fifth column within the ANC, 'those forces within our ranks which, having draped themselves in the cloak of radicalism, act to discredit and weaken the government'. Moreover, the Opposition was bent on derailing the ANC by exploiting the white-owned mass media, which was itself 'driven by fear of a truly non-racial order because of its concern to preserve its own racial status'.[12] Accordingly, the ANC had to display complete unity and straightforwardly advance black interests through affirmative action, aid to black business and so on.

It was, in effect, a separate manifesto, opposed in tone and substance to Mandela's rainbow-nation inclusiveness. Mbeki's slogans were quickly taken up by his allies such as Bulelani Ngcuka, the ANC chief whip in the Senate. Ngcuka bitterly protested that there were still too many whites in leading positions and implicitly criticized Mandela for neglecting 'his own constituency'.[13] Similarly, Peter Mokaba, a frequent cat's-paw for Mbeki, insisted that no one should be employed in the public service who could not speak at least three South African languages, a criterion intended to exclude whites.[14] Soon there were bitter accusations by ANC MPs that Joe Slovo, Kader Asmal, Dullah Omar, Trevor Manuel and Derek Hanekom (that is, the non-African ministers) were employing far too many whites, Coloureds and Indians,[15] and Tony Yengeni, another Mbeki supporter, insisted that 'affirmative action is applied equally by every Ministry'.

Several Mbeki clients – most obviously Mokaba – were used as virtual rottweilers against Ramaphosa. Ramaphosa had humiliated Mokaba by coming down hard against his continued use of the 'Kill the Boer, Kill the Farmer' slogan, so there was no love lost. But in addition Mbeki enjoyed the patronage of Sol Kerzner and used this to get Kerzner to fund Mokaba's National Tourism Forum. Mokaba pillaged these funds so that by January 1995 the Forum's books were in a hopeless mess.[16] It later emerged that in addition to his MP's salary Mokaba had taken another R400,000 p.a. from the Forum.[17] By then, however, and in part due to Mokaba's agitation, Ramaphosa had been dealt the *coup de grâce*. Mbeki was a past master of this sort of patronage play. Ramaphosa, like other UDF veterans, was simply unfamiliar with this style of politics. They were sitting ducks for Mbeki.

Mbeki's emergence as a racial nationalist working constantly to mobilize blacks against an imagined white threat came as a shock to the many whites who had seen him as a suave, cosmopolitan sophisticate. Gavin Evans was only one of many who had seen a different side of Mbeki in exile. Mbeki, he realized, 'always had something in reserve and was only revealing part of his hand . . . behind that genial half-smile was a different agenda – perhaps just a throbbing personal ambition'. Then he met people who had worked under Mbeki. One said: 'The thing about Thabo is he could put a knife in your back and you'd have no idea you'd been stabbed until you saw the point coming out of the front, and you'd never guess who'd done it. The word "evil" is not one I like to use but in Thabo's case . . .'[18] In exile, Mbeki had been seen as extremely calculating and determined, above all, to hide his own emotions. I remember a debate in the Anti-Apartheid Movement where the ANC journalist Ruth First had fallen foul of the party hierarchy for openly mentioning Joshua Nkomo's undoubted corruption. The debate to condemn her raged for hours. Mbeki sat in the front row but never by any gesture or facial expression could one guess which way his sympathies lay, though in the end he joined in the general condemnation. Those aware of his reputation in exile were surprised to hear the early enthusiasm of many white South Africans for Mbeki's open-hearted charm.

Returning to South Africa, Mbeki had little popular support and found all the major bases covered. Hani and Slovo controlled the SACP and MK. The trade unions were a world to themselves. Ramaphosa had taken over the ANC organization and Mandela stood for the non-racial traditions of the Freedom Charter. The only element unrepresented was the racial nationalism previously championed by the PAC, Azapo, the Black Consciousness movement and many bantustan politicians. Mbeki moved quickly to make that base his own. The only possible threat to ANC rule lay in divisions within the African bloc – and what better way to unite that bloc than to seek a fresh racial polarization of the electorate by warning of threats from white plots, the return of apartheid and from a mysterious but ubiquitous 'third force'?

This worked. It was so easy to translate racial nationalism into immediate demands for jobs, for money and even just for psychological revenge. Even those within the ANC who clung to the non-racial emphasis of the Freedom Charter did not find it politic to challenge this new racial nationalism, which was clearly popular. Everywhere the talk was of the urgent need for 'transformation', which meant replacing all non-Africans with Africans or, at the very least, with Indians and Coloureds. Ministers, indeed, the heads of all public institutions, made it clear that their chief objective was not so much the implementation of this or that policy in society at large, but the 'transformation' of their own workforce. Otherwise – and despite having for so long demanded the right to run the country – ANC ministers seemed little concerned with doing so. When not busy with clearing 'apartheid-era bureaucrats' from their ministries, ministers were frequently abroad, sunning themselves in the general admiration for the 'South African miracle', offering advice on how others could learn from South Africa's example, or just general 'fact-finding' and 'networking'. When asked about their future plans they would talk about the challenges ahead: bringing about a 'people-driven RDP', the staging of the 1995 rugby World Cup, the 1996 African Cup of Nations football finals, the fortieth anniversary of the Freedom Charter and the bid for the 2004 Olympics. The government was drunk on symbolism but short on work.

There were early warning signs. In October 1994 it was reported that major donor countries were upset because they had put R10 billion in aid on the table and the government was simply not using it.[19] The Japanese ambassador announced that three months earlier he had offered aid of R1.4 billion and simply could not get a response from the government. Pressed, Jay Naidoo angrily declared that, 'South Africa will set its own stringent conditions for the acceptance of any aid packages.'[20] Under this pressure, the ministries of Education, Defence, Police, Civil Service and Public Enterprises all declared that they were finding it difficult to implement their programmes. The response of the National Working Committee was to set up an intelligence committee to probe 'sabotage' within those ministries.[21]

THE BLOEMFONTEIN PARTY CONFERENCE, DECEMBER 1994

Government affairs received scant attention compared to the furious jockeying for position within the ANC itself, with all attention concentrated on the 49th party conference to be held at Bloemfontein in

December 1994. Walter Sisulu had only reluctantly accepted the post of Deputy President in 1991 to avoid a Hani vs. Mbeki fight: now he was adamant about stepping down. The ANC was also still vague about its economic strategy and the country looked expectantly to its first conference in power to chart the way ahead. In fact, the party was in a mess and Ramaphosa, the secretary-general, faced an unenviable task. During the election the party had had 4,500 paid workers. Most now had to be made redundant. The party had exercised few controls on election spending and faced a debt of R70 million. Such spending had helped the party win the elections but the Western Cape ANC leader Allan Boesak had incurred a R1 million debt while losing his province to the Nats, so his position was now under threat.[22]

Ramaphosa not only had to cleanse the Augean stables within the ANC but had also been elected president of the Constituent Assembly with the job of finalizing the constitution. There was still talk of his becoming chairman of the ANC parliamentary caucus or even ANC deputy president but Ramaphosa himself made it clear that he wanted to get out of politics altogether and go into business. He had been thoroughly worsted by Mbeki and his thankless double load was killing him. But Mbeki realized that for the man who had come second on the ANC list to drop out of politics would seem a sign of disaffection, with the blame laid at his own door. Accordingly he persuaded Mandela that Ramaphosa should not be allowed to quit. Publicly, he announced that 'Ramaphosa's deployment has not been resolved . . . We have to continue looking at the question of that deployment.'[23]

This was the first usage of the term 'deployment' in the post-election ANC. It was Mbeki's way of insisting that the tight Leninist discipline of the exile ANC still applied. In exile almost every aspect of a cadre's life had been decided by the party – where they should go, what job or course they should do, whether and to whom they could get married, and so on.

Another concern was the SACP. Now that he was no longer on the SACP politburo Mbeki was also not sure he could control what the party got up to. The fact that two of its leading cadres, Jeremy Cronin and Cheryl Carolus, had not accepted positions on the ANC parliamentary list suggested that the party wanted them to retain their freedom of action (which might be constrained by the ANC whip) and devote themselves to building the organization.

A clear sign that something major was afoot in the SACP had been its suspension of Harry Gwala in June 1994. Hani's death in 1993 had left Gwala as the dominant individual within the SACP, with a large personal following. He was a self-declared Stalinist and also a murderer on a large scale. He openly boasted of killing IFP opponents in KwaZulu-Natal – he had run hit squads since 1991 and made no secret of it – and it was common knowledge that not a few of his opponents within the KwaZulu-Natal ANC had also met sudden and violent deaths. Gwala's suspension was a sign that this Wild West era was over and that the path was being cleared for a new leadership. Cronin attempted to deny that the suspension had anything to do with Gwala's plots to kill Jacob Zuma, Ben Martin or Blade Nzimande (who was to become the new SACP leader) but this was rather spoilt by Gwala's own admission that party interrogators had discussed all these death plots with him.[24] It was a sign of the times that controlling a multiple murderer was regarded as simply a matter for SACP in-house tidying up.

The SACP had gone along with Gwala to this point, even supplying him with his murder weapons, but he was an embarrassment to the new guard now taking over. Mbeki's office displayed a lively suspicion of Cronin and Carolus for being 'too sympathetic' to trade union mass action.[25] An anonymous document, 'Unmandated Responses', was critical of Cronin and Carolus and called for complete unity behind the government. Mbeki was believed to be the author.[26]

Mbeki also did a deal with Boesak, who resigned the Western Cape ANC leadership for a promised diplomatic job. Sure enough, Alfred Nzo appointed Boesak as ambassador to the UN in Geneva, rejecting the numerous reports that Boesak had misappropriated funds and insisting that all these accusations had been thoroughly examined and found to be without substance.[27] By throwing this protective veil over his misdemeanours, Mbeki turned Boesak into yet another client.

But Danchurch, the Danish group funding Boesak's Foundation for Peace and Justice (FPJ), had done its homework and was in a state of righteous Protestant rage. Boesak had quietly siphoned off a great deal of their money to operate a whole portfolio of businesses, including a hotel in the Eastern Cape. Using his position as a trustee of the Equal Opportunities Foundation, Boesak got the Foundation to give the FPJ R500,000. Boesak had also got the FPJ to set up a Children's Trust Fund (CTF) which, amazingly, his trustees – including Archbishop

Desmond Tutu and the Black Sash leader, Mary Burton – allowed him to run for years without any audit or financial statement. Most remarkable of all, they had done nothing when in 1992 Boesak had transferred R447,112 back from the CTF to the FPJ to pay for 'staff loans', a sure signal that the CTF was merely a slush fund. Boesak had diverted 'soft' money that came his way – such as Paul Simon's R423,000 from the *Graceland* tour – into the CTF and the poor children it was intended for had seldom benefited.

Boesak had relieved many other donors of large sums – Coca-Cola, the German Otto Benecke Fund, Warner Lambert, BP, the Dutch government and the Swedish development agency SIDA – but he was a master at showing every donor the same project, so that all believed they had funded it. When the balloon went up, most donors preferred just to walk away. Danchurch alone was determined to pursue the case of the R2.7 million it had donated. Boesak went through a great show of selling off his upmarket Constantia house, as if to show poverty – in fact it was mortgaged to the hilt – and denounced Danchurch for its 'arrogance'.[28] He doubtless felt secure enough, for he had also used FPJ money to make donations to a whole raft of ANC politicians in the Western Cape, including Senator Christmas Tinto and his successor as provincial ANC boss, Chris Nissen.[29] But Danchurch, infuriated at Boesak's cleverness in hiding his crimes and at his use of threats and racial slurs against them,[30] pressed doggedly ahead with their case. Mbeki even flew to Germany to try to talk Danchurch out of their action, but to no avail.[31] Mbeki insisted that Boesak 'did not misuse funds'[32] – this was enough to keep Boesak on side for the vital Bloemfontein conference – but he could not be saved. Mbeki gave Mandela the unpleasant job of telling Boesak that he could not, after all, go to Geneva.[33]

Mandela, now one of the world's best-loved figures, seemed certain to dominate the Bloemfontein conference. Ramaphosa's supporters, including Slovo and the SACP,[34] could hardly believe that the man who had negotiated the new constitution and managed the ANC's election triumph was really going to be squeezed out. They sought desperately to push Ramaphosa for the ANC deputy presidency or at least to block Mbeki by persuading Sisulu to stay on, but in vain.

In fact Mbeki dominated the conference and both Mandela and Ramaphosa were humiliated. Mbeki had chosen the conference theme, 'From

Resistance to Reconstruction and Nation-Building', and authored the key strategy document with the same title. Mbeki sought to undermine Mandela by arguing that his concessions to the whites could only be at the expense of blacks. His paper identified 'the main motive forces of democratic transformation' as the black working class, the black rural poor and a 'significant section of the black middle strata'. Accordingly, the overwhelming need was for black unity.[35] On the eve of the conference a key (and doubtless inspired) article appeared in the Black Consciousness magazine *Tribute*, accusing all the non-African ANC cabinet ministers of appointing only non-Africans to their ministries. Ramaphosa was also vilified for having made too many concessions to the whites during the constitutional negotiations and for having marginalized Africans in his reorganization of the ANC. The only sound figure was Thabo Mbeki with his commitment to 'the all-round political, economic and social emancipation and upliftment of the black majority'.[36]

Mbeki easily carried the conference with him and was elected unopposed as the new ANC deputy president, thus formally anointing him as Mandela's successor. Ramaphosa, sick at heart, asked Mandela for a cabinet post – refused on the grounds that it would mean a war with Mbeki – and then said he wanted to resign and go into business instead. This was also refused. Ultimately Ramaphosa gave way and accepted the secretary-generalship again after a very firm lecture from Mandela. Jacob Zuma and Henry Makgothi – both Mbeki nominees – were easily elected as national chairman and treasurer-general respectively, even though Makgothi was little known and the party rules forbidding the holding of multiple posts should have ruled out Zuma, who was already chairman of the KwaZulu-Natal ANC.

Mandela had strenuously objected to all the key positions going to Africans and had launched a 'Mandela Plan' to balance off the ethnic groups by bringing the likes of Slovo, Asmal and Maharaj into the leadership team. Mbeki, who had hand-picked his list, was well aware that neither Slovo nor Maharaj trusted him an inch. Accordingly Mandela's plan was labelled 'the Indian Option' and roundly defeated.[37]

Mandela, alarmed at the conference mood of radical populism, strove hard to be reasonable. To those who talked of sweeping away the IFP leader, Chief Buthelezi, he argued that the IFP had won the election in KwaZulu-Natal fair and square. He pleaded for fiscal discipline, insisted that privatization was an economic necessity, and appealed for the payment of township rates and rents as a matter of 'the nation's morality'. His speech was far too moderate for Mbeki, who quickly briefed the press that Mandela had missed out some key points in his text (which, of course, Mbeki had written) such as the accusation that De Klerk had waged a 'low intensity conflict against black people' in 1992–3, together with expressions of all-out solidarity with Cuba and Palestine.[38] Unsurprisingly, Mandela declared that he would step down as President in 1999, the first moment possible.

Why did Mandela not resist Mbeki? First, Mbeki was the heir apparent of his old comrade, Oliver Tambo. Secondly, there was now no real counterweight to Mbeki within the top echelons of the ANC. Tambo had died in April 1993. Sisulu had retired. Hani was dead, Ramaphosa pushed out. Joe Slovo might have been an alternative voice but he was white, had cancer and was rapidly fading; he died in January 1995. The only other voices challenging Mbeki – Winnie Mandela, Bantu Holomisa and Mathews Phosa – were all outside the top leadership. Moreover, Mbeki's exile group commanded a clear majority within the NEC and its inner core, the NWC, which meant that one could not go against Mbeki without threatening ANC unity, something Mandela would never do. In any case, Mandela was old, knew nothing of economics or government and respected Mbeki's expertise. Everything conspired to put him in Mbeki's hands.

There was more than a hint of King Lear about the ANC's ageing leader. When I had met one of his comrades who had been released from Robben Island ahead of Mandela, he told me: 'I worry what will happen when he comes out. His thought processes are slow and deliberate and there is something very simple and childlike about him. His moral authority, the strength of his principles and his generosity of spirit are all derived from that simplicity. But he will be easily manipulated by those who are quicker, more subtle and more sophisticated.'[39] And so it was. The media lavished praise upon him and he moved around the country and indeed the world in a bubble of adulation. He was seen as the central figure of South Africa's life and politics but this was mainly pretence. As Jean Lacouture said of De Gaulle in 1965–8, 'He was like the ageing captain of a football team. The ball was at his feet and at every stage he was the dominating player on the pitch. And yet the game itself escaped him.' This was made plain again when De Klerk led the

Nats out of government, very much against Mandela's wishes. His continued pleas to whites not to emigrate were equally disregarded. De Klerk's exit left six ministerial vacancies up for grabs. Given the favour with which Mandela regarded Cheryl Carolus, she was widely expected to get one of them. But she was no favourite of Mbeki's and this was what counted.

For Mbeki the only fly in the ointment at the Bloemfontein conference was Carolus's election as deputy secretary-general against Mbeki's nominee, Sankie Mthembi-Nkondo. The SACP, always crucial to the ANC's organization, had insisted on having one of its own at the heart of the apparatus. But privatization sailed through the conference without demur, as Mbeki had hoped. With its old socialist options no longer on the menu the conference vented itself instead in Africanist demands for affirmative action and black empowerment. Mthembi-Nkondo, one of several younger ANC women described as being 'very close' to Mbeki, was brought into the leadership anyway, replacing the ailing Slovo as Minister of Housing.

Bantu Holomisa, the former Transkei president, topped the poll for the NEC, the ANC's only true opinion gauge. Several of the whites and Indians favoured by Mandela also came near the top, thus rather disproving Mbeki's Africanist argument: Maharaj (fourth), Valli Moosa (eighth), Dullah Omar (tenth), Ronnie Kasrils (eleventh) and Slovo (thirteenth). Terror Lekota, the premier of the Free State, came seventh despite the fact that he had just been ejected from his province's ANC chairmanship by an Mbeki-supported faction (led by Pat Matosa and Ace Magashule) for being too conciliatory towards whites.

MANDELA'S SEA OF TROUBLES

Mandela, straight from a bruising conference, faced a mess in all directions. The Boesak case had brought a sharp new focus on corruption. Donors had long complained that contributions to the ANC's main NGO, the Kagiso Trust, fell into a bottomless pit of unaccountability but it was now pointed out that R138 million given to the Association of Ex-Political Prisoners had also gone missing – had in fact been stolen to buy houses and cars for ANC and government officials, make them personal 'loans' and buy several of them small businesses.[40] The collapse of Mokaba's National Tourism Forum revealed a similar tale of looting. In the North West, Rocky Malebane-Metsing, the provincial minister of agriculture, was revealed to have illegally lent R15.5 million to a Jamaican businessman.[41] Lekota had been forced out in the Free State because he had sacked the provincial housing minister for corruption.[42]

There were, too, insistent DP (Democratic Party) and NP demands for a commission of inquiry into the Shell House shootings in 1994 in which 53 had died and 173 had been injured. Despite having a warrant to search Shell House, the police had been denied entry and while the ANC had then handed over 146 weapons to the police, ballistics tests showed that only one of these had had anything to do with the shooting.[43] Quite clearly, any inquiry would be bound to find the ANC guilty of mass murder, with possible life sentences for many of its leading officials. Mbeki accordingly declared that a commission of inquiry would be quite 'improper'[44] but in the end the only way to cut off such demands was for Mandela to put his presidential authority on the line. So he announced that he had personally instructed security personnel to 'defend Shell House if attacked, even if you have to kill people'.[45] Given that this was so out of character and that it had taken well over a year for Mandela to 'reveal' this, few believed him. In effect, he was saying 'if you want to proceed with this line of enquiry you will have to charge me with mass murder', knowing there was no appetite in any quarter for this. It was crude but it worked.

The scandal over the Association of Ex-Political Prisoners also had to be brushed under the carpet. *The Sowetan* revealed that one government official who had stolen from the fund now had four fast food restaurants in Johannesburg, while another owned two chain stores in the Cape. A furious official of the Association, Willie Sekete – himself an MK veteran – announced he was going to expose the embezzlers but it was already obvious that this would do great damage to powerful individuals in the ANC. Sekete was found murdered a few days later.[46] Sekete might usefully have reflected on the fate of several ex-MK soldiers tortured by Modise's men in Quatro, who had returned home after 1990 determined to air the scandal despite the obvious embarrassment it would cause the ANC. One of them, Sipho Phungulwa, was assassinated straight after leaving the ANC office in Mthatha. His companion, Nicholas Dyasop, escaped to tell the tale. After this Quatro victims fell silent. Sekete's assassination also had the desired effect: nothing more was heard of this scandal.

Other matters were less easily dealt with. Boesak was a particular problem. His revelation that he had brokered Malaysian donations of millions of rand to ANC election funds was hurriedly denied by the ANC. The government's response was to rush out a 3-page report by the lawyer, Mojanku Gumbi – commissioned, it was said, by Mandela, though in fact, of course, by Mbeki – which announced that the government legal team she headed had investigated Boesak and concluded that there was no evidence that he had misappropriated funds and, indeed, suggested that Boesak was still owed money by his Foundation for Peace and Justice.[47] The South African Council of Churches had already offered Boesak its 'support, prayers and care'[48] but now there was a concerted government effort to get Boesak off. Mbeki, who had actually commissioned the Gumbi report – she worked in his office and was also described as being very close to him – now declared that while 'Allan must take responsibility for the administrative mess' at the FPJ, the key thing was that 'Boesak has not stolen money'.[49] ANC spokesmen accused the press of a 'witch-hunt' against Boesak, while Mandela declared that Boesak was 'one of the most gifted young men in this country' who 'deserves a very high position'.[50] Meanwhile the President's office urged the Office of Serious Economic Offences to speed up its investigation since 'it is unfair for Dr Boesak to have to wait a lengthy, indeterminate period'.[51]

Boesak, who had already labelled his investigators 'racists', was so emboldened by this (he declared himself 'very thankful and happy that the Lord does not sleep'[52]) that he announced that he was contacting the Danish and Swedish governments to get them to make Danchurch and SIDA (the Swedish state development agency) apologize to him, withdraw their charges and open discussions with him about the 'restoration' now due to him. So scandalous was Danchurch's behaviour, he averred, that he was having it placed on the agenda of the World Council of Churches.[53] Danchurch, which had incontrovertible proof of Boesak's thieving, angrily denounced the Gumbi report as 'preposterous', 'a logical absurdity' and a flagrant attempt to interfere in due legal process. Mandela went on television to support the Gumbi report as 'a good professional investigation'. The accusations against Boesak were, he claimed, 'baseless' and he had harsh words for the bona fides of those who continued to make such allegations.[54] Once again, putting Mandela's moral authority on the line was expected to be the knock-out blow: surely Danchurch and SIDA would back down now? But whereas it was comparatively easy to bully local officials into line, the ANC had not reckoned with the force of enraged Protestant conscience.[55] The charges were not withdrawn. Boesak left for the United States with the case still unresolved.

Most difficult of all for Mandela was the case of his wife, Winnie, deputy Minister for Arts and Culture and head of the ANC Women's League. Mandela's personal animus against his errant wife was already considerable but, as with Boesak, the case was greatly complicated by the fact of her alliance with Mbeki, who tried frantically to stop Mandela sacking her from the government. Mandela was furious at Winnie's open attacks on the government from the left and sternly told her that all ministers had to support the government.[56] Winnie wrote an apology – actually written for her by Mbeki – which Mandela dismissed out of hand.[57] The situation in the Women's League was equally intolerable: virtually the whole top leadership had resigned, citing Winnie's 'undemocratic practices'. Apart from Benazir Bhutto's missing cheque, there was the fact that Winnie had involved the League in a tourism venture with the film star Omar Sharif, from which she alone drew profit[58] – and the fact that she had only secured the presidency of the Women's League because her supporters had used muti (lucky charms) and carried knives and guns.[59] Meanwhile Hazel Crane, an illicit diamond dealer, was funding Winnie on a grand scale, including the gift of a house.[60] Winnie had also not yet answered for the funds missing from the ANC Welfare Department or her failure to pay for the Learjet she had chartered to bring diamonds in from Angola.[61]

Each time Mandela wanted to sack Winnie, Mbeki played the desperate middleman, trying to restrain the President while getting Winnie to comply at least formally. Winnie then announced that she was off to Abidjan to attend a film festival. Mandela forbade it – Mbeki was his messenger[62] – but she went anyway. Mandela wanted to sack her immediately but Mbeki restrained him. While she was away police raided her Soweto house and found quantities of guns and grenades. This brought her hurrying furiously back. She angrily refused to see Mbeki, saying he had been party to the raid on her house. With this her fate was sealed and Mandela duly sacked her.[63] Nearly a year later the government was still trying to retrieve the state-owned BMW and Mercedes she had appropriated on leaving office.

Winnie's sacking caused a storm, for she was still popular in many quarters, and her family, the Madikizelas, were a major force in the Eastern Cape. Bantu Holomisa, a fellow-supporter of the populist left, was upset by her sacking. Annoyed by Mandela's assertions that the Transkei's rulers had stolen billions, he challenged Mandela to prove his allegations which, he said, were odd given that the government had not yet dealt with 'straightforward cases like Sol Kerzner',[64] a reference to the bribes Kerzner had allegedly paid to Kaiser Matanzima and other Transkei politicians in order to get casino rights on the Wild Coast (the Transkei's eastern seaboard). Such talk brought Holomisa into conflict with Mbeki, not only because of Mbeki's links to Kerzner but because Holomisa, Hani's close associate, was now the darling of the Eastern Cape rank and file, his large popular following dwarfing Mbeki's – in Mbeki's home area.[65] Accordingly, Mbeki got the ANC executive to censure Holomisa for criticizing Mandela. When Winnie was sacked Holomisa refused to join the ANC team sent to the Eastern Cape to explain this decision. He was called in by Mandela for a 'stern warning'.[66]

In February 1995 F. W. De Klerk sounded the alarm: many were worried that Mandela, buffeted and exhausted – by affairs of party, not government – would resign long before 1999.[67] But government was foundering too: none of the ANC's promises were being fulfilled. Fewer than a thousand houses were built in its first year. The land redistribution target was quickly abandoned. Sibusiso Bengu, the Minister of Education, had suffered a stroke immediately after taking office and thereafter did little. Free compulsory education never materialized but Bengu launched a disastrous scheme to cut the number of teachers by offering generous retirement packages. These were invariably taken by the best and most experienced teachers, leaving the teaching profession utterly unable to carry out the promised task of educational transformation. The situation at the Health Ministry was even worse, with Dr Nkosasana Dlamini-Zuma driving doctors abroad by the thousand while simply ignoring the Aids crisis. To the amazement of business the government had no economic policy at all. It was pure drift.

THE STRANGE HISTORY OF THE RDP

The RDP, the government's centrepiece, never really got started. Cosatu had put much energy into drafting it and put its old boss Jay Naidoo in charge. Naidoo's main skill lay in populist rhetoric. He charged about the country declaring passionately that the RDP could only succeed through popular participation – if it was 'people-driven' – but there was no way anyone could participate in it. And the RDP, however laudable, had fatal flaws. Such an ambitious programme, requiring the close co-operation of many different ministries, would require the retention of old and experienced civil servants – whereas the ANC had immediately begun winnowing them out and appointing its own. The RDP treated labour simply as a beneficiary of its programmes, making no mention of higher productivity, labour flexibility and so on. Then again, the delivery of improvements on the ground would depend crucially on local government, and no thought had been given to this. The plan mentioned only state spending but in fact its success would depend heavily on the private sector's response. The plan also failed to consider that the more successful South Africa's development was, the greater the wave of illegal immigration it would suck in. And the RDP could not work unless a modicum of law and order was restored and an end made to the culture of non-payment of rates and taxes, which crippled local administration in much of the country.[68]

The civil service was continuously purged until it had been 'transformed' into a virtually all-black body, though, since it was impossible to find enough skilled blacks, many posts were left vacant. Yet for the emergent black middle class the transformation of the public service was regarded as the government's shining success, for it had provided a large number of well-paid jobs for black people. Nothing was said about its concomitant collapse in capability. Meanwhile the various government ministries resented the encroachment of the RDP office and were extremely critical of its often ignorant attempts to intervene. It was soon clear that the RDP lacked business plans or project documents for its proposals – it was simply a large unbudgeted wish list.

Bishop Stanley Mogoba, then leader of the PAC, once told me that he was much troubled by the fact that almost none of the ANC's leaders had what he called a normal married life, by which he meant the happy life-long partnership with the same spouse. 'They have every other possible sort of thing – multiple partners, multiple divorces, marriages which are complete fictions and so on. Sometimes they seem to turn themselves inside out trying to maintain relationships, but very few of them manage to make things work.'[69] The bishop's reflections had a bearing on the RDP, for not long before taking office, the minister, Jay Naidoo, had married a white Canadian, Lucie Page, in a wedding replete with hired Rolls-Royces, which raised many eyebrows in the trade union movement. Ms Page meanwhile continued to report on South African politics for Radio-Canada despite being married to a leading South African politician. Continuously in psychotherapy and states of anxiety and depression, she brought her son from a previous marriage, her mother and her ex-husband to accompany her on her honeymoon with Naidoo. Soon after their marriage they went into joint therapy. Naidoo was, she reveals, wholly unprepared for the RDP's challenge and would pine for the 'good times': 'I miss the times that we chanted slogans in the street. It's much easier than building a country.'[70] Those who only listened to Naidoo's rhetoric about a 'people-driven RDP' would have been surprised if they had known he was in such a state of depression over his job as to require anti-depressants and continuous psychotherapy. The problem, he decided, was that his job required him 'to do a hundred and eighty degree turn with a country that has been drifting in the same direction for three hundred and fifty years'.[71] His listeners would have been more surprised had they known that Naidoo had promised his wife that he would soon emigrate to Quebec with her,[72] though whether he ever really meant this seems doubtful. Before long Lucie had gone back to Canada, taking Jay's children with her, but she failed to get him to make more than lightning visits there. Once he swapped the RDP for the Ministry of Posts and Telecommunications his depression lifted and, much against her will, Lucie returned to South Africa.

Naidoo's RDP career was a classic case of 'beware of getting what you wish'. Of the funds allocated to the RDP for 1994–5 only 55 per cent were actually spent.[73] The government's housing record in its first year[74] compared poorly with Verwoerd's. In any case, the RDP's drafters had simply ignored the fact that the budget deficit was already running at 9.5 per cent of GDP, that the state's debt was R254 billion and that interest payments were R50 billion a year. A poll in early 1995 found that 74 per cent of business executives had 'no faith in the RDP'.[75] Above all, the ANC was wholly unprepared to govern. Ministers, consumed by ANC politicking and enjoying the perks of office – luxurious foreign travel above all – behaved as if the country and economy simply ran themselves. Mandela had filled the Trade and Industry Ministry by asking round the table who was a good economist. Trevor Manuel had put up his hand and got appointed but later admitted that he had misheard; 'I thought Madiba wanted to know who among us was a good communist.'[76] In fact Manuel became a far better than average minister. Unusually, he worked hard and listened to his civil servants.

THE DISPUTE OVER ECONOMIC STRATEGY

The general sense of drift was unmistakable and investors sold the rand, which steadily fell in value. Business became increasingly concerned and, partly out of a desire to help, began to devise its own economic strategy. Mandela, after all, had admitted that he 'hadn't a clue about economics': he had made his contribution by reversing early ANC pledges of nationalization. On 1 March 1996 the South African Foundation, representing the fifty biggest companies, unveiled its 'Growth for All' plan. It advocated leaner government, anti-crime strategies, export promotion, a determined privatization drive and a dual labour market. The only solution to South Africa's mountainous unemployment, it argued, was to have a much more flexible labour market for the legions of unskilled workers.

Business expected opposition from Cosatu but was shaken by the fury of the ANC reaction. Even many years later Alan Hirsch, chief director of economic policy in the Mbeki presidency, was still full of anger at Growth for All: it was 'an analytical and political error',[77] it was 'clumsily composed' with 'brutal frankness' and it was 'non-strategically dumped into the public arena'[78] (that is, it was published). Yet it was a perfectly conventional set of prescriptions, based mainly on IMF data, and it was transparently well intentioned.

In fact business had unwittingly hit several bull's-eyes. Tito Mboweni, the Minister of Labour, had initially aimed to reach a compromise between labour and business but had completely surrendered to Cosatu. The resulting labour laws greatly increased the costs and difficulties of employment and led employers to shed labour wherever they could. But Mbeki was hypersensitive – and he wanted control, while business was saying that government should slim down, deregulate, privatize, that is, give up some control. This theme was to recur constantly. Whenever the ANC faced a choice between higher economic growth and strengthening control, it unhesitatingly chose the latter. Cumulatively, this preference was to be a large cause of unemployment. Moreover, Growth for All saw business taking a policy initiative, tantamount in Mbeki's eyes to suggesting that the ANC was unable to govern, or anyway was not governing. This was utterly impermissible. In his view the ANC had to exercise complete hegemony, with its leadership in all spheres acknowledged by all social groups. Business must, like everyone else, realize that the ANC was the only authority now and act accordingly.

But business had also unwittingly intervened in a private conversation. Ever since De Klerk had legalized the ANC and SACP in 1990 their leading lights had been locked in frantic and secret discussions about how to proceed. Although Mbeki had taken a sabbatical from the SACP, he had been a senior politburo member and his closest advisers, Essop and Aziz Pahad and Joel Netshitenzhe, were all equally dedicated and long-term party members. So were the large majority of ANC ministers who took power in 1994. In Moscow, old Africa hands from the Communist Party of the Soviet Union laughed aloud when I told them that the South African press had published solemn analyses showing that 40 or 50 per cent of the ministers were Communists, for they knew the number was far greater. Moreover, Communists predominated in the cabinet secretariat, at upper levels of the civil service, in the ANC components of the police and armed forces and, most strikingly of all, in the intelligence services where virtually all the top officials were Stasi-trained. In their internal ANC discussions, Mbeki, the Pahads and other old Communists still used all the old terminology: 'proletarian dictatorship', 'class hegemony', 'balance of class forces', 'US imperialism', 'neo-colonialism' and so forth.[79]

It was obvious that the new international balance of forces was unfavourable to the establishment of socialism, but the ANC hesitated. The direction was unclear. Obviously an ANC-ruled South Africa would strive to lead a coalition of anti-imperialist Third World forces but there was no consensus about what to do within South Africa. While the Cold War had lasted the universal assumption had been that an ANC-ruled South Africa would, effectively, be a people's republic. Alec Erwin, the UDF's economic spokesman, had, indeed, explicitly opted for the East European model for South Africa,[80] while even in 1989 there had been open ANC/SACP talk of 'building East Germany in Africa'. Debate over the nature of that socialism had been restricted to whether there would be a one- or two-stage revolution.

However, such thinking was based on the wishful assumption that the ANC would achieve military victory over its apartheid foes, climaxing in 'the seizure of power'. The collapse of apartheid would also see the collapse of the capitalist system as a whole, for capitalism and apartheid were inseparable. All of which had turned out to be wrong. There was no seizure of power and it was clear that in many respects liberation was good for capitalism, with an end to sanctions, increased access to foreign capital, improved trade opportunities and the abolition of all manner of market-unfriendly social constraints. It was clear that in the new post-Cold War world the ANC could not opt for a single-stage transition to socialism. Indeed, it was difficult even to discuss the socialist option too openly, for fear of provoking the flight of capital and skills.

The RDP had been part of the process of ANC deradicalization. In the end even the Keynesians of the left, like Vella Pillay, the long-time ANC economist who had worked for the Bank of China, lost out. He had wanted a budget deficit of 7–8 per cent of GDP, funded by foreign loans, in order to launch a comprehensive New Deal – a king-size RDP – aimed at making a large and immediate impact on poverty and unemployment.[81] This was resisted by Mbeki out of fear that such a path would end in dependence on the IMF and World Bank: again, the idea of thus losing control was unacceptable.[82] Then it became obvious that even the modest version of the RDP which had been attempted was failing badly. At this point Growth for All was published, making it embarrassingly clear that the ANC had no working economic policy at all.

The result was to jolt Mbeki into action. With the sound and fury directed at Growth for All used as covering fire and the rand continuing its slide, within a month the RDP office had been shut down, Jay Naidoo moved to another job, Trevor Manuel made the first black Finance Minister, and Alec Erwin appointed as Trade and Industry Minister.

Naidoo expressed his 'enormous relief' at no longer having to run the RDP,[83] while Erwin tried, absurdly, to claim that the closure of the RDP office was a sign of the RDP's success in integrating itself into other departments.[84] Work on a new economic policy was rushed along and in June 1996 Gear – the Growth, Employment and Redistribution policy – was introduced.

ENTER GEAR, STAGE RIGHT

The key elements of Gear were budget-deficit reduction, greater labour flexibility, accelerated privatization, a monetary policy aimed at lowering inflation and preventing further depreciation of the rand, the gradual relaxation of exchange controls, tariff reduction and the moderating of wage demands. Ironically, this meant accepting most of the aims of Growth for All; in fact the government was to be far tougher than business had dared to hope in bringing down the budget deficit. The target for that deficit, set at 3 per cent of GDP, was the same that EU countries had set themselves under the Maastricht agreement and this appears to have influenced the choice of target. In order to sell the policy to the public, projections were made showing that with Gear in force by 2000 the economic growth rate would be 6.1 per cent and that by 2000 an extra 1.35 million jobs would be created. Anyone who had seen how Margaret Thatcher's similarly tough deficit-reduction policies had, initially, collapsed public sector demand, leading both to economic contraction and higher unemployment, could only rub their eyes in disbelief.[85] Cosatu and the left were not fooled and a prolonged shout of rage went up, not just at Gear's conservatism but at the fact that it had been introduced in a sudden, top-down way, without consultation in the ANC–SACP–Cosatu alliance.[86]

The adoption of Gear was a landmark. First, one-stage socialism had been ruled out; then Keynesianism of the left; and then the RDP: it had been a rapid retreat. Many forces were pushing the government back: the exodus of white capital and skills, the collapse in both domestic and foreign private investment, the almost complete inefficacy of government itself; but for most this was summed up by the very visible and continuing fall of the rand, down 9.3 per cent in 1994, a further 5.7 per cent in 1995 and a further 13 per cent in 1996.[87] There was a real possibility of an economic meltdown which would end in social disorder and a humiliating collapse into the arms of the IMF.

The man who bore the stress of this imminent crisis was Thabo Mbeki. It was his finest hour. His problems began with the fact that Mandela, though hugely popular and enjoying vast moral authority, had little idea about economics or governance in general and often let slip unwise off-the-cuff remarks. He declared that the solution to continuing violence in KwaZulu-Natal was for everyone to join the ANC, without apparently thinking about the one-party consequences – or the impact of his words on the IFP leadership. In 1995 he told a May Day rally that if the IFP continued to resist the ANC he would cut off all funding to KwaZulu-Natal, the most populous province. This was a completely unconstitutional threat which had to be quickly retracted.[88] Similarly, when he dismissed Winnie from government he failed to read the constitution and thus had to reappoint her and later dismiss her again. Visiting Tanzania, he announced that, 'We are going to sideline and even crush all dissident forces in our country.'[89] And, just as his unplanned pledge of free health care for mothers and children had seen the collapse of medical services in the old homelands, so his favourite scheme of free meals for four million poor schoolchildren had collapsed in his native Eastern Cape as early as 1995 amidst widespread fraud.[90]

When Mandela appealed to whites, 'Don't leave, don't let us down and leave the country,'[91] he did it in terms which made African nationalists wince. Accused of going too far to pacify whites he responded angrily: 'Why should we not pacify them? Let's forget the past. Let's put down our weapons. Let's turn them into ploughshares. Let's build our country.'[92] Mandela was big-hearted enough to mean this. Similarly, his visit to the white Afrikaner homeland of Orania to have tea with Betsie Verwoerd, the 94-year-old widow of the late and unlamented Prime Minister, was a huge international publicity coup. The odd couple, all smiles, had tea, and Mandela, grinning, said, 'I feel like I'm in Soweto.'[93] For Mandela could get away with anything – even when he denounced the United States over Iran or Cuba or told it 'to go jump in the lake', President Clinton would smile and clap. Even more than Reagan, he was the Teflon President – but in a way it was not quite serious.

Mbeki, the real power in the administration but without Mandela's authority, faced the real problems. It was a lonely task. Most ANC activists were both too parochial and too ill-educated to understand how vulnerable the country was to international capital markets. Even those the ANC called its economic experts would seldom have passed muster as such anywhere else. Mbeki also faced such last-ditch pro-Ramaphosa suggestions as a dual executive of President and Prime Minister – which, at Mbeki's urging, the ANC's NEC kicked into touch without debate.[94] His impatience with the ANC's 'populists' led to increasing protest from Winnie Mandela and Bantu Holomisa. No one doubted that when Holomisa attacked ANC 'elitists' who were using intelligence circles against him, he meant Mbeki. Only Mandela's treatment of Holomisa as almost an adopted son kept the peace.[95] Mbeki had quickly lost confidence in Jay Naidoo and wanted to get rid of him as early as July 1995, but then had hurriedly to deny any intention of taking over the RDP office himself.[96] He was irritated by the sheer unreality of most of the political debate. Democracy had made people expect all sorts of miraculous things, he said, 'But we can't move at the pace we thought we should move. It doesn't mean the targets are wrong. But where's the money?'[97]

The launch of Gear prompted a fundamental debate within the tripartite alliance. The SACP and Cosatu were furious, but it caught them at a disadvantage. The deaths of Hani and Slovo had left the SACP with no commanding figure – its new leader, Charles Nqakula, made little impact, and its new chief theoretician, Jeremy Cronin, was a white poet. Cosatu had lost many cadres to Parliament and its new leader, Sam Shilowa, was untested. Their protests could not stop Gear, especially since Mbeki got Mandela to put his full authority behind it.

It was the common understanding of the alliance that South Africa was now in its 'national democratic' stage, a period of national reconstruction and class collaboration during which a new black 'patriotic' bourgeoisie would emerge. For Marxists, this national democratic revolution (NDR) was analogous to the Soviet New Economic Policy period or Mao's 'national democratic' stage of the 1950s, a period of consolidation before the second-stage leap into socialism. The guarantee of that ultimate perspective was that this interim compromise period should be constructed under the hegemony of the working class and peasantry, represented by the ruling party. But this was now in question for the SACP and Cosatu. 'This was a clear case of policy driven by panic due to the fall of the rand,' said Cosatu. They had been completely excluded from the drawing up of Gear, which had been put together by economists from the Treasury, Reserve Bank, the IMF and World Bank – what Cosatu called 'backward forces'. 'If left unchallenged, the consequences will be the emergence of a ruling bloc dominated by the bourgeoisie – including major fractions of the old [white] bourgeoisie and emergent capitalist fractions.' The ANC leadership, it suggested, believed that 'the balance of forces are not in our favour and that we therefore have to give in to the market'. The SACP even more pointedly asked: 'National democratic transformation – but under which class hegemony?'[98]

The accusation was that Mbeki had, with Gear, sold out the revolution. Indeed, Cosatu and the SACP thereafter referred to Gear as 'the 1996 class project'. Although Mbeki was careful not to take personal responsibility for this turning point and insisted that the RDP continued in ethereal form, this fooled nobody. Mbeki's reply – 'The State and Transformation', a policy document presented to the NEC in November 1996 – used the full battery of Marxist-Leninist argumentation to attack the 'ultra Left' and to argue that 'The historic and objective reality . . . is that the bulk of capital . . . is in private hands, both domestically and internationally'; that such capital was the primary source of investment and was also mobile and that the ANC accordingly had no option but to make a deal with business or, as the document put it, 'the democratic state must establish a dialectical relationship with private capital as a social partner for development and social progress'.[99] At the same time Mbeki was careful to make continuing references to the NDR, thus leaving it open to ANC activists to believe either that transformation would consist essentially of building a black capitalist class or that this was merely a preliminary to a later transition to socialism.

MBEKI VS. THE LEFT – AND HOLOMISA

Thereafter Mbeki faced the distrust and opposition of the left. He dealt with this in the classic nomenklatura manner. Shilowa was co-opted and made premier of Gauteng; Nqakula was similarly courted, quit the SACP leadership and became a loyal Mbeki-ite cabinet minister; Carolus was first blocked, then sent abroad – and discarded; Cronin was watched, denounced as a white and forced, humiliatingly, to abase himself. Other leftists were treated similarly – Philip Dexter, the communist leader of the militant National Educational, Health and Administrative Workers Union, was promoted to head the (toothless) labour–business chamber, Nedlac, while Enoch Godongwana, a Cosatu radical, was promoted into the Eastern Cape provincial government. Few radicals were able to resist Mbeki's adroit use of sticks and carrots.

Ironically – for he had counselled such policies – Gear did not keep De Klerk in the Government of National Unity. The ANC had steamrollered everything through cabinet so that neither the NP nor IFP ministers had any influence. At the same time the liberal DP under its able young leader, Tony Leon, was clearly stealing De Klerk's voters by its outspoken opposition. De Klerk first raised the demand that the GNU continue beyond 1999 but when Mbeki made clear that the answer to that was no, it was merely a question of when De Klerk would quit, which he ultimately did on 1 July 1996.

Ramaphosa was to leave Shell House in May for a career in business (he had been 'deployed' there, the ANC said). Ramaphosa, preoccupied with negotiations on the final draft of the constitution, had in practice left his party duties to Cheryl Carolus, who became acting secretary-general when he quit. Carolus had been elected against his own candidate and was close to Ramaphosa, so Mbeki regarded her with suspicion. Carolus was seen by many as having a strong claim to the secretary-generalship but the election of a Coloured woman in such a male-dominated organization was always unlikely. Mbeki put up Joel Netshitenzhe instead, but Cosatu pushed forward Kgalema Motlanthe, Ramaphosa's successor at the head of the National Union of Mineworkers. Prudently, Netshitenzhe withdrew.

A far bigger challenge came from Bantu Holomisa, who claimed that 'all my troubles began' with his election at the top of the NEC list since 'certain ANC leaders' (i.e. Mbeki) had seen him as a threat from that moment on. This was not surprising: Holomisa had been a close friend of Hani's and Winnie's and was notably independent-minded. He had come to power in the Transkei – which he ruled with considerable aplomb – as a result of a coup against Stella Sigcau, and was a leading inxile. And, as a recent ANC member, he was unused to its iron discipline.

Bantu Holomisa broke ranks before the Truth and Reconciliation Commission. The TRC, in the ANC's eyes, had been set up with the task of exposing apartheid atrocities to help make the ANC invincible in the 1999 election. To make sure the TRC was politically onside, all candidates for its membership were screened by an eight-member panel, of whom six were ANC members.[100] But Holomisa (now a deputy minister) submitted documents to the TRC showing that his old enemy Stella Sigcau, now an ANC minister, had received R50,000 from a R2 million bribe paid to the Transkei bantustan government by Sol Kerzner.[101] He also alleged that the ANC had taken a R2 million election donation from Kerzner in 1994, in return for which he was to be cleared of the outstanding bribery charges which were a huge stumbling block for him in his effort to build a career in the US casino business.[102] Under US rules anyone with a conviction for corruption is automatically disbarred from holding a casino licence.

The ANC was much discomfited by Holomisa's testimony and Mbeki was mandated to see him. However Mbeki made no move to do so[103] and instead defended Sigcau in Parliament. At this, Holomisa angrily accused Mbeki and his henchman, Steve Tshwete, of corruption and attempting to defeat the ends of justice. Kerzner had, he alleged, funded a whole series of events for the ANC. Both Mbeki and Tshwete had repeatedly benefited from Kerzner's largesse. His message to them was 'get yourselves out of Sol Kerzner's top drawer first'.[104] Angry ANC denunciations followed: Holomisa was telling 'blatant lies'; it was 'scurrilous and repugnant' to suggest that Kerzner had funded Mbeki's birthday party. Kerzner himself, now thoroughly alarmed, denied giving the ANC R2 million and called Holomisa 'a manipulative, incompetent liar'.[105] Cheryl Carolus said that Holomisa's statements were 'blatantly false, malicious and defamatory': she knew where every cent had come from in the ANC accounts and nothing had come from Kerzner.[106]

Mbeki now had to destroy Holomisa politically or suffer grave political damage himself. Moreover, Holomisa was articulating anxieties felt by many within the old UDF where Tshwete's role as Mbeki's 'Mr Fixit' was resented. Tshwete was a determined and ruthless man. He wore thick spectacles without which he was nearly blind and would blink uncomprehendingly at the world. This, together with his constant inebriation, had earned him the nickname of 'the drunken mole'. He was Minister of Sport, had been Mbeki's fellow-exile, and did much of

Mbeki's dirty work. He had led the charge against Holomisa and had also been sent to the Free State to arbitrate the fight between the popular premier, Terror Lekota, and his local rivals. Lekota was the most popular single figure thrown up by the UDF and had won the hearts of many Free State whites by his warmth and openness. He was clearly building a formidable regional base. This had to be stopped. Tshwete had insisted that Lekota reinstate his rivals (whom he had sacked for corruption) and offered him an ambassadorship if he would resign. Lekota refused, sealing his fate.[107]

Holomisa, meanwhile, was unperturbed. Kerzner, he said, was 'not a credible witness': he had taken out large newspaper advertisements denying that he had paid a R2 million bribe to the Transkei president, George Matanzima, but then admitted to the Harms Commission in 1989 that he had done precisely that.[108] From that bribe, he pointed out, Matanzima had distributed R50,000 to several of his bantustan ministers – including Sigcau. Before the Alexander Commission in 1988 Sigcau had admitted taking the money, saying, 'Knowing African tradition as I do, how could I as a leader of the Pondos reject a gift from the Tembu royalty without offending the giver?'[109] This had prompted Holomisa to carry out his coup against Sigcau, whereupon she had led a deputation to Pretoria in 1988, demanding the apartheid regime remove Holomisa by force.[110]

Holomisa's particular ire was reserved for Kerzner. Mbeki had become involved with Kerzner as soon as he returned from exile, Holomisa said, and in 1990 had come to him to discuss Kerzner's case then with the Transkei Attorney General, Christo Nel. 'He said he had been approached by Kerzner who had wanted to know if he [Mbeki] could help in his case.' Holomisa had told him there was 'no short cut' and the law would have to take its course.[111] Mandela had then called a meeting at the Captain's Table restaurant at the Carlton Centre in early 1994 where he said that Kerzner was anxious to have the bribery charges quashed and had made a R2 million donation to ANC funds to facilitate this. Holomisa replied that Kerzner should send his lawyers to see Nel. This he did, but Nel said the charges against Kerzner still stood. Holomisa accepted this and washed his hands of the matter. After the 1994 election, Holomisa continued, Mandela 'kept on asking me how the Kerzner issue could be solved', repeatedly praising Kerzner's contribution to the national economy.[112] Kerzner had been throwing largesse at the ANC elite ever since 1990 and many ANC leaders had enjoyed Kerzner's luxurious hospitality. When Mandela's daughter Zinzi got married and had her honeymoon at a Mauritius hotel in 1992, the whole event had been 'courtesy of Sol Kerzner'.[113]

But Kerzner was now under great pressure. In July 1996 the *Wall Street Journal* ran a front-page story suggesting irregularities in the way that the head of the National Indian Gaming Commission had approved Kerzner's $300 million Mohegan Sun casino resort and shortly afterwards the London *Sunday Times* ran a story suggesting that Kerzner had offered the Tory party £7 million for British citizenship. In Mauritius, where he owned extensive hotel interests, bribery allegations had led to the resignation of a cabinet minister while similar allegations were being aired in the Bahamas about the mega resort development Kerzner had started there in 1994. Given that Kerzner had actually admitted paying the R2 million bribe to Matanzima – and thus admitted he had been lying the previous year when he had told the Alexander Commission the opposite ('it's not my style') – he was extremely vulnerable to the charges being pressed by Nel. Meanwhile he was pumping money out of South Africa as fast as he could. His Sun International had exclusive gaming rights and R1.2 billion in tax breaks for Lost City alone, and other foreign-registered Kerzner companies had the management contracts for the complex, with their fees paid in US dollars.[114]

Mbeki and Tshwete, to their fury, now found themselves in the dock. They could not actually deny receiving perks but they tried to insist these came from someone other than Kerzner, and Mbeki arranged for their defence to be conducted by statements from Shell House, so they were not forced to defend themselves personally. In Tshwete's case he had received free accommodation at Sun City to watch a big boxing match. The ANC insisted this had been paid for not by Kerzner but by the boxing promoter Rodney Berman. Berman himself immediately denied this.[115] Holomisa also alleged that Kerzner had paid for Mbeki's fiftieth birthday party in 1992, a much-photographed, high-profile event. The party had been held at the up-market Houghton home of Paul Ekon, a wealthy playboy, racehorse-owner, restaurateur and diamond dealer, though Holomisa claimed to have 'privileged information' that Ekon had been merely a front and Kerzner had actually paid for the party. Ekon himself insisted that 'Sol [Kerzner], Holomisa and Thabo [Mbeki] are all good buddies of mine' and said the party's costs had been shared with the textile industrialist Charles Priebatsch and Mandela's wealthy tailor, Yusuf Surtee, who supplied the ANC elite with clothes from his Sandton boutiques. Priebatsch, who had also hosted Mandela's birthday party when he had been visited by the pop singer Michael Jackson in July 1996, said that he, Surtee and Ekon had hosted Mbeki's party too, though the (plentiful) drink had been supplied by an unknown sponsor. Ekon had, however, later told friends that he had hosted the party at Kerzner's behest.[116]

Holomisa's allegations shone a garish light on the sort of social life now led by the ANC elite, particularly Mbeki. Kerzner's exploitation of the bantustans for business gain had made him the *bête noire* of ANC activists and thus an embarrassing patron for Mbeki, but the attempt to focus the spotlight on Ekon instead backfired. Ekon, it emerged, was not only a close associate of Kerzner, Mbeki, and the deputy Foreign Minister, Aziz Pahad, but of the convicted fraudster Greg Blank.[117] Ekon was, indeed, at the centre of an interesting social circle; he had dated Kerzner's ex-wife, the former Miss South Africa, Anneline Kriel, and had been a friend of Eugene Riley, the intelligence agent who had forewarned of the Hani assassination and then been mysteriously murdered. Moreover, Ekon had to leave South Africa hurriedly in 1995 after having been implicated in a criminal investigation conducted by the police gold and diamond branch. He had returned, he said, when assured that he was no longer under investigation. The *Mail and Guardian*, relating his account, added that it had 'reason to believe this is not true'.[118] The Mbeki camp quickly realized that it was unwise to make too much of the Deputy President's friendship with Ekon.

Holomisa found few allies: Mbeki controlled a majority on the NEC and was simply too strong. The ANC Youth League was critical of Tshwete's role in the Free State[119] but only the ANC Women's League (thanks to Winnie) supported Holomisa, saying his sin had merely been 'telling too much truth'.[120] But the Women's League had problems of its own, the auditors having just discovered R7.8 million missing from its accounts.[121] Kader Asmal was chosen to chair Holomisa's disciplinary hearing and Alec Erwin named as his prosecutor – two non-Africans, a clear sign of unwillingness among the ANC's African leadership to take sides against Holomisa. Asmal quickly took advantage of Holomisa's objections to him to recuse himself.

Because of his affection for Holomisa, Mandela had been anxiously following the affair. When the tumult first erupted over Holomisa's original remarks against Stella Sigcau, Mandela had telephoned Holomisa and told him that if only he would apologize he (Mandela) would 'be able to neutralize the forces against me'. As the affair developed, within the ANC Mandela was 'always accused of protecting Holomisa'.[122] But the crunch came when ANC leaders, Cheryl Carolus in the forefront, denounced Holomisa for alleging that Kerzner had given the ANC R2 million, while Kerzner himself threatened Holomisa with legal action over this allegation. Holomisa demanded an independent audit of the ANC's books and said that in any case Mandela himself had told him about the R2 million.

To the consternation of both the Mbeki faction and Carolus, Mandela then admitted that he had indeed accepted a R2 million donation to ANC funds from Kerzner, saying that he took sole responsibility for this and that he alone had known about it. How this was possible was never explained: had the money remained in Mandela's back pocket? Mandela defended Kerzner, saying there was no proof of the charges against him. The ANC had called Holomisa 'a blatant liar' for alluding to Kerzner's donation but Mandela insisted that 'No apology will be made to Bantu Holomisa or anybody. Even if people wanted to apologize, I would not allow them.'[123] Similarly, Mandela was furious at the Women's League's support for Holomisa and ordered that all its funds be cut off except for regional officials' salaries,[124] though in both cases his action was clearly an unconstitutional suppression of free speech.

Holomisa's disciplinary hearing was a farce. None of his allegations had been disproved and, indeed, Mandela's admission had largely vindicated him. As Holomisa pointed out, given that he had been condemned by the ANC's NWC even before his hearing and that both Mbeki and Tshwete had publicly demanded his expulsion, there was no real chance of a fair hearing. At the hearing Holomisa produced a letter from Tobin Prior, Sun International's marketing director, accepting the veracity of Holomisa's claim that Sun had provided free hospitality for cabinet members. Holomisa then asked his prosecutor, Alec Erwin, if he had not also accepted such favours from Kerzner: Erwin made no reply.[125] After ninety minutes Holomisa simply walked out. The committee recommended that he be expelled both from the ANC and as an MP. He was immediately sacked as a junior minister. In a supremely cynical move, Peter Mokaba, despite the scandal of the missing millions at his

National Tourist Forum, was now brought in as Minister for Tourism, replacing Holomisa. Mbeki consolidated his position by bringing in his enforcer, Essop Pahad, as a deputy minister. But despite his position as President-in-waiting and de facto acting President, Mbeki had had a narrow scrape. He sought to ensure that nothing of the kind could happen again. From this point on he took control not just of day-to-day government matters but, to a large extent, of ministerial appointments as well.[126]

Mandela denied that the ANC was exercising pressure on Christo Nel not to prosecute Kerzner. 'I won't argue with my dad,' was Holomisa's comment on hearing this,[127] though later it emerged that Kerzner had discussed his legal problems with Mandela who, after accepting a large sum of money, told him that 'I'm going to speak to that young fellow Holomisa'. Later, Mandela reported back that he had 'had a word' with Holomisa but that he 'wasn't listening'.[128] There was widespread cynicism when Nel later reported to Parliament that he was dropping the case ('There is', Holomisa said, 'something fishy in the whole exercise'[129]) – and even more a while later when Kerzner admitted his payment to Matanzima in his testimony before the New Jersey Casino Control Commission.[130] Kerzner managed to get the Commission to take the view that the bribe had been 'a single aberration', yet, on his own evidence, he had also paid a large sum to Mandela while trying to persuade Mandela to get the court case against him called off. This would normally be viewed as a bribe to pervert the course of justice, and would have landed both Kerzner and Mandela in serious trouble.

The Holomisa affair also made a mockery of the TRC, for the ANC, shocked by Holomisa's testimony, now announced that ANC members could only tell the Commission things which had already been cleared with the ANC (that is, with Mbeki's office). The TRC could hardly take such open censorship lying down, so its chairman and deputy chairman, Archbishop Desmond Tutu and Alex Boraine, met with the ANC, who specified that this censorship applied only to statements by ANC leaders. Astonishingly, Tutu and Boraine accepted this.[131]

MBEKI'S CENTRAL APPARATUS VERSUS AN UNRULY PARTY

The Holomisa affair was ominous. The party apparatus had triumphed over the party's second most popular figure (after Mandela), whose claims had been largely vindicated. Much to Mbeki's fury Holomisa continued to be a star attraction at ANC rallies.[132] The almost metronomic efficiency with which Mbeki had disposed of rivals had, however, been widely noted. Tokyo Sexwale, the premier of Gauteng, attempted to curry favour by demanding that Holomisa apologize to the ANC for having tried to 'criminalize' Kerzner's contribution to party funds. 'I don't have time for opportunists,' was Holomisa's curt reply.[133] At Holomisa's homecoming rally in Mthatha posters portrayed Sexwale's head on a dog's body.[134]

Sexwale had sprung to prominence after Hani's death when he spoke movingly of his lost friend. As premier of the most important province, he was much in the limelight, was voted one of South Africa's sexiest men, and was talked of as a possible Deputy President – and thus Mbeki's likely successor. Other names in play for this position were Mathews Phosa, the popular premier of Mpumalanga province, Jacob Zuma, the ANC leader in KwaZulu-Natal, and Joel Netshitenzhe.

Sexwale's handicap was that rumour constantly connected him to drug trafficking, although these rumours were never substantiated. In 1994 De Klerk said that he had information which, if released, would see Sexwale 'running all the way to Japan'. On becoming Deputy President, Mbeki enquired of De Klerk whether he had been alluding to Sexwale's involvement with drugs. De Klerk was non-committal but from this point on the rumours were assiduously fed.[135] Sexwale wrote repeatedly to De Klerk, attempting to refute the trafficking claims, but De Klerk said that Mbeki had asked for and received all letters, documents and other evidence relating to these charges.[136] Sexwale then heard that 'senior ANC officials' (i.e. Mbeki) had ordered an investigation of the drug trafficking charges against him.[137] Holomisa repeated the drug allegations against Sexwale and also demanded to know more about Sexwale's relations with a particular construction company and how he had acquired a large mansion.[138] All this remained at the level of insinuation but it proved too much for Sexwale, who now declined all interest in the deputy presidency and held a joint press conference with Mbeki to make clear his complete loyalty to him.[139] Netshitenzhe hurriedly withdrew, leaving only Phosa and Zuma in contention.

The two men stood in stark contrast. Zuma, the son of a domestic worker, had received no formal instruction in English until a prisoner on Robben Island – though he too had passed through the Lenin School in Moscow. A true son of the soil, he was genial and popular at grass roots. Phosa, who was ten years younger, was the son of a nurse who had served in Europe and given her son a far more cultured background. Phosa was a star student, a lawyer, wrote poetry in English and Afrikaans and spoke many languages. He was extremely popular in Mpumalanga and the only provincial premier with a national following.[140] Zuma stood for simple, unquestioning devotion to the ANC, but Phosa was a far more independent spirit.

The left had been taking stock. In just a few months the RDP had been abandoned, Jay Naidoo had been demoted, Ramaphosa had departed, Holomisa had been vanquished, Lekota forced out of power in the Free State and Peter Mokaba had deserted. Power was now completely centralized within Mbeki's office where Essop Pahad operated as an all-powerful gatekeeper. The reversal of policy represented by Gear had been carried out so stealthily that even senior cadres had only learnt about it from the press.

Inevitably, the discontented beat a path to Mandela's door but the old man had been squared in advance. Mbeki and important white businessmen assured him that Gear was the right way ahead. In any case, it was now government policy and Mandela's highest principle was complete unity behind the ANC government. When an ANC/Cosatu workshop poured scorn on Gear, Mandela angrily declared that the movement must deal with the question of 'discipline within our ranks'. Enraged that Jeremy Cronin, the SACP deputy secretary-general, had publicly criticized ANC policy he threatened to resign from the ANC unless Cronin was expelled. Only a special meeting between Mandela, the SACP leader Charles Nqakula and Mandela's old comrade Raymond Mhlaba, the SACP chairman, smoothed the matter over.[141] An SACP militant who declared that the presence of SACP ministers in the cabinet was now 'meaningless' and the alliance was 'a meek and uncritical mouthpiece of the Cabinet', was reprimanded,[142] but the feeling was widespread.

Mandela was inevitably affected by the unhappy turmoil in the ANC. ANC MPs declared that the party was 'lurching from blunder to blunder' and expressed their unhappiness at its leadership style characterized by 'the mismanagement of crises, a consolidation of central authority and a clampdown on internal dissent'. Yet, citing 'a climate of fear', not one MP would speak on the record. 'You don't think about sticking your neck out for fear of getting your head chopped off,' said one.[143] Mandela sometimes wavered. In November he declared that it was not up to him to choose his successor, that the ANC would decide the matter. The markets panicked and the rand fell sharply at this apparent withdrawal of his support for Mbeki, though Mbeki's office issued an angry statement insisting that Mandela's position had not changed and that Mbeki was still the heir apparent.[144]

Mathews Phosa spoke for the discontent welling up within the ANC. 'There is', he said, 'no longer serious regard for the principle of collective leadership, democratic practices, criticism and self-criticism', a remark aimed at Mbeki's instinctive centralism. 'We must face the reality that the ANC constitution is being violated, the code of conduct is being violated and the level of discipline is dropping off. The politics of power, positions and money are corroding the very character of the movement.' Gear, he said, had not been discussed in fair and open debate. Instead, everything now 'starts within government and there is a danger of government marginalizing the ANC'. This trend had begun with the suspension of armed struggle without consultation and decision-making over Gear had been mere 'cabalism'. For Phosa, the key ANC tradition was 'the principle of internal party democracy. We challenge the president, we challenge anybody within the party irrespective of rank. You have to win your argument on merit.' The blurring of the state–party boundary now brought the danger that government policy would simply be imposed on the ANC.[145] Phosa, too late, realized the significance of the Holomisa affair and pleaded before the NEC that he not be expelled, but Kader Asmal moved for expulsion and it was carried.[146] Nonetheless, in a clear reference to the Kerzner affair, Phosa called on the government to act more toughly against corruption: 'we must not be seen to be covering up for each other' and warned that 'tribalism, racism, regionalism and factionalism are emerging in the ANC.'[147]

Jacob Zuma, now in the Mbeki camp, responded by flatly asserting that the ANC was above all other considerations. 'You can't say the constitution is above the ANC. Once you begin to feel above the ANC you are in trouble.' The ANC troubles in the Free State were a good lesson, he claimed: if people had to go to preserve ANC unity, no price was too high.[148] He gave Phosa a barely disguised warning: 'Some party members have grown big-headed. These people are making a fatal mistake.' Even provincial premiers 'must not forget they take instructions from the organization'.[149]

This last remark touched on a sore point. Many cadres were shocked at how Mbeki's office now intervened routinely in provincial party matters, throttling any notion of local party democracy. It had left a very bad taste that Lekota, despite his popularity there, had been bundled out of the Free State, offered an ambassadorship (which he declined) and then demoted to Senator. Mbeki's office made it clear that its replacement nominee, Ivy Matsepe-Casaburri, must be elected unopposed, though she had no local following at all. During the hearings held for her previous post as SABC chairperson she had proclaimed her undying loyalty to the ANC. Reminded that such partisanship was inappropriate, she had insisted on her political independence. Now, artlessly, she returned to asserting her undying loyalty to the ANC.

In the Western Cape, Boesak's successor at the head of the ANC, Chris Nissen, had resigned. Tony Yengeni, the populist wide-boy from Khayelitsha, threw his hat in the ring as did the white ANC activist Carl Niehaus, but Mbeki decided that the cabinet minister Dullah Omar should get the job. Similar pressure was exercised to ensure an unopposed election. The Eastern Cape premier, Raymond Mhlaba, was forced out and although Steve Tshwete, among others, coveted the post, Mbeki's nominee, the Revd Makhenkesi Arnold Stofile, was elected unopposed.

In Northern Province Peter Mokaba was desperate to gain the ANC chairmanship as a stepping stone to the premiership, but Mbeki insisted that Nelson Ramathlodi should retain the chairmanship. When Mokaba was nominated an ANC spokesman hurriedly announced that Mokaba would be 'unavailable due to his national commitments'.[150] When this did not work, Mokaba was ordered to stand down by Mandela. Mokaba, who was far more popular than Ramathlodi, nonetheless allowed his nomination to go forward. The chairman, under Shell House orders, simply refused to accept Mokaba's nomination,[151] the argument being that he was too busy being a junior minister. Yet, simultaneously,

Dullah Omar, a full cabinet minister, had been given the analogous job in the Western Cape. To the consternation of both Mokaba and Mbeki, rebellious activists then voted in the unknown George Mashamba.

The situation in KwaZulu-Natal was the most complicated of all. Harry Gwala's death had removed the greatest ANC warlord but Jacob Zuma's elevation had left a vacuum which Sifiso Nkabinde, the ANC warlord of Richmond, was keen to fill. Shell House forbade him to run against Sipho Gcabashe for the post of ANC secretary but Nkabinde went ahead anyway despite frantic attempts by the conference chairman to rule his candidacy out of order,[152] was narrowly defeated and then elected in triumph to the provincial executive. Mbeki was furious. Zuma, rather ominously, declared that 'The ANC, I am sure, knows what to do.'[153] Thus began a saga which ultimately saw Nkabinde expelled from the ANC, causing him to vent his murderous attentions onto his own old party. Many died in the minor civil war which then gripped Richmond, ending with Nkabinde's arrest and ultimately his murder by ANC activists. In jail, Nkabinde revealed that many recent bank robberies and cash-in-transit heists had been carried out with the involvement of leading ANC figures, a revelation which doubtless shortened his life.[154] Zuma had warned that party members who had grown 'big-headed' were 'making a fatal mistake': in Nkabinde's case this was literally so.

The management of ANC affairs so that there was only one unopposed candidate for each job shocked old ANC democrats. Anthony Holliday argued that the way in which Mbeki was made Mandela's heir 'without a single vote being cast' suggested that the ANC was 'dealing with a question of tribal chieftainship instead of with the governance of a modern state'.[155] Moreover, ANC membership had plummeted by over 70 per cent in a year[156] so that the ruling group now represented only some 200,000 activists in the entire country. Similarly, the use of imbongis (praise-singers) who preceded Mandela and Mbeki on public occasions led some to believe that an older, chiefly model of authority had now been installed.

Mandela certainly had a chiefly style, but real power did not lie with him. The larger point was that the Leninism of the exile ANC was now being imposed on the country as a whole. For men like Mbeki and Essop Pahad the ANC, whatever its membership figures, 'was' the masses, in the same way that Communist parties 'were' the working class. Thus the triumph of the ANC was the victory of democracy. That is, democracy was an event (the ANC's coming to power), not a process requiring constant practice and renewal, let alone checks and balances. There was no more room in this conception for grass-roots democracy or the endless consultation typical of the UDF than there was for the notion of a loyal opposition. For Mbeki and those like him, South African politics was divided between 'the progressive forces' (i.e. his supporters) and 'the forces of reaction' which, axiomatically, had to be destroyed. By definition, any party which stood up to the ANC – like the DP or even factions within the ANC – was part of the forces of reaction.

The ANC now found it was living in the uncomfortable environment of a multi-party democracy but, instinctively, the exile elite tried to maintain the ANC's 'monolithic unity', using whatever combination of blandishments, intimidation or charm was required to get the chattering classes to see things their way. To a remarkable extent this worked in the Mandela period. Mandela was the period's overwhelming personality and his charisma and charm were immensely valuable tools for the ANC. In a real sense, however, the Mandela years were a myth, for his presidency was largely a fiction. He had no control of power and could do little to direct events. Sycophantically, the media refused to believe this, although the evidence was clear enough. When Mandela came up with an idea – giving the vote to 16-year-olds was one – which Mbeki's NEC majority did not like, he was ruthlessly voted down, no matter the loss of face. Even when Mandela artlessly told the press that Mbeki was really in charge, not him – and by early 1997 he had begun to admit this quite often[157] – this was treated as a charming foible. Mandela's warm personality and inclusive spirit were stamped indelibly on the nation's heart in these years but as one examines the realities of power of the time one sees ever more clearly that his well-loved face was merely the mask of a very different regime.

4
The Mandela Presidency II: 1996–1997

Great historical transformations are always bought dearly, often after one has already thought that one got them at a bargain price. Jakob Burckhardt

It takes time to ruin a world, but time is all it takes. Bernard de Fontenelle

Mbeki was determined to impose the leadership he wanted on the provinces largely because the provincial sections had the dominant voice at the ANC's national conference. All eyes were firmly focused on the ANC's Mafikeng conference at the end of 1997. Mandela had declared he would step down as ANC president then, so this conference would see a changing of the guard, with a ten-year Mbeki presidency stretching ahead. The key question now was about who would become Mbeki's deputy president, with the clear expectation that that person would in time become President of South Africa.

As with all movements which have spent decades in revolutionary opposition, the revolutionary tradition still thrilled activist hearts. At the 1994 Bloemfontein conference the delegates had elected populists like Holomisa, Winnie Mandela and Peter Mokaba to top NEC positions. Holomisa, though still popular, had been expelled. Mokaba had become an Mbeki client, his past as a police informer overlooked. That left Winnie: sacked from government, divorced by Mandela but, despite her unsavoury reputation, still a major force on the populist left, willing to say aloud what others were afraid to say.

INTRA-PARTY TENSIONS

For the left, the period since 1990 had been one of steady retreat. But Gear represented the greatest threat, for it had been policy-making with the SACP and Cosatu simply cut out of the loop. In their eyes the tripartite alliance meant that the ANC had to submit all policy initiatives for their discussion and approval, thus guaranteeing that the national democratic revolution (NDR) would proceed in a manner which they would control. The NDR would then see the emergence of a black 'patriotic bourgeoisie' but only under continuing 'working class hegemony'. But if the ANC could simply cut its partners out when it mattered, then the working class had lost control of the NDR. It could thus fall under the sway of the new bourgeoisie and white capitalists which, the left feared, Mbeki now represented. This was the nub of the ideological dispute between the left and Mbeki, though it was seldom openly articulated for fear of frightening domestic and foreign investors and because an open fight would threaten the alliance's future.

In the 1960s and 1970s liberals had prayed for a split among the ruling Nats, knowing there was no way ahead without it. In the end it came and did indeed help to open the floodgates. So almost from the start liberals again began hoping for a split in the ruling African nationalist alliance, some even rashly predicting one. This ignored the realpolitik of the situation. Any ANC leader would want to keep the SACP and Cosatu as allies: they were the dominant force on the left and the organizational heart of every ANC election campaign. While they remained allies the ANC could not be seriously threatened from the left and nor could it be accused of selling out the revolutionary tradition. Similarly, the SACP and Cosatu leadership (there was a large overlap) had every incentive to maintain an alliance which gave it great influence, access to government and hopes of individual upward mobility for many of its cadres. But the relationship depended on the ANC believing it was the boss and the SACP–Cosatu believing that they enjoyed potentially decisive influence and that the question of a future advance to socialism remained open. Mbeki happily obliged, continually hinting that the NDR was but the prologue to socialism. The key point was that for as far ahead as one could see no other relationship offered more to any of the contracted parties than did the alliance. In this respect, of course, the ANC and the unions were merely treading in the steps of European socialist parties a century before.

The situation was complex. Mbeki had been careful merely to 'take sabbatical' from the SACP. He continued to employ Marxist-Leninist rhetoric and his ministers included many open SACP members – the two Pahads, Erwin and Kasrils, for example – as well as many other secret SACP members, though this secret-membership category was gradually to fall away. Mbeki was also assiduous in his courtship of the new SACP and Cosatu leaders, Charles Nqakula and Sam Shilowa, promising them preferment if they played along. The SACP, seeing this and noting that SACP ministers had all happily gone along with Gear, realized that not only could it not rely on such members but that they might become Mbeki's spies within the party, a notion which eventually led to the eviction of figures such as Essop Pahad from the SACP executive.

The hard core of the party crystallized around the deputy leader, Blade Nzimande, and the party's leading theorist, Jeremy Cronin. This was a large step down from the Hani–Slovo days. Nzimande, the son of a Mozambican sangoma (witch-doctor), had conducted his activist career mainly in the 'soft' world of student and academic politics and had never been banned, jailed or exiled. He had a doctorate in (of all things) personnel management. Cronin, the son of a naval officer, had actually served in the apartheid armed forces but had then got involved in student politics, studied Marxism at the Sorbonne and had known jail and exile. Within Cosatu their key ally was Shilowa's deputy, Zwelinzima Vavi.

These ideological tensions within the ANC inevitably had an ethnic overlay. In exile, Xhosa predominance had become the norm: Tambo, Mandela, Hani and Mbeki were all Xhosas and the furious IFP resistance to the ANC was rooted in the fact that 'Zulus have never been defeated by Xhosas'. Ironically, when the IFP joined the Government of National Unity (GNU), the ANC could not allow it to claim leadership of the largest ethnic group, the Zulus, so an at least matching number of ANC Zulu ministers were appointed, with the result that early GNU cabinets were Zulu-dominated. In African eyes the more significant fact was the domination of the Nguni group (comprising Zulus, Swazis, Xhosas and Ndebeles, though in practical terms it came down to Zulus and Xhosas). Since non-Ngunis make up over half of South Africa's black population, this was a sore point, made worse by the shabby treatment meted out to Lekota (South Sotho), Ramaphosa (Venda) and Sexwale (North Sotho). It also lent extra tension to the challenge mounted by Mathews Phosa (North Sotho).

Phosa also represented the spirit of the old United Democratic Front (UDF), of which he had been a co-founder before leaving for exile. The ANC boss in Mpumalanga for nine years now, he was well dug in. He greatly disliked what Mbeki was doing to the ANC. 'I am deeply concerned', he declared, 'that the ANC, as a collective and a party, has lost the sense of being the leader, the director. There is no longer serious regard for . . . collective leadership, democratic practices, criticism and self-criticism. Rumour-mongering and character assassination have replaced criticism and self-criticism, especially as vicious campaigns are not taking place within constitutional structures but in cliques and factions which are self-serving.'[1] Such sentiments were typical of the appalled view which the old UDF took of developments in the alliance it had joined in a state of starry idealism. The UDF had been endlessly consultative, had had a real sense of constituency and had been continuously in touch with grass roots. But the exile ANC of Mbeki, Modise and the Pahads had never had grass roots to worry about, let alone consult. It was simply Leninist. Phosa's was not an isolated reaction. Another provincial leader warned of 'cloak and dagger politics, cut-throat campaigns and bloodletting' and that 'backroom manipulation is rife'.[2]

But the forces making up the old UDF were poorly placed to fight back. It was already late: Ramaphosa was gone and Jay Naidoo was on the way down. Its old leaders were dispersed around the provinces, Phosa in Mpumalanga, Popo Molefe as premier of North West province, Lekota in the Free State (and now deposed even from there) and Murphy Morobe relegated to head the obscure Finance and Fiscal Commission. Archbishop Tutu had wisely stepped back from politics while Boesak was in disgrace. Moreover, the civil society institutions which had played such a large part in the UDF were now sharply cut back to size. The South African Council of Churches, for example, had played a central role when led by Tutu but his successor, the Revd Frank Chikane, abandoned the job in order to run Mbeki's office. With the head of the SACC keen to render unto Caesar whatever he wanted, little more was heard of the once-mighty Council.

There was another factor too. Sibusiso Madlala, my old MK confidant who had spent decades in exile, shook his head as he watched these developments. 'Phosa and these guys are only waking up now to what sort of movement they've joined,' he told me.

> It was the same with me in MK. Only gradually did I understand that the first duty of ANC intelligence was to spy on the ANC, that the leadership placed informers at every level of the organization, so that trouble could always be cut off at the pass. It's the same now. Although officially the ANC isn't supposed to have maintained its own intelligence organization, it has of course – I see these guys, I know them, they're still in their old jobs. You can be quite sure that someone like Mathews Phosa has his phone tapped, his letters opened and that there are people in his office reporting on him to Mbeki. The same with all the others like Ramaphosa, Sexwale and Lekota.[3]

In January 1997 an ANC lekgotla (council) was held at which the question of the party's secretary-generalship had to be faced. The work had long since devolved on Ramaphosa's deputy, Cheryl Carolus, who was ambitious to keep the job. But she was unacceptable to Mbeki, who had been furious when he learnt that Carolus had asked Ramaphosa back to party headquarters to help explain the accounts to her. This confirmed Mbeki's belief that she was too close to his erstwhile rival. So the Mineworkers' Union boss, Kgalema Motlanthe, and Joel Netshitenzhe were approached to see if they would take the job. Both declined.[4]

Accordingly, Carolus was informed that while she would be confirmed as acting secretary-general until the party's Mafikeng conference, she would not succeed Ramaphosa. Carolus collapsed in tears, accused the leadership of treating her shabbily and declared that in that case she had no interest in remaining at Shell House: she would prefer the ambassadorial post Mbeki dangled in front of her.[5] She also publicly declared that Ramaphosa had not left his post voluntarily but had been pushed out, an open accusation against Mbeki. With that, her fate was sealed. She had been one of the eleven-person ANC team in the original negotiations with De Klerk, had been ANC head of policy and had even been mentioned as a possible future President by Mandela. Now her political career was over. She became high commissioner to London but after a brief tour of duty there she was demoted to head the state agency, SA Tourism, and then found solace in becoming a multi-millionaire director of De Beers, with her SACP principles – and political career – a fast receding memory.

First, however, Carolus had to officiate at a major public defeat for the ANC leadership. She was one of a high-level team sent to 'facilitate' the Free State ANC conference, that is to say, to ensure that the new premier imposed by Mbeki, Ivy Matsepe-Casaburri, was duly elected as leader of the Free State ANC. Mbeki himself gave the keynote address, claiming that it was 'a straightforward lie' to say that the ANC national leadership had its own preferred list of candidates for local jobs. The decision to appoint Casaburri had been taken, he noted, and the party's duty was simply to implement it, and he warned of 'a disease creeping into the movement' caused by 'low levels of political understanding among some comrades', which could only play into the hands of 'our enemies'.[6] Disregarding such sophistry, Lekota's furious partisans threw out Casaburri and elected the unknown Zingile Dingane in her stead. Mbeki quickly said that this should not be interpreted as a snub to the ANC's national leadership but if he believed this, he was the only one who did.[7]

An even tougher problem was the ANC Women's League, where Winnie Mandela's autocratic style had led to wholesale resignations from the executive over her 'undemocratic practices'. Even Mandela's attempts to persuade the resigners to go back had fallen on stony ground.[8] This left the Women's League as Winnie's fiefdom, and she used it for continuous populist sniping against the government. In particular, the League's support for Holomisa had enraged both Mandela and Mbeki and at the ANC's eighty-fifth anniversary celebration in January 1997 Mandela singled out the League for 'failing the women's movement'.[9] It was obvious that nothing would change unless Winnie was displaced, so the Health Minister, Nkosasana Dlamini-Zuma, was enlisted to run for the Women's League presidency, to be decided at its congress on 28 February. Ten days beforehand a meeting of Mandela, Carolus and Mbeki's envoy, Steve Tshwete, agreed that the congress be deferred on the grounds that insufficient preparation had been done. While this was certainly true – an organizational shambles was normal under Winnie – the real point was that Dlamini-Zuma had no chance of winning.[10]

MBEKI'S DRIVE FOR CENTRAL CONTROL

Faced by these centrifugal forces Mbeki maintained an unrelenting pressure for central control. No one within the ANC could be unaware of this pressure. A minority might rebel but no one with ambition could afford to. Even Mandela made pointed reference to the changed atmosphere within the ANC in his eighty-fifth anniversary speech. The ANC had, he said, become far too concerned to deny its mistakes, far too reluctant to rectify its errors. He urged a return to the 'culture of democracy and debate'. There were complaints that the parliamentary caucus had become a mere rubber stamp, that consultation within the alliance had ceased and that dissent was being muzzled, so he urged ANC officials to return to grass roots and listen to voters.[11] Even Mbeki tried to put himself on the right side of such a critique. At a meeting of the ANC parliamentary caucus in February one of the more independent-minded MPs, Barbara Hogan, prefaced a comment with 'I don't want to make trouble but . . .' – whereupon Mbeki asked if this meant that people were frightened to speak in caucus for fear of being viewed as troublemakers. There was a thunderous chorus of 'Yes'. Mbeki professed himself to be much shocked.[12]

Such disavowals carried little weight. All power and patronage flowed from Mbeki's office and the tentacles of his office reached into every corner. Whereas the budget for Mandela's office staff for 1997–8 had fallen by 11 per cent – and many even of those staff were dealing with questions like getting Mandela's signature for autograph-hunters, arranging celebrity visits and the like – the budget for Mbeki's office had risen by 20 per cent. It already had 96 staff and a further 65 people were being recruited. Moreover, while Mandela's staffers said that 'We've been progressively reducing his workload', most of that 'workload' was little more than play. His main 'duty' was photo opportunities with visiting celebrities – in a not atypical fortnight his guests included Princess Diana, Bill Cosby, Gloria Estafan and Hillary and Chelsea Clinton. He often spent days at home doing nothing. *The Sowetan* pointed out that even his lengthy absences abroad 'have scarcely been noticed', so absent was he from the real business of government.[13]

Mbeki's office was exactly the opposite. Through Aziz Pahad he ran foreign policy. Domestically, Essop Pahad acted as an all-purpose fixer and enforcer. A whole host of commissions, agencies and programmes were also attached to Mbeki's office. Repeatedly, Mbeki attempted to set up a Policy Co-ordination Unit, with the duty of monitoring and co-ordinating the formulation of policy across all ministries – but this tended to be frustrated by the growing functional anarchy of the disparate ministries. Even senior staff in Mbeki's office found it took many months to get a file from another ministry, if they could get it at all.[14] Although Mbeki relied for his personal security on an all-white team of Afrikaners, none of his top advisers was white. Key figures were Vusi Mavimbela, Mbeki's political adviser and a long-term Mbeki client from exile days, Moss Ngoasheng, his economic adviser, a former Robben Islander who had trod the familiar road to Sussex University, and Mojanku Gumbi, an outspokenly Africanist lawyer and Azapo member, usefully connecting Mbeki's office into Black Consciousness circles.

THE PROBLEM ABOUT WINNIE . . .

The ANC Women's League finally held its conference after Mbeki and Steve Tshwete had worked hard to bring together the feuding factions (Winnie on the one hand, Dlamini-Zuma on the other). Tshwete managed to get his hands on an advance copy of Winnie's opening address to the League and was shocked to see that it criticized the government as a 'gravy train', attacking it for failing to deliver on its promises. Winnie also denounced the whole proportional representation system as a bosses' charter and laid into the ANC party bosses in particular. In a furious meeting lasting until 3 a.m. Tshwete and other ANC leaders insisted that she omit all these passages, threatening that otherwise there would be no opening speech at all – presumably by cancelling the conference. Winnie gave way but, typically, managed to smuggle the original version of her speech into the next edition of *New Nation*.[15]

The deal brokered by Mbeki was that Winnie could keep the Women's League presidency but that Dlamini-Zuma must become deputy president. The sitting deputy president, Thandi Modise, then decided to challenge Winnie for the presidency but lost heavily. Winnie accordingly swung her support behind Dlamini-Zuma for the deputy presidency but the indignant Ms Modise held on to her job by a large majority, leading Dlamini-Zuma to announce that she no longer wished to have any role in the organization.[16] Ms Modise angrily complained that Winnie had recruited a large number of thugs from the MK self-defence units who had followed her everywhere at the conference, one of them telling her that she 'would be destroyed' if she persisted with her presidential bid. For her own safety she had had to be whisked away from the conference under heavy security guard.[17] Winnie made no denial. Observers spoke of the 'pervasive tension' at the conference and reported that Winnie's supporters included two sangomas in full ritual dress – scary for many – and that she had led the singing of militant songs such as 'These guns remind me of Winnie Mandela'. At one stage she attacked illegal immigrants, especially 'foreigners from Mozambique who crawl through broken border fences', universally taken as an attack on President Mandela's new consort, Graca Machel.[18]

The Women's League thus remained under Winnie's control and she remained a threat at one remove to Mbeki. Her radical populism was largely fraudulent. She told Parliament that she had no assets to declare and that she 'was proud to be poor',[19] yet she was one of the wealthiest MPs. Besides her parliamentary salary and three houses in Soweto, her friendship with the illicit diamond dealer Hazel Crane had brought her a house in Cape Town's exclusive Bishopscourt and much else besides. She also ran 'Heroes Acre' from the house which she and Nelson had once inhabited in Soweto, where struggle pilgrims could buy soil from the property at R50 a bottle, one of a large number of money-making schemes she set up to exploit the Mandela name. She retained a large staff of bodyguards and travelled everywhere in her large white Mercedes. None of this mattered to her supporters. In a party where dissent had vanished and the revolutionary tradition was summarily curtailed, she was a rare independent voice willing to express the frustrations of the townships and squatter camps.

The centralization of power under Mbeki did not, however, translate into effective government. There was little co-ordination between ministries and many ministers did little or nothing. When Stella Sigcau died in office in May 2006 after twelve years in government no one could point to any achievement or even action she had taken in office. Mac Maharaj liberalized road and air transport but neither he nor any other Transport Minister tackled the major problems of the transport infrastructure. Indeed, it was difficult to find a minister – apart from Manuel at Finance – who did not preside over a steep fall in standards in his or her area of supervision.

DEVELOPMENTAL FAILURES: WATER AND THE IDT

The failures of government in this era were perhaps best symbolized by two areas, the Department of Water Affairs and Forestry (DWAF) and the Independent Development Trust (IDT). DWAF was publicly celebrated as one of the government's great successes, for the Minister, Kader Asmal, easily convinced the media that he was doing a sterling job. No one doubted that in a dry country like South Africa water management had great significance and that providing a sewage system and clean water to the poor was a task of the first importance. Every South African was familiar with the teetering figures of women and young girls carrying immensely heavy cans of water on their heads to their families from rivers or distant taps: it was not a job that any African man did.

The World Bank, on its initial foray into South Africa in 1994, pointed out that the country's entire industrial structure had been distorted by a failure to price water correctly. Put bluntly, neither Johannesburg nor Pretoria should really exist. They can do so only because huge amounts of water are piped to them from Lesotho and 1,820 metres uphill from KwaZulu-Natal and their residents are never asked to pay the full costs of this exercise. This was understandable when Johannesburg was the main mining centre, but had become quite crazy when that city and Pretoria came to depend mainly on manufacturing and service industries. When – and it was only a matter of time – the real price of water was charged to these cities most of these industries would migrate to the coast and, in particular, to KwaZulu-Natal, where two-thirds of the country's rain falls.

Kader Asmal was at one with his apartheid predecessors in not wishing to face this reality. But the World Bank and water experts in general had an even more important message for him. In a purely technical sense South Africa had been near the top of the class in handling its water supplies – it had a complex system of water reticulation, large dams, major reservoirs and sophisticated inter-basin transfers. Indeed, apartheid South Africa had bequeathed its successors the best water infrastructure and resource-management system on the continent. The state was responsible for bulk supply but delegated its authority to major water boards and the actual sale and delivery of water was left to local government. The glaring deficiency, of course, was the poor delivery of water to black rural communities and the mushrooming squatter camps.

Asmal now decided, however, that DWAF would take over the delivery of water schemes, and simultaneously DWAF took over all the homeland water departments, swelling in size from 10,000 to 30,000 employees. Frantically, Asmal's advisers pointed out that a central Water Ministry was a dinosaur; all international experience showed that such an animal should not exist. In the end the only water schemes that worked were those devolved either to local communities or to private water companies. Moreover, research showed that no water system was sustainable unless it was matched with the local community's ability to pay for it. There were rare cases – Durban was the only South African example – where rainfall was so plentiful, water supplies so cheap and population so dense that one could get the urban middle classes to subsidize water delivery to the poor, but most of South Africa was not like that. Water was scarce and expensive, the population (and thus the water reticulation system) was spread out and if the middle classes there were forced to pay such subsidies they would simply move away. So water schemes should not be set up by a centralized ministry. Instead there should, at most, be a ministry of a few hundred civil servants overseeing the devolution of water supply responsibilities to local communities or to private water companies. And the real costs of water delivery would have to be progressively felt in water pricing. Any attempt to buck the market by pretending that water was not a scarce resource would only produce disaster.

Within the ANC Asmal passed for an intellectual, but he simply ignored this advice. He knew there was a huge popular demand for a proper water supply for poor blacks and that many on the left talked of water being a human right, akin to the right to life. They would not accept realistic water pricing, however inevitable in the long term. There were also many ANC activists demanding well-paid jobs with the powerful water boards: the party assumed all parastatals were now part of its patronage system. Most important, if he slimmed down the ministry and decentralized water delivery Asmal might lose the opportunity for the publicity coups he craved. Accordingly, he disregarded all the expert advice, kept his ministry as fat as ever and launched centrally conceived water schemes around the country, exactly what he had been warned against.

Asmal rushed around the country opening water schemes while local women ululated and photographers snapped pictures of a beaming minister surrounded by delighted villagers. The local media naively lapped it up. Indeed, the chattering classes commonly saw Asmal as the only really effective minister. In reality it was a cynical disaster. World Bank advisers warned that Asmal was repeating exactly the mistake made in many African countries, namely, that the state paid the capital costs of the new schemes and the local communities paid for the water but no provision was made for payment of depreciation, maintenance and repair. Without this the new schemes were white elephants, destined for speedy failure. Faced by such advice Asmal merely became angry. Morale in his department plummeted, yes-men were promoted and most of the top experts left. As one water expert put it to me at the time, 'The worst thing is that really quite large resources are being pissed up against the wall and when, entirely predictably, these schemes prove unsustainable, no one is going to find it easy to marshal this enthusiasm or such resources to do the job properly.'[20]

So successful was Asmal's showmanship that at the 2000 Stockholm Water Festival he was awarded the Water Prize. It was similar to the World Health Organization award for her anti-smoking measures that Dr Dlamini-Zuma had received a year earlier – at the very time that her refusal to deal with Aids had allowed the epidemic to gather irresistible momentum.

By the time Asmal received his award he had moved on to be Minister for Education, leaving DWAF in the nick of time. Already a major report on water delivery had concluded that 'there is questioning of the permanence of the advances being made . . . It is widely reported that about two-thirds of the rural water projects in South Africa are currently not working . . . As fast as new projects are being launched, established projects are reported to be breaking down . . .'[21] The most important water board, Umgeni Water, was racked by repeated scandals, a fact, the *Mail and Guardian* reported, 'directly attributable to Asmal. The scent of corruption, inefficiency and debt is directly connected to ANC political decisions to have full control.'[22] The decision to ignore the question of affordability quickly had catastrophic consequences as water providers tried to recover their costs from consumers who were unable to pay. Inevitably, the poor took the brunt. By May 2002 'at least 10 million South Africans had had their water cut off since 1994. More than two million were evicted from their homes for the same reason . . .'[23] Worst of all, by 2000 there were major outbreaks of cholera, directly traceable to failures in sanitation and water supply. Such outbreaks had never occurred under apartheid. Despite DWAF's swollen numbers and large budget it had taken only six years to reach this nadir.

The failure at DWAF was due to the refusal to take difficult decisions. Failure over the IDT was more to do with squandering an institutional inheritance. Set up in 1990 with a grant of R3 billion from the De Klerk government, under the chairmanship of the determinedly non-political Judge Jan Steyn, the IDT set itself to address the needs of the black poor in education, health and job creation. It was independent of government and included many ANC worthies as well as businessmen among its trustees. It recruited development experts and busied itself with every sort of development programme: schemes for agricultural betterment, rural clinics, irrigation and electrification; it built community centres and thousands of new classrooms and toilets; it ran educational programmes for 140,000 teachers and school principals, set up literacy programmes, helped establish more than 20,000 new small businesses, and carried out a wide range of housing projects.[24] It was incomparably the biggest and most expert development agency in the country and soon it attracted money from foreign donors as well. The first ANC Minister for Public Works, Jeff Radebe, handed over a quarter of his 1994–5 budget to the IDT because it could spend it far more efficiently than he could.[25] The donors wanted to see properly evaluated, costed and budgeted project programmes with a well-worked-out rationale, clear timelines and impact assessments. The IDT had the expertise, had done the work; nobody else came close.

This was also the problem. With the ANC in power the RDP office was painfully aware that both the Minister and his subordinates were complete amateurs in the development business. They looked at the IDT, with its established programmes, expertise and credibility – and resented it. Inevitably, they played to their strong suit, political legitimacy, and decried the IDT as 'an apartheid creation'. They were merely representative of a far larger community of struggle activists ('strugglistas', as they were known). With apartheid dead, these activists hurriedly reinvented themselves in a plethora of 'development' NGOs, many of them with rather nebulous aims. What they really wanted was a salary, perks and patronage, and 'development' was the new thing.

The IDT sat squarely in their way. When they demanded IDT funding they were told that everything depended on their expertise in the development field and on whether they were acceptable to the rural communities the IDT were trying to help. This was bad news for the hurriedly retooled strugglistas who had no real development expertise, and were keen to maintain an urban yuppie lifestyle. Inevitably, they too denounced the IDT as an apartheid creation. They particularly disliked the fact that the IDT's chief executive, Merlyn Mehl, was a Coloured, while its senior executives included several other Coloureds and the occasional white. The fact that this merely reflected the distribution of expertise did not count with the strugglistas – and they had many allies in their relatives and friends in the burgeoning government bureaucracy in which struggle credibility was at a premium and expertise at a discount.[26]

Mbeki's office was receptive to the plaintive noise from the struggle NGOs not only because they were a significant constituency but because Mbeki and Essop Pahad were instinctive centralizers. They disliked the notion even of development patronage escaping to Jay Naidoo's RDP office, let alone to an independent NGO: they preferred a straightforward state takeover. Mbeki detailed one of his leading loyalists, Phumzile Mlambo-Ngcuka, then a deputy minister at Trade and Industry, to work with Pahad on bringing the IDT to heel.

The result was increasing pressure on the IDT and demands that it be replaced with a new national development agency more receptive to the needs of the strugglistas. Provided the IDT's trustees and managers stood firm, this could easily be resisted; the IDT had a trust deed guaranteeing its independence, had money in the bank and had credibility with foreign donors. But they did not stand firm. Wiseman Nkhulu, the IDT's CEO, suddenly resigned in March 1995 and government pressure increased. First, an interim Transitional National Development Trust was set up purely to give money to NGOs, then pressure built for the IDT's replacement by a National Development Agency (NDA).

Mbeki set up an advisory committee which invited all the major activist groups in the field to come and testify. What they wanted, of course, was an NDA whose main job would be to dispense grants to their own NGOs and which would quit doing development projects. Theoretically, this was in order to leave the field free for NGOs but in practice it was because the strugglistas who would staff the NDA lacked any of the necessary skills for such work. This would, of course, constitute a complete betrayal of the IDT's mission and of the black poor.

Winding up the IDT should have been unthinkable. Not only had it carried out hundreds of development projects, but by the end of 1997 it had spent R2.7 billion of its initial R3 billion, had committed a further R600 million – and raised another R4 billion. And the consensus was that development programmes worked best if they were upwardly led from communities and civil society. If the IDT's chair, Dr Mamphela Ramphele, and the other trustees had stood firm, they had both the legal and financial means to carry on. But Ramphele simply gave way. Mehl and the other leading Coloureds and whites resigned. The government appointed a whole raft of new trustees[27] who obediently voted considerable funds over to the NDA. Ramphele soon took off to a highly paid job at the World Bank where, however, she proved something of a disappointment. Her contract was not renewed.

The result was predictable. In 2000 the IDT was relaunched as a mere shadow of its old self, its new role being to 'enhance government's delivery capacity'. Despite repeated large advertisements in the press boasting of its achievements (all actually achieved by the old IDT), the new IDT did virtually nothing. By 2003 the Auditor-General reported that its administrative costs had risen out of control, that it was paying huge sums unnecessarily to consultants, that it was failing to spend even its much reduced budget, that projects were not completed on time, that there was no recording system for project proposals, no method for prioritizing projects or evaluating their impact, that many of its projects were high risk, lacked documents, had no budget, had no visible activities and did not record income. It was a complete shambles.[28]

The NDA was as bad. In its first year it handled its hardly onerous task of handing money out to NGOs so badly that it managed to disburse less than 10 per cent of its R340 million budget, resulting in the decimation of NGOs depending on it for delivery. Of the 280 NGOs working in adult education in 1997, for example, by 2001 only

60 remained. A R50 million grant from the EU sat in its bank account unspent, causing the EU to freeze further grants. The agency failed even to process grant applications made to it. A source close to the NDA laid the blame squarely at the door of its management including its CEO, Dr Thoahlane Thoahlane: 'He has no management skills, no management experience, a poor leadership style . . . He's inexperienced in the field and the staff he appoints don't have adequate track records in developmental areas.'[29] Thoahlane so demoralized staff that a quarter of them left during his one-year tenancy, some accusing him of racism and sexism. Ultimately the board, embarrassed by the bad publicity, requested his resignation. Thoahlane, on holiday in the United States, demanded five years' salary as a golden handshake,[30] insisting that 'it's just whites that are complaining'.[31] The board's chairman, Delani Mthembu, took over as CEO (while retaining the chairmanship) but within a year was accused of having 'created projects for friends and relatives and ignored funding procedures in allocating funds for them'.[32] The Auditor-General agreed that most of the agency's business plans had not been properly approved and that spending on them was therefore 'irregular'.[33]

In August 2003, thanks to the intervention of the Minister for Defence, Terror Lekota, the PAC leader, Thami ka Plaatjie, was given a senior job at the NDA, despite complaints that the post had not been properly advertised, that he had no qualifications and despite the fact that in his previous job as Registrar of Vista University, Plaatjie was 'accused of costing the university thousands of rands by abusing its vehicles and its telephones'.[34] By this time the chaos within the organization was such that staff salaries were not being paid on time, let alone payments to projects. In late 2003 the Minister for Social Development, Zola Skweyiya, ordered an inquiry into mismanagement, fraud and corruption and Mthembu was suspended. This left the chief operations officer, Pula Zwane, in charge, though it was then discovered that he had concealed criminal convictions on drugs charges and had actually been serving a suspended sentence even when appointed.[35] He too was suspended on full pay – for several years. Skweyiya put a new board in place, complaining that the NDA had spent more money on press advertisements for itself than on anything else, that R90 million given to the agency by the government had gone straight into the private bank account of the NDA's finance director and that it had hired a private security company to spy on its own staff and on NGOs.[36]

Mthembu resigned before the disciplinary hearing against him could be completed, but then sued for wrongful dismissal. Meanwhile allegations continued that a fire which had broken out in the NDA's filing room in July 2004 was a deliberate arson attempt to destroy files bearing on corruption charges.[37] Zwane finally resigned after receiving a golden handshake, despite charges of having paid illegal bonuses and made unprocedural hirings.[38] Skweyiya's new nominee for CEO, Marigwashi Phiyega, had to be put on hold after his previous employer, Transnet, flatly advised against his appointment.[39] Although a new board and new CEO were put in place, the scandals continued. In 2006 it emerged that R8.77 million had been stolen by a mere accounts clerk while an EU grant of R7.5 million had been irregularly spent and had to be refunded.[40] The Auditor-General reported that there was extremely poor financial control at the NDA, that the clerk had been recruited despite known lies in her CV and that procedures had not been adhered to.[41] Despite its vastly reduced role – all it had to do was pass money it was given on to others – the organization was shambolic. Its 'finances were in such a state of disarray that it was impossible to say what had happened to much of the money destined for poverty alleviation', and performance bonuses were paid to staff without any performance evaluation.[42] Quite clearly the NDA existed in order to enrich those who staffed it and no one else.

This sad story dramatizes several separate failings. First, there was an extremely cavalier approach to institution building. It had taken some time to build the IDT and it had working systems, procedures and linkages in place. Most of all, it had a history and culture of efficacy and successful delivery. It was utter folly to discard this and attempt to set up a wholly new successor institution, one which never worked. This was a mistake which the government made repeatedly in many spheres. Secondly, every person involved in the above saga claimed to be dedicated to the cause of poverty alleviation and some, at least, were sincere. Yet the result was disastrous. Good intentions are far from enough.

Thirdly, a choice had had to be made between the ambitions of an aspirant black middle-class group and the needs of the black rural poor. It was simply no contest. Despite its decades of rhetoric the new government unhesitatingly chose against the poor. Just as in the case of water, it instinctively sought a centralized solution, even though everything suggested that a decentralized solution would be far more effective. In both cases the interests of the new black bourgeoisie were identified with the extension of the central state apparatus. Finally, rhetoric was a bad guide. Both at DWAF and the IDT the new government's management led to dramatically bad outcomes for the poor.

AFFIRMATIVE ACTION

Even such egregious examples were dwarfed, however, by the policy of affirmative action, which was the government's central thrust in this period. The loss of the ANC's old socialist agenda meant that this was what it was left with, *faute de mieux*, and the political pressure for such measures exercised by the rising black middle class was all but irresistible. In effect the old apartheid job-reservation laws were reinstated, this time in favour of blacks.

Yet the case against affirmative action was strong. International studies showed that it lowered economic efficiency, that it could only help a minority and thus never hope to provide an answer to poverty, and that it redistributed away from the poor towards the middle classes. This was particularly bound to be true in the South African case. There was a vast army of black proletarians – miners, domestic workers, farm labourers – who could never benefit from affirmative action. Apartheid had also bequeathed a black labour force which was massively underskilled in the areas in which affirmative action was likely to apply. Bantu Education and the 'tribal college' black universities had increased this effect, with black graduates almost invariably underskilled compared to whites. Finally, the bantustan system had produced no less than ten homeland bureaucracies, teeming with low-skilled white-collar workers and wannabe bourgeois, who were now to be absorbed by the state. Many of these cadres had been schooled in appalling work habits, were almost unemployably unproductive and sometimes corrupt. The ease with which the ANC embraced this group – which it had formerly reviled as traitors – spoke volumes both for its knee-jerk Africanism and its instinctive siding with the embryonic middle class. It now also embraced the tribal colleges, which it had condemned previously as segregated and intrinsically inferior apartheid institutions. Now they bore the title of Historically Disadvantaged Institutions and received preferential treatment.

Affirmative action came at a high political cost. The ANC had been built on the premise of non-racialism and this was obviously inconsistent with racial favouritism. Under apartheid, Africans had longed for merit, not race, to count. This was, indeed, their very definition of fairness. Athol Fugard captured this in his famous character, Sizwe Bansi, who yearned to be his own man, to have an unjust system off his back, to be allowed to prove himself on his own merits. This spirit was the basis for the coming together of all groups to write an essentially liberal constitution.

All of which was blown away like leaves in a gale. Not only should blacks be given preference when other criteria were equal but in practice whole categories of jobs were simply closed to whites. Every institution's workforce should mirror the nation's demography, and there would be time enough to look at white job applicants when that objective had been reached. This soon led to a preference for Africans over Coloureds and Indians. So utterly racial was this preference that quite commonly black people from the rest of Africa or even from the West Indies or North America would be given preference over Coloured or Indian South Africans, although the latter had been victims of apartheid and the former had not. All that mattered was skin colour.

Racial criteria were enforced throughout the public sector to the point where whites and other minorities often simply did not apply for jobs there. But similar pressures were felt in the private sector too as companies sought desperately to achieve the 'right' demographic profile. Given the shortage of black skills, the large companies often paid exorbitant and racially discriminatory salaries to get the blacks they needed. Job-hopping by the young and over-rewarded group of black yuppies became almost the norm. Public sector institutions which could not compete with private sector salaries often simply refused to recruit at all if blacks could not be found, so national, provincial and municipal government departments soon had huge numbers of unfilled posts.

Moreover, even the achievement of full demographic representation, with 75 per cent of jobs going to Africans, would be no reason to give any of the remaining jobs to non-Africans. Thus there was, for example, fierce pressure on the national rugby and cricket teams to include more players of colour, but no pressure at all on the (mainly African) national football team to include more whites. Similarly, in 2006 the police commissioner in charge of human resources ordered that the police force be halved to under 10 per cent white by 2010[43] although this would inevitably damage police efficiency in the run-up to the 2010 football World Cup.

Affirmative action had been applied in other countries in order to make minorities feel more integrated into society, but it was quite a different thing to apply such measures where they affected not 10–15 per cent of jobs but upwards of 75 per cent. And, while Africanization policies were common in independent Africa, nowhere else had such policies been applied to a sophisticated industrial economy. This was, indeed, the crux, particularly when taken together with the lamentable state of African education in South Africa, far inferior to that in French and British colonial Africa. It was not just that Ghanaians, Zimbabweans and other English-speaking Africans were strong competitors for South African jobs. More ominously, nowhere else had the mismatch between the sophistication of the economy and the lack of sophistication of the workforce been so wide.

The decision to press ahead regardless with affirmative action throughout both public and private sectors was the greatest single disaster to overtake the new South Africa. It speedily crippled the state machine and the parastatals, collapsing the standard of services delivered. In 1997, in response to successful legal actions by white employees who had sued the government for racial discrimination against them, it was decided to amend the Public Service Act because it was 'imperative to get rid of merit as the over-riding principle in the appointment of public servants'.[44] Once this was done, racial discrimination was not only legal again but actually obligatory. It became commonplace for blacks and whites doing the same job to have different salaries, different retirement ages and different benefits. In effect apartheid-style job reservation was reintroduced throughout the public service.

The key question became whether a person or an institution had been 'historically disadvantaged': this, rather than capacity or ability, now determined who got which job, contract or grant. Indeed, the better salaries, jobs and benefits now generally went to the less qualified. This inversion of functionality carried a heavy price in itself and also made it clear to job recipients that it was their skin colour rather than their merit which mattered. Inevitably, such recipients became expert at playing the race card, but since affirmative-action appointments rapidly became synonymous with sub-standard ones, everyone insisted that they had only got their just deserts on merit.

Affirmative action meant that the new state, with its ambitious agenda, was almost immediately broken-backed. Yet ministers obstinately refused to take this into account and pushed for ever-greater powers of intervention and regulation even though their departments were quite incapable of dealing with the business thus created. The result was a growing logjam, with all departments working more and more inefficiently. There was one great exception, the South African Revenue Service (SARS). Its new boss, Pravin Gordhan, a former Communist, had been appointed with the specific aim of making whites pay far more taxes than they ever had before. In this he was prodigiously successful. This was the goose that laid the golden eggs for the rest of government and SARS worked like clockwork, hiring the best accountants it could find, regardless of race. For Gordhan had cannily made sure that SARS was not part of the public service and was not bound by government pay-scales or by a centralized union bargaining process. For the fact was that even in 2002 only 246 of the country's 19,757 chartered accountants were black.[45] If the Employment Equity Act – let alone the Public Service Act – had been applied to SARS it would clearly have been crippled. The irony was that SARS produced revenue surpluses which government departments, crippled by affirmative action, lacked the capacity to spend.

The Employment Equity Act set stiff racial targets for every level of the workforce, yet the Population Registration Act of 1950 (which had laid down racial classifications) had been abolished back in 1991. Now these old classifications had to be surreptitiously resurrected and applied: for what was to stop a person of any race proclaiming that he was 'an African'? There had to be some way of determining who was an African in the old apartheid sense. The results were often ridiculous. For example, the government tried to get the banks to keep a note of the race of their customers, insisting that racial equity principles should apply to credit extension. The banks protested that by law people were now allowed to classify themselves as they wished, that their staff were now explicitly told to make no racial distinctions and in any case there would be large numbers of people whose 'racial classification' was uncertain. The government did not want to be responsible for re-introducing racial classification, yet it needed others to do so, because an ever-increasing body of legislation depended precisely on the maintenance of racial distinctions.

The private sector was more constrained by market forces than the public sector, but despite the scarcity of skilled blacks the state exerted strong pressure on the larger private companies. For example, in 2001 Gauteng's ANC provincial government threatened to take away its R16 billion-a-year account from Standard Bank if it did not hurry to fulfil its affirmative action targets.[46] Such threats were common. Some businesses resorted to desperate measures, cutting back their numbers to less than fifty employees in order to avoid the Act, contracting out work to avoid having more employees on their own books, or hiring black executives or directors who were merely fronts. Others took their businesses private, for this made them much less visible than public companies.

Only so much dodging was possible. One continually met whites and Indians sickened by the effects affirmative action was having in their work environment, unhappily aware that promotion was now unlikely to be based on merit alone and convinced this meant there was no future for their children in the country. By 2006 a million whites and large numbers of Indians had left. The émigrés were usually young and the country's loss in talent and skills was prodigious. Mangosuthu Buthelezi, who termed the affirmative action policy 'reckless', insisted that it was a betrayal not only of non-racialism and the national interest but also of the promises made to whites which had led them to give a two-thirds majority to De Klerk's referendum to embrace democracy in 1992. Had they 'envisaged in the early 1990s the way in which affirmative action and racial classification would come to dominate the post-apartheid labour market, few would have voted yes', he said.[47] This was probably true: the De Klerk Foundation strongly objected to the way in which affirmative action was enforced.

THE UNPOPULARITY OF A 'POPULAR' POLICY

So rapid and complete was this process of 'transformation' that it was accepted as inevitable. Indeed, politically correct whites would loudly trumpet their own commitment to 'transformation', without which, one was told, 'the country would burn' and there would be 'blood on the streets', the assumption being that affirmative action enjoyed massive popular support.

This was not, in fact, the case. A post-election survey in 1994 found that 61 per cent of all voters, including 52 per cent of Africans, wanted to see appointments made strictly on merit, 'even if some people do not make progress as a result'.[48] In 1996, the Helen Suzman Foundation again tested public opinion on this and related issues. We found that only 23 per cent of voters took a hardline position in favour of affirmative action, whereas 54 per cent were clearly opposed, believing either that 'There should be special training for Africans/blacks but the best applicants for jobs should be appointed whoever they are' or that 'There should be no such policies and jobs must go strictly on merit'. A middle group of 22 per cent believed that 'preference should be given to Africans/blacks, but if others are better qualified, they should get the job'. Thus 76 per cent regarded merit, not race, as the overriding criterion.

In June/July 2000 after affirmative action had been in force for several years, backed up by unrelenting government pressure and propaganda, we tested opinion on the same question again. We found that white opinion had noticeably softened, while African opinion had actually hardened. This time only 22 per cent took a hardline position in favour of affirmative action, while 56 per cent took a hardline position against it, with the middle group declining to 19 per cent.[49] This African majority resistance to affirmative action contrasted with the passionate commitment of the educated minority who benefited from it. Such findings were so unpopular with government that no newspaper was willing to reproduce them. Yet they were hardly surprising: affirmative action offered nothing to the black majority other than worse services. Here too the crucial question was whether to prioritize the interests of the poor black majority or those of the educated minority. There was never the slightest doubt of the answer. When we asked what kind of people had benefited most from the changes made since 1994, only 14 per cent said 'the mass of the ordinary people', while 28 per cent said 'the new people who have got jobs in government', another 22 per cent said 'better educated people' and 8 per cent said 'politicians'.[50]

Mandela had nothing to do with the development of such policies. They were Mbeki's policies, but they were also part of the spirit of the age. All channels of African opinion were dominated by the better educated, the middle-class aspirants, the great beneficiaries of affirmative action. Their support for such measures was vehement and unanimous: no wonder most whites mistook them for a majority. The only Africans who might have resisted this trend were the industrial working class, but their trade union membership was falling and Cosatu was increasingly dominated by white-collar unions. So Cosatu joined in this Africanist chorus as well, even attempting to outdo the ANC in its commitment to 'transformation'.

This inflection of ANC policy towards the interests of an acquisitive black middle class was covered by a continuous but dishonest rhetoric about its commitment to the poor. Those aghast at the damage being done often felt compelled to remain silent not only because criticism would be regarded as racist but because it was clear that the policies favoured by the left would be even more disastrous. Indeed, when visitors asked what the differences within the ANC were about, the jocular reply often given was that the ANC wanted to ruin the country, but Cosatu and the SACP wanted to achieve this far more quickly. Certainly, the left's red-shirted militancy was a boon to Mbeki: white capitalists concluded that it was better to endure a crazy policy of affirmative action if that was the price of keeping Mbeki in power and the Reds out.

PREPARING THE TRANSITION FROM MANDELA

The impending transition from Mandela gripped all minds. The South African National Civic Organization (Sanco) kicked off by formally backing Mbeki, claiming, absurdly, that Mbeki enjoyed the same 'overwhelming popularity' as Mandela.[51] Sanco was an empty vessel. During the 1980s many civic associations had been members of the UDF. The ANC, in typical centralist style, federated these into a single ANC-affiliated body but with the great transition now over many such associations had collapsed and anyway no national body like Sanco could reflect their essentially local nature. But Mbeki ensured that Sanco had some money, its own investment arm, Sanco Investment Holdings – and thus patronage. Mlungisi Hlongwane, Sanco's long-standing president, was naturally an Mbeki loyalist, allowing Mbeki's office to use Sanco to fly political kites. In 2006, in a similar manoeuvre, Hlongwane proposed a third presidential term for Mbeki.

Mandela insisted that for reasons of ethnic balance the deputy presidency must go to a non-Nguni,[52] suggesting a short list of Terror Lekota (Southern Sotho), Joel Netshitenzhe (Venda), and Tokyo Sexwale and Mathews Phosa (Northern Sotho). Sexwale, whose confrontation with Mbeki had forced him to abandon politics for the business world,[53] speedily withdrew. Phosa was popular but was unacceptable to Mbeki, as was Lekota, who also withdrew.

Netshitenzhe was Mbeki's choice and thus the favourite.[54] He was bright, modest, and, if Mbeki served two terms as President, Netshitenzhe would, in 2009, still be only 53. Netshitenzhe, knowing Mbeki's visceral dislike of rivals and crown princes, knew better than to throw his hat into the ring. Mbeki was determined to block Phosa, so ultimately he got the NEC to instruct the ANC Youth League to withdraw its nomination of Phosa and nominate Netshitenzhe instead.[55] Mbeki also lined up single candidates for all the other major offices: Jacob Zuma for ANC national chairman, Kgalema Motlanthe for secretary-general and another Mbeki client, Mavivi Myakayaka-Manzini, for his deputy.

The SACP launched its expected onslaught against Gear – and Mbeki. Blade Nzimande denounced Mbeki's rationale for Gear as 'opportunism'. The interests of the poor could only be advanced by a 'developmental state'. Gear, instead, aimed at the creation of a new ruling-class coalition composed of 'major fractions of the old white bourgeoisie and and new emergent capitalist fractions' of the 'patriotic [black] bourgeoisie'. Gear was thus a neo-liberal prescription aimed at stabilizing the new social order based upon a 30 per cent privileged group which would oppose 'the excluded 70 per cent as a threat to newly acquired privilege and power', and would thus inevitably result in a new authoritarianism. This clear-cut attack stirred anxiety even within the SACP, however, for it was unmistakably 'a personal assault on Mbeki'.[56] Cronin added fuel to the fire by insisting that ANC structures must assume political primacy over all legislative and government institutions. The ANC must make policy and instruct the government, not the other way around.

Mbeki responded, inevitably, by demanding party unity against the usual mythic monsters. The TRC conveniently summoned a special session to hear Mbeki's speech, which alleged that a 'Third Force' of apartheid-era intelligence agents was still active, and the anti-apartheid struggle was not yet over. The former ANC warlord Sifiso Nkabinde had been working 'for elements within the SA Police Services'. The Third Force was responsible for all political violence in South Africa, having even stage-managed the war between the IFP and ANC.[57] Those who criticized the ANC leadership were themselves possible apartheid agents. Mandela helpfully took up this cry, announcing – with no evidence – that the little war around Richmond, set off by Nkabinde's expulsion, was the work of Third Force elements in the police. Indeed, he went further, pointing his finger at senior policemen and announcing the unlikely proposition that 'Greater Pietermaritzburg is the headquarters of all Third Force elements in South Africa. Let them be warned that the power of the people will root them out from where they hide.'[58] Needless to say, no such thing happened and the situation only quietened down after ANC partisans finally managed to murder Nkabinde.

Cronin's claim that Mbeki was building a new 70/30 class coalition against the black poor (the so-called '1996 class project') found echoes throughout the ANC, where millenarian dreams that 'economic democracy' would follow on the heels of political democracy were still strong. This had to be more directly countered. As usual, Mbeki used racial cleavages to undercut class. Netshitenzhe, at Mbeki's suggestion, put forward a conference paper in which he argued that although South Africa had to be a multi-cultural and non-racial society there must be 'African leadership' in all ANC and state structures, with the aim of building 'a new African nation'. At the same time a document was circulated round the ANC parliamentary caucus arguing that Mandela's 'rainbow nation' concept was 'a temporary phenomenon' and that 'the culture and values of the African working class' must 'constitute the core of the new South Africa'.[59] This was preceded by allegations[60] that the minorities, particularly Indians, were far too numerous in the ANC leadership. For Mbeki had surveyed his opponents and realized that such a campaign would undermine and wrong-foot many of them: the cabinet ministers Valli Moosa (Indian) and Trevor Manuel (Coloured), both old UDF figures and therefore, in Mbeki's eyes, suspect; the clearly disaffected Cheryl Carolus (Coloured) and Jay Naidoo (Indian); the once-powerful figure of Mac Maharaj (Indian), who had thrown in his lot with the old UDF elements against Mbeki;[61] and, not least, Jeremy Cronin (white).

Racial slanging was dirty work not befitting a Deputy President so Peter Mokaba took the lead, promoting discussion of the party's racial balance, with the usual vilification of 'Mandela's Indians'. Mbeki's Indians, the Pahad brothers, were without doubt the most unpopular and powerful Indians in government but Mokaba steered the discussion in other directions. It had, he claimed, been outrageous of Mandela to favour Carolus for ANC secretary-general and even more outrageous for him to put forward Maharaj as a possible president. Most impertinent of all, when Oliver Tambo had died in 1993 Mandela had nominated Kader Asmal to succeed him as national chairman. Mokaba had nominated Mbeki who won 18 : 3 after a three-line whip had been put on all Africans present to oppose the outrageous presumption of having an Indian preside over the ANC. Kader Asmal's egotism was well known and it was universally assumed that he had talked Mandela into proposing him. There seemed no end to the sheer cheek of these Indians, argued Mokaba: why, the Speaker, Frene Ginwala, had also had cabinet ambitions and was only kept out with some difficulty.[62] In arousing anti-Indian sentiment among African nationalists Mokaba was ploughing a fertile field. Asmal and the Justice Minister, Dullah Omar, were so offended that they boycotted a caucus meeting where the agenda was to 'bash minorities'. Mokaba high-mindedly declared that the agenda was not racist but merely 'trying to achieve the unity of the African people . . . to defeat the hierarchy of oppression'.[63]

At this point Sexwale's resignation as premier of Gauteng opened up a succession battle which once again showed the power of the populist left. Gauteng, which includes Pretoria and Johannesburg, is by far the richest province. There were initially five candidates for the succession, including Frank Chikane, the head of Mbeki's office. But once the local stalwart, Amos Masondo, was chosen by Mbeki, enormous pressure was exerted to force all the other candidates to stand down. Three did, but the populist Mathole Motshekga refused. He had a clear majority: six of the province's ANC regions had nominated him against only one for Masondo. Motshekga was put under such extreme pressure to withdraw that he simply vanished for a while, keeping his cellphone switched off. When voting was due to take place and it was realized that Motshekga would win there were last-minute attempts to change the electorate by adding more Masondo supporters. When this failed, voting was postponed for several weeks. A fruitless attempt was made to persuade Sexwale to stay on to block Motshekga. Everyone agreed that Motshekga's work in the provincial legislature was dreadful – but he had the votes. Like Winnie, his strength lay in the squatter camps where his attacks on 'sell-outs' in the ANC leadership went down well.

An attempt was made to get Mandela to order Motshekga to stand down but the President refused to take sides. Motshekga was then deliberately given the wrong time for the nomination meeting so that he might arrive too late to be nominated. The election was repeatedly postponed and an additional 100 ANC branches were hurriedly set up to try to increase the anti-Motshekga vote. In the end Masondo withdrew and Chikane ran against Motshekga. Although, characteristically, Mbeki denied he was behind Chikane, he kept his director's job on hold for him, as clear a sign of approval as there could be.[64] Chikane was the ideal Establishment candidate: he came from Soweto, had Mbeki behind him and was internationally famous. Despite that, Motshekga utterly trounced him, 343 to 179. The result sent shock waves through the entire ANC, for Winnie Mandela and the Women's League had campaigned for Motshekga. The populists had shown their strength.

MATHEWS PHOSA'S BATTLE FOR THE SOUL OF THE PARTY

Motshekga's victory, a serious blow for Mbeki, was followed by a more significant challenge. Mathews Phosa, furious at what he termed 'the back-stabbing and cut-throat jockeying for party positions' and the centre's undemocratic interference in the affairs of the provinces, decided to challenge the party Establishment and run for the post of deputy president. Phosa was widely popular and it was clear that Mbeki's candidate, Joel Netshitenzhe, would be hard pressed to stop him. Mbeki put such strong pressure on his Mpumalanga provincial ANC not to nominate Phosa that its spokeman, Jackson Mthembu, was reduced to saying, 'We have done nothing wrong by nominating premier Phosa. The ANC constitution says anybody within the party can be nominated for a leadership position.'[65] The province was unhappy that the ANC NEC should be composed 'solely from one faction',[66] for Mbeki had turned the NEC into his pliant instrument.

Phosa's bid was challenge enough but it awakened a further nightmare. Winnie now also decided to run for deputy president, despite a directive from the NEC ordering that she not be nominated.[67] When, a fortnight later, Motshekga scored his resounding victory in Gauteng, the leadership's worst fears seemed to be confirmed. Winnie might win – and if she did not, Phosa surely would. Phosa was friendly with both Mandela and Winnie and had taken care not to take sides when they divorced, so there was no animosity between the Phosa and Winnie camps. They were rivals but united in their detestation of Mbeki's centralist rule.

Phosa's challenge was the more significant, for his was the last principled stand of the UDF traditions of democratic consultation against the iron-clad discipline of the exile ANC. Phosa was outraged at the degradation of ANC internal politics – and said so: 'Look at some of our meetings – in some cases comrades draw weapons which can inflict grievous bodily harm. And some comrades are too happy to launch assaults at each other in the mass media. Who suffers? The movement suffers, the interests of the people are betrayed as we each want to be the chairperson, mayor, premier, councillor, deputy president and president.' Throughout the party, Phosa declared, democratic processes were being hijacked. The ANC's backbone had always been its principle of collective leadership. The tendency of some ANC leaders only to 'pay lip-service to the principle must be stopped. Individualism is fast killing collective leadership, with the movement clearly being used as a stepping stone to personal glory, self-aggrandizement and enrichment. The leadership contest for top positions in the ANC is being fought with back-stabbing and vicious character assassination.'[68] Phosa was also a Mr Clean, determined to clean up the notoriously corrupt Mpumalanga administration, and spoke strongly against nepotism, a touchy subject amongst the ANC elite where husband-and-wife teams and extended family networks were common.

Phosa bitterly criticized the way provincial elections for premiers and party chairmen were being managed: the leadership was 'promoting puppetry'. Rumour campaigns and spying were being used to discredit others. 'Highly questionable' memoranda were used to smear individuals: the real motive was 'to say – remove them out of the way'.[69] Shortly after it was revealed that in addition to the ANC department of intelligence and security, Mbeki was also using a secret undercover police unit reporting directly to him. This unit – headed by Andre Lincoln, formerly in an intelligence cadre – stirred the interests of the regular police by its apparent association with criminal circles, including the notorious mafioso, Vito Palazzolo. It emerged that Palazzolo, who had absconded from a Swiss jail where he had been held on drugs charges, had had links in ANC intelligence since the early 1990s, leading to a drugs probe which saw two of Mandela's bodyguards sacked.[70]

Phosa did not mention Mbeki but was clearly running against his whole style of governance. He was challenging not just Mbeki's methods but the notion of a central cabal allowing only one candidate to go forward for each job. The decision about whether he would be elected, Phosa said,

> is not in my hands, neither is it with the national executive of the ANC. The structures and branches of the ANC have the right to nominate and debate the names of the incumbents for vacant positions in the party. Let me put the record straight. Nobody has yet asked me not to stand. In any case individual members and groups within the NEC have a right to lobby support for a particular person. However, they cannot decide who should be the kings and cannot stage manage the election of a new leadership. They may have particular preferences about whom they want for certain positions but they have no right to manipulate who gets what position. What is the purpose of democracy if the leadership appoints and anoints its own candidates?[71]

MBEKI VS. PHOSA

Mbeki responded swiftly to the dual challenge of Phosa and Winnie. Pressure was exerted on the ANC Youth League, which obediently dropped Netshitenzhe as a candidate for deputy president and replaced him with Jacob Zuma, also speedily nominated by the ANC in KwaZulu-Natal. There were many reasons for this: Netshitenzhe, with no popular following, was too obviously an Mbeki client; he anyway preferred a backroom role; and Mbeki was doubtless uneasy about having a declared crown prince standing ready to take over. Zuma, on the other hand, was a true man of the people with a large popular following. Whereas the Venda, where Netshitenzhe's origins lay, were a small and rather despised group, Zuma would have the enthusiastic support of Zulus delighted to see one of their own among the top ANC leadership. Zuma was, moreover, already a close Mbeki ally and his background as the boss of ANC intelligence had its uses.

But many greeted the idea of Zuma – probably the least educated member of the ANC elite – becoming the country's No. 2 with virtual stupefaction. His many wives and innumerable children by these and other women were a part of the old Africa that the young modernizers of the ANC hardly wanted to see up-front. Moreover, he had been an administrative disaster as a provincial cabinet minister in KwaZulu-Natal. 'It was apparent that he'd never run an office and needed to be told, this is a filing cabinet, this is a desk and you can use a secretary to dictate letters,' one exasperated local politician told me at the time.[72] Mandela also cautioned Mbeki that Zuma was seen as so close to him that to choose him would only reinforce Mbeki's reputation for wanting only yes-men. The best candidate, Mandela averred, would be independent-minded and young enough to be a potential successor.[73] This advice was, of course, ignored.

Yet Zuma was a genial and sympathetic man who had, crucially, won the good opinion of Chief Buthelezi and had made peace in KwaZulu-Natal. Moreover, Zuma had all the working-class grass roots and sensibilities that Mbeki lacked. He loved leading the singing on ceremonial occasions – he had a fine voice and was greatly in demand at funerals – and he had the popular touch. Best of all, no one could possibly imagine Zuma as President, so Mbeki thought he could safely pick him with no fear that he would ever be seen as an alternative President. Zuma was anyway two months older than Mbeki, so the idea of him following Mbeki after 2009 was also unthinkable. Indeed, Zuma had told journalists before the 1994 election that he planned to retire in 1999.[74] And if Zuma was not the non-Nguni Mandela had wanted, at least he was a Zulu and not another Xhosa. Zuma was, of course, happy to accept Mbeki's invitation and keep his mouth shut: he refused to give interviews or even return journalists' calls.[75]

Mbeki needed to neutralize the left, which was backing both Phosa and Winnie. This meant facing down the anti-Gear challenge from the SACP and Cosatu. First, Mbeki got Mandela to confront Cosatu head-on at their Congress, at which Gear was fiercely attacked until Mandela rose to give a completely uncompromising defence of government economic policy, making it clear that he expected their loyal support. There was stunned silence: the union leaders knew that their members would not wish to go flatly against Mandela. The ANC leadership knew the same for it had secretly commissioned polls which showed that the large majority of Cosatu members were ANC supporters first and union members second. This was the crux.

Secondly, a paper under Peter Mokaba's name was circulated in which he questioned whether the SACP's position in the tripartite alliance was still appropriate. 'The SACP has become a mere caucus within the ANC, rather than an independent partner in the alliance. Meetings of the communist party have simply become meetings of some ANC members to the exclusion of others.' Mokaba compared the SACP to other pro-ANC NGOs and asked whether it should really have the privilege of being regarded as a separate third wing of the alliance. The present situation, he argued, smacked of 'ill-discipline or opportunism'.[76] The implicit suggestion was that SACP members might have to choose between the party and the ANC. No one had made such a suggestion for over forty years. Inevitably this reawakened all the old Africanist complaints that the alliance with the SACP allowed white and Indian communists to exert disproportionate influence on the movement.

The fact that Mokaba's document was presumed to have been authored by Mbeki gave particular significance to his suggestion that in future the ANC should minimize the role of elections within its ranks. NEC positions, he argued, should be ex officio rather than elective, while all major posts in the ANC should be appointed by the ANC president – ministers and deputy ministers, provincial premiers, parliamentary committee chairpersons and everyone else of significance right down to the chairpersons of local party branches.[77] This was the first warning of how an Mbeki presidency would seek to extinguish internal democracy. At the time it seemed too far-fetched for anyone to take it seriously.

Even more provocatively, Mokaba suggested that the ANC abandon any idea of carrying the national democratic revolution through to a second, socialist stage. What was wrong with accepting that this was as far as the NDR would go? 'We don't need isms: we can't eat isms. Socialism was unable to evolve and therefore failed. The ANC cannot build socialism. It can only build a market economy which is capitalism. What I have seen is every country in the world embracing the market. China is growing on the basis of acceptance of markets. Capitalism is not a swear word.'[78] Mokaba also boldly asserted that 'The ANC has never had socialism as its goal. It never was a socialist or communist organization. Its programme simply seeks to establish the most democratic capitalist society based on a mixed economy.'[79]

This last point was also provocative. Technically it was quite correct that the ANC had never committed itself to socialist goals, but everyone in the movement knew that this had been for tactical reasons, to preserve the image of a broad national movement. In practice it was extremely difficult to find ANC leaders in the 1980s who were not vehement socialists. But the purpose now was, of course, to pick a fight with the SACP, preferably with a white like Jeremy Cronin. Like a fish rising unwisely to the bait, Cronin attacked Mokaba's paper. Mokaba replied in deliberately insulting terms. Cronin was an embarrassment and 'stupid' and 'must learn to read and understand issues before he makes comments'.[80]

Both the SACP and Cosatu decided to beat a tactical retreat or, at the least, to bide their time. Mafikeng was to be Mandela's last conference and the moment when the torch would be passed to the next generation, a deeply emotional occasion. Whatever the reason for it, the grass roots would never understand or support disunity at this point. In effect the left was told if they did not like the situation, they could leave. No one wanted that. Everyone had, meanwhile, seen how Ramaphosa and Sexwale had been snapped up by the corporate world. Clearly, they were both soon going to be rich men. Their example had changed everything, breeding a spirit of *enrichissez-vous*.

Mbeki was well aware of this. He leant heavily on the belief that power alone could bring wealth and that possession of the political kingdom thus gave a new and fundamental form of leverage. The ANC had always been a hard school but power and wealth had brought a new ruthlessness right into its heart. It had itself become a rich organization, with large sums solicited by Mandela abroad pouring in, complemented by large sums skimmed off the arms deal. The cynicism behind such transfers was transparent. Thus Mandela bestowed South Africa's highest honour, the Order of Good Hope, on both Libya's Qaddafi and Indonesia's Suharto, leading to outraged criticism from the Opposition, for it was quite clear that these were simply rewards for large donations to ANC funds. Mandela, disgracefully, suggested that such complaints were racist – and thus refused to face the issue, which was that he had used state visits, and now national awards, to solicit party funds.

No one inside the ANC was ignorant that large sums were pouring in. One particular consignment from Malaysia at this time saw huge amounts of cash brought back in trunks, with ANC employees making repeated trips to Kuala Lumpur to bring all the trunks in.[81] The legality of such transfers was dubious. Often they consisted of 'hot' or laundered money in the first place and no one seems to have bothered with foreign exchange regulations or other such niceties. The secrecy surrounding such donations and the fact that they were usually in cash made them tempting targets for criminals, for the ANC could not risk a public row if money went missing. Inevitably, very little of the Malaysian money reached the ANC's account. Instead huge sums were deposited into private trusts. An ANC official, Stanley Yakobi, then investigating the 'disappearance' of some forty ANC vehicles (vehicle theft occurred frequently in government and ANC-run organizations), was given the job of enquiring into the missing money. He was almost immediately gunned down in an execution-style killing outside the ANC's Shell House headquarters.[82] The matter was speedily hushed up as if the existence of gangster networks inside party headquarters was just another sad fact of life, like pilferage in a supermarket.

Mbeki's pressure had silenced the left but in the end Phosa and Winnie had to be confronted directly. Phosa would clearly win a free election for the deputy presidency and was determined to resist Mbeki's pressure, so Mbeki convinced Mandela to tell Phosa to withdraw. Phosa said in that case he would run for the post of national chairman, but Mandela said he must not do that either.[83] Phosa, realizing that Mandela had been mobilized by Mbeki simply to squeeze him out, angrily confronted Mbeki and refused to withdraw. Phosa then set off on a trip to the Netherlands where, to his utter consternation, he heard that Mandela, then attending the Commonwealth Heads of Government summit in Edinburgh, had simply announced as a fact that Phosa had withdrawn his candidacy for the deputy presidency.[84] Mandela had no authority to change nominations made by ANC structures but Phosa, not wishing to contradict Mandela publicly, announced after agonized consideration that he would not run for any ANC post or even for the NEC. Privately, he felt Mbeki had betrayed him and considered quitting politics altogether.[85] Mbeki did not want that: he was already widely blamed for driving Ramaphosa and Sexwale out of politics. Accordingly, Cheryl Carolus announced that notions of Phosa quitting were 'far from the truth' and again insisted that neither the NEC, Mandela or Mbeki had any preferred candidates for ANC posts, though, as *The Citizen* showed, this was far from the truth.[86]

MBEKI VS. WINNIE

Dealing with Winnie was more difficult. She would clearly not listen if either Mbeki or Mandela asked her to withdraw her candidacy. However, with wonderfully convenient timing, the TRC summoned Winnie before it. The TRC had its own reasons for this: grilling Winnie would helpfully counter public perceptions of its pro-ANC bias. But it could not have acted in a manner which suited Mbeki better: at the perfect moment in the run-up to the Mafikeng conference the most discreditable parts of Winnie's past were to be examined in the full glare of national and international publicity.

When, in 1991, Winnie had been tried for the murder of the young activist Stompie Sepei, the ANC had tried to hush things up. Many ANC members who knew a great deal about Winnie, notably Albertina Sisulu, stayed silent and the key witness against her, Katiza Cebekhulu, was kidnapped on ANC orders and later found in a Zambian jail. Nonetheless, Winnie was found guilty of kidnapping and assault, although the assault conviction was dropped on appeal and the kidnapping jail sentence softened to a fine. No judge, it seemed, was willing to risk sending Winnie to jail. Joe Slovo and numerous other ANC leaders had attended her trial, giving clenched-fist salutes outside the courtroom and making it clear that saving Winnie from jail was still part of the anti-apartheid struggle. In fact they were perfectly aware of Winnie's record, but Winnie and Boesak had played leading roles in the struggle. If both were shown up as scoundrels the ANC risked losing the moral high ground.

This time, however, the opposite was true: it suited the ANC leadership for Winnie to be discredited, so tongues were loosened. Cebekhulu, Jerry Richardson, the former 'coach' of the 'Mandela United Football Club', Winnie's band of thugs, and Albertina Sisulu all came forward with the most serious allegations about Winnie's role. The chief of police now said the police might reopen investigations against Winnie while the Attorney General's office said it was studying the 'new information' about her. The press was so agog with this news that it never asked how Richardson was suddenly free to give television interviews from prison or what incentive he could possibly have had for incriminating himself in another murder.

The aim of this offensive was to drive Winnie to apply for amnesty before the TRC, which she could do if she either admitted to the crimes she was accused of or at least took moral responsibility for the activities of the Football Club. Only if she applied for amnesty, it was argued, would she be safe from legal action by the state, which could cost her millions of rand to defend. This, however, Winnie utterly refused to do, saying that any application for amnesty by her was bound to be seen as an admission of guilt – and she insisted she was wholly innocent on every count. She was shrewd enough not to be bullied by the threat of legal action, rightly believing that neither the state nor the judiciary would have the nerve to put her in jail. She also realized that the Mbeki leadership group was behind the ramp mounted against her and furiously rounded on them, claiming that they had thrown her to the wolves, and that they were way out of touch with popular opinion. Let them test that, she suggested, by calling a referendum on the death penalty – knowing full well that all polls showed 85–90 per cent of voters would like the death penalty restored.

This led to a furious denunciation of Winnie by Mbeki's crony Steve Tshwete, who called her 'a charlatan who needs help'.[87] Cheryl Carolus, joining in the chorus, called her 'a coward'.[88] In an unprecedented display, the Minister for Safety and Security, accompanied by the chief of police and a whole posse of police detectives, met with the TRC to assure them that no stone would be left unturned in rounding up witnesses against Winnie. Meanwhile her charge sheet before the TRC had lengthened to one involving eighteen full-scale atrocities.[89] All of which was intended to frighten Winnie into applying for amnesty. Her appearance before the TRC was a charade, as the commissioners tried energetically to get her to make the admission of guilt that both the media and the government wanted. She called their bluff, resolutely refusing to accept fault on any point, let alone apply for amnesty. In the end it was Archbishop Tutu who cracked, not her, for he ended her fruitless grilling by giving her a large, pardoning hug.

Winnie's TRC appearance had nonetheless served its purpose, for it enabled the ANC leadership to mount a large media campaign against her, accompanied by fierce pressure against her candidacy. Zuma, for his part, kept the lowest of profiles, insisting that he had no views of his own or any personal ambitions. 'The ANC will decide on who is deployed where – it will happen.'[90] This stance was doubtless maintained on Mbeki's instructions, for Zuma was not an impressive candidate. Everywhere the anti-Winnie pressure was strong: even in Winnie's stamping ground, the Eastern Cape, senior ANC leaders attempted to get the province to nominate Zuma not Winnie, but met with great resistance. 'There is little respect for Zuma here,' *The Star* reported Eastern Cape leaders as saying. 'Phosa was a better and intelligent alternative. Really, Tata [Mandela] can't be serious about Zuma.'[91] In every province branches and regions nominated Winnie, but everywhere the local leadership, under instruction from the centre, insisted on choosing a single 'consensus' candidate, thus avoiding a vote. Only in North West Province did these tactics fail to produce a nomination for Zuma and a vote ensued, with a number of branches absent or abstaining, which Zuma won 72 : 63. But, the *Financial Mail* reported, 'strong feelings remain within the ANC that Zuma is not fit to be deputy president; that he is too subservient to president-to-be Thabo Mbeki. This sentiment is reflected in moves to prevent the deputy president of the party automatically becoming deputy president of the country.'[92] In the end the leadership was able to prevent Winnie from being nominated by any province. In the Eastern Cape the provincial leadership managed this only by filing its own nominations first, pre-empting the branches, and then furiously lobbying them into line. Even in Zuma's native KwaZulu-Natal it was touch and go and only after extensive lobbying by both provincial and national ANC leaders did Zuma beat Winnie by the narrowest of margins.[93] This left her depending on a nomination from the conference floor, so the rules were hurriedly changed, with the proportion of delegates required for such a nomination to be valid increased from 10 per cent to 25 per cent. Similarly, when Popo Molefe, premier of North West Province, announced he would run for ANC treasurer against Mbeki's candidate, Mendi Msimang, the rules were altered to make this a full-time post, thus ruling Molefe out.

THE SHOWDOWN AT MAFIKENG

When the Mafikeng conference finally met further pressure was exerted on Winnie not to stand – in vain. The NWC demanded that she defend her public criticism of the ANC leadership (a possible disciplinary offence) before the NWC (she would not) – and Cheryl Carolus again branded her as 'cowardly'.[94] Winnie's supporters were warned that they too might find themselves in disciplinary trouble if they persisted in supporting her. Nonetheless, she was greeted with a crescendo of chants and songs as she arrived and conference memorabilia celebrating Winnie out-sold even those commemorating Mandela himself.[95] There was a near-riot in the Free State caucus when delegates demanded to be allowed to change their vote from Zuma to Winnie. Winnie seemed to be supported by nearly half the conference delegates, though undoubtedly at least some of this support was an expression of resentment at the treatment of Ramaphosa, Sexwale, Phosa, Holomisa and Lekota, the restriction of debate over Gear and the general style of top-down discipline.[96]

When the time for the election of deputy president came Mbeki made sure that he himself was in the chair. Winnie was nominated from the floor but when the hall was asked whether the nomination was seconded only a small group of delegates dared to raise their hands. Winnie, knowing she had far more support than that, asked for more time, which Mbeki refused. Winnie turned to him: 'Comrade Thabo, I think I do understand what is happening' – and declined the nomination. It was decided not to count the 127 votes cast for Winnie, though Cheryl Carolus insisted, against all the evidence, that 'The ANC has never been afraid of the democratic process'.[97] Later, many delegates said they had been waiting for Winnie to accept nomination before declaring their support.

The debate on Gear was a similarly damp squib. Trevor Manuel, who was nervous ahead of the debate, kept emphasizing that the RDP was still alive and had not been replaced by Gear, and argued that 'it would be unfair – and disempowering – to ask conference delegates to endorse Gear'.[98] In fact the debate was over in less than fifteen minutes, with neither the SACP nor Cosatu opposing the resolution, which merely recorded that conference was in favour of macro-economic stability and that 'Gear provides a basis for that stability'.[99] Yet any proper debate on Gear would undoubtedly have seen a large majority vote against it, just as Phosa would easily have been elected deputy president had he stood. Neither he nor Tokyo Sexwale would even accept nomination to the NEC.

Nonetheless, the conference kicked against the straitjacket Mbeki had imposed. Ramaphosa was elected to the No. 1 position on the NEC, making it clear how strongly delegates disapproved of the way he had been forced out. Mokaba, on the other hand, dropped from No. 3 to No. 19 in the rankings and no less than seven of the top ten placings went to non-Africans, a sharp rejection of Mokaba's demand for Africans-only leadership. Kgalema Motlanthe, who had emerged as the consensus candidate for secretary-general, was also the left's man: he was a senior figure in Cosatu and on the SACP executive. Mbeki had, however, counted on getting his nominee Mavivi Myakayaka-Manzini in as deputy secretary-general, but she was handily beaten by Thenjiwe Mthintso, a hardliner from the SACP. Most striking of all, Mbeki's nominee for national chairman, Steve Tshwete, was beaten by more than 2 : 1 by Terror Lekota, a demonstration both of Lekota's popularity and the widespread sympathy over his unfair treatment. Lekota's key political opponent in the Free State, Ace Magashule, failed even to get elected to the NEC.

Thus although Mbeki was elected unopposed as ANC president, pushed in the deputy president of his choice and guided Gear through unscathed, every time there was anything like a free vote the conference demonstrated its resentment against him and those seen as his puppets. Lekota's election was ecstatically greeted, almost all the delegates bursting into song, although everyone knew this was a victory against the leadership. Later, Lekota unwisely remarked that his victory had been a defeat of the Xhosas by the Sothos,[100] but immediately he spoke only of 'a certain level of vindication' and how it was 'fantastic that the leadership allowed the election like it ran'.[101] In fact the leadership had had quite enough of democracy and managed to slip though a motion making ANC national conferences a quinquennial rather than triennial event in future. Moving this motion, Kader Asmal claimed that national conferences cost too much money and energy and disturbed the stability of the ANC. Instead, in mid-term there would only be a national general council. This change also extended the terms of the NEC and all its officers from three years to five, thus accentuating the hold of the top leadership over the organization.[102]

Mbeki was quick to emphasize the ANC's endorsement of Gear. Delegates had, he claimed, decided that 'the policy directions are right' – namely, that there must be budget cuts, that jobs could only be created in the private sector, that inflation must be conquered – and that the Reserve Bank governor must be the sole arbiter of interest rates.[103] Mbeki declared that Gear would not be forced through without discussion by the ANC's allies, but also, paradoxically, that their discussion would not be allowed to change the terms of the strategy.[104]

Thus the business of government was cursorily dealt with, almost as an afterthought – which in a sense it was since the leadership's attention was overwhelmingly focused on internal ANC politics. The tensions and contradictions which had surfaced in the wake of the ANC coming to power had, for the moment, been dealt with. The left had been shut up, the populists seen off, and the power of patronage and government confirmed. The price had been a victory for top-down discipline over anything resembling democracy – and the selection of an unsuitable deputy president.

MANDELA'S MAFIKENG SPEECH

The entire conference was overshadowed by Mandela's effective retirement; the old man now refused even to serve on the NEC, excluding himself from all the party's inner councils. His retirement was in turn overshadowed by his conference speech, which effectively ended the age of reconciliation and rainbow optimism.

Needless to say, the speech had been written for Mandela, mainly by the usual Mbeki–Netshitenzhe team, and it saw the President treated like a ventriloquist's doll. Thus while Mandela himself had been forthright about the fact that the ANC had made serious mistakes in power which it must acknowledge and learn from, the speech began with a denial that 'any serious mistakes [have] been made' and a reference to 'occasional mistakes, if any'. And while Mandela's constant theme had been reconciliation, neither the word nor the concept had any place in the speech. Instead there was a paranoid recitation of all the forces allegedly working for 'the destruction of the ANC'. The Nats, despite having voluntarily handed power to the ANC and shared a government of national unity with it, were now said to have maintained intact a covert intelligence system and special forces to perpetrate a counter-revolution. The Democratic Party and Bantu Holomisa's United Democratic Movement were as bad. (The latter would try to 'infiltrate agents . . . into the structures of our movement'.) Those liberal NGOs who had dared set themselves up as independent watchdogs,[105] Mandela said, were being used by sinister outside forces like USAid to promote the agendas of foreign countries. The mass media, 'an instrument to protect the legacy of racism', 'has set itself up as a force opposed to the ANC' and was conducting a propaganda campaign suggesting that ANC rule had brought a crime wave with it. This produced calls for the restoration of the death penalty which were 'in reality, calls to hang those who are black and poor'.

While Mandela's speech nominally upheld multi-party democracy, in practice it depicted all opposition parties as mere 'agents of the counter-revolution' and even linked them with organized crime. There was no room for reconciliation because 'the leaders of the apartheid system, who perpetrated a vile crime against humanity . . . have made the point very clear that they neither regret the evil they visited on our country nor are they willing to commit themselves to a political culture informed by respect for human dignity', for they were still 'driven by their old arrogance which derived from attachment to ideas of racial superiority and their capacity to impose their will on the people through resort to terrorism'. Occasionally the speech lapsed into complete craziness: 'According to the UNDP's Human Development Report 1977, the corporate spies of General Motors as well as those of Ford Motor Company exceed our Gross Domestic Product.'

Mandela also called for complete national unity to 'join in a common offensive to create a new moral base that will inform the rebirth of our nation'. Not only should all political parties join in this effort but so should 'religious, business, trade union, women, youth, student, professional, cultural, media and other organizations and various personalities, such as the traditional and other leaders and creative workers, including sportspeople'. This would 'not happen spontaneously' but would be led by 'we, who are the vanguard'. It was a clear hankering for Leninist single-partyism.

The advent of ANC rule had coincided with an unprecedented crime wave, growing public sector corruption and all the characteristic sins of African nationalist rule elsewhere in Africa, the natural corollary of suddenly promoting to the leadership of a complex and relatively wealthy society a subaltern culture of acquisitive patriarchalism. This could not be looked in the face. Instead, the speech spoke of how 'colonial and apartheid domination' together with 'the modern market mechanism' were responsible for 'the collapse among the Africans of a system of social behaviour informed by the precepts of humanism which, historically, have informed African culture'. This was said to explain public sector venality, fraud and corruption, low tax morality, white-collar crime, corruption in the criminal justice system, rape and child abuse, disrespect for human life and the easy resort to force, robbery, mendacity in public affairs and contempt for law and the state. So everything that was going wrong was still the fault of apartheid.

All of which was to be redeemed by 'the advance towards an African Renaissance'. The overarching theme of the Mbeki period was then laid out in its full ambition: the OAU must 'reorient itself' towards this objective, as should all African political organizations and governments, and not only should 'the masses in all African countries' be 'similarly mobilized' but so must 'the intelligentsia, the professionals, trade unions, business people, the religious and traditional leaders, cultural workers, the youth and women, the media and so on'; the same single-party vision, but this time amplified on a continental scale. Moreover, South Africa must work for 'cohesion among the countries of the Third World' and seek to democratize all 'the international institutions of governance', such as the UN and IMF.

These were 'revolutionary tasks', Mandela said, so 'we need battalions of revolutionaries'. In turn this caused one to review the 'revolutionary alliance' of the ANC, SACP and Cosatu. The two latter organizations represented particular special interests while 'the ANC represents the people as a whole, and the African working masses in particular' – and thus, inevitably, had to play the leading role.[106]

Mbeki had two motives in getting Mandela to make this speech: to legitimate in advance the key projects of the Mbeki presidency and to protect against the possibility that Mandela's rule might be contrasted as more liberal-minded than Mbeki's. The speech could, if necessary, be used to justify one-party rule and the complete suppression of opposition. It sought to maximize party unity by reinventing the struggle –

against long dead bogeymen. And, since the conference had to adopt Gear, the more 'revolutionary' rhetoric, the better.

Mandela loyally gave this speech, bitterly hostile to the whole ethic of reconciliation he had preached, because his loyalty to the ANC was boundless. He often joked that if, when he died, he found himself in heaven, his first request would be to join an ANC branch there. But he tried to soften the speech a little by inserting a fatherly lecture (not included in the prepared text circulated to the press) – clearly meant for Mbeki – on the leadership traditions of the ANC, warning that there could be no place for the settling of personal scores or the marginalization of opponents within the movement. Mandela's words, though carried by no newspaper, were caught on film by the SABC – which also showed Mbeki shifting nervously and uncomfortably as the old man spelt it out. His words did not appear in print until 2006:

> One of the temptations of a leader who has been elected unopposed is that he may use that powerful position to settle scores with his detractors. He may marginalize them and, in certain cases, get rid of them and surround himself with yes-men and women. His first duty is to allay the concerns of his colleagues in the leadership, for them to be able to discuss freely without fear within the internal structures of the movement. Any subject should be discussed from all angles and people should even be able to criticize the leader without fear or favour. Only in that case are you likely to keep your colleagues together. There are many examples of this, allowing differences of opinion, as long as those do not put your organization into disrepute. Surround yourself with strong and independent persons who can, within the structures of the movement, criticize you and improve your own contribution so that when you go outside your policy your decisions are foolproof and they cannot be criticized by anybody successfully.[107]

The overall effect of the speech was so disastrous that Mbeki wandered through the ranks of foreign journalists telling them that they must not take it too seriously. But the deed was done and it cast a pall. Although Mandela was to grace the stage for a further two years, his Mafikeng speech clearly marked the end of the post-1994 euphoria. Unused to criticism, Mandela bridled at the inevitable media reaction, which he put down to white racism. When it was pointed out to him that many of the country's newspaper editors were now black he insisted that such editors were 'mere tokens'.[108]

It was a sad end for Mandela. It is difficult to blame a man who had suffered so much and was already old and frail. But he had made poor use of his immense authority. He had failed to grasp the task of government and presided over many blunders and lost opportunities. He had helped prevent any democratic election for either of the ANC's top posts in the ANC, had forced the best-qualified candidate out of the race, had backed up Mbeki's manoeuvres all the way, with dire implications for the future of intra-party democracy, and had ended by giving a disgracefully illiberal speech. Above all, he had settled the succession in favour of Mbeki, a fateful step whose wisdom he was clearly in some doubt about. As always with Mandela, all these sins were instantly forgotten by the hero-worshipping media. It is far from certain that history will be so kind in the longer run. Happily, the lasting legacy of Mandela was his spirit of generosity and reconciliation. The real tragedy was that, as with so many struggle veterans, including his closest comrades, Oliver Tambo and Walter Sisulu, for him liberation had come too late.

5
The Age of Mbeki I: Building the New Order

The tumultuous love of the populace must be seized and enjoyed in its first transports; it will not keep. The Earl of Chesterfield

With the Mafikeng conference Mbeki was openly in charge. His office had started with a staff of ten but by early 1998 this number had increased more than tenfold and had already begun to merge with the Office of the President.[1] Mbeki found it hard to delegate and thus clustered around his office innumerable other functions. Already his office had set up structures to deal with youth, gender equality, the disabled, children, HIV/Aids, NGOs, government communications and the bi-national commissions with the United States and Germany. In addition, Mbeki chaired the cabinet, many cabinet and inter-ministerial committees, the NWC and the NEC. His director-general, Frank Chikane, flatly announced that 'This office is responsible for the executive management of government', making it clear that Mandela's day was done.[2] Special units had also been established in the office: the Programmes Unit, dealing with programmes cutting across multiple ministries, the Operational Unit to intervene actively in provincial matters, a unit to manage the social and diplomatic lives of Mbeki and his wife, Zanele, and the Co-ordination and Implementation Unit (CIU), headed by Pundy Pillay, to co-ordinate policy across all ministries.

Although journalists used phrases like 'presidential power-house' and the 'Mbeki super-presidency', this structure was a lot less impressive in reality. The advisers were, without exception, chosen as loyal servants and yes-men: none had powerful independent minds. Mbeki liked to announce with great fanfare the launch of impressive-sounding conclaves – his International Investment Council, including many international business stars, his International Marketing Council, various gatherings of black intellectuals, and so on – but they had a limited impact. Mbeki was not prepared to countenance much of the advice international investors gave (liberalize labour markets, make it easy to import needed skills, do not force companies to give away large chunks of their equity to black empowerment rent-seekers). Similarly, Mbeki's stance on Aids and Zimbabwe soon undermined whatever the International Marketing Council might try to do.

The CIU never really got off the ground. After two years Pundy Pillay admitted that the job was all but impossible.[3] Like most actors in the new government he seemed almost to pride himself on the fact that nobody on his staff knew how such tasks had been managed in the pre-1994 order. From 1994 to 1998 there had been no provision at all for policy co-ordination. Ministers had become completely used to developing policy on their own. They were, indeed, 'very concerned' when the idea of a CIU was mooted and insisted that it remain small.

They need not have worried: Pillay never had the capacity to do his job and left it in 2002. Little was heard of it again until Netshitenzhe took it over in 2006, running it in tandem with his job as the government's chief spin-doctor, though public relations was clearly the real focus of his work. By 2006, indeed, government policy was as little co-ordinated as ever and large parts of the government machine had virtually ceased to work at all. Someone was needed to play the full-time and exhausting role of Prime Minister, insisting that ministers did their jobs and that policy was properly co-ordinated, but no such post existed and Mbeki showed no interest in the task.

The Pahad brothers, Essop and Aziz, who had been with Mbeki since their days at Sussex University, were men with whom Mbeki felt absolutely safe because, as Indians, they could never be rivals or even develop independent constituencies. By making Aziz deputy Foreign Minister, Mbeki could exercise complete control in the area which interested him most. Essop operated principally on the domestic front. He was widely unpopular, regarded by many as a bully and suspected of running the government's 'dirty tricks' department, but he was effective. Both men were so perfectly suited to carrying out Mbeki's elliptical and indirect style of management that they were 'in many ways, an extension of Mbeki'.[4] Much the same could be said of Joel Netshitenzhe, the third key insider.

Mbeki also maintained links with those who might prove useful in the business world, especially Saki Macozoma and Patrice Motsepe. Mbeki tended to consult Tito Mboweni and Alec Erwin over economic issues, although Trevor Manuel was overwhelmingly the most important (and successful) Economics Minister in government. Mboweni bore watching, for many saw him as a possible future President, while Erwin made it his business to be more Catholic than the Pope in his loyalty to Mbeki. He was, indeed, a remarkable Vicar of Bray, having once led the Federation of South African Trade Unions (Fosatu) in opposition to any links with the ANC or SACP; had then somersaulted into a position with Cosatu, formed when Fosatu came within the ANC fold; had then abandoned his principled opposition to links with the ANC by joining the party and, in order to prove his radical credentials as a white, had then joined the SACP, though as tension grew between the party and Mbeki, he left that too. He was, quite simply, a weathervane.

Mbeki was keen to cut back the influence of radical whites and (especially) Indians within the government and to increase the number of women. Within Mbeki's office itself there were no whites and a heavily Africanist bias. The new NWC appointed after Mafikeng reflected these predilections. The party's six top office-bearers and the heads of its Women's and Youth Leagues were ex officio members of the NWC, effectively the ANC's politburo, with a further fifteen members elected from the NEC. Of the twenty-three, nine were now women but there was only one white (Gill Marcus) and one Indian (Frene Ginwala). The contrast with Mafikeng, where non-Africans had taken seven of the top ten places on the NEC, reflected careful organization by Mbeki's camp. Disgruntled members of the minority groups naturally took their grievances to Mandela. He in turn issued a warning, clearly intended for Mbeki: 'I want to caution the ANC not to be arrogant, not to fall into the temptation of a majority party, to brush aside the concerns of the minorities.'[5]

This was, of course, ignored but Mandela was clearly uneasy at the direction Mbeki was taking: 'If I am convinced that the course they are embarking on is going to lead to disaster, to a lack of trust and confidence on the part of the public, I will speak out,'[6] he said, already sounding like an ex-President. Indeed, in January 1998 Mandela had cut his schedule right back as part of the handover to Mbeki. It was clear that he considered himself to be at least semi-retired already. Indeed, Mandela, now 80, said he planned 'to be relieved of all government duties', a statement he was forced to retract when it was pointed out that as head of state and government he could not constitutionally avoid certain duties and functions.[7]

From the outset the stress of Mbeki's new political order was on achieving complete ANC control over every aspect of the nation's life. The ANC might have felt content to control the executive, both legislative houses and seven out of nine provinces, and to share power with the IFP in KwaZulu-Natal. But it rankled greatly that the Nats still controlled the Western Cape: Mbeki announced that ensuring ANC victory there was 'a key national issue'.[8]

Within the ANC the victory of the exiles was now complete. Ramaphosa was gone and Cheryl Carolus was in London. Jay Naidoo soldiered on as Minister of Posts and Telecommunications, rewarding himself with a huge trip around Africa just before the 1999 election, knowing he was about to lose his job. He parachuted happily into a business career, all trace of his previous radicalism eclipsed.

Given Mbeki's predilections, there were question marks over the remaining Indians in cabinet, Kader Asmal, Valli Moosa (another UDF leader) and Mac Maharaj. Maharaj was a successful Minister of Transport but he was too powerful, too independent and was sympathetic to the inxiles.[9] A whispering campaign began suggesting Maharaj was corrupt and that his Ministry was exclusively staffed by Indians. Valli Moosa, a competent technocrat, and the bombastic Kader Asmal were careful to stay onside with Mbeki but none of the three Indian ministers lasted beyond the end of Mbeki's first presidential term.

Mbeki's sole opposition within the movement came from Cosatu and the SACP. It hardly helped that the new ANC secretary-general, Kgalema Motlanthe, continually quoted Mandela's admission to the 1997 Cosatu congress that Gear had been introduced without consultation. Motlanthe, an old-style communist, made it clear that he distrusted politicians, that he never wanted to be an MP and that he was continually tempted to return to the trade union world. He told ANC cadres that their job was to teach the youth 'to hate capitalism'.[10] Such views were enunciated without any regard as to how they affected investor confidence, already fragile after a drop in the gold price and the emerging markets collapse of late 1997.

THE DRAMA OF THE RAND

Mbeki had lived in Britain through Harold Wilson's long struggle to defend the pound and was conscious that a depreciating currency represents an international vote of no confidence in a country. The rand had been at R2.50 to the US dollar when Mandela walked free in February 1990. By the time Mandela became President it was R3.50, a decline of 40 per cent. The week after the 1994 election, when I suggested a devaluation to Alec Erwin, he told me, 'No, it's already happened.' It had not. By February 1996 the rate was R4.20 to the dollar, a further 20 per cent decline. Whenever Mandela caught a cold things got worse, for the markets worried that the rainbow-nation stability he had brought would disappear with him.

The governor of the Reserve Bank, Chris Stals, was a traditional Afrikaner inherited from the P. W. Botha regime but confirmed as governor by Mandela in 1994. Stals was experienced, stolid and dull. Theoretically, the Reserve Bank was completely independent of political control but, as Stals said in his retirement speech in 1999, 'after all is said and done, a central bank can only be as independent as the government of the day wants it to be. From my experience I have learnt that, without regular contact and close co-operation with the Minister of Finance, the life of a central banker can be very lonely.'[11]

When De Klerk announced the end of apartheid in February 1990 the foreign exchanges started to panic. Stals faced a classic conundrum: on the one hand foreign reserves were down to around $2 billion but on the other hand the rand was one of the most heavily traded secondary currencies, with dealings of some $10 billion a day. This meant that there was no possibility of supporting the currency by simply selling dollars or pounds, so Stals began to gamble – doubtless after due consultation with De Klerk – by buying forward contracts on the rand. This had two advantages: first, one could buy on margin, thus multiplying one's intervention five- or tenfold; and secondly, the market, aware of these large forward contracts, would think twice about shorting the rand. It was a form of gambling, for it meant opening a net open forward position (NOFP); that is to say, the forward book contained contracts to supply foreign exchange far in excess of the Bank's reserves.

These were casino tactics, but initially the gamble worked well: from an NOFP of $16 billion at the start of 1994 the figure soared to over $25 billion by end 1994 but was then successfully brought back down to under $10 billion by the end of 1995. Then as the currency crisis of 1996 took hold the NOFP soared back over $20 billion. Thereafter, the NOFP was gradually winched down to just over $15 billion by early 1998, when the emerging markets crisis struck with full force. Stals now had little ammunition left but simultaneously brought the NOFP back up to $23 billion while forcing real interest rates up from 14.8 per cent in April 1998 to 21.8 per cent in August that year. Despite these extraordinary measures the rand sank to R6.84 to the dollar.

Real interest rates of over 20 per cent caused a hideous crisis throughout the economy. None of Gear's promises of higher growth and more jobs were coming through. Instead, job losses mounted all the time and growth fell to under 1 per cent in 1998. This hideous squeeze, combined with the high crime rate, pushed white emigration to new levels – and with every emigrating white family went another five or six jobs. Worst of all, Stals had not only torpedoed growth, employment and Gear but he had failed horribly in his gamble. He had failed to stop the rand's fall and now had to meet some hideous gambling debts, for the forward contracts had to be honoured with huge losses incurred on each of them. Yet the government not only uttered no word of criticism but publicly backed Stals.[12]

This pretty much gave the game away. Stals' strategy had not really been his own. Mbeki was deeply sensitive to the rand's fate, seeing it as an implicit vote of no confidence in an ANC government – indeed, it was the rand's fall which had prompted the introduction of Gear and the tough Mandela–Mbeki line against Gear's critics. Stals was in no doubt about Mbeki's determination to defend the rand. Perfectly aware of the fate which awaited a white Afrikaner who torpedoed the economic policies and election promises of the first black government, he was careful to stay onside with Mbeki. Indeed, the strategy adopted was probably more Mbeki's and Manuel's than Stals': the mistakes made were those of naive beginners. When the policy went wrong it naturally suited Mbeki and Manuel to deny responsibility by asserting the independence of the Reserve Bank governor – and Stals played along. Hence the oddity that Stals was allowed to retire in 1999 with every honour. Mbeki even went out of his way to show his regard for Stals in 2005 by making him a member of the Nepad African Peer Review's Panel of Eminent Persons.

Stals had done enormous damage and left the rand – and his successor, Tito Mboweni – in a parlous position, with a huge NOFP still hanging over the currency. Somewhere down the line, the Bank would have to supply billions of dollars to the market that it did not have. In practice, the Treasury had to go to the bond market to raise the money, which was then instantly given away. This created an implicit bias against the rand, storing up trouble for the future. Mboweni ruled out intervention to prop up the rand and was blunt about the 1998 debacle: 'The central bank made a big mistake to intervene in the currency market to support the currency,' he said, adding that over $10 billion had been spent on intervention. 'A lesson was learnt then.'[13] The real oddity was the absence of a culprit.

THE WAR AGAINST THE LEFT

Economic contraction and job losses produced a major showdown at the Cosatu congress in June 1998, where both Mandela and Mbeki frontally attacked the critics of Gear. The policy was non-negotiable and the ANC would not reserve places for SACP and Cosatu members on its 1999 election lists unless their opposition abated – a virtual threat to tear up the tripartite alliance. This was followed by a repeat performance at the SACP congress. But the party was no pushover. The new general secretary, Blade Nzimande, like Zwelinzima Vavi at Cosatu, belonged to a younger generation which had not been in exile and did not defer to Mbeki. When Mandela departed from his prepared speech to tell the delegates that it was their duty to support the government, Thenjiwe Mthintso, who was presiding, acidly thanked him for his 'unmandated' comments, adding amidst stony silence that when it came to Mandela's spontaneous remarks 'delegates must ignore that part of the speech'.[14] Mthintso was also ANC deputy secretary-general, and her act of *lèse-majesté* provoked bitter comment. Mbeki soon booted her into touch by making her ambassador to Cuba. Meanwhile the SACP resolved that Gear's 'overall thrust must be rejected'.

In response to the left's threat Mbeki had already launched an ambitious plan to expand his support in the centre by wooing Mangosuthu

Buthelezi and his Inkatha Freedom Party. The IFP had led KwaZulu-Natal with the ANC as its junior coalition partner since 1994 but political violence had continued until the joint efforts of Jacob Zuma and Buthelezi produced an effective truce from late 1995 on. Thereafter political violence diminished considerably. Now Mbeki enrolled Zuma and Mandela in a new move. Talks were held at which a merger of the two parties was discussed, the two options being that Buthelezi should dissolve the IFP and lead his followers into the ANC or that the parties should simply share a joint election list.

Neither proposal appealed to Buthelezi, who knew perfectly well that once he gave up his independent base he would have nothing left to bargain with, but he was much flattered by Mbeki's charm offensive and by the frequent occasions when he was made Acting President while Mandela and Mbeki were out of the country. Buthelezi was also gratified by the fact that the ANC at last accepted that he represented the old, non-violent Luthuli wing of the ANC and that it was time for these currents to be reunited at last. I interviewed Buthelezi during this period and he was extremely warm in his appreciation of Mbeki, saying that his relationship with him was proceeding far better than his relationship with Mandela ever had.

The logic of Mbeki's initiative was several-fold. He wanted to make race the key political cleavage in future, for this would guarantee ANC power indefinitely. By bringing the IFP within the ANC fold he would achieve complete black political unity, for he had already attracted several Azapo and Black Consciousness adherents (like Mojanku Gumbi) into his entourage. Such a move would greatly strengthen the ANC's hegemonic project but it would also give the tripartite alliance a fourth (IFP) leg, thus reducing the significance of Cosatu and the SACP. By promoting Buthelezi as Acting President, Mbeki could also dangle the deputy presidency before him. If Buthelezi could indeed displace Zuma as Deputy President then Mbeki, with his dislike of having any heir apparent at all, would have the ideal No. 2: someone who could never possibly be a presidential successor.

Naturally, the left viewed a possible IFP merger as a threat and played it down, as did Motlanthe, the ANC secretary-general.[15] But Mbeki had an even greater threat: that if the SACP and Cosatu persisted in their dissent they might find themselves booted off the ANC election list in 1999. It was now announced that a vetting process would ensure candi-

1. The official launch in Soweto of the SACP as a political party in South Africa, 29 July 1990. Winnie Mandela, Nelson Mandela and Joe Slovo.

2. Protesting miners, September 1990. Members of the National Union of Mineworkers and ANC marshals marching with SACP, pro-NUM and Cosatu banners.

3. Mbeki's fiftieth birthday party, June 1992. Front row: Sol Kerzner, Joe Slovo, Thabo Mbeki, Max Borkum, Helen Suzman.

4. President Nelson Mandela with IFP leader Mangosuthu Buthelezi on 23 June 1993 at a meeting in Johannesburg to discuss how to quell continuing political violence.

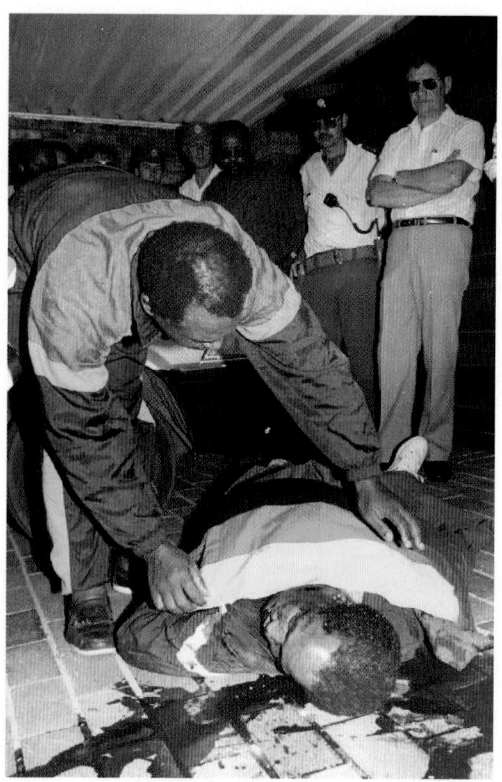

5. Tokyo Texwale covers the body of the assassinated SACP leader Chris Hani, 10 April 1993.

6. Joe Modise.

7. Funeral of an unidentified young woman Aids victim, Izingolweni, southern KwaZulu-Natal, October 1999.

8. Gerry Adams, leader of Sinn Fein, at the grave of Joe Slovo, with members of the ANC Women's League, Soweto, June 1995.

9. Cyril Ramaphosa, October 1998.

10. Nelson Mandela, two days after standing down as president, with his wife Graça Machel at a wreath-laying ceremony to commemorate the 1976 Soweto uprising, 16 June 1999.

11. Winnie Madikizela-Mandela at the funeral of Makgatho Mandela, Nelson Mandela's son by his first wife Evelyn Ntoke Mase, Qunu, Eastern Cape, January 2005. Nelson Mandela disclosed that his son had died of AIDS.

dates were compliant with ANC policy, while other reports circulated that the national leadership would select 75 per cent of the candidates, with only 25 per cent chosen by the membership.[16]

Mbeki was determined to reverse Motshekga's election in Gauteng. He commissioned the National Intelligence Agency (NIA) to investigate allegations of financial fraud against Motshekga and old accusations that he had been an apartheid police informer, despite the ANC's dislike of such divisive witch-hunts: after all Joe Modise and Peter Mokaba would head most lists of apartheid spies. Soon Mbeki had the intelligence report in his hand and by April 1998 parts of it were leaked to the press.[17] Meanwhile opposition to Motshekga within the Gauteng provincial executive was organized and reinvigorated. Squabbling within other provinces continued, so in August Mbeki pushed through a resolution that in future provincial premiers, instead of being elected, would be chosen by the ANC president (i.e. himself).

THE CONSTITUTION – AND THE JUDGES

Mbeki's sights were already fixed on the 1999 election. Given Mandela's vast popularity, which always far outran that of the ANC, in contrast to Mbeki, who always trailed his party by a large margin, there was clearly a danger that the ANC vote would fall back from its 1994 level. This was unthinkable: it would weaken the Mbeki presidency at birth and would undermine the ANC's hegemonic project. Accordingly, the cry went up that the ANC must aim at a two-thirds majority. The Eastern Cape premier, Makhenkesi Stofile, explained that this would be necessary so that 'many' things in the Constitution could be changed, claiming, absurdly, that such amendments were necessary to get rid of treacherous civil servants. But Stofile had other targets in mind too. Like many Eastern Cape Xhosas, he was a close sports follower (all Sports ministers without exception came from this milieu). Louis Luyt, the boss of the South African Rugby Football Union, was, Stofile insisted, using the Union to carry out apartheid policies. He also called for Grahamstown (in his province) to become 'the cultural capital of Africa', a most unlikely eventuality.[18] The press had fun at Stofile's expense, leading him to attack the media bitterly. In South Africa, 'Bra' (brother) is common slang and the local press labelled the premier 'Bra Stoff' (brassed off).

Stofile's call was taken up by others, including the ANC secretary-general, Kgalema Motlanthe, who said what was needed was an ANC government 'unfettered by constraints'. In particular he took aim at the judges and the Judicial Services Commission which advised the President on the appointment of judges, the Attorney General, the Auditor-General and the governor of the Reserve Bank.[19] Tony Leon, the DP leader, asked Mandela what the ANC intended to do with a two-thirds majority if they got it. Mandela insisted that the ANC had no intention of amending the Constitution,[20] thus contradicting Mbeki's supporters. But many ANC activists disliked the judiciary. There was now a black President, a black cabinet and a huge black majority in Parliament. Only the judges were still mainly white – and were not bound by the ANC line. The judiciary was sensitive to this situation and keen to avoid collisions with the government, but judicial independence was a constant irritant to the ANC.

Hence the Boesak case witnessed Mojanku Gumbi's bizarre attempt to pre-empt legal proceedings and clear Boesak. Then the Minister of Justice, Dullah Omar, when told that Boesak was to face fraud charges complained bitterly that 'neither the president, the deputy president, the cabinet nor the Minister of Justice were asked for their views with regard to possible prosecution'.[21] Controversially, Boesak hired the country's top lawyers to defend him – while applying to the Legal Aid Board for help. When Boesak explained that he could do this because a 'mystery donor' had donated R1 million to top up whatever the Legal Aid Board put in, the Opposition argued that the Board had no business helping people with R1 million to spend on legal advice. Mandela then offered to raise funds for Boesak's defence and said he doubted whether there was even a prima facie case against Boesak for fraud and theft. This brought strong protest from Frank Kahn, the Western Cape Attorney General, at the President's clear political pressure on the case: had anyone else said this they would have faced a contempt of court charge. Mandela was forced to apologize.[22]

There were other irritants, too. A long list of black 'struggle lawyers' – including a member of the ANC NEC and close friend of Mbeki, the Durban attorney Linda Zama – were struck off for their misuse of monies held in their trust accounts. Typically they attempted to insist that white racism lay behind their disgrace and the National Association of Democratic Lawyers, an ANC front, defended them as 'good lawyers'.[23] Attempts to transform the judiciary resulted in many appointments going to affirmative action candidates of such dubious quality that lawyers tried hard not to appear before them, also leading to charges of racism. When Judge Vuka Tshabalala, who was known to be fond of a drink, was nominated as deputy judge president of KwaZulu-Natal in April 1998 fourteen white judges petitioned against the appointment. A furious ANC reaction saw Tshabalala confirmed and the judges forced to apologize. Judge President John Hlope of the Western Cape repeatedly accused his white judicial colleagues of racism, allegedly gave a case to one white judge because Hlope was sure 'he would fuck it up' and referred to another judge as 'a piece of white shit'.[24] Judge Siraj Desai, an open ANC partisan, was regarded by many as inappropriately political. He refused to step down even after he had been the subject of rape charges and despite the fact that he had lied to the police.[25]

The most difficult issue, though, was judicial independence. In 1997 the Minister of Justice announced that apartheid-era judges were to undergo a compulsory reorientation programme 'to eliminate the culture of racism, repression, sexism and intimidation' in which, apparently, they wallowed.[26] The TRC claimed the judges had made 'a bigger contribution than all the state's assassins' to shoring up apartheid, while Kader Asmal argued that all judges appointed under apartheid should be compelled to reapply for their positions.[27] Such suggestions that the judges were little better than criminals who needed Mao-style re-education programmes hardly created a happy environment.

Judicial independence came under greatest pressure when courts failed to reach the verdicts the ANC wanted. When the ANC renegade Sifiso Nkabinde was acquitted of all sixteen charges against him, the ANC was furious. He was murdered soon thereafter. Similarly, the ANC campaigned for one of their greatest *bêtes noires*, the former army boss and Defence Minister, Magnus Malan, to be brought to trial but Tim McNally, KwaZulu-Natal's director of public prosecutions, was reluctant to press charges, believing a conviction unlikely. This merely added to a long list of ANC grievances against McNally. When McNally finally acceded to this pressure to try Malan, Malan emerged unscathed as charge after charge was dropped – for the prosecution had tried to rig evidence by inserting long, identical passages into the testimony of several witnesses. The result was an explosion of rage against McNally.

Mbeki responded by creating a National Director of Public Prosecutions, an anomalous post given the provincial structure of the country's judicial system. The first director, Bulelani Ngcuka, previously the ANC chief whip in the Senate, founder of the National Association of Democratic Lawyers and Mbeki intimate, swore not to allow politics to influence his work – yet his first act was to sack McNally because 'everywhere I go people say there are problems with that office'.[28] Ngcuka became a key arm of Mbeki's new order and set up a new elite police unit, the Scorpions, under his office, giving it enormous muscle. Mbeki thus took a large step towards politicizing the prosecution service and the police.

The most embarrassing case of all arose over South Africa's unofficial religion, rugby. Louis Luyt, the boss of the South African Rugby Football Union, had long been a pet hate of ANC activists, to whom he symbolized the brutish Afrikaner power of the old days. Under Luyt, South Africa had impeccably hosted – and won – the 1995 Rugby World Cup, but Luyt, who had behaved with extreme boorishness at the victory celebrations, was widely disliked. Given the rich takings the game provides in this rugby-mad nation, there was no shortage of aspirants for Luyt's job and one of them, Brian Van Rooyen, a Coloured businessman who had been sniping at Luyt for a long time, forwarded a dossier of complaint to the Minister of Sport, Steve Tshwete. Tshwete set up a commission of inquiry into the Rugby Football Union with the clear intention of bringing rugby under political control. Luyt objected that only the President had the right to set up commissions of inquiry, so Tshwete's Director-General, Mthobi Tyamzashe, issued a press statement in which he said that Mandela had 'happily responded' to Tshwete's request for a commission and told him that 'a commission is yours if, in your best judgement, it is opportune'. Luyt then objected that the President had clearly not 'applied his mind' to the subject.

The result was a political disaster. Both Tshwete and Mandela swore under oath that the conversation alluded to by Tyamzashe had never taken place. Tyamzashe accordingly denied the press statement and said all copies of it had been lost. Luyt then produced an original copy of the statement, whereupon Tyamzashe admitted that he had been lying under oath. There were, he said 'honest lies' and 'dishonest lies': his had been honest ones. Steve Tshwete praised this perjury and also denied all manner of comments and statements attributed to him in the press. He even denied having given the interview on which one article was based, though he later had to retract this denial.

The judge, Justice William de Villiers, who later found that Tshwete too had perjured himself, decided that the only way to settle the matter was to subpoena Mandela. Mandela cut a poor figure in court, refusing to call the judge 'your Lordship'. In his judgment, de Villiers found that the President's testimony lacked credibility. 'That may be due to a lack of veracity or unreliability or a combination of these factors . . . The President's overall performance on the witness stand was less than satisfactory. His overall demeanour, to my mind, is subject to material criticism. He flatly refused to answer a number of questions and to some extent the court was used as a podium for political rhetoric.'[29] Given Mandela's legendary political trials many years before (when, however, he had also simply given political speeches and avoided all cross-questioning) this was a terrible come-down. De Villiers set aside the commission of inquiry. Luyt had won, game, set and match.

The ANC fell into a paroxysm of fury, labelling de Villiers 'an apartheid judge' and threatening an international boycott of South African rugby unless Luyt resigned, saying it would 'block the airports' to prevent a Springbok rugby team touring abroad.[30] The government's National Sports Council demanded that Luyt and the whole Rugby Football Union executive resign, and Cosatu threatened mass action unless this occurred. The Union's sponsors panicked and also demanded the executive's collective resignation. Ultimately the Constitutional Court rallied to Mandela's side and Luyt was forced out. The Union apologized for having Mandela subpoenaed and agreed to a commission of inquiry into itself, but the government lost interest in such an inquiry once Luyt had gone. Political pressure had reversed a court judgment, throwing the case to those who had openly committed perjury, and vilifying the judge who had dared assert his independence.

At almost exactly the same time the TRC issued its Report, which was greeted with a furious blast of hostility from the ANC. As Essop Pahad was later to explain to a Chilean colloquium on truth commissions, the ANC had assumed the TRC would simply do its job of analysing apartheid as 'a crime against humanity', and had been disconcerted to find that, however pro-ANC most commissioners were, the TRC had nonetheless developed a will of its own.[31] The ANC demanded a special session with the TRC to discuss – and vet – the Report before it was published. To Mbeki's annoyance, by a narrow majority the TRC refused, fearful that other parties would demand the same. The ANC was further angered when De Klerk successfully went to court to force certain changes in the way the Report dealt with him.

The TRC Report had found – it could hardly find otherwise – that the ANC had been involved in the torture and execution of suspected traitors, the killing of civilians in bomb and landmine attacks and fomenting political violence. It highlighted the atrocities committed in the ANC camps in Angola and elsewhere and the persistent refusal of the ANC leadership over many years to face up to and take responsibility for these terrible acts. Although the great weight of the TRC Report was directed against the apartheid regime and the IFP, the Commission knew that failure to mention these obvious facts would remove any remaining claim it had to impartiality.

The 25-page denunciation of the TRC issued by the ANC claimed that the TRC had 'grossly misdirected itself', that its findings were 'capricious and arbitrary' and in general that the Commission had failed to understand the difference between 'gross violations of human rights' and legitimate forms of anti-apartheid struggle.[32] The ANC also objected that it had not been allowed to discuss and lobby about the Report in advance; with its long history of forcing 'consensus' on less than fully willing partners, it was outraged that it had been placed on the same level as other parties.

However, Mandela made it clear that personally he was happy to accept the Report, thus creating some confusion. If the ANC statement did not represent its own leader, who was behind it? The answer, of course, was Mbeki: a hegemonic party could hardly allow that an external authority higher than itself not only existed but could use that position to find moral fault with the ANC. Mbeki also wanted to maintain his alliance with Joe Modise and the others in charge of the MK camps, the ANC group most disgruntled by the Report. Mbeki prudently stayed silent as, with Mandela's support, the Report sailed through. For Mandela had had two major objectives on taking office, the first to leave the country with a new Constitution and the second to effect a lasting reconciliation. This gave the TRC's work a particular importance in his mind. But for this, ANC pressure would doubtless have overthrown the TRC Report just as it had overthrown the judgment in the Luyt case.

ANC HEGEMONY – AND THE ID BOOK SCANDAL

Given Mbeki's objective of complete ANC hegemony, it was quite unacceptable that both KwaZulu-Natal and the Western Cape had resisted the ANC's onward march.[33] Motlanthe, echoing such thinking, said that what the ANC wanted was 'unfettered power'.[34] In its determination to exceed even Mandela's 1994 vote, the ANC leadership hit on the idea of making the possession of a new bar-coded ID book necessary to register to vote in the 1999 election. But ANC backbenchers reacted badly when this bill was presented: surely it would be wrong to deprive the many citizens lacking such ID books of the vote? Judge Johann Kriegler, the head of the Independent Electoral Commission (IEC), declared that he felt the same. The ANC NEC emphasized that it was up to citizens to procure the new ID books from Home Affairs and that even applications for such IDs would be sufficient to vote.

The issue sounded technical but was not. Under apartheid, Africans had all been defined as citizens of this or that bantustan and had thus received bantustan IDs. With the incorporation of the bantustans they were automatically the first in line for the distribution of new South African (bar-coded) IDs. But whites, Indians and Coloureds had all been citizens of the old South Africa and thus tended to possess the old ID books. Not many had bothered to queue at Home Affairs offices to acquire the new bar-coded ID books; the old ones were still perfectly legal so there had been little incentive to change them. Under the new rules these non-African groups were thus the most vulnerable to disenfranchisement, and since these were the very groups most likely to vote for Opposition parties, the new rules would inevitably favour the ANC, helping it gain its two-thirds target. Moreover, surveys showed that 2.4 million South Africans had failed to obtain even the old ID books and such citizens would also be automatically excluded from the vote.[35] The ANC, conscious that this number included many white foreign nationals registered as permanent residents (who had been allowed to vote in

1994 but would be disenfranchised this time), nevertheless pressed on. Its backbenchers were brought to heel and the bill rammed through.

Home Affairs estimated that there were 2.5 million people without the new ID books and promised to process applications at 280,000 a month. Since Home Affairs' inefficiency was legendary, few believed this. In any case a Markinor/Idasa study commissioned by the SABC showed that the number lacking the new IDs was well over five million.[36] The Opposition parties, now aware of the massive foul about to be perpetrated against them, threatened to go to the Constitutional Court to stop it.

The historical symmetry was exact. The Afrikaner nationalists, determined to consolidate the power they had won in 1948, had cut every legal corner to disenfranchise the Coloured vote by the next election, in 1953. Now African nationalism was doing the same, disenfranchising millions of Opposition voters. The Opposition could hardly credit this surpassing act of cynicism and Marthinus Van Schalkwyk (who had succeeded De Klerk as leader of the New National Party (NNP), as it was now called) volubly expressed his own disbelief until Mbeki walked across to his office and explained that it was only months since the ANC had made the new regulations law. The Nats and DP were demanding that they now rescind that law but this could never happen. 'Don't you understand, Marthinus? If we pass a law one way one minute and then vote to repeal it the next, in effect we are saying Africans can't govern – and the ANC is never going to accept that.'[37]

So the Opposition went to the Constitutional Court. The matter seemed straightforward: the ANC was making a fundamental right (the franchise) dependent on the possession of a discretionary document. It was as if the right to vote had been made dependent on the production of a driving licence.

THE PECULIAR POLITICS OF THE CONSTITUTIONAL COURT

The Constitutional Court stood at the apex of the new legal order and enjoyed great prestige. Yet its position was peculiar: in a black-run state, six of its eleven members, including its president, Arthur Chaskalson, were white. Conscious of the growing ANC clashes with the lower judiciary, the Court knew that were it to stand up to the government on a major issue, it would undoubtedly come under strong political attack in which the fact of a white majority on its bench was bound to feature prominently.

In fact the Constitutional Court was most unlikely to behave thus, for the ANC government, following the example of American presidents down the years, had done its best to pack the court. Chaskalson was a long-time ANC supporter and had helped defend Mandela at the Rivonia trial (1963–4). Ismail Mohammed had a similar anti-apartheid activist background and his brother, Ismail Ayob, was Mandela's personal lawyer. Johann Kriegler, Lawrie Ackermann and John Didcott were all independent-minded, though Didcott nourished a passionate and outspoken dislike of Chief Buthelezi, which did him no harm with the ANC. Pius Langa (who was to succeed Chaskalson as Chief Justice[38]) was a strong ANC man and a former president of the National Association of Democratic Lawyers, while the other two black judges, Yvonne Makgoro and Tolly Madala, could generally be relied on to be ANC-sympathetic. Kate O'Regan, the statutory woman, also had a struggle background but could be notably independent. This set of judges alone would have guaranteed a safe pro-government majority but to their number had to be added Albie Sachs, a Communist Party apparatchik: at the hearings preceding his appointment, there had been strong adverse comment about his failure to criticize the human rights atrocities in the ANC camps. Finally, there was the politically correct Richard Goldstone.

An extremely able lawyer, Goldstone had attracted criticism within the legal profession even on his way up as an advocate, when he had socially entertained at his home the attorneys who might bring him cases. Such behaviour, seen as touting for custom, was greatly frowned upon. Throughout his career he had been criticized for his sheer ambition; De Klerk noted how 'some of his colleagues criticized him for being over-ambitious' and how it was rumoured that he saw himself succeeding Boutros Boutros-Ghali one day as UN Secretary-General, leading to his nickname 'Richard Richard-Goldstone'.[39] Under apartheid – unlike most of the other judges on the Constitutional Court – he had been careful to avoid anti-apartheid activism. Indeed, his decision to take silk in 1980 had drawn criticism from liberal circles, for many anti-apartheid lawyers refused promotion to the judiciary where they would have to apply apartheid laws.

Under De Klerk, however, he had made up for lost time and had led the high-profile Goldstone Commission into the causes of violence. Goldstone was supposed to report to De Klerk and to Mandela but in 1992 he carried out a surprise raid on a branch of military intelligence and issued a dramatic statement to the media suggesting that the military was involved in illegal partisan activities. De Klerk was furious; he 'did not like the sensational manner in which Goldstone had publicized preliminary and untested findings',[40] though of course this manner of proceeding made Goldstone the ANC's favourite judge. The upshot was that De Klerk fired twenty-three senior SADF officers. Though evidence for their guilt was not immediately forthcoming, it was promised that it soon would be. In fact it never was and many of the officers successfully sued De Klerk, who later had to apologize and retract.[41]

The most remarkable fact about the Goldstone Commission was that while it was supposed to investigate all armed groups, it simply failed to investigate MK or any form of violence organized by the ANC.[42] This was *Hamlet* without the prince, for MK continued to be active, recruiting, training, managing arms caches and carrying out hundreds of attacks, murders and other armed actions. Both the IFP and the security forces laid plentiful evidence before the Commission on these matters but Goldstone concentrated his attentions on other groups involved in violence, an attitude which naturally endeared him to the ANC. Goldstone was adamant, however that, contrary to the ANC's repeated allegations, there was no evidence for the existence of a 'third force' organizing violence against them. Then, just weeks before the 1994 election, Goldstone dramatically reversed himself, pointing to a systematic and silent war waged by the police from a farm called Vlakplaas against the ANC and its allies.[43] Goldstone implicated three police generals, all of whose careers were effectively ended, though Goldstone made no attempt to put the allegations against them to the three men, nor allowed them to defend themselves or test these accusations through cross-examination.[44] Goldstone said he had decided to bring out a report on these allegations, prior to further investigation, in order to bring them to public attention before the election, and indeed the timing was perfect for the ANC's election campaign. It thus came as no surprise when Goldstone was appointed to the Constitutional Court.

Thus the Court started life with a built-in pro-ANC majority and with enough members of legal distinction to enjoy considerable prestige. This was not, however, uniformly true. Judge Didcott, one of the court's ablest members, found, to his indignation, that several of his fellow-judges were unable even to write out a proper judgment. He found himself having to help others write their judgments or, in some cases, take on the whole job himself. He was especially indignant that not all those who needed such help were black, a reference to Albie Sachs, who had not practised law for decades before becoming a judge.[45]

One of the Court's first duties was to rule on the sensitive issue of the death penalty. In the 1980s South Africa had regularly executed more than 1,100 people a year, the third-highest execution rate (after Iran and Iraq) in the world,[46] but in 1990 De Klerk had suspended the death penalty. The government made it clear that it would like to see the death penalty abolished. Politically, De Klerk had given it little choice for it was unthinkable that the ANC should reintroduce the harshest penalty in the book after the Nats had seen fit to suspend it, particularly since the death penalty in South Africa has very largely involved white men executing black men. On the other hand, only Colombia has a higher murder rate than South Africa: in South Africa one is twelve times more likely to be murdered than in the United States and fifty times more likely than in the EU. In the decade 1994–2004 there were more than 215,000 murders in South Africa and reported rapes occur at over 1,000 a week, with many more unreported. Not surprisingly given such figures, all opinion surveys showed large majorities favouring the death penalty, with Africans emphatically most in favour.

The government was correspondingly reluctant to abolish capital punishment, so in 1995 the buck was passed to the Constitutional Court, which ruled that the death penalty was a cruel, degrading and inhuman punishment and in conflict with the rights to life and dignity enshrined in the Constitution.[47] This was, of course, massively unpopular – 'a dirty trick', Judge John Didcott thought, 'getting us to carry the can because the government didn't have the guts to do it'.[48] In terms of the court's executive-mindedness it was just the beginning.

In 1996 the court was presented with the final draft of the new Constitution, which included several striking innovations. Although the Interim Constitution had expressly forbidden any substantial reduction in provincial autonomy, the new draft did exactly that. Although the court objected, in the end it let through the new principle of 'co-operative governance', which, in effect, gave the national government the last word. Similarly, it had been agreed that only 'universally accepted' human rights should go into the Constitution's bill of rights, but the new draft not only included the socio-economic rights which were typically found only in the constitutions of socialist states but actually extended these to include the rights to access to housing, health care, food, water and social security. This too the court accepted, despite grave reservations expressed by many lawyers, for such provisions were obviously unenforceable. Modifications to the Judicial Service Commission, potentially allowing greater political interference in the selection of judges, also sailed through. Most remarkably of all, so did the revolutionary new doctrine of horizontal rights (that is, making the bill of rights binding on private persons as well as the state). The court itself had previously warned against this doctrine, which would erode both the justiciability of rights and the separation of powers, both of which were enunciated as constitutional principles. Many other dubious cases were accepted by the court, for example the introduction of a new right to 'make decisions regarding reproduction' (that is, allowing abortion on demand) although this clearly conflicted with the principle that only 'universally acceptable' rights should be in the bill of rights.

Not just the court's executive-mindedness was on display here but the ANC's fundamentally different attitude to law-making. For decades its programme and great shibboleth had been the Freedom Charter, whose ringing phrases many could recite: 'The doors of learning and of culture shall be opened!', 'The People shall govern!', etc. But the Freedom Charter was, so to speak, a constitution in the sky. Not only could it not be applied in apartheid South Africa but, as the inmates of the MK camps in Angola were indignantly to attest, in practice the ANC leadership paid no attention to it, so that detention without trial, torture, execution and other denials of civil rights were perfectly normal. Moreover, even within the exile ANC beyond the camps there was no allowance for the freedom of speech and publication which the Charter promised; indeed, cadres even had to seek party permission for such private matters as getting married.

Thus the Charter was like a family heirloom, wheeled out with great pride in speeches at rallies, but not something for everyday use or even for much use at all. The same attitude now inspired the ANC to produce a clearly impractical Constitution, as also endless codes of conduct, mission statements and wordy declarations galore, but it became obvious that not even government ministers paid much attention to the Constitution in practice, let alone lesser laws and codes.

The next great political issue before the court was the appeal to overturn the de Villiers judgment in favour of Luyt and the Rugby Football Union. This was now redundant, for everything of substance had already been conceded, but the government could not bear the idea of being worsted by the hulking figure of Luyt, the unpopular epitome of the old-style Afrikaner. So it asked the Constitutional Court to reverse the judgment. As Luyt said, 'the deck was stacked against us. Here was a court appointed by Mandela himself, consisting largely of people who were heavily involved in the Struggle, now being asked to rule over the findings of a man branded publicly as "an apartheid judge" – someone who had the temerity not only to find in favour of Luyt . . . but to cast aspersions on the veracity of Mandela.' Luyt then infuriated Chaskalson even more by suggesting that he really ought to recuse himself since he had a close lawyer–client relationship with Mandela dating back to the 1960s, by mentioning the ANC affiliations of various other judges, and by asserting (correctly enough) that they were all friends of Mandela. Chaskalson furiously dismissed the idea of recusal and the court duly reversed De Villiers' verdict – an outcome, as Luyt put it, 'about as surprising as hearing that the All Blacks had beaten Japan. We had had no real chance.'[49] Luyt had seriously discomfited the court which, besides trumpeting its independence, was greatly seized of its own political righteousness. In the new South Africa it was a badge of honour to have defended Mandela at Rivonia, to have had one's arm blown off in the struggle (Albie Sachs), to have been an ANC adviser at the constitutional talks (Pius Langa) or to be a frequent ANC defendant in political trials (Zac Yacoob). Luyt's point was that political righteousness was nonetheless political, thus out of place in a court, and an obstacle to impartial justice.

Even this paled in significance compared to the challenge the court faced over bar-coded IDs. Under other circumstances the fact that millions of voters who had permanent residence permits and had all been allowed to vote in 1994 but were disenfranchised this time would have been a major issue. But now at stake was the disenfranchisement of millions of full citizens: a study by the (government-funded) Human

Sciences Research Council showed that up to 5.3 million citizens would be disbarred by the bar-coded ID decision. Everyone knew that it was way beyond the capacity of Home Affairs to issue such a number of IDs in the time available (even seven years later in 2006 they were still 1.5 million IDs behind) and that the vast queues at Home Affairs offices were a huge and unreasonable incentive to accept disenfranchisement as a lesser evil. The DP also showed that to insist on bar-coded IDs would favour the ANC and heavily penalize opposition parties, young people and racial minorities.[50] Above all there was the sheer unreasonableness of making the most basic constitutional right depend on a discretionary document; the centrality of the struggle for the franchise in South African history; and the clear echo of the curtailment of Coloured voting rights by the Nats.

The DP and the NNP had made it clear that they would have to go to court over the matter and Judge Kriegler announced that to persist with the bar-coded ID requirement would so mar the election that he would have to resign as head of the IEC. At this point President Mandela intervened: he knew that even within the ANC there were many who worried that not just the smooth running but even the legitimacy of the election could be threatened, so he offered to meet the opposition parties and implied that he was willing to review the government's stance. All the opposition was asking, after all, was that other forms of ID be allowed in addition to the bar-coded ID. However, when Mbeki heard of this initiative Mandela's offer was withdrawn without explanation.[51]

The IEC was supposed to guarantee the integrity of elections, so Judge Kriegler now led a group of his fellow-commissioners, together with senior IEC staff, to meet with Mbeki and other cabinet ministers. Kriegler insisted that by this highly partisan alteration to the franchise the government had effectively undermined the IEC's independence, contrary to the clear requirements of the Constitution. Mbeki and his team dismissed such arguments out of hand and, to his horror, Kriegler found that his fellow-commissioners, led by his deputy, Brigalia Bam, immediately swung over to Mbeki's side. This was unsurprising: even in 1994 the IEC had been stuffed with ANC supporters and this tendency had only increased since then. In effect Mbeki was cracking the ANC whip and Ms Bam and her fellow-commissioners obediently fell into line. Mbeki's team attacked Kriegler as having a questionable commitment to 'transformation' and said that Ms Bam had 'a more appropriate understanding of the role of the IEC'.[52] Kriegler resigned and was succeeded by Bam.

Thus by the time the question of bar-coded IDs came to the Constitutional Court Mbeki had, over the same issue, already faced down ANC backbenchers, the parliamentary committee on Home Affairs, the Opposition, Mandela and the IEC: it was a non-negotiable matter. The court was hardly willing to stand up against that. To its everlasting discredit it took Mbeki's side with only Justice O'Regan dissenting on the ground that the decision 'betrays a disregard for the importance of the right to vote'.[53] Yet two weeks earlier the court had accepted the ANC suggestion that prison inmates should have the vote[54] – since most prisoners were black this was likely to favour the ANC. In finding for the ANC case the court insisted that 'The vote of each and every citizen is a badge of dignity and personhood. Quite literally, it says that everybody counts . . . whoever we are, rich or poor, exalted or disgraced, we all belong to the same democratic South African nation.'[55] Accordingly, where there was any doubt one had to come down emphatically on the side of enfranchisement.

Yet when it came to depriving millions of people of the vote in the bar-coded ID case, the court changed its normal procedures so as to avoid examining the infringement of rights, said there 'was no point in belabouring' the importance of the vote and insisted that the key question was simply whether Parliament had acted 'reasonably', not whether it had infringed the fundamental rights of citizenship. It said the onus must be on the complainants to show that the government had no way of granting the bar-coded IDs in time, but then declared that that matter was in any case 'irrelevant'. In any case, it claimed, the law had given people six months to acquire the necessary documents (this was untrue: it had given them six weeks). The majority of the court insisted on the superiority of bar-coded IDs, but then said that in any case temporary registration and ID documents could be used, ignoring the fact that these temporary documents would actually be less secure than the old IDs and that Parliament had, in 1997, expressly recognized the older IDs as valid for all purposes, including registration and voting. No wonder O'Regan, in her dissenting judgment, called the majority verdict 'too deferential'.[56] It was worse than that – a hotchpotch of circumlocution, factual omission, misstatement and sheer evasion.

The Constitutional Court's failure to stand up to the ANC government on critical questions of law was of great moment. During the struggle the ANC had defied the law on principle, as was only natural for a clandestine movement. Government required respect for the law from the governing party. Mandela understood this and was notably principled in defending judicial decisions even when they did not suit the ANC. But the Constitutional Court had a vital role to play in educating the ANC government at large to respect the law and judicial independence. Pandering to it when it cut legal corners was a true *trahison des clercs*.

The publication of the ANC election lists for Parliament and the provincial legislatures in February 1999 was greeted with uproar, for it revealed a clear disrespect for the law. The ANC had promised that it would exclude from its lists anyone with a conviction for theft or corruption or who had violated the party's code of conduct. Yet its candidates nonetheless included Winnie Mandela, despite her four convictions for assault and kidnapping, and despite still not having refunded the R100,000 she had spent on an unauthorized trip to Ghana while travelling on a diplomatic passport she had no right to; Pat Matosa, with a conviction for attempted murder; sundry Mpumalanga politicians with convictions for corruption; the deputy Speaker, Baleka Mbete-Kgositsile, despite her having conspired to gain an illegal driving licence; and sundry other provincial politicians with convictions for theft and corruption such as the former North West provincial minister for education, Mamokoena Gaoreteletwe, who had spent R500,000 on a trip to the 1996 Olympics which had included her husband and a personal bodyguard.[57] Mbeki tried to quell the storm by insisting the lists would be modified but both Winnie and various others survived the process.

THE FALL OF MATHEWS PHOSA – AND PROVINCIAL DEMOCRACY

Mpumalanga had from the outset been plagued by corruption, the most striking case being the attempted sale for R25 billion of a fifty-year lease to the Dubai-based Dolphin group, giving it a commercial development monopoly over Mpumalanga's game reserves, including the Kruger National Park. The secret deal, authorized by the provincial minister for the environment, David Mkhwanazi (a former bantustan minister), was quashed once it came to light. Mkhwanazi was only forced out later when it emerged that he had hired as senior officials his wife, daughter, brother and sister-in-law. He left office with the Auditor-General still unable to find the R19 million which had gone missing during his term of office.[58] Also disgraced by the scandal were the leader of the local ANC Youth League, James Nkambule, and the Parks Board boss, Alan Gray. Other corruption scandals forced the appointment of the Moldenhauer commission of inquiry.

Magistrate Heinrich Moldenhauer took particular aim at the provincial minister for safety and security, Steve Mabona (another bantustan ex-minister), for issuing two fraudulent driver's licences to the deputy Speaker of Parliament, Baleka Mbete-Kgositsile. Mabona, cornered, claimed the allegations were due to 'evil spiritual forces doing the devil's work'. Moldenhauer found that Mabona had lied (and not just about the devil), recommended his immediate removal from public office and called on the police and the Heath Commission to probe Mabona's use of state funds to finance his luxurious lifestyle.[59] Amazingly, Mabona was allowed to remain a backbencher and the deputy Speaker brazened it all out, becoming speaker of the provincial parliament. Meanwhile the provincial finance minister, Jacques Modipane, had, in a R1.3 billion promissory note deal, allegedly signed notes illegally using thirty-two local game reserves as collateral for massive offshore loans.[60] Mathews Phosa, the provincial premier, cracked down on all these miscreants, suspending them from office.

After the Mafikeng conference Mbeki was keen to get rid of Phosa and happily received a delegation, led by James Nkambule, of disgruntled Mpumalanga officials dismissed by Phosa. Inevitably, they sought to claim that it was Phosa, not they, who was corrupt. Nkambule became Phosa's chief accuser and after a series of damaging press leaks, all casting Phosa in a poor light, the Mpumalanga ANC set up a commission of inquiry to investigate the situation. This might well have uncovered a rich seam of intrigue, for Nkambule had received substantial cash payments from Alan Gray's Parks Board and the documents released as part of the 116 charges of misconduct against Gray showed how Nkambule and Gray had bankrolled a lavish lifestyle for themselves and their cronies out of Parks Board funds.[61]

Mbeki quickly squashed this initiative, appointing a national ANC commission of inquiry instead, headed by his close confidante, Nosiviwe Mapisa-Nqakula, wife of the cabinet Minister Charles Nqakula. The commission's mind was already clearly made up: it was determined to take a 'vicious' line against Phosa.[62] Realizing what was happening, Phosa tried twice to resign but was dissuaded by Mandela, who was much concerned at losing a man of his stature. The commission then recommended that the suspension of those sacked for corruption by Phosa be lifted and also tried to forbid Phosa to speak to the media. Phosa indignantly said he was merely defending himself from his detractors and that he could not understand how the commission could place faith in the testimony of 'criminals'. The commission found that Phosa and January Masilela were the chief cause of factionalism in the provincial ANC, but Masilela was then co-opted onto the ANC NEC as a sign of favour, while the commission recommended that Phosa be 'redeployed'.[63]

Already it had been announced that the NEC would in future 'hand-pick' provincial premiers, which meant, in practice, that the NWC would choose them – which in turn meant that Mbeki would do the choosing. Sure enough, in April 1999 Mbeki announced to a stunned NWC that he was axing both Phosa and Gauteng's Motshekga. Mbeki displayed such intense hostility towards Phosa that all but one of the NWC members were cowed into silence.[64] It was a crucial moment, for Motshekga had been voted in at the head of the Gauteng list and had received more branch nominations than anyone else,[65] while Phosa had been unanimously supported by every branch in Mpumalanga. Provincial democracy was now dead.

Mbeki replaced Phosa with Ndaweni Mahlangu, yet another former bantustan minister, who promptly reappointed Mabona, Masilela and Modipane. Mbeki was so determined to get rid of Phosa that in effect Mpumalanga was turned over to bantustan ex-ministers with known records of corruption. Mahlangu speedily distinguished himself by admitting that he had lied about some things, but said this was something a politician quite normally had to do. An embittered Phosa announced he was quitting politics. Mbeki did not want headlines about him driving out yet another ANC leader, so efforts were made to persuade Phosa to become an MP and accept the chairmanship of a parliamentary committee. Phosa was having none of it and returned to his law practice, though he remained an ANC NEC member. During the 1999 election Mbeki campaigned in Mpumalanga, warning of 'thieves who joined the government' (clearly meaning to imply Phosa).[66] It was a classic example of the Mbeki style, for he had just installed several doubtful figures in the province's government. He also appointed Sam Shilowa, the former Cosatu boss, as premier of Gauteng. Shilowa, who rapidly developed a taste for cigars and a luxurious lifestyle, became a devoted Mbeki supporter.

The premier of the Free State earlier imposed by Mbeki, Ivy Matsepe-Casaburri, had proved such a failure that she and most of her cabinet failed even to be nominated by the local party branches, which placed Ace Magashule at the head of the list. Mbeki could hardly continue with Matsepe-Casaburri, but he was most unwilling to see the province depose his candidate for one of its own. So, to general stupefaction, Winnie Direko, a 66-year-old community worker, was imposed as the premiership candidate.[67] Magashule was 'redeployed' to Parliament. Direko found herself utterly without support from either the ANC provincial executive or even her fellow list-members. So Mbeki went personally to the Free State to introduce Direko to the local party, pointedly refused to meet the provincial executive and over half the ANC list was sacked and replaced.[68]

THE 1999 ELECTION

The ANC which approached the 1999 election was a juggernaut, greatly strengthened by five years of control over state institutions and resources. Mandela had continued to use his foreign state visits as ANC fund-raising expeditions, even telling one public meeting that in the last year alone he had raised $20 million from Saudi Arabia and the United Arab Emirates. This produced embarrassed disclaimers from Luthuli House (as ANC headquarters was called from 1998), unused to such frankness.[69] Moreover, Mandela admitted that King Fahd's donation came on top of an initial $50 million he had given in 1990 and that he had also relieved Indonesia's President Suharto of $60 million and Malaysia's premier, Mahathir Mohamed, of $50 million. Qaddafi had also given generously, while many donors remained undisclosed. Overall, the ANC had received at least R1 billion from such foreign leaders since 1990.[70] In addition, the ANC received large donations from most South African companies, desperate to remain on side with the new regime. The often shambolic ANC organization was overflowing with money: at least one businessman found, to his amazement, that the cheque he handed the ANC for R1 million in 1999 remained uncashed (and had presumably been lost). Facing fresh requests for an election donation in 2004 he quietly cancelled the old cheque and wrote a new one for the same amount.[71]

The ANC secretary-general, Kgalema Motlanthe, found that grass-roots party organization was a complete mess. Branch leadership was, he admitted, 'very weak' and while the ANC might claim some 400,000 members, many activists had either allowed their membership to lapse or found themselves waiting for three years and more for delivery of their party cards. ANC membership was now a route to power and patronage so that 'If you have enough money, you can pay membership for a group, start your own branch and get elected as leader', Motlanthe admitted.[72] Within the party's upper echelons the get-rich-quick mood was palpable.

The old populist left had fallen silent: Winnie had sunk from view, Harry Gwala was dead, Holomisa was gone, Peter Mokaba was now a strong Mbeki-ite and Tony Yengeni, the communist rabble-rouser of Khayelitsha, was now recruited to the Mbeki cause (he was appointed chief whip), professing himself an ardent supporter of Gear and privatization and keen to declare that 'there is nothing wrong morally or politically for black people to become millionaires'.[73] There was no political reflection of the fact that unemployment, poverty and inequality were all far worse than in 1994. Cosatu and the SACP, having surveyed the balance of forces, had postponed their battles to another day and loyally campaigned for the ANC. Mbeki, in return, quietly buried his threat to kick them off the ANC's election list.

The party manifesto repeated the old slogan of 'A better life for all' but this time there was no mention of 1994's key slogan, 'Jobs, Jobs, Jobs'. Having failed to fulfil almost all its promises of 1994, the ANC gave few concrete commitments though, absurdly, it did promise to create a national public health system by 2004. Its manifesto announced that 'The time has come for Africa's renaissance', and Mbeki promised to clamp down on indiscipline, permissiveness, corruption and disorder and demand a faster pace of service delivery[74] – though exactly the opposite was already happening.

What saved the election from being simply a coronation – and Mbeki's inauguration ceremony outdid even Mandela's in its munificence – was Tony Leon's tiny DP. Despite having only seven MPs it had easily outperformed the NNP as an Opposition, a performance for which Leon himself was largely responsible. The DP, with minimal resources, decided on a bold gamble: it would launch its 'Fight Back' campaign (against crime, corruption and the ANC's hegemonic ambitions), aimed at rallying the discontented minorities, and spend almost all its tiny budget in the first fortnight. The ANC played into its hands, furiously claiming that this meant 'Fight Black', providing the DP with massive extra publicity, so that the party, which had scored just 1.7 per cent in 1994, loomed disproportionately large in the campaign.

Leon demanded to know what the ANC wanted a two-thirds majority for. In truth, it was simply part of the ANC's self-image that the party must always be seen to be advancing, never retreating. And Mbeki was determined to surpass Mandela's 1994 score so as not to be in his shadow. This was what the whole fuss over bar-coded ID books was really about. But Leon could also point to an ANC document which spoke of the movement's need to extend its control 'over all the levers of power: the army, the police, the bureaucracy, intelligence structures, the judiciary, parastatals, and agencies such as regulatory bodies, the public broadcaster, the central bank and so on'.[75] Moreover, the ANC had set out on its website a document, 'Cadre Policy and Deployment Strategy', which spoke of how the ANC would deploy cadres throughout every crevice of the state and civil society in order to achieve complete party hegemony. Leon had little difficulty in arguing that this would subvert the entire constitutional order, create untold opportunities for manipulation and corruption, scare off foreign investors and, in effect, create a new ANC Broederbond. The ANC, having published the document, found itself having to back-pedal.[76]

The results wholly vindicated Leon. The ANC gained 66.35 per cent, but had contracted an alliance with Amichand Rajbansi's Minority Front, just sufficient to give it two-thirds – though at quite a price. Rajbansi, who had headed the apartheid-era House of Delegates, had behaved in such a manner that the 1989 James Commission had concluded that he was 'ruthless, unscrupulous . . . and unfit for any public office that required integrity'.[77] But the DP had won 9.56 per cent, overtaking the IFP (8.58 per cent) and the NNP (6.87 per cent). The

NNP had lost 70 per cent of its vote since 1994 and clung on only in the Western Cape, thanks largely to a loyal knot of Coloured support, but its days were clearly numbered. Leon's achievement was historic. Under universal suffrage, and despite the deliberate bias in the franchise against minorities, a liberal party had emerged as the official Opposition. Neither Alan Paton nor Helen Suzman had hoped for as much.

Although the IFP's vote fell it held on as the largest party in KwaZulu-Natal. Mbeki offered Buthelezi the deputy presidency – provided he handed over KwaZulu-Natal to an ANC-led coalition. Realizing full well the importance of keeping his base, Buthelezi refused. The project of uniting the IFP with the ANC was dead.[78] When I interviewed Buthelezi again in 2002 I found him wholly disillusioned with Mbeki.

MBEKI'S SUPER-PRESIDENCY

Under Mandela, the Deputy President's office had been far bigger than the President's. Now the two offices were combined and Zuma's brief was simply to fulfil whatever tasks the President allocated to him. Zuma told me: 'I didn't mind at all – I was happy just to be on the team.'[79] At Luthuli House, the party presidency had 'only existed in name' under Mandela[80] but once Mbeki became ANC president he moved in Smuts Ngonyama, hitherto a provincial minister in the Eastern Cape, as head of the party president's office. The office ran the political life not just of Mbeki but of Zuma and the party chairman, Terror Lekota. Ngonyama also took over responsibility for the party's departments of information and publicity and international affairs (Mbeki's key interest), which Mavivi Myakayaka-Manzini, an Mbeki adviser, was drafted in to run.

Several moves reflected the new, ultra-centralist Mbeki style. First, Nkosasana Dlamini-Zuma, having proved her reliability by taking flak for having carried out Mbeki's wishes at Health, was now put in charge of Foreign Affairs. Secondly, the Intelligence portfolio was elevated to a full cabinet ministry – something common only in totalitarian states. Essop Pahad, Mbeki's key henchman, was given cabinet status as Minister in the Office of the Presidency – effectively Prime Minister. In charge of Safety and Security (that is, the police) Mbeki put another key confidant, Steve Tshwete. At Health, a key ministry given Mbeki's stance on Aids, he put Manto Tshabalala-Msimang. Mbeki had, as a young man, fled into exile with her and they had always remained close. She was to serve him with complete fidelity, destroying her own reputation as a result. The previous year Mbeki had set up a government information service, Government Communication Information Systems, and this he now took in hand. The *Mail and Guardian* commented: 'Thabo Mbeki sits at the centre of a web of power not experienced in this country since the paranoid heyday of apartheid.'[81]

Ngonyama, who was to play a key role in Mbeki's presidency, was also an example of how Mbeki sought to neutralize the challenge from the left. For, despite his private-school (Hilton College) background, Ngonyama had been the No. 2 man in the Border region of the SACP. Charles Nqakula, the former SACP general secretary, was now Mbeki's parliamentary counsellor, while his cabinet included many SACP figures who in practice placed their loyalty to Mbeki over their loyalty to the party: Alec Erwin (Trade and Industry), Geraldine Fraser-Moleketi (Public Service and Administration), Ronnie Kasrils (Water and Forestry), Sydney Mufamadi (Provincial and Local Government) and Jeff Radebe (Public Enterprises), who also headed the policy unit at Luthuli House. Such figures, as also Mbhazima Shilowa (premier of Gauteng), Aziz Pahad (deputy Foreign Minister) and his brother, Essop, could all be relied upon to speak up for Mbeki's position within the SACP.

Mbeki arranged ministries into 'clusters' managed by the President's own office while the director-general of the presidency chaired the forum of directors-general from all departments, effectively setting the cabinet's agenda. Within his own office Mbeki appointed Parks Mankahlana – yet another Eastern Cape Xhosa – as his spokesman and chief director of communications, an appointment which went down badly with the press, who had taken to referring to Mankahlana as 'Pinocchio' following the straightforward lies he had told about Mandela's wedding to Graca Machel.

In October 1999 Sifiso Nkabinde, the former ANC boss of the KwaZulu-Natal Midlands, began to provide information to the press about how he and his associate Bruce Mhlongo, in company with various other ANC leaders, had carried out a number of major bank robberies and cash-in-transit heists.[82] Nkabinde told the press that he was not bothered about going to jail, for he was sure he would be killed within a few days anyway. And so it was: he was murdered in January 1999, just in time to prevent any further damaging revelations. Ultimately eight men were brought to trial for his murder, including Mhlongo, who had actually organized the 'hit' – at, he claimed, the behest of the ANC in KwaZulu-Natal, who had hired him for the job. Mhlongo was a man with a serious criminal record, but was also a frequent and acknowledged police informer. He made no bones about the fact that he had played a part in many robberies and in-transit heists, each time getting off by turning state's witness. He had been named at the TRC as a man with a record of great criminal violence and was under investigation for no fewer than twenty-eight murders.

Nkabinde's murderers had used R5 assault rifles traced back to the Pietermaritzburg police's murder and robbery unit, apparently stolen by Mhlongo's close relative, Bongani Ndlovu, then a police sergeant in that unit. The rifles had been stolen in 'highly suspicious circumstances', having been removed without any sign of forced entry. The assumption was that there had been police collaboration in the theft. Superintendent Clifford Marion opposed bail for Mhlongo, saying that he was suspected of having already killed two witnesses to the Nkabinde murder and was planning to kill a further three witnesses in the case. Marion said Mhlongo was not only a hit man and professional bank robber but a menace to the trial itself. At which point Chris McAdam, deputy director of the Organized Crime and Public Safety Unit, backed up by the National Directorate for Public Prosecutions, announced that all charges against Mhlongo were being dropped in return for his turning state's witness against the other seven accused, a decision which met 'with outrage in the legal community and the public'.[83] Thus a man accused of numerous murders and armed robberies, who himself admitted he had been hired by the ANC to assassinate Nkabinde, was allowed to walk free, avoiding further embarrassment for the ruling party, as a result of decisions by politically appointed state prosecutors. It was an early indication of how the state prosecution service was to be used under Mbeki.

As Tony Leon had pointed out, the ANC was committed to extend the party's control 'over all the levers of power' in society.[84] Now, with the election over, ANC deployment committees were set up at both national and provincial level and this policy was so thoroughly followed out that by October 1999 the SACP magazine, *Umrabulo*, identified the police as the only state institution not under full ANC control and called for further efforts to enforce complete ANC hegemony over civil society. 'This area is critical,' *Umrabulo* continued, 'because even though we may have made material progress, unless the forces for change are able to exercise hegemony, it will impact on our capacity to mobilize society. The transformation of the SABC did take much longer than we thought. With regard to the print media, the ownership structures remain a problem. The movement also needs to look at universities, research and policy institutes, culture etc.'[85]

In fact by this stage only three determinedly liberal NGOs were left.[86] Within the English-speaking universities it had already become clear that no vice-chancellor could be picked who was unacceptable to the ANC, although under the Nats these universities had routinely picked anti-apartheid vice-chancellors and defied the government. Such pluralism was now unthinkable, but, given the atmosphere of ANC-mindedness, it was also politically incorrect to make such comparisons. Within days of the *Umrabulo* article, the cabinet appointed Jackie Selebi, a senior ANC figure, as Police Commissioner while the Stasi-trained Vusi Mavimbela took over the National Intelligence Agency.

This new nomenklatura also represented the colonization of the state – and, increasingly, the private sector too – by a narrow elite of, at most, a few score ANC families, many of whom had interlocking alliances with one another. Thus, for example, Mbeki's new ambassadors to Washington and Paris respectively were Ms Thuthukile Mazibuko-Skweyiya and Ms Sheila Sisulu. The former was the wife of the cabinet minister, Zola Skweyiya – and was also the ex-wife of another cabinet minister, Jeff Radebe. Mr Radebe's new wife, Bridgette, was the sister of Patrice Motsepe, the multi-millionaire head of African Rainbow Minerals, another of whose sisters in turn was married to Cyril Ramaphosa, the ex-ANC secretary-general and now too a big businessman. Ramaphosa's ex-wife, Nomazizi Mtshotshisa, was chairperson of the Midi television consortium. Sheila Sisulu was the daughter-in-law of Walter and Albertina Sisulu – the greatest of all the ANC families, for Walter had been Mandela's mentor and his wife, Albertina, the patron of the UDF. Sheila's sister-in-law, Lindiwe Sisulu, was at that time deputy Minister of Home Affairs, later serving as Minister of Intelligence and then of Housing. Her brothers, Max and Zwelakhe, were also major ANC figures: Zwelakhe had been the editor of the radical *New Nation* (1986–93), then chief executive of the SABC, chairman of Savannah Resources and a director of Aquarius Platinum of Afrimineral Holdings, while Max, having served as ANC chief whip, became head of Denel, the defence industry parastatal, general manager of Sasol, the giant oil company, and a director of Matsepe's ARM. Sheila Sisulu was also a major shareholder in Worldwide Africa Investment Holdings – alongside Judge Louis Skweyiya, Zola Skweyiya's brother. Thus the ANC, the South African state, the parastatals and even private companies were rapidly becoming a sort of extended family business. Such a development was, of course, quite opposite to that prescribed by the Freedom Charter.

Mbeki's immediate concern was the problem with Cosatu and the SACP, whose resistance had been strong enough to ensure that very little of the privatization – and none of the labour flexibility – promised by Gear had actually taken place. They remained bitterly resentful of Gear's 'class project' while Mbeki nursed the usual Soviet-style ambitions of achieving organizational and political hegemony over the labour movement.[87]

At an ANC NEC meeting in November 1999 Mbeki tabled a paper prepared, under his direction, by two of his acolytes, the Northern Province premier, Ngoako Ramathlodi, and the KwaZulu-Natal provincial minister, Dumisane Makhaye, entitled 'The Role of the Progressive Trade Unions – a New Mandate'. Referring to unions in the usual Leninist style as 'economistic' and 'syndicalist', the paper accused the unions of being a labour aristocracy, comfortably esconced above the 40 per cent unemployed and the large number of informal-sector semi-employed. The problem, the paper concluded, was that the unions had 'embraced the struggle tactics of the past without absorbing the political basis of our struggle'.[88] The remedy was for Cosatu to accept the leadership of the political vanguard, namely, the Mbeki leadership.

The unions and SACP had played a large organizing role in the 1999 election but were keenly aware that Mbeki occupied the political high ground. The government had, moreover, shown itself willing to use tough tactics in the recent public service strike. On top of that Mbeki had co-opted many trade union and SACP leaders while sending members of the 'awkward squad' off to peripheral jobs where they could do no harm. The great fear within Cosatu was that Mbeki would use his position of strength to start appointing union officials in just the way that he now picked all ANC provincial premiers and the directors-general of the various ministries.[89] Such takeovers of the unions by ruling nationalist parties had often taken place elsewhere in Africa.

Instead, Mbeki promised that government would bring in major welfare grants as income support for the poor in return for various Cosatu concessions, including a deliberate effort to build up the ranks of the black bourgeoisie. 'His underlying message to the alliance,' the *Financial Mail* commented, 'was "I'm the boss".'[90] The SACP and Cosatu decided that it would be folly to fight Mbeki at this point and when, the following month, he established a new alliance 'monitoring structure' of the top two of each of the three partners under his chairmanship, they were happy enough to go along and leave their battles to another day.[91]

A SETTLING OF ACCOUNTS

Although Mbeki had effectively run the government for the previous five years he had immediately concentrated far more power in his hands than either he or Mandela, even in combination, had ever had before. He had improved on the parliamentary majority Mandela had won in 1994 and had assumed unheard-of powers of patronage. Very soon the NWC was less in evidence, for the real purpose of this inner group had been to defeat rebellious elements and to control Mandela. Mbeki chose instead to relate to the NEC, which was far too large to meet frequently, to operate as an inner cabinet or to constitute a serious brake on presidential power.

Mbeki liked to give orations and make gestures on a high level of abstraction – about the African Renaissance, the African Union, the New Economic Partnership for African Development (Nepad), the decade of struggle against racism, South–South relations and the like. But when it came to practical decisions Mbeki wanted both to micro-manage and to avoid responsibility. Time after time decisions would be taken in secret and delegated to intermediaries to announce (if they were announced at all), so that Mbeki was left with complete deniability, smiling and aloof, apparently above the battle. Foreign diplomats professed themselves utterly at sea. Elsewhere in the world they would know exactly how decisions were made and who made them, 'but here we do not know who is making policy'.[92] Often this meant Mbeki himself was making policy. Underlings would be pushed forward to give speeches, sign letters or take initiatives, and Mbeki's authorship would never be acknowledged. It was the politics of Richelieu and Mazarin, of knives behind the curtain and spies behind the arras. In modern terms it often meant dirty tricks.

THE LAND BANK SAGA

Among the first to feel the new style's sting was Helena Dolny, widow of the SACP leader, Joe Slovo, and head of the Land Bank, a crucial institution within the South African farming world. Dolny had made a considerable success of the post: she was an incorruptible workaholic and greatly increased the Bank's sphere of operations and profitability while simultaneously 'transforming' it in approved ANC style. But there had been no love lost between Slovo and Mbeki, who had in any case decided to make agriculture a showcase of his Africanist intentions. A hit list was drawn up of whites who had to go, starting with the Minister of Agriculture, Derek Hanekom, and many white radicals whom Hanekom had recruited. Almost coincidentally this introduced a policy change: Hanekom and his advisers had been principally concerned to help farmworkers and the rural poor, albeit in a blinkered and self-defeating way,[93] while their black successors were more interested in promoting a black rural bourgeoisie.

Dolny was a more difficult case. She was an exemplary worker and her husband had been a struggle hero, with squatter camps named after him all over the country. Sacking her would produce an embarrassing political confrontation and would make it hard for Mbeki to deny responsibility. So she had to be smeared – by someone else – and then had to go of her own accord. Dolny's first inkling that she was in trouble came when she failed to receive an invitation to Mbeki's inauguration and was then disinvited from attending a Mandela farewell banquet.[94] In later years those to whom such mishaps occurred were quick to realize that they were in the cross-hairs, but Dolny plodded on. While she was on holiday after the 1999 elections, a letter written about her to Mbeki by Bonile Jack, the Land Bank chairman, was leaked to the press: Jack accused her of racism, nepotism, mismanagement and corruption. It was neatly done: she was away, unable to reply, and the story appeared in the press replete with photographs and was the well-prepared lead item on the state-controlled SABC News.

Dolny later recorded her ensuing travails in a book of heartbreaking naivety: how she was prevented even from seeing a copy of Jack's letter; how key board meeting tapes had mysteriously disappeared from the safe; how crucial board minutes had also disappeared; how her office doors were left open by someone who obviously had a key; how well-informed leaks always checkmated her in the press; how the new minister was not going to go ahead with disciplinary proceedings but then, after a meeting with Mbeki, how, suddenly, she was; how there were threatening telephone calls and a bullet shot into her kitchen; and a great deal more of the same until she finally accepted the inevitable and accepted her golden handshake. Her friends at the Bank were quickly purged. She described what had happened to her as 'ethnic cleansing', a remark for which she had repeatedly to apologize.[95]

Bonile Jack had been an unsuccessful applicant for Dolny's job and was a former bantustan politician with a past to live down. With Dolny felled, Jack went on to enjoy presidential patronage and an increasingly wealthy career, while Dolny, ironically for the widow of an SACP leader, became a middling executive of a commercial bank. Dolny's book treats Jack as the main villain of the piece but does not consider why his attitude towards her changed so suddenly or the possibility that he may have written his letter of complaint against her at the behest of the President's office. Similarly, she reports that the journalist who came up with the story against her was Mthatha Tsedu, without ever reflecting on how close Tsedu was to Mbeki. During the 1999 election, while journalists followed Mbeki around in a bus, Tsedu alone had shared the presidential limousine.

At the Land Bank disaster soon followed. Repeated qualified audits drew attention to the Bank's appalling mismanagement in the post-Dolny era. One notable scandal revealed that the Bank had lent R800 million to Pamodzi Investment Holdings in which the ANC Secretary-General, Kgalema Motlanthe, and the one-time ANC premier of the Northern Cape, Manne Dipico, held shares. Staggeringly, this amounted to 33 per cent of the Bank's total capital base, an extraordinary concentration of risk in a loan to a single lender – merely to help Pamodzi buy a stake in another company.

By 2006 the Bank's capital had fallen from R3.1 billion to R1.1 billion, due to impairment provisions and bad debt write-offs, and so much money had been wasted or diverted into the pockets of cronies that the directors were forced to note 'uncertainties which may cast doubt on the Land Bank's ability to continue as a going concern'. This panicked the government into forking out R1.5 billion to bolster the Bank's capital reserves. Naturally, this merely encouraged all the wrong things and by March 2007 the government had to intervene to suspend three senior Land Bank officers (all of whom received salaries Dolny might have envied) and to pump a further R700 million into the Bank.[96] By April 2007 the government admitted defeat, recalling a retired white Afrikaner, Nallie Bosman, to oversee the Bank. A whistleblower within the bank who provided the auditors with information about corruption at the bank, including R1 billion in loans made for non-agricultural purposes, received death threats and survived an assassination attempt. In July both Bosman and the bank's CEO, Alan Mukoki, resigned, Mukoki commenting that the bank 'will be in turnaround for a long time to come'.

This was a euphemism. Healthy under Dolny, the Bank was now a basket case and had had more CEOs in ten years than any other South African bank.[97] All told, bank officials had siphoned off more than R2 billion, which, despite legal advice to the contrary, they had used to fund projects quite unrelated to the Bank's stated purpose, such as the construction of an up-market equestrian estate on the KwaZulu-Natal North Coast and a luxury golf estate in Midrand. The beneficiaries of these loans included not only black business friends of leading executives of the Land Bank but Paul Baloyi, chief executive of the state Development Bank. Both Bank employees and directors had benefited from these and similar loans. One such loan of R770 million had been made to Patrick Sokhela, a sugar tycoon, to purchase a sugar mill and to buy professional league status for Sokhela's football club. Sokhela had defaulted on the loan and become unobtainable, so the bank had had to attach the sugar mill. An audit suggested that criminal charges be preferred against Mukoki and various others. In effect a major state institution had collapsed completely in a welter of theft.[98]

This was paralleled within the same ministry by the situation at the Agricultural Research Council where financial mismanagement costing R150 million had led to the suspension of the chief financial officer, Lazarus Gopane. Audit reports also pointed out the unsatisfactory position of the Council's chief executive, Ms Nthoana Tau-Mzamane, who, through being continuously absent from work, had failed to exercise any financial control. The farming community was outraged at the decline of the Council, Africa's only agricultural research institute, hitherto known for its research excellence. A year later government had merely reinstated Gopane as finance officer.[99]

All ministers of agriculture kept up a high-decibel rhetoric about the undoubted inequity of land-ownership patterns and the need to restore land to black communities. In general white farmers agreed with this but the sight of the major institutions under the ministry's control collapsing under the weight of theft and mismanagement bred a cynicism and contempt which hardly made the cause of land reform easier.

THE CELL C SAGA

Shortly after the election a similar settling of accounts took place with Nape Maepa, chairman of the independent South African Telecommunications Authority (SATRA), who had dug in his heels over the award of the lucrative third cellphone licence to the Cell C consortium. At the root of the matter stood a R7 billion arms sale to Saudi Arabia negotiated by Joe Modise in 1997, a deal which remained stalled despite the payment by Denel, the state arms manufacturer, of a R100 million 'commission'. This was embarrassing to Mbeki, not only because he sought to back up Modise's deals but because the ANC had developed close relations with the Saudi royal family, and had received a $60 million Saudi donation to ANC funds. To help push the deal through a promise had been given that Cell C (in which the Saudis were majority shareholders) would get the crucial licence. Cell C had then taken on black empowerment partners in South Africa, including Schabir Shaik and his brother Yunus, Jakes Gerwel, Mandela's tailor, Yusuf Surtee and various others. So while SATRA was supposed to weigh up the competing bids for the licence, Mbeki was determined that it had to go to Cell C. And Nape Maepa was being difficult, insisting that Cell C was by no means the best bidder.

In May 1998 Mbeki's appointee, Snuki Zikalala, was suddenly jumped from a junior to a top job at the SABC and, simultaneously, press leaks accused Maepa of nepotism, maladministration and corruption. Zikalala, who had a Bulgarian Ph.D. in journalism and a Soviet ruthlessness in controlling the news, was rapidly advanced to control all radio and television news in the run-up to the 1999 election. With the election over, Zikalala turned on Maepa, claiming on air that a forensic audit had found him guilty of corruption and mismanagement. This was untrue. No such audit had been completed and there was no evidence against Maepa. Nonetheless, the parliamentary communications committee went into closed session to discuss these allegations, while ignoring the fact that Maepa's deputy, Eddie Funde, was outspokenly pro-Cell C and had connections with Cell C's shareholders. Mbeki's spokesmen did their work in the closed session and the committee called for the Auditor-General to investigate Maepa. The anti-Maepa campaign reached a climax which included death threats and forced his recusal from the selection committee just on the eve of its final decision – which, of course, went in favour of Cell C despite two independent evaluations, both unfavourable to Cell C.

Mbeki also ordered the NIA to investigate bidders for the licence – in effect, an intimidating investigation of those bold enough to challenge Cell C – and the Minister of Posts and Communications, Ivy Matsepe-Casaburri, stopped the Auditor-General from investigating alleged irregularities in the selection of Cell C. Moreover there were reports that the Minister, her lawyer, and Mbeki's chief enforcer, Essop Pahad, were all at the secret venue where SATRA made its decision. SATRA members were apparently told that Cell C 'had' to win the contract in the national interest though the usual tape recording of their proceedings was mysteriously found to be blank on this occasion. Thereafter Maepa tried to resume his position on SATRA but Mbeki's legal adviser, Mojanku Gumbi, intervened to stop him.[100]

The manipulation of the tendering process for this multi-billion rand project was so obvious that it became a major impediment to foreign investors: it was one of the three greatest factors contributing to the 43 per cent drop in foreign investment in South Africa in 2000.[101] But the President had had his way, just as he had over the arms deal. Yet he had uttered no public word about either Dolny or Cell C. It was a new style of government. Mandela had led from the front, something Mbeki carefully eschewed – and it could, if necessary, get quite rough: a bullet into Dolny's kitchen and death threats against Maepa. Nobody, of course, could possibly connect the President with such tactics. Yet the lesson was not lost upon those who followed events. *Business Day*'s editorial on Dolny's resignation spoke of how 'Mbeki likes to operate by remote control . . . there can be little doubt about his involvement.

What one might call smiling assassination has become the hallmark of Mbeki's leadership. He gives no hint of his displeasure – until, without warning, the guillotine descends.'[102] Similarly, Howard Barrell, editor of the *Mail and Guardian*, referred to Mbeki as 'smiling death'. The Dolny and Maepa cases both occurred in Mbeki's first few months as President but more such cases followed until it was soon accepted that anyone who opposed the new President did so at his peril. The hidden nature of the sanctions against those who stepped out of line led to an atmosphere of fearful conformity not only within the ANC and the state machine but far into the media, the business community and civil society.

Officially, though, no one wanted to admit this. The happy embrace of the new South Africa which had characterized the Mandela years continued, though it now covered a real anxiety about the consequences of annoying the new President. People like Tony Leon who spoke out freely were anathematized to such a degree that even journalists, whose profession demanded a certain neutrality, would keep their distance from such 'trouble-makers' – or, often, join in the vilification. Those who had experienced apartheid's apogee recognized the atmosphere of intimidation and nervous compliance.

For a while this served to magnify Mbeki's power. It seemed as if nothing could stand against him. And yet, largely as a result of his own actions, within two years his presidency was brought so low that his very survival seemed in doubt. It was a crisis from which he was never fully to recover.

6

Paranoia and the Plague

There is no national science just as there is no national multiplication table; what is national is no longer science. Anton Chekhov

Paranoid Personality Disorder: *Individuals with this disorder assume that other people will exploit, harm or deceive them, even if no evidence exists to support this expectation ... They are preoccupied with unjustified doubts about the loyalty or trustworthiness of their friends and associates ... Individuals with this disorder are reluctant to confide in or become close to others ... They read hidden meanings that are demeaning and threatening into benign remarks ... They may view an offer of help as criticism that they are not doing well enough on their own ... Individuals with this disorder persistently bear grudges ... Minor slights arouse major hostility, and the hostile feelings persist for a long time ... They are quick to counterattack and react with anger to perceived insults ... They may gather trivial and circumstantial 'evidence' to support their ... beliefs.* American Psychiatric Association, *Diagnostic and Statistical Manual of Mental Disorders* (2000)

To understand the story of Aids in South Africa one has to start with Frantz Fanon's analysis of 'the colonial personality'. What Fanon had to say about the division between the worlds of the settler and the colonized – a division which was not just social and geographic but profoundly marks the psychology of the colonized – has particular force in South Africa, where white settlement took place for longer and settlers were more numerous than anywhere else in Africa. 'The colonized people are utterly transformed by colonialism and know it. It is not just that they have been "detribalized", urbanized or proletarianized: their entire mentality is shaped by the generations that have lived under colonialism. The settler is right when he speaks of knowing "them" well. For it is the settler who has brought the native into existence and who perpetuates his existence.'[1] The native is convinced of his own inferiority. He grows up being treated as a lesser being and, more damagingly still, has to watch his parents being similarly belittled. 'The settler makes history and is conscious of making it' – that is, the white world is dynamic and creative, skyscrapers arise, new inventions pour forth, while the black world is timeless and immobile, a world of torpid passivity.[2]

However much they resist colonialism, the colonized are swamped by it, accepting its values and judgements, including a negative valuation of themselves. 'When confronted with the world of the European the black would experience a dreadful anxiety at the prospect of revealing his innate inferiority. His greatest fear is that of behaving "like a nigger" . . . Each day of his life he is faced with the reality of his social and ultimately his existential inferiority.'[3] The result is a complex mix of destructive complexes and emotions: above all those of guilt (for failing to match the world of the whites), inferiority, self-hatred, an 'exceptional sensitivity', with rage never far from the surface, and paranoia, since it is clear that the white man is not only a superior but also a vastly cunning opponent.

Such feelings last well into the independence era. Although the liberation elite espouses universal values and human rights it will, Fanon suggests, quickly lapse into its own racism, for 'the racial prejudice of the young national bourgeoisie is a racism of defence, based on fear'.[4] Its paranoia is deeply inbred and the white world beyond has still to be confronted.

All of these traits have been on prodigious display in the new South Africa. Moreover, many African states still see South Africa as essentially a white country, utterly dependent on white know-how and expertise, with just a cosmetic black elite on top. Insecurities engendered by such notions underlie much of the behaviour of South Africa's new elite. There is, inevitably, much anti-white racism and occasional displays of anti-Indian and anti-Coloured racism too. Many of the new elite seemed to lose touch with reality as, propelled by affirmative action, they moved from one top job to the next in different fields as if they were all multi-talented. Promotion to high office frequently seemed to cause the egos of those promoted to swell like balloons, resulting in extravagantly patrimonial, even monarchical displays of self-regard. Mbeki's regal inauguration in 1999 set the tone. The inaugurations of black university vice-chancellors became coronations, with choirs, bands, displays and dance-troupes.

The liberation struggle's older generation, men like Tambo, Sisulu and Mandela, were secure in their own personalities but many of the following generation exemplified all the insecurities of 'the colonial personality'. Many had been convinced by apartheid, even while the struggle against it provided the principal meaning of their lives. With the struggle and apartheid suddenly over, they had lost their psychological moorings. Many ANC leaders and activists found security in a defensive rage, clinging to their victimhood, no matter that some of them were now rich and powerful. This treasuring of victimhood was accompanied by a comprehensive paranoia, a sense of self-righteousness and of entitlement. The white capitalist world would always be the enemy. The struggle against it was the struggle of the just and they should now inherit the earth. The furious assertion of the superiority of African ways merely reflected feelings of inferiority and status anxiety.

This paranoia was first visible in the ANC conviction that De Klerk's offer of negotiations was merely a trick and then, when it became clear that it was not, that he would never surrender power. For several years after the ANC took power ministers asserted that the ANC was in government but not yet in power. Every failure of the government was attributed either to apartheid or a 'third force' whose existence was never proved. Mbeki warned at the outset that should an ANC government fail, it would be the fault of the whites. Within months of taking office Mbeki warned that 'opposition forces' would wage a merciless struggle to 'destroy the ANC' and cautioned that 'the network established by the counter-insurgency forces, the spearhead of the counter-revolutionary offensive against the democratic movement, has never been dismantled'. These forces would encourage the formation of an ultra-left critical of the ANC, carry out assassinations, destabilize government, use agents provocateurs and carry out disinformation campaigns. These themes were taken up by other ANC spokesmen, warning of assassinations to come and 'a secret government operating alongside us'. Such fact-free, evidence-free assertions told one far more about the speaker's psychological state than about the actual situation. Even Mandela sometimes echoed such nonsense, warning, for example, that a threatened public servants' strike was due to infiltration by 'elements who want to undermine the government'.[5]

Paranoia was not just a matter of rhetorical style. It ran deep and was a particular problem with Mbeki. Soon after the ANC had taken power the South African Foundation, representing the country's top fifty corporations, held a dinner to introduce its members to Mbeki. The general theme was that business and government were inevitably partners. As part of the proceedings, the corporate bosses were asked to come up with ideas as to how they could best help the government.

One suggestion was that the government, through no fault of its own, was inevitably short of management expertise and that each company present should second two of its top managers for the government to use in whichever way it liked. Mbeki took grave offence: the Foundation was suggesting that 'Africans can't govern'. For a long period thereafter relations between the Foundation and the Deputy President's office remained frozen solid.[6]

Mbeki's paranoia was not unrepresentative. Anyone who criticized the government was quite commonly accused of seeking to reimpose apartheid. When FIFA selected Germany over South Africa to stage the 2006 football World Cup Mbeki called it 'the globalization of apartheid', while the commentator Xolela Mangcu declared the decision was 'the vicious intersection of money and race'.[7] When Mbeki's refusal to meet an HIV-positive child, Nkosi Johnson, provoked criticism, one ANC spokesperson, Weziwe Thusi, labelled the furore 'a conspiracy' which used the child's suffering 'as a weapon to firstly neutralize, then isolate and destroy Mbeki completely', generating propaganda such that 'this immoral President has to be condemned even by Nazis' as a 'worse-than-Hitler President of the 21st century'.[8] Or again, the ANC leader in KwaZulu-Natal, S'bu Ndebele, refused to answer Opposition questions about the sky-high hotel and transport expenses of provincial ANC ministers on the grounds that the Opposition would use such information to mount assassination attempts against them.[9] Paranoia was a key part of the ANC's world view, a fact of catastrophic importance once the Aids pandemic began.

AIDS BEGINS

The first two South African Aids cases were diagnosed in 1982 but the disease remained within a white, homosexual ghetto until 1987 when the first African case was diagnosed. By 1990 the HIV rate (judged by figures from ante-natal clinics) had risen to 0.7 per cent and by 1992 to 2.2 per cent.[10] There was already a large body of expertise enabling one to predict a number of outcomes in the South African case,[11] but it was also clear that there was considerable cultural resistance to dealing frankly with the coming holocaust. When I tried to raise the subject with black audiences in those years I faced audience walkouts, incomprehension and a feeling that public discussion of such matters was unseemly. Moreover, already in 1988 *Sechaba*, the official ANC organ, had questioned the African origin of the virus, arguing instead that it had been hatched 'in the secrecy of the laboratories of many imperialist countries'.[12]

African society found the public discussion of sexual matters generally unpalatable and many African men did not appreciate having fidelity, let alone condom use, preached at them. So a lot would depend on bold political leadership making sure that such instincts were not pandered to. Chris Hani, who had been shocked by the devastation wrought by Aids elsewhere in Africa, was admirably outspoken[13] but other ANC leaders tended to duck the issue. Mandela, warned that his mentioning the issue could cost him votes, decided to drop the matter.[14] Nonetheless, by 1992 the National Aids Convention of South Africa (Nacosa) had devised a practical anti-Aids plan. Drs Nkosasana Dlamini-Zuma and Manto Tshabalala-Msimang had helped draft the plan and soon after the 1994 elections this was endorsed as the National Aids Plan. Everything seemed set fair.

It was not to be. To Nacosa's stupefaction, Dr Dlamini-Zuma, now Health Minister, ignored the plan, which was never implemented.[15] Indeed, she ignored the whole subject of Aids as far as possible. Instead she spent her time on new anti-smoking legislation and bitter attacks on the big tobacco companies; on berating the medical schools at the formerly white universities to increase their black intake; on grandiose schemes to increase primary health care, sharply cutting the budgets of the top hospitals, now criticized for their preoccupation with 'diseases of the rich' (such as heart transplants); and in strong criticism of the big pharmaceutical companies (known as 'Big Pharma') for profiteering at the expense of the poor. She was steered in this direction by Mbeki (who was already effectively running the government), though his own attitudes towards Aids remained diplomatically hidden.

Dr Dlamini-Zuma thus did what was congenial to a struggle politician: attacking the white and the rich in the name of 'the masses'. Doctors, appalled by the damage to hospitals and medical schools, emigrated in droves – the so-called 'Zuma refugees' – whereupon she imported Cuban doctors and made service in rural areas obligatory for all trainee doctors. This merely increased the emigratory flow. The idea of improving pay and conditions for doctors (and nurses) in order to make them stay was anathema to the Minister, for that would have meant 'pampering' the largely white medical corps.

The Aids pandemic doubled in two years – from 7.6 per cent in 1994 to 14.2 per cent in 1996[16] – while the government did nothing. In 1995 a huge outcry greeted the news that the Health Department, ignoring normal tendering processes, had given R14.3 million to Bongani Ngema's musical, *Sarafina II*, on the grounds that it would be a popular educational tool against Aids. In effect, Dr Dlamini-Zuma had simply thrown away a large chunk of the Department's anti-Aids budget as a gift to a 'comrade' (and fellow-Zulu), while far worthier anti-Aids initiatives went unfunded. She tried to defuse the crisis by claiming that a mystery donor had footed most of the bill, but three years later there was still no sign of any such donor or his money. She then said, untruthfully, that the play had been funded by the EU – and then sacked her chief civil servant, Dr Olive Shisana, for refusing to take the blame. Meanwhile fraud charges were laid against Ngema.[17] Judge Willem Heath, investigating the matter, called Dlamini-Zuma 'reckless' and 'negligent'.[18] But she was Mbeki's client and therefore unsackable.

VIRODENE AND AZT

Mbeki and Dlamini-Zuma enthusiastically promoted Virodene, a quack 'cure' for Aids, actually consisting of a toxic industrial solvent. Despite the fact that Virodene's inventors had ignored all the ethical and procedural protocols for drug research and that the Medicines Control

Council had condemned their product as dangerous, Mbeki and Dlamini-Zuma got the Virodene researchers, Olga and Zigi Visser, to address the cabinet in January 1997, an occasion Mbeki described as 'moving'. (Zigi Visser argued that Mbeki should pump unlimited funds into Virodene to help develop the drug which 'he knew his own cabinet ministers were cured with'.[19]) Mbeki and Dlamini-Zuma denounced the Medicines Control Council as merely the tool of the international pharmaceutical companies. But as the facts about Virodene leaked out Dlamini-Zuma and Mbeki were forced to back down under the scorn of the medical profession and a torrent of DP criticism. They reacted with typical paranoia, Dlamini-Zuma shouting that 'the DP hates ANC supporters. If they had their way we would all die of Aids' while Mbeki pointed to the millions of Africans already dead of Aids and wondered if 'those who kicked up all these dust-storms' about Virodene 'did not have precisely these results in mind'.[20] Mbeki authored an article entitled 'The War against Virodene', in which he spoke of a large conspiracy between the Medicines Control Council and nameless others to subvert the Vissers' work so that 'in our strange world those who seek the good for all humanity have become the villains of our time'.[21]

The arrival of AZT, a drug which cut mother-to-child HIV transmission by 50 per cent, brought new hope. Moreover, a woman raped by an HIV-positive assailant could nullify the infection if she took AZT within forty-eight hours. Yet in 1998 Dr Dlamini-Zuma announced that she and the provincial health ministers had decided against making AZT available, because they wished to focus on prevention instead. When it was pointed out that AZT was a preventive drug, she said it was too expensive. When AZT's makers, Glaxo Wellcome, cut the drug's price by 70 per cent she said it (and its successor, nevirapine) was toxic and that those advocating its use were just trying to poison blacks. Clearly, any excuse would do.

With 5,000 HIV-positive babies born every month, the decision against AZT meant condemning 30,000 children to death every year. In addition, South Africa has the world's worst rape statistics: in 2004–5, for example, there were 55,114 reported rapes, 40 per cent of them against children,[22] but since most rapes went unreported the police thought the real figure was three times that. Anti-rape activists put the figure higher still. Since rape is by definition a traumatic event, it leads to blood-to-blood transmission far more often than ordinary sex and thus accounts for numerous new HIV infections. Here too the decision against AZT was bound to cost thousands of lives. There was outrage at the sight of a Health Minister denying life-saving drugs to the sick and the Treatment Action Campaign (TAC), consisting largely of disgruntled ANC-aligned Aids activists, was formed in reaction to this decision.

International opinion was equally shocked by the AZT decision, for South Africa now had more Aids victims than any other country. The crucial difference between South Africa and other affected African countries was the transport system. In Uganda, for example, limited movement between remote country districts and Kampala meant that rural rates of HIV infection never approached those seen in the capital. South Africa, however, had an excellent road network and, thanks to minibus taxis, a fast and cheap means of moving people around. As a path-breaking study at Carletonville (a mining town) showed, this in turn led to the equalization of HIV rates between rural and city areas.[23] By 1999 life-expectancy for a baby born in Zululand was down to twenty-eight years, the same as at the time of King Shaka in the early nineteenth century.[24]

While Mandela remained President the world saw South Africa in a rosy glow, so when Dlamini-Zuma attended the World Health Assembly in 1999 all the talk in the corridors was of declaring South Africa a global medical emergency, but what the Assembly actually did was to say nothing and to give Dlamini-Zuma an award for her anti-smoking campaign. Dlamini-Zuma was then at war with Big Pharma, seeking to avoid the World Trade Organization's Trade Related Intellectual Property Rights Agreement in order to import cheap generic drugs. All she needed to do to circumvent the agreement was to declare Aids a national emergency. But Mbeki was determined not to admit that South Africa, just five years into an ANC government, was in a state of emergency.

Mandela said nothing, did not even demur over the decision against AZT. Given the galloping rate of HIV increase it was easily predictable that if the pandemic went unchecked the hospitals would fill up with Aids patients and these would crowd out all others. By July 2001 this finally happened in South Africa's (and the world's) biggest hospital, Chris Hani-Baragwanath Hospital in Soweto, where the head of the department of medicine, Professor Ken Huddle, spoke of his and the hospital's 'feeling of hopelessness, major hopelessness', knowing that Aids cases would double in the next five years.[25] If the nightmare vision of the public health system collapsing under the ever greater weight of Aids was to be avoided, it was absolutely essential that firm action be taken in the early years of the Mandela government. But Mandela did nothing, a huge failure of leadership.

Mandela was openly longing to retire; that Mbeki, as early as January 1997, could line up the whole cabinet behind Virodene speaks volumes about how little control Mandela really had over government. In retrospect it is easy to see that Dlamini-Zuma was in fact doing Mbeki's bidding throughout this period, although Mbeki's own views on Aids remained hidden. Once Mbeki took over as President he not only promoted Dlamini-Zuma to Foreign Minister but even hinted that he would like to see her as President one day, since he was keen to reward her for taking the flak up-front for what were in fact his own policies. This became clear in October 1999 when he announced that his own late-night internet searches had convinced him that AZT was toxic.

MBEKI'S AIDS DENIALISM REVEALED

The new Health Minister, Dr Manto Tshabalala-Msimang, had a good reputation among Aids activists. Within weeks of her appointment she met with Nacosa, making it clear that she shared their concerns. One leading Aids activist told me how he had congratulated her at the time on her more enlightened views and told her that he looked forward to her reversing the decision on AZT – at which she looked deeply troubled and said that 'it would be more than my job is worth to do that'.[26] And, indeed, shortly after Mbeki's own anti-AZT speech, she suggested that AZT weakened the immune system and could lead to crippling 'mutations' in babies.[27] This caused utter consternation among Aids activists, who had never previously suspected her of such views. The long-time ANC activist and Aids specialist Professor Hoosen Coovadia broke ranks to talk despairingly of the government's 'amazing statements with no basis in fact'.[28] When, in 2000, the government's long-awaited South African National Aids Council was set up, it was stacked with government ministers (all Mbeki loyalists) and included two 'traditional healers' (witch-doctors) – but had no representative from the TAC, the Medicines Control Council or the Medical Research Council, nor any scientist or medical practitioner.

By early 2000 it emerged that Mbeki's hostility to AZT was only part of the story. He had found an alternative explanation for Aids in the writings of Aids dissidents like Peter Duesberg and David Rasnick, who claimed that the disease simply did not exist. To the horror of the medical profession, both Duesberg and Rasnick were invited to South Africa to sit on a 'Presidential International Panel of Scientists on HIV/Aids in Africa'. Mbeki simultaneously dispatched a letter to President Clinton, Tony Blair and the UN Secretary-General, Kofi Annan, arguing for a fresh look at Aids – this 'specifically African' epidemic – and suggested that the Aids dissidents' views had to be strongly considered. In a flight of wild paranoia he described them (and, by inference, himself) as being terrorized and persecuted for their views, likening their fate to those who had struggled against 'the racist apartheid tyranny'. Soon, he suggested, such dissidents would not only see their books burnt but would themselves be burnt at the stake. Clinton thought the letter so mad that he sent it back to the State Department, suggesting it was a hoax. When the letter's contents were leaked, causing both mirth and amazement internationally, Mbeki saw this as proof that his paranoia was justified.

Mbeki's certainty that he was right, his intellectual arrogance as many called it, was a major part of the problem. The ANC mainly consisted of poorly educated, parochial people and its few intellectuals were old-style communists for the most part, hardly people with supple minds. Mbeki had got an ordinary degree at Sussex where 'none of us would have said he was particularly bright' as one former fellow-student put it,[29] but he was shrewd and smart and had mixed with a diverse, cosmopolitan company. This put him streets ahead of most others in the ANC and he was used, perhaps over-used, to being the cleverest person in the room.

Mbeki claimed to write and speak with complete authority on any subject he chose: the 'science of Aids', the biochemical effects of specialized medicines, the economy, international affairs, the theory and practice of 'the national democratic revolution', the arcane calculation of deep-level mining costs, South African history, all manner of literary trivia and much else besides. Having uttered on any such subject, it was impossible for him to retract or admit error, for being right had immediately become a matter of defending his dignity. To admit that he had been wrong about anything would mean that his 'enemies' – his critics – had worsted him. His difficulty in delegating, his tendency to micro-manage, his pretence to specialized knowledge in every field and his extreme sensitivity to criticism were all classic paranoid traits.

Thus Mbeki continued to attack those who demanded AZT to prevent mother-to-child transmission of HIV – claiming to be taken aback by how many South Africans were willing 'to sacrifice all intellectual integrity to act as salespersons of the product of one pharmaceutical company'[30] – long after he had agreed to open the Aids 2000 conference in Durban. To argue that those trying to prevent unnecessary child deaths were merely lackeys of Big Pharma was bound to provoke the large numbers of scientific specialists and Aids activists attending the conference. But Mbeki relied entirely on his own rightness and the majesty of his office to quell such critics. Professor Coovadia (the conference chairman), together with other leading medical experts, pleaded with Mbeki on the conference eve that he should keep clear of scientific debates.[31] This merely produced a furious counter-attack by Tshabalala-Msimang and two other ministers, questioning the academic credentials of those who had made the plea and alleging that they were 'frontline troops of the pharmaceutical industry'.[32]

Four days before the conference all 5,000 attending scientists, Nobel Prize winners, medical researchers and academics, published the Durban Declaration, clarifying the relationship between HIV and Aids. The Declaration was bitterly attacked by Tshabalala-Msimang as 'elitist' while Parks Mankahlana, the President's communications chief, warned that if anyone handed a copy of the Declaration to the President it would find 'its comfortable place among the dustbins of the office'.[33] Yet all the conference wanted to hear from Mbeki was a simple admission that HIV caused Aids.

The conference was a disaster for Mbeki, who, basing himself on a long-outdated WHO report, argued that the real killer was extreme poverty. He was to return to this theme frequently, arguing that Aids was just a disease of poverty, so that poverty, not Aids, was the root cause one had to tackle. It was absurd: South Africa, with the largest number of Aids victims, is a middle-income developing country and all the poorest African countries have lower Aids rates. The only country with a higher Aids rate than South Africa, Botswana, also has a higher per capita income.

His speech was met with expressions of disgust and walk-outs. Nkosi Johnson, the child Aids activist, became a major star of the conference and there was further criticism when Mbeki refused to meet him. There was furious applause for speakers who criticized Mbeki and for the statement of Mamphela Ramphele that for government to give official sanction to Aids dissidents was 'irresponsibility that bordered on criminality'.[34] Mandela, anxious to repair some of the damage caused by his own inaction while President, closed the conference with a plea for complete unity in fighting Aids. He too was applauded to the echo, a painful contrast with Mbeki's reception. At conference end, South Africa's two leading Aids scientists, Professors Coovadia and Salim Karim, were warned by Health Department officials that Mbeki was extremely angry with them for the way the conference had gone.[35]

Mbeki, clearly stung, dug in his heels – and so, perforce, did Tshabalala-Msimang, who had now completely internalized her own spear-carrier role, though, her behaviour suggested, not without considerable cost to herself. Moreover, Mbeki had so damaged his own position domestically and internationally as to create serious resistance within the alliance. Both Cosatu and the SACP stated publicly that HIV caused Aids and that questioning of that fact was unscientific and damaging to the anti-Aids effort. Ultimately, in October 2000 Mbeki was forced to announce that he was 'withdrawing from the public debate' over HIV/Aids.[36]

This was not a happy formula, for Mbeki meant that there was an ongoing 'debate' over Aids, that the issue had not been settled. The problem it left was twofold. First, all African experience suggests that strong political leadership from the top is essential in combating Aids, a requirement which would hardly be met by Mbeki remaining silent. Secondly, Mbeki was left smarting from what was perceived as a public defeat, which, given his personality, meant that he was bound to return to the issue. Meanwhile he had become a hero of the Aids dissident movement which prominently boasted of his allegiance to their cause.

In 2001 the Presidential Aids Advisory Panel issued its report, putting the recommendations of the Aids dissidents on an equal footing with those of the general scientific community. Orthodox medical opinion was incensed, while Aids activists warned that the whole 'debate' was hugely damaging. As Catherine Campbell showed in her book *Letting Them Die*,[37] the first instinct of many people, faced with the terrifying threat of Aids, was denial, pure and simple. Only strong, outspoken leadership from the top could puncture this grass-roots denialism, which would seize on any ambivalence in public messages over Aids to conclude that safer sex and HIV testing were unnecessary. Among black miners in Carletonville 'there were even more misapprehensions about HIV' in 2000 than there had been in 1995, with a corresponding growth in conspiracy theories and the disparagement of condom use.[38] Such disparagement fed on gestures such as the government's refusal to accept the gift of one million free HIV test kits from a US drug company.[39] Perhaps worst of all, Campbell claimed, Aids denialism at the popular level,

> has often gone hand in hand with the vicious stigmatization of people living with HIV/Aids, leading many ordinary people to distance themselves from the problem.... This stigmatization has driven the disease underground ... and served as a major obstacle to HIV prevention efforts, given that HIV-positive people are far more likely to disclose their status and seek help and advice if they live in communities that are tolerant and supportive of people carrying the virus. People living with HIV/Aids often prefer to hide the nature of their problem out of fear – fear of rejection, but also in many contexts fear for their personal safety. People whose family members die of HIV/Aids often prefer to tell people that they died of other causes. As a result of the taboo nature of the topic, their friends and relatives will often collude in this HIV/Aids denial as a gesture of support towards the affected individual or family. This distancing is but one local example of a more general tendency – at every level of South African society – to deny collective ... responsibility for the epidemic.[40]

Public attitudes towards Aids remained woefully ignorant, with witchcraft commonly blamed as the cause of Aids deaths in rural areas. Even among army recruits – young men with at least ten years of schooling – 4 per cent said people with HIV had been bewitched and another 22 per cent were uncertain whether or not this was the case; 23 per cent said that Aids was just 'God's way of punishing sinners for their immorality'; 4 per cent said Aids did not exist; 12 per cent said it could be cured and 9 per cent said that 'healthy young people do not get Aids'. Some believed that Aids could be contracted by touching, swimming with, or eating food prepared by an infected person.[41]

April 2001 saw the government win its battle against the pharmaceutical industry, which had challenged South Africa's determination to use parallel imports and compulsory licensing to force its access to cheap drugs, which all thirty-nine major international pharmaceutical companies said was a violation of their intellectual property rights. Under intense pressure, the companies withdrew their suit. Aids activists celebrated wildly: at last cheap anti-Aids drugs would be available. Tshabalala-Msimang hurriedly squashed this prospect, saying the drugs were still unaffordable and possibly unsafe, and that the infrastructure to distribute them was lacking. It was clear, as *Business Day* put it, 'that government is more interested in scoring points off the multinationals than providing care for millions of poor HIV/Aids sufferers'.[42] The ANC website immediately warned about the great dangers of using anti-retrovirals (ARVs)[43] while Mbeki went on television to say that 'I think it would be criminal if our government did not deal with the toxicity of these drugs' – and to refuse to take a public HIV test, as other political leaders had done, saying that to take a test would be to 'confirm a particular paradigm',[44] the paradigm in question clearly being that HIV did cause Aids.

The government, having won its case against Big Pharma, now dug in to refuse AZT or its successor, nevirapine. Tshabalala-Msimang angrily said that nevirapine was too expensive, so its manufacturer, Boehringer Ingelheim, announced it would make the drug available free for five years. She denounced the company for making such statements 'without consultation', and said that South Africa would never accept special treatment: the drug must be free to other developing countries too. Boehringer Ingelheim immediately agreed even to this proposal, infuriating the Minister. The government continued to find every means possible to stall ARV-distribution. Worse, Mbeki had issued instructions to his followers to prevent NGOs from distributing ARVs too. Thus in Nelspruit (Mpumalanga) a project to help raped women avoid Aids was repeatedly harassed by the provincial health authorities and the local health minister, Sibongile Manana, accused the project of trying to poison black people and 'overthrow the government'. Similar pressure against using ARVs to help HIV-positive pregnant women not to pass their infection on to their children forced the resignation of a number of doctors who said their Hippocratic oath compelled them to save lives if they could.[45] Newspaper articles about Aids frequently quoted doctors 'who ask not to be identified for fear of victimization'.[46]

Despite its allegations that ARVs were toxic and had not been properly tested, the government exhibited a cavalier attitude to medical ethics with the quack cures in which it continued to take an interest. Olga and Zigi Visser, the inventors of Virodene, had incurred the wrath of the Medicines Control Council by conducting illegal human trials of their highly toxic drug in 1997–8,[47] and continued to conduct illegal trials on human guinea pigs in Tanzania, where their clinic was visited in 2001 by Tshabalala-Msimang – just before an indignant Tanzanian government deported the Vissers.[48] Meanwhile Enerkom, a subsidiary of the government's Central Energy Fund, invested R80 million into another would-be Aids cure, oxihumate-K, made out of burnt coal. This wholly unproven drug was also tested on Tanzanians, in an attempt to evade scrutiny in South Africa.[49] When Enerkom officials brought ten bottles of the drug for trial at Johannesburg Hospital they were thrown out by angry doctors.[50] The next year – before oxihumate-K could be commercialized – the Central Energy Fund hurriedly sold off Enerkom at a big loss, clearly desperate to get clear of the wreckage.[51]

Another ANC-linked Aids 'cure' was Hypo-Plus, in which the MK Military Veterans Association was involved. Hypo-Plus contained extracts of African potato and mopani worm, 'Africanist' materials favoured by the Health Minister. The recipe for Hypo-Plus, which was sold through a pyramid-selling scheme, allegedly came to its inventor, Mr Des Pretorius, 'as a vision from God'.[52]

Despite Virodene's denouement in 1997, the Vissers (by now divorced) continued research and testing for another four years, inviting the question of where their money came from. Moreover, in 2005 Virodene went on sale on the internet as a drug 'for the management of HIV/Aids and other auto-immune diseases'.[53] Although Mbeki had repeatedly denied that the ANC was financing Virodene, there is a suspicious paper trail suggesting exactly that. A court application from one of the Vissers' discontented shareholders unearthed the fact that a 6 per cent shareholding was earmarked for the ANC and a further 1 per cent for Joshua Nxumalo, a former ANC underground operative, for 'ANC introductions work'.[54]

At least R17 million – and perhaps R35 million – had been passed to the Vissers (much of it in dollar bills) by Max Maisela, an Mbeki intimate and adviser-turned-businessman and former head of the Post Office.[55] Another Virodene investor was Karim Rawjee, an associate of

Joe Modise's who had allegedly paid off ANC politicians for state contracts he had won.[56] The ANC treasurer, Mendi Msimang (husband of Manto Tshabalala-Msimang), was also allegedly involved. Another investor was Wafiq Said, a Syrian tycoon who had come to prominence in 1985 when he received a £120 million commission for helping to sell British Tornado fighters to Saudi Arabia. Said was particularly close to Prince Bandar al Saud, a personal friend of Mbeki's, who had lent Mbeki his plane, put him up in his UK home and who had also developed an interest in the South African arms industry.[57] Said (who, thanks to Mbeki, attended Mandela's wedding to Graca Machel) and Rawjee were both businessmen Mbeki had met as a result of his friendship with Joe Modise.

There was, indeed, a classic 'struggle accounting' arrangement to fund Virodene, replete with large payments in cash and go-betweens in the arms trade. Moreover, the Vissers soaked up money. They lived the high life – their divorce papers revealed a large company drinks account, various nude high jinks and a great variety of sexual behaviour. Letters from Olga Visser to Mbeki also came to light, begging him for more money, reporting on Virodene's progress and warning that AZT was toxic.[58] And although Tshabalala-Msimang said she had visited the Virodene laboratory in Tanzania almost by accident, in another letter Olga Visser made careful arrangements for just such a visit. Thus despite Mbeki's denials, the ANC's involvement with Virodene did not stop in 1997.

THE 'CAUSES OF DEATH' DISPUTE

Mbeki could not stay away from the Aids issue. Questioned by the BBC's Tim Sebastian over his Aids stance in 2001, he tried to play down the disease's significance (Sebastian had cited official figures predicting seven million Aids deaths in the next ten years) by saying that in fact the main cause of death among South African men aged 16–45 was violence: 54 per cent had died in road accidents, from suicide, murder and other non-natural causes. This was mere sophistry. Mbeki's figures came from a 1999 study in which Aids deaths reflected the far lower numbers who had been HIV positive five to ten years before. The real point was that Aids in South Africa was a runaway pandemic, where future death rates could be predicted with some certainty. But Mbeki had now pronounced and official data now had to be 'corrected' to ensure his views were not contradicted by the facts.

This launched a new chapter in the deliberate falsification of the real statistical facts. When a World Bank-funded report recommended ARVs for pregnant mothers and warned that by 2010 even 40 per cent of hospital staff would be HIV positive, the minister simply sat on it.[59] Having discovered how useful out-of-date statistics were, Mbeki wrote a public letter to Tshabalala-Msimang in September 2001 in which he cited 1995 WHO figures showing that only 2.2 per cent of recorded deaths in South Africa were due to Aids. He argued that in the light of these figures not only did the country's Aids statistics and medical research programmes require revision but so did the government's health and social policy priorities. He insisted that 'a virus cannot cause a syndrome', predicting, with pre-emptive paranoia, that those who had already settled on 'the misperception' that Aids was the largest cause of death would mount 'a concerted propaganda campaign' against him.[60] This was deliberate obscurantism. His figures were clearly chosen for being out of date, and 'causes of death' statistics invariably underestimated Aids because victims died of opportunistic infections (for example, tuberculosis) and doctors were under pressure to omit references to Aids on death certificates. Similarly, Mbeki liked to cite all-Africa statistics because the inclusion of North Africa, with its minimal rate of HIV, diluted the horrendous figures for sub-Saharan Africa.[61]

Mbeki knew that what he said was untrue. The head of the Medical Research Council (MRC), Professor Malegapuru Makgoba, had told the Presidential Aids Advisory Panel early in 2000 that MRC research showed that Aids was now the largest cause of death, and he warned that the disease would kill five to seven million people by 2010, 'which compares with the Holocaust figure of six million'.[62] In fact by mid-2003 the first million were already dead and another 5.3 million were HIV positive. By 2007 there were 1 million Aids orphans and 2.5 million were predicted for 2010. The government tried hard to prevent the release of these figures but late in 2001 they were leaked, showing that by 2000 40 per cent of deaths of 15–49-year-olds were due to Aids and that already 25 per cent of all deaths (including child deaths) were Aids-related.

Tshabalala-Msimang and two cabinet colleagues tried to pooh-pooh these figures, claiming that authoritative data could come only from the (official) Statistics South Africa.[63] Their letter was utterly paranoid, talking of 'lynch mobs', 'the delirium of witch-hunts', 'the tearing of hairs', 'beating of drums' and 'a sense of hysteria all round'.[64] Mbeki was equally furious, insisting that poverty was 'the predominant feature' of the country's patterns of disease and death. Anyone arguing otherwise was part of a conspiracy, 'a determined and aggressive attempt to hide the truth about the direct and immediate relationship between poverty and health'.[65]

Mbeki blamed Makgoba for the leak so Tshabalala-Msimang now accused the MRC of having put itself 'in a hostile position vis-à-vis the government and it will be necessary for this serious situation to be attended to'.[66] Mbeki got the ANC NEC to declare the MRC report 'not credible', while Tshabalala-Msimang launched a witch-hunt to find the report's leaker. Under government instruction, Statistics South Africa issued its own report to challenge that of the MRC but its work was so defective as not to be taken seriously. Once again, the integrity of a major public institution, in this case Statistics South Africa, had been suborned for political purposes. The Statistician-General, Pali Lehohla, actually came to the offices of the Government Communication and Information Service to make his 'presentation' – an all-out attack on the MRC's evidence, methodology and modelling.[67] Rob Dorrington, Professor of Actuarial Science at the University of Cape Town, described the presentation as 'riddled with half-truths and misunderstandings'.[68] Already, moreover, the health departments of (ANC-controlled) Gauteng and Free State had reported that Aids was indeed by far the largest cause of death in both provinces.[69]

In September 2000 Tshabalala-Msimang circulated to provincial premiers and health ministers a chapter from William Cooper's *Behold a Dark Horse*, in which Cooper, who advertised himself as 'America's leading UFO expert', argued that HIV had been specially devised by the world's ruling elite to reverse population growth. Cooper, the originator of 'unified conspiracy theory', which explains world events as the result of a conspiracy between the Jews, the CIA, the Freemasons, secret societies and aliens, was the leader of the far-right Arizona militia and a frequent attender at Ku Klux Klan rallies, describing the latter as 'misunderstood patriots'.[70] Tshabalala-Msimang was clearly desperate for reinforcement and not particular about her sources.

UNEASY BEDFELLOWS: CASTRO HLONGWANE AND THE CONSTITUTIONAL COURT

The discomfiture with Mbeki even within ANC ranks was palpable. He told Parliament that government policy was 'based on the thesis that HIV causes Aids' but eight days later, addressing the ANC caucus in October 2000, he warned that he (personally) and the ANC government were being targeted by the CIA and international drug companies because he had the temerity to question the link between HIV and Aids and because South Africa was challenging the world economic order. The TAC, he said, was funded by US drug companies and a leading agent in the campaign against him. He demanded the support of ANC ministers and MPs but ANC MPs, appalled by his paranoia, leaked the speech to the *Mail and Guardian*, whereupon Mbeki's spokesmen claimed the reports were rubbish and accused the newspaper of illegitimately taping the caucus meeting. This latter accusation was, of course, an admission that the story was true.[71]

The NEC rallied round Mbeki, claiming that the Aids controversy resulted from 'a massive propaganda onslaught against the ANC, its president and its government',[72] but many ANC leaders – including Mandela – felt deep concern at Mbeki's direction. Even as the ANC caucus and NEC were giving Mbeki their backing, it emerged that scores of ANC MPs were taking ARVs to contain their HIV-positive status.[73] In November 2001 a parliamentary committee dominated by ANC MPs and chaired by the ANC MP Pregs Govender, recommended that ARVs be made available to all rape survivors and pregnant mothers.[74] Cosatu maintained its critical position and the TAC filed a case demanding that the government be compelled to observe its constitutional duty to protect the people's right to life by making ARVs available to prevent mother-to-child transmission of HIV/Aids.

Mandela and Archbishop Tutu pleaded for a more rational policy, as did the American ex-President Jimmy Carter on a visit to South Africa in March 2002. Mbeki made no reply but the ANC spokesman, Smuts Ngonyama, denounced Carter's 'interference and contemptuous attitude' and accused him of being 'willing to treat our people as guinea-pigs in the interest of the pharmaceutical companies'.[75]

The NEC, under Mbeki's direction, now announced that it was as yet unproven whether ARVs should be given to rape victims or health workers infected by chance with HIV. No government decision on the use of ARVs would be made until an evaluation process, which would only start in December 2002, was complete.[76] So drugs now routinely available elsewhere would have to await a separate South African (i.e. Mbeki's) assessment. The NEC statement boasted that South Africa would 'not be stampeded into precipitate action by pseudo-science, an uncaring drive for profits or an opportunistic clamour for cheap popularity'.

In December 2001 Judge Chris Botha in the Pretoria High Court ruled in the TAC's favour and ordered the state to report back to the court by 31 March 2002 on how a comprehensive plan for prevention of mother-to-child HIV transmission would be implemented. The government immediately asked the Constitutional Court for leave to appeal, though Mbeki and Tshabalala-Msimang were in no mood to accept judicial interference of any kind. Tshabalala-Msimang, asked whether she would abide by Judge Botha's judgment, replied 'No', while the Minister of Justice, Penuell Maduna, insisted that Botha's judgment would apply only to provinces in the old Transvaal (a jurisdiction which had ceased to exist).[77] This merely revealed that the Minister of Justice had no idea how the law worked: a few days later he had to back down. Tshabalala-Msimang insisted she did not have to obey the court until the TAC got a court order compelling the Minister to execute its previous order. Meanwhile Judge Botha issued an advice to the Constitutional Court that it should not hear any appeal against his judgment, for the Constitution was quite categorical on the matter.[78]

This judgment provoked a hysterical reaction in Mbeki. He now refused for many months to take calls from Mandela, who was deeply concerned at the cul-de-sac the government had got itself into.[79] Finally, Mandela broke ranks and appealed for ARVs to be made available in all public hospitals. Mbeki's furious response took the form of an extraordinary document, allegedly the work of Peter Mokaba, 'Castro Hlongwane, Caravans, Cats, Geese, Foot and Mouth and Statistics: HIV/Aids and the Struggle for the Humanization of the African', circulated to the NEC in March 2002. The document insisted that no one had seen the human immunodeficiency virus; ARVs were poison; and poverty was the fundamental cause of Aids. Orthodox explanations of Aids were a conspiracy pushed by an 'omnipotent apparatus', posing as friends of Africa but with the real aim of dehumanizing Africans. A conspiracy existed to push the idea of an African Aids epidemic (which, he said, did not actually exist) in order to sell ARVs. Africans must stand up against such 'mental colonization' and reject the whole idea that there was such a disease.[80] The Aids drugs were themselves deadly and the fiction of the epidemic had been created by the big pharmaceutical companies as a way of terrorizing Africa, a propaganda campaign assisted by so-called Aids researchers who were in fact financed by Big Pharma.[81]

Mbeki, who later admitted that he was the document's real author, had it circulated throughout the ANC as his response to Judge Botha and Mandela.[82] Simultaneously, 60,000 copies of an 8-page Aids dissident leaflet were distributed as a newspaper supplement in the Eastern Cape and KwaZulu-Natal. Again, this was allegedly paid for by various donors but was clearly an Mbeki initiative.[83] The *Mail and Guardian* also showed that a letter signed by the Limpopo province premier, Ngoako Ramathlodi, attacking the MRC's Professor Makgoba for insisting that HIV caused Aids, had also been written by Mbeki.[84] Mbeki was known to spend the midnight hours surfing the internet, which was how he kept abreast of Aids dissident views. The Hlongwane document was a meandering, obsessive and poorly constructed paper, 115 pages long – and later was further extended. It tells one much of Mbeki's intellectual and mental state.

The Hlongwane document claimed that Mbeki's spokesman, Parks Mankahlana, who had died of Aids in 2000, had actually been poisoned by ARVs – at the time Peter Mokaba had denounced 'the vultures of the press' for 'diminishing the stature' of the deceased by linking his death to Aids.[85] The dying Mankahlana, himself an Aids dissident, had lapsed into hysterical tirades of Aids denial. Mokaba himself died of Aids soon afterwards. It had been a strange career: radical activist, youth leader, police informer, peculator, junior minister, Mbeki confidant and Aids dissident. Like many in that condition, he fought a hysterical personal battle of denial. Mokaba's death produced a macabre quarrel over his ill-gotten gains in which the ANC was intimately involved.[86] Mbeki insisted he had never known anyone with Aids, yet two of his intimates, Mankahlana and Mokaba, had died of Aids. This too posed questions about Mbeki's mental state.

The government angrily insisted that it did not need to obey Judge Botha's ruling unless and until that judgment was confirmed on appeal to the Constitutional Court. In early April the Constitutional Court insisted, inevitably, that the government must obey the court. Mbeki's wild and paranoid response depicted the TAC as the villains of the piece:

> We will not be intimidated, terrorized, bludgeoned, manipulated, stampeded or, in any other way, forced to adopt policies and programmes inimical to the health of our people. . . . Some individuals engaged in politics and public health have achieved and seek to obtain public prominence on the basis of loading an extremely harmful and unacceptable campaign to deny our people all information and knowledge about the incidence of diseases of poverty in our country. . . . Despite the propaganda offensive, the reality is that the predominant feature of illnesses that cause disease and death among the black people in our country is poverty.[87]

Mbeki and the Constitutional Court were clearly on a collision course. The Court was squeezed. On the one hand it had a large pro-ANC majority, had deferred to government on all major matters, and Mbeki was clearly determined to get his way. Judge Botha's judgment had already led to a Health Department statement that 'such critical issues as the role of the judiciary in relation to executive policy decisions' had to be resolved. More threateningly still, Joel Netshitenzhe had announced that 'The whole matter of the judiciary and the part it plays in deciding on matters of government will have to be thrashed out. If there is a fear that the courts are the ones that are deciding on state policies rather than the government of the people, then this issue will have to be thoroughly aired.'[88]

A warning shot was the government pressure brought to bear on the Human Rights Commission, whose independence was guaranteed by the Constitution's Chapter 9. The HRC had since 1997 taken the view that the distribution of ARVs to HIV-positive sufferers was a human right and had strongly supported the TAC. The HRC's chairman, Barney Pityana, had arranged that it would participate as 'a friend of the court' on the TAC's side, saying that the HRC had unique evidence to contribute, based on government documents to which it had exclusive access. On the eve of the court case Pityana got a call from Marumo Moerane, senior counsel acting for the state.[89] Moerane clearly made Pityana an offer he couldn't refuse, for Pityana immediately withdrew the HRC from the case and sent an e-mail to his fellow-commissioners saying he had done this because, despite his earlier statements, the HRC had nothing to add. He then resigned as HRC chairman, but was soon thereafter installed with great pomp as vice-chancellor of the University of South Africa, a post which he could not have obtained without government goodwill. Pityana's career as chancellor of Venda University had hardly been distinguished and had climaxed in a stinging legal judgment against him, but he was a man of brazen ambition. Astonishingly, he later attempted – unsuccessfully – to take over the Anglican archbishopric of Cape Town.

With the HRC thus taken care of, the Constitutional Court could have no doubt how high the stakes were. Arthur Chaskalson, the Chief Justice, a long-time ANC supporter, was certainly keen to avoid confronting government if at all possible. On the other hand the justices were aware that to take the government's side over Aids would irretrievably ruin the Court and all their own individual reputations. The Court would be written off for ever as a mere government lackey and would lose all respect internationally. For the judges, who liked to preen themselves before international opinion and even set their caps at international appointments, this was a prohibitive price.

At this point a remarkable evolution took place. Despite his earlier promise to retire from the Aids debate, Mbeki was now right back in it, bitterly denouncing the conspiracy afoot as 'a studied and sustained attempt to hide the truth about diseases of poverty', by those with 'particular agendas' who, if they got their way, would produce a further deterioration in the nation's health. His peroration built up to a classic affirmation of victimhood: 'We are both the victims and fully understand the legacy of centuries-old and current racism on our society and ourselves.'[90] Then on 17 April the cabinet suddenly reversed itself, recognized the efficacy of ARVs and recommended that they be made available to rape victims. The Health Department announced it was preparing a plan for the universal roll-out of ARVs. The announcement was greeted with universal jubilation: at last Mbeki and the ANC had seen the light. A new and hopeful era could begin.

This was over-optimistic. Mbeki had been making Aids-denialist noises right up to the eve of the cabinet announcement. So what had happened? Clearly, there had been signals from the Constitutional Court that it was bound to dismiss the possibility of a government appeal, in which case it would be better for the government to moderate its position in advance rather than be humiliated by the Court. In addition, within the cabinet Buthelezi had become an outspoken critic of the government's Aids policy. But the most urgent reason stemmed from the visit to South Africa of the Canadian premier, Jean Chrétien. Chrétien, who was due to host the G8 summit in Canada in June (which Mbeki would attend), was a supporter of Mbeki's Nepad proposals but had grilled Mbeki hard over Aids and warned him that his stance was endangering Nepad.[91] This impression had been powerfully reinforced when Canadian journalists travelling with Chrétien had given Mbeki a torrid time over his Aids policies at a joint press conference with Chrétien.[92] Already in January Foreign Minister Dlamini-Zuma had told the cabinet that South African diplomatic missions abroad were struggling against a barrage of negative publicity over the government's handling of Aids. So urgent was the need to send a different signal internationally that top South African diplomats were informed of the policy change before the cabinet.[93]

The apparent policy change of 17 April ensured that Mbeki's attendance at the G8 summit went smoothly – but at home nothing changed. The Trade Minister, Alec Erwin, said that before ARVs could be introduced prices for them had first to be negotiated with the drug companies: sixteen months later the companies said the government had yet to contact them.[94] In July 2002 the Constitutional Court earned the plaudits of liberal opinion by refusing the government leave to appeal, thus confirming Judge Botha's judgment. Those who so ringingly celebrated this decision as proof of the Court's sturdy independence would have done better to take note of the dog that did not bark in the night: this time there was no angry reaction from Mbeki. For the Court had quietly let the government off the hook by releasing it from any need to report back to court on progress towards the prevention of mother-to-child HIV transmission. As the judges knew perfectly well, this was an open invitation to the government simply to ignore Judge Botha's decision, which it could now do with impunity, and which indeed it did.

It was, without doubt, the Court's most fateful decision – playing to the gallery by seeming to stand up for Aids victims while in fact betraying them. Moreover, the Court, the highest in the land, was subtly but clearly aiding the government to disregard a major judicial decision. As the years went by and the government continued to take advantage of the loophole the Court had so thoughtfully given it, millions more were infected, hundreds of thousands more died and the Court's decision weighed heavily upon the land. For the 'great change' of 17 April was nothing more than a cruel hoax, a feint to enable Mbeki to sidestep his domestic and foreign critics. In practice government policy changed not an inch, nor did Mbeki's opinions. For a while the sidestep enabled Mbeki to regain the initiative but as euphoria turned to confusion and then to bitter disappointment, the result was a corrosive cynicism.

THE ANC BECOMES AN AIDS DENIALIST PARTY

ANC leaders and cabinet ministers had to decide what to do. On the one hand Aids was killing their friends, families and voters at an accelerating rate. On the other hand, Mbeki's word was law. The terrible result was the transformation of the ANC, the party of liberation, into a party that averted its eyes while Africans died on a hitherto unknown scale. For Mbeki demanded obedience on the Aids issue. Pregs Govender, having rebelled, now had no political future and retired from Parliament. But Dipuo Peters, the Northern Cape provincial health minister who denounced the local hospital for providing ARVs to a nine-month-old baby which had been raped and sodomized, was rewarded by being made premier.[95]

To their undying shame ANC leaders decided to back Mbeki up. Parks Mankahlana had opposed the provision of ARVs to prevent mother-to-child transmission of HIV because 'Who is going to look after the orphans of AIDS mothers, the state?'[96] Essop Pahad denounced medical experts as 'pseudo-scientists'.[97] Alec Erwin gaily announced that Aids had 'no impact on the South African economy or workforce'.[98] When the *Mail and Guardian* quizzed cabinet ministers about the link between HIV and Aids only Membathisi Mdlalana publicly agreed that HIV caused Aids (and was later booed as a traitor at an ANC caucus meeting). It was of critical importance that the Education Minister should take a stand. Yet the Minister in question, Kader Asmal, was only willing to say that 'HIV may cause Aids'. All the other ministers refused to respond.[99]

ANC provincial politicians took the hint, so that the national anti-Aids budget was underspent by 40 per cent in 1999 and by 30 per cent in 2000[100] while provincial education departments underspent their Aids education budgets by 60 per cent in 2001.[101] Even much of what was spent was deliberately wasted: in Mpumalanga a third of the Aids budget was spent on football matches, plays and prayer days and in building huts for a local chief.[102] Yet the awful impact of Aids was ever more apparent. In the worst-hit province, KwaZulu-Natal, the impact on education was clear. Children of HIV-positive parents dropped out of school, not only because they were needed at home to nurse their parents and perform other tasks, but because family structure and discipline tended to collapse. In addition, health and funeral costs took the money which would have gone on school fees, uniforms and transport. By July 2001 enrolment in Grade 1 in the province had – unprecedentedly – fallen 20 per cent in four years.[103]

Inevitably, the political cost grew: every child rape (and, given the myth that sex with a virgin cures HIV, believed by 30 per cent of South Africans,[104] there were many such rapes) became a test of government policy. Mbeki was under insistent pressure on the issue. The South African Medical Association gave its support to doctors who prescribed ARVs for rape victims or in cases of mother-to-child HIV transmission and there was talk that 'doctors under the current government increasingly feel that they are facing the same conflicts as doctors in the apartheid era'[105] when the dilemma had been how to deal with victims of police torture such as Steve Biko. The DA provincial government in the Western Cape and the IFP-led coalition in KwaZulu-Natal both announced they would distribute ARVs and so did the ANC government in Gauteng. The Health Minister condemned Gauteng's move as against ANC policy and the ANC labelled it as 'opportunistic'. The Gauteng premier, Sam Shilowa – a self-styled 'Mbeki yes-man' – immediately backed down.[106]

Despite the court ruling requiring the government to distribute ARVs, Tshabalala-Msimang, on Mbeki's instructions, fought a determined rearguard action. When, in 2002, the TAC brought a contempt of court application against the Mpumalanga provincial health minister,

Dr Sibongile Manana, for refusing to distribute ARVs, Tshabalala-Msimang responded, 'If she [Manana] goes to prison, I'm going with her.'[107] But the Minister, after making such outrageous statements, would simply deny ever having made them. This was the case, for example, with her outburst on hearing of the Constitutional Court ruling: she insisted that the Court was saying that 'I must poison my people'.[108] When the Global Fund for HIV/Aids, Tuberculosis and Malaria tried to give $72 million to KwaZulu-Natal she blocked it, accusing the Fund of 'trying to bypass the democratically elected government'.[109] In order to delay and obstruct the distribution of ARVs the Minister used a variety of excuses: legal problems, cost, the need to put a proper dispensing infrastructure in place and negotiations with the drug companies. When asked by *The Guardian* how there could be not enough money for ARVs when South Africa was spending so much on arms, including wholly redundant submarines, she said South Africa had to defend its coastline. 'Look at what Bush is doing. He could invade.'[110]

Tshabalala-Msimang's behaviour became increasingly eccentric. In 2003 she appointed the leading Aids denialist Dr Roberto Giraldo as her adviser. She showed an increasing antagonism to the international agencies involved with Aids, saying she would be embarrassed to receive money from the Aids Global Fund when other South African Development Community (SADC) members got no such money – though actually five of them were receiving such funds.[111] When the UN Special Envoy for Aids in Southern Africa, Stephen Lewis, warned that governments which allowed the epidemic to continue could be held accountable for 'mass murder by complacency' she accused him of 'arrogance of the first order' and suggested he criticize developed countries instead. Lewis said he had 'rarely seen such a litany of inaccuracies' and pointed out that he had indeed criticized developed countries; his speech had been made in New York.[112] When Professor Richard Feacham, the Global Fund's director, arrived to sign a $165 million anti-Aids grant to South Africa, enormous sums were channelled from the country's Aids budget into five-star banquets, gala events and receptions for him but the Minister declared herself unready to sign. Feacham was sent away 'terribly disappointed',[113] his chequebook unopened.

There were increasing murmurs that Mbeki and his Health Minister were guilty of genocide. One Cape Town businessman refused to sit next to Tshabalala-Msimang on a plane for this reason. The angry minister twice shouted at him to 'Fuck off'.[114] The minister became increasingly reluctant to release her department's own annual HIV/Aids survey, showing yet further increases in the number infected. In 2003 the Minister was 'too busy' to release the results so the DA forced the issue by using the Promotion of Access to Information Act. Thereafter, the same pantomime was performed annually, with each year the figures worse.

In 2003 the Health Minister announced the 'astounding results' of her department's research: that olive oil and garlic wonderfully boosted the immune system. Soon she was also boosting the virtues of the African potato, lemons, beetroot and sundry other vegetables, effectively as substitutes for ARVs. This was, she averred, the (superior) African way and she particularly recommended the African potato (hypoxis). When Stellenbosch University tested these vegetables a premature halt had to be called when patients receiving hypoxis extract became ill, suffering severe bone-marrow suppression. Animals fed with the extract succumbed to Aids far more rapidly than those not fed with it. The university also cautioned against the efficacy of the Minister's other panaceas.[115] The African potato, it emerged, significantly reduced the effectiveness of ARVs.[116] (Earlier, Stella Sigcau, the Minister of Public Works, claiming that 'traditional medicine' (i.e. witch-doctors' concoctions) helped fight Aids,[117] developed a 'secret' herbal medicine out of peach leaves that would 'help cure Aids', which she eagerly dispensed. The government made no move to restrain her.)

In July 2003 the TAC leaked a report prepared for the Health Minister in April but which she had not released. It revealed that 1.7 million lives could be saved by 2020 if ARVs were made available on need. This would also prevent 1.8 million children from becoming Aids orphans.[118] Despite public indignation, the Minister declined to take the report to cabinet. Meanwhile the TAC's campaign had won worldwide support, with protests staged at South African embassies all round the world, reminiscent of the anti-apartheid demonstrations of yore. The TAC also laid charges of culpable homicide against Tshabalala-Msimang and Alec Erwin for deliberately failing to prevent Aids deaths. When the WHO endorsed nevirapine after tests in Uganda proved that the drug halved mother-to-child transmission of HIV, Dr Kgosi Letlape, head of the South African Medical Association, demanded that ARVs be made available immediately and spoke openly of 'genocide'. However, the

Medicines Control Council – now firmly under Health Ministry control – announced that it rejected the Ugandan research and that it was considering banning nevirapine as unsafe.[119]

But the pressure continued to build. In July 2003 a World Bank report suggested that Aids could lead to complete economic collapse once the cumulative generational effects were added in. 'If nothing is done to avert the epidemic then countries like South Africa . . . could suffer a 50 per cent decline in their per capita GDP over three generations'[120] – a verdict immediately attacked in South Africa. An IMF report estimated that South African life expectancy would drop from 64 in 1994 to 37 by 2010.[121] According to Loewenson and Whiteside by 2000 the figure had already fallen to 43.[122]

As the 2004 elections approached ANC leaders found all their meetings dominated by the question of Aids. It seemed certain that 'the issue of ARVs was likely to cost the ruling party greatly in the coming elections unless something was done urgently to address it'.[123] So in August 2003 the cabinet instructed the Health Minister to prepare a plan to roll out ARVs to the public as a matter of urgency. This plan was unveiled in November: ARVs would be provided free, with 50,000 people treated in the programme's first year. The press happily greeted the announcement as a final admission by Mbeki and Tshabalala-Msimang that they had been wrong about Aids.[124] Again, it would have been wiser to keep the track record in mind.

This got the government through the election, with only the TAC still doubtful that the government did not mean what it said. The TAC – whose leaders were now dying of Aids at a rate of twenty-five a month[125] – threatened further legal action if ARVs were not rolled out immediately and its leader, Zachie Achmat, demanded that Mbeki visit Aids patients in hospital.[126] Given that the Clinton Foundation had brokered a deal giving South Africa the world's cheapest ARVs with a 70 per cent price reduction,[127] it was hard for the government to make cost an issue. It was forced, resentfully, to procure a supply of ARVs to head off the TAC's suit.

By now the TAC was routinely harassed by NAPWA, the National Association of People Living with Aids, an organization financed by the Health Department for precisely that purpose. NAPWA, echoing the Health Minister, denounced ARVs as poison and attacked the TAC for being run by Coloureds and whites, claiming that Africans in its leadership were only 'window-dressing'. For Mbeki was irked by the TAC's constant resort to the courts and irritated that Achmat had been nominated for the Nobel Peace Prize. NAPWA was the government's answer: a tame NGO to harass the other Aids NGOs.[128]

ARVS, SANGOMAS AND SNAKE-OIL

It was soon clear that the promise to roll out ARVs was way behind target. The government had promised to get the drugs to 53,000 patients (although medical opinion suggested that 500,000 needed them), but by June 2004 only 3,593 had them.[129] Professor Hoosen Coovadia spoke sadly of a 'lack of will' in government over Aids, pointing out that key anti-Aids posts in the Health Department had been left unfilled for months.[130] The next month, at an International Aids Conference, Tshabalala-Msimang publicly attacked Stephen Lewis, the UN Special Envoy on HIV/Aids in Africa, who had suggested that the government roll-out of ARVs should be accelerated. Back home, the Medicines Control Council loyally announced that it could not recommend nevirapine and would de-register the drug,[131] thus placing in jeopardy the government's entire anti-Aids programme. Although the Council later climbed down the TAC now took court action demanding disclosure of the Health Department's timetable for its ARV roll-out. There was, it emerged, no timetable – that would only have encouraged 'undue expectations'.[132] Tshabalala-Msimang naturally criticized this 'total pre-occupation with the number of people on ARVs'.[133]

The TAC applied for punitive costs against the Health Department, pointing out that it had incurred large legal costs in making eleven separate requests for the non-existent timetable. This led to a bitter attack on the TAC in Mbeki's online *ANC Today*, accusing it of being motivated by 'an academic desire to test the limits of the constitution'. The TAC immediately experienced acute difficulties with one of its constituent members, the Traditional Healers' Organization (THO). This had teamed up with the Aids dissidents, including Anthony Brink and the German vitamin-vendor, Matthias Rath. Rath's Health Foundation energetically promoted vitamin 'cures' for Aids and led demonstrations against the TAC as a front organization for Big Pharma – demonstrations in which the THO joined.

The Mbeki presidency had been cultivating the sangomas ('traditional healers' or witch-doctors) for some time. Anyone visiting the 2002 World Earth Summit in Johannesburg could see that sangomas selling herbal cures for Aids had been allocated prime position next to Mbeki's stands on the African Union and Nepad. The very fact that the THO had been formed and was suddenly in funds was itself suggestive: South Africa's 200,000 sangomas had never remotely looked like organizing themselves before. The hidden hand of Mbeki's office was generally suspected. Later, Anthony Brink revealed that in 2003 he had been approached by a Professor Mhlongo, another prominent Aids dissident and a close confidant of Mbeki, to say that Mbeki 'desired the establishment of a dissident AIDS activist organization to serve as a counterweight to the TAC'. Indeed, Brink said he had been secretly consulted by the Health Minister and by the ANC 'at the highest level'.[134]

The way in which the Mbeki government reacted to the challenge of the TAC tells one a great deal. Mbeki's South Africa, like Mao's China, witnessed repeated political campaigns launched by the government, during which NGOs, churchmen and 'community leaders' would lend their support. The SABC would relay the message as a form of news, companies would show willing by distributing campaign buttons and literature to their staff, the Post Office would hand out millions of free pamphlets and nominally independent front organizations would be set afoot to relay the government's message. Thus, for example, the 'buy South African' organization, Proudly South African, which tended to equate patriotism with Mbeki personally. As Mbeki came under fire from Zuma's angry supporters in 2005–6, Proudly South African took out innumerable and expensive newspaper advertisements consisting of full-page colour photographs of a smiling Mbeki. The press happily took the advertisements and refrained from pointing out what was going on.

Many such campaigns – for example the annual '16 Days of Activism for No Violence to Women and Children' – were unexceptionable in their aims, but they were also exercises in which the ANC 'mobilized' the obedient masses, habituating them to its hegemonic leadership. The TAC was loathed by Mbeki, not only because of its critical stance towards government, but because of its moral leadership in the Aids field. Mbeki's typical response – that the offending organization was an apartheid supporter – was not possible with the TAC. The Health Minister tried her best on this front by singling out white and Coloured

12. Thabo Mbeki (*right*) with President Teodoro Obiang Nguema Mbasogo of Equatorial Guinea, Pretoria, July 2004.

13. Thabo Mbeki with Robert Mugabe of Zimbabwe, Harare, July 2008.

14. Tony Leon and supporters at a DA rally in Durban City Hall during the 2004 election campaign.

15. Convicted businessman Schabir Shaik leaves Durban High Court, July 2005.

16. Tony Yengeni with supporters outside Pollsmoor Prison before beginning his jail sentence, August 2006.

17. Finance Minister Trevor Manuel giving his budget speech to the South African Parliament, February 2007.

18. Jacob Zuma (*centre*) elected ANC president, with Thandi Modise (*left*), SACP chairman Gwede Mantashe (*second from left*), national party chairman Baleka Mbete (*third from left*), treasurer Mathews Phosa (*second right*) and Kgalema Motlanthe (*right*), December 2007.

19. Nelson Mandela at the Hyde Park concert for his ninetieth birthday, June 2008.

20. Nelson Mandela at the ANC celebration for his ninetieth birthday, Loftus stadium, Pretoria, with Jacob Zuma (*left*) and Thabo Mbeki, August 2008.

21. Jacob Zuma marrying his fourth wife at his rural homestead, Nkandla, KwaZulu-Natal.

22. Essop Pahad.

23. Jacob Zuma arriving with supporters at the Pietermaritzburg High Court, August 2008.

24. Jacob Zuma supporters outside Pietermaritzburg High Court, September 2008.

25. Jacob Zuma with the Zulu king Goodwill Zwelithini ka Bhekuzulu, Kwadukuza, KwaZulu-Natal, September 2008.

TAC activists for racial attack but nothing could change the fact that most Aids sufferers (and TAC supporters) were black. Hence the resort to attack-dogs, ANC front organizations created for that purpose.

The government also tried to dominate the Aids field by sponsoring LoveLife, South Africa's best-funded Aids organization. LoveLife spent its large budget on mass advertising campaigns aimed at preventing HIV among teenagers but, since it deferred to Mbeki's views on Aids, its slogans were of a bewildering generality and were often a celebration of ANC themes. Naturally, it operated in splendid isolation from other Aids organizations. Its biggest donor, the UN's Global Fund to Fight Aids, Tuberculosis and Malaria, decided in 2005 to cut off its funding because LoveLife had no discernible impact. LoveLife's CEO then rather gave the game away by claiming that the cut was due to the influence of 'American right-wing ideology' and reactionaries 'critical of the South African government'.[135] But the word was out in the international donor community about Mbeki's fronting tactics. Very obviously, the Gates and Merck Foundations spent lavishly on Aids in Botswana but stayed clear of South Africa, as did the Clinton Foundation, despite Clinton's strong ties with Mandela.

THE WAR AGAINST THE TAC

None of this was lost on Mbeki who in *ANC Today* had claimed that the United States had used Africans as guinea pigs for nevirapine and that NGOs under the control of Big Pharma had, in collusion with the Constitutional Court, forced the government to roll out nevirapine. Achmat retorted that 'Mbeki does not have the courage to declare his views on HIV publicly'.[136] The inevitable riposte was mass press advertisements by the THO attacking the TAC as a 'dinosaur bound for extintion (*sic*)', commending the government and arguing that South Africans rightly only had confidence in their traditional healers.[137] Nobody could believe that the THO had found the funds for such expensive advertisements without government help. But then nobody could have imagined that an ANC government would take the side of the witch-doctors against the doctors.

War thus commenced between the government proxies, the THO and the Rath Foundation on the one hand, and the TAC on the other.

Although Matthias Rath attacked Big Pharma, his special venom was reserved for the TAC. In March 2005 Rath, with the help of the ANC's alliance partner, Sanco (the South African National Civic Association) – which, it turned out, it had paid[138] – plastered all the Cape Town townships with vitriolic anti-TAC posters. A furious TAC claimed that some people had been frightened off ARVs by Rath's propaganda, at grave risk to their lives. The TAC launched a defamation suit against Rath and by threatening legal action forced the Medicines Control Council to launch an investigation into Rath. This quickly led to open street clashes, with THO activists in traditional African dress carrying posters proclaiming their support for Rath and Tshabalala-Msimang.

For by then the Health Minister had come out in Rath's support, despite the condemnation by both the WHO and UNAids of Rath's claims as 'wrong and misleading'.[139] She also declared that ARVs were killing people and that she was 'not happy' with her own department's figures that 42,000 people were now taking ARVs. She was roundly condemned by mainline medics for her 'careless and dangerous' talk. Professor Salim Karim pointed out that his centre had 400 people on ARVs, that less than 1 per cent had withdrawn, none had died and that 'our patients have gained weight, gone back to work and led normal lives'.[140] In fact many of those receiving ARVs were getting them from NGOs; fewer than 30,000 were getting them from the Health Department.

Although reputable medics denounced Rath, his Foundation built exactly what the government wanted, an alliance of NAPWA, THO and Sanco to counter the TAC and cloud the issue. Tshabalala-Msimang admitted that she had met Rath and refused to disavow him as long as it could not 'be demonstrated that the vitamin supplements he prescribed are poisonous'. This missed the point, which was that Rath opposed the use of ARVs, which did work, in favour of vitamins, which did not.[141] In November 2005 the TAC and the South African Medical Association, supported by Cosatu, launched legal action to force the Health Minister to stop Rath campaigning against ARVs and testing his own remedies on HIV-positive patients.

The South African Medical Association and the TAC compared what Rath was doing with Nazi medical experimentation on concentration camp prisoners, but Rath's simplistic propaganda had lent the Health Minister fresh heart. She now announced that HIV patients should be given the choice between ARVs and 'traditional medicines', which were 'cheaper than western treatments',[142] and launched into fresh panegyrics about the curative effects of garlic, olive, beetroot and the African potato. The DA (again) reported the Minister to the Health Professions Council for 'conducting what could amount to medical malpractice by telling patients to use medicines for which no evidence of efficacy exists'.[143] Meanwhile the DA noted the government's increasing tendency to sit on reports about Aids. The 2000 survey of ante-natal clinics had been published in March 2001, the 2001 survey in June 2002 and the 2002 survey – after DA legal action – only in September 2003. By the end of September 2004 the 2003 survey had still not been published so again the DA took legal action to compel publication. Similarly, despite multiple requests the Department of Public Service and Administration would not divulge the results of two reports it had commissioned into HIV/Aids in the public service. When these were leaked they showed that between 100,000 and 120,000 of the government's 1 million employees were HIV positive.[144] As anyone who has worked alongside HIV-positive workers can attest, the recognition of the disease has terrible consequences. Victims become anxious, depressed, and suffer a whole range of bipolar, compulsive, eating and substance-abuse disorders. Such people become aberrant colleagues, neglect all civic and other duties and have a suicide rate thirty-six times the normal.[145]

The newly 'transformed' civil service had been dysfunctional before Aids struck but this was the *coup de grâce*. The disease had appalling results among teachers: by 2005, 12.7 per cent of the country's 350,000 state-employed teachers were HIV positive.[146] Further investigation revealed that the Eastern Cape provincial government had suppressed a report revealing both the extent of the disease in the province and the utterly inadequate state response to it, while in the Western Cape the National Prosecuting Authority had suppressed a report on rape in the province.[147] This was merely the tip of the iceberg: at every level of government there was a concerted attempt to hide the effect of Aids, though even the Health Department admitted that the number infected with HIV had increased from 5.6 million in 2003 to 6.29–6.57 million in 2004.[148] Mbeki refused to believe the civil service faced a crisis: 'People die from anything. No one has sounded the alarm where I work in the Presidency. Nobody has said there is a particularly alarming tendency of people dying.'[149]

Estimates of those needing ARVs were now around 700,000 but the actual number receiving them (many from NGOs) was stuck at around 125,000. The government clearly had little intention of living up to its promises. In practice it would get away with the smallest distribution of ARVs possible and most HIV-positive people would simply be left to die. Its principal energies were focused on suppressing the facts and fighting the TAC. Zachie Achmat, speaking at the TAC national conference in September 2005, made this clear:

> The TAC has been under sustained attack. NAPWA, THO, ANC Today, the Rath Foundation – there is one thing they all have in common and that is the Health Minister and the President's Office. It is a strong allegation we are making. What we are saying is that the Health Minister, with the support of the President, has met with Rath, has met with Anthony Brink, has used NAPWA against us, has used the traditional healers' organization against us.[150]

Mark Heywood, the TAC Treasurer, said, 'We hear from very senior officials, including cabinet ministers, that they have been told by Mbeki "Don't work with TAC".' And the TAC was being singled out. Two years previously the TAC conference had been attended by a number of government and provincial officials, but this time all such representatives had declined invitations.[151] One figure who did attend the TAC conference was the Cosatu secretary-general, Zwelinzima Vavi. He was blunt. 'This lack of government leadership is a betrayal of our people and our struggle. We are sitting by while the biggest threat to our nation since apartheid is ruining our families and our communities.'[152] The Health Department denounced Vavi as 'irresponsible' and a mere mouthpiece of the TAC.[153] At the same time, it emerged, the Health Minister was attending the National Health Council, listening to the Aids dissidents she had invited. 'They seem hell-bent on de-railing their own programme', the South African Medical Association commented.[154]

It was an apt description. For ARV distribution to work, a system of monitoring and evaluation had to be put in place, but nearly two years after the government had announced the roll-out of ARVs no such system was in place. NGOs set up their own monitoring forum but despite endless confirmations that they would attend, no public health officials turned up, for the Health Department was operating a three-line whip against such involvement.[155] By 2005, as WHO/UNAids noted, South Africa was falling far behind target, with only 10–14 per cent of those needing treatment actually receiving it. Tshabalala-Msimang predictably denounced 'this unjustified vilification of the South African government'.[156] Not surprisingly, an opinion survey published in October 2005 showed that 90 per cent of blacks thought the government should do more to supply medicines to the HIV-infected.[157]

ANOTHER FALSE TURN: 2006

Aids deaths impacted ever more heavily on African communities, increasing anxiety and discontent over the government's policies. Every family had losses – Mandela and Buthelezi had both publicly admitted losing children to Aids. When Mandela's grandson, Mandla, got married in 2006 in front of a crowd which included Mbeki, the bride and groom clung to one another crying as they told how both of them had lost both parents to Aids.[158]

Officially, Tshabalala-Msimang claimed that progress was being made and that the rate of infection was no longer increasing so fast. But this had always been predicted: once a high proportion were already infected it simply became arithmetically impossible to keep the infection rate from increasing. The bankruptcy of government policy created a great lake of despair in the midst of society. Inevitably charlatans moved in to fill the gap, promoting all manner of ridiculous folk remedies in order to fleece the dying and their relatives. The Health Minister herself, quite unpardonably, was at the forefront of such initiatives, preaching the wondrous nutritional effects of beetroot, garlic and the African potato. But it was worse than that. In KwaZulu-Natal, the worst-affected province – HIV rates of 66 per cent were recorded among pregnant women there[159] – a folk remedy called Ubhejane was promoted by Zeblon Gwala and Professor Herbert Vilakazi, a special adviser to the province's premier, S'bu Ndebele. Gwala sold R40,000 worth of Ubhejane every weekend and the promoters claimed that pre-clinical trials at the local university had been extremely promising, although this was denied by the university. Tshabala-Msimang, the provincial health minister Peggy Nkonyeni, and the mayor of Durban, Obed Mlaba, also promoted Ubhejane and tried to get Deputy President Phumzile Mlambo-Ngcuka's mother, Sabbath Mlambo, to administer it to HIV-positive patients.[160] It was sad to see such quackery reinforced by leading community figures. Vilakazi had been one of the country's leading African sociologists, though my own confidence in him had taken something of a knock after he tried to convince me that Karl Marx was black.

Increasingly the government found itself in the dock of international opinion. In 2006 the UN General Assembly was to hold a special session on Aids and the government tried to prevent Aids NGOs like the TAC from attending, provoking a furious reaction from Stephen Lewis, the UN Special Envoy on HIV/Aids: 'How do you keep the leading voice on Aids from the country with the highest infection rate from speaking?' The Health Ministry accused the TAC of having 'used such platforms to vilify the government and particularly President Thabo Mbeki'. The TAC replied that 'We live in a democracy and the government has to accept that it will be criticised for some of its policies'.[161] Under intense international pressure the government sulkily had to give way, and tried to play the race card, praising the TAC's African spokesperson, Khensani Mavasa, whom it contrasted with the 'unbecoming behaviour of Zachie Achmat', the TAC's Coloured president.[162]

Unabashed, at the 16th International Aids Conference, held in Toronto in August 2006, Tshabalala-Msimang had a stall stocked with garlic, beetroot and lemons. This immediately became the main conference talking point, the object of great scorn and hilarity until the stall was trashed by angry demonstrators. Stephen Lewis did not spare the Minister, describing her and Mbeki as 'obtuse, dilatory and negligent' and referring to South Africa as 'the only state in Africa whose government continues to propound theories more worthy of a lunatic fringe than of a concerned and compassionate state', adding that 'The government has a lot to atone for. I am of the opinion that they can never achieve redemption.'[163] Mark Wainberg, the conference chairman, said the world had been 'watching South Africa continue to deteriorate' under denialist leadership. 'It is something that burns a hole in my heart.'[164] At conference end a large group of HIV-positive South African women sought asylum in Canada.[165]

Meanwhile in KwaZulu-Natal Judge Chris Nicholson warned of a 'grave constitutional crisis' if the government continued to defy court orders to make ARVs available to prison inmates.[166] Due to Aids, deaths in prison had soared fivefold since 1996.[167] Despite that, the government had sought to deny ARVs to the desperate prison population. However, the watershed for the government was the Toronto conference, which climaxed with eighty-two leading Aids scientists appealing for an end to the government's 'disastrous pseudo-scientific policies' and asking Mbeki to sack his Health Minister, 'who now has no international respect'.[168] Mbeki went to the UN to make his usual denunciation of the rich nations who 'insist on an unequal relationship with the poor'[169] but in his absence the cabinet revolted. Zola Skweyiya led the criticism of Tshabalala-Msimang, for his department had to deal with the ever-increasing number of Aids orphans.[170] Aids was taken away from her and entrusted instead to Deputy President Phumzile Mlambo-Ngcuka and the deputy Health Minister, Nozizwe Madlala-Routledge, resulting in a more rational government attitude. Both women emphasized that HIV causes Aids and that the distribution of ARVs was essential. The Toronto conference had upset ministers because it was such an exact replay of the apartheid years, with the South African government held up simultaneously to opprobrium and ridicule.

But, as with previous such turning points, less had changed than had been hoped. Both Mbeki and Tshabalala-Msimang remained in office, exercising a malign, foot-dragging influence – and Nozizwe Madlala-Routledge was sacked a year later. ARV distribution remained massively behind target, the mortality figures continued to deteriorate and the pit of despair continued to deepen.

WHY?

Thus the unhappy story of Mbeki, the ANC and Aids. No other policy or event did more to damage all the actors involved. By 2008 2.5 million South Africans had already died of Aids, often in misery and ostracism, many deliberately deprived of medicines which could have saved them. This regiment of the damned included huge numbers of small children, innocents put to the slaughter. This ruined not only Mbeki's reputation but the reputations of cabinet members who supported him or refused to dissent while countless lives were lost. It also showed up the new elite's callous attitude towards the African masses, whose interests they claimed to be pursuing. Even the ANC's long crusade against apartheid was devalued, for apartheid never committed a genocide like this. Aids was also largely responsible for South Africa's fall down the rankings of the UN Human Development Index, from number 85 in 1990 to 120 in 2004.[171]

Internationally the damage was vast. Pathetic attempts were made to shore up Mbeki's standing by getting foreign celebrities such as Harry Belafonte and Jesse Jackson to voice support for Mbeki's stance on Aids[172] but this simply diminished the visitors. Similarly, the University of Cape Town's decision to honour Mbeki with a special award for presidential leadership, the citation actually mentioning Aids, was damaging to the university rather than truly helpful to Mbeki. What could one say when the government of the most developed country in Africa sided with the witch-doctors against the doctors? Stephen Lewis was more typical when he spoke of the universal bewilderment among Aids activists about Mbeki's policies. His relationship with Tshabalala-Msimang was, he said, probably not 'mendable'[173] and she seemed unwilling to invite him to South Africa again.[174]

But the great question remains: why did this happen?

The Aids monitor, Virginia Van der Vliet, suggests that Mbeki believed passionately in an 'African Renaissance' and 'the African Century' and that it was simply impossible for him to hold to these visions while accepting that tens of millions of Africans were being snatched away by a pandemic having an even greater effect than the slave trade. (The slave trade is, Van der Vliet warns, the most accurate parallel: other epidemics tend to carry off the old, the weak and the babies, but Aids, like the slavers, targets the young, strong and vigorous.) 'Faced with such a painful reality,' she argues, 'denial, or grasping at the prospect of some alternative explanation, is understandable.'[175] Mbeki saw Aids as a 'uniquely African catastrophe' and therefore thought that 'a simple superimposition of Western experience on African reality would be absurd and illogical'. He was always looking for an 'African solution to an African problem', which in turn led to misplaced enthusiasm for Virodene and other folk 'remedies'. Professor Salim Karim explained Mbeki's enthusiasm for Virodene thus: 'Africans can do this. Virodene became our redemption.'[176]

This may be part of an explanation but it is not enough. All the improvements in health care in Africa, from smallpox eradication to mass inoculation campaigns, were, after all, a welcome 'superimposition of Western experience on African reality'. It seems more sensible to place Mbeki's response to Aids in the context of the peculiar psychological deformation of the 'colonial personality'. The key traits of that personality – paranoia, an overwhelming sense of victimhood and thus also of righteousness and entitlement – are prominent elsewhere in Africa, which is why Mbeki's attitude to Aids was not unique. Many African governments tried to ignore Aids and Mbeki was not alone in viewing Aids as a conspiracy: Namibia's President Sam Nujoma, for example, was even more outspoken in that direction.[177] Moreover, Nujoma, like Robert Mugabe, also exhibited a primary homophobia, conflating that with his response to Aids.

To understand Mbeki's response as a 'colonial personality' to Aids one must bear several things in mind. The first is the fact – burningly conscious in the popular mind but almost never articulated – that the incidence of Aids is so racially distinct. Although South African Aids statistics avoid any mention of the sufferers' ethnicity, the University of Cape Town's Centre for Actuarial Research compiled data[178] showing Africans as six times more likely to contract HIV than Coloureds and eight times more likely than whites. Earlier research had shown that the majority of HIV-positive whites and Asians were men, for among them Aids was still confined to a homosexual ghetto. Once this is taken into account, the African predominance within the heterosexual population is even more striking. Among Coloureds the HIV rate had actually declined from 1997 to 1999, while the rate among Africans continued to increase rapidly. Moreover, the University of Cape Town's data showed that when education, skill levels and income were held constant, Africans were still overwhelmingly more likely to contract HIV.

It is, of course, ridiculous that the sheer sensitivity of the issue has prevented researchers from determining why Africans are more vulnerable to HIV. However, this knowledge vacuum has no impact on the popular consciousness, where it is firmly established that heterosexual Aids victims are, overwhelmingly, Africans.

This posed an agonizing dilemma for a racial nationalist like Mbeki. The peculiarity of Aids was that it was not like measles or chickenpox. With the exception of rape victims and accidental infection, Aids was a disease which one could choose not to get. On the whole it seemed clear that whites, Indians and Coloureds had accepted the necessity of safer sexual practices, while large numbers of Africans had not. Because of the taboo nature of this topic we do not really know why this was but the resulting gap in our knowledge left the field open to prejudicial stereotypes on all sides, though these were seldom openly expressed. In the same way, there was no doubt that South Africa's extraordinary incidence of rape – and of child rape – was a predominantly African phenomenon: with Africans making up three-quarters of the population it could hardly be otherwise.[179] Fifty per cent of all cases before South African courts are for rape.[180] Moreover, the ANC's coming to power coincided with an extraordinary 63 per cent fall in the numbers of those convicted of rape.[181] All of which led to a widespread, though unproven, perception that Africans are particularly liable to commit rape.

Mbeki was deeply troubled by this stereotype. This first emerged in 2000 during an exchange of letters with the DP leader, Tony Leon, who, fatally, had offered to stand alongside Mbeki on political platforms in a joint campaign against Aids (fatally, for offers of help are particularly resented by the paranoid). In his long, rambling reply Mbeki cast himself as the victim of a sustained campaign – 'no amount of pressure, however virulent, strident and sustained, will persuade me to betray', etc. – and singled out for attack the journalist Charlene Smith, herself a rape victim, who had talked of South Africa as having 'a culture in which rape is endemic'. This, in Mbeki's hands, immediately became 'the gravely insulting statement made by Charlene Smith about rape being "endemic" in African culture'.[182] No amount of insistence by Smith that Mbeki, not she, was doing the racial stereotyping made any impact. But Smith is right: South Africa does have a culture in which rape is endemic. A survey of 300,000 young South Africans found that 58 per cent believed that forcing sex on 'someone you know' was not sexual violence and that 71 per cent of girls had been forced to have sex.[183]

One of the appeals of Aids dissidence is that such concerns need not be confronted. If Aids does not exist, or is unrelated to HIV, then the difficult question of why some seem more willing to adopt safe sexual behaviour than others need not be explored. But clearly this was a deeply troubling area for Mbeki and other Aids denialists. Their way of dealing with it was not to argue for their own views but to depict themselves and other Africans as the victims of white racist stereotypes, and then to argue against those (imagined) stereotypes. This was evident in Mbeki's speech in 2001 where he attacked those who wanted to see Aids higher up the political agenda for believing that 'we [Africans] are but natural-born, promiscuous carriers of germs . . . [and] that our continent is doomed to an inevitable mortal end because of our unconquerable devotion to the sin of lust'. It was evident, too, in his 'Castro Hlongwane' paper:

> Yes, we are sex crazy! Yes, we are diseased! Yes, we spread the deadly HIV through uncontrolled heterosexual sex! In this regard, yes, we are different from the US and Western Europe! Yes, we, the men, abuse women and the girl-child with gay abandon! Yes, among us rape is endemic because of our culture! Yes, we do believe that sleeping with young virgins will cure us of Aids! Yes, as a result of all this, we are threatened with destruction by the HIV/Aids pandemic! Yes, what we need, and cannot afford because we are poor, are condoms and anti-retroviral drugs![184]

Similarly, in 2004 Mbeki attacked Kathleen Cravero, the deputy executive director of UNAids, as a racist for having written that many women in Asia and Africa did not have the option to abstain from sex. 'Clearly,' Mbeki raged, 'the view is that as African and Asian men, we are violent sexual predators.' An ugly scene followed in Parliament where Mbeki accused Charlene Smith of writing that black men were 'rampant sexual beasts, unable to control our urges, unable to keep our legs crossed, unable to keep it in our pants'.[185] Mbeki said that he could not keep quiet while racists 'accuse us, the black people of South Africa, Africa and the world, as being, by virtue of our Africanness and our skin colour – lazy, liars, foul-smelling, diseased, corrupt, violent, amoral, sexually depraved, animalistic, savage – and rapist'.

One can only guess at what late-night fantasies produced such prose, all the more so since Mbeki had always been quite famously a ladies' man. The journalist Max du Preez earned great hostility by referring – on air – to Mbeki as 'a womanizer', a perhaps old-fashioned pejorative term. Suffice it to say that Mbeki's anguished soliloquies about the sexuality of the African male were, in part inevitably, about himself. But to put racist accusations in the mouths of others and then to denounce those others is merely a way of avoiding having to answer some difficult questions.

The best way to understand the logic of Mbeki's position is to ask what he *should* have said about Aids. Inevitably, this would have involved a sermon to African males, not only that they should respect women, refrain from rape and wear condoms but, above all, that to avoid Aids the first requirement is that one takes responsibility for oneself, that one acknowledges that (unless one is a rape victim) this is a disease one can choose not to get. But this would involve preaching a philosophy of individual responsibility, of self-discipline, of not blaming others, of not trying to excuse one's behaviour by reference to the patterns of the past or external influences.

Gay communities in the developed world, where Aids first struck, have, in the main, behaved in just such a manner, taking responsibility for their behaviour and firmly altering it, which is why HIV rates have declined in those communities. ARVs can make being HIV positive a condition one can live with but, in the absence of an anti-Aids vaccine, the only way of bringing down HIV rates is behavioural change. One merely has to articulate this alternative path to see that Mbeki would have refused it like a horse refusing a jump. Such a speech was impossible for Mbeki because Aids was a metaphor for the entire African condition. The ANC did not believe in an assertive citizenry of individuals. Instead, it talked of 'mobilizing the masses': the masses were the object of their leaders who decided when and how to mobilize them. Endlessly, the masses were instructed that their role was to be disciplined, to receive instruction, to listen to their vanguard and obey. If they behaved correctly they would rise, not on their own merits but as a result of being 'deployed'; if they behaved badly they would be 'sidelined', but in any case they would be passive.

Aids was also a metaphor in a grander sense. Mbeki's whole posture was one of victimhood, of castigating white guilt for colonialism, racism and apartheid – all rolled into the single, timeless term 'oppression'. This victimhood led inevitably to a huge sense of entitlement: the white developed world must acknowledge its guilt – which could then be expiated via contributions to Nepad, debt relief and an endless stream of other paybacks. This is why Mbeki wanted to see Aids as a disease born of poverty, for, in his view, African poverty could only be the result of Western capitalist exploitation and pillage. If Aids was a disease of poverty then, by definition, the blame lay with colonialists, capitalists, in a word, with whites.

What was unbearable – quite literally – about the conventional view of Aids was that it located responsibility (or, if one stigmatized the HIV-positive condition, blame) in the black community itself, that it argued that the danger was primarily that of becoming a victim of one's own behaviour, and that a bottomless indignation against whites and capitalism was simply irrelevant and misplaced. Such conclusions were psychologically so abhorrent to Mbeki that he naturally searched for any other explanation to fill the gap. The Aids dissidents were what he lit upon, sending him down that particular troubled road, but almost any alternative explanation would have served. In the beginning was denial; dissidence merely followed.

Thus Mbeki's Aids denialism derived from an intense sense of paranoia and victimhood. Yet if such feelings were merely personal to Mbeki it would not have been possible for them to be sustained as state policy for years on end. But in greater or lesser degree these feelings were widely shared within the ANC and, indeed, beyond. One should not forget Dr Nkosasana Dlamini-Zuma's careful selection of powerful, white capitalist enemies – Big Pharma, the formerly white medical schools, the tobacco companies and so on. Each of the ensuing clashes could be seen as heroic struggles by black victims, fists up against the white, capitalist world. That was the stance in which not just Mbeki but she and many others felt most comfortable. The doctrine of individual responsibility, self-discipline and behavioural change required to fight Aids not only did not sit easily with such a posture but it threatened to undermine the sense of victimhood which underlay Mbeki's (and the ANC's) response to the whole gamut of policy issues.

Thus Mbeki's attitude to Aids was not an isolated aberration nor was it a purely individual matter. Sadly, Aids is indeed a metaphor of the wider African condition. The denialist attitudes to which it has given rise are simply the most powerful sign of how disabled, irrational and self-referential black consciousness in South Africa had become during its long, unequal struggle against white supremacy.

7
The Age of Mbeki II: From Triumph to Disaster

Exile immobilizes to some degree the minds of those who suffer it. It imprisons them for ever within the circle of ideas which they had conceived or which were current when their exile began. For the exile, the new conditions which have been created in his native country and the new ways of thinking and behaving which have been established there do not exist. Alexis de Tocqueville

Mbeki's presidency ran into early and almost fatal trouble over Aids and over Zimbabwe. Although Dr Dlamini-Zuma's inaction on Aids had dismayed Aids activists, few suspected the truth: that she was doing Mbeki's bidding, a fact later confirmed to me by her former husband, Jacob Zuma.[1] As Mbeki's own Aids denialist views emerged there was stupefaction: even among the ANC faithful, one saw a shaking of heads, a questioning of the President's sanity. Equally shocking to many was his clear siding with the Mugabe regime in Zimbabwe. Here too, had attention been paid, there had been forewarning in the shape of the earlier crisis in South Africa's relations with Nigeria.

THE CRISIS OVER ABACHA

It had always been obvious that Africa's giant, Nigeria, would be both South Africa's key rival and key partner in Africa. Nigeria had always seen itself as the leader of African opinion, which was why even the conservative regime of Sir Abubakar Tafawa Balewa took an uncompromisingly tough stand against South Africa's continued Commonwealth membership after Verwoerd's Republic was declared. Even radicals like Kwame Nkrumah were willing to compromise to keep South Africa in, but Nigeria's hard line settled the issue.[2] The exiled ANC received strong Nigerian backing and was well aware of the key nature of the relationship and of Nigerian sensitivities about playing second fiddle to an economically stronger South Africa. But relations were complicated by the fact that General Sani Abacha, who had seized power in November 1993, was the most corrupt and brutal of all Nigeria's military leaders. Mashood Abiola, who had won the 1993 elections, was thrown into jail by Abacha, as, too, was ex-President Olusegun Obasanjo, who had been part of the Commonwealth Eminent Persons Group to visit Mandela in jail. Abacha plundered the country to great effect, spiriting away no less than $4.3 billion.

The Mandela government maintained good relations with Abacha while seeking to persuade him towards democratic reform. The situation was complicated by the ANC's acceptance of $5 million from the Nigerian government in 1990 and another $5 million from Abacha in 1994.[3] In 1995, after ex-President Jimmy Carter had managed to broker a deal whereby Obasanjo was released from jail to house arrest, Mandela sent Archbishop Tutu to broker a similar deal for Abiola. The respite was brief: almost immediately Abacha re-arrested Obasanjo and many others for allegedly plotting a coup. A military tribunal sentenced thirteen 'plotters' to death and Obasanjo and ten others to life imprisonment. Mandela, appalled, pleaded for clemency. In July Mbeki visited Nigeria and was greatly fêted by the Abacha regime. Mbeki said Nigerians hoped that South Africa would be able to assist the return of democracy in Nigeria and that the Nigerian government was 'sensitive to the concerns we and many others have raised with regard to clemency', Abacha having assured him that no immediate action would be taken against the 'coup plotters'.[4]

Mbeki's mission was thrown into confusion by the news that forty-three 'coup plotters' had been shot by firing squad. To save embarrassing its visitor further the status of the forty-three was changed to 'armed robbers', and Mbeki, who refused to comment, departed. He told Parliament in Cape Town that no hostile moves or sanctions should be taken against Abacha. Instead, South Africa should use diplomacy, 'engaging the leadership of Nigeria to bring about democracy as soon as possible'.[5] Mbeki had learnt from his mentor, Oliver Tambo, to avoid criticizing other African governments. After such behaviour had led to the ANC's ejection from Zambia and Tanzania, Tambo had ordered that 'nobody speaks about what they see in Africa'.[6]

Mbeki's 'quiet persuasion' did not work but it remained Pretoria's official line until the Commonwealth Heads of Government Meeting (CHOGM) in New Zealand in November 1995. The South African issue had dominated so many preceding CHOGMs but now South Africa was back in the Commonwealth and Mandela was welcomed with open arms. Hanging over the conference, however, was the fact that the Ogoni writer and human rights activist Ken Saro-Wiwa, together with eight other Ogonis, had been condemned to death. Saro-Wiwa's son, together with the Nigerian Nobel laureate, Wole Soyinka, urged the CHOGM to impose the same sanctions which had been used to end apartheid. Soyinka was critical that Mandela, whom he saw as the decisive figure on this issue,[7] had not already taken a stronger line. Mandela insisted that 'quiet persuasion' was preferable.[8] Nigeria then confirmed the death sentences, causing both Mandela and Zimbabwe's President Mugabe to threaten sterner measures if the sentences were carried out, Mandela making a ringing declaration that South Africa would never 'stand aside when any people anywhere in the world become victim to systematic racism, oppression and tyranny'.[9] The news then arrived that all nine men had been hanged.

The Commonwealth was wearily used to the sight of its African members refusing to condemn even outrageous human rights abuses committed by other African regimes and now looked with concern at Mandela. If he behaved the same way, all hope of upholding human rights in Africa would collapse. To their relief, Mandela demanded Nigeria's expulsion from the Commonwealth and the imposition of sanctions, including an oil embargo. Cyril Ramaphosa, the ANC secretary-general back in South Africa, loyally supported the notion of expulsion but Mbeki, whose relations with Abacha remained warm, steered the cabinet merely into calling for the restoration of democracy in Nigeria. Mandela was furious: the 'quiet persuasion' policy had been made to look foolish. Moreover, he was deeply conscious of the fact that he and the other Rivonia trialists might well have been hanged back in 1963. By refusing that option the apartheid regime had left open the door to eventual change – but Abacha had done the opposite. The CHOGM resolved to suspend Nigeria's membership and give it a two-year deadline to reform or face expulsion. Mandela's bold stand on principle had an ironic result. Mozambique, finding itself entirely surrounded by Commonwealth members, had asked him if he could gain

Commonwealth membership for them too. It was an incongruous idea: Mozambique had no previous connection to the British Empire. Mandela now introduced the application – which went through on the nod, such was the gratitude and relief the older Commonwealth felt for him.

Had the conference been in South Africa Mbeki would doubtless have used the ANC apparatus to bring Mandela to heel. But Mandela, off-base and interacting continuously with foreign leaders, had made policy on his own for once. From the first Mbeki worked furiously to reverse Mandela's stand, for he was sure that his own ambitions of continental leadership would be damaged by a head-on fight with Nigeria which most African states were unlikely to join. It was a self-fulfilling prophecy, because it was soon clear to other African states that Mbeki and the deputy Foreign Minister, Aziz Pahad, were actively seeking to undermine Mandela. Thus while Mandela phoned the British Prime Minister, John Major, and President Clinton asking (in vain) that they apply oil sanctions against Nigeria, Pahad declared that South Africa's trade with Nigeria was far too small for it to be able to lead to any call for economic sanctions, let alone an oil embargo. South Africa had already recalled its high commissioner to Nigeria, said Pahad, claiming that this 'was one of the strongest diplomatic steps a country could take', and adding that 'We don't forget the role Nigeria played in our struggle.'[10]

Mandela continued to insist on stronger measures, saying the Commonwealth deadline was too distant.[11] Archbishop Tutu supported Mandela, as did Ramaphosa, calling for an embargo on Nigerian oil and urging Shell to pull out of Nigeria.[12] Not surprisingly, Abacha took aim at Mandela personally; he was hanged in effigy at a rally in Abuja and Abacha said that 'Because probably [on account of] being incarcerated for decades, he knows nothing about modern world diplomacy'.[13] Worse still, from Mbeki's viewpoint, the Nigerian Foreign Minister claimed that Mandela was betraying Africa and that South Africa was not properly African at all; in reality it was still a white-run state with a small black elite nominally in charge. Abacha castigated Mandela as 'a threat to African unity'.[14] It rapidly became clear that Mandela was out on a limb. In December he called a meeting of SADC in order to galvanize regional support for his appeal for a boycott of Nigerian oil but failed entirely to carry SADC with him – for the OAU secretary-general,

Salim Ahmed Salim, had already made it clear that he would not support any campaign to isolate Nigeria.[15] There was suspicion that Mbeki had undercut Mandela by quietly letting it be known that the ANC was not behind him on the issue.

By year end voices within the ANC were publicly raised at the complete confusion in foreign policy. Mandela insisted that South Africa must continue to recognize Taiwan (because of its generous donations to the ANC) but also that it wanted good relations with Beijing. While he regarded Bill Clinton as a close friend, Mandela also maintained close ties with Libya's President Qaddafi, denounced by the United States as a terrorist sponsor. But it was the Nigerian crisis where confusion was greatest, for while Mandela maintained his tough line and Ramaphosa tried to organize a boycott of Shell service stations in protest at Shell's refusal to withdraw from Nigeria, Mbeki continued to row back as hard as he could. Thus it was now agreed that South Africa, the only African state to withdraw its diplomatic representative from Nigeria, would nonetheless maintain a 'two-track' policy, including continuing contacts with Abacha. When Abacha announced that he was withdrawing Nigeria's team from the African Cup of Nations tournament in South Africa, frantic efforts were made to dissuade him.

Within Nigeria, however, Mandela's stand had made him massively popular, for Abacha's brutal rule was much resented.[16] Within South Africa a solidarity committee supporting the restoration of Nigerian democracy was set up, dominated by Cosatu and SACP. Given the ferocity of the repression within Nigeria, the anti-Abacha opposition, led by Wole Soyinka, necessarily had to base itself outside Nigeria and looked to South Africa for support. When Soyinka decided to try to bring together the scattered opposition forces, he was loath to hold the conference in Europe or America and, feeling it was important to emphasize the opposition's authentically African nature, elected to hold the conference in Johannesburg on 30–31 March 1996.

I was astonished to find this event held in a sleazy downmarket hotel in a dangerous part of town. The event bore the heavy stamp of the SACP; the conference hall was dominated by a poster showing Abacha as the mere puppet of Shell (a perspective not shared by the Nigerian delegates) while outside the works of Marx and Lenin were on sale on a table draped with the hammer and sickle. The attendance was surprisingly sparse, the atmosphere strained and peculiar. Jeremy

Cronin, the SACP deputy secretary-general, welcomed the Nigerians, as did his comrade, Cheryl Carolus. Cronin said how much he appreciated their need to be based on African soil and that really the only proper place for the conference was in Nigeria itself. This produced an explosive response: several Nigerians declared that the situation in Nigeria was far worse than anything South Africans had known under apartheid. Had they attempted to hold such a conference there they would all have been killed. Several suggested, indeed, that the ANC had been lucky for, by comparison, the apartheid regime had fought a relatively gentlemanly fight. Cronin, showing signs of strain, rapidly excused himself on urgent other business, an example swiftly followed by Carolus. Wole Soyinka then appealed to delegates not to allow their anger at the circumstances surrounding the conference to prevent them focusing on the real objective, Abacha; things must not be allowed to deteriorate into a tirade against their hosts.

Gradually I got the real story out of the delegates. The South African government, fearing that the conference would infuriate Abacha, had carefully set out to cripple it by refusing visas to those on Nigerian passports. Thus the only delegates attending were those travelling on British, American or Canadian passports (who did not need visas), and hence the poor attendance. Then, on the last day before the conference, visas had been granted to the rest – too late for them to attend but enabling Pretoria to deny that it had refused visas to delegates. Mbeki's machiavellian handiwork was unanimously suspected. Cronin and Carolus had come along to steer the proceedings in an anti-imperialist direction, making it difficult for the delegates' furious indignation to break surface, but they had both clearly sensed that it might do so at any moment, hence their desperate desire to leave. No wonder Cronin had wished the conference was being held somewhere else; and no wonder, too, the fury against his suggestion of a venue in Nigeria, for delegates from Nigeria had been precisely the ones unable to attend. The real beauty of this manoeuvre was that even in the unlikely event of Mandela hearing of this sabotage and demanding an explanation it would have been easy to throw the blame onto low-level bureaucratic bungling. I published the whole story in *The Times* (London) next morning, which led, I was told, to some exasperated remarks by Carolus in that day's solidarity meeting with the Nigerians. The only South African journalist present decided that it was too risky to write about such things. Not a word appeared in the South African press about this remarkable story.

On 4 June 1996 the Foreign Minister, Alfred Nzo, announced that South Africa was abandoning its hard line because a South Africa vs. Nigeria conflict would breach 'the norms of African solidarity'.[17] On the same day came news that Mrs Kudirat Abiola, the wife of Mashood Abiola, who had campaigned in favour of Mandela's anti-Abacha campaign, had been assassinated. Abiola's own death occurred not long afterwards. Almost certainly, Abacha was emboldened to kill them both by the relaxation of South African pressure. South Africa's opposition to Abacha now ceased and a resumption of full diplomatic relations was expected once Mbeki became President – but, almost immediately, Abacha died of a heart attack: in bed with three Asian prostitutes, he had overdosed on Viagra.

Mbeki joined in the general chorus of acclamation about the restoration of Nigerian democracy. He had, in fact, displayed no concern about human rights or democracy when it mattered. Within the ANC the line taken by Mbeki-ites such as Mavivi Myakayaka-Manzini was that Mandela had been 'manipulated by the imperialist powers' into taking a mistaken position on Nigeria: they had got South Africa to do their dirty work for them, a mistake which must never be repeated.[18] This was clearly Mbeki's own interpretation, one which was to be of great significance when the Zimbabwean crisis erupted only nine months into his presidency.

THE AFRICAN RENAISSANCE

Mbeki's great theme was the 'African Renaissance'. With South Africa's liberation the whole continent had now cast off the chains of colonialism and conditions were ripe for the twenty-first century to be 'the African century'. This Renaissance was to be achieved by a new compact with the rest of the world in order to increase aid and investment flows to the continent to the tune of $64 billion a year – a programme which was ultimately to find issue as Nepad. Also part of this project was Mbeki's proposal that the OAU, now utterly discredited, must be replaced with the African Union. The AU would then endorse Nepad and the African Renaissance and would move towards full continental unity, just as the

EU had in Europe. Mbeki would devise the institutions and write the script for the whole continent, becoming its leader, unifier and representative to the world.

Thus the dream. In Mbeki's vision only colonialism had held Africa back and, freed of that, it would naturally gallop ahead – provided it could first achieve peace. To this end – and it was the most praiseworthy side of his presidency – Mbeki invested great efforts in trying to end conflicts all round Africa, though the idea that such conflicts were mere vestiges of colonialism could not long survive acquaintance with reality. Crucially, there was no notion that Africa could develop along Asian lines, depending essentially upon its own resources. The whole idea of Nepad was that Africa could not develop without external capital inflows, and it was assumed that Africa would continue to receive aid. Indeed, it was clear that even in terms of its own health Africa could not manage without outside help. Aids had struck the continent savagely and there was no prospect of the continent inventing an Aids cure or greatly reducing the impact of the disease by changing sexual mores. The only hope lay in outside help.

Domestically, the dream of an African Renaissance played well. It was, after all, voting for motherhood and apple pie. Meanwhile, business anxiously noted that most of the elements of Mbeki's domestic economic policy had yet to be achieved. Gear had never really been implemented. Government debt had been fiercely wound down but bitter opposition from Cosatu and the SACP had halted privatization, while plans to increase labour flexibility were quietly shelved. And while Mbeki spoke enthusiastically of using market forces to create a new black bourgeoisie, many ANC activists felt uncomfortable with this objective. When Mbeki opposed a Cosatu strike against unemployment, Kgalema Motlanthe, the ANC secretary-general, supported it. Mbeki, aware of such resistance, backed off from the really tough decisions. Instead, he displayed a penchant for empty symbolism. He loved making high-sounding speeches ('I am an African') and announcing the creation of high-prestige advisory councils on investment, on information technology, indeed, on anything at all fashionable, and would recruit great names such as George Soros or Carly Fiorina to sit on them. The idea was that Mbeki, the philosopher-king, would preside over important meetings of the great and the good, thus confirming his image as an internationally recognized and supremely intelligent leader.

At the outset Mbeki had the ball at his feet and might have forced through the rest of Gear had he been determined enough – but the moment and momentum were lost. Internationally, Mbeki aspired to be the leader of the South – and, indeed, he achieved the chairmanship of the defunct Non-Aligned Movement – but South Africa could not really be mentioned in the same breath as Brazil, India and China unless it achieved far higher growth rates. Mbeki was loath to face the social sacrifice and political conflict necessary to achieve that.

In many ways Mbeki resembled Anthony Eden. Like him, he had had to live in the shadow of a giant (Churchill/Mandela); like him, he could be personable and charming: and, like him, his strong suit was foreign affairs. But just as Eden was rapidly undone by foreign affairs in the shape of Suez, so Mbeki was to meet his Waterloo over Zimbabwe.

THE ZIMBABWEAN CRISIS BEGINS

When the Helen Suzman Foundation carried out a survey throughout southern Africa in 1997 we were struck by the extent to which urban opinion in Zimbabwe had utterly rejected not just the Mugabe regime but the whole set of cultural assumptions on which the ruling Zanu-PF was based.[19] It was no surprise to see this movement take organized form with the foundation of the Movement for Democratic Change (MDC) in late 1999 and we immediately set out to test opinion there again. As it happened, President Mugabe chose to call a constitutional referendum – giving himself yet more power – at exactly the same time that our survey was in the field. Although the MDC had barely campaigned and the result was universally seen as a foregone conclusion, the 'No' vote won 55.9 per cent. Our survey showed that over 63 per cent said they wanted change and only 36 per cent wanted Zanu-PF to stay in power. By comparing the results at regional level we were able to show that the vote had been rigged in a pro-Mugabe direction in a number of provinces. Only in Harare and Bulawayo, where rigging was more difficult, was the vote certainly fair. Clearly, the ballot stuffing in rural areas had been done to order but when the huge 'No' vote came pouring from the cities it simply capsized all previous calculations.

Mugabe had lost a referendum rigged in his favour.[20] His regime was now clearly doomed. The MDC, buoyed up by the momentum of their referendum victory, were certain to win the mid-year parliamentary elections, probably by a landslide. Mugabe graciously conceded defeat on television, but he had no intention of quitting power. Within two weeks of the referendum result the invasion of white-owned farms by Mugabe thugs, the so-called 'war veterans', began, the objective being to drive white farmers off the land, even at the cost of destroying Zimbabwe's farm-based economy.

Mugabe's tactic was widely misunderstood. The hegemony of Zanu-PF, though contested by urban-dwellers, was secure as long as it commanded the rural masses. To be sure, the two Matebeleland provinces, still traumatized by Mugabe's massacres of the 1980s which left 20,000 dead and many more beaten and tortured, would never be safe for Zanu-PF, but in the other six Shona-speaking provinces the key point was that in every drought or famine the ruling party would distribute food only to those who held a party card. It was 'the politics of the belly' in its crudest form: the Shona peasantry were kept in a state of feudal dependence on the ruling party bosses. However, on the 4,000 white-owned farms farmworkers lived with their extended families, so that on average 600 or more people lived on every farm. Since these farms were highly productive, well irrigated and well managed, they were pretty much proof against famine or drought. The bottom line was that no farmworker or his family would starve. Most of the farmers who had stayed after independence were people determined to make a success of the new Zimbabwe: they ran farm schools and special schemes for Aids orphans. Thus some 2.5 million Africans lived under the umbrella of this reasonably benevolent white paternalism – and, to that extent, were not vulnerable to Zanu-PF pressure. So when they lost faith in Mugabe they felt free to vote against him.

In 2000 the farmers ferried their workers to the polls, voting alongside them against Mugabe. Mugabe assumed that the farmers had manipulated the farmworker vote and determined to destroy this oppositional nexus for ever. The farmers would lose their farms and the farmworkers would learn the terrible lesson of what happened to feudal serfs who rebelled against their lord. They were the real target: they had voted 'No' massively and had influenced many other rural folk to vote 'No'. The whites were chased away but the farmworkers were subjected to months of beatings and torture during which they were made to sing Zanu-PF songs and repent of their error of believing that anything could protect them from Mugabe's wrath. Those who survived were spat out upon the roadside, brutalized and terrified. The farm schools, the clinics and the Aids orphan schemes were all wiped out.

The pretence was that what had happened resulted from frustration over the lack of land reform. This was untrue. In our repeated surveys of Zimbabwean opinion we found the land issue was nowhere near the top of people's concerns. Mugabe himself had torpedoed early attempts at land reform, handing out farms only to wealthy cronies and completely disregarding the poor, and this was why the British government, which was funding the exercise, withdrew in disgust. Thereafter Mugabe showed scant interest in land reform save as an occasional issue to wave over the heads of the farmers. Every farmer who sold land had to offer it to government first but the government seldom bought it. Mugabe always had a 'third chimurenga' (revolution) at the back of his mind, the first chimurenga being the resistance to colonial settlement, the second the guerrilla war for independence. During that struggle Mugabe and his warriors had often dreamed of how they would extirpate the whites root and branch but such dreams had been set aside on independence in 1980, partly because independence was brokered and guaranteed by the British government, and because the white farms were the key motor of the economy, feeding the population, financing the Zimbabwean state and supplying its need for exports and foreign exchange.

The guerrilla war had taught Mugabe a fundamental lesson: his guerrillas had been the heroes of the peasantry but they had also killed and tortured them if they suspected their loyalty. In 1980, ignoring the settlement terms, Mugabe had kept his guerrillas in the villages, utterly dominating the peasantry – who had voted for him in a mood of fear and euphoria. This was exactly the relationship he sought to preserve, using every opportunity to remind the peasants of their dependence on the whim of their masters. When the populist Edgar Tekere broke with Zanu-PF and briefly threatened Mugabe's rule, Mugabe suddenly rediscovered the land issue, threatening land seizures from white farmers, for he understood that the key to remaining in power was to reduce everyone to the status of suppliant.[21] As the MDC leader, Morgan Tsvangirai, once bitterly observed to me, 'Mugabe came to power talking Marxism-Leninism. Now he never mentions the workers. He hates us because trade unions can stand up against power. He wants to reduce us all to peasants – unorganized, at his mercy and pathetically grateful even for crumbs.'[22] In fact, Tekere's party never really got off the ground and Mugabe happily forgot land reform, ignoring the land reform proposals put to him by the white farmers. But the notion of land seizures was always his ultimate recourse should his power be threatened, which, after February 2000, it was. The beauty of the tactic was that the image of African nationalists fighting for land reform against settler colonialism played well before an African audience and even internationally.

MBEKI'S REACTION TO THE ZIMBABWE CRISIS

Even before the referendum Mbeki had become anxious about the stability of Mugabe's regime. Mugabe's military adventure in the Congo and his huge pay-outs to his party's war veterans had helped push inflation up to 58 per cent while the lack of foreign exchange produced fuel and electricity shortages.[23] Mbeki was, indeed, more anxious than Mugabe: he took the initiative, telephoned Mugabe and suggested he fly up to Harare on referendum eve, where he announced an R800 million aid package in an attempt to sway the vote Mugabe's way.[24] He spent no less than six hours in talks with Mugabe.[25]

When Mugabe lost the referendum Mbeki's worst fears were realized. The trade union movement had powered Frederick Chiluba to overthrow Kenneth Kaunda in Zambia not long before. Cosatu was threatening Mbeki at home and now the trade-union-backed MDC had defeated Mugabe: the pattern was clear. Worse, Mbeki feared the effect on African opinion throughout southern Africa of the sight of a national liberation movement being ejected from power by a popular revolt. The fall of Portuguese rule in Angola and Mozambique in 1974 had had an elemental effect on black opinion throughout the region by showing that white rule was not invulnerable after all. Suddenly, everything was thinkable. If Mugabe fell there might be a similar *prise de conscience* against the national liberation movements elsewhere. This had to be prevented at all costs.

Mbeki tried to heal the breach between Mugabe and the IMF but Mugabe was resistant. In his view, 'the IMF is targeting the Harare government and ... it all boils down to an international white conspiracy'.[26] Mbeki offered that South Africa would intercede for Mugabe at the IMF: Mugabe wasn't interested. So Mbeki suggested that South Africa place its capital markets at Mugabe's disposal, floating a rand-denominated bond for Zimbabwe, which South Africa would guarantee.[27] This ran into immediate trouble. 'It just doesn't make sense,' one banker told me. 'Mbeki's gone to all this trouble to manage down his own foreign debt and cut borrowing costs. Now he comes up with a proposal which will increase foreign debt, increase his own borrowing costs and give a guarantee to a bankrupt foreign government when Pretoria refuses to guarantee bonds even for its own state-owned utilities like Eskom and Telkom.'[28] Such schemes reflected Mbeki's desperate anxiety to shore up the Mugabe regime, but none came to fruition.

Violent land invasions continued across Zimbabwe as the campaign began for the June parliamentary elections. Mbeki, too anxious to wait for that, immediately summoned a secret summit of southern African liberation movements in Johannesburg, the first of several such meetings. For Mbeki, these were virtual councils of war. Many African nationalist parties called themselves liberation movements but Mbeki's definition included only those parties which had fought armed struggles against white colonialism: Zanu-PF, the Angolan MPLA, Frelimo (Mozambique), Swapo (Namibia) and the ANC. Protocol required that Mbeki could not participate unless all the other presidents attended, but when they failed to do so Mbeki simply dispensed with protocol and lectured the delegations on the meaning of Mugabe's referendum defeat.

The liberation movements were revolutionary by nature and it was a fundamental objective of world imperialism to defeat them, to turn the clock back on their victories. This was the meaning of Mugabe's referendum defeat: utilizing the services of its local cat's-paw, the MDC (an analogue of the IFP in South Africa), imperialism was bent on overthrowing Mugabe. This had to be resisted at all costs, for if successful, imperialism's agenda would be extended to all the southern African countries in turn. The sight of Zanu-PF losing power would undermine faith in all the other liberation movements, a situation which the imperialists would inevitably exploit. And the defeat of the liberation movements could only mean the triumph of their old enemy – colonialism, apartheid or, at least, capitalism on white terms. The triumph of the national liberation movement (that is, themselves) represented the triumph of the masses, a culmination, a righteous ending to history. This was why Mbeki was so anxious over events in Zimbabwe: he interpreted them as the first move in an imperialist manoeuvre which would have as its next target the eviction of the ANC from power in South Africa. He saw them, in other words, as a direct threat to himself.

All the delegations responded enthusiastically. The end of the Cold War had left them confused and rudderless but they remained strongly convinced of their own righteousness and tended automatically to view the West, the IMF and World Bank and globalization as their natural enemies. The fact that there was no practical possibility of the return of colonialism or apartheid was not the point. The point was that anything which threatened their own permanent dominance was simply not in the script. They shared much of Mbeki's instinctive paranoia, his tendency to see hidden enemies and a hostile grand design – rather than their own mistakes – behind every setback. And although, like him, they had diverged in practice from implementing socialist policies, Marxism-Leninism still provided the only intellectual framework within which they felt comfortable. They were perfectly happy, African-style, to fit almost any event into this framework. Thus when the Queen had visited South Africa in 1995 ANC ministers delightedly swarmed aboard her yacht, *Britannia*, with communists like Ronnie Kasrils happily accepting the royal benediction as the world's legitimation of the South African revolution.[29]

This split personality had, of course, long been second nature to exiles like Mbeki. On the one hand they were trained in the Lenin School, on the other hand they had to charm Western liberals. They had, for decades, to practise the skills of that famous South African phenomenon, *tweetalige jakals* – two-tongued jackals. The Zimbabwe issue required the same sleight of hand. Although Mbeki did not say so publicly, he desperately wanted to keep Zanu-PF in power and frequently appeared hand in hand with Mugabe as an expression of that fraternal solidarity. But he knew that to side openly with Mugabe's racism, his use of violence and his open rejection of property rights and the rule of law would be extremely damaging. Out of this contradiction was born the notion of 'quiet diplomacy'. This was essentially a confidence trick. Publicly, Mbeki would claim that he was attending to the crisis of Zimbabwe with sensitive action behind the scenes, insisting that 'megaphone diplomacy' was useless. After all, Zimbabweans must determine the future of Zimbabwe, South Africa could do no more. In fact Mugabe, or preferably a younger successor, would be fully supported while he crushed the MDC and guaranteed Zanu-PF rule into the indefinite future. Mugabe, like Namibia's Sam Nujoma, was to echo Mbeki's analysis of the situation time and again. He quickly understood the rules of the game and exploited them to his own ends, refusing to make way for any Zanu-PF successor, making the prolongation of his personal rule synonymous with that of Zanu-PF.

Mbeki decided that he must take Mugabe's side over land, pretending that the villains of the piece were the British for withdrawing their financial support for land reform and thus ignoring the fact that this 'reform' had simply transferred land to Mugabe's cronies. Shortly before the election Mbeki met with the other liberation movement leaders at Victoria Falls, at the end of which Mozambique's President Joaquim Chissano was pushed forward to announce their common position. Mugabe was, he announced, a 'master' and 'a champion' of the rule of law and was committed to halt violence and solve the land problem peacefully – this at a time when reports of murder, torture and mass beatings on the farms were a daily occurrence. Journalists pressed Chissano: surely he knew that the British and other donors had said they stood ready to fund a transparent land reform programme which did not just give land to Mugabe's rich cronies? Chissano said that such thinking was very dangerous. 'What you are telling us is very grave. It is creating ill feelings in our hearts. You are saying it is a sin to be a freedom fighter. It is grave if the British government thinks like that.' When this produced incredulous hilarity Mbeki quickly stepped in to say the British should have continued to negotiate: 'I don't think it is correct for anybody to walk away from this,' adding that South Africa was intervening with the IMF to get it to fund Zimbabwe's land reform.[30] This was, of course, absurd: the IMF would want all the same assurances which the British had failed to get.

THE BIRTH OF 'QUIET DIPLOMACY'

The run-up to the June 2000 parliamentary elections in Zimbabwe was marked by a rising crescendo of farm seizures and intensified violence against the MDC. Every day brought fresh outrages, fresh abuses of the state-owned broadcast media, more beatings, more torture, and more than thirty murders. The incident which remains in my own mind was the account in the (independent) *Daily News* of a farmworker suspected of MDC sympathies forced by his Zanu-PF tormentors to sit down on a red-hot paraffin stove, with an accompanying photograph of his bottom, horribly grilled meat. But I was also a trustee of an anti-torture NGO and saw many other victims up close.

The various international observers were – mainly – appalled at this travesty of a free election. Few of the observers and none of the journalists believed that the MDC would not have won the election overwhelmingly had anything like 'free and fair' conditions obtained; as it was, the electoral register and the count were also extremely suspect. Despite which Zanu-PF came away with only 63 seats, the MDC 56 and Independents 1. The Helen Suzman Foundation managed to carry out an exit poll, which cast the gravest doubt on these results. Thirty-three per cent of voters said that they thought at least some of their neighbours would vote against the party they really preferred, while 12 per cent said this was what they themselves had done. Given the intimidatory pressures against such frankness, we believed both figures ought, in reality, to have been higher. But even if one allowed only for an extra 12 per cent for the MDC – and the responses could not mean anything else – there should have been an MDC landslide, with from 87 to 91 MDC seats out of 120.[31] The truth was almost certainly more dramatic. Despite the intimidation we found clear MDC majorities even in the Zanu-PF heartlands of Mashonaland Central and Mashonaland West: there were no safe Zanu-PF seats.

The (dominant) ANC component of the South African parliamentary observer mission made it clear from the first that it was there to find the elections free and fair come what may. This had been made clear to the ANC delegates as a matter of party discipline before they set out. Many of them were severely discomfited by what they observed but they were under the command of the ANC chief whip, Tony Yengeni. Back home Mbeki repeatedly declared in advance that the elections would be free and fair, and, on the eve of the poll, he summoned Yengeni back to South Africa for a last-minute briefing. Kgalema Motlanthe also announced before the election that it 'would be free and fair', insisted that reports of violence were deliberate press exaggeration and endorsed Zanu-PF's stand on the land issue, saying that the British had given

Mugabe 'no choice' but to take action. The war veterans' land invasions were, he said, merely 'a protest action'.[32]

Mbeki was unwilling to utter any public criticism of Mugabe, but what both the markets and international opinion wanted was a clear statement that South Africa would uphold human rights, property rights and the rule of law – preferably in Zimbabwe, but certainly at home. Yet Mbeki refused to give any such assurances when he addressed the nation on 4 May, and the rand, which had already begun to slide, crashed as investors sold South African assets and capital fled from the country. The rand had nearly touched R6 to the dollar in January, but by late April it was at R6.60, and by the end of May it had fallen to nearly R7.20. As one market analyst put it on the evening of 4 May, 'It's Mbeki's Rubicon – and he hasn't crossed it'.[33] Mandela, meanwhile, could not contain his feelings about Mugabe, whom he referred to, without naming him, as 'the tyrant'. Some African leaders, he said, had liberated their countries but overstayed their welcome. 'They want to die in power because they have committed crimes.' When journalists asked whether he meant Mugabe he replied angrily 'Everybody here knows who I am talking about.'[34]

Only on 10 May did Mbeki make the reluctant admission that he would not allow copycat farm invasions in South Africa, but he refused to criticize Mugabe. The damage to confidence was profound: even the ANC's parliamentary liaison officer, Pieter Venter, resigned in horror. He had sat in on ANC strategy meetings, asking himself, 'If the ANC's hold on power was ever threatened in the way that Zanu-PF's is being, would it behave in the same way? From my observation of some people in these meetings and in the caucus, I eventually came to the conclusion we could easily see the ANC behave like Zanu-PF.'[35] But Mbeki had rightly judged that many journalists would be so keen to believe the best of the ANC that he fed them a steady diet of hints and reassurances that 'quiet diplomacy' was gradually working, allowing them to believe that the ANC had not entirely forsaken the defence of democracy and human rights. Despite all the evidence to the contrary, they swallowed the bait.[36]

THE LOST LEADER

The loss of confidence in Mbeki was severe. The damage done by the Zimbabwe issue came on top of the revelation of Mbeki's denialist views on Aids. In July came the further revelation of how Mbeki had joined the Aids denialists' lobby. Anita Allen, a South African journalist with no medical expertise, had somehow decided that HIV and Aids were unconnected and sent Mbeki a dossier full of Aids denialist nonsense. Three months later Allen was working near midnight when her fax machine began to chatter with a handwritten fax from Mbeki saying he wanted to discuss the subject with her the next morning. They met and he took her advice, summoning an Aids panel full of Aids dissidents.[37] It also emerged that much of Mbeki's own 'knowledge' on the subject had been accumulated in late-night internet trawls. The notion of a President foolish enough to bank his reputation on bits and pieces picked up in this amateur way in the small hours did little for public confidence.

There was an uncomfortable atmosphere within the ANC. Whereas under previous leaders the party had been a broad church there was now 'a culture of sycophancy'. Quietly,

> many within the ANC bemoan the demise of debate within the organization, a process that began in the Mandela years but which has accelerated after Mbeki took over ... This demise ... was abetted by the ANC's assumption of state power, a move that gave the leader the added power of patronage. [And] Mbeki was able to utilize patronage to maximum benefit. Internal ANC dissent against Mbeki grew in the meantime, but [it] was merely whispered in the corridors. Only trade union leaders, buttressed by an army of organized workers, had the courage and the strength to speak out against the President's views.[38]

Thus no prominent ANC member uttered a dissenting word over either Zimbabwe or Aids. Yet throughout the country people were aghast and there was uneasy questioning: what sort of man was the President?

I put this question to one of his old girlfriends from his university years, who had lived with him and knew him better than most. She was emphatic that he was not a racist, that most of his friends had been white or Asian, that any anti-white attitudes were either a later development or, perhaps, play-acting for political reasons. He was, she said, very guarded and kept many elements of his life secret. While he loved his mother, he had been in awe of, and frightened of, his father. In practice, the ANC was the only family he had. Although not a particularly diligent student himself, he had a considerable respect for intellectuals and intellectualism. He was greatly impressed by a number of white communist intellectuals, the most striking of whom had the habit of beginning his expositions with well-chosen quotations from English literature, a habit which Mbeki imitated. But he was both too disorganized and otherwise preoccupied to excel himself. His life was a succession of essay crises, of last-minute scrambles to cobble things together, often in the small hours – for he was already a night bird. He was hopeless with money, always in debt, endlessly borrowing from Peter to pay Paul; his cheques tended to bounce. He had a considerable sense of entitlement, heightened by a sense of being a representative of a righteous and suffering people. His girlfriends were wont to be shocked by the realization that he felt himself free to start affairs with others while maintaining previous amorous relationships as well.

He had a heroic self-image ('Once I put on some chamber music and he switched it off saying "those of us involved in great struggles prefer symphonies"') yet also, ironically, a horror of confrontation of any kind, let alone blood and gore, from which he utterly shrank.

> He was completely unable to tackle things head-on. If something annoyed him, he wouldn't say so or signal it directly. You had to intuit if he didn't like something: he'd just go very quiet. But he had a large sense of self. Indeed, there was a streak of narcissism, though mainly, of course, he was calm, charming and had a sense of humour. Just occasionally this calm would be punctured and he would burst out in wild tempers at real or imagined slights to his ego. But when he was told by the movement that he must train to fight with MK he went into a complete panic, he was beside himself, quite shattered. He did the training in Moscow but got out of fighting by pulling strings somehow. He couldn't face such a possibility.[39]

There are tantalizing hints here. For all his machiavellian ruthlessness in political manoeuvre Mbeki was not very strong, would back away from tough challenges, trying to find a way under or around. There was, too, always a hint of fragility, as was inevitable in someone lacking a supportive family background, who was black, physically small and in some ways a Walter Mitty, dreaming of being a commanding intellectual, a great leader, a hero of the struggle. Political power gave him the chance to live out some of these dreams. He would show he was a master of every subject, even making his own rules over Aids, quoting from literary classics and pretending to an encyclopedic knowledge of Third World history. Because he had learnt the skills of diplomacy and image-projection, he seemed to believe he could use spin doctors to revise reality and his own biography at will. Over and over again the President's office volunteered the story of how the young Mbeki, desperate to join the struggle, had volunteered to fight in MK – though Essop Pahad, in charge of that office and Mbeki's university companion at the time, knew better than anyone that this was untrue.

Similarly, there was a bizarre grandiosity about Mbeki, the undistinguished student, always behind with his essays, projecting himself as the philosopher-king of Africa. There was also a wilfulness, an egocentricity that sometimes parted contact with reality. His correspondence with Tony Leon over Aids revealed someone unwilling to take into account the context from which his quotes were taken to a degree at which he often stood his sources on their head in order to squeeze out of them the meaning he wanted. Within the ANC, a movement of very poorly educated people, it was not difficult for him to get away with such things, but he seems not to have understood that when attempted on a larger stage, such behaviour could not pass muster. This was peculiar in a man of such sophistication. How could he not see that his behaviour over Aids and Zimbabwe would ruin his reputation abroad, torpedoing whatever hopes he had of a prestigious international job after his presidency?

Mbeki liked announcing new policies with grand éclat – the policies would have an impressive name and an acronym suggesting high seriousness – but there was often little follow-through. First there was Gear, then Nepad, which, though an absurdity from the first, was treated seriously by a credulous press. The plan was predicated on annual capital flows from developed countries to Africa of over $64 billion a year, and a Nepad bureaucracy was set up to plan the implementation of projects on the fondly imagined day when this money would start rolling in. Yet, of course, the money which arrived was either private investment, bilateral aid or loans, none of which could be channelled through such a bureaucracy. Another early announcement related to the government's 'Integrated and Sustainable Rural Development Strategy' – but eighteen months later there were still no details of what the strategy might be.

Land activists concluded that it was a 'phantom strategy'.[40] It faded away without ever being fully explained, let alone implemented. The year 2006 saw the launch, amid great fanfare, of 'Asgisa' (Accelerated and Shared Growth Initiative for South Africa), the idea being to raise the economic growth rate to 6 per cent or more by increasing the skills pool available and removing obstacles to growth. Asgisa was born of excitement at the growth spurt of 2004–5, occasioned by a commodity-price boom, but hardly had it been announced than power cuts began, slashing the growth rate and causing many more skilled personnel to emigrate. The government also promised a new industrial strategy but a year later no strategy had appeared. Thereafter the talk was of 'the developmental state', although by this time the state was failing on every front, having neglected infrastructural investment for years. Yet these acronyms and mantras were breathlessly repeated by credulous academics and journalists: not many were willing to notice that the king had no clothes.

A similar grandiosity and credulity enveloped Mbeki's ambition that South Africa might gain a (temporary) seat on the UN Security Council, and for years on end it was suggested that South Africa might soon be a permanent Security Council member, with a veto. This was of a piece with the carefully cultivated notion – taken quite seriously by the South African press – that Mbeki might succeed Kofi Annan as UN Secretary-General. Both notions were non-starters. The only country the United States was willing to accept as a new Security Council member was Japan (which the Chinese were determined to veto). And the UN secretary-generalship always rotates between continents so there was never the slightest possibility that Annan would be followed by another African. Mbeki also had the ambition of arbitrating the Middle East conflict, doubtless conscious of the enormous kudos attaching to those, like Jimmy Carter, who managed to achieve progress in this intractable area. This too was a non-starter: neither side in the Middle East took these attempts seriously, both because ANC policy was straightforwardly pro-Palestinian and because only a superpower able to back up its role with muscle and money had any chance of playing arbiter. Yet Mbeki's vision of his role in world politics often required that his cabinet waste days on end considering its non-existent role in Middle East arbitration.[41] The same grandiosity made it impossible for Mbeki to admit that he had been wrong or publicly to change course. Once he had pronounced he had to continue insisting he was right. As Mondli Makhanya put it, 'a hallmark of the Mbeki presidency has been what can only be described as an intellectual superiority complex. Behaving almost like a benevolent dictator, Mbeki has nursed the notion that he knows what is right for South Africa to such an extent that no amount of lobbying and public pressure can divert him from a chosen path.'[42]

In the 1980s and early 1990s many of the white elite who had rubbed shoulders with Mbeki had come away charmed and impressed, often believing they had made a new friend. The revelation of a very different Mbeki once he had achieved power came as a nasty shock. It was not just a matter of Aids and Zimbabwe. They were shocked by his repudiation of Mandela's one-nation legacy, by his pronouncement that there were two nations, one rich and white, the other poor and black, and his constant willingness to use the race card. In his determination to protect the arms deal from scrutiny he alleged that those who wanted the deal to be investigated by Judge Willem Heath's Special Investigation Unit were guilty of racism and made clearly paranoid charges that such demands were the work of hostile forces conspiring against South Africa. Then, in a televised outburst, he produced two organization charts linking him, Jacob Zuma, Essop Pahad and Joe Modise to various companies involved in the arms deal, and suggested that these were among the falsely incriminatory documents Heath was working from. In fact they were merely reproductions culled from *Noseweek*, South Africa's rather pale imitation of *Private Eye*. None of this inspired confidence.

Mbeki's grandiosity made him arrogant, aloof and inaccessible. Many who had counted him as a friend now found they had no access at all. De Klerk once told me how he had spent months waiting for an interview, only to be fobbed off with an underling when the day duly arrived. Even Mandela found that for months Mbeki, who preferred the company of acolytes and yes-men, would not see him or even take his calls.

THE EARLY CRISIS OF THE MBEKI PRESIDENCY

By late 2000 the collapse in confidence in Mbeki was visible in the polls. Mandela had always run well ahead of the ANC in the polls: in June 1995 he had the confidence of 76 per cent of all South Africans, a figure which improved to an incredible 85 per cent in the month before he retired, 20 per cent ahead of the ANC's score. Mbeki had started well with an even larger ANC victory, though his own ratings never did better than mirror the party's; indeed, he clearly rode on the party's coat-tails rather than vice versa. By July/August 2000 an Idasa poll found that only 50 per cent approved of him as President and the next month a Research Surveys poll found that only 46 per cent of black women thought he was doing a good job, compared to 69 per cent in February 2000. The Idasa poll showed, moreover, that only 41 per cent trusted him and that most people believed he was uninterested in their lives or opinions.[43] Another survey in 2000 among the nation's youth found that while Mandela easily topped the list of role models among all races, Mbeki was a role model for only 4 per cent, trailing behind a list of pop and sports stars. Even Hansie Cronje, the disgraced former cricketer who had taken bribes to fix matches, rated higher among the young than Mbeki.[44]

Although one of the remedies recommended by his desperate spin-doctors was that the President cease comment of any kind about Aids (a policy he found hard to observe), the damage was already well and truly done: even after this 'no comment' policy had been in force for some while polls found that overwhelming majorities believed that Mbeki was a closet Aids dissident who believed Aids was harmless and that drugs supposed to treat Aids did more harm than good.[45] For many people this came close to saying that the President was crazy. Already there was much murmuring that perhaps even the uneducated Jacob Zuma would make a better President. Already such gossip had ignited Mbeki's paranoia and after only a year in office Zuma discovered that he was already under informal investigation to see whether he had been corruptly connected to the arms deal, something which could not possibly have occurred without Mbeki's backing.[46]

The collapse in public support for Mbeki climaxed around Easter 2001. A Markinor poll commissioned by the SABC in March 2001 found that among all voters 15 per cent supported the DA but 28 per cent trusted Tony Leon as leader, while 52 per cent supported the ANC but only 42 per cent trusted Mbeki.[47] These were sensational results: whereas there had been a 56 per cent gap between the ANC and DP in 1999, the gap between their leaders was now only 14 per cent – despite the huge ANC effort at demonizing Leon. Moreover, the 42 per cent who now trusted Mbeki contrasted with a 60 per cent figure supporting him at the time of his election and the even higher numbers who had routinely supported Mandela. The ANC electorate was stable at 67 per cent. If one assumed that the 42 per cent who still trusted Mbeki were all ANC voters, it meant that three out of every eight ANC voters had lost confidence in their new President after only eighteen months in office. The poll results were so bad that they were quickly snatched off air by the SABC, doubtless under orders from the presidential office.

Then, in a live SABC interview, Max du Preez, a journalist, said that the debate over Mbeki's leadership was caused partly by his stance on Aids, 'but also because he is seen as a womanizer. It is publicly known . . . that the president has this kind of personal life. I'm not saying it's scandalous. He's a womanizer.' The result was complete uproar. Geraldine Fraser-Moleketi, a cabinet minister, issued a statement on behalf of all women ministers and deputy ministers denying that they had earned their positions as a result of sexual favours to Mbeki. ANC spokesmen attacked du Preez as a racist, 'a commissar of apartheid' who had committed 'hate speech' and 'declared war' on the South African people. Dumisane Makhaye, an Mbeki henchman, called on the ANC to 'take any necessary step' against du Preez, who was, indeed, assaulted by an unknown assailant shortly afterwards.[48]

Days later the *Mail and Guardian* led with the headline, 'Is Thabo Mbeki Fit to Rule?', claiming that 'we ask [this question] in the knowledge that it is on the lips of many South Africans, many of them dedicated members of the ANC, the SACP and the trade unions'. The paper added, 'His 22 months in power have been disastrous. And he has no one to blame but himself.'[49] This produced further shrill denunciations but there was no doubt that Mbeki was on the ropes.

THE FIGHT BACK FROM THE BUNKER

Mbeki and his henchmen plotted a desperate recovery strategy. This had several elements. The presidency was further strengthened with more staff and Joel Netshitenzhe was given an even more central role. A 'religious working group' of prominent clergymen was set up to advise Mbeki on poverty alleviation and social development, and to launch a campaign for 'moral renewal'. The real purpose was to try to pull back to Mbeki's side clerics who had criticized his position on Aids and the deepening inequality and poverty which higher unemployment had brought. New legislation was announced to enforce black economic empowerment with the process driven from the presidential office – music to the ears of the aspirant black bourgeoisie.

Mbeki's image was held to be in a bad way because of a uniquely hostile local press. This was fantastical – the press was often downright obsequious – but Mbeki's attitudes to Aids and Zimbabwe had damaged his international image to the point where on every foreign trip, no matter what its purpose, he was endlessly questioned by journalists on these two damaging topics. In the presidential view, 'since foreign journalists and diplomatic observers derive their original perceptions about this country and its leadership from reportage and analysis that originates locally, South African journalists and their editors must by hook or by crook be brought into line'.[50] A series of meetings was held with the South African National Editors' Forum – attended not by the presidency's highly paid spin-doctors but by the President, Essop Pahad and high-ranking cabinet ministers, who would harangue the press and insist that a single common view be hammered out. The fact that the press naturally reflects a plurality of views was not considered. The claim was repeatedly made that the press was white-controlled and that racism was the core of the matter, with the corollary that black editors and journalists who dared criticize were racial traitors.

Mbeki also gave extended interviews to selected foreign journalists (never to local journalists with local knowledge to hand). The result was often absurd: thus Magnus Linklater, interviewing Mbeki for *The Times* (London), stated as a matter of fact that 'the South African media have begun a war of attrition against Mbeki, accusing him of arrogance and insensitivity'.[51] Linklater followed up with a highly sympathetic article about Mbeki's Aids policies, swallowing whole Mbeki's assertion that he had never said that HIV was not a cause of Aids and speaking admiringly of how Mbeki had 'briefed himself in formidable detail' on the issue.[52] Anthony Sampson, whose position as Mandela's biographer had made him a sort of ambassador for the ANC, saw his role as promoting Mbeki's image internationally. In his interview with Mbeki, an inevitably friendly affair, he treated with similar seriousness Essop Pahad's assertion that the press was involved in 'the most vile and vicious campaign against a head of state' and that this meant that Mbeki faced 'a different kind of opposition to what we're used to in Western Europe'.[53] In fact, the Independent Newspapers group, owned by the Irish baked beans magnate Tony O'Reilly, by far the largest press group in the country, were so slavishly pro-government as to trigger repeated protests by the Opposition about their biased coverage. Sampson, who sat on the Independent Newspapers international advisory board, repeatedly used his influence in the British media to discourage any attempt at a 'warts-and-all' profile of Mandela and would attempt to intercede with newspaper editors not to publish correspondents whose reportage he regarded as insufficiently pro-ANC.

A key objective of Mbeki's media offensive was to neutralize the Aids issue. First, Mbeki tried to avoid further comment on the issue. Secondly, he claimed that he had never actually said HIV was not a cause of Aids (that is, one cause among others – allowing Mbeki to maintain that poverty was the real killer). And thirdly, Mbeki's refusal to allow the distribution of nevirapine, at that stage the only effective anti-Aids drug, was explained as resulting from the need for South Africa to carry out its own tests of the drug's safety. All of which was absurd. Mbeki had told Parliament that 'a virus cannot cause a syndrome', a straightforward denial that HIV caused Aids. He had also told *Time* that 'the notion that immune deficiency is only acquired from a single virus is unsustainable'.[54] In addition he had written to world leaders in April 2000 comparing Aids dissidents to heretics burnt at the stake. He had also declared on television that he would never take an Aids test because that would mean accepting a particular paradigm of Aids (i.e. that it was caused by HIV) and he had attacked the use of nevirapine as comparable to 'the biological warfare of the apartheid era'.[55] He had also insisted he knew no one who suffered from HIV or Aids and that Aids was not the principal killer of South Africans aged 16–45, despite a mountain of evidence to the contrary. The 5,000 Aids scientists who signed the Durban Declaration the year before did so precisely because they felt progress was impossible until Mbeki accepted the link between HIV and Aids. Linklater's willingness, despite all this, to swallow Mbeki's assurances about Aids policy simply showed why Mbeki gave all his interviews to foreign, not local journalists.

As things went from bad to worse the mood within Mbeki's core group – the Pahad brothers, Smuts Ngonyama, Parks Mankahlana, Joel Netshitenzhe and Steve Tshwete – became increasingly embattled. Hardly accidentally, two of his top five aides – Pundy Pillay and his economic adviser, Moss Ngoasheng – left in the first year. Mbeki's first thought was to put his most trusted lieutenants in charge of intelligence and security – Tshwete, as Minister of Safety and Security, in charge of the police; his former adviser, Vusi Mavimbela, as director of the NIA, and Lindiwe Sisulu as Minister of Intelligence. Trained by the KGB and with a long career in ANC Intelligence, Sisulu was a considerable expert. Many of this top layer were, like Mbeki, Eastern Cape Xhosas: Tshwete, Ngonyama, Mankahlana and Sisulu. Mbeki also appointed Jackie Selebi – despite his somewhat unsavoury reputation – as Police Commissioner and Siphiwe Nyanda as head of the army. Finally, Mbeki had spies in every ministry – sometimes just the directors-general, who now reported to him, but sometimes (notably at Home Affairs to watch Buthelezi) he made sure that the directors-general themselves came from intelligence backgrounds. Inevitably, the paranoia grew as the situation deteriorated.

The more Mbeki and his key advisers saw their mishaps as the result of dark conspiracies, the more they struck out at phantoms and lost their balance. If paranoia had led Mbeki into the camp of the Aids dissidents, they in turn worked to increase it. The prominent Aids dissident David Rasnick argued that

> The involvement of the FBI, CIA and NSA in Aids represents a far greater threat to our freedom . . . Mbeki and SA stand alone in all the world in questioning the underlying assumptions about Aids. That makes Mbeki and SA threats to the business interests, prestige and US global hegemony. Overtly, the world's scientific press, as well as the general media and press, are working together to isolate and neutralize Mbeki and SA's government. Covertly, millions of US dollars are

being spent to monitor and neutralize Mbeki and other African leaders. Much of this money is used to 'orchestrate' the public media and press.[56]

Mbeki found this sort of rhetoric sufficiently appealing to appoint Rasnick to his Aids advisory panel, defying a storm of criticism over Rasnick's technicolour views.

The true believers, yes-men to begin with, tended to idolize Mbeki and encourage him to believe ever more in his unique genius. Smuts Ngonyama was not alone in comparing Mbeki to Jesus. The plots against him were akin to Judas Iscariot's betrayal. 'It's the same. Out of all the disciples around him, everyone is loyal and openly supports him. But one of us will betray him and it will hurt because it is one of us who is selling out.'[57] In May 2001 eleven black businessmen took out a whole page advertisement in the *Sunday Times* (its cost – more than R160,000 – caused many to believe the government was secretly paying) to argue that criticism of Mbeki was an 'apartheid-style disinformation campaign', the disloyal work of whites, 'liberals' and racist right-wingers. The advertisement praised Mbeki as 'intelligent, circumspect and passionate about the condition of our people'. Exactly the same line, hardly coincidentally, was taken in Parliament by Essop Pahad ('So vicious, so underhand and so sustained have the attacks on [Mbeki] been that even fair-minded patriotic whites have started asking serious questions about the motive behind these attacks').[58] Nat Kekana, another ANC speaker, took the same line, arguing that the Opposition, whites and the media really objected to being 'governed by black savages' and were out to 'vilify and crucify the leadership of our country'.[59] Mbeki did not discourage these comparisons of himself with the crucified Christ, emanating from a core group who were mainly atheists or Muslims.

THE 'PRESIDENTIAL PLOT'

Given the paranoia at the heart of the Mbeki group, his recovery strategy inevitably consisted of pre-emptive attacks on anyone considered a possible threat or rival. The NEC meeting of March 2001 was the catalyst which finally brought this strategy into the open. Mbeki's disastrous start had triggered discussion that he might serve only one term as

President and in North West Province an anonymous pamphlet, 'One President, One Term', had been circulating. At the NEC Mbeki, placing a copy of the pamphlet on the table, demanded to know who its author was. There was a long silence, finally broken by a torrent of tributes to Mbeki's leadership, denunciations of the media, the whites and the usual list of enemies, and the hostile citing of Ramaphosa, Sexwale and Phosa, the names which got mentioned as possible replacements in the event of a one-term presidency.[60] This in turn led 'the inner circles at Luthuli House' to posit, on the basis of no evidence, that the three men had been meeting secretly to plot the destabilization of the Mbeki regime 'by spreading negative rumours about Mbeki'.[61] As the NEC ended the news broke that Tony Yengeni, the ANC chief whip, had, while serving as chairman of Parliament's defence committee, acquired his Mercedes 4 × 4 from a company involved in the arms deal. This was roundly denounced as part of a media 'witch-hunt' against ANC leaders – though it was entirely true and, five years later, resulted in Yengeni going to jail.

The first casualty was Jacob Zuma who, only days later, was forced to make a humiliating public declaration that he had 'no intention or desire to stand for the position of President'. This was not enough and the National Prosecuting Authority (and the special police unit, the Scorpions, which fell under it) now began a formal investigation of Zuma's possible involvement in corruption linked to the arms deal. This investigation, which continued year after year, involving an enormous commitment of the scarce time, money and manpower of an already overstretched police force, could not possibly have started – or continued – without strong presidential backing. No ANC minister (the National Prosecuting Authority fell under the Minister of Justice, Penuell Maduna) could risk launching an investigation into the party's No. 2 man unless he had the unequivocal support of the No. 1 man.

Steve Tshwete then announced on television that he was investigating Ramaphosa, Phosa and Sexwale to see if they were involved in a plot he had uncovered to oust Mbeki, who, he said, might be in 'physical danger'. A foreign intelligence service (read: CIA/MI6) might be involved. The principal informant about the plot was the disgraced Mpumalanga youth leader James Nkambule, though Tshwete said he had also uncovered corroborating evidence from others who had signed affidavits saying they had been used to plant false stories about Mbeki in the media, ranging from his alleged womanizing to his alleged involvement in the Hani assassination. Again, it was obvious that Tshwete was acting at Mbeki's instigation. Moreover, it emerged that the police investigation of the 'plot' had actually begun the previous year.[62] This tallies with Zuma's statement that even in 2000 he was aware that he was being investigated informally. In this respect Mbeki's presidency resembles that of Richard Nixon, who was no sooner elected than he began setting illegal wire-taps and compiling an 'enemies list'.

Nkambule was a deeply suspect witness: he was facing seventy-seven charges of fraud and theft and had already admitted to stealing R2.3 million from the government. By his own account, in August 1999 he had been working for ANC intelligence (which was supposed no longer to exist) and had been sent by Mbeki to spy on Mathews Phosa. Most of Nkambule's affidavit and report to Mbeki concerned events in late 1992 when an arms shipment for the ANC from Eastern Europe had arrived in Maputo, which led to a meeting in the Mozambican capital attended by the Mozambican premier, Mathews Phosa, Chris Hani, Joe Modise and a Teddy Coleman. Using the good offices of President Daniel Arap Moi of Kenya and a Kenyan Asian arms dealer, Ketan Somia, the arms were sold to the MPLA in Angola for $2.5 million. By March 1993 this led – as we have seen – to an angry confrontation between Hani and Modise about the fact that the money was never transferred to the ANC's account.

Nkambule asserted that Phosa was attempting, together with Winnie Mandela and Tokyo Sexwale, to link Mbeki to the Hani assassination, and that Phosa had been mandated to see Hani's assassin, Janus Walus, in prison in order to get him to retract his previous testimony and implicate Mbeki. In October 2000 Phosa had telephoned him to tell him he now had an affidavit from Walus saying that he and his fellow-conspirator, Clive Derby-Lewis, had been involved in ivory dealing with Hani and Mbeki; that Hani had owed them money; that Mbeki had then contacted Walus, telling him Hani was about to betray him and also seize the ANC leadership, sidelining Mbeki, and that they were thus both threatened by Hani; and that Mbeki had then provided Walus with both the murder weapon and the details of Hani's security arrangements. (Walus and Derby-Lewis denied all of this.[63]) Phosa had told him, Nkambule said, that he had shared this affidavit with Cyril Ramaphosa, with Jacob Zuma, who was 'disappointed and feeling betrayed', and with sundry African ambassadors. The anti-Mbeki group was now planning to feed these allegations and other black propaganda against Mbeki to the international media and to mobilize opposition within the ANC against Mbeki's autocratic leadership style in order 'to destroy the President'.[64]

Nkambule's story was ridiculous. The notion that Walus and Derby-Lewis had been business partners of both Hani and Mbeki was absurd, as was the idea of Mbeki getting involved with guns, actually handing a murder weapon to Walus and confiding his political worries to him. Mbeki was not a man for guns, was legendarily tight-lipped and was always careful to maintain complete personal deniability by doing things through subordinates. Quite apart from Nkambule's own unreliability, one must reckon with the fact that these documents were released to the press by Mbeki with the notion of swinging opinion his way, and that they were very likely doctored with that purpose in mind. Strong pressure was put on Sexwale and Ramaphosa to state publicly that they welcomed being investigated, thus isolating Phosa, the principal target.

Nkambule, once Phosa's supporter, had become Mbeki's faithful foot soldier. Doubtless the fact that he had been caught stealing large sums made Nkambule vulnerable to pressure from anyone who could promise him a way of avoiding prison. He now became the key witness against Phosa before the ANC commission sent to investigate 'disunity' in Mpumalanga. Chaired by Mbeki's loyal client, Nosiviwe Mapisa-Ngakula (chair of the parliamentary intelligence committee), the commission recommended that Phosa be sacked, though its proceedings were never made public. Nkambule reported to ANC intelligence based at Luthuli House under Tito Maleka, to Smuts Ngonyama in the President's office, and to the Police Commissioner, Jackie Selebi. Selebi, who had been hand-picked by Mbeki, took the unusual step of participating personally in the investigation of Phosa – who was, of course, also accused of having been an apartheid police informer.[65]

The Mbeki–Tshwete strategy failed completely. Mbeki's anxieties had fastened on the fact that Ramaphosa was still supported by his old allies in the SACP and Cosatu and he was worried by the idea that a resurgent left might make Ramaphosa its presidential candidate. To this end Mbeki's men had lobbied unsuccessfully to stop Zwelinzima Vavi becoming secretary-general of Cosatu and Blade Nzimande becoming secretary-general of the SACP.[66] The SACP and Cosatu were now outside his control and the attempts by Mbeki's men to get the two organizations to agree to Tshwete's investigation of Ramaphosa, Sexwale and Phosa failed miserably. This should have made Mbeki realize that he was far overreaching himself by attacking the three men together. They were all extremely popular within the ANC. It might just have been possible to attack them one by one, but attacking all three together meant mobilizing a large majority within the ANC in their defence. All three vehemently denied the allegations: Ramaphosa said they were 'ludicrous and insane', Phosa that they were 'really crazy' and Sexwale that they were 'complete hogwash'. Moreover, Mandela rallied to their defence ('The three comrades that have been mentioned I will always hold in high esteem') and even spoke of Ramaphosa as 'one of the right people to lead South Africa'. Mandela quickly added, though, that he would back Mbeki for a second term.

Both Cosatu and the SACP condemned the investigation as 'a witch-hunt'. Kgalema Motlanthe, while defending Tshwete's right to carry out such an investigation, nevertheless said that he himself did not believe in the existence of a plot to oust Mbeki and warned that 'If you begin to believe these conspiracies we will paralyse our organization'.[67] The only ANC figures to stand up for Tshwete were Mbeki's inner group and the Police Commissioner, Jackie Selebi. The Opposition and the media denounced the notion of the plot as ludicrous and an editorial in *The Economist* twice labelled Mbeki as paranoid.[68] Cosatu denounced Tshwete for using the state security apparatus as a weapon in intra-party squabbles and demanded that he apologize to the three men. Mbeki had imagined that once the allegations were aired, opinion would rally to his side. Exactly the opposite occurred. It was a huge self-inflicted disaster.

Mbeki quickly tried to distance himself from the disaster – typically, through an interview with a foreign journalist, the ITN's Jon Snow. He said he did not really believe Ramaphosa wanted to 'harm me', that the whole affair had originated with the media and that perhaps Tshwete should not have mentioned names – but that it was a very serious matter to suggest the President had been involved in plotting Hani's murder.[69] Snow gave him an easy ride, not even mentioning that the NIA, doubtless on Mbeki's instruction, had released a report the year before linking Ramaphosa to an alleged plot by the CIA and MI6 to overthrow Mbeki.[70] The idea, transparently, was to suggest that Ramaphosa was an imperialist agent and that his (imagined) presidential candidacy was really the work of London and Washington.

Thereafter Tshwete and Mbeki twisted and turned frantically. Tshwete said he was really investigating whether Mbeki had 'stage-managed the assassination of Chris Hani', though for the police to investigate anyone a charge had to be opened against them and none was opened against Mbeki. Tshwete then said the point was that, given Hani's popularity, allegations of this kind could endanger Mbeki's life. Indeed, Mbeki's bodyguards were quadrupled and placed on 'code red' and his driver instructed to drive at 125 mph.[71] Meanwhile, Mbeki, seeing that his ally, Ngoako Ramathlodi, the premier of Northern Province, was under local pressure, had the entire provincial executive of the ANC dissolved.

Mbeki refused to talk to the local media about the plot: 'Don't ask me, ask Tshwete, he's the one talking about these things,'[72] while Mbeki's spokesmen continued to claim that the media was to blame for the whole affair: 'The SABC managed to get the minister to say what they themselves couldn't say'.[73] Smuts Ngonyama, who often referred to Mbeki as 'Mr Commitment and Devotion', went on air to warn that imperialism never slept: it had killed Patrice Lumumba and Laurent Kabila in the Congo and Nkrumah in Ghana (*sic*), so 'the nation must worry'.[74] When the Opposition tried to question Tshwete about the 'plot' in Parliament he screamed that they were 'liars', 'cowards', 'spies' and 'stupid'.[75] The PAC secretary-general, Thami ka Plaatjie, commented that 'There is something wrong with [Tshwete]. He behaves like a jilted boyfriend. Tshwete is a clown and should perform at a circus. He is a drunkard.'[76] Mbeki tried hard to defend Tshwete but finally conceded that it had been wrong of Tshwete to cite names before the investigation had been completed.

Six months elapsed before it was finally admitted that there was no evidence against any of the three 'plotters'. Tshwete, under strong ANC pressure, apologized to them. In fact there had never been a proper investigation (none of the three men were ever questioned by police), any more than there had been an investigation into Mbeki's alleged role in Hani's murder. All that had happened was that Mbeki had panicked, first at the release of a letter by Winnie Mandela detailing his 'womanizing' and specifically his late-night soirée with Wendy Luhabe, the attractive young wife of the Gauteng premier, Sam Shilowa, and then at the 'One President, One Term' pamphlet. All this had been spun together with a paranoid insistence that everyone from Mac Maharaj to Jacob

Zuma, Max du Preez and the three 'plotters' were involved in a vast conspiracy against him. The ANC Youth League and Women's League had loyally rallied to Mbeki, insisting they wanted him to run for a second term. Certainly the affair had ensured there would be no challenger to Mbeki in 2004. But the price was high. Mbeki gave two more suave UK interviews – to *The Guardian*'s Hugo Young[77] and *The Independent*'s Magnus Linklater[78] – in which he skated around the matter but the affair left lasting resentment within the ANC. Three years later James Nkambule admitted that he had lied, and apologized to the three accused for 'the dissemination and publication of such falsehoods'. He claimed that he had been 'manipulated by politicians' into making the accusations and said he felt 'like a used condom'.[79]

STEVE TSHWETE: LAW AND ORDER OUT OF CONTROL

Thami ka Plaatjie was right: there was something badly wrong with Tshwete. Like all too many exiles he had become an alcoholic. The struggle had been a rough school and Tshwete was now a man willing to say and do whatever was required to get his way. If, the next day, his words were exposed as lies, no matter, they had served their purpose. He would shrug off any opprobrium with the next drink. It was a measure of what Mbeki's paranoia had reduced him to that he had become so reliant on a man who was not just reckless but, in large measure, out of control. Tshwete was not a wholly unpopular figure – as Minister of Sport, he had happily caroused with cricketers and rugby players – but he was a notorious liar and was well known for his drunken bluster. Whenever a particularly egregious crime took place he would announce that he knew who the culprits were and that the net was fast closing upon them, though no arrests ever followed. But the fact that Mbeki relied so much on him and that he had the President's ear made him one of the most powerful ministers.

A graphic illustration of Tshwete's power came, indeed, in the midst of the 'presidential plot' when Tshwete summoned the ministers of Defence, Intelligence, Justice and Foreign Affairs and rammed through a new clause to a bill regulating the private security industry, excluding all foreign investment or control. This amendment – which Tshwete did not take either to cabinet or the ANC caucus – was then pushed through the parliamentary safety and security committee, whose chairman, Mlukeki George, another Eastern Cape Xhosa with ambitions to take over the South African Rugby Board, was a close ally of Tshwete's. George announced that no foreigners would be allowed to hold shares in any private security business or run such companies, insisting that 9/11 had made it more important than ever that security companies remain South African-owned and run. National security, no less, was at stake.[80]

This extraordinary proposal seems to have resulted from one of Tshwete's drinking bouts with his old MK buddies. Former MK operatives always tended to think first of careers in the armed forces or in the security business. And the inefficacy of the police had made private security a profitable industry: it employed three times as many people as the police, and middle-class South Africa paid through the nose for its 'instant armed response'. British companies (ADT, Group 4, Securicor and Chubb) and the American Tyco had spent nearly R3 billion to take over a host of little local companies. The UK companies had relied on the 1998 UK-SA Investment Promotion and Protection Agreement, which specifically forbade such asset-grabbing as Tshwete was proposing, while Tyco had received specific assurances from the ANC that its investment was safe.[81] But Tshwete knew that budding black businessmen wanted to get their hands on this lucrative business and that if he could hand it over to them he would be handsomely rewarded. Cleverly, Tshwete had chosen for his coup a moment when the ministers of both Finance (Trevor Manuel) and Trade (Alec Erwin) were abroad.

The Opposition DA pointed out the ruinous effects the move would have on foreign investment. Manuel returned and was furious. The UK High Commission pointed out that such a move would threaten all British investment in South Africa and produce a major diplomatic and trade crisis with South Africa's biggest foreign investor. This was too much and Tshwete was forced to back down completely. Luckily, he found this relatively easy to do for, as a practised and brazen liar, he was used to claiming that he had never meant his own previous statements – or, indeed, made them at all. Suddenly, it emerged, national security was not at stake after all. The foreign companies took the hint and promised black empowerment deals to bring in some of the hungry black businessmen on the sidelines. Interestingly, Tshwete had felt able to take such initiatives without any fear of dismissal or public disavowal by the President.

SPLITTING THE DA

With the 1999 election the DP had become the official Opposition – and a serious thorn in Mbeki's side. It now had 38 seats in Parliament but punched well beyond its weight. Buoyed by its years as the main parliamentary Opposition to apartheid, the DP was well organized, vocal, and experienced in exploiting every parliamentary opportunity to question and embarrass the government. Also, Mbeki was failing badly, and the DP leader, Tony Leon, was extremely sharp in pointing this out. Mbeki's exile experience had given him no preparation for this. Mandela had liked Leon, laughing and joking with him, even visiting him in hospital when he had an operation. But Mbeki was prone to imagine as his enemies all manner of people who never spoke a hostile word to him. Faced with someone whose whole *raison d'être* was to criticize him as publicly as possible, Mbeki simply couldn't cope. He couldn't even bring himself to call Leon by name, referring to him only as 'the white politician'.

In all parliamentary democracies there is a necessary relationship between the government leader and the leader of the Opposition. In South Africa, through the hardest years of apartheid, this had always remained the case, with regular leadership-level meetings, an attempt to achieve consensus on at least some issues. Now this relationship lapsed completely for Mbeki could not face one-on-one meetings with Leon. He always shrank from direct, face-to-face confrontations and since Leon was also cleverer, better educated, tough and direct, meetings with him were likely to be difficult. So Mbeki refused to meet, relenting only when Leon announced his retirement.

The DP continued to trounce the NNP in municipal by-elections but it was obvious that if the two parties fought one another in the December 2000 local elections they would split the opposition vote – so they came together to form the Democratic Alliance (DA). Opposition voters were delighted and rewarded the DA with 23 per cent of the vote, enabling them to win a whole slew of towns, especially in the Western Cape and

KwaZulu-Natal. The ANC held its own but was acutely annoyed by the DA gains. It was part of the ANC's hegemonic self-consciousness that it should always be seen as going from strength to strength, as befitted the party of the righteous. Headlines about a white-led party winning towns back from the ANC were just not part of the script. Worse still were the polls showing Tony Leon gaining strongly against Mbeki in the presidential stakes.

In fact the DA was an ill-conceived marriage. The DP, with its strong anti-apartheid record, had compromised itself by bringing in the rump of the Nats. All it had bought was overnight municipal success. The DP had been on the verge of annihilating the NNP and winning over its voters: the alliance meant it also had to make room for the NNP elites at local and national level. The result was acute indigestion, particularly since the NNP insisted on keeping its own separate organization within the alliance.

The worst situation was in Cape Town where the DA – in fact NNP – mayor, Peter Marais, soon proved a loose cannon. Marais, a Coloured populist, decided to rename several of Cape Town's most famous streets and, when the popular verdict was hostile, simply rigged the vote. Reports of every other sort of irregularity swarmed around his person and private DA polls soon showed that his effect on the party's standing was strongly negative. Leon showed increasing irritation with Marais, who was, he felt, letting down the DA cause, while the NNP leader, Marthinus Van Schalkwyk, attempted to protect Marais. Tensions were greatly inflamed when a laptop belonging to Leon's assistant, Ryan Coetzee, was stolen and correspondence with Leon on the machine was leaked, showing how little the Leon camp trusted the NNP.

This theft was the first of a series of 'dirty tricks' mounted against the DA, almost certainly by the NIA or ANC intelligence. There were recurrent scares over the bugging of DA conference and caucus rooms, with strong circumstantial evidence pointing to the NIA as the culprit. Confidential conversations were leaked to the media,[82] exacerbating tensions within the DA camp.

Meanwhile it emerged that the NNP owed Absa Bank R5.2 million. Absa (Associated Banks of South Africa) made it clear that they expected repayment from the DA, although the parties had agreed that neither would bring any debt into the alliance. The significance of this news was that the NNP clearly could never again contest an election on its own.

Modern campaigns are fought on overdrafts, paid off by post-election fund-raising, but more than two years after the election the NNP could not clear its debt and would therefore be unable to obtain credit to fight any future campaign. Absa said it was not levying any interest on the debt because 'the NNP does not have the capacity to service interest or the capital'.[83] The once-mighty party of Afrikaner nationalism which had ruled the country for forty-six years was bankrupt. And since the NNP could never secure credit again, any future NNP campaign would have to be funded by the DA – or the ANC.

Matters came to a head in October 2001 with Leon and Van Schalkwyk publicly at odds. Leon then fired Marais as mayor of Cape Town and had him suspended from the DA. Van Schalkwyk protested – and promptly announced that the NNP was leaving the DA and had struck a deal instead with the ANC. For secret negotiations had been going on with Mbeki for some time: suddenly the dirty tricks against the DA appeared in a new light, part of a campaign which had not been understood at the time. The immediate effect of the NNP–ANC deal was that the two parties, now in concert, had a majority in the Western Cape provincial assembly and ejected the premier, Gerald Morkel, a Coloured former NNP member who had stayed loyal to the DA, with an ANC-led administration replacing him. Morkel was then made DA mayor of Cape Town in Marais's place. Van Schalkwyk, hitherto to Leon's right, now accused Leon of having 'reduced opposition politics to an angry white voice' and of only being concerned to protect white privilege, placing it above loyalty to the country.[84]

Mbeki's deal with Van Schalkwyk puzzled many: the NNP was a discredited shell, frightened to challenge the DP/DA even in municipal by-elections. The ANC had angrily denounced the DP for embracing 'the party of apartheid' – and yet now it did just the same itself. Immediately, all that it got out of it was a share of power in the Western Cape – hardly that significant when the ANC held power almost everywhere else. Yet the deal was a major watershed. The DP – and then the DA – had developed considerable momentum in 1994–2000. This was now stopped in its tracks. Moreover, for Mbeki the extinguishing of the DA provincial government in the Western Cape was a major gain. It had been by far the most dynamic and successful government of any province, had scored striking successes in the war against crime and had defied national policy by starting the distribution of ARVs to Aids sufferers.

So successful was the provincial government that the ANC-led provinces sent delegation after delegation to Cape Town, asking for help and advice, for the Western Cape was seen as a successful model, a beacon to the rest of the country. Mbeki could not stomach this.

Mbeki had hired apartheid-era security operatives to investigate the alleged scandal of the bail-out of Absa (whose consortium included the principal Afrikaner bank, Volkskas) by the Reserve Bank back in the 1980s. They reported that Absa had indeed gone bust and been illegitimately handed R3 billion by the Reserve Bank to keep it afloat. Absa had owned up and offered to pay it back over four years at R750 million a year. Mbeki did not accept this offer, however; he had already decided that he must seek a deal with Afrikaner interests and this way he could be sure that Absa would do him favours when required.[85] He was quite right. First, Absa surfaced the fact of the NNP's debt at a moment when it was likely to do most damage within the DA. However, it then treated this loan with remarkable charity, declining to charge interest on it, and finally wrote it off altogether. It is difficult not to view Absa's successive moves as having been choreographed in the President's office, particularly since it also emerged that Absa had given R2 million to fund Ronald Suresh Roberts, an unconditional Mbeki-admirer, to write a hagiographical work on 'Mbeki's intellectual heritage' – a remarkable sum for a bank to give to a private individual. It later emerged that Roberts had received the grant thanks to the direct intervention of the Minister in the President's office, Essop Pahad – although Pahad tried to hide this fact, having earlier denied to Parliament that he had played any such role.

The NNP–ANC deal saw the NNP MPs in Parliament and their members of the provincial legislatures break their alliance with the DA, but NNP municipal councillors could not do this since they had been elected on a DA ticket and were not allowed to cross the floor. The Western Cape provincial government was thus handed over to an ANC-led coalition (with Peter Marais as premier) but Cape Town remained a DA bastion. Mbeki was determined to put an end to this and immediately announced that legislation would be brought in to allow floor-crossing at every level, though the rules were carefully calculated to favour the ANC.[86] Mbeki had been alarmed by the DA's municipal sweep and Leon's progress in the polls: it was now a major objective to kill his momentum. As the SACP's No. 2, Jeremy Cronin, explained to his comrades, it was necessary to welcome Van Schalkwyk, a former apartheid spy, into the alliance because 'The key thing is that this co-operation offers the possibility of defeating the Tony Leon project.'[87]

THE ATTACK ON THE DA

The anti-DA offensive moved into higher gear in April 2001 when the German con-man Jurgen Harksen – a fugitive from justice, shortly to be handed over to the German authorities – alleged that he had given the DA more than R1 million, and that he had had close personal links with Morkel to whom he had given more than R100,000 for his personal use. Morkel, though protesting his innocence, was forced to stand down as mayor while the provincial government set up the Desai Commission to probe it for months on end. Even Peter Marais's resignation as premier – facing allegations of sexual misconduct and possible criminal charges – was overshadowed by the so-called Harksen affair, for the DA had earned a squeaky clean reputation through its exposure of government corruption, a reputation which the ANC was determined to overturn.

The split within the DA had left some dynamite lying around. The old NNP, particularly in the Western Cape, had been a byword for every possible sort of jobbery and chicanery. Now, however, with Van Schalkwyk's fraction of the NNP in alliance with the ANC, it was not difficult for its members to come up with plausible allegations against their erstwhile comrades who had remained in the DA. Moreover, long before the split the DA provincial government had realized that it was under attack by the NIA and had turned for help to the government's chief civil servant, Niel Barnard, the former head of the apartheid-era National Intelligence Service. Barnard, who had won warm commendation from Mandela for his exemplary behaviour during the transition, recruited some of his own former operatives to help the provincial government and also advised on the setting up of counter-intelligence measures to prevent it from being spied upon. This involved the setting up of a secure room, proof against eavesdropping equipment, the regular sweeping of offices for bugs and the purchase of a hi-tech machine, the Watchdog, able to detect bugs and snoop on conversations up to four kilometres away.[88]

I interviewed both Barnard and Hennie Bester, the DA leader in the

Western Cape, at that time and asked Bester if he had reservations about employing old apartheid spooks. No, he said, they had helped crack the urban terrorism which had long plagued the region. And meanwhile ANC-ruled provinces were sending representatives to learn from the DA in the Western Cape. This was, I reflected, a toxic mix. Mbeki was bound to be infuriated that ANC-ruled provinces looked to the sole DA province as their model. And for the DA administration to use apartheid-era spooks and eavesdropping technology would provide the ANC with an opening it was bound to seize.[89]

And so it turned out. Once the NNP–ANC coalition took over the province Peter Marais set up the Desai Commission with the mandate of inquiring into spying on the provincial government. When the Harksen scandal broke he broadened the terms of reference to enable Desai to go into that too, for the Commission's real job was simply to rake up whatever dirt it could find on the DA. Judge Desai, a former ANC branch chairman and a close friend of most of the Western Cape ANC leadership, was only too happy to do this. Having initially stated that it was not within the Commission's terms of reference to determine whether Harksen had given money to the DA, he then proceeded to lead witnesses to precisely that question. When it emerged that Harksen had given at least equal sums to the ANC, Desai showed no interest. And so on. The possibility that Harksen might have agreed to blacken the DA's reputation in order to curry favour with Pretoria, and thus perhaps prevent or delay his extradition to Germany, was never examined. Although everyone agreed that Harksen was an inveterate liar, his accusations against the DA were treated as gospel while statements he made about funding the ANC were disregarded.

The Desai Commission, whose life was repeatedly extended, produced continuous headlines linking the DA (especially Morkel and another ex-NNP figure, Leon Markowitz) to charges of corruption and did the party great damage. In May 2002 Bester resigned from political life, disgusted with Morkel's refusal to stand down, while the Minister of Justice announced that he was investigating the DA on charges of money-laundering.[90] The Scorpions began investigating possible criminal charges against Morkel and Markowitz[91] and repeatedly gave off-the-record media briefings suggesting that the arrest of prominent DA figures was imminent. They also staged raids during which DA materials were confiscated which would later be leaked to the media or fed to

Harksen to bolster his evidence. The party had no doubt that the Director of Public Prosecutions, Bulelani Ngcuka, was behind the Scorpions' campaign. Such partisan abuse of the Scorpions and the national prosecution service was to become a frequent weapon against Mbeki's opponents, most notably Jacob Zuma.

No DA figures were ever arrested but a potent atmosphere of threat was maintained and the party was quite visibly on the ropes. The DA chief whip, Douglas Gibson, called the Desai Commission a 'kangaroo court conducted in a prejudiced and malicious manner by a man who is acting more like the ANC branch chairman he used to be than the independent investigator he is obliged to be now'.[92] Inevitably, the DA was criticized for failing to show respect for the judiciary. The agony continued all the way into 2003, by which time both Morkel and Markowitz had been relegated to the DA's back benches.[93]

Meanwhile a series of burglaries of party and parliamentary offices and DA members' homes across the country targeted the party's computers. Other valuable items were often left untouched. The aim, transparently, was to destabilize the DA, spy on it and rob it of its databases. Among the sensitive data stolen were the identities of donors, records of the party's telemarketing, its bank records, membership lists and position papers setting out the party's strengths and vulnerabilities. One of the MPs I interviewed told me that the Nats had been told by the ANC that they had to bring over DA members with them, particularly during the floor-crossing exercise, and that, sure enough, the Nats were clearly using mailing lists off the stolen computers in their attempt to fulfil this demand.[94]

After a series of leaks to the media from confidential meetings, the DA also became worried about the security of its parliamentary caucus room. Already in December 1999 a security sweep had revealed that a ray was being beamed onto the caucus window from the NIA building opposite, thus enabling electronic eavesdropping to take place. Security consultants now found that the amplifier box in the caucus room had been tampered with in the last few days: almost certainly a listening device had been removed. As a result the DA were reduced to taking security measures even within Parliament – a 'white noise' producer was played at caucus meetings, MPs were instructed not to use telephone landlines and members would frequently walk outside to hold confidential discussions.[95]

The continuing computer thefts were clearly carried out by professionals: no thieves were ever caught. In July the DA asked the Police Commissioner, Jackie Selebi, to investigate the matter and the issue was also raised with the Special Investigation Unit and with Bulelani Ngcuka. This had no effect: the thefts continued. Finally in September, following the seventeenth such theft, Douglas Gibson requested an urgent meeting with the Minister of Intelligence, Lindiwe Sisulu. The DA, Gibson said, was 'being subjected to an ongoing, politically motivated and carefully orchestrated series of break-ins': it simply could not 'stand by and allow itself to be the target of a dirty tricks campaign aimed at undermining the democratic process'.[96]

For once the DA were in luck. Lindiwe Sisulu, though an intelligence expert, was also a human rights activist. A well-educated woman with a string of degrees from British universities, as a member of the remarkable Sisulu family she enjoyed a special and independent status within the ANC. She was shocked by the implications of what Gibson had to say and the computer thefts stopped immediately. It seems likely that the burglaries had been orchestrated from sources high up in the ANC but that Sisulu had been left out of the loop. The fact that she had the power to terminate the thefts speaks volumes but it may not have pleased Mbeki. After the 2004 election Sisulu was, to her mortification, sacked as Minister of Intelligence and made Minister of Housing instead. Unsurprisingly, she ended up in Jacob Zuma's corner against Mbeki.

THE ASSAULT ON THE DA ON THE CAPE FLATS

The assault on the DA had a further dimension in the Khayelitsha squatter settlement, outside Cape Town. Here the DA had made inroads thanks to the tireless activism of township workers fed up with the warlord-rule of local ANC councillors. This in turn led to brutal reprisals. On 21 April 2002 one ANC councillor, De Poutch Elese, held a meeting in Crossroads, where his DA opponents attempted to speak about Elese's alleged abuse of his housing allocation powers to punish DA supporters. Elese drew a gun and in full view of the crowd shot six of the DA activists, wounding five and killing one, Kenneth Ndayi. The police, however, declined to lay charges against Elese. Helen Zille, a local DA leader who had helped to organize DA branches in the townships, issued a statement saying that the shooting 'was the latest in a series of attacks that are increasing in frequency and severity' and that the ANC was 'spearheading a campaign of violent intimidation against its political opponents in Xhosa-speaking areas', and she alleged ANC–police collusion. Instead of preventing violence against DA supporters the police had carried out 'the repeated arrest of DA activists on spurious and frivolous charges, often before a long weekend, so they have to spend five days in jail before the bail application', whereas even serious and well-substantiated charges against ANC office-bearers were seldom followed up, dockets containing the charges were repeatedly 'lost' or 'misplaced' and the charges 'were often withdrawn without reasons being given'.[97]

These accounts closely resembled the scenes I had previously witnessed in Zimbabwe, where the democratic opposition to Mugabe was repeatedly and violently attacked by members of President Mugabe's ruling Zanu-PF while the police stood by or joined in the assault. So I went to Khayelitsha to see whether the comparison really held. One DA activist I met, Lungwisa Gazi, had never supported the ANC. 'When the necklacings started in the 1980s, I said that's not for me. Also the ANC forces people to attend its rallies. No other party does that.' When her eldest son was murdered in 1996 the local ANC 'just dismissed the case – I was an opposition supporter after all'. When, in 1998, she persisted in opposition activities her younger son, Boyboy (17), was seized by the ANC and tried for murder by a kangaroo court. Fearing for his life, she called the police but the ANC councillor and ex-mayor, Vuyani Ngcuka (brother of Bulelani Ngcuka), ordered them to leave – and they did. Boyboy was then beaten till he was unconscious and had to be hospitalized.

Gazi laid charges against the local ANC leaders but both they and the police put enormous pressure on her to drop them. The police inspector investigating the case told her that he was under great pressure to drop it and had been threatened and placed under surveillance. Ultimately he was transferred. When Gazi persisted with the case an ANC mob burnt down her house in Khayelitsha, looting all her possessions. She had to run for her life – and had been running ever since: wherever she moved the local ANC street committee would threaten to burn her out again. In April 2000 the ANC finally caught up with Boyboy. He was shot and killed, another case which was never properly investigated. 'We were much better off under apartheid,' said Gazi. 'Then you could call the cops and they would try to do their job. Now they take the side of those who are threatening you.'

Gazi began establishing DA branches as the only counterweight to the ANC big men. The Langa township branch soon had more than 300 members and the nearby Joe Slovo squatter camp – where Gazi ran a soup kitchen – became a DA stronghold. The ANC saw this as a major provocation and ANC trucks roamed the area, denouncing the DA over loudhailers while fires were started. The whole settlement burnt down, the ANC loudhailers cheering the destruction of 'the DA soup kitchen' and declaring that 'We'll never have this again'. Normally fire victims received R500 each in relief from the city council but the squatters now found this was blocked and when they tried to get new ID documents necessary to vote in the 2000 local elections these too were refused. When the DA polled more than 500 votes in Langa a campaign of threats began against DA supporters.

In 2001 Gazi joined with two other DA stalwarts, Regina Lengisi and Mambele Makeleni, to launch a DA branch in Langa. This ended with more than 100 houses of DA supporters being burnt down. Makeleni's house was destroyed and the three women were repeatedly summoned before kangaroo courts. The ANC, having stolen the DA membership list from Makeleni, tried her and Lengisi for using witchcraft 'to persuade black people to join a white man's party like the DA'. She was sentenced to having to leave her home in Langa for ever unless, of course, she rejoined the ANC. Gazi and Lengisi said that the kangaroo court was a major ordeal in itself. 'There are often two or three hundred people there, all shouting for your blood,' Gazi said. 'After a while you begin to feel terribly guilty no matter how innocent you are.' 'The worst thing is the way young people are encouraged to shout insults and obscenities at you,' added Lengisi. Proceedings were only halted by Helen Zille's appearance at the court with a lawyer and a court injunction. The fact that Zille was able to conduct the defence in fluent Xhosa merely increased the hostility with which she was regarded by the ANC. Zille grew outraged as she recounted other cases in which women had been raped as a punishment and the police had refused to accept their complaint. 'The police just say, if the DA comes and organizes in an

ANC area, you must expect trouble. Don't then come and complain to us,' she said.[98]

When I contacted the local ANC its response was simply to 'reject with utter contempt' all the DA's multiple allegations and affidavits. The ANC provincial secretary, Mcebisi Skwatsha, accused Zille of 'opportunistically sneaking into townships and working together with disgruntled and destructive elements . . . whipping up emotions of poor people and then retreating to her ivory towers (*sic*), not worried about the consequences of leaving behind a bitter and divided community'.[99] For Zille and Gazi this was effectively a denial of multi-party politics. 'The ANC believes it owns poor areas and has a copyright on their vote. Thus the intervention of any other party there is illegitimate,' said Zille.

The ANC's blank rejection of Zille's charges, indeed its refusal to discuss them seriously at all, was not just due to embarrassment. Its Western Cape section had been headed by a succession of Coloured politicians who did not live in the squatter camps or go there. Most of the black elite behaved similarly, moving out of Khayelitsha as soon as possible to middle-class suburbs. 'The gap between those at the top and those at the bottom,' said Zille, 'is just as wide as it was under apartheid. I never see Skwatsha or any of the other leading ANC Africans out here in Crossroads or Khayelitsha.' Gazi was adamant that the ANC leadership was responsible for the denial of multi-partyism in the Cape. 'The worst was Steve Tshwete. He used to come down here and urge them "to get rid of these bastards, clean them out" and he would even appear on TV, speaking in Xhosa, to say the same, sometimes using words I don't want to repeat.' The fact that Tshwete was Mbeki's confidant and the Minister in charge of the police certainly left local ANC enforcers with the impression that they had backing right from the top for their war against the DA. Tshwete's behaviour was, at best, wildly irresponsible, at worst, murderous.

The death of Kenneth Ndayi lifted the confrontation to a new level, with the DA leader, Tony Leon, angrily accusing President Mbeki of complicity in 'a campaign of intimidation, harassment and violence'. SABC television sent a team to cover these events but no such footage was ever screened though the SABC gave continuous coverage to ANC–NNP propaganda attacks on the DA – exactly the sort of behaviour which had characterized the SABC at the height of apartheid. The comparison with Mugabe's Zimbabwe was, I realized, accurate enough.

THE FLOOR-CROSSING DEBACLE

These pressures on the DA were merely the prelude to floor-crossing. Back in 1996 when the new constitution was being certified the DP had argued that an MP must be free to cross the floor if his conscience so dictated but the Constitutional Court delivered a long and reasoned argument as to why floor-crossing was both immoral and inappropriate. When in 1998 the DP introduced a parliamentary motion in favour of such a measure, the ANC vehemently opposed it, quoting the court's judgment. Now, however, such a law was necessary to give full effect to the ANC–NNP deal and so the ANC pushed through its own variant of floor-crossing. Then in 2002 the minor parties in Parliament went to the Constitutional Court asking it to declare the new law unconstitutional. Having so recently taken such a strong position on the issue the Court seemed to have no option but to do this. Even the Court's most ardent offenders were embarrassed when, instead, it made a 180-degree turn and declared the new law entirely constitutional: the ANC had changed its position and so the Court felt obliged to do the same. Even the Court was too embarrassed to argue against the position it had taken six years before, contenting itself instead with the simple statement that floor-crossing was not unconstitutional.

Given the pro-ANC majority in the Court, its lack of courage and principle was not truly surprising, for the ANC was clearly hell-bent on exploiting its new alliance with the NNP to reverse the DA's sweeping gains in the 2000 municipal elections. This was not an area of marginal interest: if the Court were to stand up to the government on this it would have meant a head-on confrontation with a determined President. And the Court had its own worries: all year long the ANC had been making threatening noises about 'white racist judges' and demanding faster transformation of the judiciary. But, as Van Zyl Slabbert pointed out, the Court's job was 'to see to it that the Constitution acts as a check on the possible abuse of power'; instead it had preferred 'to avoid political controversy'[100] – which, in the new South Africa as in the old, meant not annoying the government. Yet what was about to happen under the name of floor-crossing was as clear a definition of the abuse of power as one could get.

For when floor-crossing went ahead it was a completely cynical exercise in which the ANC bribed and suborned representatives to change sides. As a result, the DA lost Cape Town and a whole raft of municipalities throughout the Western Cape while many IFP gains in 2000 were reversed by similar tactics in KwaZulu-Natal. Typically, IFP or DA or minority party members were visited at their homes by night by ANC intermediaries who offered them positions on the ANC list, well-paid jobs or committee positions with generous allowances if they would switch sides. It was true that the large majority of NNP councillors elected on the DA ticket stayed with the DA – and those who defected were generally reviled by popular opinion – but this merely reflected the fact that the ANC was buying back control of municipalities it had lost. Once it had bought enough councillors to give it control of a municipality, and the patronage that went with it, there was no incentive to buy any more.

Tony Leon, the DA leader, claimed that there was 'a serious, considered, determined attempt to destroy real opposition in South Africa. And the leadership driving this comes from the top of the ANC,'[101] but perhaps his greatest frustration was with the press which seemed wholly unwilling to grasp the drama unfolding before it. For the press, like the Constitutional Court, had its own interests to consult. The ANC continually insisted that the press was racist, white-controlled, served reactionary interests and was not serving its proper ('progressive') role, charges the press was desperate to rebut. It wanted to embrace the new South Africa and it wanted, if possible, the government's friendship or at least its acceptance. So while it was willing to criticize the ANC from time to time, it tried to adopt a determinedly 'progressive' stance. But if what Tony Leon was saying was taken seriously the implication was that the ANC, and President Mbeki in particular, were potential totalitarians, actively attempting to subvert the democratic system. In which case it was clearly the job of the press to sound the alarm and to defend democracy and the constitution – which would mean head-on collision with the government.

This was, however, not on the agenda of the press, and particularly not of the largest press group, Tony O'Reilly's Independent Newspapers. Ergo, the only thing to do was to refuse to take seriously the arguments made by Tony Leon and the DA. The shameful result was a sort of deliberate non-journalism which carefully avoided looking at the evidence – the extraordinary behaviour of the Desai Commission, the mass shack-burnings and intimidation of DA supporters in Khayelitsha, the seventeen computer thefts, the outright bribery of floor-crossing, the complete moral collapse of the Constitutional Court and so on – and instead treated Leon and the DA either as if they were just making a noise about things as politicians always did, or even as people suffering delusions.

Thus, for example, the interview with Leon by John Battersby, group political editor of Independent Newspapers, in June 2002. Leon was described as a man in the grip of 'two key obsessions', the spinelessness of the media and President Mbeki's anti-democratic tendencies. 'Throughout the interview,' Battersby reported, '[Leon] revives the alleged conspiracy.' Leon's 'draconian forebodings' played to the minorities' racial fears of the black majority (and were thus implicitly racist). And while 'Leon does not give out any of the signs of a leader who is breaking under the strain', this was clearly a scenario Battersby wished his readers to have in mind. His conclusion was that 'Leon is a "yapdog" rather than a lapdog and . . . is on the country's scariest political roller-coaster ride. High highs and low lows.'[102] Thus a well-supported case about the undermining of constitutional democracy was turned into an eye-rolling psychological portrait of the complainant. This was not atypical.

But with the conclusion of floor-crossing the anti-DA campaign effectively stopped. The ANC had got what it wanted, Lindiwe Sisulu had called the NIA to heel and, not least, foreign correspondents based in South Africa had begun to write highly critical articles about what was going on. This last was taken seriously. Under apartheid the ANC had enjoyed the moral high ground with the international press, and exiles like Mbeki had become used to the notion that they were portrayed as victims and heroes, men of great moral stature and authority. The ANC was deeply attached to this international image and when warning signs began to flash that they were endangering that status, the warning was taken.

These were hard years for South Africa's young democracy. One by one its new democratic institutions were tested – and failed. In the course of the row over the arms deal the Speaker, the Auditor-General and the Public Prosecutor had all been successfully diverted into partisan behaviour. The Constitutional Court had repeatedly failed to stand up to the government, even to protect the franchise or to prevent wholesale political bribery and corruption. The NIA had been used to spy on the official Opposition – even inside Parliament itself, and both the Scorpions and the National Prosecuting Authority had been abused for partisan ends. In addition, the struggle over Aids had seen the politicization of bodies such as the Medicines Control Council, Statistics South Africa and the Medical Research Council. Where Mandela had respected the independence of the judiciary and other institutions, Mbeki had suborned one institution after another. Within the ANC, provincial democracy had been largely struck down and even government ministers were spied upon.

Worst of all, most of the watchdogs were not barking. The Constitutional Court, the press and most NGOs were loath to notice what was going on, let alone stand up against it. Quite understandably they – and many others, especially foreign visitors – liked to celebrate the spirit of '94, racial reconciliation, the rainbow nation and the still-wonderful fact that the transition to democracy had been peacefully achieved. They did not want their celebration interrupted by jarring notes suggesting that, even as the party went on, the butler was making off with the silver and that there might soon be little left to celebrate. Those who sounded such notes were denounced as reactionary, negative, even racist. It was a hard time to be a conscientious democrat, particularly since those now endangering democracy were those who had been loudest in their denunciation of past oppression and in their insistence that 'the people shall govern'. James Thurber counselled that 'You can fool too many of the people too much of the time.' More pertinent still was Napoleon's warning: 'Among those who dislike oppression are many who like to oppress.'

8

The Truth and Reconciliation Commission and the Problem of Hegemony

The world overcomes us, not merely by appealing to our reason, or exciting our passions, but by imposing on our imagination. Cardinal Newman

Man is what he believes. Anton Chekhov

The first attempt to transform the moral and cultural climate of the new democracy was made by the Truth and Reconciliation Commission. It was a peculiar, if necessary body. Originally the ANC had dreamt of Nuremberg trials where the guilty men of apartheid would be arraigned and judged. The Nats, while naturally determined to avoid that, could not but agree that many bad and unjust things had happened under apartheid and, they would add, there were many skeletons in the ANC cupboard too. It was obvious that some sort of ritual of exorcism and cleansing had to be performed if the new democracy was not to be hopelessly dogged by demands for revenge. There had to be some way to expose the horrors of the past – in return for which society as a whole could say Amen and move on.

The result was the TRC. It was widely hailed as a great success and adopted as a model in many other countries, and yet it was in every sense deeply flawed. First, it was given the Herculean job of examining the political killings and abuse of human rights from March 1960 to May 1994 – in just eighteen months. Even though this period was extended by a year, it was a ludicrously short time, and had been decided for political purposes. Secondly, this was clearly a job which required the labours of historians and political scientists well versed in the period and in the research techniques appropriate to contemporary history, supplemented by help from professional detectives. The commission lacked any such figures. It was headed by Archbishop Desmond Tutu, who was deputized by Alex Boraine (former president of the Methodist Church), and it included several other ministers of religion. Boraine himself spoke of 'the strong religious and largely Christian emphasis of the commission'.[1] Boraine was in many ways the TRC's critical figure, for Tutu, though more famous, was a legendarily poor administrator. If the TRC was not to be a complete shambles, it needed a strong No. 2, someone who could handle organization, procedures – and a prima donna. Boraine was exactly that. Otherwise the commission was composed largely of lawyers and political activists, with a strong ANC bias.

It was thus a microcosm of the way the new South Africa tended to organize itself: it had a ridiculous timetable, it deliberately avoided picking people with the necessary skills, and its staff was politically heavily biased. This situation was compounded by the appointment of Charles Villa-Vicencio, head of the Department of Religious Studies at the University of Cape Town, as the TRC's research director. He was politically partisan and had no experience of the contemporary historical research required. His research team was equally unsuitable. Worse still, people with the most impressive credentials for the job were turned down.[2]

From the first the TRC was a peculiar mix of religion (there was much praying and invocation of the Almighty), theatre, quasi-legal process and a great deal of raw emotion as thousands of apartheid victims told their stories, often of the most shocking brutalities, amidst a great deal of weeping which sometimes included the commissioners. The TRC received worldwide publicity, and Tutu, in particular, had a considerable gift for cultivating it. Hence the two undoubted merits of the commission: on the one hand it allowed thousands of ordinary people to express their often very painful experiences, bringing catharsis for many, and on the other hand it publicized many of the horrors of apartheid so that thereafter no one could possibly plead ignorance. While a seasoned anti-apartheid campaigner like Helen Suzman maintained that she had not learnt a single thing from the TRC which she did not already know, there were many sheltered and parochial white folk for whom the hearings were a painful revelation. For the millions who had suffered under apartheid it was also a therapeutic vindication, a sign that these evils had now been recognized by all South Africa and denounced for ever. The TRC had many weaknesses but it is impossible to weigh, let alone disregard, these diffuse merits.

FOUR KINDS OF TRUTH AND THE PROBLEM OF BIAS

The TRC worked on the questionable theory that reconciliation could only be achieved by everybody telling and facing the complete truth. Van Zyl Slabbert's point that a quick visit to the divorce courts would soon heal one of such illusions was never faced. In any case the TRC was too much of a rush job. It did not bother looking at many important events and at the end no one could claim that the complete truth had been told. More worrying still was the fact that the TRC was heavily influenced by Mr Justice Albie Sachs, who expounded the notion that there were four different kinds of truth. First, there was factual and verifiable truth, that is, the only sort the law courts dealt with. Secondly, there was 'personal or narrative truth'. Everybody had his or her own truth and listening to this led to 'the creation of a narrative truth' that 'captured the widest possible record of people's perceptions, stories, myths and experiences'. Thirdly, there was 'dialogue or social truth', 'the truth of experience that is established through interaction, discussion and debate'. Finally there was 'healing truth', which was 'the kind of truth that places facts and what they mean within the context of human relationships, both among citizens and between the state and its citizens'.[3] Ignoring the fact that the politest description of truths 2–4 was hearsay, the TRC enthusiastically embraced this transparent nonsense.[4]

The TRC's interim five-volume Report was effectively its final report, despite the fact that only 8 per cent of amnesty applicants had been heard when it was written. It contained just enough material critical of the ANC for Mbeki and the hardliners to object to it but thanks to Mandela's enthusiastic support it was accepted by Parliament. The commission essentially ignored its obligation to prepare a corrected final report: in effect the interim Report was just reissued. This was, perhaps, just as well, for the TRC received a very good press both domestically and internationally and the sheer size of the Report (and its lack of an index) successfully defeated most readers. Had a final Report been properly compiled it would have had to take account of any mistakes which had come to light in the earlier Report and this would have been a very embarrassing business indeed, as Anthea Jeffery showed in her concise but deadly work, *The Truth about the Truth Commission.*

The trouble started with the fact that the TRC was supposed to be impartial but was not. There was a large pro-ANC majority among the seventeen commissioners with just two old-order representatives and none representing either the IFP or the DP. True, Boraine had once been a DP MP but his name evoked a response of hilarious cynicism in DP circles. The story told in such circles was of how, when Van Zyl Slabbert had suddenly resigned both from Parliament and the DP leadership in 1986, Boraine had spent some days canvassing his own chances of succeeding Slabbert as leader. Only when it became clear that this could not succeed did he also resign 'on principle'. Many Methodists had had a somewhat similar shock when Boraine had earlier abandoned the Church's presidency to which he was appointed in 1970, first in order to join the Anglo-American Corporation (1972) and then to become an MP (1974). This series of radical changes had left many wondering where Boraine really stood. About Tutu there was no mystery: he was close to Mandela, and his wife, Leah, had canvassed for the ANC in the 1994 elections.

This impression of bias was speedily confirmed by the TRC's actual behaviour. When the TRC faced a witness it did not like, such as Brigadier 'Oupa' Gqoza or F. W. De Klerk, commissioners found it impossible to disguise their feelings. Even Tutu was forced to intervene, in Gqoza's case, to warn commissioners that to say what they did in a public hearing was undermining any claim to even-handedness. In De Klerk's case he was treated so rudely that Tutu and Boraine were forced to apologize publicly. But it was no good. On each subsequent occasion commissioners would betray their feelings so publicly that before long the TRC had lost the confidence of non-ANC voters, who, polls showed, saw them as hopelessly biased.

All told, the TRC received some 21,300 victim statements detailing almost 38,000 gross violations of human rights. However, only the 10 per cent or so who appeared in person gave their evidence under oath, so that, in Dr Jeffery's words, the other 90 per cent 'had an evidentiary status lower than an affidavit'.[5] Moreover, in order not to upset victims, some of whom were clearly traumatized, there was little or no cross-questioning. On top of that, many of the statements dealt with events that had happened to others, not to the victim him- or herself, so that they were really just untested hearsay. Dr Jeffery gives some of the results – one woman insisting that after she had seen police open fire on protesters she had counted 175 graves when a judicial commission of inquiry had given the figure of two deaths. The TRC itself gave the figure of two, or sometimes (inexplicably) three, deaths in this encounter.[6] In another instance of a police shooting in 1985 a judicial inquiry had given a figure of twenty deaths. Victims attested that thirty-four people had been killed and the TRC itself gave the number as twenty or (inexplicably, at another point) forty-three deaths.[7]

Thus the TRC itself implicitly accepted that victim statements might be wide of the mark but so sloppy was its Report that it was often internally inconsistent on even such an important matter as the number of people killed. Moreover the TRC decided that it would be satisfied with 'a relatively low level of corroboration' of victim statements and in practice often failed to provide any corroboration at all. This made it impossible for the TRC to base its decisions on 'factual and objective evidence', as its founding statute required.

A further problem uncovered by Dr Jeffery was that the victims who came forward to give testimony were far from representative. The IFP, reasonably enough given the composition of the TRC and its research department, had concluded from the outset that the commission was hostile to it. Accordingly, in KwaZulu-Natal, where the fiercest conflict between the UDF/ANC and IFP had occurred, the TRC received many more statements from ANC victims of violence than from IFP victims – and then concluded that the IFP had killed three and a half times more people than the ANC had.[8] Worse, it emerged that the research department had determined which cases it wanted to cover and that victims were often deliberately sought out in terms of the researchers' own preconceptions.[9] This had grave results for the commission's impartiality and the markedly lesser coverage it gave to massacres in which the IFP was the victim.

Yet the TRC continued to argue as if the victims had all come forward spontaneously, justifying its own concentration on violations committed by the government's security forces rather than by the liberation movements by insisting that '90 per cent of statements had demonstrated the involvement of security forces in human rights violations'[10] – a considerably less impressive argument when one realizes that many statement-givers had been sought out precisely in order to focus on those violations. Although several submissions to the TRC had drawn attention to the horrific impact of attacks by the liberation movements on black policemen and town councillors, to the large-scale coercion accompanying any form of mass action, the hundreds of 'necklace' (burning tyre) executions and to the deaths in bomb attacks of hundreds more who failed to do as ordered by the liberation movements, the TRC paid only the most cursory attention to such phenomena. Moreover, the TRC appeared to show open partiality for the ANC – as, for example, when its amnesty committee granted collective amnesty to thirty-seven ANC leaders even though they had not made full disclosure of their violations, despite the commission's founding legislation requiring full disclosure and also specifically refusing the notion of 'collective amnesty'.

The TRC research department established national and regional chronologies of events in which violations had occurred and then devoted its resources to researching these. There were, Jeffery points out, some remarkable omissions, including:

the killing in 1987 of workers who refused to take part in strikes called by Cosatu, including the necklacing of five men during a strike;
the killing of around 100 people as part of the coercive measures to enforce an anti-VAT stay-away called by the ANC in 1991;
the KwaShange massacre in which thirteen IFP Youth Brigade members were killed near Pietermaritzburg in 1987;
the massacre of thirteen IFP supporters near Hammarsdale in March 1990;
the execution of an IFP leader and his entire family at Patheni in August 1992;
the massacre of eight IFP supporters at Patheni in 1993;
the hand grenade attack on the home of an IFP leader in Umlazi in August 1986, in which his wife was killed and his three children injured;
the massacre of twenty-three IFP supporters at Crossroads and Zonk-izizwe in 1992.

These omissions all reinforced the picture of partisanship. Even more remarkably, the TRC made no mention of several key events which were part of the historical record and which resulted in many deaths and human rights violations. Chief among these was the ANC's adoption of the 'people's war' doctrine in 1983, which involved targeted assassinations and the use of lethal coercion to achieve results. The ANC had also made numerous calls for the use of violence (including murder) against 'collaborators' such as black municipal councillors, policemen, political opponents and anyone suspected of being an informer. And in May 1992 it had adopted the 'Leipzig Option' involving the attempted violent destabilization of the KwaZulu, Bophuthatswana and Ciskei homelands. The problem was that the ANC felt complete self-righteousness about its use of violence, an attitude which, despite their formal commitment to impartiality, was shared by many within the TRC.

The NP, which had thrashed out the terms of the TRC, insisting that it really should be impartial, made lengthy submissions to it, as did the security forces. *Inter alia*, they pointed out that within eighteen months of the outbreak of revolutionary violence in September 1984 the 'people's war' strategy had resulted in the destruction of 3,000 houses and more than 1,200 schools, the widespread disruption of black education and the deaths of 573 people, 295 of them by necklacing. The NP also pointed out that its decision to abandon apartheid and open the way for democracy had been greeted by unprecedented black-on-black violence as the ANC fought the IFP for supremacy both in KwaZulu-Natal and on the Reef. The NP further pointed out that various ANC members – not just Winnie Mandela but Chris Hani and Ronnie Kasrils – had cheered on or at least excused the use of the barbaric 'necklacing' of opponents. They also noted the role of the 'people's courts' in the townships, which had dispensed a very rough form of justice, often leading to summary executions by necklacing. Moreover, the ANC's Radio Freedom called for the elimination of 'anybody who mobilized the Zulu-speaking people',[11] following which more than 400 IFP office-bearers were killed, as were thousands of other IFP supporters. All this was essentially ignored by the TRC, pushed onto the UDF (exonerating the ANC), or dismissed as the 'unintended consequences' of UDF action.

The NP also argued that the government, faced with the onset of revolutionary violence, had had to maintain order and that, particularly during De Klerk's presidency, it had tried hard to avoid abuses on behalf of the security forces, though such abuses had undoubtedly occurred. This the TRC simply disregarded, not surprisingly given that many of its members shared the classic struggle perspective that there could be no moral equality between those fighting against apartheid and those fighting to preserve it. But the point was that apartheid had ended because De Klerk had abolished it, well before the ANC came to power, and the new dispensation had been reached by mutual agreement. The whole point of Mandela raising De Klerk's hand in triumph at the conclusion of negotiations was that there had been a national consensus on reaching a democratic settlement, and thus no more victors and vanquished. It was in this context that the TRC had been founded and its job was not to take sides but to examine objectively the history of killings and gross human rights violations. The TRC was thus simply not at liberty to dispense with the NP's (or any other party's) point of view. As Jeffery puts it, the TRC 'was mandated to take the NP's viewpoint into full account. Instead the commission failed even to record it, let alone to discuss it and give reasons for rejecting it.'[12]

ABOVE THE LAW AND LEGAL PRINCIPLE

The TRC's mandate obliged it to make its findings 'in accordance with established legal principles'. The commission was unhappy about this. For a start, it meant that it had to take account of all relevant evidence (impossible when its Report was written with 92 per cent of amnesty applications still to be heard) and also to verify that evidence, something clearly in conflict with its decision to avoid cross-examination of witnesses and to opt for only 'low-level corroboration' of witness statements. These principles also meant that the commission had to operate in an open and transparent manner, in practice clearly contradicted by its holding of a number of closed sessions. The TRC was never willing to reveal what had happened in these secret sessions or allow any public scrutiny of them. But the problem was a far wider one. Most of the commissioners were either political activists or political clerics. They were simply not used to behaving or thinking like judges. Thus one commissioner, Dumisa Ntsebeza, stated at an early stage – before he had seen much of the relevant evidence – that 'nine out of ten cases' of violence had been committed by the apartheid state, while Alex Boraine similarly stated that 'the overwhelming majority of misdeeds had been committed by the security forces of the previous government'.[13] Given the fact that by far the majority of political killings occurred in the struggles between the UDF and ANC on the one side and its various black rivals – IFP, PAC and Azapo – on the other, these statements were extremely questionable. But the real point was that judges should not prejudge matters coming before them, let alone openly declare their prejudgements.

At an early stage the Chief Justice ruled that the commission must observe the legal principle of *audi alteram partem* (hear the other side). This upset the commission, which argued that if alleged perpetrators of human rights abuses were allowed to testify alongside their accusers this would make the TRC seem 'too perpetrator-friendly'[14] and make the whole TRC process 'too legalistic and formal'. Perpetrators might even demand the right to cross-examine their accusers, increasing the trauma they had already suffered.[15] The commission's concern that victims should not have to come face to face with those who had (for example) tortured them sounds reasonable until one realizes that the TRC was thus deciding in advance that all accusers definitely were victims, an obviously untenable position. Moreover, the accusers quite routinely made allegations of murder, torture or other equally serious crimes, so the notion that the accused should be deprived of any right of reply or any chance to rebut these accusations was equally untenable. The commission itself behaved poorly when tested on this score. It named F. W. De Klerk as a perpetrator of gross human rights violations. When he objected, they ignored him. So he applied for a court order compelling them to take into proper consideration his own side of the story. In the end the commission backed down entirely, removing its finding against him from its Report. Had it followed legal principles, it would hardly have needed to undergo such humiliation. But how many other of its findings would have stood up against a determined legal challenge? In some cases the commission was cavalier with the rights of the accused to a degree which would have astounded any court. Some 200 such accused were supposed to submit their objections to findings against them – on the very day when the finalized text of the Report was presented to the commissioners.[16]

Finally, the TRC departed radically from legal principles in the way it reached and presented its conclusions. In any court a judge has to give a reasoned account of how he reached a decision, weighing up the competing evidence, showing which parts of it can be corroborated, explaining why some evidence must be given more weight, why only some evidence is to be regarded as substantiated, and then to provide a final rationale for reaching his final conclusion. The TRC did not do this. Often it merely mentioned allegations by unnamed accusers, without even explaining whether these were amnesty applicants or victims, and then reached a summary conclusion. In many cases the commission had simply decided that the accusers were indeed victims and that what they said was true – often despite a lack of cross-examination or corroborating evidence. To be sure, the TRC made a point of saying that its standards were not those of criminal law – that is, of establishing proof 'beyond reasonable doubt' – but only those of civil litigation, that is, of establishing a balance of probabilities. Even so, this hardly excused the commission for failing to explain why it came down on one side rather than the other. This was a remarkable failing given that the commission was using these methods in order to find individuals accountable for major crimes, including murder.

These various handicaps made the TRC a highly fallible body, a situation worsened by the fact that it was supposedly examining violations across a forty-four-year period. Moreover, the commission had an exceptionally good opinion of itself. There was always a danger in setting up such a tribunal and staffing it with people used to making moral and political rather than legal judgements, and giving them the power of amnesty: an operation performed on a confessional model, so that only sinners willing to make a clean breast of their sins could obtain a plenary indulgence, a full pardon. Moreover, many commissioners were ministers of religion, used to laying down the moral law to congregations who seldom argued back.

Thus many commissioners individually and the TRC corporately tended to act and speak as if they occupied not just the moral high ground but some sort of moral Everest. Archbishop Tutu, for example, acted as if he were the nation's confessor, repeatedly appealing to all whites to apologize for apartheid, revealing, remarkably, that he believed in the doctrine of collective guilt. The objection to this was not just that numerous whites had opposed apartheid. Worse, the doctrine of collective guilt has been used to justify anti-Semitism (the Jews were collectively guilty of killing Christ, etc.) and other potentially genocidal creeds down the ages. It is strongly rejected, not only by jurists, but by all Christian theologians, a fact of which Archbishop Tutu seemed blithely unaware.

So great was this feeling of self-righteousness that the TRC clearly believed itself superior to ordinary courts of law. Indeed Tutu declared, 'The commission can claim, without fear of being contradicted, that it has contributed more to uncovering the truth about the past than all the court cases in the history of apartheid.'[17] The TRC also often criticized the criminal courts which had normally tried the sort of cases they were now examining. They took too much time and cost too much. They often required 'large teams of skilled and highly competent investigators' – bizarrely, the TRC thus turned its own relative lack of such staff into a virtue. Worst of all, the courts required too high a standard of proof – 'proof beyond a reasonable doubt' – thus leading to the acquittal of people like General Magnus Malan, the head of the army, the SADF and Minister of Defence. For, to the ANC's fury, Malan, along with eleven other senior SADF officers, had been tried in 1996 on two charges, both relating to his alleged involvement in illegal IFP activities, and found not guilty. This combined the ANC's two greatest hate objects, the IFP and Magnus Malan. Malan symbolized all that the ANC had been fighting against throughout the struggle, and for many ANC activists he was the very personification of evil. To find him not guilty was thus an outrage; to find both him and the IFP not guilty was beyond an outrage; it was a provocation.[18] The TRC felt much the same.

FINDING AGAINST THE IFP: AN UNEQUAL ADJUDICATION

No part of the liberation struggle in South Africa was more intensely ideologized and contested than the struggle between the IFP and, first, the UDF and then its ANC successor. This war was essentially fought in two places, in the great townships and hostels of Gauteng, where the IFP had considerable support, and in KwaZulu-Natal, where it was the power in possession. It had installed itself as the single party of the KwaZulu homeland with IFP candidates usually elected unopposed because no one cared to face the wrath that would follow upon attempts at real political competition. In the 1980s the UDF charged into this world, bussing in young Gauteng activists to start school boycotts, using straightforward coercion when necessary. From then on the battle was waged, with the UDF and ANC picking up most support in urban areas (where chiefly power was largely absent) and the IFP remaining dominant in rural areas, where the traditional chieftaincy was an integral part of the movement. The UDF and ANC, following the Vietnamese model, targeted many of the IFP chiefs and headmen for assassination, while the IFP fought back with vigour.

I was in KwaZulu-Natal for a good part of the 1980s and 1990s, saw a great deal of this struggle at close quarters and wrote about it. There was a huge propaganda attempt by the ANC – successful with many journalists – to depict the struggle as one between IFP aggressors and UDF/ANC victims. This was ridiculous. For a start the IFP was the power in possession and it was the UDF and ANC who had to take the initiative if that was to change, which often meant they initiated violence. Once battle was joined both sides gave as good as they got, or tried to. In KwaZulu-Natal, at least, the struggle had the nature of a Zulu civil war so both sides were bonny fighters.

The big difference was that the ANC had the support not only of many 'progressive' journalists but of ANC-aligned NGOs, human rights organizations and 'violence monitors', who faithfully took the party line. Since the ANC anyway had the support of the better-educated urban blacks, the result was that the ANC version of events was thoroughly articulated both nationally and internationally. The IFP's supporters tended to be the least educated and had no such backing chorus of NGOs and would-be opinion leaders, something about which they were angrily but silently conscious. Anyone who viewed the struggle as a fifty-fifty matter and tried, at least, to maintain some sort of professional objectivity came under fierce pressure to abandon such reactionary positions. The key point for many was that Buthelezi was the leader of the KwaZulu bantustan and was thus seen as an apartheid creation. This was unfair: Buthelezi had at every stage asked for and received the ANC's agreement for him to take power in KwaZulu. The IFP had in effect merely been an internal ANC, using its colours and anthem. And Buthelezi had taken the ANC line in refusing independence for KwaZulu, an act which did much to wreck apartheid.

Because the propaganda battle was so overwhelmingly one-sided, the 'progressive' side often became convinced by its own propaganda.

Buthelezi and the IFP, for example, were viewed as mere apartheid puppets who would collapse once white power was not there to support them. This myopic view simply refused to take into account how deeply the IFP was embedded within Zulu culture, of which it was indeed an expression, and ignored the fact that the *amakhosi* (chiefs) were the key base of both IFP and rural Zulu society. The result was seen in 1994 and 1999 – long after the fall of white power – when the IFP defeated the ANC in both provincial and national elections in KwaZulu-Natal. In the end IFP predominance there was to be ended (in 2004) only by classic pork-barrel politics and some fairly sharp electoral practice.

Another key 'progressive' belief was that the IFP was responsible for most of the violence and was, with the help of the security forces, operating hit squads against the ANC. This was not so much wrong as bizarrely one-sided, for MK was concurrently mounting the biggest hit squad operation in South Africa's history against IFP office-holders and cadres. A key part of this accusation was that in 1986 Magnus Malan's SADF had provided a number of IFP cadres with training in the Caprivi strip as hit squad operatives. Substantial documentation was submitted to Mr Justice Jan Hugo at Malan's trial in 1996, alleging that Malan had illegally helped train such men as assassins, but Hugo dismissed the evidence as flimsy, found that the documents were capable of an innocent interpretation and found Malan not guilty on the charge.

The TRC, on the other hand, found that 'the SADF conspired with Inkatha to provide it with a covert, offensive paramilitary unity (hit squad) to be deployed illegally'. In order to justify this complete reversal of the court's verdict the TRC made a number of criticisms of the trial – none of which, on examination, stand up – and asserted that Hugo had found fault with the prosecution case for its failure to call military witnesses whose expertise could have been decisive. In fact Hugo made no such assertion. The TRC, indeed, offered no valid reasons for disregarding Hugo's thorough examination of the Caprivi allegations (which took up 55 pages of his judgment). The commission's finding has every appearance of blind prejudice.[19]

Malan and his nineteen co-defendants were also accused of responsibility for the massacre of thirteen people in KwaMakhutha in January 1987, the idea being that Caprivi hit squad trainees had attacked the house belonging to Willie Ntuli and killed all those inside, including four children, and that Malan and the SADF had thus aided IFP assassins to murder their opponents.[20] This was a strange accusation for anyone who knew the KwaZulu-Natal South Coast, for KwaMakutha was an IFP stronghold. The mayor was IFP; one of Buthelezi's praise-singers lived there; and Willie Ntuli was an IFP member, as were several others of those killed. Moreover, there had been earlier attacks that month on IFP leaders and members in KwaMakutha (killing one person) and the attackers had used AK-47s – MK's weapon of choice; Inkatha tended to use different weaponry. When news of the KwaMakutha killings first surfaced, the assumption of all those who knew the terrain was that this was a textbook MK assault on an IFP stronghold, taking out key cadres and headmen in the approved manner. So embarrassingly obvious was this conclusion that there was considerable local derision when the *Weekly Mail* suggested, somewhat hopefully, that perhaps the attackers had wanted to kill the Ntulis' 21-year-old son, Victor, a UDF activist. This was a very long shot. Not only were UDF activists thin on the ground in the village but Victor had not been home for many weeks – ever since the rough stuff began.

Only ANC zealots could believe that the KwaMakutha attacks had been mounted by the IFP – and now, believing their own propaganda, they attempted to pin this on Malan. It was odd. Malan was a tough guy whose era included many cruel and bloodstained events. There must, surely, have been other incidents in his career which offered the prosecution a better chance than trying to pin KwaMakutha on him. Judge Hugo had thrown the whole thing out. It hardly helped that the main witness for the prosecution was, he said, unreliable and a liar whose evidence was 'contradictory, improbable and absurd', or that the prosecution had coached witnesses and even inserted whole portions of one witness's statement into another by computer cut-and-paste, or that it had 'inveigled' one witness to give evidence designed to mislead the court, 'probably deliberately so'.

The TRC ignored the whole trial and found that IFP Caprivi trainees had launched an attack on 'the home of UDF leader Mr Bheki Ntuli' (*sic*), the implication being that Malan's SADF had trained the attackers and was thus complicit. The TRC made no reference to all the weaknesses Hugo had found in the prosecution case and gave no explanation for its remarkable finding, which was clearly a matter of pure ideological prejudice. It was the same when the TRC examined the assassination of the pro-ANC Chief Maphumulo, gunned down in the driveway of his home in 1992. A judicial inquest heard allegations that this was the work of a hit squad but Mr Justice N. S. Page found that these allegations were fabricated and untrue. The chief had had many enemies and it was impossible to say who had killed him. The TRC simply asserted that Maphumulo had been the victim of 'a planned hit-squad operation', ignoring Judge Page's findings.[21] Again, no reasons were provided: it was simply the assertion of ideological true believers.

REVERSING THE VERDICTS OF THE COURTS AND COMMISSIONS

Armed with a righteousness confident enough to reverse even such rulings, the commission then began to reverse the verdicts of many courts and commissions of inquiry, even though these had normally spent far more time and deployed far more expertise than the TRC had in the examination of their individual cases. Thus, for example, the Boipatong massacre of 1992 in which forty-five people, many of them ANC supporters, had been killed. The ANC's immediate accusation that the NP and the police were implicated in the killings was not upheld by the Goldstone Commission which investigated it, nor by the independent British police experts sent out to give their own report. All these authorities found that there was no evidence at all of either NP or police involvement. There was no doubt on any side that the IFP residents from the nearby KwaMadala hostel played a leading role in the massacre – this after a protracted period in which the hostel-dwellers had found themselves under attack from their political opponents in Boipatong. Despite this the TRC found that 'the police colluded with the attackers', that 'white men with blackened faces participated in the attack', and that the police who 'were biased in favour of the IFP' thus shared responsibility for the massacre.

This was a remarkable finding, especially since the police successfully prosecuted seventeen of the IFP residents for murder. According to Jan-Ake Kjellberg, the Swedish policeman serving with the TRC, the commission had conducted no real investigation of its own, nor had it found any new testimony or any new witnesses.[22] What it had done was simply to lift its findings almost verbatim from an ANC-aligned NGO which had rushed to judgement on the matter long before Goldstone or the British investigators had completed any of their exhaustive work on the case. The guilt of the police and the De Klerk government had become an article of faith for ANC activists and the TRC merely recycled this highly partisan rush to judgement. The ANC had used Boipatong as its reason to launch 'rolling mass action' and had frequently (though erroneously) asserted that constitutional negotiations had broken down as a result of the massacre. (In fact the ANC had already broken off negotiations shortly before that.) To have concluded that there was no police or government involvement would have amounted to saying that the entire ANC posture in the wake of Boipatong had been, at best, mistaken. The TRC had no appetite for such a clash with the ANC. Yet the TRC was wrong, as its own amnesty committee later acknowledged when the offending KwaMadala residents came before it. Repeatedly questioned as to whether there had been any involvement by police, whites or the government, the residents stolidly replied that they alone had been involved.

The TRC made an equally remarkable finding over the Trust Feed massacre of 1988 in which the police captain, Brian Mitchell, had been found guilty by a criminal court on eleven counts of murder. Mitchell, sentenced to death, commuted to thirty years in jail, applied for amnesty and although there were many problems with his testimony and there was no denying that he had ordered his special constables to attack the house where the eleven victims (all IFP supporters) were killed, he was nonetheless given amnesty. Even more remarkable was the case of Mitchell's subordinate, Sergeant Neville Rose, who had escaped any blame by the criminal court, which found the evidence against him unreliable. Despite the fact that the TRC had no new evidence, it declared Rose guilty of being an accessory to murder, without explaining how it reached this conclusion or how it justified its rejection of the criminal court's finding.

Sometimes the TRC's reversals of previous judicial findings seemed quite wilful and careless. The Sebokeng shootings of March 1990, for example, had been the subject of an earlier commission of inquiry under Judge Goldstone. He found that the crowd of 50,000 protesters had been badly marshalled and led, that it had failed to communicate its plans to the police and was in part responsible for the confused confrontation in which the police blocked the crowd's path. In a chain reaction begun by a nervous constable, some sixty shots were fired, killing 5 people, with 161 injured. Although Goldstone strongly criticized the police, including their commander, Captain du Plooy, he found du Plooy not guilty of any criminal conduct. The problem, rather, lay in the undisciplined behaviour of individual policemen, nine of whom were later charged, six of them with murder.

The TRC made no mention of Goldstone's critical remarks about the protesters but found du Plooy 'directly responsible for the deaths and injuries that occurred' – which it put at 13 dead and 400 injured, though elsewhere in its Report it says 17 were killed and later 'at least 13', and later still that there were 8 dead and more than 300 injured. The Report also said that 'no action was taken' against the police, thus contradicting its acknowledgement elsewhere in the Report of the nine policemen sent for trial. Once again, the TRC gave no reasons for departing from Goldstone's much more thorough verdict and mentioned no evidence which led it so dramatically to reverse his finding about du Plooy. The Report's repeated self-contradictions suggest gross carelessness about a matter of life and death.

Later in the same year there was further violence at Sebokeng, this time the subject of a judicial inquest by Judge E. H. Stafford who found that IFP supporters, who had been forcibly evicted from their hostel by ANC supporters, then turned on the latter, killing 38 of them. The SADF were ordered in to prevent further violence but once again a nervous soldier fired off a shot which was followed by 160 more. Stafford found that no order to fire was given but that the SADF's undisciplined behaviour had been inexcusable. He found, however, that press reports that the SADF had killed 11 people were false: in fact they had killed four people.

The TRC downplayed the extent to which the IFP supporters had been provoked by their opponents' earlier behaviour, and asserted that the IFP attack had killed 23 and the SADF 15. No reasons or new evidence were cited for this reversal of Stafford's findings. The TRC had simply divided the initial figure of 38 casualties into components of 23 and 15, omitting the further 4 (not 15) deaths caused by the SADF.

Similar hostilities between IFP hostel-dwellers and ANC township residents at Phola Park in Tokoza led to a massacre in September 1991, again investigated by the Goldstone Commission. Goldstone found that a group of hostel-dwellers proceeding towards the local stadium had come under fire by three AK-47 wielding gunmen, who killed 16 and injured 13. Almost simultaneously another group of hostel-dwellers near the stadium came under attack by a group of men wielding guns, axes and other weapons, killing another two hostel-dwellers. The police quickly brought the area under control, preventing any retaliatory attacks. Goldstone could not identify any of the attackers though he chanced upon one Mncugi Ceba, who was both a Phola Park leader and a police informer. Goldstone said that while using informers like Ceba hardly created trust in the police, 'no offence on the part of the police was proved'.

The TRC told a very different story. It said 23 (not 18) people had been killed in the initial attack, for which it exclusively blamed the three men with AK-47s, whereas it was clearly a co-ordinated attack by two groups. It then claimed that 42 more were killed and at least 50 injured in a wave of retaliatory violence, whereas Goldstone had found none. The TRC blamed Mncugi Çeba (whose name it misspelt) and thus indirectly the police for the massacre. Again it gave no explanation for these radical rejections of Goldstone's findings. In places the Report deliberately distorts Goldstone's findings to suit its own version.

The TRC's examination of the Shell House shootings of 1994 posed the question of how it would deal with an incident where the IFP had been the victims. The shootings took place during an IFP march through Johannesburg on 28 March, demanding recognition of the sovereignty of the Zulu king over KwaZulu-Natal. Ten people (eight of them Zulu demonstrators) were gunned down at Library Gardens, following which another eight Zulu marchers were shot dead by ANC marksmen operating from the top of ANC headquarters at Shell House. There was no fighting, no ANC casualties, just a one-sided massacre.

The subsequent judicial inquiry under Mr Justice Robert Nugent heard that the demonstrators had launched attacks on Shell House and that the ANC guards had acted defensively to save their own and their leaders' lives. Nugent rejected this completely, saying that the evidence offered to support this allegation had been 'fabricated after the event'. He found that there had been no justification at all for the shooting, that no warning had been given and that the guards had continued firing into the crowd even after it had turned and run.

The TRC found that around 50 people had been killed and more than 300 injured during the events, caused by the demonstrators launching a series of offensives against Shell House. The commission gave no reasons for ignoring the judicial inquest or overturning its findings. The victims were thus found responsible for their own massacre, a truly spectacular conclusion.

Finally, hundreds of people had been killed (often by being thrown off moving trains) and many more injured in the Gauteng train violence of 1990–93. The Goldstone Commission examined some 100 such attacks in the 1991–2 period and, while it referred to the concurrent ANC–IFP violence, the commission could see no link between the violence and either the ANC or IFP or that it had served any political purpose. The ANC tried to blame the police but the commission explicitly repudiated this. Finally, since a 'third force' was alleged to be behind the violence, Goldstone had invited anyone with evidence to that effect to come forward. No one had stepped forward, so no finding could be made on that score. The TRC, on the other hand, found that the IFP were 'centrally involved' in the train violence which had in the end killed 572 people, concerting their activities with the security forces in an effort to prevent the ANC coming to power. To reach this remarkable conclusion the TRC relied on evidence (covering only five out of 600 incidents) given to Goldstone which his commission had disregarded as uncorroborated and unreliable. The TRC simply forgot that it had earlier admitted that the train victims came from all political persuasions and that the attacks had no clear political objective.[23]

THE TRC REPORT

How could the TRC adopt such a hugely deficient Report – and fail to explain why the greatest upsurge of violence came in 1990–94, after the abolition of apartheid? The Report argued that apartheid and racism were at the root of all the violence, but manifestly rivalry between black political groups (one of which, the UDF, was led by the TRC chairman, Archbishop Tutu) had been a greater cause of fatalities. The Report was written by the TRC's research department – but was there no process of fact-checking, comparison with earlier findings or simple evaluation? The Report was also often internally inconsistent to a degree which invalidated even the highly biased findings it reached. These were failings which any ordinary court would have turned up. The Report is, as a result, unusable as evidence. Its bias and incompetence are so pervasive as to undermine confidence in the work as a whole.

The Report was, in the first instance, the responsibility of Charles Villa-Vicencio, a responsibility which he obviously failed to discharge. For an academic used to examining theses for errors and internal consistencies it was an extraordinary failing. But what of the other commissioners? They had to sign off on the Report and accept public responsibility for it. Did they not read it? Did none of them realize how badly flawed it was? Perhaps their minds were not on it. The TRC was big international news and its leading figures were celebrities, continually travelling abroad to star at international conferences. They had a large interest in boosting the 'truth and reconciliation process', recommending it for all manner of other countries. The last thing they wanted to hear was that the TRC process was deeply flawed and its Report riddled with errors and prejudice. In effect the commissioners seem to have gone for the easy applause of an international community which badly wanted to believe in the validity of the TRC process. They did this instead of doing their jobs and at the cost of a finished product which is historically indefensible.

All this was revealed by Anthea Jeffery. Her work was meticulous and no one tried to argue with any of her criticisms of the TRC. Other authors who wrote about the TRC, often wanting to draw large philosophical conclusions about it, were simply unable to cope with her work. Richard Wilson wrote, 'The TRC was not simply a rubber stamp on an ANC version of the past as Jeffery and others have claimed.'[24] Such a dismissal allows Wilson to ignore the larger implications of Jeffery's work, but Jeffery made no such claim. Similarly, James Gibson gives Jeffery's work less than a sentence in a book of 482 pages.[25] Others who wrote about the TRC simply omitted all reference to her.

Yet Jeffery's work was widely sold and read. Boraine's own account makes no mention of Jeffery at all, but he is extremely careful to avoid any mention of the various examples she has given of the TRC's bias and errors.[26] The same approach is adopted by Terry Bell[27] and also by John Allen.[28] Jeffery's work is clearly the elephant in the room: once its points are admitted for debate a great deal of the philosophizing about the TRC simply falls away. So no one wanted to admit those points or even argue against them. This merely shows how much writing about South Africa is still heavily ideological, with the TRC, in particular, a holy cow.

The opinion polls left the TRC in no doubt from an early stage that it was widely regarded as biased, especially by whites – a serious matter for the TRC since it could hardly perform its healing role if it was seen merely as a tool of the ANC. This was undoubtedly why the TRC paid some attention to the atrocities committed in the ANC's camps in Angola and why it grilled Winnie Madikizela-Mandela at length (though, as we saw, this was at a juncture when this was useful to some ANC politicians, led by Thabo Mbeki). Nonetheless, such confrontations were important in allowing the TRC to make at least some claim to even-handedness – and its criticisms of atrocities in the ANC camps were enough to alienate Mbeki and the ANC hardliners. But before this a major drama had erupted within the TRC itself.

THE DRAMA OVER NTSEBEZA

In May 1997 the police captain John Lubbe, seconded to the TRC, informed the black activist lawyer and commissioner Dumisa Ntsebeza that he had found a file note suggesting that Ntsebeza had been involved in the Heidelberg Tavern massacre of 1993 when Apla[29] gunmen killed four and wounded five of the tavern's customers. Ntsebeza's white Audi had, he said, been seen ferrying the men to the tavern and its registration number noted. Ntsebeza dismissed the whole report as rubbish but placed the matter before Tutu and Boraine, who concurred that it was nonsense: after all, the file note was dated 1994 and no action had been taken. In July, however, the news became public, creating a sensation, particularly since Tutu was away in the United States, so Ntsebeza had become deputy chairman of the TRC. Boraine hurriedly announced that Ntsebeza had recused himself from the inquiry. Lubbe then located Bennett Sibaya, a gardener who claimed to have seen Ntsebeza and his car at the scene of the attack.

The inquiry continued into September when, to his horror, Ntsebeza heard there was discussion within the TRC that it would be best if he resigned in order to limit the damage to the commission. Yet Ntsebeza had not even been interviewed for the inquiry or his alibi checked, and his resignation would be taken as an admission of guilt, permanently damaging his career. All this was without due process of any kind: Ntsebeza was finding out in the roughest possible way how different

TRC justice was from the kind dispensed by the courts. He declared that resignation was out of the question. Lubbe then left the TRC, taking all the documentation about the case with him. (This was not unusual – TRC staffers frequently walked off with documents.[30]) Then it was suggested that the TRC's investigations unit (which Ntsebeza headed) be shut down, thus disposing of the inquiry. This too would leave Ntsebeza in limbo and he opposed it.

The TRC hearings on the Heidelberg massacre opened on 27 October. No one could figure out Bennett Sibaya, who was quite some gardener. He spoke a number of languages, including fluent Russian, knew the Marxist classics, had travelled widely, owned valuable property and was arranging to buy more. Yet before the TRC Sibaya acted as if he only knew isiXhosa, and had everything translated for him. He positively identified Ntsebeza. By this stage media fascination with the case had exercised considerable pressure on the TRC's reputation and staff. Tutu (who was in Lesotho) now rang Ntsebeza and suggested he take leave until the whole affair blew over. Indeed, Tutu had had a press release prepared to that effect. Ntsebeza was stunned. To 'take leave' at this juncture would be interpreted as a resignation *manqué* and he knew that he could never recover from that. In effect he was being thrown to the wolves simply for PR reasons. He protested that the other commissioners had not considered the matter. Tutu said the matter was just between the two of them (Boraine was in Denmark).

Ntsebeza's lawyer was horrified. What about innocent until proved guilty and what about due process? And why had no one spoken to him? Ntsebeza had the press release torn up, and Tutu announced he would fly back to convene an emergency TRC meeting. Things might have gone very badly for Ntsebeza – except that Bennett Sibaya suddenly recanted all his evidence, saying he could not, after all, identify Ntsebeza as the man at the scene of the crime. With that the case collapsed. Not just Ntsebeza's good name was saved but, quite likely, that of the TRC. For the commission to have forced out one of its senior black members in such a fashion would have led to enormous trouble – and it would not have looked good in court. Tutu and Boraine had known of the matter since May but had not communicated it to the other commissioners. Lubbe had been allowed to walk off with all the key documentation. Pressure had been repeatedly brought to bear on Ntsebeza to act in a way deeply damaging to his interests and due process had not been observed.[31]

EVERYONE MUST APOLOGIZE AND ALL SHALL HAVE PRIZES

Although the TRC's coverage of the human rights violations of 1960–94 was extremely patchy (it left the job less than half-finished), the basic methodology was quickly established. Perpetrators of abuses must apologize before the commission and make full disclosure of their crimes, in return for which they would (or might) receive amnesty, forgiveness and perhaps even a hug. This model did not meet with universal satisfaction. For example, Steve Biko had been beaten to death and the Biko family wanted ordinary justice as dispensed by the courts, with the perpetrators jailed. They were not interested in apologies. Or hugs.

There was also controversy over the fact that, to qualify for amnesty, violations had to be politically motivated. Some apartheid security police units had been so completely out of control that they had committed crimes of every kind, often for profit. Did they qualify? On the other hand, Chris Hani's assassins, Walus and Derby-Lewis, had clearly acted for political reasons and were thus suitable candidates for amnesty. This was highly inconvenient: the SACP would simply not tolerate their hero's killers walking free, so it was decided, on the basis of no evidence, that they had not made full disclosure.

The TRC thus arrogated to itself a sort of supreme moral high ground from which it, and it alone, might dole out or refuse forgiveness and amnesty to anyone it chose. This not only placed it above even the highest court in the land but seemed to put it almost on a par with St Peter at the pearly gates, deciding who was to go to heaven or hell. On top of that came Tutu's idiosyncratic showmanship – clowning, praying, sometimes weeping on camera – creating a telegenic mixture as compulsive as any soap opera.

The main problem was a shortage of hoodlums to confess their desperate deeds. For the minority who had already been convicted the TRC presented a fantastic second chance, and some tried that, with occasional success. For the majority of those who had killed and tortured to 'preserve white civilization', the idea of appearing on 'the Des and Alex Show' (as some irreverently termed it) to confess their sins and have their names written in the Good Book was not attractive, however. For a start, if you did not own up, chances were they would never find out. Secondly, you never knew what might happen: Tutu was mercurial and the TRC seemed able to make up its own rules as it went along. It was easier to be off in the Congo, Iraq or wherever else the dogs of war were gathering. But a surprising number quietly went to ground in South Africa. One would come across them running guest houses in remote beauty spots or becoming resourceful multi-tasking businessmen in small towns.

LOOKING FOR VILLAINS

With few attractive villains in sight the commission looked further afield. Its greatest coup lay in securing F. W. De Klerk's attendance. He was grilled for hours, not allowed any smoke breaks, and treated far more roughly than one might have imagined, given that he had abolished apartheid and democratically handed power over to the ANC. But many within the TRC had scores to settle, wanted to haul their old enemies before it, wanted to see them squirm – and apologize. This ritual of penitence was both a symbolic humiliation of their enemies and a reaffirmation of their own moral supremacy. There was a hunger – given voice by Tutu's repeated demand for whites to apologize – for the entire old order to go down on bended knee and acknowledge its crimes. So, despite the TRC having had to apologize to De Klerk for its rough behaviour, it longed to repeat the performance, this time with P. W. Botha or Chief Buthelezi in the dock. Realizing exactly what was in store for them, both men refused to attend.

Buthelezi had appeared before the commission early on, making a three-hour statement of his views and presenting a 750-page memorandum. He denounced the ANC, accused the TRC of bias and was particularly cutting about political clerics like Tutu, pointing out that they had never appeared at the graveside of any of the thousands of murdered IFP supporters or sought to comfort their widows and children. He abhorred violence, he said, but apologized for past hurts on behalf of his followers.[32] With that he was gone.

This was hardly satisfactory to the TRC. Many commissioners wanted to summon him, grill him and hold him and the IFP responsible for most of the violence in the fighting between the UDF/ANC and the IFP, and they also wanted to find him guilty of collaboration with 'third force' elements. But Buthelezi and the IFP were now in the government of national unity, the recipient of many overtures from Mandela and Mbeki; indeed, on eleven separate occasions Buthelezi was appointed Acting President while both Mandela and Mbeki were simultaneously abroad. Whatever the ANC might have said about Buthelezi once, it seemed to have swallowed it now. Moreover, after 1995 the joint peace-keeping efforts of Buthelezi and Jacob Zuma had seen the long Zulu civil war gradually peter out. Did the TRC really wish to disturb that delicate balance? In any case, how could Buthelezi be made to attend? He would ignore a subpoena and if, as a result, the authorities tried to put him in jail for contempt, anything might happen. Not only would the TRC's work in KwaZulu-Natal become impossible but, it was remembered, although both John Vorster and P. W. Botha had wanted to lock Buthelezi up they had never dared do it for fear of a violent Zulu reaction.

The TRC thought about it – and backed off. Instead, it settled for giving Buthelezi a bad press. It even held hearings in camera so that Walter Felgate, for many years Buthelezi's adviser and speech-writer, could denounce his old boss and accuse him of all manner of dastardly acts. The author Richard Wilson is, indeed, concerned that the TRC did not make more of Felgate's allegations.[33] Personally, I was sorry to see Walter pour such vitriol on his own life for decades past. I had known Walter since we were students together – I remember him riding round on powerful motorbikes with Fatima Meer, later Mandela's biographer, on the pillion. In the 1970s he was a busy go-between, moving between Buthelezi, Oliver Tambo and Steve Biko. He used to say he was ready to die for the IFP and demanded that I join it, a request I had to disappoint. When he finally betrayed Buthelezi he did so with great self-righteousness and stole a huge volume of Buthelezi's correspondence and papers. He brought these to me at the Helen Suzman Foundation, wanting me to store them and also to write them up. I had to disappoint these requests too. He had been well paid to work with Buthelezi and he was well paid by the ANC to defect. His TRC appearance was the last throw of the dice. With his usefulness to the ANC then over, it treated him with scant respect. Unlike Wilson, I suspect the TRC knew what it was doing: it allowed Felgate to blacken Buthelezi's name (his 'secret' session was immediately leaked to the press) but did not risk relying on what he said.

If the TRC was, in the last analysis, scared of Buthelezi, it was determined to summon P. W. Botha – *die Groot Krokodil* – before it. Botha did not need F. W. De Klerk's example in order to say no. He sat in retirement in Wilderness (a beautiful village near George, in the Western Cape), angrily dismissed the TRC as 'a circus' and laughed at it. Tutu tried to persuade him, in vain: Botha was courteous but adamant. So the TRC subpoenaed him. Botha ignored the subpoena, was convicted of contempt and given a suspended sentence. This was overturned on a technicality, leaving Botha as the clear victor. It had been a foolish fight to pick. In the end the TRC could not make an 82-year-old ex-President do what he did not want to do, nor could they put him in jail.

THE LONG MARCH THROUGH THE INSTITUTIONS

Frustrated over both Buthelezi and Botha, the commission, which had already held hearings on the political parties, conscription, youth and women, announced that it would now summon before it representatives of the legal world, business and labour, the Churches, the health sector, the prisons and the media to account for their behaviour under apartheid. This alarmed some of those concerned. They argued that the TRC had been set up to examine gross human rights violations, not to come after sections of civil society and demand apologies from them. The decision was certainly questionable given the huge gaps in the TRC's coverage of human rights violations, its primary business.

It also meant that the TRC set itself up as judge and confessor above every other legal and moral authority in the country, with even churchmen having to come and confess their sins before it. The judges, whose opinion of the TRC may well be imagined, adamantly refused to go before the commission, arguing that this would call judicial independence into question. Alex Boraine says he argued against subpoenaing individual judges to appear but that he now considers this to have been wrong and that judges should have been subpoenaed simply to show that there was no one in society who could not be called to account by the TRC.[34] He does not explain how the commission would have dealt with the delicate problem of jailing those judges who refused their subpoenas. In fact, the hearings into 'the legal community' consisted largely of testimony by ANC-aligned legal NGOs, denouncing the judges bell, book and candle.

The media had its reservations, but took its medicine. The TRC denounced the English-language press for appeasing apartheid, the Afrikaans press for supporting it and the media in general for racism. This was by no means fair, as there had been anti-apartheid editors and journalists of great distinction. Moreover, the whole of the press was now eagerly appeasing the Mbeki government and using racial criteria to make affirmative action appointments. That is, the behaviour of the press towards the apartheid and ANC governments was in many respects identical but no one thought this worthy of mention, let alone criticism.

Labour naturally took its chance to denounce business, with the ANC joining in and the TRC sympathizing but business was thoroughly taken aback by its summons. Boraine concluded that 'business leaders failed to admit that they had deliberately moderated their critique of the government's racial policies' – and was particularly hard on the mining industry because of

> its creation and support of the migrant labour system, which has been responsible for the breakdown of family life, the emergence of social ills such as alcoholism, prostitution and crime, and the stunting of the development of the workers . . . workers were regarded as replaceable labour units rather than human beings. The fact that nearly 70,000 miners died in accidents during the twentieth century and more than one million were seriously injured starkly reveals the lack of basic care, let alone compassion in that industry.[35]

What was missing was any admission that Boraine had worked in the mining industry himself.

The Anglo-American and De Beers empire was naturally in the front line, particularly since Bobby Godsell, the CEO of AngloGold, was also president of the Chamber of Mines. He and Nicky Oppenheimer would clearly have to attend and apologize for their companies' sins. This occasioned a lively debate within Anglo. Godsell was in a particularly odd position. As a devout young Methodist in Durban, Godsell had been greatly influenced by Boraine, then the president of the Methodist Church, and they had often debated how a good Christian should respond to living in an apartheid society. Godsell had been taken aback by Boraine's decision to give up the Church's presidency for a job at

Anglo in 1972 but Boraine had convinced him that being at Anglo actually gave one considerable power to do good – and encouraged Godsell to join Anglo himself. This was how Godsell had come to occupy his present position. There was thus a considerable irony in now being held to account for his corporate sins by the TRC, with Boraine a leading inquisitor.

Moreover, on being elected to Parliament in 1974, Boraine had reasoned with Anglo that it was in the public interest for people like himself to be in Parliament. Anglo agreed. The problem was, Boraine pointed out, that his parliamentary salary would be considerably lower than what he received as a senior Anglo executive: would the company care to top up his salary? Anglo generously agreed to do this, so that throughout his parliamentary career Boraine had received a handsome retainer from Anglo on top of his salary, a remarkable deal for someone who had only worked for the company for two years. This was now the subject of heated debate within Anglo. Some were in favour of publicizing these details in order to expose what they saw as Boraine's hypocrisy: how dare he stand in judgement on the company and force it to beg for (his) forgiveness? If he had earlier seen a job in Anglo as an opportunity to do good, how could he now round on the mining industry as the root of all evil? And if it was evil, how could he have taken its money for all those years?

Anglo is a sophisticated company, and in the end its corporate wisdom held that to expose Boraine would be seen as an attack on the TRC. Quite irrespective of the rights and wrongs of the matter, the resulting fallout might damage the company. So it was better to grit one's teeth, swallow hard and take what came. And thus it was.

There was, however, a memorable moment. Anglo and De Beers pointed out to the TRC that they had been by far the biggest philanthropists of all South African companies and they had contributed financially not only to the opposition Progressive Party and its heirs[36] but to all manner of anti-apartheid conferences, publications and individuals – including Steve Biko. In so doing they had frequently incurred the wrath of the apartheid government. The commissioners quoted back at them the accident rates in the mines, the rates of silicosis among ex-miners, the relatively low wages of miners over a long period and the company's general compliance with the apartheid labour system.

This sort of dialogue was batted back and forth for quite a while.

When Nicky Oppenheimer took the stand, appearing entirely relaxed, he easily admitted that the companies could have done more against apartheid. When pressed further he simply agreed with his inquisitors: 'Of course, in retrospect it's clear we should have done more. But there we are. Sometimes one only knows these things in hindsight. One always comes back to the gospels, John 8: 7. That says it all. John, chapter 8, verse 7.'

There was muttering among the commissioners. No one was sure quite what he was talking about. What did John 8: 7 say? Oppenheimer's reply was a high lob to the back of the court. 'Really, gentlemen, I thought it was you who were the men of the cloth, not me. It's where Christ is on the Mount of Olives and they bring forth the woman caught in adultery in order to stone her to death. Christ stops it, saying "Let him who is without sin cast the first stone".'[37]

AFTERMATH

Great claims were made for the TRC and some of its members made a career out of preaching the need for and lending their expertise to other TRCs all over the world. The TRC enjoyed a huge international media success. Its activities often provided good copy and wonderful sound bites and film clips. The effect was to play into the vast international pleasure and relief felt at the peaceful ending of apartheid. Now, as in a morality play, these good and godly men of the TRC had come forth to expose evil and to shrive South Africa. This they had done by their indefatigable commitment to bringing out the whole truth in all its painful reality – and in true mystical fashion this alone was enough to heal the rainbow nation. The title Boraine chose for his book, *A Country Unmasked*, echoes this view, as if the truth about apartheid was unknown until the TRC revealed it. The leading commissioners, especially Tutu, could spend the rest of their lives receiving honorary degrees and giving homilies about truth and reconciliation. Boraine set up the International Center for Transitional Justice in New York, handsomely funded by American foundations, and held a variety of US academic posts. Dumisa Ntsebeza became a judge and then chairman of the international company Barloworld.

Yet the TRC was deeply flawed. Its procedures were dubious, its

Report frequently told untruths, nor did it really dispose of South Africa's painful history, enabling everyone to go on, unscarred by the past. The philosophy behind it was clearly unsound. The relationships between truth, healing, reconciliation and achieving closure are simply a lot more complex and difficult than was allowed for. One must look at the experience of other countries who had to deal with the aftermath of such painful wounds in their societies: post-war Europe dealing with its collaborators and local fascists, the inconsistent and incomplete attempts to deal with Nazi and Japanese war criminals after the war, the Soviet Union dealing with de-Stalinization, and the post-1990 attempts in central and eastern Europe to come to terms with the damage wrought by Communist totalitarianism. In every case one finds angry commentators claiming that history is being falsified, that the guilty are escaping, that the victims have gone unavenged. One realizes that invariably these societies have not really put their painful histories behind them, that they will still have to deal with them, perhaps for generations to come. That is simply the nature of human history. It would be very convenient if quick fixes like the Nuremberg trials, the *épuration* in France or the TRC in South Africa really worked, but the fact is that they cannot and do not.

The TRC Report roundly criticized all whites for having supported apartheid – a 'crime against humanity'. As the commission faded away this was what was left hanging in the air. Indeed, Boraine saw the whole process as almost endless: 'the process will not be completed until all South Africans who benefited from apartheid confront the reality of the past, accept the uncomfortable truth of complicity, give practical expression to remorse, and commit themselves to a way of life which accepts and offers the dignity of humanness.'[38]

There were, of course, quite a few whites who did feel guilty, though when they were asked what particular abuses or violations they had committed they always said that they had committed none, that they felt collectively guilty about a past from which they had benefited but which they had always striven against. It was a strange sort of guilt, felt largely on behalf of others who had behaved differently from themselves.

But many whites felt little or no guilt. By 2009 any white aged 30 had been only 11 when apartheid was abolished in 1990. For such people, apartheid was something they had hardly known and had never voted for. Many of those old enough to remember had simply been apolitical, and still were. In addition there were many who said, 'I always voted against apartheid, I always treated blacks well, what more could I have done?' Nevertheless, the demand for a white apology was the TRC's insistent legacy.

In January 2001 a group led by Carl Niehaus, a former ANC MP, launched the 'Home for All' initiative which invited whites to sign a declaration acknowledging 'the white community's responsibility for apartheid', 'our debt to fellow black South Africans' and accepting that it was whites' 'failure to accept responsibility for apartheid [which] has inhibited reconciliation and transformation'. A Development and Reconciliation Fund was also to be established as part of the initiative, which clearly enjoyed the ANC's blessing. The initiative followed straight after the suggestion made by the Minister of Justice, Penuell Maduna, backed by Mbeki's lawyer, Mojanku Gumbi, that affluent whites and businesses should pay reparations for apartheid 'initially on a voluntary basis'.[39]

The initiative betrayed a considerable state of intellectual confusion. Religious leaders of every kind, including the Chief Rabbi, endorsed this latest variant of racial collective guilt as if unaware that this doctrine had been repudiated by all their churches and had been the scourge of Jews down the ages. Richard Goldstone signed the declaration and was also a trustee of the Development and Reconciliation Fund. Earlier, as chancellor of Wits University he had told a graduation ceremony that graduates must not expect the top jobs any more because, quite rightly, 'the sins of the fathers' would be counted against them. When it was pointed out that he was not only encouraging young, skilled whites to emigrate but endorsing the doctrine of collective guilt, he had hurriedly denied that he accepted that doctrine. Yet here again he was clearly accepting it. Disturbingly, several TRC commissioners, who had presumably thought a bit more deeply about the matter, also accepted the doctrine of collective racial guilt. Signatories included Alex Boraine and Mary Burton, Charles Villa-Vicencio, and prominent lawyers such as John Dugard, Kate O'Regan and Richard Rosenthal.

The Home for All initiative quickly ran into strong opposition. De Klerk would not sign, saying the declaration was simplistic and that he rejected the idea of loading collective guilt onto whites: all South Africans – not just whites – had to work for reconciliation.[40] DA spokesmen were equally dismissive. Joe Seremane said he could not accept that just one group was responsible for the country's history. 'I don't see the ANC coming forward with apologies for necklace murders. I also don't see any disclosures over the atrocities committed at their military bases,' he said.[41] The DA MP Dene Smuts simply replied that 'it would be inappropriate to participate in any whites only initiative'.[42] An opinion poll soon found 80 per cent of whites opposed to signing such a declaration,[43] after which the initiative effectively collapsed.

Mbeki himself did all he could to highlight real and imagined instances of white racism, frequently dreaming up instances of whites despising blacks as licentious, dirty and disease-ridden. His readiness to play the race card was naturally copied all the way down the social scale and had a socially poisonous effect. Mbeki's aim was clearly to consolidate a black racial bloc behind him and to keep whites on the defensive. Given that they were the best-educated group, serving in many leading positions, whites were still natural opinion-leaders so it was essential to keep them on the back foot, if possible excluding them from the debate altogether. This continuous attempt to inflame racial feelings was the very opposite of the reconciliation the TRC had theoretically aimed at.

The idea of collective white guilt was tenacious. Tutu would occasionally – and passionately – repeat his demand for a racial apology, and any black spokesman who cared to make such a demand was assured of considerable publicity. Thus in February 2008 Jody Kollapen, the chairperson of the official Human Rights Commission, declared that Mandela had gone too far in the direction of reconciliation, which had made whites complacent about their collective racial guilt. 'It's not too late,' he announced, 'for whites to say sorry for apartheid.' Really such an apology should have been offered 'at the appropriate time' but 'even if it didn't happen then, it is never too late'.[44] This time the resultant reaction was much less and only a few pious whites from the African Christian Democratic Party volunteered to apologize. None of the Home for All signatories showed any interest in apologizing this time. Indeed, a glance at their signatories list showed that since 2001 a number had found their 'home for all' somewhere else and quietly emigrated.

Whites had now generally understood the game they were in, a game in which blacks play the (by now already ritualized) 'victim', 'entitlement' and 'white guilt' cards at them and in which they respond in a number of equally ritualized ways. As Kollapen rightly said, 'it is never too late'; that is, there is no real ending to this game in sight. No matter what goes wrong (especially in government), it will be said to be due to apartheid or, as apartheid recedes over the distant horizon, it will be said to be due to the 'heritage of apartheid'. This move seeks to throw all blame – even for power cuts or the government's failure to deliver services – onto the whites. Whites will respond with arguments or perhaps a partial admission of guilt but then the next card will be played, and so on. In effect this is really a bargaining process, with the desired result being an endgame in which certain adjustments are made, extra resources are acquired from the whites and a new status quo reached with goodwill ('reconciliation') all round – until the next round of bargaining begins.

In this debate over 'white guilt' one can see similarities with the United States, despite the fact that South Africa's blacks are an 80 per cent majority and America's a 12 per cent minority. The black American intellectual Shelby Steele writes of how the concepts of 'black victimization' and 'white guilt' fit together: 'You must never ever concede that only black responsibility can truly lift blacks into parity with whites' because to do so would be to give up control over white guilt. In politics, blacks wear either the mask of the challenger or that of the bargainer. The purpose of these masks is to enable blacks to gain things from the white majority by 'manipulating their need for racial innocence'. Because whites are 'stigmatized with past racism, blacks have a monopoly over racial innocence and believe, as only the oppressed can, that this is their greatest power in America'.

In a passage which also has strong echoes in South Africa, Steele writes that 'the post-sixties black identity is essentially a totalitarian identity' – a tremendously debilitating force in black culture. 'This identity wants to take over a greater proportion of the self than other identities do . . . "it" wants you think as a black, not as yourself. Moreover, this is a policed consciousness . . .' Barack Obama has also written tellingly about this, recalling how 'most of us were tired about thinking about race all the time'. He remembers how a mixed-race girl on campus nearly cried when she said that black people were trying to make her choose sides, that it was black people who made everything about race. Obama found himself wondering if only 'white culture' could be non-racial, neutral and objective. 'Only white culture had individuals.'[45] This is the cul-de-sac into which racialized identity, collective victimhood and collective racial guilt leads.

The TRC's influence on South Africa's development was ambivalent. While it enabled society to claim that the past had been dealt with, it did so at the cost of a very flawed and inaccurate process. Racial reconciliation did not really happen, partly because Mbeki made its rejection a cornerstone of his policy but also because the TRC's whole model was wrong. Reconciliation, if it is achieved at all, grows slowly as a result of living together over time. The past, in its different versions, continued – inevitably – to haunt the present and future. The dialogue between the alternative, bargained realities of 'white guilt' and 'black victimization' was stale and unprofitable. The whites could, if they wanted, apologize, but the more they apologized, the more they got blamed.

THE ANC AND HEGEMONY

The ANC saw the TRC as merely the first step in a far larger change it wished to effect in the country's moral and cultural climate. During the struggle years the ANC had assumed that its 'seizure of state power' would be followed automatically by a transformation of the national culture in its own image. When in fact the white regime amicably handed over power through negotiation much of the old society – and the 'natural' cultural dominance of its mainly white educated class – remained intact. The ANC was accordingly much concerned with gaining 'hegemony' over society. It was helpful that the TRC had thrown whites onto the defensive but the ANC, in explicitly Gramscian fashion, wanted the whole society to view reality through an ANC lens.

The Italian communist theorist Antonio Gramsci believed that the bourgeoisie was able to rule not just because it had the state machine behind it but because the lower classes voluntarily assented to its rule. Italian peasants and workers willingly consented to bourgeois rule because they were under the sway of the cultural and intellectual hegemony of the Catholic Church, which in turn owed its power to the activities of legions of religious intellectuals: priests, bishops, theologians, Catholic writers, newspaper editors and so on. This intelligentsia spun a web of beliefs such that the poor interpreted reality through it and could conceive of no other way of thinking. Ultimately, this hegemonic culture served the interests of the ruling class, preaching that 'the poor will always be with us', that the poor 'should render unto Caesar what is Caesar's', and in general that the existing social and religious hierarchies should be respected. Acceptance of these beliefs meant that the ruling class ruled confidently and easily as a 'natural' fact, for they and the ruled shared a single set of axioms, paradigms and ideas.

This in turn led Gramsci to consider the crucial role of the intelligentsia. There were 'traditional intellectuals' who thought and wrote within an established intellectual canon and who were largely outside the world of political debate. Most religious intellectuals were of this kind, as were writers and artists interpreting a received literary or cultural tradition. But there were also 'organic intellectuals' who derived their significance from the organic way in which they related to the interests of a particular class, whose vision and strategy they were constantly concerned to articulate. In the end, he believed, the workers' cause could not triumph unless its intelligentsia could achieve the same intellectual and cultural hegemony that the old Catholic intelligentsia had previously enjoyed. Only when everybody – not just the workers – saw things through their eyes, their lens, their definitions of reality, would the working class win the uncontested supremacy it sought.

Initially the ANC saw hegemony mainly in institutional terms; it must put its cadres in charge not just of government but the army, civil service, broadcasting, the police and every other socially commanding height. This coincided happily with the desire of the new black bourgeoisie to have all these jobs and salaries for itself. There was, indeed, no limit to its appetite any more than there was to the ANC's hunger for hegemony. Once Mbeki took over, the second leg of the strategy was made clear: the ANC's organic intellectuals must establish political and cultural hegemony, with Mbeki cast as the country's foremost black intellectual.

Moreover, Mbeki wanted to apply this Gramscian model to the entire continent. Thus he told the Association of African Universities in Cape Town on 22 February 2005 that the days were gone when African politicians treated intellectuals as 'a voice of the enemy'.[46] He spoke of the colonial era when 'the educated native' – a group to which, he said, he had himself belonged – had been 'detached from his or her people because he or she is educated and aspires to be something other than a native because he or she is educated'. Now, African intellectuals must renew their organic connection to their people and realize that there was now 'an enormous space for the intelligentsia to resume its place in the vanguard of the process of change'. There could be no African Renaissance without intellectuals.

Famously, René Dumont in his *L'Afrique noire est mal partie* (1962) spoke of the new 'bureaucratic bourgeoisie' which so deformed development. But South Africa's case was far broader. The new elite was not just based in the civil service and a few parastatals, but encompassed appointments on state quangos, NGOs, a vast and often well-paid class of provincial and municipal representatives, affirmative appointments throughout the worlds of commerce and professional practice, and in the worlds of health, justice and education, as well as on the boards of directors and in the middle management of every sort of private enterprise. When Sasol, the country's largest industrial concern, chose a new chief executive on simply meritocratic grounds it was fiercely denounced by the government. Sasol must be 'punished' for daring thus to place its own corporate interests higher than those of political rent-seeking.[47]

INSTITUTIONAL HEGEMONY WITHOUT CULTURAL HEGEMONY

While this takeover proceeded apace in every sphere of life, allowing for the almost complete institutional hegemony of the ANC, there was no corresponding ANC cultural and intellectual hegemony. To be sure, the ANC monopolized the airwaves, turned public holidays, anniversaries and state ceremonial occasions into ANC celebrations, and bullied the press and the business sector into acquiescence. But the black intelligentsia was largely missing. Too many of this tiny group had been psychologically damaged, by apartheid, by exile, by 'the movement', by political violence or just by being unable to keep their balance on becoming suddenly middle class. Although some struck aggressive anti-white postures, it was not difficult to discern complex feelings of inferiority and self-hatred beneath. In a word, too many were prey to the self-defeating dramas of the colonial intellectual of which Frantz Fanon remains the most penetrating analyst.

This hollowness was evident, too, in the continuing concern with a very narrow canon, essentially to do with race – W. E. DuBois, Steve

Biko and other 'Africanist' writers whose stock in trade was merely self-assertion, denunciation of white colonialism and, often, insupportable claims of African primacy in the world of learning. As with the African intellectuals described in Shiva Naipaul's *North of South*, too often the point of the associations they formed was simply to exist. Thus organizations like the Natives Club (a discussion group), the Forum of Black Journalists, the Black Lawyers Association, the Black Management Forum and so forth were happy to create controversy by being (unconstitutionally) racially exclusive and by attacking their multi-racial counterparts, but otherwise they played no part in the real debates within their professional milieux. They were far outmatched by their professional peers, let alone by the long and well-established traditions of English and Afrikaans-speaking 'white' culture, which remained utterly dominant. The ease with which Ronald Suresh Roberts, an abrasive West Indian carpet-bagger, was able to emerge as Mbeki's leading propagandist spoke volumes about the paucity of talent available to the ANC. The party desperately wanted a newspaper of its own but lacked both the organizational and journalistic talent to launch one.

The result was what the black writer Aubrey Matshiqi termed 'the crisis of hegemony facing the ANC'. The ANC, he pointed out, 'seems to rely too much on Mbeki's intellect even when he is wrong' and Mbeki was, as Matshiqi delicately put it, 'susceptible to perceptions of intolerance and paranoia'. Mbeki and his group, he argued, behaved 'like a besieged minority that seeks to stifle critical thought through the paranoid labelling of its critics'. The result was that 'intellectual independence and excellence have become synonymous with opposition to, and criticism of the ANC'.[48] Essop Pahad, Minister in the President's office, often declared that nowhere else in the world did a democratic government face such vicious press criticism as in South Africa. This was, of course, nonsense, but no bad indicator of the paranoid atmosphere in that office during the Mbeki presidency. In exile the only press that Mbeki and Pahad were used to was the ANC's own *Sechaba*, the *African Communist* and the *World Marxist Review*, which Pahad edited from Husák's Prague. Mbeki's view of the world had shallow social roots in a country which is overwhelmingly Christian, socially conservative and consumerist. Government ministers often expressed anxiety at the difficulty of getting a good audience for ANC speeches even on major struggle anniversaries, at the political disinterest of the young, and at the collapse in the study of African languages through lack of demand since 1994.[49] Even securing a good crowd for President Mbeki to address on Freedom Day (27 April) depended on the handout of food parcels and flags to all who attended.[50]

CHRISTIANS ESCAPE

Most Christian churches (with the exception of the Dutch Reformed Church) played a prominent part in the anti-apartheid struggle and many supported the UDF. This enabled the ANC to establish considerable influence and even control over such key institutions as the South African Council of Churches (SACC) and, via Archbishop Tutu, the Anglican Church. The Catholic Bishops Conference took at least an equally strong anti-apartheid line but retained greater institutional autonomy. By 1990 there was an almost automatic assumption among the ANC leadership that the Christian churches were part of the 'progressive movement' and should, accordingly, accept the general political leadership of the ANC. The SACC, in its mission statement of 1995, said that 'the churches are committed to stand in critical solidarity with the government',[51] but there was, in general, a great deal more solidarity than criticism. The fact that Frank Chikane could give up the SACC leadership to work in Mbeki's office spoke volumes about the churches' subordination to the ANC. Throughout the Mandela period the churches remained part of the ANC 'family', hugely strengthening the party's hegemonic position. Only with Mbeki did the ties begin to loosen.

A remarkable testament to just how completely the churches had been co-opted came in 2001 when the SACC chairman, Molefe Tsele, delivered a speech on how 'The Church must once again become a nuisance to the nation'. This followed increasing tension as the SACC criticized the government over Aids and demanded free ARVs and nevirapine for all pregnant mothers. The SACC had also asked for the arms deal to be abandoned and the money spent on the poor instead. In his speech Tsele said,

> We must run away from an incestuous cohabitation with the government, for to do so will be suicide to our mission as a church. We will cease to exist as an autonomous entity. To be in alliance with a persecuted political movement is one

thing, but to become its ally in government is another. The problem for South Africa is that the government tends to see non-support as opposition, and even such opposition is construed in such terms that make an 'anyone who is not with us is against us' dichotomy.

The ANC, he said, 'tends to instrumentalize the Church. The Church is generally seen as a nuisance that must be appeased by handouts. I often get hot under the collar when I see Church leaders treating political leaders like African royalty, sometimes even interrupting a church service because the premier or a Cabinet minister has arrived.' Tsele also remarked that Kader Asmal's 'attack on churches' earlier that year (when he had described 50,000 Christians attending a prayer rally against crime as 'sectarian, divisive and non-inclusive') was 'not easily forgotten by many Christians'. The question, Tsele said, was, 'Are we useful tools for the ANC agenda of ascendancy to power, remembered only when needed, or do we have our [own] agenda?'[52]

Mbeki strongly reprimanded Tsele and spoke of religious communities which 'had come to the conclusion that the end of white minority rule had also brought to an end their own obligation to be involved in the continuing struggle to address the terrible legacy [of apartheid]'.[53] Mbeki also referred to Desmond Tutu as being among other 'patriots and religious leaders', implying that Tsele and those like him were not patriots. Quite clearly, in the ANC's view, the Church leaders were simply part of the 'mass democratic movement' and must accept its discipline. To reinforce the point the KwaZulu-Natal ANC attacked Tsele's speech as 'satanic and evil'.

Tsele was no conservative. A Black Consciousness activist who had been detained in the 1980s, a member of various ANC front organizations and previously an adviser to the ANC premier of Northern Province, he stood well to the left of the ANC. Like Tutu's successor, the Anglican Archbishop Njongonkulu Ndungane, he demanded the cancellation of 'the apartheid debt', thus forcing the government, to its great embarrassment, to side with the bankers in resisting the demand.[54] Tsele was a strong opponent of globalization and took it as axiomatic that the World Bank and IMF were evil institutions. While opposed to the government's Aids policy and offended by the sight of BEE millionaires, he tended to support Robert Mugabe – how could taking land from white farmers be other than God's work? – and the SACC under his leadership declared Mugabe's rigged presidential election of 2002 to be 'legitimate'.

Such clerics, like many critical intellectuals, placed themselves to the left of the government because anything to the right of the ANC was, simplistically, identified with the old apartheid regime. But the key point was that the clerics were contesting with the ANC what was almost its proudest possession, its occupation of 'the moral high ground'. The split widened inexorably with the growing Mbeki–Zuma divide. Desmond Tutu spoke for many other Church leaders when he roundly criticized both men and insisted that Zuma was morally unfit to be President. This was a clear sign that the churches had irretrievably escaped from ANC control. In a society which is over 90 per cent Christian the consequences for the ANC's hegemonic ambitions could only be negative.

BACK TO THE FUTURE

Mbeki's ideology was, in any case, archaic, almost antique: exile and the Cold War had left ANC thinking frozen in the past. Emerging into the light again after 1990 it made a few essential adjustments (the abandonment of nationalization, the conditional embrace of black capitalism) but all Mbeki's political instincts – a reconstituted pan-Africanism, a knee-jerk anti-Americanism, the pursuit of the leadership of the Non-Aligned Movement – harked back forty years and more.

Indeed, Mbeki's African Renaissance consisted largely of trying to revitalize dead horses so that Mbeki could ride them. The OAU had long since faded into insignificance and bankruptcy. Its failure to stand up for human rights and its de facto toleration of even the worst African tyrants had robbed its windy liberation rhetoric of much meaning. The developed world paid it no attention and many African states refused to pay their dues. Mbeki resurrected this dead horse as the AU, had himself made its president (its founding conference was held in Durban, largely at South Africa's expense), and its Pan-African Parliament (PAP) sat in Midrand. The whole exercise depended on South African subsidy; the initial sessions of the PAP were largely taken up with laughable proposals for raising the revenue necessary for it to continue sitting by taxing the developed world. Anything to avoid asking African states to pay for a powerless parliament which they all knew was a waste of time.

It was the same with the Non-Aligned Movement, the offspring of the 1955 Bandung conference. What, after that, was this Movement now non-aligned between? Despite that – and the glaring fact that Asia's growth had left Africa far behind, making Afro-Asian solidarity increasingly improbable – Mbeki revived it, made himself its president, and held its reconstitutive conference in Durban. South Africa again picked up the tab. Predictably, Mbeki seized on the fiftieth anniversary of Bandung to try to revive the Bandung conference, whose reconstitutive meeting was also held in South Africa at the expense of the long-suffering South African taxpayer. There was, too, the pantomime of Alec Erwin being elected president of UNCTAD, the UN Conference on Trade and Development. Development issues had, for over a generation, largely escaped to the World Bank and IMF, while trade issues were dealt with first by GATT, the General Agreement on Tariffs and Trade, and then by the WTO. This left UNCTAD with nothing to do. The fact that the major Western states made no objection to a Communist Party member like Erwin assuming UNCTAD's presidency was sign enough of how irrelevant it had become. Even so accomplished a rider of pantomime horses as Mr Erwin was unable to breathe fresh life into this poor old nag.

The ANC had, moreover, not come to terms with why its earlier heroes – Kwame Nkrumah, Sekou Toure, Julius Nyerere and Samora Machel – all failed. Similarly, its Marxism knew nothing of Eurocommunism, let alone glasnost or perestroika. Mbeki gave much the same speeches about pan-Africanism and non-alignment that Nkrumah and Nyerere had once given, about the West's need to assuage its endless guilt with equally endless handouts, and how Africa's time had come ('the African century'). The whole creaky enterprise was not just old-fashioned but showing its age.

One is reminded of Régis Debray's account of the lasting effect of his induction into the world of Marxism-Leninism in the 1960s:

In effect, 'Marxism-Leninism' had the privilege of being spoken from Hanoi to Caracas by way of Rome and Brazzaville, unifying a multilingual diaspora of believers in the illusion of a shared destiny. I continued to practise this dead language long after I had lost the faith . . . I spoke 'Marxian' for twenty-odd years, eventually using that language of the head to satisfy a heart unwilling to divorce *militants*, a spectral community that survives in today's France only through the obstinacy of a few balding, jargonizing Blimps of progressivism. The

> joke is that this obsolescent Sanskrit ... deprived the celebrant of any real resonance ... [What they clung to was the idea of] *the* Revolution ... Majestic but evanescent, the planetary-Platonic Idea ... still floated above its locally disappointing epiphanies – Algeria, Vietnam, Cuba, Guinea and so on – like a worldwide effort of imagination.[55]

Mbeki's ANC was caught in exactly this trap. It was there for two reasons. Part of the African nationalist wave of the 1950s, it had been preserved in exile, as in aspic, waiting to fulfil its long-postponed destiny. The lengthy persistence of white minority regimes in southern Africa meant that the nationalist movements there had to wait till the 1970s, 1980s or even 1990s to achieve what their confrères had in the 1960s. Secondly, the ANC lacked an intelligentsia able to face up to how much the world had changed in the generation that had grown up as it waited to fulfil its 1960s 'moment'. So when the ANC came to power it still spoke – and thought – in this 'obsolescent Sanskrit': not just calling everyone 'comrade', but the same tired old terminology of 'the national democratic revolution', 'the motive forces of the revolution' and 'the national liberation movement', quite oblivious to the fact that all of this had gone down with the Berlin Wall and the Soviet *Titanic*.

Little wonder then that the ANC and Swapo (which had come to power in Namibia after a similarly protracted period in the deep freeze of exile), together with Frelimo and the MPLA, rallied to the defence of Mugabe's Zanu-PF in 2000. The advance of democracy and modernity threatened them all. Mugabe was so marooned in the past that he pretended he was fighting against the attempted reimposition of British colonial rule, a chimera embarrassing even to his friends. All these 'national liberation movements', thanks to the isolation of being on the southern tip of the least developed continent and to the peculiar retardation of its history, inhabited a Jurassic Park all of their own. Dinosaurs all, the climate of the twenty-first century as it unfolds is unlikely to be favourable to them.

ALWAYS YESTERDAY

The ANC's archaic ideology is, of course, an exact analogue of Afrikaner nationalism, whose confrontation with the international world was as stark as it was precisely because it too enshrined an antique ideology. Henry Kissinger, after meeting with South Africa's Prime Minister, John Vorster, in 1976 claimed that he had been dealing 'with a character from the Old Testament', so amazed was he to talk to a man in charge of a developed capitalist economy who quoted the Bible and spoke about the intrinsic inferiority of the black race in a way no modern politician would have. But as Christopher Hope puts it, 'It is always yesterday in South Africa. [The nationalist], otherwise such a Neanderthal political thinker, genuinely considers himself to be the Future . . . He wishes to move forward into the future by returning to the past . . .'[56]

ANC ideologists have tried to equate apartheid with Nazism but the comparison is ludicrous. Under apartheid, African life expectancy and per capita income rose steadily and although it was a cruel and wicked system it killed relatively few people. What affronted the civilized world about apartheid was simply its antique nature. It projected into the 1980s the doctrines of segregation and white supremacy which had been standard fare in the Western world of the early 1900s. Its very archaism held up an embarrassing mirror to a shameful but common Western past. For such a political antique to linger on was possible because of South Africa's physical isolation, but even there it was ultimately undone by the forces of globalization. The same is bound to be true, though rather more quickly – South Africa is more integrated into the global order now – for Mbeki's antique ideology. The ANC pretends, of course, that it is still fighting apartheid, but what the ANC has to fear is not a resurrected Boer far right but the rise of a South African version of Zimbabwe's MDC.

Many regimes in Africa have shared the ANC's old-fashioned mixture of Marxism and nationalism. Those which attempted to build socialism collapsed in the 1960s, 1970s or 1980s, while others (Tanzania, Mozambique) abandoned their original ideology. Those that did neither ended up with low or negative growth (Namibia, Zimbabwe). The sole exception is Angola, where investment has poured into the oil enclave economy and where the ruling group exhibits the most spectacular corruption in Africa. But not one succeeded in turning this ideological mix into a successful development model.

And how much harder to make such a mixture work in the twenty-first century ... For the ANC, just like the old Nats, have tried to steer South Africa back in time. As Christopher Hope put it, for nationalist ideologues 'the best place for the past was firmly ahead of them'.[57] Mbeki's speeches dealt obsessively with a simplistic view of South Africa's (and Africa's) past, flattening it all out into one long continuum of oppression and struggle, a long parade of past injustices, slights and suffering.[58] The racism which gave rise to colonialism and apartheid was, he insisted, still alive but otherwise there was little room for the present, let alone the future. The past thus presented was a renovated, ANC-defined past, with a great deal smoothed over and left out – but there was no forward vision of the society the ANC was supposed to be building other than frankly incredible glimpses of a utopia in which poverty, injustice, inequality and racism have all disappeared. Most religious sects give more details about heaven than the ANC does about what comes next.

FAULTS IN THE GRAMSCIAN MODEL

The failure of the ANC's hegemonic project now seems virtually certain. There is, one realizes, a fault in the basic Gramscian model. How can a party representing the least educated really achieve intellectual and cultural hegemony over groups which are better educated, more sophisticated, are backed up by a vast cultural inheritance and whose assumptions receive continuous implicit support from developed world opinion more generally? Such a project has succeeded only in societies where the hegemonic party was backed by terror, omnipresent surveillance and political constraints of every kind. But there is no precedent for a hegemonic party succeeding against such odds in a multi-party system like South Africa's, where a liberal constitutional order has been maintained.

In its 'Strategic and Tactical Approaches to the Opposition' (2005)[59] the ANC saw itself as engaged in a 'battle of ideas' to defeat the counter-revolution, characterizing the situation as follows:

a begrudging acceptance of the new order and a constant search for opportunities to weaken the ANC among most of the established media;

a predominance of the ethos of an individualistic and materially focused mindset with the values of a caring society struggling to assert themselves;

artistic and cultural struggles for indigenous and humane forms to assert themselves in the midst of an overwhelming onslaught of imported expressions or imitations thereof; and

intellectual discourse and endeavour in the social sciences barely able to represent, profoundly critique and sharpen social transformation praxis.

The document suggested that overall 'the creation of a democratic society has proceeded well; but it rests on shaky economic foundations (too much capital still in white hands) and its spiritual sustenance is deficient. The irony of this challenge is that, small as the support for the white-oriented opposition parties may be, these parties appeal to forces that have inordinate power and influence precisely in the spheres of economics and ideology.' To fight this threat and that posed by NGOs not aligned with the ANC, the party launched a hegemonic 'people's contract'. 'We seek to ensure, at least, that all South Africans, individually and in their organized formations, become part of the people's contract.' Smaller political parties must be absorbed or co-opted so that the ANC would grow to become 'a movement of the whole people'. Since the DA, at least, would inevitably refuse such co-option, the ANC would have to show 'that a "fight back" challenge to the cause of transformation does not pay; that a mind-set of co-operation . . . is in the best interest of each political formation'.

This was a straightforward prescription for single-partyism, excluding only the DA, which, together with other liberal forces, would be demonized as anti-patriotic and subjected to pre-emptive attack. The attempt to make the celebration of the Freedom Charter and the people's contract into the focus of national not party loyalties, was an early example of such tactics, with the DA cast as the sole 'anti-democratic and unpatriotic' force. But the hostile references to individualism, materialism and imported cultural expressions suggested a far wider cultural struggle against Western influences – perhaps comparable to those waged by the old Soviet bloc or fundamentalist Islam. Such a struggle could hardly be waged, let alone won, without a wholesale disregard of the present constitution.

This perspective was not just Mbeki's. Thus, 'Fighting the Stranglehold of Neo-liberalism', a paper by the cabinet minister and SACP member, Sydney Mufamadi,[60] echoed the same themes, arguing that 'the neo-liberal orthodoxy sits as a tyrant on the throne of political-economic policymaking. The dominant social and economic forces are doing their utmost to hegemonize the discourse' – in particular by trying to diminish the role of the state in development. There is, accordingly, the imperative of constructing a broader counter-hegemonic perspective for one must take into account the fact that 'in the so-called failed states, it is the imposition of the neo-liberal orthodoxy that has undermined the state and contributed directly to the descent into anarchy and civil war'.

It is hard to imagine that anyone could honestly believe that the fate which befell Somalia, Liberia, Sierra Leone or the Congo derived from their adoption of liberal ideas or economics, so the significance of this passage doubtless lay more in the way the whole discussion of 'failed' and 'rogue' states has alarmed Third World radicals who view the notion of states such as their own 'failing' as a nightmare, seeing in it only a rationale for First World intervention.

Mufamadi inveighed against 'the confidence of liberalism': the left must deploy 'its background of experience in organization and ideology' to build 'a broad coalition of social forces' against this threat. He warned that the left must 'not be seduced into posing the state and "civil society" in a dichotomous relationship. Such a dichotomy is false and for the state and society it leads to results that are mutually enfeebling.' Thus in building its broad coalition the progressive state would seek to commandeer everyone, not allowing any private sphere of 'civil society' to be off-limits to the state. The totalitarian impulse is again quite clear.

As with many ANC documents, there was a strong defensiveness, even paranoia, in Mufamadi's paper (which Mbeki probably ghosted) – liberalism is 'a tyrant' and 'confident', the ANC's movement is under 'neo-liberal attack' and liberalism uses the IMF, the World Bank and the World Trade Organization 'to shape the discourse within which policies are defined, the terms and concepts that circumscribe what can be thought and done'. Even in relationship to its home-grown media, the ANC sees itself as under siege and nowhere is the sense of threat greater than in the field of cultural hegemony. This defensiveness was the key to the call for the mobilization of almost single-party unity, a project Mbeki clearly had in mind for his third term.

LIBERAL INSTITUTIONS UNDER PRESSURE

The South African liberal tradition dates back well over two hundred years. It has been an insistent minority voice, usually threatened, sometimes almost underground, but resilient and continuing. Whether this tradition can survive through the ANC's hegemonic period will depend in large part on the strength of liberal institutions: the constitution, the press, universities and NGOs, and the main liberal political party, the DA. Of these, the DA has been by far the most successful in the new South Africa, growing by leaps and bounds after 1994 thanks to Tony Leon's tough-minded leadership. Leon's great achievement was to make the DA the official Opposition, a status which it may well retain.

The press has fared less well. In some newsrooms discussion has become both so jejune and so politically correct that experienced journalists find it hard even to find a way of phrasing their concerns. But the newspaper business is a competitive one and, as Matatha Tsedu found at the *Sunday Times*, if his Africanist ideology collided with the market he would pay the price. Of course we have seen many editorial betrayals and a shameful lack of backbone and objectivity but ultimately the whole conception of being a proper newspaper is antipathetic to the ANC's hegemonic project. Some of the strongest resistance to that project came from black voices in the press – from Mondli Makhanya, editor of the *Sunday Times*, Barney Mthombothi, editor of the *Financial Mail*, and the columnist, Xolela Mangcu, loud in his criticism of 'the nativist siege mentality of the Mbeki era'.[61]

The constitution is vulnerable because the Constitutional Court hardly inspires confidence, but the achievement of a liberal constitution is acknowledged by almost everyone as one of the key achievements of the Mandela era, making it difficult to attack. The liberal institutions in the greatest danger are the universities – ultimately just public-sector institutions subject to the same mismanagement, political manipulation and disastrous affirmative action as the rest of the public sector – and the liberal NGOs. Their number has shrunk as several previously independent NGOs adopted an ANC-aligned political correctness or just decayed. The few that remain are vital. They have generated a fund of authoritative information on the South African situation, provided a platform for liberal intellectuals and, by being willing to risk political unpopularity, have pushed the edge of the envelope for many others.

On the other hand, the liberal tradition may merely need to survive in order to win. The Zimbabwean example is important here. After independence in 1980 Zanu-PF enjoyed nearly twenty years of effective single-partyism: African nationalist hegemony seemed complete and permanent. There was no liberal press but the anti-Smith liberals of the UDI era had a lasting influence and many of them stayed on while a few liberal NGOs carried the flag. More and more black Zimbabweans imbibed these values, rose to prominence in the NGOs and in the end formed the nucleus of the MDC, a majority African party with a liberal democratic philosophy, able to win any free election from 2000 on. Despite its current travails the liberal democratic cause is still the only plausible successor to the Mugabe regime.

The lesson for South Africa is clear. The hegemony of the ANC's antique form of African nationalism probably reached its apogee in 1994–2000. Decline lies ahead. The obvious failures of ANC delivery and the general ageing of the 1994 political alignment is bound to weaken it further. Moreover, African nationalism is South Africa's third and last wave of nationalism. The early years of the twentieth century were dominated by a jingoistic Anglo-nationalism, which was gradually superseded by Afrikaner nationalism and now by the last wave, African nationalism. No further nationalist wave is imaginable. As the last wave gradually subsides, some variant of the liberal tradition may well be the sole political alternative left within the system. Liberals face many problems; they have been persecuted by all three waves of nationalism, just as Zimbabwean liberals were persecuted by both Smith and Mugabe. But the failure of the ANC's hegemonic project almost certainly presages more fundamental problems for that party. The question is simply whether the ANC will then attempt to emulate Robert Mugabe and cling to power by undemocratic means or whether it will accept, as its English jingoist and Afrikaner nationalist forerunners had to, that its day is done.

9
Facing the World over the Zambesi

Had he never been emperor, no one would have doubted his ability to reign.
Tacitus

The Mandela presidency saw a great deal of what one might call celebratory diplomacy, in which the great man travelled the world to huge acclaim. Innumerable foreign visitors also made their way to South Africa in order to seek new opportunities in the post-apartheid state and cement their own liberatory credentials by being photographed with Mandela. This was extremely popular despite the large and semi-obligatory donations which often followed such photo opportunities.

THE STRANGE WORLD OF FOREIGN AFFAIRS

None of this was serious. What was serious was that no one understood foreign affairs. Even Mbeki, the ANC expert in foreign affairs, had so little understood the situation that he had overlooked the fact that South Africa's overwhelming foreign interest was to negotiate a new trade treaty with the EU – the source of two-thirds of the country's trade and most of its foreign investment – as quickly as possible, gaining the freest possible access to the world's biggest market. By the time Pretoria awoke, it was too late. A South African trade agreement meant easier access for its fruit and wine but the EU had signed the Maastricht Agreement with a 1997 deadline, which entailed tough public spending cuts, and no EU government was going to risk infuriating its farm lobby on top of that. So the talks with the EU dragged on and on. The Trade

Minister, Alec Erwin, bullied and threatened (bluster he had learnt in his trade union days) to no avail, for his EU counterparts were vastly more experienced and expert. Each year Erwin announced that the trade agreement with the EU would definitely be concluded soon, ending with an absolute promise that it would be fact by 2000. But it was not. Further years slipped by in squabbles over detail and the lengthy process of EU countries individually ratifying the agreement.

Oddly, despite the fact that less than 2 per cent of South Africa's population are Muslims, there was a strong Muslim presence in foreign affairs. Mandela's Foreign Minister, Alfred Nzo, was ineffectual and Mbeki, together with Aziz Pahad, the deputy Foreign Minister, had a predominant influence from the first. Once Mbeki became President, his confidant, Essop Pahad, made his influence felt across the whole field of government policy. Yet another Muslim, Kader Asmal, chaired the committee on arms exports, while Abdul Minty was director-general of the Foreign Affairs Department. Minty and the Pahads were all Muslim communists. In both capacities they had for decades regarded the Israelis with deep enmity, apartheid allies and worse. Mbeki was keen to take the Muslim side in general, not only because of donations to the ANC from the Arab world, but because his ambitions to leadership of the Third World made sensitivity to Islam essential. Early on the NIA was caught spying on the German and Israeli embassies, for both were regarded as enemies.[1]

As elsewhere, there was a speedy clear-out of competent whites but the damage ran deeper in Foreign Affairs. First, the South African Foundation, which had effectively provided an alternative foreign service in the field of trade promotion, was summarily wound up, with an irreplaceable loss of expertise. Secondly, the ANC used ambassadorships as spoils for distribution to party stalwarts, and the notion of a trained diplomatic corps virtually disappeared.

But thirdly, Mbeki, on becoming president, appointed Dr Nkosasana Dlamini-Zuma as Foreign Minister. In her previous Ministry, Health, officials had found her impossible to work with. This experience was now repeated. Within months her staff were utterly demoralized, with one official noting that at least 'it is bringing black and white colleagues closer together because they experience the same kind of humiliation'. The Minister actively sought to keep desk officers in the dark about her dealings with countries in their regions, frequently disregarded the briefs she was given and rearranged her own foreign flights so frequently (once changing her flights twenty-seven times in a week) that her officials often had no idea where she was or what she was doing. She complained bitterly about not being properly briefed even after she had disregarded her brief, telephoned officials at all hours with bizarre requests and micro-managed her department so that all foreign postings and promotions had to come through her, with resulting long delays and vacancies in key foreign missions.[2] Even high-level ANC cadres like Jackie Selebi and Sipho Pityana did not last long around Dlamini-Zuma. All those who could flee the department, did so.

The result was disastrous. Despite Dlamini-Zuma's efforts to shield envoys who were political appointees, there was an increasing number of scandals in embassies abroad. By 2001 three full ambassadors and nine junior officials were under investigation for 'unbecoming behaviour', ranging from financial fraud to sexual harassment and insubordination, while the country's high commissioner to Ghana was found guilty of 'persistent drunkenness'.[3] This was, however, merely the tip of the iceberg, for Dlamini-Zuma frequently ignored evidence of misbehaviour. Thus the ambassador to Indonesia, Norman Mashabane, was found guilty of sexual harassment of twenty-two different women. But Dlamini-Zuma nonetheless kept him in office for years more. Mashabane had uncovered a car scam conducted by some of his embassy staff, and Dlamini-Zuma suggested that, as a result, all twenty-two women had colluded against Mashabane, despite two separate disciplinary hearings having concluded that there was no link between the two matters. In the end Mashabane was found guilty by a court – after which he was soon touted for a top job in the office of the Limpopo premier.[4] Similarly, the former ambassador to Brazil, Mbulelo Rakwena, was promoted to head the Latin American desk in Pretoria despite two damning reports finding him guilty of malversation of funds and large-scale expenses fraud.[5] Given the Minister's willingness to employ men of this calibre, it may be imagined what excesses were necessary to get even a dozen diplomats investigated for their misdemeanours.

Meanwhile, foreign diplomats in Pretoria found the department so unresponsive to approaches of any kind that they feared their relations with South Africa were on the rocks, only to find that this was a normal situation for all diplomats. Diplomats, traditionally unwilling to make public complaint, were vocal about the department's lack of knowledge in every area of policy, and the same was true of the departments of Trade, Industry and Defence. Many simply found it difficult to get any official to pick up a telephone, let alone return their calls. The US ambassador, Eric Bost, lost his temper after months of failing to get any of the appointments he requested. He repeatedly warned officials that the United States was South Africa's biggest aid donor and that it was intolerable that he could never see the Foreign Minister, her deputies, or any other minister to discuss how that aid should be spent; if this was not remedied, he would go public. In the end he did so, in a great roar of rage. Other diplomats were delighted: 'He has spoken for us all,' said one. Other major aid donors complained of arrogance, incompetence and ingratitude.[6] Foreign Ministry officials professed themselves wholly unaware of the problem. 'South Africa's foreign service is just a joke, a disgrace,' one diplomat told me. 'Many countries which are far smaller and poorer are much better represented.'[7]

Mbeki was a foreign policy President, soon acquiring at great expense his own presidential jet, something which even the British Prime Minister did not stretch to. He was constantly travelling around the globe and seemed to volunteer for roles – chairman of the AU, head of the Non-Aligned Movement, and mediator in Ivory Coast or Zimbabwe – which took him abroad. Many of his foreign trips, to attend foreign funerals, address Caricom in Jamaica or attend such obscure bodies as the Diamond High Council in Antwerp, were clearly quite unnecessary, as if he was seeking reasons for travel. Some commentators concluded that he was bored with South Africa and its problems, that he had found South African blacks brutalized, barbarous and a great disappointment, and that he was voting with his feet for a continued life in exile. His speeches frequently gave more prominence to entirely symbolic events in international affairs than to something as pressing as the Aids crisis or unemployment back at home.

The centrepiece of Mbeki's foreign policy was supposed to be the interconnected themes of the African Renaissance, the African Union and Nepad. A necessary preliminary was that Africa had to be at peace: hence his frantic attempt to extinguish conflicts around the continent, the most praiseworthy part of his presidency. But it was obvious from the start that the dream was stillborn. Just as he sought to put out the fires in Burundi or the Congo, so new conflicts would erupt in Ivory Coast, Somalia, Eritrea and the Sudan. There was no end in sight: several other states, including the giant of the continent, Nigeria, simmered on the edge of civil conflict. The uncomfortable truth was that before the advent of colonialism Africa had been racked by endless wars and disputes and that with colonialism and its enforced peace removed, conflicts had mushroomed again. Mbeki insisted his task was to put out the last smouldering conflicts left by colonialism. In truth he had taken on an endless job.

THE AFRICAN UNION: DREAMING ON

The OAU had been Kwame Nkrumah's brainchild. No sooner had Ghana won independence in 1957 than he began to dream of uniting all of Africa. Quite why dreams of continental unity appeal to Africans but not to Asians, Middle Easterners or Latin Americans is not frequently asked, though it is a good question. But what made Nkrumah's dream truly unrealizable was the way in which he scorned the sort of gradual building process which had worked for the likes of Cavour and Bismarck in the nineteenth century: it had to be achieved all at once by a simple resolution of African presidents. The result was complete failure. The only principles the OAU stuck by were a respect for colonial boundaries and non-interference with whatever the despot next door got up to. It was happy to vote through twenty-one treaties and conventions but only thirteen of these were ratified and none enforced. Member states chronically failed to pay their dues.

Meanwhile, by 2000 independent Africa had been the recipient of over $1 trillion, with very little to show for it, and was collectively in debt to the tune of $334 billion, again with no one able to point to much that had been achieved with all these resources. But even as they channelled resources abroad into Swiss or Malaysian bank accounts, Africa's rulers – including ageing despots, killers and torturers by the score – continued to pay lip-service to African unity. Meanwhile 60 per cent of the UN Security Council's agenda focused on African disputes and as Kofi Annan put it, 'I don't think this is something we should be proud of.'[8]

Mbeki was the continent's dominant voice. Fascinated by the success of the EU, he could have used the South African Customs Union free trade area (South Africa, Namibia, Botswana, Lesotho and Swaziland) as his base, endowed it with a Treaty of Rome and gradually incorporated one southern and central African state after another. Instead, he opted to follow in Nkrumah's footsteps: all or nothing and all at once. At a summit in Lusaka in July 2001 the OAU transformed itself into the AU. If the new organization was to succeed – and foreign donors were vital from the start – there had to be recognition from the outset that Africa needed a constructive relationship with the developed world. This in turn meant facing down those still wedded to ranting against colonialism rather than recognizing their own faults.

Mbeki had no stomach for this. And, as one observer put it, 'it suits autocrats like Gaddafi and Mugabe to continue shadow-boxing with the ghosts of long dead men in pith helmets'.[9] The new AU, concluding that the OAU had failed because it was just an elite club of leaders, announced that it would cater for the participation of African people through two new institutions, a Pan-African Parliament and an African Court of Justice. There was also to be an African central bank and a single currency (eliciting a quiet 'not in my lifetime' response from many African central bankers, including South Africa's Tito Mboweni[10]), an Economic, Social and Cultural Council and an AU Commission, as well as a Peace and Security Council and specialized technical committees.

Later, the AU considered a common policy on defence and security and a single African army. Samuel Johnson said that one should refuse to contemplate 'six impossible things before breakfast', but Africa's presidents had no such inhibitions. They happily voted through the creation of an African Monetary Fund, an African Investment Bank and the target date of 2030 for a single currency, despite the fact that less than 10 per cent of African trade is with other African countries. Meanwhile the AU had inherited the OAU's debts (only sixteen of the organization's fifty-three members had paid their dues in full, despite Libya's habit of buying votes by paying other countries' dues) and there was so little confidence that member states would pay their dues that there were immediate proposals for the AU to fund itself by special taxes on foreign mining companies and non-African airlines overflying Africa.

This ran up into a brick wall, for the AU depended heavily on foreign donors, especially the EU. The donors were insistent that independent

Africa had squandered its first forty years because of poor governance and warned that everything now depended on the new organization showing not only an improvement in governance itself but a completely different attitude to member states run by dictators or guilty of human rights atrocities.

Mbeki was elected the first president at the AU launch in Durban in July 2002, a moment of triumph, for it acknowledged his success in positioning himself as *the* leader of Africa. He told delegates, 'Let us proclaim to the world that this is a continent of democracy and good governance.'[11] There was all manner of spectacular symbolism: a fly-past, a military parade, Zulu regiments and an appearance by the Senegalese football team which had done so well in the previous World Cup. (The team had also earned huge publicity on its way home via Taipei where a record thirty-two prostitutes were sent up to service the team in their suite.[12]) All told, South Africa paid R100 million to host the event. But the bad old ways were all still in place. Madagascar's new President, Marc Ravalomanana, was banned from attending the AU, theoretically because it had decided that his election was not valid (despite the opinion of Madagascar's High Constitutional Court to the contrary) but in reality out of solidarity with the defeated President, Didier Ratsiraka, who had ruled for thirty-three years. Quite clearly, the AU was still an old boys' club of leaders. The fact that Ratsiraka had fled to France and tried to organize a mercenary invasion to bring down his successor was ignored.

In fact Mbeki achieved little during his AU presidency: ratification of the various protocols setting up the new AU institutions was extremely slow and although South Africa picked up many AU expenses (and funded the Nepad secretariat), the new organization began to run into debt and heads of state began to ignore AU meetings. By early 2004 membership arrears already exceeded the AU Commission's annual budget despite the fact that donors were paying for over 70 per cent of the AU's Peace and Security Council. The Council set its initial task as intervening to prevent civil wars or genocide, for Africa is a continent where one needs to provide against future genocides. By the time of the AU's third summit in Abuja in 2004 the organization had managed to collect dues amounting to only a quarter of the previous year's (tiny) budget and when President Olusegun Obasanjo told the assembled heads of state that the budget needed to be increased twelvefold he was met by helpless giggles. Only fifteen of fifty-three members ratified the protocol on an African Court of Human Rights but it was difficult to know where, if anywhere, such a proposal would go, for the AU immediately voted to merge it with the African Court of Justice, another non-functioning body.

Mbeki's pursuit of empty symbolism was at its most obvious in his determined battle to make South Africa the seat of the Pan-African Parliament (PAP). No one could possibly take such a body seriously: no African leader was willing to cede much power to a parliament and many did without parliaments altogether. A fortiori, no continental parliament was going to be more than decoration. Yet Mbeki solemnly told South Africa's Parliament that he expected the PAP to gain full legislative powers over the whole continent,[13] something which was considerably less likely than finding fairies at the bottom of one's garden. Indeed, those countries that ratified the PAP did so precisely on the assumption that it would be impotent. No one would otherwise have agreed that every state, regardless of population, should have the same number of representatives (five), and nor would bloodthirsty dictatorships like Equatorial Guinea have agreed to join anything that resembled a real parliament.

When the PAP met for its first (three-week) session in Johannesburg in 2004 there was the usual feast of symbolism: African dancers, poetry readings, concerts, religious blessings, ethnic regalia, rows of flags, VIPs rolling up in huge limos, and a vast security presence. Mbeki told the PAP that 'the African masses' were looking at it expectantly to help them 'escape from the jaws of poverty and . . . the clutches of under-development'.[14] The notion that the well-dressed delegates alighting from their Mercedes at Johannesburg's swish international hotels had really come for this reason would have surprised anyone who saw how much time they put into shopping.

Reality soon broke in. Lack of funds forced the PAP to end its session a week early and it petitioned the AU for more money, a procedure considerably less hopeful than sending a letter to Santa Claus. Thereafter the PAP's meetings became obscure minor events, barely noticed in the press. That it survived at all was a minor miracle, for, South Africa apart, no African country was interested in paying for it: Germany and the UN were more important donors. Inevitably, angry voices were soon raised in the PAP that South Africa was reneging on its promises. The

200 computers initially provided by South Africa for the PAP were all quickly stolen and there was no internet access, nor even any calculators.[15] Delegates made it clear that at least they had hoped to slake their thirst for consumer electronics while in Johannesburg. Already the PAP had become an embarrassment. It was, accordingly, ignored.

THIRD WORLD LEADERSHIP AND THE PROBLEM OF ISRAEL

Mbeki's grandiose ambition was to be the leader of the Third World, championing the South against the North. This too was more about symbolism than reality. Until Mbeki revived it (and paid for it), the Non-Aligned Movement had ceased to exist because with the Cold War over, non-alignment was meaningless. Mbeki sought to suggest that South Africa was one of the dynamic giants of the future along with India, Brazil and China; thus he flew to attend President Lula's inauguration in Brazil, while ignoring President Kibaki's contemporaneous inauguration in Kenya. He even suggested that South Africa might club together with Brazil and India to build commercial jetliners, an enterprise for which South Africa had no capacity whatsoever.[16] The larger truth, of course, was that headlong growth meant that much of Asia was leaving the Third World. One could descry a future in which Africa might be the only poor continent.

Mbeki's fascination with Israel grew out of the notion that, with apartheid gone, Israel was the last white, Western colony in the Third World. His idea of 'solving' the Arab–Israeli problem was that his mediation might help pressure Israel's rulers into abdicating power, just as the Afrikaners had done. It was a grandiose fantasy, for the ANC saw Israel as a 'racist state' and saw itself as eradicating 'apartheid practices on a global scale'.[17]

Israel, naturally, saw the idea of South African mediation as laughable, but this did not deter Mbeki. In 2002 he held a conference of Palestinians and Israeli doves (the Israeli government was unrepresented) after which John Battersby faithfully, if untruthfully, reported that this 'has secured a central role for South Africa as a facilitator in the Middle East peace process'.[18] With ironic simultaneity, the Israeli government and the

Jewish Agency announced that Jewish immigrants from South Africa would now receive the subsidy packages reserved for 'countries of hardship and persecution'.[19] Undiscouraged, in 2003 Mbeki led a ministerial mission to meet Israeli officials 'to share the South African experience of conflict resolution',[20] again with the notion that everything should be handed over to the Palestinians as it had been to the ANC.

Throughout 2004 Aziz Pahad and Mbeki spent enormous energy in leading the charge against Israel at the UN and touring the Middle East in an attempt to isolate Israel. The Israelis showed their disgust by shutting their trade office and announcing that relations were at an all-time low because of South Africa's 'hardline anti-Israeli' position, a move Pahad angrily denounced as Israel trying 'to impose sanctions on us'.[21] In fact, trade between the two countries had fallen and the Israelis considered breaking off diplomatic relations entirely. Pahad and Mbeki hailed Hamas's victory in the 2006 Palestinian elections and immediately launched talks with Hamas, with Pahad setting off for the Middle East again to 'facilitate the peace process'.

Given that the United States, the EU and most Western countries refused to meet Hamas until it renounced violence and accepted Israel's right to exist, Pretoria's attitude put it into a group which Israel frankly regarded as its enemies. Israel immediately scuppered Mbeki's mediation ambitions by announcing that it would refuse to meet foreign officials who met with Hamas. It was hardly an exaggeration to term South Africa an enemy of Israel: South Africa's Minister for Intelligence, Ronnie Kasrils, visited Iran in 2006 where he 'lauded the great victories of the Lebanese Hezbollah against the Zionist forces' and appeared to encourage them to attack the Israelis again, arguing that 'the successful Lebanese resistance proved the vulnerability of the Israeli army'.[22]

RACISM – AND TERRORISM

Ironically, Mbeki's enthusiasm for the Palestinian cause created a major foreign policy debacle in 2001. In 2000, at Mbeki's instigation, the South African Human Rights Commission had held an anti-racism conference, a veritable festival of white-bashing, to give vent to Mbeki's departure from Mandela's inclusive vision of a rainbow nation. Henceforth, Mbeki's slogan of 'two nations, one white and rich, one black and poor' was to be the guiding motif. So fervent was the conference's anti-white rhetoric – and fresh attempts were made to get whites to confess their collective guilt – that there were complaints that Mbeki was installing a new form of black racism. The government's reply was given by Mbeki's legal adviser, Mojanku Gumbi: although black racism was technically possible, in practice it never really occurred and was so rare that one could not truly speak of it. Thus the only real racism was white racism.

The decade 2000–2010 – that is, the whole of Mbeki's presumed two-term presidency – was declared to be the decade of the struggle against racism, clearly foreshadowing a constant diet of anti-white rhetoric. This notion had an international dimension: the whole white world must atone for its historical sins by paying reparations for slavery and colonialism. This would take the form of Western funding for Nepad, Mbeki having settled on a figure of grants to Africa of almost $1 trillion over fifteen years. Thus Mbeki would assume the leadership of the entire Third World in demanding that the West apologize, atone and pay. And this would be achieved at a special UN World Conference Against Racism, to be held in Durban in September 2001. In its eagerness, the government volunteered not merely to host the conference but to pay most of its costs.

In the conference run-up there was high excitement that it would see a rebuke to the West of historic proportions. 'Indigenous people' were invited from all over the world and the cause of ethnic minorities anywhere in the West was taken up with great indignation. Arriving in Durban for the conference, I found what could only be described as a crazed atmosphere of millenarian expectation and furious blaming. Black Americans, Roma, Inuit and many other minorities were there in strength and were all, apparently, angry. Even many of the whites attending the conference were anti-white. A great theme was the rights of indigenous peoples but this did not seem to work for all. Thus whites were condemned for colonialism abroad, and were also blamed for not making ex-colonial people welcome enough in their own countries. I asked many delegates whether there was anywhere that whites had rights as indigenous people themselves. There was apparently no such place.

A 7,000-strong NGO forum preceded the conference proper and quickly fastened on the Arab–Israeli dispute. It adopted a draft declaration in which Israel was denounced not merely for racism but for ethnic cleansing and genocide. Israeli and Jewish delegates were tolerantly willing to accept much of this provided there was a balancing section condemning the evils of anti-Semitism. This, however, was thrown out, and the forum now lobbied the conference to adopt its declaration too. At which point Israel walked out, swiftly followed by the United States, effectively ruining the conference. The accusation of anti-Semitism now hung over the whole meeting. Worse, the whole idea had been that the most powerful white nation, the United States, must attend in order to be condemned, to be allowed to apologize – and become the biggest reparations donor. But this cause had gone badly awry. Black Americans indignantly argued that reparations should be paid to them, not to independent Africa. Nigeria, the biggest black nation, opposed the whole notion of reparations while President Abdoulaye Wade of Senegal said the idea was 'rubbish' and 'an insult to Africans'. The conference had decisively shifted away from the agenda Mbeki had wanted and his proffered leadership of the South against the North was not accepted.

The EU delegates had had their backbones considerably stiffened by the United States' withdrawal. While many of them had earlier seemed to be willing to offer apologies, this hope now vanished. Moreover, it was clear that the United States blamed South Africa for the debacle: it was the host, it had encouraged an anti-Israel and anti-American atmosphere and it had by far the largest number of delegates and activists at the conference. This became a major grievance in the cold war between Mbeki and Colin Powell. Mbeki's response was furious and immediate: it was announced that it would not, after all, be possible for the flagship of the US fleet, the USS *Enterprise*, to dock in Cape Town. The visit had been long planned and Cape Town was happily anticipating 6,000 free-spending US sailors. But the carrier was nuclear-powered, which meant it needed permission to dock from the South African National Nuclear Regulator, whose chief executive, Ms Louisa Zondo, had previously promised to give authorization in good time. Suddenly she found she could not consider the matter for another month, effectively sabotaging the visit.[23]

Just three days later the cataclysm of 9/11 occurred, utterly wrongfooting Mbeki's anti-American stance. Mbeki immediately declared the event a 'terrible tragedy' and offered humanitarian aid. Mandela denounced the terrorists in even rounder terms. In the emotional atmosphere of the time President Bush got Mbeki to agree to full co-operation between the countries' respective intelligence agencies in hunting down terrorists. But almost immediately Aziz Pahad began to sound a note strongly critical of the US/UK strikes into Afghanistan and, as Muslim opinion hardened, so did that of the South African government. More than a thousand South African Muslims left to fight for the Taliban, with many more volunteering.[24]

By January enormous pressure had been brought to bear on Mandela, causing him to recant publicly his earlier support for the war in Afghanistan: he now apologized for his views as 'one-sided and overstated'. The new line was that Osama bin Laden should not be blamed for 9/11 until he had had a proper trial, that is, never. By this time it was easy to buy a T-shirt on the streets of Durban with a picture of bin Laden and the slogan, 'Innocent Till Proved Guilty'. (I still have one.) Only three days after Mandela's statement, Deputy President Jacob Zuma was pushed forward to make a notable alteration in the government line. Speaking at a Durban mosque he accused the United States of double-standards and equated the war in Afghanistan with 9/11: both involved acts of terrorism.[25] By March government ministers were openly accusing the United States of 'war hunger', and urging 'rebellion' against the hegemony of Western interests and ideology in international life.[26]

THE TREACHEROUS WATERS OF THIRD WORLD DIPLOMACY

South Africa gave great prominence to its relations with Cuba and Libya and embraced any new anti-American Third World leader, such as Hugo Chavez in Venezuela or Evo Morales in Bolivia. On the eve of the Iraq war Aziz Pahad went to Baghdad and posed next to anti-American slogans, clearly currying favour with Saddam Hussein. Soon South Africa was again refusing to allow US warships to dock at South African ports – in March 2005 the ruse of the National Nuclear Regulator was again used to deny such rights to the USS *Harry S. Truman* and its supporting flotilla, despite the fact that this meant a loss of more than R100 million for local merchants. The ANC exiles who had spent their entire careers as members of 'the international progressive movement' could not adjust to the end of the Cold War. Instinctively, they pursued a continuing struggle against 'the imperialists' (pre-eminently the United States and Britain), clutching at any straw to keep the struggle alive.

Thus Pretoria sustained warm relations with North Korea and soft-pedalled its reaction to Pyongyang's acquisition of nuclear weapons; led a group of nations at the UN which prevented the censure of Sudan for human rights abuses in Darfur; was one of only five nations to abstain from the decision of the International Atomic Energy Agency to report Iran to the Security Council; supported Libya to chair the UN Commission on Human Rights; and recognized the breakaway movement Polisario's Saharawi Republic, thus killing off its diplomatic relations and burgeoning trade with Morocco. Such decisions put South Africa in the company of states which were both political dinosaurs and among the world's worst human rights offenders. The disingenuous reason given for this was that such states had supported the anti-apartheid struggle. This was an evasion: so had many other states who were now horrified by the ANC's abandonment of its human rights tradition. The real point was that in Pretoria's eyes what determined whether a state was 'progressive' was not whether it tortured its citizens or allowed free elections but whether it took an 'anti-imperialist' stance.

To some extent appearance masked reality. The United States remained South Africa's biggest trading partner by far, and Mbeki gave the United States the one thing it really wanted in the wake of 9/11: intelligence co-operation against terrorism. South Africa was in some respects an ideal haven for al-Qaeda, with its significant and wealthy Muslim population and its sophisticated banking and communications facilities. But the NIA co-operated with the CIA, and one of the key suspects from the bombing of the US embassy in Kenya, Khamis Khalfan Mohamed, who had fled to South Africa, was caught and handed over to the United States, despite a Constitutional Court ruling that this was unlawful. Other terrorist suspects followed, including Khalid Mahmood Rashid, a Pakistani national flown out of South Africa in 2007 before any court hearing could be arranged, to be handed over to the Pakistani authorities, by whom, undoubtedly, he would be tortured.

In agreeing to such renditions Pretoria had shown that, whatever its anti-American rhetoric in other spheres, it was perfectly willing to earn US brownie points if this merely meant ignoring human rights.[27] In addition, the CIA was allowed to operate relatively freely within South Africa – in 2001–3 I came across considerable CIA activity in Pretoria linked to attempts to prevent South African know-how in nuclear and bio-chemical warfare from leaking abroad to terrorist groups. Indeed, CIA agents roamed around freely, interviewing suspects and even setting up 'sting' operations without any NIA participation. The real consistency lay in Mbeki's grandiosity: he liked strutting on the big stage with Bush and however much he wanted to denounce 'the imperialists', he also wanted to be in the G8 summit photo with Blair and Bush.

Mbeki's strategy was that South Africa, exploiting its South–South contacts, would win the leadership of Africa and then of the entire Third World, which it would then represent at the top table, talking to the G8 on behalf of the world's poor and underprivileged. Having assumed this leadership position, South Africa would use its leverage to transform the entire structure of international relations by insisting on much stronger Third World representation on the UN Security Council, all affiliated UN bodies, the World Bank and the IMF. And since South Africa would lead this transformation of 'the international architecture', South Africa itself (and thus Mbeki himself) would be given a leadership position in all these organizations.

Mbeki pursued these objectives by according an abnormally large role to ideology and symbolism. Hence his bizarre decision to link the celebration of South Africa's first decade of democracy with Haiti's bi-centennial celebration of independence. The link was that Toussaint l'Ouverture's successful slave revolt in Haiti, producing the first independent black state, was the first step in a long emancipatory process which had climaxed with the ANC's accession to power in South Africa. In addition, Mbeki continually sought to give expression and leadership to 'the black diaspora'.

Diplomats expressed astonishment that Mbeki should seek to associate himself with the poorest, most corrupt and least successful state in history. Moreover, Haiti's President Jean-Bertrand Aristide had drawn criticism from human rights groups for electoral fraud, the use of violence and intimidation against opponents and complicity in drug running. But Mbeki announced that he would not only attend Haiti's celebrations (making a gift of R10 million to Aristide) but he would also mediate between Aristide and his opponents. The navy ship SAS *Drakensberg*, replete with helicopters, armoured vehicles and 133 military personnel, would support the visit. He was the only head of state in the world to accept Aristide's invitation to attend.

Everything went wrong. The Haitian opposition construed South Africa's military presence as support for Aristide. One of the helicopters was fired on, as was Mbeki's motorcade. Mbeki had to cancel his attendance at the principal celebration, abandon his attempt at mediation and scuttle back home amidst Opposition mockery and uproar. No amount of retrospective media spin could disguise the complete shambles.[28] Moreover, while Mbeki insisted that he had not taken sides between Aristide and his opponents, it emerged that large shipments of arms and anti-riot equipment had been illegally[29] sent from South Africa to prop up the embattled Aristide regime. Before they arrived, however, Aristide was deposed and flown out of Haiti by US forces, who accused him of involvement with a Colombian drug ring.

Colin Powell rang Mbeki to ask that he give asylum to Aristide. Mbeki angrily refused, saying he would not 'legitimize a coup d'état',[30] though shortly thereafter he reversed himself and welcomed Aristide. He insisted so strongly on the event's significance that, uniquely, a virtual instruction was issued, demanding that all ambassadors be present to welcome Aristide. A number of African ambassadors went but the rest of the diplomatic corps showed its feelings by ignoring the event. Thereafter Aristide and his entourage lived in luxury in South Africa, at the taxpayer's expense.

PEACE-KEEPING AMBITION AND THE BROKEN SWORD

Mbeki realized that the African Renaissance, his leadership of the AU and his hopes of a UN Security Council seat all depended on South Africa taking the leading role in African peace-keeping. In theory South Africa was perfectly equipped for this. Under apartheid the South African Defence Force was generally reckoned the world's tenth best army, comparable to the Israelis, and it was far better equipped than any other African force. The reality was very different, however. The armed forces were undermined by affirmative action and corruption and by the need to integrate cadres from the old homelands, the ANC, the PAC and the Defence Force into a single new South Africa National Defence Force

(SANDF). Moreover, the first Defence Minister, Joe Modise, was too busy getting rich to bother about the state of the SANDF.

The result was a rapid spiral of declining capacity, low morale, lack of cohesion between the various elements of the force, corruption and maladministration. In 2000 an audit found that large sums of money had disappeared within the Defence Department and that there had been 'mismanagement of almost criminal proportions'.[31] By 2001 the International Institute for Strategic Studies commented that the SANDF's fighting strength had fallen behind even that of Botswana and Zimbabwe and that it was doubtful if it any longer even had the capacity to repeat its 1998 intervention into Lesotho, 'let alone engage in robust peacekeeping elsewhere on the continent'. Its logistics system was 'in complete disarray', troops on deployment received minimal support and their food supply was 'extremely bad'.[32] The new Defence Minister, Terror Lekota, never got on top of his job and was frequently criticized for his failure to meet his constitutional obligation to discuss peacekeeping missions with the parliamentary defence committee. Like other ministers, he was focused on 'demographic representivity', not actual performance. He was thus greatly cheered that by 2003 whites constituted only 24.7 per cent of the SANDF, a number still shrinking fast.[33]

Within the armed forces there was the usual tendency to view state institutions as part of a spoils system, rather than institutions run for the benefit of others. And so by 2002 the army had 207 generals. Since the army had shrunk from 124,000 in 1994 to 70,000, this amounted to one general for every 338 soldiers, compared to 1 : 4,000 in the US Army and 1 : 18,000 in the Swiss Army – and whenever Lekota managed to get extra funds, the result was yet more generals.[34] Seventy per cent of the defence budget went on salaries and many of the spoils-system beneficiaries were quite middle-aged. By 2002 the army had 'an average age somewhere in the region of 40' and the average age of combat troops was 32, against an international norm of 18–22. Many officers were fat and overweight. Fifty-three per cent of all troops were either too sick or too old to be deployed, with only one battalion available for deployment abroad on a sustainable basis.[35] Sickness was often a synonym for Aids. In one sensational test, 89 per cent of an SANDF volunteer group proved to be HIV positive. Lekota argued passionately that this was unrepresentative and that the real figure across the force was only 22 per cent. This was not exactly reassuring, particularly since the UN forbade the deployment of any HIV-positive personnel on peace-keeping missions. In 2004 Lekota finally forbade the recruitment of HIV-positive personnel and set the target of having a force where 'only 10 per cent' would be HIV positive.[36]

The result was a witches' cauldron, with unceasing pressure for more black senior officers, with white officers disaffected by what they termed racism and with generally declining capacity. The most dramatic situation existed in the SAAF where in 2003, despite affirmative action, over 90 per cent of pilots were white and only 7 per cent black. SAAF generals admitted that there was no hope of their achieving the target of 64 per cent black pilots by 2012, because of poor maths and science standards among black applicants. Lekota's reponse, to the horror of aviation professionals, was to lower the pass levels required of trainee pilots,[37] but many officers had already taken matters into their own hands and started cheating in their military exams. This produced a scandal in 2002 when Brigadier-General Lennox Matyila, the fourth-highest ranking officer in the SANDF, was found cheating and was dishonourably discharged, while Colonel Sithabisa Mahlobo, Colonel Stanley Khumalo and Brigadier-General Alice Temba were all demoted for cheating. Ten others faced fraud charges related to cheating and the problem was admitted to be widespread. What added piquancy to the case was the fact that Temba had been the SAAF's first black woman officer, Mahlobo had commanded the peace-keeping force in the Democratic Republic of Congo (DRC) and Matyila had been Commander of the Ciskei (homeland) army.[38]

Nonetheless, there was insistent pressure to Africanize the force faster with whites given strong incentives to quit. This led to mass resignations of white pilots and aircraft technicians in 2004–6, with the result that the SAAF lacked enough pilots to fly its planes. The head of the SAAF, Lt.-Gen. Carlo Gagiano, admitted that the force would be unable to make full use of the new Hawk trainers and Gripen fighters so expensively purchased as part of Modise's arms deal and that there was no early likelihood of the missing pilots being replaced.[39] Similar pressures in the navy produced a shortage of men to man the expensive new submarines.

Corruption and mismanagement within the Defence Department were now endemic. In 2006, for the fifth year in a row, the Auditor-General reported large-scale unauthorized expenditure, a failure to monitor losses and damage to equipment, arms and ammunition, storage of arms and equipment in the wrong conditions, general maladministration and poor internal controls and the large-scale disappearance (i.e. theft) of guns and ammunition. Lekota was furious when *The Star* reported that the peace-keeping force in Burundi had 'mislaid' large numbers of vehicles, armoured cars, ambulances and forklift trucks, even larger numbers of guns, bombs and grenade launchers, and 1.5 million rounds of ammunition, some of which had found its way to the rebels attacking the Burundi capital, Bujumbura. Lekota insisted that the army knew where all the vehicles were (not that it had recovered them) but seemed unaware that an official inquiry had already admitted the losses.[40] The army could not explain how one of its lieutenants had been deployed to Burundi as a peace-keeper while out on bail on a murder charge. This recruitment followed the appointment of a Director for Military Prosecutions who himself had several criminal convictions.[41]

Inevitably, peace-keeping operations were affected. In 2003 Lekota visited the South African contingent in the DRC after troop complaints of lack of medical support and slow delivery of equipment and the court martial of a major on charges of sexual misconduct. Somewhat unwisely, he lashed the troops for complaining and 'behaving like animals': they should try to be more like Mandela and 'your commander-in-chief, President Thabo Mbeki' who had spent thirty years in exile without seeing his family.[42] This latter reference brought a roar of laughter from the troops, for few thought of Mbeki as having had a hard life in exile.

When the AU then asked South Africa for more peace-keepers, this time for Liberia, Lekota declared it was impossible: the SANDF was already overstretched. Mbeki publicly tried to overrule him but no mission was sent. Meanwhile, there was considerable embarrassment over the involvement of SANDF troops in the sexual abuse of minors and other forms of misconduct in the DRC. Despite this, a small SANDF force was sent to Darfur and in 2005 Mbeki volunteered yet more peace-keepers, this time for Somalia.

Mbeki had also become embroiled in mediating the conflict in Ivory Coast but here he was far out of his depth, drawing sharp criticism from President Jacques Chirac of France, who accused him of not understanding 'the psychology and soul' of West Africa. Mbeki had to retire, bruised, from the fray. When fierce fighting erupted in Somalia in 2007 there was deep disquiet, but South Africa's capacity was clearly exhausted. Mbeki could only fume while 10,000 highly trained South Africans from the old SADF served in Iraq in their private capacity, the third largest group after the Americans and British. The most heavily recruited groups were the crack troops of the old apartheid special force units – 32 Battalion, the Parachute Brigade and Koevoet. The contrast between their expertise and that of the new SANDF was painful.

By 2006–8 little was heard from Mbeki about the African Renaissance and Nepad. There was no sign of any renaissance. Conflicts continued to erupt across the continent. Nepad was, effectively, a dead letter. The African Parliament had ceased to meet and there was no sign of the AU becoming a reality. Mbeki's ambition of becoming the leader of all Africa had not worked. He had met strong resistance from Libya, Nigeria, Senegal and Egypt and there had been a bruising contest for a permanent seat on the UN Security Council in 2006. This ended in farce, with the AU demanding, ridiculously, not one but two seats for Africa, replete with a veto, plus five more non-permanent members of the Council of which two should be African. Mbeki, knowing that such demands were unacceptable even to Africa's supporters elsewhere in the world, tried to moderate them but was voted down at an AU summit. His failure to carry even this 'home' constituency wrecked his case. Unsurprisingly, the whole project of Security Council 'reform', let alone altering the 'international architecture', simply collapsed.

When South Africa presided over the Security Council for a month in January 2007 it merely compounded the damage. South Africa used its chairmanship to prevent the Council from discussing the denial of democracy in Burma or human rights atrocities in Zimbabwe and to obstruct UN sanctions against Iran for its refusal to terminate its nuclear enrichment policy. It also abstained on a US motion for a tribunal to investigate political killings in Lebanon and opposed Western pressure for sanctions against Sudan over Darfur. Pretoria declared that it did not see sanctions as an appropriate response in almost any instance, an attitude which Jendayi Frazer, the US Assistant Secretary for State for Africa, described laconically as 'ironic, given their own history'. Describing South African–American relations as going through a 'rough patch', Ms Frazer said this was 'partly because they see themselves as a global power, partly because they see themselves as the voice of the developing world'.[43]

Mbeki's ambition to transform the international order had been the emanation of a personality with grandiose illusions. South Africa was a middle-income developing country of less than fifty million people. The idea that it could be a key initiator of change in the world system – or even the leader of the Third World – was absurd. The exiled ANC had passed motions and lobbied – and lo! the miracle had happened. Mbeki seemed to believe that the same tactics could wreak the further miracle of changing the international system. This was not one but many bridges too far.

THE ELEPHANT IN THE ROOM: ZIMBABWE

One foreign policy issue dominated all others: Zimbabwe. Mugabe's human rights abuses were so flagrant and his destruction of the country's economy and social fabric so devastating that there was no escaping its primacy – and by forcing Ian Smith to accept majority rule in 1980 John Vorster had shown that South Africa had overwhelming leverage over its neighbour when it wanted to use it. By adopting the pretence of 'quiet diplomacy' Mbeki had managed to deflect some of the criticism aimed at his stance on Zimbabwe but only at the price of accepting that he shared the same objectives as the rest of the international community, namely the restoration of democracy and human rights there. His real aim, the maintenance of Zanu-PF in power, was in practice quite incompatible with these objectives.

This contradiction could never be got round and as the situation in Zimbabwe continued to deteriorate it undermined South Africa's credibility in all other spheres. How could Mbeki be taken seriously about world problems if he would not attend to the pressing problem next door? How could South Africa bid for funds for Nepad or a place on the UN Security Council if it refused to take good governance and human rights seriously even on its doorstep?

The sight of Mbeki's government taking Mugabe's side, despite his recourse to violence, his election-rigging and his flouting of property rights and the rule of law, had alarmed investors and produced a run on the rand. While this reinforced Mbeki's determination to dissimulate his real policy behind the fiction of 'quiet diplomacy', not all ANC leaders were so successfully devious. In 2000 the Minister of Agriculture, Thoko Didiza, called a conference of provincial ministers of agriculture to discuss an offer of 'support' from her Zimbabwean counterpart to advise them on how to settle new black farmers on the land. The DP, well aware of the bloody reality such 're-settlement' entailed, described her statement as 'absolutely ominous'. The markets took the same view, with the rand hitting R8.46 to the dollar in September.[44]

A full-scale run on the currency now developed. In October Deputy President Zuma expressed satisfaction with Mugabe's explanation of his land reform and even suggested that the 'reform' would not affect commercial farming. The Reserve Bank governor, Tito Mboweni, hurriedly insisted that Zuma had not meant to sound approving of Mugabe's policy,[45] but by month end the rand had fallen to R9.40. Mbeki's attitude to Zimbabwe was clearly the root cause, which was why panicking big business leaders agreed in November to take out advertisements in the local and British press pledging support for Mbeki's policy and protesting against the 'massive misrepresentations' which portrayed Mbeki as supporting violent land invasions.[46] The rand continued to plummet, reaching an all-time low of R13.10 on 20 December. Although it then recovered slightly, the markets had delivered an unmistakable vote of no confidence. Mbeki's response was to set up a commission of inquiry stacked with Africanist ideologues to ascertain whether the rand's collapse had been due to racism in the markets.

The Western powers were seriously concerned. Chester Crocker, the former US Assistant Secretary for African Affairs (1981–9), warned, 'If South Africa ducks the challenge on Zimbabwe, there will be enormous costs.'[47] Similarly, the British minister Peter Hain, while visiting South Africa in 2001 said, 'I sometimes wonder whether the leadership of southern Africa understands the gravity of the situation. Constructive engagement seems to have failed.' Reflecting that he had earlier been keen to support Mbeki's 'African Renaissance' and that he had tried to encourage investors to put their money into South Africa, he said that Zimbabwe had 'hammered confidence the most' and spoke of how the freedom struggle there had been 'so badly prostituted' that he was now quite unable to persuade investors back to South Africa. 'I wonder if the sub-continent's leaders have truly fathomed how serious it is and what their responsibilities are,' he added.[48]

Dr Dlamini-Zuma sent a furious letter to Hain's superior, the Foreign Secretary in London, saying that Hain had shown his contempt for the government and that the relationship between the two countries was now seriously in question.[49] When journalists asked why South Africa could not exercise pressure on Zimbabwe as Vorster had done, Dr Dlamini-Zuma responded with the standard government line: 'You are advising that we go to war with Zimbabwe. We are not prepared to go to war.'[50]

MBEKI AND THE INTERNATIONAL POLITICS OF ZIMBABWE

Mbeki himself tried to avoid the subject of Zimbabwe. When the Opposition called a parliamentary debate on Zimbabwe his office hurriedly said the President was 'too busy' to attend, though it could not say what his other commitments were. Instead, his acolyte, Mavivi Myakayaka-Manzini, head of the ANC international affairs department, insisted that South Africa could not condemn Zimbabwe: 'We did that with Nigeria when Madiba took a position without consulting the Commonwealth, without consulting the SADC, without consulting the OAU, and what happened? Everyone stood aside and we were isolated because it was a terrible mistake we made . . . we acted as this bully.' Accusing the media and the Opposition of 'dictating to the ANC', she insisted that the ANC could never condemn Zanu-PF. 'These are our comrades we fought with in the struggle. Our relations have been sealed in blood.' When asked how she felt about Mugabe's dismissal of the country's chief justice she insisted: 'People have lost confidence in the judiciary.'[51] Her remarks, including the sharpest attack on Mandela ever heard from an ANC leader, undoubtedly reflected Mbeki's thinking.

Although Mbeki was guarded in what he said about Zimbabwe, there was no doubt that he controlled foreign policy, particularly in this key area. The rationale of supporting a fellow liberation movement against imperialism had been internalized by the ANC, so statements to that effect repeatedly issued from lower-level ANC figures, but given that the policy actually required careful dissimulation, with different messages for different audiences, Mbeki did not trust anyone else to show the necessary finesse. Dr Dlamini-Zuma tended to take a straightforwardly hard line. Visiting Cuba in 2001, she was effusive in her praise of Cuba's democracy and human rights ('you'd be amazed by how democratic it is'). Journalists read her a recent report by Human Rights Watch detailing the lack of a free press or a multi-party system there, and a long list of human rights abuses. 'Who is Human Rights Watch?' she asked. When told that they had campaigned against apartheid, she replied, 'They were not our supporters.'[52] On Zimbabwe, she simply insisted that South Africa would 'never criticize' its neighbour.

As the Zimbabwe crisis grew in amplitude, Condoleezza Rice named the country 'an outpost of tyranny'. This, to many ears, had ominous undertones of Bush's 'axis of evil' and thus the possibility of forcible regime change. Mbeki tried to insist, in effect, that Zimbabwe was within South Africa's sphere of influence, and tried to prevent the issue being discussed at the AU or UN, forums in which 'the imperialists' might get their way. So while he was normally keen to refer all matters to the UN, where the Afro-Asian bloc was strongest, he mobilized African support to keep Zimbabwe off the UN's agenda. Mbeki also obtained the co-operation of black Africa's other key leader, Olusegun Obasanjo of Nigeria – who tended to defer to Mbeki's judgement on the Zimbabwean issue – and tried to establish himself as the indispensable intermediary through whom others would relate to that issue. He was particularly sensitive to any direct British or American intervention in the situation: this conjured up fears of 'imperialist aggression' in southern Africa. Hence the extreme reaction to Hain's remarks and also the icy reception for the first black US Secretary of State, Colin Powell.

It might have been expected that Powell, the world's most powerful black man, would have been fêted and given a state reception when he visited South Africa in May 2001. In fact the opposite was the case. Powell expressed strong concern about Zimbabwe's crisis, warning that it risked unravelling all the democratic gains in southern Africa. Although publicly he praised Mbeki effusively, he clearly disapproved of South Africa's support for Mugabe (by now South Africa was supplying Mugabe with electricity on credit). Remarkably, his hosts had not provided Powell with any platform from which to speak during his visit, so Powell decided to take the bull by the horns and give a speech at Witwatersrand University. Mbeki's office seems to have taken this as a challenge. Powell's visit to Wits quickly became a nightmare. He was heckled and was held a virtual hostage for an hour by left-wing students, many of whom belonged to the ANC-affiliated South African Students Congress (Sasco), holding placards reading 'White House Nigger'.[53] Yet the ANC was usually able to control its Sasco allies and, more generally, what went on at Wits.[54] Had the government really wanted to stop a visiting dignitary receiving such offensive treatment, it would certainly not have happened.

Anyone who believes that this attributes too much to a conspiratorial hidden hand has to explain the remarkable fact that Powell received identical treatment on his next visit in 2002, for the World Summit on Sustainable Development in Johannesburg. Powell was due to speak at 11 a.m. (a prime spot) but the South African chairman suddenly shifted him from this spot, allocating it instead to the Palestinian Foreign Minister, Farouk Kaddoumi, who gave a bitterly anti-American speech. The displacement of the foreign minister of the world's only superpower by an obscure functionary of a semi-state amazed most of those present. Later all became clear. By the time Powell rose to speak in his later slot the public gallery had been packed with anti-American activists, who howled Powell down. South Africa was strongly criticized in diplomatic circles for having set Powell up for such treatment. This was formally denied by Deputy President Zuma but for those who knew the Mbeki style it merely confirmed the suspicion that this slap in the face for Powell had been planned in the presidential office. Then, as usual, the hapless Zuma, who had doubtless had nothing to do with it, was pushed forward to face the music.[55]

With the Zimbabwean situation still deteriorating, both the EU and United States began to threaten targeted sanctions and, increasingly, voices within the Commonwealth demanded Zimbabwe's suspension. Clearly, the presidential election in Zimbabwe in March 2002 would be the acid test. Mbeki, who had received withering criticism for his approval of the rigged election in 2000, had hoped that by now the opposition MDC would have been crushed, allowing an orderly and peaceful Zanu-PF election victory, preferably with a younger successor to Mugabe. But Mugabe was determined to run again and his behaviour was quite unbridled – violent, homophobic and sometimes anti-Semitic.[56] When Mbeki hinted that he would be embarrassed if he again had to defend an obviously unfree election, Mugabe's *Herald* hurled abuse at him as a 'Judas Iscariot' who was not properly African and who was siding with the British against the liberation forces.[57]

It was the same tactic that Abacha had used and, once again, it worked. South Africa declared that it would oppose sanctions against Zimbabwe, attacked both the MDC and Zimbabwe's independent press as 'agents of foreign interest' and claimed that the West, by attaching 'strenuous conditions' to aid for land reform, was responsible for the country's land crisis.[58] South Africa then rallied the whole SADC group behind Mugabe, causing John Makumbe, head of the Zimbabwe Crisis Committee, to claim that they had effectively given 'Mugabe a green light to go flat out with violence and intimidation to win re-election'.[59]

THE ZIMBABWEAN PRESIDENTIAL ELECTION, 2002

Mugabe needed no encouragement: violence against the Opposition escalated with mass beatings, torture and occasional murders. Mugabe, who was himself receiving generous aid from Libya, made it illegal for the opposition MDC to receive any similar outside help. This was a problem for me since I had agreed to carry out opinion surveys for the MDC candidate, Morgan Tsvangirai. These were foreign-funded and thus, under the new law, illegal. We decided to press ahead. The surveys had to be carried out in frightful conditions with even the interviewers, let alone the interviewees, at grave risk. I had repeatedly to sneak into Zimbabwe and meet Tsvangirai secretly at remote venues in order to brief him on the polls. These were undoubtedly favourable to him, but Mugabe's terror campaign had created a great fog of fear, resulting in record non-response rates. People were just too frightened even to talk about the election, let alone vote. During the campaign one of the MDC leaders who knew about the polls was arrested and tortured for several weeks. He never divulged my name. I owe him my life.

Mugabe meanwhile announced that he would not accept any election observers from Britain, Germany, the Netherlands, Sweden, Denmark or Finland since they were all biased in favour of Tsvangirai – an action supported, remarkably, by the AU secretary-general, Amara Essy. When the EU observers arrived Mugabe refused to give accreditation to their mission head, the Swede Pierre Schori, and expelled him. Aziz Pahad, equally remarkably, called on the EU not to take this amiss but to 'look at the bigger picture'.[60] The EU unsurprisingly spurned his advice, withdrew their observer mission and announced targeted sanctions against selected regime members. Pahad complained bitterly that the media 'internationally and at home' was 'demonizing' Mugabe and this 'constant criticism' must stop[61] – a forlorn hope when Mugabe was trying to keep out even South African journalists.

The South African Observer Mission, led by its ambassador to Zimbabwe, Sam Motsuenyane, had barely arrived when some of its members found themselves on the receiving end of Zanu-PF violence. They were caught in the MDC offices in Kwekwe which were attacked and heavily stoned, though the police prevented the observers from talking to any of their attackers. Meanwhile Sir Garfield Todd, the 93-year-old former Prime Minister whose championing of majority rule had earned him house arrest under the Ian Smith regime, was now deprived of his Zimbabwean citizenship and thus of the vote. He said that, although 'I say it through tears', he was glad his wife was no longer alive to see the 'suffering, torture and humiliation of the Zimbabwean people and the undermining of our constitution'.[62] Todd's plight spoke volumes. Mbeki, ignoring all this, said he was sure the election would be free and fair.

A Commonwealth Heads of Government Meeting (CHOGM) convened in Coolum, Australia on the eve of the Zimbabwean poll. The British Prime Minister, Tony Blair, proposed that Zimbabwe be suspended from the Commonwealth for its open flouting of democratic principles. Although he was strongly supported by Australia, Canada and New Zealand, Mbeki rounded up the African bloc – one-third of the Commonwealth's fifty-four members – to oppose him. Instead it was decided that a three-member commission, consisting of Mbeki, Australia's John Howard and Nigeria's Obasanjo (the past, present and future CHOGM chairmen), should make a recommendation based on the report of the Commonwealth mission observing the election in Zimbabwe.

The election culminated in farce, with a wholly inadequate number of polling stations provided in strong opposition areas, producing huge queues of voters unable to vote. Mugabe was declared the winner by 400,000 votes, with voting figures which were quite impossible given the small number of voters registered. Clearly the ballot had been stuffed. Later I came across cigarette smugglers who confessed to having ferried into Zimbabwe truck loads of ballot papers printed in South Africa, already marked with a cross against Mugabe's name. I could not verify this claim but they had no reason to lie.

The South African Observer Mission, though avoiding the phrase 'free and fair', announced the election was 'legitimate'. Hardly coincidentally, this expressed exactly what Mbeki wanted out of the election, a confirmation of Zanu-PF's continued legitimacy in power. The Commonwealth observers came to the opposite conclusion, as did all the other Western observer missions allowed into the country. (In 2000 the Commonwealth observers had issued a hopelessly lame report after a long internal tussle with a black power Maori who had taken Mugabe's side. The Commonwealth had learnt its lesson: this time its report was sharp and unequivocal.) Even before the election S'bu Ndebele, the premier of KwaZulu-Natal and an Mbeki client, made the ANC view clear by accusing 'Western powers and interests of desperately trying to impose their President on the people of Zimbabwe'.[63] The rand fell 3 per cent on the news of Mugabe's victory.

Blair was outraged that Mbeki was trying to block Commonwealth action against Mugabe, playing the race card quite openly to do so. This would set at naught everything the Commonwealth stood for. Blair's frustration at trying to help democracy in Africa only to be blocked by African leaders accusing him of racism was not lessened by the sheer lunacy of some of the African rhetoric. Thus the Commonwealth had given an award to Uganda's President Yoweri Museveni for his country's campaign against Aids. Museveni declared that one reason for its success was that Uganda had no homosexuals, when in fact Uganda had been listed by human rights activists as guilty of maltreating and torturing its homosexuals.[64] So when Blair's motion to suspend Zimbabwe was defeated and the decision handed instead to the Commonwealth troika of Howard, Obasanjo and Mbeki, Blair bluntly told Mbeki, 'OK, Thabo, you've got what you want – two blacks and one white. But remember, you can have Nepad or you can have Zimbabwe but you can't have both.'

Until this point Mbeki had managed to play the Third World radical with the Non-Aligned Movement and the intimate of the mighty at G8. But now it was quite clear that Britain, the United States, the EU, Australia and Canada were all firmly lined up on Zimbabwe and that if he succeeded in protecting Mugabe he would pay a high price. Mbeki was profoundly shaken: nothing in exile politics had prepared him for this either/or. In exile the ANC had taken a Soviet line – supporting the Soviet invasion of Czechoslovakia in 1968, for example – but it still remained the darling of Western liberals, still receiving their money, even their hero-worship. The ANC could be trained by the Stasi, run guns to the IRA, side with Castro – and even then Reagan's America would vote for anti-apartheid sanctions and give scholarships to ANC exiles. It was a long, unconditional free ride. Whatever they did the ANC were still the good guys. There were no either/ors. Now there were, and all that deference had gone.

Mbeki returned from Coolum furiously denouncing Blair for having described the troika as 'two blacks and one white' and alleging that both the Commonwealth and the international media were inspired by 'white supremacy' and 'a stubborn and arrogant mindset' which insisted that 'at all times the white world must lead'. He was in full paranoid flow: 'If the decision-making process in the Commonwealth is going to be informed by this kind of thinking, then obviously it is not worth maintaining the association. It cannot operate on the basis of the humiliation of, and inflicting of insult on, some members by others. Alternately, those inspired by notions of white supremacy are free to depart' if they felt they were being dictated to 'by inferior blacks'. What particularly upset Mbeki was that the white Commonwealth had treated the denial of democracy in Zimbabwe as axiomatic and had regarded attempts to defend Mugabe as crazy and contemptible. They behaved, he said, as if the white minority view was 'intrinsically and obviously correct ... simply because the minority is white' or because it thought in terms of 'a primitive black and a generic African tendency towards dictatorship'.[65]

Mbeki had planned to rely on the South African Observer Mission's report but found it laughed to scorn in the press. Key members of the mission, like Bobby Godsell, the AngloGold boss, dissociated themselves from the report. When Motsuenyane launched the report in Harare journalists jeered and diplomats walked out. Motsuenyane sat stunned and flustered: when he claimed that the MDC had endorsed the election by participating in it he was met with laughter. Moreover, the SADC parliamentary observer mission had condemned the election, pointing to torture, murder, arson and false imprisonment amidst a 'prevailing climate of fear'.[66] Their report made the mission look even worse.

THE CONSEQUENCES OF COOLUM

As Mbeki flew into London to attend the first troika meeting, he found himself the object of condemnation in both the international press and diplomatic circles. Blair rang him to say that, while he personally still supported Nepad, 'after the position of Africa on Zimbabwe, other Western leaders would laugh [Nepad] – and him – out of court if he pretended there was no concern' about Zimbabwe.[67] The Canadian premier, Jean Chrétien, who was hosting the next G8 summit, rang to say that the G8 would refuse to work with African leaders on Nepad if they did not change tack on Zimbabwe. When the troika sat down to business the Commonwealth secretary-general, Don McKinnon, tabled the emphatic report of the Commonwealth observers and Howard read out the agreements made at Coolum as to the sanctions which must flow if the Zimbabwean election was adjudged not to be free and fair. This greatly irritated Mbeki, whose spokesman later accused Howard of being 'schoolmasterish'.[68]

Mbeki insisted that no action be taken against Mugabe, but after two hard hours Obasanjo caved in, agreeing that some action was needed. Zimbabwe was of marginal importance to Nigeria and, apart from wishing to stay onside with the G8, Obasanjo's main concern was the success of the next CHOGM, to be held in Nigeria. With this Mbeki was lost. All he could do was bargain for Zimbabwe's suspension to be for one year only (Howard wanted indefinite suspension) and for the provision of food aid to Harare. A beaming Howard announced the measures at a press conference. Obasanjo smiled but said nothing. Mbeki looked distraught.[69] Returning to the Dorchester hotel, he was told by his doctor that he had been overworking and over-travelling. But this was the only world Mbeki knew: he took an early morning flight to a development finance conference in Mexico.[70]

Mbeki returned home in a ragged state and to a farcical situation. The ANC was steeled against the expected media onslaught when it supported Mugabe's re-election, but now Mbeki himself had been partly responsible for Zimbabwe's suspension from the Commonwealth. Equally embarrassing was the praise-singing from around Africa. President Arap Moi's Kenya – a byword for corrupt and undemocratic rule – hailed Mugabe's re-election. The Namibian observer mission congratulated Mugabe. The AU observers declared the election 'transparent, credible, free and fair'.

ANC Today published a statement by Mbeki that 'the will of the people of Zimbabwe has prevailed', but Smuts Ngonyama then explained that this was 'a mistake': the statement had been issued by the ANC, not Mbeki.[71] Kgalema Motlanthe accused Blair of leading a conspiracy to force Mugabe from power – his reference to 'the hostile forces in the US and UK who are mobilizing to determine who the ruler [of Zimbabwe] should be' being a clear echo of Mbeki's 'imperialist aggression' theory.[72] Mbeki said nothing but got the cabinet to affirm its belief in the 'legitimacy' of the Zimbabwe election while ANC parliamentarians, on the very day that Zimbabwe was suspended from the Commonwealth, declared that the election was 'a credible reflection of the people's will'.[73]

The NEC mandated Dumisane Makhaye to explain party policy to the faithful. He demanded full support for Mugabe's 'liberation struggle' against the Western powers who were intent on recolonizing southern Africa. 'The West wants to impose presidents of their choice on our region. Zimbabwe is only a strategic hill. The real objective is South Africa. The gross interference in the internal affairs of Zimbabwe by Western powers is a dress rehearsal for South Africa.'[74] This was

> part of an offensive by Western powers against the very independence of Africa. Zimbabwe is only a testing ground. For South Africa's white establishment the demonization of the Zanu-PF leadership was a warning to the black leadership in South Africa: 'You dare touch white privileges anywhere, the whole world will pounce on you!' The objective of Western powers is to ensure governments and parties of former national liberation movements are weakened. The talk about the need for a strong opposition is part of this strategy.

Everywhere 'imperialism was bankrolling opposition to national liberation movements. But the people of Zimbabwe voted for the president of their choice' so that 'the forces of recolonization have suffered a strategic defeat in Zimbabwe' but 'their first counter-offensive has been to declare the will of the people of Zimbabwe unfree and unfair'.[75]

Makhaye was his master's voice. In terms of Mbeki's 'imperialist aggression' theory any party that opposed a national liberation movement – in Zimbabwe the MDC – was, by definition, an instrument of counter-revolution. Thus ANC members were regaled with the complete fiction that the MDC met regularly with Renamo (the opposition to Mozambique's ruling Frelimo), the NNP and other right-wing parties in the region. They were also told that the MDC was effectively the same thing as the white Commercial Farmers Union and that it had close relations with South Africa's DA (it did not: Tony Leon had made one ten-minute courtesy call on Morgan Tsvangirai); and that it was closer to the West than to Africa.[76]

This was all nonsense. The MDC was based on Zimbabwe's trade unions; its white supporters had passionately opposed Ian Smith, while Smith's most notorious allies and arms-suppliers such as Billy Rautenbach, John Bredenkamp and Andre Holland were Mugabe's allies. The MDC sought good relations with the ANC, but was cold-shouldered. Instead the MDC maintained friendly relations with Cosatu, who, like the SACP, opposed Mugabe because of his hostility to the trade unions.

Mbeki meanwhile used South Africa's presidency of the Non-Aligned Movement to build a Third World coalition which blocked attempts to bring the Zimbabwean issue before the UN General Assembly or its Human Rights Commission. African states introduced 'no action' motions on the basis that there could be no debate on human rights until the prior land issue had been dealt with. Ignoring the obvious, the South African press still displayed an extraordinary credulity towards the fictional policy of 'quiet diplomacy'.

Mugabe had little difficulty exploiting the situation to stay in power himself, knowing that Mbeki would never be willing to use South Africa's overwhelming leverage against him. Mugabe was, indeed, willing even to flirt with al-Qaeda, though he knew this could only embarrass Mbeki. Not only was Mugabe one of the few people given a forewarning of the events of 9/11 but he had actually allowed al-Qaeda militants to fly into Zimbabwe in the week following 9/11 to get fitted out with false Zimbabwean passports.[77] For Zimbabwe was now a rogue state and Mugabe was willing to dine with the devil, especially if it brought foreign exchange his way.

THE FIGHT WITHIN THE COMMONWEALTH: ROUND TWO

Mbeki still deeply resented the way he had been defeated by Howard and Blair and determined to reverse that defeat at the troika's meeting of March 2003, when the one-year suspension period would be up. In January 2003 Malusi Gigaba, president of the ANC Youth League and a frequent conduit for Mbeki's views, launched a long diatribe against Britain and Australia, 'the white section of the Commonwealth', who were guilty of 'sickening hypocrisy' in their dealings with Zimbabwe when all they were really concerned about were their own white 'kith and kin'. Again, it was his master's voice. The Australians denounced the document as an 'ignorant and abusive rant unworthy of circulation in a great political movement like the ANC'.[78]

Another ventriloquized statement followed. Abdul Minty, director-general of the Ministry of Foreign Affairs, astonished an audience of twenty Commonwealth heads of mission by a blistering attack on John Howard's behaviour as troika chairman. One diplomat described Minty's performance as 'very discourteous and embarrassing. There seems to be a co-ordinated drive to delegitimize Howard, split the Commonwealth on race lines and force the Australians out of the game on Zimbabwe. A whole anti-West thing seems to be going on.'[79] Minty also denounced as racist Australia's issuance of travel advisories warning tourists about potential dangers in South Africa, thus exactly repeating Mbeki's own allegation in *ANC Today* (a complaint ridiculed by one diplomat as 'completely paranoid'). Minty also denounced Howard for disclosing a telephone conversation he had had with Mbeki and Obasanjo – a clear sign that Minty, too, was speaking on Mbeki's behalf.[80]

Howard had been trying to extract a clear commitment from Mbeki and Obasanjo to attend a troika meeting on the anniversary of Zimbabwe's suspension. Australia and New Zealand had both imposed targeted sanctions against Mugabe and his cronies meanwhile, for the situation in Zimbabwe had continued to deteriorate and none of the Commonwealth's conditions for the restoration of democracy and human rights had been met. In such circumstances Howard had regarded the renewal of the suspension as virtually automatic and had been greatly surprised, while en route back from a visit to the United States, to get a telephone call in Honolulu from Mbeki and Obasanjo in which they said that they could not see any purpose to the troika meeting again.

A letter from Obasanjo to Howard was then published, seeking to justify Mugabe's position in general and making a number of astonishing assertions: the Zimbabwean police had apologized for torturing an MDC MP and promised to take action against the perpetrators; those guilty of abuses in the land reform programme had been brought to book; and Mugabe had set aside a huge sum with which to compensate white farmers who had lost their land.[81] None of these things was true and observers concluded that, following his normal penchant, Mbeki had drafted the letter for Obasanjo, whose grasp of Zimbabwean realities was weak.

Mbeki had assumed that if the troika did not meet Zimbabwe's suspension would simply expire. He had forgotten the old French saying, 'Les absents ont toujours tort.' Don McKinnon had prepared an utterly damning report for the troika, detailing Mugabe's appalling human rights record and how the 'fast-track land reform' was actually the mere stealing of land by the already rich.[82] McKinnon now announced that after consulting widely with Commonwealth members he was extending Zimbabwe's suspension until the next CHOGM. Worse, he assumed Mbeki and Obasanjo had, by their absence, agreed to go along with the majority decision.

Mbeki had, again, been comprehensively and publicly outwitted. His anger was patent: in London South Africa's high commissioner, Lindiwe Mabuza, acting on Mbeki's instructions, insisted that McKinnon had cheated. She demanded to know 'precisely what countries were consulted and what positions they communicated to the Secretary-General', arguing that none of the ten African Commonwealth states, nor any of the Non-Aligned Movement states would have voted to suspend Zimbabwe. McKinnon's decision was, she said, 'a political and procedural travesty'. Aziz Pahad demanded a review of the decision. But Mbeki had far overestimated his influence with other African states and members of the Non-Aligned Movement. They might agree with him when he was there demanding their support but when they were left to make up their minds under pressure from their biggest trade partners, investors and donors, the result was very different. Obasanjo quickly professed himself keen to move on and not fight the decision, leaving

Mbeki spitting fire against McKinnon all on his own. Not a single other African Commonwealth member queried the decision. Several of them, indeed, had secretly voted for Mugabe's continued suspension.[83]

The problem, again, was Mbeki's grandiosity. He had assumed too easily that his long experience of ANC politicking made him a match for Blair and Howard. It did not: he was outclassed. They had working foreign services, which he did not, and they had seen him coming a mile off. Equally, he had overestimated his ability to control Obasanjo. This broke down on the harsh fact that Nigeria had very different interests. And he had too easily assumed he could control the smaller African states too. Worse, his failure was public. Although the pretence of 'quiet diplomacy' went on, Mbeki had failed to protect Mugabe from sanctions and ostracism. He had twice been publicly defeated within the Commonwealth and found himself wholly isolated. Western diplomats were unanimous that the Zimbabwe issue had seen Nepad become a dead letter. As one put it, Africa and South Africa have to 'get their house in order and then we can take them seriously and commit to development aid and promoting investment. [Nepad] is a wonderful idea but it all falls down at the Zimbabwe hurdle.'[84] Worst of all, the premise behind supporting Mugabe was not working. It did not lead to the quick suppression of the MDC and the re-stabilization of the country under Zanu-PF rule, the MDC would not go away, the situation continued to deteriorate – and stabilization was not in sight.

THE FIGHT WITHIN THE COMMONWEALTH: ROUND THREE

At its conference in Stellenbosch in 2002 the ANC gave a rapturous reception to Emmerson Mnangagwa at the head of a Zanu-PF delegation, for Mnangagwa was seen as Mugabe's likely successor. The fact that Mnangagwa had been blacklisted by the UN as one of the main plunderers of the wealth of the war-torn DRC cut no ice with the ANC any more than did Mnangagwa's bloodstained record as head of the secret police (the Central Intelligence Organization) during the Matabeleland atrocities of the 1980s. The UN had detailed the criminal nature of the Congo's plunder 'through a variety of criminal activities, including theft, embezzlement, diversion of public funds, undervaluation of goods, smuggling, false invoicing, non-payment of taxes, kickbacks to public officials and bribery'.[85] Mnangagwa was, nonetheless, hailed as a 'fellow progressive' at Stellenbosch. A year later South Africa blocked a UN vote condemning human rights abuses in Zimbabwe. Dr Dlamini-Zuma insisted that the Mugabe government was easing its most draconian laws and offering land back to evicted white farmers. Neither of these things was true. Worse, when evidence was presented of hundreds of cases in which opponents of Mugabe had been tortured, Dr Dlamini-Zuma dismissed this as due merely to 'over-zealousness' by the security forces.[86]

The Iraq war, which started in March 2003, was a nasty shock for both Mbeki and Mugabe. They had both subscribed to the notion that the imperialist powers were plotting regime change in southern Africa and here, as if to bear them out, was a public demonstration of Anglo-American might to secure regime change in an even more contested corner of the Third World. Thereafter Mugabe worried that a coup against him might be launched by British special forces based in South Africa, while Mbeki was anxious lest Mugabe's continued antics would give the imperialists the excuse they wanted to launch the first stage of a programme of regime change by force in southern Africa.[87] Within weeks of the war government insiders were expressing fears that 'It would be dangerous for the region and the African continent if the West started interfering in our governance issues', that 'the West could gain a foothold in the region' or that Mugabe might be removed from office and brought before an international tribunal like Slobodan Milošević.[88]

President Bush sought to lay such fears to rest during his visit to South Africa in July 2003, praising Mbeki's attempts to find a solution to the Zimbabwean crisis. Mbeki infuriated the MDC by claiming publicly that Mugabe was talking to his Opposition about a settlement – a blatant untruth. Behind closed doors Mbeki also gave Bush his solemn promise that Mugabe would be gone within a year. Bush was greatly relieved.[89] But in any case obtaining South African help in the rendition of terrorist suspects far outweighed the importance of Zimbabwe for Bush.

Mbeki was determined to reverse his earlier defeat and lift Zimbabwe's suspension from the Commonwealth. Two months before the CHOGM due to be held in Abuja, Nigeria, Mbeki's spokesman, Bheki Khumalo, announced that South Africa saw no reason for Mugabe not to be invited to Abuja and would formally ask President Obasanjo to ensure that such an invitation was extended. This had to be snatched back the next day, however, when it became clear that Obasanjo had no intention of thus picking a fight with the Commonwealth majority.[90]

Mbeki's attempts to get other African countries to refuse to attend CHOGM unless Zimbabwe was invited were similarly unsuccessful – McKinnon was lobbying hard the other way – so Mbeki decided to punish McKinnon by putting up an alternative candidate for his job, the Sri Lankan, Lakshman Kadirgamar. Commonwealth officials were unusually outspoken in response, pointing out that it was impossible to readmit Zimbabwe given that the regime's behaviour had continued to deteriorate and that it had refused entry to Commonwealth officials. They queried why South Africa was trying to unseat McKinnon. 'Is it pique at the Zimbabwean issue? If so, why? What results has its position [of quiet diplomacy] yielded?'[91]

Mbeki was routed. Zimbabwe's suspension was maintained and the question of reviewing Zimbabwe's future membership handed to a seven-member panel, chaired by Nigeria and including South Africa, Mozambique, India, Jamaica, Canada and Australia – thus diluting South Africa's leverage while maintaining an Afro-Asian majority. McKinnon was thumpingly re-elected by 40 : 11. Again, the struggle over Zimbabwe came down to a bitter confrontation between Mbeki on the one hand, and the Commonwealth's white leaders on the other – indeed, Blair's spokesman squarely blamed Mbeki for the difficulties: 'The problem appears to be that South Africa does not accept that Zimbabwe should remain suspended.'[92] But it did not work. McKinnon produced a memo setting out a long litany of Mugabe's further human rights abuses. Faced with that, Mbeki's arguments for readmitting Zimbabwe – even his public promise that the whole Zimbabwe problem would be solved by June 2004 – were met with derision. Mugabe then solved the issue by walking out of the Commonwealth, claiming that Zimbabwe was being persecuted by white racists in its ranks.

In mid-CHOGM South Africa's Foreign Ministry, on behalf of the SADC group, issued a statement insisting that the Commonwealth's entire future hung in the balance if Zimbabwean membership was not restored. To Mbeki's fury no one took this seriously and the statement was simply brushed aside. Mbeki issued his own broadside, quoting the SADC statement (which he had drafted) expressing 'our displeasure and deep concern with the dismissive, intolerant and rigid attitude displayed by some members of the Commonwealth',[93] while his spokesman, Abdul Minty, blamed McKinnon, arguing that the Zimbabwe issue should never have been taken away from the troika. Mbeki's furiously bitter statement ran to thousands of words and ended with a typical peroration: 'Our poverty and underdevelopment will never serve as reason for us to abandon our dignity as human beings, turning ourselves into grateful and subservient recipients of alms, happy to submit to a dismissive, intolerant and rigid attitude of some in our country and the rest of the world, towards what we believe and know is right, who are richer and more powerful than we are.'[94] Thus, a plea in favour of Mugabe's tyrannical and brutal regime somehow transmuted by the end into a heroic statement of victimhood, struggling for human dignity against the rich and the powerful. The text not only gave away the true authorship of the phrase 'dismissive, intolerant and rigid' in the SADC document but one would imagine the author to be someone on the edge of destitution rather than the President of a considerable state. Such rhetoric revealed both Mbeki's enormous self-righteousness – how could a victim be wrong? – and the reasons why the major powers at the CHOGM could not take him seriously.

Mbeki had gravely embarrassed Obasanjo, at one point suggesting that the report of the Commonwealth election observers be rewritten in line with South Africa's view, at another threatening that the whole of the SADC would walk out of the Commonwealth together with Mugabe. Obasanjo resisted both suggestions and was embarrassed when Mbeki expressed his anger at the leaking of the vote on the secretary-generalship (which had shown the weakness of his position). Then, when Mbeki's promise that a Zimbabwe settlement was imminent was greeted by laughter from other delegates, Mbeki furiously sought to prolong discussion and had objected when Obasanjo, who could see this was getting nowhere, had brought the debate to an end. The result was a distinct coolness between Mbeki and Obasanjo.[95]

Again, Mbeki had greatly overestimated his strength. A whole flock of African states had voted to maintain Zimbabwe's suspension: Kenya, Botswana, Ghana, Gambia, Sierra Leone and Malawi. Moreover, the decision to put up Kadirgamar had been a disaster: indeed, it left the candidate himself and Sri Lanka bitter that most of the promised African bloc votes for him never materialized. Jean Chrétien, the Canadian premier, typified the attitude of the major Commonwealth states: 'There was a candidate who stood against McKinnon. I don't know him. I've never met him and if I did, I don't remember.'[96]

Mbeki returned from his second humiliation at a CHOGM to face a broadside from the churches. Desmond Tutu warned that if South Africa ignored human rights abuses in Zimbabwe, it would end up ignoring them at home. He was, he added, 'baffled', both that Mbeki could denounce CHOGM's procedures as undemocratic when they had been settled by overwhelming majority vote and also by the demand for Zimbabwe's suspension to be lifted: suspension had been meant to make Mugabe respect the rule of law and refrain from violence, but this he had not done.[97] Other Church leaders denounced the use of torture in Zimbabwe, giving specific and ghastly details of victims having red-hot needles pushed into their armpits and shoulders, their genitals beaten to a pulp, and so on.[98] The Revd Frank Chikane, the President's director-general and a former head of the South African Council of Churches, was dispatched to do battle with the clergy, making the most contemptuous accusations against them.[99] This attack on fellow-churchmen seeking to speak up for victims of torture was perhaps the most extraordinary statement ever issued by a South African cleric.

THE ZIMBABWEAN ELECTION OF 2005

Mbeki had always said that a key reason for 'quiet diplomacy' was to protect the Zimbabwean economy, for South Africa would bear the brunt of any meltdown, starting with inevitable large flows of economic refugees. By now it was apparent that these were precisely the results of his policy. Zimbabwean GDP shrank by 40 per cent in the wake of Mugabe's onslaught on commercial agriculture. Shortages, soaring unemployment and inflation sent Zimbabweans streaming into South Africa by the million. Despite this, regular high-level summits between the ANC and Zanu-PF continued. The proceedings were always secret except for a statement that the two parties had 'a shared vision in the region', though some reports claimed that the ANC had agreed to help Zanu-PF in the forthcoming 2005 election,[100] Mbeki having now admitted that his promised June 2004 deadline for a resolution to the crisis would not be met. South Africa continued to protect Zimbabwe from discussion of its human rights abuses at the UN – indeed, so bizarre did the proceedings of the UN Commission on Human Rights become that the major Western powers decided to make the Commission's reform an early priority.

As the 2005 Zimbabwean parliamentary election neared there were the familiar ANC claims that the election would be free and fair, though the day after Dr Dlamini-Zuma made such a prediction the MDC's elections director, Ian Makone, was arrested.[101] Mbeki was outraged that Condoleezza Rice should list Zimbabwe as one of six 'outposts of tyranny' (alongside Cuba, Belarus, Burma, North Korea and Iran) but his policy was now so discredited that not even the pusillanimous South African business community supported him; indeed, that community's main paper, *Business Day*, ridiculed Mbeki's prediction of a free and fair election: 'Mbeki is talking nonsense. The forthcoming election in Zimbabwe is already unfree and unfair.'[102] Elinor Sisulu, daughter-in-law of Walter Sisulu, also dissented, arguing that Mugabe was a world champion at rigged elections and that there was every sign that the South African Observer Mission would arrive at the election with its mind made up that it was free and fair irrespective of 'anything they may witness on the ground'.[103]

The election went exactly as Sisulu had predicted. The MDC lost 15 of its 56 seats in an election the South African Observer Mission termed 'legitimate and fair' but which the rest of the world treated as a farce. Even the usually tame South African Council of Churches attacked the mission's report as 'morally questionable' and said its tone was 'almost as if the perpetrator [of violence] was being congratulated and rewarded'.[104] Mugabe immediately launched 'Operation Murambatsvina' (Clear out the Shit), a pre-emptive strike against suspected opponents, destroying homes and businesses and rendering nearly two million people homeless. The Murambatsvina – which cost an estimated hundred thousand lives – was condemned around the world, though Mbeki refused to criticize it. The ANC used its majority to prevent Parliament from discussing the South African Observer Mission's report, which the Murambatsvina had made an embarrassment. Mugabe had been advised to carry out the Murambatsvina by the exiled Ethiopian dictator, Mengistu Haile Mariam, now a welcome guest in Harare, despite his being found guilty of genocide by an Addis Ababa court. Mbeki also hosted Mengistu (who came to Johannesburg for medical treatment), apparently guaranteeing that he would not be handed over to justice.[105]

Despite such obvious indications that Mbeki was little concerned with human rights, the South African press continued fondly to imagine that Mbeki's aim in Zimbabwe was the restoration of democracy. Even the well-known commentator Allister Sparks found it too painful to face the truth about Mbeki and Mugabe. Sparks, whose reporting had been so pro-ANC that he had been nominated for their election list in 1994, criticized Mbeki for giving 'the impression of support' for Mugabe but noted: 'Some read Mbeki's reticence as an indication that he was secretly supportive of Mugabe . . . this was certainly not true.'[106]

Yet the facts of that support were always clear. Ever since the decisive March 2000 summit of liberation movements there had been repeated summits, sometimes just between the ANC and Zanu-PF – as for example in June 2004 when the Zanu-PF chairman, John Nkomo, led a top-level delegation to meet the ANC in Johannesburg. The ANC's delegation showed the importance it attached to such meetings: it was led by Mbeki himself, flanked by Deputy President Jacob Zuma, ANC chairman Terror Lekota, secretary-general Kgalema Motlanthe and treasurer-general Mendi Msimang.[107] Mugabe himself, in mid-Murambatsvina, thanked Mbeki for his 'solidarity and comradeship', adding that 'South Africa is part of us and we share ideas with President Thabo Mbeki almost on a weekly basis'.[108] When Phumzile Mlambo-Ngcuka succeeded Jacob Zuma as Deputy President she remarked that 'We learnt a few lessons from Zimbabwe (on land reform) – how to do it fast. We may need some skills from Zimbabwe to help us.'[109]

COUNTING THE COST

By now the costs of Mbeki's Zimbabwe policy were beginning to be felt. The Zimbabwean economy continued to nosedive, sending some three million migrants pouring into South Africa. Zimbabwe, historically always South Africa's largest trading partner in Africa, fell behind first Mozambique and then Zambia in significance. Relations with Britain and other major Commonwealth countries were badly strained, a situation not helped by Mbeki's decision to boycott the 2005 CHOGM in

Malta, sending the Deputy President instead. This was unprecedented: Commonwealth leaders always attended unless prevented by last-minute emergencies. The piqued Mbeki announced he would not be going seven weeks in advance.

Mbeki had also damaged South Africa's relations with Nigeria, increasingly cool in the wake of Abuja. In 2005 the South Africa–Nigeria Bi-national Commission failed to meet even once. Mbeki, still involved in mediation attempts in Ivory Coast, was roundly criticized in Nigeria for failing to report back on his efforts to Obasanjo, the AU chairman, as protocol demanded. Feelings frayed further as South Africa and Nigeria competed for a possible African seat on the UN Security Council, with Nigeria openly questioning South Africa's authenticity as a black state, suggesting that it was 'too white' to represent Africa properly.[110] Ms Dayo Oluyemi-Kusa, director of the Institute for Peace and Conflict Resolution, a think tank based within Nigeria's presidency, told the press that 'We have real blacks, unlike Egypt and South Africa', adding the crucial rider that 'South Africa might seem to be the favourite because it is technologically more advanced, but the foundation was actually laid by whites under apartheid'.[111]

Writing off Obasanjo, Mbeki was the first African leader to congratulate his successor, Umaru Yar'Adua, on his election as Nigeria's President, attending his inauguration in May 2007, despite the fact that the election had been condemned far and wide as fraudulent. By now even black commentators like Barney Mthombothi, editor of the *Financial Mail*, were vocally critical:

> Mbeki has done more than anyone else to legitimize the electoral fraud that produced Yar'Adua . . . as if to cock a snook at the rest of the world the man was flown to South Africa for a well-publicized parade and a presidential handshake. A view is slowly gaining currency that the new South Africa, contrary to received opinion, has so far not been a good thing for the continent. It has not been a force for good . . .[112]

The Zimbabwean issue had also cost South Africa dear over Nepad and the AU, for the foreign donors on whom everything depended made it clear that the whole question of Africa's attitude to good governance would stand or fall on the issue of Zimbabwe. In December 2001 the AU's Commission on Human and People's Rights tabled a report criticizing Mugabe's human rights record but South Africa and

Zimbabwe invented pretexts to stop the AU from considering it: first that it had not been translated into French, then that Zimbabwe's government had not been consulted.

Similarly, when the Pan-African Parliament (PAP) met it had been decided in advance it would not discuss the Zimbabwean issue. To ensure this result Pretoria had broken the PAP rules obliging member states to send delegations representative of their own parliaments, thus preventing the possibility of delegations sent from the ruling party alone. The ANC used its parliamentary majority to ensure that the official Opposition, the DA, was not represented in South Africa's PAP delegation; the DA would certainly have raised the Zimbabwean issue.

When the AU summit in Banjul in July 2006 discussed a charter on good governance and democracy, Mugabe was observed to be fast asleep in his seat. He could afford to doze, for the AU rejected the charter precisely because it sought to sanction presidents who, like Mugabe, manipulated their constitutions to stay in power indefinitely. Embarrassing such presidents-for-life would never do.

All of this had a price. Foreign donors were perfectly aware of this institutional cheating aimed at shielding the Mugabe regime, just as they were aware that during the peer review of governance, Nepad's most crucial component, Pretoria had manipulated the process to rig the review document on South Africa. The final draft was, nevertheless, not uncritical, infuriating the government, which tried in vain to persuade the panel to change its report. It then angrily rejected 149 of its 150 recommendations, insisting that whatever was wrong was actually the fault of apartheid. It particularly disliked the panel's reported worries about the emasculation of Parliament, threats to judicial independence, the driving out of competent whites by affirmative action and the abuse of immigrants' human rights: such criticisms, it claimed, revealed the panel's 'ideological and value-laden' approach.[113]

Not surprisingly, by 2007 none of Nepad's twenty flagship projects had obtained the requisite foreign funding. Senegal's President Abdoulaye Wade was biting: 'Expenses adding up to hundreds of millions of dollars have been spent on trips, on hotels. But not a single classroom has been built, not a single health centre completed. Nepad has not done what it was set up for.'[114] Blair's remark that 'you can have Nepad or you can have Zimbabwe but you can't have both' had been prescient. Mbeki had made support for Zanu-PF his top priority – so Nepad was a dead duck.

Such a priority seems extraordinary to anyone not sharing Mbeki's essentially Marxist-Leninist world view, shared by at least some of the top ANC elite. In private it was not difficult to hear ANC MPs expound their bottomless regret at the collapse of the Soviet Union and, especially, East Germany, their fears of a landing by US Marines and even their lament that the Soviet working class could not have been 'more patient' so that the Soviet Union would have survived to help them build a People's Republic in South Africa. Only if one accepted this logic did it make sense to give priority to defending brother liberation movements like Zanu-PF against imperialist assault. In this, as in many other senses, the ANC continued to live in the world of the 1960s. Like covert flat-earthers in an era when everyone else believed the world was round, they carefully camouflaged their beliefs most of the time, but underneath the belief remained not just alive but primary.

THE ZIMBABWEAN ELECTIONS OF 2008

Mugabe met Zimbabwe's economic crisis by simply printing money, so inflation escalated to over 100,000 per cent by March 2008. A split in the MDC took some pressure off Mugabe but as 80 per cent unemployment, food shortages and the collapse of the country's health facilities took their toll, life expectancy plunged to only 37 for men and 34 for women – a halving in only ten years. Inevitably, and despite fierce repression, political unrest grew and with it cracks within Zanu-PF. An increasingly cornered Mugabe determined to crush the Opposition once and for all so that, whatever happened to the regime, it could never take over. In March 2007 dozens of Opposition leaders, including Morgan Tsvangirai, were arrested, beaten and tortured, producing an unprecedented international protest. Mbeki said nothing. The ANC issued a statement vaguely referring to 'alleged assaults on Opposition leaders in police custody' and expressing the hope that 'these allegations will be thoroughly investigated' – this at a time when television images of a prodigiously battered Tsvangirai, with both eyes closed from his beating, were seen around the world.

So great was world pressure this time – it reduced Aziz Pahad to a sort of hysterical indignation about the media's 'unfairness' – that a special SADC summit admitted for the first time that there was a Zimbabwean problem. However, the meeting expressed no public criticism of Mugabe, who bounced out of it declaring that 'We got full backing, not even one criticized our actions. Yes, I told them [Tsvangirai] was beaten but he had asked for it.'[115] This gave the lie to the statement he had submitted in advance to the summit in which he had asserted that Tsvangirai had 'at no time [been] assaulted in police custody'.[116] Mbeki, whom the SADC had entrusted with the role of mediator, began his task. He gave an interview – typically, to a British paper – in which, absurdly, he expressed confidence that Mugabe would step down willingly and talked confidently about free and fair elections in Zimbabwe in March 2008.[117] In fact Mugabe stood, yet again, as Zanu-PF's presidential candidate – if he lived, he would still be president at the age of 90.

A truer reflection of Mbeki's attitude was the fact that SABC journalists were forbidden to listen to SW Radio Africa, the independent station which broadcast the unvarnished truth about Mugabe's misrule.[118] Mugabe revealed what Mbeki had actually told the SADC summit: 'He said "The fight against Zimbabwe is a fight against us all. Today it is Zimbabwe, tomorrow it will be South Africa, it will be Mozambique, it will be Angola . . . And any government that is perceived to be strong and to be resistant to imperialists, would be made a target. So let us not allow any point of weakness . . ."'[119] Thus seven years into the Zimbabwe crisis Mbeki's analysis, though often masked from view, remained as it had been at the outset.

Mugabe now launched an all-out assault on the MDC, swearing publicly that his main objective was to ensure that it could never come to power. Hundreds of MDC activists were detained, beaten and tortured. Mbeki made no comment, although this already precluded any possibility of a free and fair election in 2008. Those who dared report the truth about Mugabe's repression were also targeted. Edward Chikombo, the cameraman who had filmed Tsvangirai's injuries, was hunted down and murdered.

Mbeki's mediation was aimed at producing elections which could confer at least minimal legitimacy on Zanu-PF. There was a new constitution and amendments to other laws. The number of parliamentary seats was increased from 120 to 210, the President's right to name thirty extra MPs was abolished, and it was determined that to win a presidential election a candidate must win at least 50 per cent on the first round or, failing that, face a run-off within twenty-one days. SADC emphasized that it did not wish to be embarrassed again by the murderous state violence which had marred previous Zimbabwean elections. Mugabe, in return, allowed in election observers only from SADC and other friendly states thought likely to sign off on a Mugabe victory as 'free, fair and credible'. Despite protests by the MDC that conditions in the country made free elections impossible, Mugabe pushed ahead with parliamentary, presidential and local elections, all to occur on 30 March 2008.

The election was, as the SADC had demanded, peaceful. Simba Makoni, a former Zanu-PF Finance Minister, entered the presidential race with Mbeki's support, for Mbeki badly wanted Zanu-PF to present a more acceptable face to the outside world. Mugabe, an octogenarian megalomaniac, was irretrievably tarnished. The SADC election observers were predictably disgraceful. The Opposition was denied access to the state-controlled media and was not allowed even to see a copy of the electoral register, which included thousands of dead and non-existent voters. Mugabe changed the electoral regulations by decree at the last moment, allowing police inside polling stations to 'assist' voters. Yet the observers hurriedly proclaimed the election free, fair and credible and left the country before any result was declared. Even as their mission head gave his blessing to the election, some of his team could be seen shaking their heads.

'Sure, Mbeki thought Zanu-PF – whether Makoni or Mugabe – would win and SADC was quite happy with that,' Willias Mudzimure, an MDC MP for Harare, told me.

> They had seen how Mugabe had the rural vote locked up solid and the idea was that by increasing the number of parliamentary seats, there would be a large increase in the number of rural seats, all of which Mugabe would win. And because there'd been such a reign of terror in those rural areas in past elections, frankly we couldn't get good candidates to stand for us there – people were just too scared. Also, they knew the MDC was split and that we'd wanted the election put off to June. They didn't think we had a chance.[120]

But it all went wrong. Taking advantage of the more peaceful conditions, the Tsvangirai forces successfully penetrated the rural areas, staging huge rallies there and winning hitherto safe Zanu-PF seats. In previous elections Zanu-PF had distributed food and seeds to those with Zanu-PF cards: if you didn't vote Zanu-PF you didn't eat. Now the state simply had no more resources. And SADC's drafters had quietly inserted Section 64 (1) E into the new Electoral Act, requiring all votes to be counted at the polling station where they were cast, with the results, witnessed by the party agents, then posted publicly outside the station. This gave the Opposition a virtually foolproof way of detecting cheating. 'Mbeki didn't read the fine print of his own agreement,' laughed Chris Mbanga, Tsvangirai's chief of staff. 'He can't have realized how crucial Section 64 (1) E would be, nor that the changes to the Public Order Act made it much easier than before for the MDC to hold meetings with its local activists.'[121]

As the results trickled in, the Zimbabwe Electoral Commission quickly briefed the Zanu-PF politburo. Not only had the MDC and its allies easily won the parliamentary elections but, according to initial estimates, Tsvangirai was way ahead with 58 per cent, Mugabe trailing on 27 per cent and Simba Makoni had 15 per cent. In fact these estimates, based on an unrepresentative sample, were too favourable to Tsvangirai but the message was clear: Mugabe had lost. The politburo hit the roof. Mugabe then ordered the Electoral Commission to declare him elected with 53 per cent and that the 'traitor' Makoni's vote be reduced to 5 per cent. This produced resistance both from the Electoral Commission and from the army, police and intelligence chiefs; the Commission objected that manipulation of the results on such a massive scale would be both difficult and obvious, while the security chiefs were concerned that the country might become ungovernable if the popular will was so brutally flouted.[122]

Mbeki was continuously on the telephone from Pretoria and had his emissaries in Harare. Out of Mbeki's discussions with the Zanu-PF politburo, the Electoral Commission and the security chiefs came the notion that the results should be 'adjusted' so that Tsvangirai was brought back under the 50 per cent mark, perhaps to 47–49 per cent, while Mugabe could get 41 per cent and Makoni 10–12 per cent. With no candidate over 50 per cent this would make a run-off necessary. Mugabe should then withdraw, leaving Zanu-PF to rally behind Makoni. The security forces would play a strong role in organizing the run-off and Makoni could then be given just over 50 per cent and Tsvangirai kept out. For Mbeki, like Mugabe, regarded the election figures as entirely manipulable.

As word that Mbeki had been heavily involved spread into the South African media, Mbeki's office quickly denied that he had been involved at all. The MDC were aghast at Mbeki's cynicism but torn between being diplomatically polite towards a powerful neighbour and making unprintable remarks about him.

The deal stitched together by Mbeki might have worked. 'We were saved from this outcome', an MDC MP told me, 'by our most reliable ally, Robert Mugabe, who absolutely refused to stand down.' Mugabe clamped down on the release of the presidential results, ordered a recount, launched a new terror campaign against the MDC and, ignoring the constitutional requirement for a run-off within twenty-one days, scheduled a run-off for 30 June. It was clear that the elections would be stolen, whatever it took. Mbeki flew to Zimbabwe, appearing hand in hand with Mugabe to insist there was 'no crisis' in Zimbabwe, a statement which was ridiculed and condemned both at home and abroad. The MDC now wrote to Mbeki saying that his disgracefully partisan behaviour meant they could no longer accept him as a mediator. Mbeki's office denied getting this letter and suggested it did not exist. The MDC angrily redelivered it.

THE TRAGEDY OF MBEKI'S FOREIGN POLICY

Mbeki's basic assumption, that Mugabe could crush his opposition and then restabilize Zimbabwe under permanent Zanu-PF rule, had proved false: destabilization continued apace. And, with a population continually stressed by food shortages and man-made crises, deaths from hunger and Aids continued to soar. The population was falling so fast that there was increasing talk of genocide; on the crudest calculation there had been at least two million 'abnormal' extra deaths since 2000 and the real figure might be much larger. It was not an ethnic or religious genocide (though clearly MDC supporters suffered most), more a general mass culling of the population as a result of deliberate and malign government policy. Mbeki, repeatedly accused of genocide at home as a result of his Aids denialism, accused of shielding a genocidal regime in Sudan and of giving a free pass to another mass murderer, Mengistu, now found himself complicit in yet another genocide. In a few short years he had travelled a long way from the euphoric emancipatory promise of 1994.

The new South Africa's foreign policy began with the enormous advantage that in 1994 the country and its leader were extraordinarily popular throughout the world. This was largely squandered: in many ways Mbeki's presidency seemed more like a throwback to the bad old apartheid days. The government became defensive about international criticism and used many of the same marketing ploys abroad that the Nats had deployed to fend it off, with the same low level of success. Like the apartheid regime, it blamed its Opposition at home and exiled South Africans for bad-mouthing it, for like the Nats it conflated criticism of the policy of the ruling party with attacks on the country. Like the apartheid regime, its only real friends abroad were international pariahs, and, like that regime, it was pig-headed. It knew best, refused to change its policies and tried merely to massage the response to them.

Strangest of all, the new regime's foreign policy bore no relationship to the country's national interests. Its major trading partners and foreign investors were given short shrift and continually affronted. Instead, the government courted Cuba, Libya, North Korea, Iran and Saddam Hussein's Iraq, which could do it great harm and little good. Even when Mbeki exulted in his relationship with China there was no recognition that this was a new and deadly competitor. China quickly wiped out most of South Africa's textile industry and its whole stance was projected towards forcing South Africa backwards into being a mere commodity supplier, buying up South Africa's raw chromite, for example, in order to make itself the chief supplier of stainless steel goods.

Even within its own region, Pretoria's policies were peculiar. Its clear interest was in the maintenance of a strong, prosperous and democratic Zimbabwe, its most important neighbour. Yet Mugabe, shored up by Mbeki, had led Zimbabwe back to a point where per capita income was far below 1965 levels and where life expectancy was back to its pre-colonial nadir. This cost South Africa a great deal in direct economic terms and also depressed the investment climate throughout the region. Moreover, there was nothing remotely progressive about what Mugabe's regime had become: to identify it with 'national liberation' was simply bizarre. The Zimbabwean Parliament had done away with its Speaker and instead built a massive stone throne for Mugabe, to acknowledge his position as head of the legislature, judiciary and executive, like the chiefs of old. Mugabe and his wife lived in luxury while his people starved. Politically he was no more than an African 'Papa Doc'.

A clearer view was that of the IMF's Africa director, Abdoulaye Bio-Tchane: 'The question is how far [Zimbabwe] can fall. It seems that Mugabe and [Reserve Bank governor] Gideon Gono are not able to halt the economic collapse. The whole of the sub-continent is being held back and this is holding the whole of Africa back.' Mugabe's Zimbabwe would have already collapsed but for secret assistance, he said. 'We do not have evidence of the sources but clearly they are receiving assistance'[123] – and who, if not Mbeki's South Africa, was meant by that?

It is extremely rare for governments to thus ignore their own national interests. This was, indeed, a key dividing line between Mandela and Mbeki. Instinctively, Mandela adopted the national interest as his. He did not want skilled whites to emigrate; he sided with the Commonwealth against Abacha and with the civilized world against Mugabe. Mbeki took the opposite view because he was, at heart, still devising policy not for a government but for an exiled party which knew no national interest.

10

Dream On: The Strange World of Language Politics in South Africa

Skepticism is the chastity of the intellect. George Santayana

If language had been the creation, not of poetry, but of logic, we should only have one. Friedrich Hebbel

If race has been the dominant factor in South Africa's difficult history, language has come a close second. Generations of Afrikaners remembered how, in Lord Milner's South Africa, an Afrikaans-speaking child was made to sit facing the wall wearing a dunce's hat. More than sixty years later the South African Post Office was still stamping every letter with the slogan 'Die Wonder Van Afrikaans'. And while the apartheid government was able to jail Mandela in 1962 and intimidate his supporters into fearful silence it went a step too far by trying to insist on Afrikaans tuition in township schools in 1976. The resulting explosion inaugurated an era of popular protest which never really stopped until apartheid was toppled.

When the new constitution was drafted African nationalism mingled fatally with the new political correctness to produce a perfectly mad language policy: there were to be eleven official languages as well as special measures to promote and expand the almost dead languages of Khoi and San. The eleven – isiZulu, isiXhosa, Afrikaans, Sepedi, English, Sesotho, siSwati, tshiVenda, XiTsonga and isiNdebele – had to enjoy 'equitable treatment and parity of esteem'.

The new policy was necessarily hypocritical. The French, when weighing the question of British entry to the EEC, worried that 'three languages mean one'. That is, while French–German bilingualism was perfectly viable, once English was admitted any gathering of three nationalities would quickly lapse into English because it was the only international language everyone knew. And thus it proved: today English is by far the EU's dominant language. But if three languages mean one, then eleven do so even more certainly. The ANC elite invariably spoke English. The space occupied by Afrikaans in the broadcast media shrank to a fraction of what it once was and manufacturers quietly removed Afrikaans instructions from their products. You could use any language you liked in Parliament but 90 per cent of the proceedings were in English and Hansard appeared only in English. English was reinforced at every turn by the familiar forces of the Anglosphere and by the arrival of satellite television, English soccer, the internet and South Africa's re-entry to the Commonwealth. Even next-door Namibia and Mozambique, Commonwealth members both, were striving to become English-speakers. Since 1994 South Africa has rapidly and irreversibly moved towards becoming an English-speaking country.

Yet English is only the country's fifth language: 22.9 per cent have isiZulu as their mother tongue, 17.9 per cent isiXhosa, 14.4 per cent Afrikaans, 9.2 per cent Sepedi and only 8.6 per cent English. And theoretically the country is supposed to be moving towards 'the equal use of all official languages', including their use as languages of science and research at university level.

THE TUSSLE OVER AFRIKAANS

The main problem lay with Afrikaans, whose twentieth-century achievements were undeniably remarkable. From being the lingua franca of downtrodden ex-slaves (the Coloureds) and of the beaten and divided Boer nation in 1902, the language progressed to a point where, well before 1994, a huge volume of literature had been translated into Afrikaans, which had also generated its own impressive corpus of poetry, novels, history and biography. There was a thriving Afrikaans press, television and radio, and five Afrikaans language universities (Pretoria, Stellenbosch, Potchefstroom, Free State and Rand Afrikaans universities) and another bilingual one (Port Elizabeth). Afrikaner nationalism was by far the most successful form of African nationalism that the continent has seen and by the end of the apartheid era the vast bulk of Afrikaners were modern middle-class people, appalled at their own racist past and keen to make their peace once and for all with their fellow

South Africans. Happily, the old animosities separating Afrikaners from Anglophones have disappeared and whereas forty years ago you often met Afrikaners who could not speak English, today no such person exists.

Ironically, given their history, Afrikaners now sought new, urban homelands. Once formerly white high schools became racially integrated they normally became English-speaking, so Afrikaners wanting their children educated in their home tongue were forced to quit rural and small-town communities and congregate in larger agglomerations still able to support viable Afrikaans schools. If you drive through Limpopo province you can see how one small dorp after another has been abandoned by whites, now congregated in a few larger centres like Louis Trichardt, Potgietersrus, Pietersburg and Pretoria – and even these have been renamed, respectively, as Makhado, Mokopane, Polokwane and Tshwane. The result is far fewer Afrikaans high schools than before but more Afrikaans matriculants. To see towns commemorating such trekker heroes as Louis Trichardt and Andries Pretorius lose those names breaks many an Afrikaner heart. As in Christopher Hope's poem, 'Kobus Le Grange Marais', the statue of Oom Paul (Kruger) in Church Square, Pretoria, weeps salt tears now, no keeping those impis at bay.

Rand Afrikaans Universiteit became the University of Johannesburg and, like all the other Afrikaans universities, became bilingual or even predominantly English-speaking. The sole, contested exception was Stellenbosch, the intellectual cradle of Afrikanerdom and the jewel in the crown, set amidst the Cape winelands. Those concerned about the survival of Afrikaans, led by the great historian of the Afrikaners, Hermann Giliomee – a man victimized for his liberal views under apartheid – argued that it was crucial that at least one Afrikaans university remain. Their research into how some small language groups survived gave a clear-cut answer.

First, all Flemings (for example) had to be fluent in a major international language so that they were not handicapped through being Flemish-speakers. Secondly, they had to be able to send their children to Flemish-language primary and secondary schools and there had to be at least one Flemish university. This was critical: the propagation of a culture requires the continuous reproduction of an intelligentsia which writes its books and newspapers, gives its sermons, translates works from other languages, teaches in its schools and produces its radio and television programmes. If tertiary-level education was only available in, say, French or English, this quickly became an argument for these languages to take over at secondary and primary level. Moreover, while international language texts would predominate at postgraduate level, it was vital that arguments for bilingual or parallel language instruction at undergraduate level be resisted, for experience showed that if such arrangements were allowed between a minority language and a major international language they became a mere staging post en route to the complete victory of the international language.

These arguments gave the battle over Stellenbosch a wider significance. Chris Brink, the Rector who pushed for more English-language instruction, was forced out by a massive referendum victory for Giliomee and those who wished to protect Afrikaans, but this has not settled the issue. The government exerts strong pressure on Stellenbosch to 'broaden access' and while the university happily accepts Afrikaans-speaking black and Coloured students, most Africans and many middle-class Coloureds want to be taught in English. Thus in 2006, 82 per cent of Stellenbosch students were still white, and the only way to change this would be for the university to offer more or all courses in English. With language rights guaranteed by the constitution, the university could hold out on this but – and this is the critical factor – a considerable number of Afrikaners would rather expand the role of English, whatever the impact on Afrikaans, than remain outside the new South African mainstream.

Ignoring the constitution, the government forced this integrationist logic on many Afrikaans-speaking high schools. But where once such deliberate suppression of Afrikaans language rights would have led to virtual insurrection, now it does not. Yet the ANC remains wary of Afrikaners. When the song 'De La Rey' (commemorating a Boer War general) became a hit in 2007 the ANC reacted with some alarm. 'De La Rey' was seen as a possible precursor of a new wave of Afrikaner nationalism, a phenomenon for which ANC politicians feel both fear and respect.

Accordingly, the old Afrikaans universities (even if most are bilingual now) were allowed to keep choosing Afrikaans-speaking and often white vice-chancellors in a way that was unthinkable at the English-speaking universities. Quite often the impulse for change came not from the government but from within. Afrikaners are Christian folk and many now carry a great load of Calvinist guilt about having inflicted apartheid on the country and are correspondingly very uncomfortable about doing anything which carries echoes of apartheid – such as maintaining a mainly white university. Such feelings are powerfully reinforced by a wish to stay on the right side of government. But their anxiety is more existential. So long and so loudly did the apartheid government make Afrikaans the language of racism and oppression that many Afrikaners are now reluctant to assert their own Afrikaner identity or culture, in much the same way that after 1945 many Germans became uncomfortable with any assertion of German national identity. Many Afrikaans families now have children in London or Sydney and even back home some send their children to English-language schools. When Professor Giliomee and others who wished to keep Stellenbosch an Afrikaans university insisted that if this pass was not defended Afrikaans would retreat back from the public realm into being merely a kitchen language, they often encountered Afrikaners whose response was merely a shrug of the shoulders and a 'Que sera, sera.'

IF AFRIKAANS SUFFERS, THE REAL LOSERS WILL BE AFRICAN LANGUAGES

But if the future of Afrikaans is in doubt then, a fortiori, all the other African languages are under greater threat. None of them, after all, has a fraction of the accumulated literature or institutional support that Afrikaans has. When the apartheid government set up bantustans the first act of each new homeland government was to adopt English as a medium for education. Similarly, none of the tribal universities then created even considered using anything but English, and although the government of the time was keen to provide resources for it, none of these universities made any serious effort to promote or develop indigenous African languages. Ironically, now the homelands have been scrapped, the successor African nationalists, though viewing tribalism as a reactionary force, have committed themselves to promoting these indigenous languages in a way apartheid bureaucrats could only have dreamed of.

This commitment is, moreover, made in the teeth of market forces. All university departments of African languages report steady and dramatic declines in student numbers to the point where keeping them open is a purely political decision. Similarly, although educationalists are unanimous that children do best if other subjects are learnt through their mother tongue, black parents are equally unanimous in resisting this option. Limpopo, the only province to introduce African-language (Sepedi) mother-tongue education, has faced fierce scenes with black parents angrily accusing the school authorities of 'academically damaging' their children. They, like their Afrikaans counterparts, have thoroughly understood that proficiency in English is the key to the job market. In a country with 40 per cent unemployment this has an urgency bordering on obsession.

The workaday reality is that the courts still use just English and Afrikaans (though black judges, who often do not know Afrikaans, would prefer an English-only system) and provinces teach at least two of the official languages in their schools. What this boils down to is that schools continue to offer English and Afrikaans as before but now also offer isiZulu in KwaZulu-Natal, isiXhosa in the Eastern and Western Cape, SeSotho in the Free State and so on. This induces a sense of equity, but at a price. There is a huge shortage of qualified African language teachers. The curriculum is crowded with three languages of which two will only ever be of use in South Africa and then often only in one province. This also leaves no room for other international languages or even for the other main languages of Africa, French, Swahili and Arabic.

The Ministry of Education has, however, asked all universities to submit plans for how they will promote and develop African languages. Most universities have submitted plans of such vagueness that the Ministry has asked them to redo the task but since doing anything serious would be expensive and since higher education is cash-strapped, such plans get parked on a back-burner anyway. African journalists and intellectuals like to agonize over the future of African languages, but not in a way which advances the cause. For the only way to do that is to carry out the back-breaking task of translating large numbers of classic works into the local languages. Until then, the only way to become well educated is to leave the local languages behind. There is little sign of such labours. One is reminded of how black students often made ringing speeches demanding the teaching of African history at their universities. When it was pointed out that African history had been taught for many years, they would be taken aback – but would then make another speech demanding the introduction of African history. For the real point was to belabour the 'white university'. Those who made such speeches were themselves generally little interested in taking courses on African history.

THE SMALL WAR OVER ISIZULU

The rhetoric surrounding the future of African languages is similar: a stick to beat the 'white languages' rather than a matter of serious intent. There is one thunderous exception, the University of KwaZulu-Natal, the country's second biggest, where the vice-chancellor, William Makgoba, is both a committed Africanist and a man looking for a fight. Makgoba left Wits University in 1995 after a storm in which he stood accused of maladministration, bringing the university into disrepute and falsifying his CV. At one point he purloined his accusers' personal files, using them to make all manner of allegations (all later proved groundless), and, despite his training as a medical scientist, boasted that he rubbed himself all over with lion fat every morning, the better to vanquish his enemies. In his autobiography, where he describes himself as 'a first-rate, world acclaimed African scientist', he also admits that he consulted sangomas (witch-doctors) for special potions with which to scare his enemies. He writes of 'my unquestioned brilliance as a scholar and [my] pioneering achievements, with few equals in my field and even fewer superiors'.[1]

Certainly, Makgoba's inauguration as vice-chancellor was that of a monarch, with massed bands, choirs, operas, recitals and presentations at four different centres. He swiftly granted himself a salary considerably larger than President Mbeki's and festooned the campus lamp-posts with banners describing his university as 'the premier university of African scholarship'. Although a majority of the university's academics were still white males, Makgoba soon launched a broadside in which he compared white males to displaced senior apes and insisted that they must learn to speak, sing, eat and dance like Africans if they were to find any hope of acceptance. The key theme of his inaugural address was the promotion of isiZulu, and the university soon announced that it would introduce compulsory Zulu courses for all students and make all academic and administrative appointments conditional on fluency in isiZulu.

These plans met with strong resistance. Academics pointed to the entire lack of Zulu textbooks or journals and the absence of many academic concepts in isiZulu. If Makgoba's plans went ahead they would turn the university of 60,000 students – Anglophone since its inception – into what one professor called 'an academic wasteland and a global joke'. Even the proponents of such a change found it so difficult to conceive that the plan they drew up for its implementation stretched over twelve years. Most academics ignored the plan, hoping it would just fade away.

I spoke to the Professor of Zulu about the project. She was warmly sympathetic. She was sure that the resistance to Makgoba's plans was entirely due to white racism, indeed one of her students was writing a thesis proving that point. I pointed out that if she was serious then a vast task of translation lay ahead – not just of literary classics but of textbooks of every kind, so that subjects really could be studied in isiZulu. She agreed heartily: this was a work of many years. Was she planning to play her part in that? Yes, indeed. She would shortly retire and would then devote herself to translating Bollywood films into isiZulu because 'there's good money in that'.

Yet the idea deserves some sympathy. Already in 2006 over 50 per cent of the university's students were Zulu-speakers – though many of them insisted on speaking English, seen as more 'cool' and modern. Moreover, isiZulu is the best developed and most widespread of all the African languages. There are three Zulu newspapers but none in any other African tongue, and Zulu-language radio and television have large audiences. And isiZulu is an Nguni language, so it can be understood without too much difficulty by other Ngunis, namely Swazis, Ndebeles and Xhosas. In Soweto, the language used on the street is *tsotsitaal*, a strange mixture of Zulu and Afrikaans. In other townships you can find other such amalgams, though always with a Zulu base.

In Kenya and Tanzania, the post-independence governments favoured Swahili-based education, with the result that this single lingua franca is now strongly entrenched in East Africa, and far beyond. Had the South African government taken that route, it would have had to choose isiZulu as its vehicle, trying to encourage its broadening into a sort of pan-Nguni language, but even to sketch such an alternative is to see its political impossibility. For non-Zulus this would be seen as nothing less than a continuation of Shaka's forcible incorporation of vanquished tribes into the Zulu nation. Xhosas, who predominate in the ANC leadership, would strongly resist, as would all the branches of the Sotho (including Sepedi-, Sesotho- and Setswana-speakers). It would, in a word, reawaken the spectre of tribalism, of which the ANC is extremely scared. So the constitution-makers bolted for the politically more correct, though crazy, solution of eleven official languages.

AND SO ENGLISH MARCHES ON

While that constitutional provision actually guarantees the shrinkage of most of the languages it pretends to protect, the oddity of the language battle in South Africa is that pretence is almost everything. At Stellenbosch those who wish to expand the role of English pretend that this will not be at the expense of Afrikaans, though quite certainly it will be. If you tell Zulu- or Sotho-speakers that their languages are under threat and could one day disappear they simply do not believe you. In 2005 I attended the film premiere in Durban of the touching *Yesterday*, a full-length feature film set in the foothills of the Drakensberg, where Aids ravages black communities as badly as plague once ravaged London. The producer, Anant Singh, told a rapturous audience how he had decided to 'dump English' and shoot the film in isiZulu with English subtitles. One Zulu luminary after another, including the provincial premier, followed him to the podium to emphasize this triumph of the Zulu language and the vital importance of promoting Zulu. They were all applauded to the echo – yet every one of them spoke in English and nobody even giggled.

An inverse case at the University of KwaZulu-Natal was that of the threatened French, German and Latin departments. It was decided to group them together in a Department of European Studies. But 'European' is an unhappy term for South Africans, conjuring memories of park benches stamped 'Europeans Only' or 'Non-Europeans'. Thus today the university boasts a department of 'Europe Studies' – and, again, nobody laughs. For, despite an otherwise well-developed national sense of humour, South Africans are immensely solemn about race and language.

Language is such a protean reality that this pretending surely cannot last, but its utility is that it masks reality while English gallops ahead. Samuel P. Huntington claims that the proportion of the world's population who speak English is in decline while Mandarin, Hindi and Arabic make gains.[2] This may be so on a world scale, but Africa has not heard about it and few in South Africa wish to acknowledge what is going on. Only occasionally does an African voice point out the truth – as, for example, in early 2008 when the ANC advertised a post at Luthuli House, the key qualification being excellence in spoken and written English. No other language was mentioned, which, it was pointed out, meant that none of the graduates of the Previously Disadvantaged Universities (that is, the old bantustan tribal colleges) could even think of applying, for their English would not be good enough.[3] Such voices of protest are few and do not deflect the ANC one iota, though one of the new recruit's tasks will doubtless be to draw up ringing declarations about the need to promote indigenous languages, in, of course, his or her excellent English.

So the pretence goes on. If you point out that the biggest African country, Nigeria, has adopted English as its official language, that China is launching whole new universities with English-language instruction, that proficiency in English has been made obligatory at the University of Maputo in next-door Mozambique, and that South Africa cannot escape these trends, you will be met with a smile and much confident claptrap about the rosy future of our eleven official languages. When I wrote an earlier version of this chapter as an article in the British journal *Prospect*, the SABC was so stung that it carried a half-hour programme denouncing my views. I was not invited to participate. The general gist was that there were eleven perfectly equal languages; that nothing was more certain than the renaissance of African languages; and that it was very wicked of me to suggest otherwise. It was, presumably, this wickedness which accounted for my failure to be invited.

In the United States, in the early years of the Reagan administration, no one wanted to admit how gigantic the budget deficit was going to be since the administration was supposed to believe in balanced budgets. The result was a series of remarkable statistical contortions in the Office of Management and Budget where each year projections for the year ahead were made showing little or no deficit, a result achieved by taking the rosiest possible scenario in every case. No amount of huge deficit outcomes changed this. It was said that the most powerful woman in the White House was not Nancy Reagan but a young lady called Rosie Scenario, for she always got her way on everything.

Similarly, Rosie Scenario now dominates language policy in South Africa. According to Rosie the promotion of indigenous languages is bound up with human rights and the respect for all cultures which characterizes the rainbow nation. This is the unchallengeable fruit of the revolution, so all eleven languages (and several extra sub-languages or dialects) are bound to survive and thrive. It would be almost unbearably painful to many South Africans to realize that this is just not so, and that a language which is the mother tongue of just 8.6 per cent of the population is taking over completely and will gradually exterminate most or even all of the other ten languages. And one really is talking of extermination. The ancestors of South Africa's one million Indians arrived here 120 years ago speaking only Indian languages. The last university department of Indian languages has long closed and few Indians can speak any Hindi or Gujerati. They are now almost uniformly English-speaking. Well, nearly. In Port Shepstone recently I heard Indian merchants speaking an Indian language and enquired what it was. None of them could say. They made various guesses and then gave up. It was just 'the slang we use'. This is the very last stage of a kitchen patois.

The notion that African languages in South Africa are on course to emulate the fate of the Indian languages has not yet struck home. Such an outcome would seem like a final triumph of colonialism over African nationalism. In the past people have fought and died over much less. Given these alternatives one has to feel relieved at the current pretence, ludicrous though it is, and to hope that the country continues to dream on.

11

Black Economic Empowerment, or How to Succeed in Business Without Really Trying

A man that should call everything by its right name would hardly pass the streets without being knocked down as a common enemy.

The Marquis of Halifax (George Savile)

In 2007 the Swiss-based Institute for Management Development brought out its annual competitiveness survey of the world's leading fifty-five industrialized economies, showing that South Africa had fallen from thirty-eighth to fiftieth place, by far the biggest drop of any country. The main reason for this, the Institute said, was that business executives surveyed had highlighted 'discrimination', including both black economic empowerment (BEE) and affirmative action, as a major weakness. Despite strong government protests that such opinions 'did not reflect the country's majority'[1] (they were not supposed to – only executives were polled), the Institute stood its ground. The poll result in 2007 had been 'much worse', it said: discrimination had been a major problem in South Africa down the years and the country now stood plumb last out of fifty-five in this respect. The ANC government's sense of injured indignation that the world should reach a negative judgement about its discriminatory practices exactly mirrored how apartheid governments had behaved, for both governments parochially regarded their form of discrimination as normal and justifiable. The major difference was really just that the apartheid government had legislated to favour whites while the ANC government legislated to favour blacks.

THE HOLCIM SAGA

This sense of injured surprise was the more striking given that the previous month, April 2007, had witnessed the Holcim saga, the biggest BEE deal to date. This began in 2006 when Holcim Switzerland, the parent company, announced that it was to sell 85 per cent of its 54 per cent interest in Holcim South Africa to a BEE consortium, AfriSam, headed by Elias Links, a former South African ambassador to the EU. The announcement was greeted with surprise, for the country was enjoying a construction boom which was expected to accelerate thanks to many large infrastructural projects, and Holcim South Africa, the country's largest cement-maker, was making excellent profits. Effectively the Swiss had decided to disinvest from South Africa despite the boom, disguising their intent behind an announcement about facilitating BEE. Foreign companies disliked BEE, with its requirements that they sell off a quarter or more of their equity, usually at a heavily discounted price, to BEE partners: a survey of European companies had shown that 56 per cent viewed BEE in a negative light and 8 per cent saw compliance as threatening the survival of their business.[2] Holcim Switzerland's partner, South Africa's biggest construction company, Aveng, which held 46 per cent of Holcim South Africa, bitterly resisted the move, which threatened to leave them with partners they had not chosen, who had no experience of the construction business and whose sole claim to title was that they were senior ANC figures enjoying the President's patronage – for Mbeki had intervened energetically on AfriSam's side. AfriSam would have to fund the R6.82 billion purchase price through bank loans, and the banks felt far more secure knowing that Mbeki backed the deal.

But Aveng and Holcim each had a preferential right to buy out the other's stake and Aveng stuck fast, blocking the deal. Carl Grim, Aveng's CEO, was furious. Aveng had been the first major construction firm to do a BEE deal, he pointed out. A charter spelt out every industry's BEE requirements and Grim had told Holcim that in terms of the mining charter it was obliged to sell off at least 15 per cent of its equity to BEE interests by 2009 and 26 per cent by 2014, if it were to have its mining rights renewed. Holcim had done nothing – and now preferred to exit completely rather than comply. 'Do we,' asked Grim, 'fall down in the face of someone stealing an important asset from Aveng shareholders?

No.'[3] Yet only a week later Aveng capitulated: it would now sell its entire stake to Holcim for R7.4 billion. They in turn would sell 85 per cent of Holcim South Africa to AfriSam for R14.2 billion. Grim admitted that Aveng had come under strong political pressure not to exercise its right to buy out their partner. 'We can't operate in a vacuum,' said Grim. 'The political reality is a reality and it impacts on decision making.'[4] There was much cheering by the BEE lobby: hitherto BEE had brought blacks 20–30 per cent shares but this deal gave them instant control over a major sector.[5]

But the deal had other lessons. R14 billion would leave the country. A major international company had preferred to disinvest from a booming industry rather than comply with BEE rules. Its South African partner had done the same. AfriSam brought nothing to the deal except bank loans – and the banks were willing, at a nod from the President, to double their loans to AfriSam overnight. Links and his partners had nothing to offer save their own sincere willingness to be rich and neither Aveng nor Holcim wanted them as partners; Holcim would sell its remaining 15 per cent share of the business as soon as possible. (Typically enough, Holcim Switzerland issued a statement, as it exited the country, about how it 'would remain committed to South Africa'.[6])

The deal also explains what the Institute for Management Development poll meant by 'discrimination'. Dogged in their everyday business life by affirmative action rules requiring any enterprise of fifty or more employees to mirror, at every level, South Africa's demography, executives were also faced not just with legislation requiring them to sell large chunks of their business to black partners but with political intervention to push through deals on racial grounds, which took no account of how profitability or even viability were affected. Thus discrimination creates a wide extra-legal penumbra in which political and other pressures may be felt; in which employees may be encouraged in errant behaviour by the notion that they are racially privileged, while others are demoralized by the same phenomenon; and in which no attention is paid to the absolute shortage of worthwhile racially designated employees or business partners. Such factors can make the South African workplace almost impossibly difficult. Executives could say this anonymously to a pollster but publicly they would not risk mentioning their reservations. Their lip-biting silence in turn – indeed, their pretended happiness with BEE and affirmative action – allowed politically correct commentators to express amazement at the Institute's survey's 'biased results'.

The Holcim deal was a clear distress rocket across the sky yet President Mbeki greeted it in his online *ANC Today* as a great victory for 'transformation'.[7] So he was happy. Holcim Switzerland declared themselves happy and Aveng said they were happy to have received a good price for their shares. The BEE commentators were happy – the deal was hailed as 'one of the greatest BEE successes so far'.[8] Elias Links and his associates were happy: as the new bosses they could award themselves handsome salaries and expenses. Hence the rosy glow which surrounds empowerment deals. But what would happen to Holcim South Africa whose new management knew nothing of the business, who had bought it at the top of a stock market boom and were burdened with R14.2 billion of debt?

HOW TO BUILD A NEW BUSINESS CLASS

Despite strong liberal opposition, the apartheid government discouraged the growth of an African middle class by forcing the closure of (good) mission schools, by segregating the universities, by job reservation and by making it difficult for Africans to urbanize. Only in the 1970s and 1980s did the Nationalists belatedly realize the desirability of creating a black middle class, and even then the quite strong redistributive trends in the last few decades of apartheid owed more to market forces than the government.[9] Even so, the ANC inherited a racially skewed and extremely unequal distribution of wealth and income.

South Africa's Indian population were an object example of what needed to be done. Not handicapped by Bantu Education or threats to their urban status, and motivated by strong entrepreneurial and educational traditions, the Indian community had built up its own schools and family businesses, so that despite racial discrimination throughout the apartheid period, the Indian community grew and prospered, producing a wealthy and well-educated merchant and professional class and many skilled artisans. Indeed, by 2000 the top decile of the Indian community had overtaken its white counterpart. It was not, though, an easy act to follow. One of the oddities of South Africa is that the groups best endowed with the Protestant ethic have always been East European Jews and Indian Muslims and Hindus – and Africans lacked the Indians' educational traditions. So the creation of an African middle class was always likely to require state intervention of some kind. Clearly the most promising route would be via decisive improvements in the quality of African education, housing and health and the deployment of non-African professionals to pass on their skills to young blacks.

Such a path was either ignored or rejected. There were substantial improvements to African housing thanks to the mass building of RDP houses and the upgrading of many squatter camps, but health and education both went backwards. Life expectancy fell sharply among Africans and South Africa actually went backwards down the UNDP Human Development Index. The township and rural schools attended by the overwhelming mass of Africans stagnated at best and higher education was damaged by affirmative action, the loss of many leading academics and, in some cases, egregious maladministration by new black management appointed on political rather than educational grounds. Non-African professionals were pushed out and often driven abroad. The new black elite was unmoved by such losses; indeed, many cheered them and actively opposed attempts to recruit more such professionals abroad.

The development of a broad middle class through better training and education was also too gradual a strategy for the ANC, requiring decades before the full effects were felt. Instead, public sector 'transformation' and affirmative action in the private sector promised hundreds of thousands of well-paid jobs right away. But that was hardly enough. Most societies have a representative figure of success, aped by upwardly mobile groups. In industrial Britain successful factory-owners, press barons and pop stars all bought themselves country seats and tried hard to live the life of the rural gentry. In Zimbabwe the central figure was the prosperous white farmer, so the new black elite aspired to farm ownership, a Range Rover and other such accoutrements. South Africa's masters of the universe were big business bosses with large salaries and share options, driving Mercedes and living in vast suburban mansions. Top of the heap were the randlords, the great mining moguls. So this, inevitably, was what the new elite aspired to copy – and to be.

However, even Cecil Rhodes and the Oppenheimers had been well educated and had served apprenticeships, both of which the new would-be moguls wanted to skip. And since the point of a business career was to support a lifestyle to which they wished to become immediately accustomed, there was also often a tendency to take too much out of a business too soon. There was simply no established business culture among Africans to prevent this. Indeed when apartheid ended there was virtually no African business class at all: there were taxi bosses, football bosses and shebeen operators, herbalists selling potions and magic cures, and those who ran the spaza shops (tiny retail outlets) in townships. That was about it.

THE FRUITS OF THE POLITICAL KINGDOM

All the early BEE aspirants grew directly out of the ANC. Thus Thebe Investments was set up in 1992 by Vusi Khanyile, the ANC's head of finance, with Tokyo Sexwale one of its directors. Even more striking was Kagiso Trust Investments (KTI). The original Kagiso Trust was set up in 1985 by Eric Molobi, a former Robben Island prisoner, to act as a conduit of EU funds to apartheid victims, though Molobi soon arranged for Communist-bloc funding to flow through it as well.[10] Molobi described the Trust as 'a department of a government-in-waiting'.[11] It was the biggest paymaster of ANC-connected causes, disbursing over R1.2 billion, much of it for educational purposes. Although Molobi was personally regarded as an honest man, EU donors were in a constant state of despair over the Trust's 'struggle accounting'; large sums disappeared, as into a black hole. This was simply how things worked in those days: EU money given for training Cosatu shop stewards (for example) actually funded the purchase of an office block, with the requisite paperwork in this one celebrated instance retrospectively faked. Even many of the 'scholarships' often funded ANC cadres doing some notional degree while in fact working full time as activists. It was unsurprising that many of the beneficiaries later turned up with fake degrees on their CVs – some of them my own students.

After 1990 foreign donations to the Kagiso Trust dried up so, using $15 million from JP Morgan as seed capital, Molobi founded KTI, which soon spawned many divisions and subsidiaries. Given the Kagiso Trust's reputation for dodgy accounting, the mystery of how a humble NGO transformed itself into a large corporation inevitably set tongues wagging, but such criticism was ignored. Because KTI was close to the ANC, business keen to earn ANC goodwill offered handsome discounts while KTI became a large-scale rentier, buying stakes in one company after another. Molobi, a humble radio technician by training, helped devise ANC housing and education policy, became chairman of Telkom and Metropolitan Holdings and a director of many other companies. His appointment as vice-chairman of the R32 billion a year Imperial Group provoked speeches typical of many such empowerment ventures. What exactly had Molobi brought to Imperial? 'He has guided us particularly well and given us outstanding advice on empowerment matters,' said the CEO, Bill Lynch; that is, he used his ANC networks to the company's advantage. Molobi, like many other BEE directors, had to make a virtue of the fact that he had no formal business skills: 'The divisions almost run by themselves. Management does not interfere much,' he said happily, describing himself as 'a continuous learner'. His forte was, he explained, not the company's day-to-day business. 'I look beyond the assets as such, but to the horizon to help the company survive and to cope with the ever-changing environment.'[12]

Much of the initiative for BEE lay with South Africa's corporate giants who were keen to earn government goodwill and prove their own progressive credentials by selling off assets to empowerment partners, though this was often also a graceful cover for a policy of disinvestment from South Africa and diversification abroad. Anglo-American, South Africa's biggest company, led the way. It sold off assets in order to create African Rainbow Minerals (run by Patrice Motsepe), Mvelaphanda Resources (run by Tokyo Sexwale), Shanduka (run by Cyril Ramaphosa), Ponahalo (run by Cheryl Carolus and Manne Dipico, former ANC premier of the Northern Cape), Eyesizwe Mining (run by a number of prominent blacks, recruited mainly from state bodies[13]) and Exxaro (run by Sipho Nkosi and others). Simultaneously, Anglo swallowed De Beers, listed in London and invested heavily abroad, reducing its South African exposure.

Such divestments were risky. Although the sellers sold at a discount the buyers, lacking any capital themselves, had to take enormous bank loans to purchase their new assets and then use dividend flows to pay off the loans. Often the new buyers only had minority stakes and thus depended on the old (essentially white) management to keep the company running sufficiently well for this to be possible, but where they themselves gained significant control of a company, they were reliant on their own untested management abilities. This proved problematic, often leading to disastrous corporate governance. The new BEE moguls developed luxurious lifestyles and took large sums out of the business, through high salaries, lavish expense accounts and share options as well as dividends. An economic downturn could leave them badly exposed and many then resorted to selling off productive assets merely to generate revenue.

The initial BEE flagship, Nail (New African Investments Ltd.), a consortium headed by Dr Nthato Motlana, Mandela's doctor, was set up in 1993 when the Afrikaans insurance giant, Sanlam, sold off 10 per cent of Metropolitan Life to Nail. Nail quickly put together a job lot of assets including the radical *New Nation* newspaper, and a stake in the cellphone group MTN. Although there was much press coverage about BEE's golden future, it was notable that one of the leading consortium members, Jonty Sandler, was white and that Motlana had many business failures behind him. In 1996 Anglo-American sold off the Johnnic conglomerate to the National Empowerment Consortium, led by Nail – with the Consortium demanding a 20 per cent discount on Johnnic's market price.[14] Nail also acquired Radio Jacaranda and *The Sowetan*, the biggest black newspaper. Although Nail was a public company the directors devised an extraordinary structure of voting and non-voting shares such that they continued to exercise complete control with only a fraction of the equity. Despite the Africanist hype Nail closed down *New Nation* in 1997, and was an unfocused conglomerate of stakes in white-run companies with no real value added by Nail itself. Four directors, finding that their dreams of enrichment were on hold, decided to loot the company by simply voting that R134 million in shares be transferred from the company to their private accounts. The public outcry was so great that Motlana and Sandler were forced to resign, though not before taking R100 million each out of Nail. Sandler was soon dogged by various other scandals, including charges of homosexual rape, and of paying starvation wages to the illegal immigrant workers on his farms.[15] He emerged unscathed from all these charges.

In an attempt to improve Nail's corporate governance, Saki Macozoma was brought in as CEO. Macozoma had been an ANC spokesman and MP who had become managing director of Transnet, grouping all the state-owned transport facilities. He quickly became a ubiquitous figure on innumerable company boards and university councils, the charming face of black business. Yet Macozoma had few real achievements. During his management of Transnet, Sipho Nyawo, head of Portnet, was fired for company credit card abuse of over R100,000; Joe Ndhela, another director, was suspended for 'gross misconduct', while Zukile Nomvete took over South African Airways and steered it from a R240 million profit in 1995 to a R1 billion loss by 1998. Macozoma then hired Coleman Andrews to run SAA on a contract which cost the state a R232 million payout when Andrews left, causing the Transport Minister, Jeff Radebe, to erupt in bitter criticism of Macozoma.

Nothing fazed, Macozoma, using Safika Holdings (which he ran together with Moss Ngoasheng, Mbeki's economic adviser), acquired 25.2 per cent of Stanlib, the asset management arm of Standard Bank and Liberty Life, becoming chairman of Stanlib. White businessmen hastened to offer him deals: he was, after all, known to be an intimate of Mbeki's. But at Nail Macozoma simply sold off one asset after another. He tried to take over Kagiso Media, which would have produced a clearly illegal monopoly, and professed great disappointment when Icasa, the regulatory authority, inevitably turned him down, as if he had expected the rules to be ignored for a BEE operation. In fact Icasa was ready to bend the rules if Nail could make convincing promises of improved media content for black people, but the authority highlighted Nail's 'lack of any clear promises of performance'.[16] Worse, *The Sowetan* floundered, losing 100,000 readers under Nail's direction. Macozoma's response was to blame the 'unjust' entry of the *Daily Sun* into the market. Nail's headline earnings per share declined by over two-thirds between 1997 and 2001 and its net asset value was heavily discounted. In the end Nail simply auctioned off its assets. In 2003 Macozoma put the whole company up for sale – and then put in a fire-sale bid from Safika for its assets. To the end Macozoma and his fellow-directors drew large emoluments from this sinking ship. Despite this large symbolic disaster Macozoma continued to rise without trace.

Nail told a fearsome story. As one financial journalist pointed out:

> Almost a decade later, having spent huge fees on financial advisers and lawyers, Nail is being broken up . . . Nail's only claim to success will be as a case study in how to destroy black empowerment aspirations . . . Despite generating nothing for its shareholders, all four executive directors of Nail have managed to walk away as multi-millionaires. Huge final payouts were made on top of generous remuneration packages . . . about 40 per cent of the funds are attributable to blacks. This means the largesse doled out to high profile empowerment individuals is being 40 per cent financed by some of the lowest paid workers in the country . . . an appalling way to redistribute wealth.[17]

The story was to be repeated ad nauseam.

THE WILD WEST WORLD OF BEE BUSINESS PRACTICE

Safika also had a chequered history. Ngoasheng had built the company together with Vulindlela Cuba, provoking much comment over his obvious conflict of interest, until he resigned from the presidential office in 2000. He remained, however, a director of the state Industrial Development Corporation, which had bought 36 per cent of the local operations of Siemens. Ngoasheng, ignoring the obvious conflict of interest of being both the buyer and, as an Industrial Development Corporation director, a seller, determined to acquire this, causing his Safika associate, Eric Phillips, to write a bitter letter to Siemens, exposing Ngoasheng's management style. He and Cuba had illegally taken R2 million each out of Safika (without consulting the board of directors) although Phillips, a 10 per cent stakeholder in Safika himself, avowed there were no profits to take. At first Ngoasheng and Cuba described their payout as a restraint of trade consideration, then, when this did not work, as a dividend – but since there were no profits from which to pay a dividend, that too had to be dropped. Then the money was described as a loan, but that had to be abandoned because of tax implications. In the end it was described as a special reward for risks taken. The real point was that they had decided to raid the company and any excuse would do. Phillips, finding his attempt to call a board meeting blocked, invoked the Companies Act but, at the meeting's conclusion, found Ngoasheng and Cuba had arranged for him to be arrested on specious grounds.

When he managed to convince the police he had done nothing wrong, he was subjected to a campaign of harassment including death threats. In the end his stake was bought out in return for a promise not to press criminal charges against Cuba and Ngoasheng. Siemens, hearing his story, snatched back their 36 per cent from the Industrial Development Corporation and refused to have Safika as a partner.[18]

The new world of BEE was factious and fractious: no-holds battles between black entrepreneurs were common and sometimes revealed hair-raising glimpses of Wild West business practices. That these clashes did not get completely out of hand – as in the bloody wars fought by taxi-owners and football bosses – was due to the fact that the BEE world was that of a tiny elite who were both politically connected and often related to one another. In 2002, for example, Safika waged a bitter struggle against Tokyo Sexwale's Makana Trust, a benefit fund for ex-Robben Island prisoners. The two outfits had got together to acquire MTN shares in 1997; Makana's founding trustee, Sothomela Ndukwana, also held 4 per cent of Safika and it was obvious that a consortium including Mandela's old prison comrades would likely win the BEE competition for the allocation of the shares. But then Makana bid for the third cellphone licence, a vastly more lucrative possibility, renouncing its MTN interest to avoid a conflict of interest. Safika happily took over full ownership of the shares, which had fallen in value. However, when Makana's bid failed and the value of MTN (now M-Cell) shares soared, Makana's bosses bitterly regretted surrendering their shares and claimed they had not really meant to surrender them at all but that Safika had just been 'holding' them pro tem, in effect an admission that Makana had been faking the legal requirements to avoid a conflict of interest. Ndukwana now charged Safika (i.e. Saki Macozoma and Moss Ngoasheng) with fraud and theft, a situation further enlivened by the fact that Ngoasheng, Ndukwana, Sexwale and Macozoma had all been political prisoners and that Ndukwana was a cousin of Macozoma's wife. Insults and defamation suits were flung about as well as accusations that Ngoasheng and Cuba had been looting Safika while it was running at a loss.

The whole affair was suddenly settled on an undisclosed basis, with all sides claiming to have rediscovered, in mid-battle, their prisoner camaraderie. Both sides withdrew and apologized for their allegations against one another, gravely regretting that these exchanges might have appeared as 'a threat to the economic empowerment of previously disadvantaged peoples of South Africa'.[19] They denied there had been any political pressure on them to settle, but the opposite was true. There had been concern in the presidential office that the public mudslinging was damaging the BEE cause and the reputations of many of its leading exponents linked to the ANC. Not only was Kgalema Motlanthe kept aware of the negotiations but there had been forceful interventions by Essop Pahad, Jeff Radebe, the Minister of Public Enterprises, and Bulelani Ngcuka, the National Director of Public Prosecutions.[20] The latter's involvement saw many legal eyebrows raised, for Makana's allegations had led the Johannesburg High Court to order the Department of Trade and Industry to inspect Safika on suspicion of 'grave impropriety'.[21] Both Radebe and Ngcuka were ex-political prisoners themselves, but the DPP's intervention inevitably brought suspicion that a deal had been reached under threat of prosecution, for there were many clear or alleged illegalities on both sides.

A hardly happier fate attended Anglo-American's sale of Johannesburg Consolidated Investments, subdivided into the conglomerate Johnnic and JCI, a mining finance house. There was much celebration when JCI was bought by a BEE consortium headed by the buccaneering Mzi Khumalo: Barney Barnato's old company, the world's fourth biggest gold producer, had passed into black hands. A former petrol pump attendant, MK activist and Robben Island prisoner, Khumalo, the youngest of eleven children in a poor family, had done an economics degree in prison. He was smart, without illusions and in a hurry. From the start there were fierce boardroom battles between Khumalo and his white backers; I spoke to one of the directors at the time who confided that he was resigning because of 'corporate governance issues' so alarming that he feared getting involved in illegality if he stayed on. But the trouble continued, greatly worsened by the fact that JCI had been bought at an inflated price in the first place. In the end Khumalo was forced to resign in a great cloud of acrimony over a deal not authorized by the board. JCI had to be broken up and sold off, a total failure for BEE.

Meanwhile Johnnic had been sold off to Ramaphosa's National Empowerment Consortium in a deal popularly likened to Anglo's decision to sell off some of its mines to Afrikaans interests fifty years before. Now Anglo was doing for the ANC what it had earlier done for Afrikaners – for the Consortium was stacked with ANC-aligned personalities. They were, however, wholly lacking in business experience. 'The problem with the NEC,' said the director, Mashudu Ramano, 'is that most of the people on the NEC have never run a spaza shop.'[22] Soon there was muttering that Nail might stage a coup and seize control, so the board hurriedly decided to get rid of 'old economy' assets and concentrate on hi-tech, cellphones and media. A huge asset sale began and just as it finished the US hi-tech bubble burst. Johnnic shares plummeted in sympathy and suddenly the Consortium's members could not repay the loans with which they had bought the company. The wounded company staggered on but in the end it was taken over by Hosken Consolidated Investments and Ramaphosa left. Hosken was itself a BEE company – it had started life as the textile workers' benefit fund and it was run by a white and a Coloured, Johnny Copelyn and Marcel Golding, both shrewd businessmen – but it was hardly what had been intended. Hosken wanted Johnnic in order to consolidate its casino interests, for one lesson learnt from the apartheid era was that casinos were a licence to print money.

White businessmen who failed as badly as Mzi Khumalo at JCI or Cyril Ramaphosa at Johnnic would have found it difficult to restart their careers but both Khumalo and Ramaphosa continued making one new BEE deal after another. In 2002 Khumalo's Metallon Corporation led a consortium to buy out Global Resorts for R1 billion, and in 2003 Khumalo pulled off a breathtaking coup whereby he somehow got the Industrial Development Corporation to lend him the money with which to acquire from them 10.7 million shares in Harmony Gold at a discount, shares he immediately sold on at a profit of R1 billion. Accusations were made that Khumalo had hijacked another BEE deal, that he had manipulated other BEE groups into giving way to him, that he had hidden his ownership of the BEE vehicle (Simane Ltd.) used for the operation, that he had seduced officials of the Industrial Development Corporation with loans and positions at Metallon, and that he had avoided exchange controls by transferring R700 million abroad. All of which might have been true but hardly mattered: Khumalo was laughing all the way to the bank.[23] He was a close friend of Bulelani Ngcuka, and the state made no move even to investigate Khumalo. He was now one of the richest men in the country and stories of his luxurious lifestyle were legendary. At the 2004 Athens Olympics he hired the Onassis yacht, declaring it money well spent. He also bluntly declared that he was not much interested in BEE, merely in his own business career. He even suggested that the plea for 'broad based BEE' (that is, bringing in large numbers of poorer shareholders) was racist. This was, he said, a question only black businessmen faced. No one would make that demand of a Jewish businessman.

A BRAVE NEW WORLD: THE FUTURE IS BLACK

Although the Mandela government supported BEE, it was the Mbeki government which openly spoke of the need to build a black bourgeoisie and took legislative steps to push BEE. BEE firms were privileged in public sector procurement. In tenders up to R500,000 the evaluation of tenders allowed 20 points for bids from HDIs (historically disadvantaged individuals) and 80 points for price. Above R500,000 a 90 : 10 ratio would apply. This led to shouts of indignation from black business groups, who demanded a far greater HDI weighting. In fact, as anyone knows who has sat on any committee in the new South Africa, once the principle is established that merit/price is not enough, there is a steep and slippery slope to the exercise of a straightforward racial choice. Certainly, this was how the new system worked in practice: after six months the government happily announced that even in contracts awarded on a 90 : 10 basis no less than 66 per cent had gone to BEE companies.[24]

Companies sought hard to qualify as 'black-empowered'. The basic qualification was to have black-owned equity of at least 25.1 per cent and 'substantial management control' by blacks. An elaborate points system gave companies incentives to direct as much of their own procurement as possible towards BEE companies, to appoint black executives and ensure that blacks played a real role in decision-making and at operational level. One economic sector after another, supervised by the relevant government minister, adopted its own BEE charter committing itself to various BEE goals. These were often extremely detailed. The financial sector's charter, for example, set numerical targets for black representation at board, executive, senior, middle and junior levels of every enterprise, set similar procurement and ownership targets, committed itself to extend financial services to the poor and lending for low-income housing, black small business and 'transformational infrastructure and agriculture' projects, and committed the sector to annual corporate social spending on black groups of 0.5 per cent of all post-tax profits.[25]

The government announced its overall target of placing at least 35 per cent of the economy into black hands by 2014. At the same time any 'white' company that was thought to be dragging its feet could expect merciless public criticism from the government and its associates. Bitter attacks were also levelled at 'fronting', that is, the co-option of token but relatively powerless blacks to decorate a company's image. Businesses were desperate to avoid legislation which intervened directly in a company's ownership structure or operation, and thus volunteered their compliance. Hence the beauty of the system: had it relied on government enforcement it would have failed, for government was simply unable to monitor and police such a complex set of moving targets. But business was far more efficient and business itself took over the job of policing and enforcing BEE, with a great deal of the impact lying in the insistence on BEE procurement, so that every business would demand BEE credentials from those it gave business to. In addition, businesses had the overwhelming feeling that 'the future is black' and that it behoved them to show that they were keen to be part of the change.

Business was also aware that quite apart from the small elite of black super-rich there was a burgeoning black middle class and that black consumers were an increasingly powerful force. Research showed that by 2000 black consumers had out-spent whites for the first time. Moreover, already 23 per cent of the richest decile of the population were black, a figure that was growing explosively.[26] The change was pervasive: even the smartest fashion shops now featured black mannequins – usually Naomi Campbell lookalikes; Oprah was ever-present (she visited South Africa frequently); so were Beyoncé, Kelly Rowlands and other black performers. The age of the big fat momma, the African earth mother, ended abruptly and the smarter malls teemed with slender young African women, hair straightened, and dressed to kill. Which all contributed to an exciting atmosphere of change and opportunity. The old restraints had gone, anything was possible, anyone might get rich and, as likely as not, they would be black.

This was, for most, the economic meaning of South Africa's

democratization. It was too easy, especially for those who had been exiles, to forget that much of the 'silent revolution' had occurred under apartheid. White disposable income had peaked in 1960 at triple that of blacks. For whites it had been downhill all the way from there. No one gave the apartheid government any credit for it, but racial differentials – even in state benefits such as pensions – had narrowed continuously through the 1970s and 1980s. Anyone who had known South Africa in that period knew that even the bad old days had gradually got quite a lot better and that democratic South Africa had its roots in apartheid South Africa. The new changes mainly saw a huge leap in processes already begun. But this was not what the government wanted to believe, nor the advertisers or the Oprah-watchers: they wanted to believe it was all a big hey presto, flash-of-lightning thing, the explosion of the new. And that was how many experienced it. There certainly had not been anything like BEE before.

The result was a BEE frenzy, with companies competing to grab headlines with BEE deals and continually boasting of their 'BEE credentials'. The government kept up the pressure, always talking as if white businessmen were all covert racists eager to escape their BEE duties. The ANC termed the process 'the elimination of apartheid property relations' and called for 'an element of sacrifice' by white capitalists. Max Sisulu, head of the party's Economic Transformation Committee, said that 'everybody would have to die a little to live a little longer'.[27] Exactly as with affirmative action, there was much talk of BEE as being essential if a revolution was to be avoided, of how a failure to push it to ever higher levels would somehow produce blood in the streets – for, bizarrely, BEE was said to promote the upliftment of the poor, though how exactly the poor benefited from watching Tokyo Sexwale or Mzi Khumalo become billionaires was not explained, nor why the poor might riot or revolt if such egregiously wealthy citizens were not given yet more assets.

Initially there were hopes – trumpeted by some early BEE beneficiaries – that blacks joining company boards would somehow create more jobs. That such simple-minded notions could gain any currency merely illustrated how many ANC leaders and their followers perceived the market economy only through a foggy mixture of Marxism and racial nationalism. In Mbeki's terms, of course, the new black bourgeoisie was the 'patriotic bourgeoisie' required by the national democratic revolution. It was on this basis that Cosatu and the SACP gave black empowerment their support, the assumption being that the entire bourgeoisie, black and white, would ultimately be cast aside by the socialist revolution. (Blade Nzimande, the SACP leader, had actually written his Ph.D. thesis on the concept of the patriotic bourgeoisie.) Certainly, there were expectations that black businessmen would do more than make money. 'We don't want people to go into the boardrooms and blend in. This is not a time to fit in. You are a generation that must change the paradigm,' Phumzile Mlambo-Ngcuka, then Minister of Minerals and Energy, told black businessmen, saying that they must 'create footholds and meaningful benefits for others through BEE deals and relationships'.[28] Bheki Sibiya, head of Business Unity South Africa, formed by the amalgamation of the previously separate white and black business associations in 2004, took much the same line, claiming that one out of every four black company directors were purely decorative and, knowing this, were in no position to do what proper BEE beneficiaries should, which was to engage in the 'robust debate' needed to push employment equity, skills development and transformation.[29] Sibiya made it clear that he regarded anyone cautioning that affirmative action might have adverse economic consequences as simply a racist.

'AFRICAN LEADERSHIP' – AND NEPOTISM

Yet there were concerns in the black community too. Reuel Khoza, the chairman of Eskom, spent a good deal of public money on a project on African leadership. Khoza argued that 'heavy reliance by Africans on Western models of leadership had undermined Africa's agenda for renewal'. Eskom's chief executive, Thulani Gcabashe, echoed the same idea. Africans who took up leadership positions 'have to ask themselves whether they are agents of change or are simply going to perpetuate the existing ethos of their organizations', he said. The African Leadership Study itself talked of 'the black donut' model, by which was meant the tendency of African CEOs or executives to depend on a middle management layer which was largely white and which took most of the real operational decisions. It seemed that even

African executives do not believe that fellow Africans are capable of managing. In a self-alienated manner they present themselves to their white junior colleagues as exceptions to the 'African problem'. Such African executives are far more comfortable being surrounded by white managers than African ones . . . new African managers are debilitated by the knowledge that white middle managers have occupied their positions for long periods and therefore know the job. When African middle managers fail to deliver, African executives are often prompted to turn to and rely on white managers, which perpetuates the myth of African incapacity and white excellence.[30]

The Leadership Study concluded that 'African leaders need to do some serious introspection to determine whether they are agents of transformation or new faces presiding over an old order'.[31] It was taken for granted that African models of leadership ought to be substituted. The study commented that at present many South African institutions could be transplanted anywhere in the Western world without having to change the way they operated and that accordingly 'the country suffers from an identity crisis'. Quite why anyone should believe this is mysterious: the modern company, pioneered as an institutional form in England centuries ago, has, after all, been transplanted to most countries of the world without producing any sort of 'identity crisis'. What was undeniably droll was that Ms Mlambo-Ngcuka, Reuel Khoza and Thulani Gcabashe were at that very moment all central actors in a colossal failure of leadership: the decision to ban the building of new electric power stations, to get rid of whole layers of competent white technicians from Eskom and hand over its coal procurement to BEE suppliers unable to provide the coal necessary to keep the power stations burning. Taken together, these measures were to produce swingeing power cuts and cost many thousands of jobs and billions in lost production.

Modern South Africa is a rich field for Fanonist psychological studies. Undoubtedly that is where the African Leadership Study belongs. In an unusually frank comment on the study Mathatha Tsedu insisted that there was a genuine crisis of African leadership. He told story after story of African corruption and dereliction of duty and how the only cure was to call in white replacements. He related how an African cabinet member had

told me about the frustrations of getting into government and hiring African people because that is the right thing to do, only for them not to deliver in the majority of cases. 'When you come from where we come from and you then have to realize that if you want something done quickly you have to rely on whites, it is really debilitating. You bleed internally, but our very own comrades do not work. There is generally no work ethic. Documents will not come on time or they will be sloppy. That is the painful truth.' The reality today is that people in this country who are indigenous Africans are prone to irrational behaviour fed by greed and irresponsibility. The numerous corruption and fraud cases involving esteemed African leaders are worrying issues.

Yet Tsedu too concluded that the problem was that 'African leaders are today forced by the legacy of colonialism to operate outside their cultural heritages' and that one would have to go 'back to pre-colonial times to try to find the lost moorings that made the ancestors tick'.[32]

The conclusion that the answer to a lack of the Protestant work ethic and a tendency to underperform in a modern bureaucratic environment is to search back into pre-colonial times may seem bizarre. But Tsedu too was searching for an answer in 'intrinsic' racial terms rather than looking at the large differences in education, training and experience between the blacks and whites he was comparing. Resort to such simplistic racial explanations was common. Since the 'old' standard answer, that if you want to get things done you must appoint people on merit, is, a priori, ruled out as racist and wrong ('hiring African people . . . is the right thing to do'), this leaves one few places to go.

Reuel Khoza's use of public funds to promote this 'African Leadership' vision was not unusual. ANC appointees throughout government bodies, parastatals and quangos all adopted the BEE cause as a public good. Thus the Industrial Development Corporation (IDC), originally created to promote economic growth and industrial development, now altered its focus to creating jobs, promoting small business and 'accelerating BEE'. Given the extremely narrow nature of the new ruling elite – really only a few hundred families – and its colonization of all state institutions, this was inevitably problematic, for members of exactly the same families were seeking to become BEE fat cats.

One gets the flavour of a good deal of contemporary South African life by looking at the Competition Tribunal hearings on Anglo-American's increasing its stake to a controlling 49 per cent in the country's biggest iron ore producer, Kumba Resources, in 2003. The IDC's chief executive, Khaya Ngqula, and its vice-president for BEE, Raisebe Morathi, lobbied strongly to stop this and instead to give control to an un-named BEE consortium. Anglo's request to know the identity of the mystery BEE company was refused but it then emerged that leading consortium members included Reuel Khoza and Moss Mashishi. Eyebrows were raised that Khoza, the CEO of Eskom, a parastatal, should be thus involved. Mashishi had also led a BEE consortium which acquired 20 per cent of the advertising agency Ogilvy and Mather, his partners including Mandela's wife, Graca Machel, and Wendy Luhabe, wife of the Gauteng premier, Sam Shilowa. But Luhabe was also the chairperson of the IDC . . . and other IDC officials were suspected of being consortium members too. These revelations raised the spectre of legal action and the possible exposure of high-ranking officials. Moreover, Anglo now threatened to walk away from Kumba altogether – and without its expertise Kumba would not work. Luhabe then denied that the IDC planned to take over Kumba either for itself or on behalf of a BEE consortium,[33] thus disavowing what Morathi and Ngqula had been forcefully urging for days beforehand. Clearly there had been some hurried family meetings behind the scenes.

Ngqula was also a partner of Phutuma Nhleko, the boss of MTN, in Worldwide Africa Investment Holdings, a secretive company with stakes in oil, electronics and financial services worth over R4 billion in 2005 when Mbeki's adviser, Wiseman Nkhulu (who also headed the Nepad secretariat), and Max Maisela were brought in as junior partners. In 1998 Worldwide received a R130 million loan from the IDC, provoking strong criticism not only because Ngqula was then the IDC's CEO but because the money was used for a pure equity trade. Further controversy erupted in 1999 when Alec Erwin, then Trade and Industry Minister, was forced to issue a gentle reprimand to his good friend Ngqula, after the IDC boss had received gifts amounting to R65,000 from an IDC subsidiary – though soon afterwards Erwin, as Minister of Public Enterprises, appointed Ngqula to head South African Airways.

THE STRANGE FAILURE OF SMALL BUSINESS PROMOTION

Clearly, if BEE was going to do more than create a class of wealthy rentiers among the ANC elite, then the key lay with the promotion of black small businesses. In addition to the IDC the state created the National Empowerment Fund (NEF), the National Small Business Council, Khula Enterprise Finance and Ntsika Enterprise Promotion to provide help to small businesses but they were all dogged by disaster. For the world of small black business was difficult, wracked by violence, large patriarchal 'big man' egos, endless quarrels and, often, shallow business skills – all features of life within Nafcoc (the National African Federated Chamber of Commerce), the main black business association. If one added the fact that all these agencies were staffed with people who were themselves on the lookout for economic opportunities, one had an explosive mix. The National Small Business Council was wound up in 1998 after it had been the scene of chronic leadership struggles, allegations of financial mismanagement and a plunge into debt. Ntsika was a similar story. Its first head resigned in 1996 amidst fraud and mismanagement allegations, borne out by a subsequent audit, but by 2000 the situation was much the same, with staff turnover at 100 per cent and a staff petition claiming that the agency was in a 'continuous state of disarray' and demanding a forensic audit of its CEO. A consultants' report revealed utter chaos: weak leadership, a lack of trust, an entitlement culture, poor management, poor attendance and time-keeping, and low motivation.[34]

The first head of the NEF, Khanya Motshabi, simply failed to get it off the ground and by 2003 it had still to announce any significant projects or, indeed, fulfil its statutory duty to file an annual report. Motshabi was replaced by Sydney Maree, the former world-record miler. By June 2004 he and other senior employees were suspended for 'irregular payments' and the NEF, supposedly the prime vehicle for launching new black businesses, was left paralysed. Maree was later jailed.

By 2001 Khula was also fighting to retrieve misappropriated funds in several different cases and the ANC Youth League called for both it and Ntsika to be wound up, claiming that they and another government initiative, the Umsobomvu Youth Fund, had failed to fulfil their mandates or have any impact. A good part of the problem is that small businessmen need multiple skills: marketing, distribution, entrepreneurial risk assessment and accounting. Such combinations of skills are not common and most Africans lacked the necessary educational background to perform well. As usual, the government overlooked this educational factor, for education takes time and once its significance is admitted one has to accept that change can only be gradual – a politically unacceptable answer.

Instead, the government decided that the key variable for small business success was access to finance and credit, addressed via the various (failed) initiatives mentioned above. Yet there is a much higher rate of small business success among (better educated) whites and Indians, who get no government financial assistance. Indeed, so many economically active whites were squeezed out of government jobs by affirmative action that by 2006 more than a quarter of them were self-employed, many using their severance packages to launch successful businesses. Similarly, many white managers, realizing that affirmative action and BEE placed barriers in their path to advancement, bailed out to start their own businesses, often successfully.[35]

The failure to promote small black businesses did not unduly disturb the ruling elite, for its heart was elsewhere, with the big, high-profile rentier capitalists – Sexwale, Ramaphosa and the like – to whom it had ties of kinship or friendship. At the lower social level, the government was simply going through the motions, for the ruling elite had very little connection to the world of black small business. Thus although, when awarding public contracts, the ANC would privilege 'black empowerment contractors', this was often a dubious gain, for the government paid its bills so late that many went bust. Thus the black small builder hired to renovate Mbeki's presidential residence in Pretoria went bankrupt because the Department of Public Works had still not paid him four years later.[36]

Despite its populist rhetoric, there was a huge social gulf between the new ruling elite and the lower reaches of black society. Indeed, the ANC leadership were uncomfortably aware that black society at that level contained many untameable creatures: football bosses, shebeen owners, taxi bosses, the squatter camp 'big men', vigilante leaders, gangster bosses and sangomas who traded human body parts for 'muti'. Such men carried guns, routinely settled disputes by violence and were beyond the government's reach. ANC leaders, who migrated as fast as possible from the townships to the old white suburbs, only ventured into that nether social world at election time and were distinctly nervous about trying to get anyone there to pay taxes, improve taxi safety or clean up the corrupt world of South African football.

THE HEART OF THE MATTER: THE MINES

The big question was what the ANC would do about the mining industry. Services and industry may provide over half of South Africa's GDP, but mining is still South Africa's beating heart. Mining stocks, even before the commodity boom, accounted for 30 per cent of the Johannesburg Stock Exchange and over 50 per cent of exports. In exile the ANC believed that mining was the past: after all it accounted for only 10 per cent of GDP. But the uncomfortable truth is that wages were relatively high, productivity relatively low so that, as one World Bank official put it to me, 'no one wants to make anything in South Africa'. Indeed, the key reason for unemployment being so high was the great hole in the economy where a far larger manufacturing sector ought to be, for South Africa suffers from 'Dutch disease', its currency always inflated by the high value of the minerals it produces.

Unwilling to be told that, however exploited workers might have been, they were not, in international terms, exploited enough, Mbeki engaged leading Harvard academics to come and say that the only way out was to cut wages or have a huge currency devaluation, otherwise no one would want to manufacture anything in South Africa. Local manufacturers tended to aim for the bottom of the market or, in the case of motor cars, benefited from an export subsidy scheme. Agriculture and tourism remained competitive but textiles, electronics and most other industries were painfully uncompetitive. No one wanted to face these awful truths, let alone act on them and the trade unions were opposed to anything which might cut wages. This left mining as the country's only really competitive international industry, dependent on South Africa's fabulous geological inheritance and earning most of the country's foreign exchange. Without those earnings the rand would immediately plummet to R30 or R50 to the dollar. Mining was simply the heart of the matter.

The ANC, like the Nats before them, had vowed to nationalize the mines but this commitment had melted away each time like snow in spring. The state had no means of running such a massively complex industry and nationalization would imply compensation payments of hundreds of billions of rand. But the idea lingered that the state could nationalize the underlying mineral rights and turn mining concessions into leases. The mining companies pointed out that this would throttle investment and do huge damage to the industry. Surely no one wanted to strangle the goose that laid the golden eggs?

No sooner was Mbeki elected President than he appointed Phumzile Mlambo-Ngcuka Minister for Minerals and Energy and she was instructed to begin work on a Mineral and Petroleum Resources Development Bill. The horrified mining industry pointed to the damage it would do. The Minister, unable to win the argument, lost patience and simply published the bill anyway. The bill put all mineral rights in the hands of the state, including the expropriation of all existing mining rights. Instead, the state would grant twenty-five-year mining licences, revokable at any time if the minister believed that any of innumerable conditions was being infringed or simply if she/he believed it was in the national interest to do so. All existing mining companies would have to reapply for the right to continue to mine and the minister might decide that they could only continue if they brought in a BEE partner of the minister's choice. In fact, no BEE partner, no licence.

The mining industry was appalled. The Ministry was to become a vast patronage machine, handing out lucrative opportunities to BEE enterprises, and effectively existing mining rights were to be unconstitutionally expropriated without compensation. In future, preference would be quite flatly given to BEE companies; the security of any mining venture would depend on mere ministerial whim; the minister was given virtually unlimited powers of intervention in the industry; the bill proposed new royalty charges which could threaten marginal mines, and mines would have no power to 'hoard' resources – if they did not use their rights they lost them. Mining companies warned that few would risk the vast investment required to sink new shafts with such little security. Moreover, throughout Africa mining laws had been progressively liberalized in recent years in an attempt to attract investment but the new bill marched in exactly the opposite direction. Undoubtedly its real inspiration lay in the Freedom Charter of 1955: 'the mineral wealth beneath the soil, the banks and monopoly industry shall be transferred to the ownership of the people as a whole.' Few knew or cared that this clause had been sneaked into the charter by Rusty Bernstein and its other white communist drafters as a disguised bit of socialism. In 1955 the idea of an ANC government enacting such legislation had been a far more distant prospect than a man on the moon.

Another striking innovation in the bill was that in future no minerals could be exported for beneficiation elsewhere without ministerial consent. It annoyed the ANC that precious metals (gold, platinum, diamonds and semi-precious stones) were taken to Israel, Belgium and India to be polished, turned into jewellery and sold at great profit: why should not such beneficiation be done in South Africa? In vain the mining houses tried to explain about the unique skills of orthodox Jewish communities in such matters, the far lower wage rates in India and the virtual impossibility of using relatively expensive and less productive South African workers to compete in such a niche market.

To the ANC's ears, the mining companies' objections were redolent of white racism. In vain the CEO of the Chamber of Mines, Mzolisi Diliza, pointed out that individual racism was hardly the point: 50 per cent of the mining companies was owned by pension funds and 40 per cent by foreign institutions.[37] The 'use it or lose it' principle caused anxiety too. Clearly the government wanted to maximize immediate employment but there was great concern in international mining circles that this would flood the market, pushing prices down.[38]

The mining world was in tumult over these changes but the mining companies, the sophisticates of the business world, had long since learnt that confrontational opposition was often counterproductive. Mining executives were far better educated and more cosmopolitan than their government counterparts but demolishing them in argument or, worse, taking them on legally and winning would inevitably elicit a wild racial populism. For although the new South Africa likes to boast of its fine new constitution the government frequently behaves unconstitutionally and its opponents quietly decide not to appeal to the Constitutional Court. For the Court would almost certainly lack the courage to stand up to the ANC government if feelings were running high, so it was better not to test it too hard: it would then just rule in favour of the government, creating a disastrous piece of jurisprudence and further undermining its credibility. So although the mining companies considered legal action – expropriation without compensation was a clear violation of constitutional property rights – ultimately none of the big companies took such action.

Ms Mlambo-Ngcuka, the only minister whose record was as bad as that of Manto Tshabalala-Msimang, seems never to have understood how disastrous her bill was. Simultaneously, she was vetoing, for five long years, the construction of any new power stations, despite Eskom anxiously pointing out that whereas there had once been over 40 per cent spare capacity, they were now down to 15 per cent and falling. This was to cost the country billions in lost production and billions more in lost investment. She seemed almost not to understand the objections to her Minerals Bill. Her early agreement that 'old order' rights would be automatically converted into 'new order' rights – the so-called Mbulwa Agreement – was cast aside without explanation. When it was pointed out that the World Bank's code on mining regulation specifically recommended against the granting of ministerial discretion over mining rights she said she would never use her discretion to expropriate, but then could not say why her bill gave her such powers. She claimed, absurdly, that the difficulties between the government and the mining companies was all due to lawyers who 'wasted everybody's time and tried so hard to sustain the tension'.[39]

But this was a gut issue for ANC ministers: they were convinced, despite their own increasing wealth, that they represented the black poor and that the mining companies were the enemy. Mlambo-Ngcuka explained her own intransigence thus: 'I have never seen my cabinet so militant. They are so angry. They feel the mining companies have pushed us too far.'[40] Needless to say, black business continued to insist that the bill did not go far enough and even demanded state guarantees for any loans they took out to buy into the mining industry.[41]

The government thought the mining companies were bluffing. They were not. BHP-Billiton, the world's biggest mining company, decided to invest billions on building a new aluminium smelter in Mozambique while simultaneously shelving its plans for a zinc smelter in South Africa. Other companies quietly made similar decisions, as their institutional shareholders now demanded, diverting huge investment flows away from

South Africa. As Ilja Graulich pointed out, 'it seems extremely unlikely that BHP-Billiton will be lured to increase its interests in SA. Neither will any other of the big mining houses. Although about R70 billion is being spent in the next five years on SA mining industry expansion, new projects outside of platinum are few and far between. Most of the investment is going towards upgrades and renewal of current operations.'[42] Chris Thompson, CEO and chairman of Gold Fields, declared that the gold mining industry's future lay 'outside the country'[43] – despite South Africa having been by far the world's largest gold producer for over a century. But industry leaders mainly said nothing. Platinum, now far more valuable than gold, was the great exception because 89 per cent of the world's supplies (and its associated metals such as palladium, rhodium and beryllium) are found in South Africa: those who wanted to mine it had no choice but to invest in South Africa, no matter what the mining legislation.

For the same reason, Impala Platinum early on announced a BEE deal for 20 per cent of its Winnaarshoek mine, half of which went to Mmakau Mining, run by Bridgette Radebe, wife of the cabinet minister, Jeff Radebe. Bridgette Radebe was an influential figure in both government and mining circles – she headed the Junior and Small Scale Mining Committee, had been put in charge of the state-owned (and loss-making) diamond mine Alexkor, and was on all the right panels and boards. She described the Mineral Development Bill as 'music to my ears' and despite the large investment cutbacks, declared her optimism about the future of the mining industry.[44] She had reasons to be cheerful – she was becoming very rich – but her deal was only possible because the Canadian company Platexco had decided to disinvest from South Africa, a fact which might have given pause for thought.

The world of the new ANC–BEE elite is a small one: when Bridgette took over Alexkor the mine actually fell under the supervision of her husband. Only a month after the Impala deal with Bridgette, Anglo Platinum announced a similar deal with Bridgette's brother, Patrice Motsepe, head of African Rainbow Minerals, so despite all the talk of giving economic power to the African masses, the two biggest platinum companies had concentrated their deals on just one already privileged family (for Patrice and Bridgette are the children of a Tswana princess). Moreover, Bridgette is also the sister-in-law of another BEE mogul, Cyril Ramaphosa, giving that family a degree of financial and political influence rivalling the Oppenheimers.

BEE moguls were expected to contribute heavily to ANC funds and be helpful to the President. Moreover, since their newfound wealth was politically derived, the moguls stayed within a small, closed, ANC circle; Cyril Ramaphosa, like Tokyo Sexwale, remained on the NEC. When one considers that the minister behind the Minerals Bill, Mlambo-Ngcuka, was married to Bulelani Ngcuka, the Director of Public Prosecutions, a key Mbeki confidant and later himself a major BEE beneficiary, one saw how, behind the rhetoric of 'power to the people', power was now more tightly held by a smaller group than ever before in South Africa's history. For while, under white rule, the Afrikaner nationalist elite had often intermarried and sometimes felt like one big family, economic power was always held by an English-speaking (and often Jewish) business elite. Now, for the first time, both political and economic power were centralized in the same tiny group. It was extraordinary enough that each new deal which further enriched this tiny group was greeted as a step towards 'democratizing the economy'; the claim that social revolution might ensue without more such deals was pure chutzpah.

Immediately, there was a swarm effect. Mzi Khumalo (heading Mawenzi Resources) quickly became a player, as did Paseka Ncholo (heading Khumo Bathong), while Bridgette Radebe acquired a stake in the fourth-biggest gold producer, Durban Roodepoort Deep, and a controlling share in its Crown Gold Recoveries operation. 'It's a lemming mentality,' said Phinda Madi, a professor of business studies. 'The mining sector is fashionable, almost a status symbol.'[45] During the excitement generated by this gold rush Mlambo-Ngcuka drafted a BEE Charter for the mining industry, which was leaked to the media in January 2002. The result was calamitous: the draft proposed 51 per cent black ownership of all new mines and 30 per cent black ownership of the whole mining industry within ten years, an extraordinary figure since the industry's total value was around R750 billion, suggesting that new BEE entrants were somehow going to borrow R225 billion to acquire this stake. This was clearly impossible, so the market drew the conclusion that the government had especially targeted the mining companies and that the companies would be forced to sell their shares at a steep discount. Moreover, with 70 per cent of Anglo's shares now held abroad, the 51 per cent black ownership target implied large-scale disinvestment from South Africa. Anglo-American shares fell 14 per cent. Overall, mining stocks lost 12 per cent in a day or some R90 billion. Even after a market bounce back there was a net loss of R60 billion. Mlambo-Ngcuka belatedly declared that the document had been only a draft but Mbeki was sufficiently alarmed to call in the big mining companies to ask them to help calm the market, though many ANC voices suggested that the market was 'racist'.

The companies, the government and a number of smaller players (including Bridgette Radebe) hammered out a new charter. This emphasized that foreign capital had played a key role in the development of mining throughout the country's history and that it was vital that it continued to do so. Empowerment benefits were to be more widely spread and the companies had to achieve 40 per cent black and 10 per cent female representation in all levels of management within five years. The bottom line was 15 per cent black ownership of the mines within five years and 26 per cent within ten years, though clearly such a target would depend on the banks: no less than R195 billion would need to be raised. Although AngloGold welcomed the charter, it was noticeable that Anglo shares dropped 2 per cent on the news, with sentiment not helped by the companies' commitment to helping BEE interests get loans on favourable terms. This could only happen if the companies guaranteed such loans, increasing their risk profile.

PAPERING OVER THE INVESTMENT DISASTER

With the charter's publication the media took the view that all was well. As John Battersby put it, 'The future is black. Which is good . . . The government is more comfortable to face the people and post-apartheid South Africa is more stable as transformation moves from the political to the socio-economic spheres.'[46] This was a remarkable interpretation of a process aimed at enriching a tiny elite at the cost of huge damage to the country's key industry and its international investment profile. There would doubtless have been a furious media reaction if the apartheid government had ever dared take similar measures to enforce the enrichment of a small number of its own members, their wives and supporters. So how to explain the supine nature of the media in the face of the strangulation of the mining industry, with its vast negative knock-on effects throughout society? The politically correct answer to this was that it was right to have double standards. As Battersby put it, explaining his switch from journalism to government propagandist, 'suddenly going from criticizing one government to criticizing another by the same standard seemed unfair to me'.[47] Future historians, without the benefit of living through these strange times, may have difficulty understanding this.

Yet already there were ominous signs. In 2004 the Foreign Investors Mining Association threatened legal action against the government. They had assumed that as existing enterprises within South Africa they must transfer 26 per cent of their equity to BEE partners but got a shock when they found that, if they discovered more minerals on their existing concession, BEE investors must be given an immediate 51 per cent share. They felt that the 'empowerment noose' had tightened since the 2004 election. They were, they made it clear, hardly likely to cough up the huge investment necessary to exploit these new discoveries if they lacked ownership and control over their assets. They would far rather quit the country than comply.[48] Reluctantly, the government climbed down: it had just been a try-on. Key actors within the government were adopting an aggressively opportunist stance, continually floating the toughest possible BEE positions to see what would fly – and getting away with whatever they could. This thoroughly alarmed mining executives. The Foreign Investors Mining Association warned that 'There is a lack of clarity and things continually seem to move. For a foreign investor this doesn't create a favourable investment climate. Foreign companies will be reluctant to enter the ring here.'[49]

Gold Fields immediately announced a merger with IAMGOLD of Toronto, since the fact that it was subject to the South African authorities meant that its shares were discounted by between 20 per cent and 45 per cent compared to its international peers and it was desperate to escape from that shadow. Chris Thompson, CEO of the merged entity, described the step as 'a major liberation'.[50] Gold Fields announced that it would henceforth concentrate new exploration on countries outside South Africa.[51] BHP-Billiton also announced the cancellation of plans to spend $50 million sinking South Africa's first deep-water oil exploration well, for no one could feel happy about committing capital in such an environment. 'We have learned historically that you tie up these things up front,' as one analyst put it.[52] But given the huge field of ministerial discretion over mining rights and the clearly moveable goalposts of BEE, it was hard to see how such things could be settled up front.

With the Mineral and Petroleum Resources Development Act (MPRDA) now law, Mlambo-Ngcuka brought in a new set of royalty payments, charged on top of all the corporate taxes paid by the mines. Despite the blandishments of the International Marketing Council, the mining world took sharp note. When the independent Fraser Institute brought out its 2004–5 annual report ranking countries according to the investor-friendliness of their mineral policies, South Africa had sunk to fifty-third place out of 64, far behind such erstwhile socialist states as Ghana (26th) and Tanzania (31st). Moreover, in Africa only Zimbabwe (64th) had more investors saying that they simply would not consider investing there.[53] The general trend towards greater investor-friendliness was exemplified by Nigeria, where President Obasanjo had liberalized mining laws, removing government from any role in the regulatory process and giving full legal title to investors.[54] South Africa, one expert noted, 'does not easily inhabit this investor-friendly world'.[55]

Investor confidence was further hit by the aggressive sallies against the mining companies of the deputy Minister for Minerals and Energy, Lulu Xingwana. She had made her name early on by bitter parliamentary speeches attacking the 'white capitalists who have looted South Africa's mineral wealth'. She bitterly attacked De Beers' decision to appoint Gareth Penny as its new managing director, another 'lily-white male', as she put it. When Anglo-American appointed Lazarus Zim as the first black CEO of its South African operations she denounced the company for not making him boss of its entire global operation. As the companies carried out BEE deals one after the other she declared herself unsatisfied. Insisting that the companies were not acting in good faith but were carrying out dirty tricks, she announced: 'We intend to get to the bottom of those tricks and also on top of them.' When BEE partners who could not come up with extra capital to pay their share of new mining investments found their shares diluted, she attacked the companies for 'daylight robbery'.[56] This Punch and Judy display would have been laughable except for the fact that Ms Xingwana was now a power in the land, and that such speeches had led Mbeki to promote her to deputy Minister and, later, to be Minister of Agriculture, where she immediately became the scourge of the farmers, accusing them, without evidence, of crimes against their workers. For mining companies which had to decide whether to commit billions in new investment, Ms Xingwana personified all their worst fears.

THE COMMODITY 'SUPER-CYCLE' TO THE RESCUE

Economic growth under Mbeki had been way behind the developing country average, for obvious reasons. Around 40 per cent of the work-force was unemployed and thus unproductive. The investment rate stayed stuck around 16–17 per cent (as against the 27 per cent achieved in the 1960s) and foreign direct investment (FDI) remained low. What inward investment there was tended to be foreign takeovers of South African businesses rather than new green-fields investment. The one great exception, the Daimler-Chrysler plants in the Eastern Cape, were the product of a large-scale government subsidy scheme. Mbeki took great pride in the export of Mercedes cars from South Africa but it was always clear that this investment was tenuously based on a subsidy which prevented Daimler-Chrysler from being caught in the usual high wage–low productivity trap. (When Mbeki approached Jurgen Schremp, the then head of Daimler-Chrysler, about the possibility of a BEE deal, he was told 'Don't even think about it'.[57]) What Mbeki had done was to bring down the national debt, 64 per cent of GDP in 1994, to 35.1 per cent in 2005, with foreign debt just 19.1 per cent: South Africa thus needed no help from the IMF or World Bank. The budget deficit, 5.1 per cent of GDP in 1994, fell to 2.3 per cent in 2004 and then gradually became a small surplus. The days of double-digit inflation – normal in the last two decades of apartheid – seemed to be over.

But to make any serious dent in the unemployment figures a growth rate of around 6 per cent would be necessary and growth remained far below that – 2.7 per cent in 2001, 3.6 per cent in 2002 and 2.8 per cent in 2003. Improvement on that looked difficult: higher investment rates would depend largely on more FDI, which seemed a distant prospect. Cosatu and the SACP urged a policy of government-led economic expansion, but the problem with that was that South Africans have a high import-propensity (an inevitable result of the country's weak manufacturing base), so any expansion quickly saw the balance of payments surge unsustainably into the red. The alternative, sporadically urged by Cosatu, was a policy of greater autarchy, with higher import tariffs and direct import controls, even if that meant forgoing FDI. The problem was twofold. Ever since the discovery of diamonds and gold South Africa had relied on FDI: it was unthinkable for the country to turn its back on the way the economy had worked for the whole period of its industrialization. Secondly, the ANC government had moved steadily in the opposite direction, liberalizing tariffs and (up to a point) exchange controls, joining the World Trade Organization and becoming steadily more integrated into the world economy. The ANC might not like globalization (which it viewed as synonymous with American imperialism) but in practice it accepted it as inevitable.

This situation prevailed throughout the ANC's first decade in power. It was obvious that the resulting social balance – with ever-growing unemployment and Aids – was unsustainable. But, as the old saw has it, South Africa progresses via political disasters and economic windfalls – and thus it was again. For Asia's explosive growth triggered an unprecedented commodity boom. The *Economist* commodities index, taking 2000 = 100, showed that by May 2007 the price of all food commodities was 155.9; the price of all commodities 202.9; and the real bonanza, in minerals, stood at 321.2. No country stood to gain more than South Africa. Suddenly, investments made in mining were revalorized threefold. The stock market more than tripled and growth took off – to 3.7 per cent in 2004, 4.3 per cent in 2005 and 4.9 per cent in 2006. Naturally, the balance of payments constraint kicked in, but FDI, attracted by these higher rates of growth, flowed in to make a quick buck and these inflows covered the deficits easily. Within the country these higher growth rates translated quickly into housing, car purchase and hire purchase booms. The government, naturally, took credit for the boom – though in fact its policies had prevented a far bigger boom. Carried away by the tide of affluence, Mbeki launched Asgisa – the Accelerated and Sustainable Growth Initiative for South Africa – whose target was 6 per cent growth. Asgisa was supposed to mean the systematic removal of barriers to higher growth, though naturally all the real barriers to growth, such as affirmative action, BEE, the MPRDA and the huge difficulties put in the way of bringing in foreign skilled labour, were regarded as sacrosanct.

In most mineral-rich countries the commodities boom naturally triggered huge new investment but in South Africa, thanks to the MPRDA, the opposite happened. Between 2004 and 2006 mining investment actually fell by 32.7 per cent, with the loss of 20,000 jobs.[58] The new Minister of Minerals and Energy, Buyelwa Sonjica, shaken by this data, announced her suspicions that the mining industry was trying to evade its obligation to do BEE deals, though the Chamber of Mines' own research showed that almost invariably respondents were worried by the new regulatory constraints, that there were long delays in the processing of applications for the new mining licences, that more than 15 per cent of applications had been refused (often because the Ministry judged them insufficiently BEE-friendly) and that the long delay in determining the new royalty rates had put others off.

For the new Act had made the industry dependent on South Africa's weakest point, its government bureaucracy. The Minister's own figures were particularly telling. Of the 5,454 applications for new prospecting licences, only 1,926 had been granted; of the 733 applications for new mining licences, only 174 had been granted and, most striking of all, of the 374 applications for the conversion of old prospecting licences into new ones, only 299 had been granted, and of the 377 applications for the conversion of old order mining rights into new licences, only 48 had been granted.[59] Yet when the Australian diamond company Tawana Resources announced that it would have to lay off all its workers at its mine near Kimberley if the Ministry did not issue it with a mining licence (for it could not continue operations without legal title), Sonjica was furious: 'They are trying to blackmail us and make us yield to them. It is totally unacceptable.'[60] Lazarus Zim, the president of the Chamber of Mines, who put the investment loss at around R10 billion a year simply through mines lacking legal title,[61] pointed out that the railways and ports (both part of Transnet) had also proved woefully inadequate to deal with the new demand for minerals.

The government was clearly shaken and the forceful Maria Ramos was dispatched to cleanse the Augean stables at Transnet. In addition, Sonjica tried to expedite the processing of applications and many 'junior' miners emerged to take advantage of the boom, resulting in a small (7 per cent) increase in mining investment in 2006,[62] though this still left investment over 25 per cent below its 2003 level. Despite frantic oil exploration all over the rest of Africa, investors showed an almost complete lack of interest in offshore drilling for oil and gas in South Africa, although the prospects for such finds are quite promising. Given the decision of the big mining and oil companies not to attract government wrath by criticizing the key assumptions behind the new mining and petroleum legislation and the government's equal determination to pretend that the new legislation was not problematic, there was instead a sort of comic conspiracy to find alternative reasons for the investment collapse. Sandile Nogxina, the director-general of the Minerals and Energy Department, who had driven the new Act, admitted that South Africa was losing out on mining investment though he put the figure at only R5 billion a year and suggested the reasons were inadequate infrastructure, the strong rand and a lack of skilled workers. The Chamber of Mines, for its part, continued to point a finger at bureaucratic delays while Sonjica said the problem lay with the fact that South Africa's mines were so far from the sea.[63] Only occasionally did others suggest, with deliberate vagueness, that there was something wrong with the new legislative 'architecture'.

Lurking behind such talk were the real reasons: the lack of secure property rights, not being allowed to employ the skilled expatriates needed, being forced to take on unwanted BEE partners – and the fear that ere long those partners would be allowed to grab control of one's assets. Sonjica promised new legislation to remedy the previous Act's errors, but the new bill she produced actually moved further away from allowing secure property rights. Meanwhile several small companies launched a suit against the government for expropriating their old ownership without compensation. The companies, headquartered in Luxembourg and Italy, pointing to their countries' investment protection treaties with South Africa, won their right to compulsory arbitration by the World Bank's International Centre for Settlement of Investment Disputes. The case was crucial. A judgment in favour of the companies would apply to the entire industry and the government would have to pay compensation amounting to half the country's GDP – and face a complete climb-down and loss of face to boot.[64]

The decision by the big mining companies not to take suit against the MPRDA was based partly on the assumption that in practice the transfer from 'old order' to 'new order' rights would proceed seamlessly. But this was far from the case. In 2007 the government disclosed that less than a quarter of all conversion applications had been finalized; that less than half all prospecting and mining rights applications had been granted in the previous year; and the position was worsening. Of 453 applications for mining rights lodged between December 2006 and November 2007 just five had been granted, and in June–November 2007 only one out of 1,163 prospecting rights had been granted.[65] The result was a growing crisis with both mining production and investment badly down. 'It's a real shock,' said Fred McMahon of the Fraser Institute, 'that in a place like South Africa, with great mining potential, investment is at its weakest levels.'[66]

For while the commodities boom had brought over $200 billion of new investment into mining worldwide, in 2006 investment in South Africa's mines was still well below its 2002 level. The reason was reflected in the Fraser Institute's policy potential index, comparing different legal and regulatory frameworks and their effect on mining exploration. Botswana scored twice as highly as South Africa, which was also far behind Ghana, Namibia and Zambia. South Africa was in fact level with the DRC – a war-torn country in which little worked – and higher only than Zimbabwe, a rogue state.[67] Moreover, these figures applied to the period before the mines began to be afflicted by major power cuts as the electricity crisis kicked in. In 2007 South Africa finally lost its position as the world's biggest gold producer to China. It had held the No. 1 spot ever since 1905 when it overtook the United States. Industry experts predicted that South Africa would fall further behind in 2008.[68]

THE NEW GOLD RUSH – BEE-STYLE

Amidst this turmoil in the mining industry, Patrice Motsepe and Tokyo Sexwale emerged as the biggest winners: of the R30 billion of BEE deals announced in 2003, two-thirds involved just these two men. Motsepe, young, charming and worldly-wise, cut a dashing figure. His African Rainbow Minerals was by 2004 the largest (R7.7 billion) black-owned company, controlling the country's biggest nickel mines, as well as substantial interests in gold, platinum, coal and iron ore. In addition, a BEE group he led bought 10 per cent of Sanlam, the country's biggest life insurer. He also owned the champion football team, Mamelodi Sundowns, and headed Nafcoc. Motsepe had strong links with the government.[69]

Sexwale was far more extrovert and gregarious, a crowd-pleaser who liked to be at the centre of the action. After the 2006 football World Cup final Sexwale invited the French captain, Zinedine Zidane, and the Italian defender he had head-butted, Marco Materazzi, to South Africa so that he could reconcile them. (They refused.) Naturally, he sat on the local organizing committee for the 2010 World Cup. His Mvelaphanda (Venda for 'progress') Holdings owned 22 per cent of Trans Hex, 15 per cent of Gold Fields and 10 per cent of Absa Bank while Sexwale also chaired Northam Platinum and Wingate Capital and was a director of many other companies. But, bizarrely, Sexwale also often got deals because he was 'historically disadvantaged'. Thus in 2004 Cape Town's ANC-controlled city council agreed to sell the prime Big Bay real estate to Sexwale's BEE consortium despite receiving two bids which were 30 per cent higher.[70] Yet at the same time white capitalists often offered shares at a discount to the BEE moguls – Motsepe's Sanlam deal cost other shareholders up to 4.7 per cent of their holdings.[71] So what was gained on the swings was doubled up on the roundabouts.

The same mutual reinforcement applied to the involvement of ANC luminaries in BEE deals. The government was happy at the increasing placement of ANC cadres on company boards. This showed that companies were deferring not just to black interests but specifically to the ANC, increasing the party's reach into the private sector and strengthening its hegemony over civil society. And the companies were happy because taking on ANC-connected people increased one's political leverage and one's chances of government contracts.

BEE consortia were, accordingly, constructed with an eye to political rather than economic appeal. Thus Savannah Resources, which bought a 26 per cent share of Aquarius Platinum in 2003, with half the money put up by the IDC, was chaired by Zwelakhe Sisulu. Other partners included Mandela's daughter, Zenani Mandela-Dlamini, and Steve Biko's widow, Nontsikelelo Biko, thus grouping the three most famous struggle families. When Western Areas appointed Gill Marcus as their executive chair, *Business Day* commented that this 'will likely raise eyebrows because she has no mining background'[72] – she had previously been No. 2 at the Finance Ministry and at the Reserve Bank. No one bothered to point out that it would have previously been unthinkable for a major gold mining company to appoint a Jewish woman with a lifetime career in ANC politics.

Even more striking was De Beers' R3.8 billion BEE deal with consortia whose leading members included ANC heavyweights Cheryl Carolus, Thandi Orleyn, Dolly Mokgatle, Moss Mashishi, and the former premier of the Northern Cape, Manne Dipico. The unveiling of the deal was a typical 'new South Africa' occasion with Carolus, though herself a Coloured, wearing African-style dress instead of her regulation mini-skirt and no mention of the fact that Mokgatle had performed so poorly as head of the railways that she had not survived Maria Ramos's spring cleaning at Transnet. By now, however, such deals had begun to encounter considerable public cynicism, the *Mail and Guardian* referring to the women as 'WaBenzi' (an old tribal insult) while one angry letter-writer greeted the deal with 'Another day, another sickening BEE transaction'.[73] Within a short time their Peotona ('seeds of greatness') company had added large chunks of LaFarge cement and Reunert electronics in consecutive BEE deals. There were angry comments at Reunert's AGM about the way R465 million in shares were simply handed to four already wealthy women, with the financing costs borne by the company itself.[74]

Carolus was offhand about her rapid transformation from SACP activist and acting secretary-general of the ANC. 'I was in the struggle for freedom. I wasn't in politics', and in any case, 'I'm a frontiers person, not a maintenance person.' Though professing herself concerned about growing social inequalities – of which she is a striking example – she simply shrugged that 'I can't be held responsible for all the problems in the world'.[75] Perhaps Ms Carolus deserved marks for her frankness: many of the ANC new rich continued to talk a now entirely hollow left-wing populism. Ms Carolus's husband, Graeme Bloch, continued to speak of how 'the poor need to build hegemony',[76] as if unaware that his own family was now a substantial obstacle to that.

There was by now a stampede to join the BEE gold rush. Anglo-American were shocked when their first black CEO, Lazarus Zim, resigned after only a year to lead a BEE consortium but even more dramatic was the realization by leading ANC figures that their status was now a highly marketable commodity. Considerations such as conflict of interest were simply ignored in the unseemly rush towards the golden age of BEE.

CRONY CAPITALISM FOR THE COMRADES

One of the most barefaced carve-ups came in telecommunications. Telkom is one of the most powerful and most-hated institutions in South Africa. Repeatedly, investors complained – in vain – that South Africa's version of broadband was the world's slowest and most expensive, and that sky-high telephone charges were preventing the country from developing its call-centre and business-processing opportunities. A corporate monopoly whose board exploits its monopoly position to award itself colossal salaries and bonuses, its service is poor and it jealously prevents any independent attempt to secure truly rapid broadband.

The key man at Telkom was Andile Ngcaba, the Communications Ministry's Director-General for almost a decade. A formidable figure who had headed the ANC's IT department and been in charge of MK's telecommunications, he had a string of degrees, and had helped set up the country's first two cellphone networks. His Minister, Ivy Matsepe-Casaburri, was a legendarily hopeless figure while the sector's regulator, the Independent Communications Authority (Icasa), was emasculated by lack of funding and political interference. So, Ngcaba, hard-driving, politically well connected and far abler than his Minister, dominated easily. He also became a BEE partner of South Africa's biggest home-grown hi-tech company, Dimension Data (DiData), and chairman of its local operation. At the same time, however, the US-Malaysian Thintana Communications sold off the 30 per cent of Telkom it had bought in 1997 during Mbeki's short-lived attempt at privatization. Just over half of these Telkom shares (15.1 per cent) were bought by the civil service pension fund, the Public Investment Commissioners (PIC). But Ngcaba, knowing in advance of these developments, had positioned his consortium to bid for the whole 15.1 per cent worth R9 billion.

The deal provoked outrage: Ngcaba was taking large commercial advantage of a situation he had himself created and the PIC was simply warehousing the shares, as if its duty was to make Ngcaba rich. Moreover, despite the fact that DiData was, like Telkom, heavily involved in the cellphone market in the rest of Africa, Ngcaba, ignoring the obvious conflict of interest, insisted on keeping the DiData job despite the fact that he would now join Telkom's board as well. Remarkably, the ANC's chief spokesman, Smuts Ngonyama, would make hundreds of millions of rand from the deal for 'facilitating' the ultimate arrangement between Ngcaba's consortium (which included the likes of Dali Tambo, son of the former ANC leader) and another BEE consortium led by Gloria Serobe, an Mbeki client. When asked about his role, Ngonyama, an Mbeki confidant and a powerful NEC member, answered with the immortal statement that he 'hadn't joined the struggle in order to stay poor'.[77]

The DA's Dene Smuts was typical of many critics (including Cosatu) in saying that the deal 'took crony capitalism to new heights'[78] while *Business Day* editorialized that this was 'the least mass empowering and most individually enriching exercise in the redistribution of wealth imaginable in a developing country with a majority of extremely poor people'.[79] Ngonyama professed himself 'hurt and astonished' by the criticism; he had expected 'to be praised for a successful bid to bring back a national asset'.[80] He had acted out of 'patriotic responsibility' and had 'a very strong patriotic passion about the shares that are out there'.[81] But such deals were now souring relations between the ANC and those to its left. Increasingly, embittered and penniless ANC activists, gazing at the new multi-millionaires, were saying, 'I didn't join the struggle for this.' Ngonyama's words about not joining the struggle in order to stay poor reverberated endlessly; for someone whose day job was as a public spokesman, it had been a remarkably maladroit slip. Moreover, Cosatu indignantly pointed out that the PIC's money was actually the workers' pension funds, whose trustees had not been consulted about the deal. Both the Finance Minister, Trevor Manuel, and his deputy, Jabu Moleketi, were highly critical and pushed Mbeki to reduce the BEE consortia's holdings to 10.1 per cent, the PIC keeping the other 5 per cent.

The Telkom deal was done in a blaze of publicity but usually the trading of political influence for financial gain – which is what BEE often amounted to – was conducted less visibly. Thus it only emerged much later that Ngonyama had quietly intervened to get Bato Star, a fishing company controlled by his family, out of trouble after its trawler, *Sandile* (which had a capacity far exceeding its legal fishing quota), had been arrested for illegal fishing. Bato Star grouped a series of ANC interests from Ngonyama's native Eastern Cape, including Joe Jongolo, the company's CEO and a member of the mayoral committee of Amatole municipality there, Gladman Boltina, a former Mbeki adviser, Barend Hendricks, who was part of the Telkom consortium, and Sam Kweleta, the Eastern Cape housing minister. It was a classic demonstration of how an ANC notable consolidated his local base.[82]

The fishing industry was a 'natural' for BEE because it was heavily regulated, with quotas obviously susceptible to political manipulation. Chris Nissen, formerly the Western Cape ANC leader, headed Sea Harvest, a large white-fish company, and also the BEE fishing company, Umoya, as well as accumulating multiple directorships (Tiger Brands, Woolworths, Standard Bank, Randgold and Exploration and Boschendal Properties, which he chaired), while remaining on the ANC NEC. Like Allan Boesak, Nissen had been a radical Coloured cleric in UDF days. The poignant aspect of his success was that Boesak would doubtless have been at least as well rewarded had he not been too greedy too soon. Given that fishing wealth depended on government licences and quotas, it was also unsurprising that the husband of Lindiwe Hendricks, Minister of Minerals and Energy, was a director of Sea Vuna fishing company and that the Minister herself not only owned shares in two fishing companies, Phambili and Vuna, but actually launched a trawler, *Harvest Lindiwe*, named after herself. But at least these companies fished. Other BEE companies bid for fishing quotas which they then immediately sold, paid themselves huge dividends and then had no employees or business until it was time to bid for more quotas.[83]

Criticism grew that BEE deals were not broad-based and always favoured the same few politically well-connected people. This shamed some companies into distributions of shares to employees, though on a racially discriminatory base: in Standard Bank's BEE deal white staff got 100 shares each but 2,500 black staff got forty million shares between them. A few whites, paradoxically, made fortunes out of BEE by putting together consortia and supplying business expertise which their black partners lacked. Thus in the Standard Bank deal the big winners were eight men who together received over R1 billion in shares, including such usual suspects as Cyril Ramaphosa, Moss Ngoasheng, Saki Macozoma, James Motlatsi and Vuli Cuba, but also a white, Marc Behr, who also scored heavily in the BEE deal of the insurance giant, Liberty Life. Similarly, the cellphone giant MTN's BEE deal saw 50 per cent of the shares go to five people, including two whites. Or again, the driving force behind the Peotona consortium's many BEE deals was a white woman, Wendy Lucas-Bull. Cosatu expressed unhappiness at such deals, though individual trade unionists sometimes did well – James Motlatsi was the former president of the National Union of Mineworkers, while the (former) trade unionist Irene Charnley scooped R456 million from the MTN deal.

The term 'crony capitalism' originated in the Philippines, where many of the most lucrative deals went to men close to President Ferdinand Marcos. This was true in South Africa too, where presidential advisers like Ngoasheng, Titus Mafolo and Gladman Boltina as well as Mbeki's spokesman, Ngonyama, featured prominently in BEE deals. When Murphy Morobe became deputy Director-General of Communications in the presidency, he immediately benefited from a deal whereby he and Max Sisulu acquired a large stake in the Resolve Group, a management consultancy. Resolve's chairman, Eric Molobi, expressed his delight that the group would be greatly strengthened by this 'buy-in by such prominent members of our community'.[84] Others who were useful to Mbeki also tended to do well. Thus Jacob Zuma's downfall as Deputy President was largely engineered by two men, the then Justice Minister, Penuell Maduna, and the Director of Public Prosecutions, Bulelani Ngcuka. It was, then, no surprise that when South Africa's largest property company, Growthpoint, cut its BEE deal a consortium led by Maduna and Ngcuka acquired more than R1 billion in shares – with Lazarus Zim, leading another consortium, also scoring heavily. Ian Davidson, a DA MP, described the deal as 'a prime example of everything that is wrong with the way empowerment deals are conducted'.[85] There was also adverse comment when the BEE company Phatsima Aviation bought 20 per cent of the profitable Aerosud Holdings: the BEE partners included presidential adviser Titus Mafolo, Ronnie Mamoepa, a spokesman first in the presidency and then at Foreign Affairs, Jackie Modise, widow of Mbeki's great ally Joe Modise, and Hlengiwe Mkhize, Mbeki's appointee as ambassador to the Netherlands.

No amount of adverse comment made much difference. Sun International, with renewal of its Sun City and Lost City casino licence depending on a BEE deal, pushed through a deal which brazenly broke all the rules. Shares in Sun held by the old Bophuthatswana bantustan had passed to the North West Development Corporation and thence back to Sun, though on condition that Sun would carry out a BEE deal for disadvantaged people who 'shall be resident or situated in the North West Province'.[86] The lion's share actually went to the Lereko consortium led by the previous Minister for Tourism, Valli Moosa, and Popo Molefe, previously ANC premier of the North West, although neither of them lived in the North West. The shares, sold at a 30 per cent discount, had just been warehoused until the two men left their offices – offices intimately involved with overseeing the hotel, gaming and leisure industry of Sun City/Lost City. Other smaller consortia were also involved (though Molefe's wife owned 30 per cent of one of those), as were the usual suspects, Titus Mafolo, Eric Molobi, Murphy Morobe and various government and parastatal officials. The next year Sappi, the pulp and paper giant, sold off 25 per cent of its plantation holdings to Lereko. By then Valli Moosa was also a director of Sanlam, Eskom and SAA, while Molefe was chairman of two private companies and two parastatals, Armscor and PetroSA.[87]

No one had been louder than the ANC in condemning Sol Kerzner's bantustan-based 'casino capitalism' under apartheid, but Kerzner's success had deeply impressed the ANC elite with the wealth to be gained from gambling, so much BEE activity focused on casino licences. Kerzner's fun-palaces had always been far more efficiently run than the bantustans in which they were situated, where government was invariably corrupt and incompetent. Now with the reincorporation of the bantustans, the country took on the aspect of a giant bantustan. Government was increasingly corrupt and incompetent. Casinos proliferated as did spanking new malls and hotels, many of them featuring the garish Afro-kitsch style which Kerzner had pioneered. Kerzner himself must have worried that he would be publicly hanged if the ANC came to power but managed to grease the rails well enough to leave the country with his body and assets intact. No one imagined South Africa would see him again but news of the country's bantustan-ization must have reached him, for suddenly he was back, talking new investments. It was entirely appropriate: he was as much a founding father of the new South Africa as Joe Modise.

Naturally, there was a BEE-run national lottery, Uthingo, which, given South Africans' love of gambling, made easy profits. When Uthingo's licence came up for renewal, however, the government announced, after secret meetings behind closed doors, that the new Gidani consortium would displace Uthingo. Gidani was secretive: seven of its eight directors had been appointed only days before the bid-deadline and the company refused to explain how it would install a new infrastructure allowing computerized betting at more than 8,000 points of sale in just seven months before it took over the lottery. Gidani's shareholding structure was also secret – though it emerged that key players included three NEC members, Cyril Ramaphosa, Chris Nissen and Max Sisulu, together with the chair of the Independent Electoral Commission, Brigalia Bam, and another of her commissioners, as well as the ANC ladies heading the Women's Development Foundation and the Commission on Gender Equality and the ex-chairman of Transnet, Bongani Khumalo.[88] This secrecy sat ill with the fact that the lottery involved only public money but the Trade and Industry Minister, Mandisi Mpahlwa, in announcing that Gidani had won the contract, declared that it 'would not be correct or fair to evaluate the companies in a public forum'.[89] And thus it remained. Inevitably, the handover was a disaster. Gidani was not ready in time and for some while the gambling public had to manage without a lottery.

BEE AND POLITICAL RISK

BEE had many critics, none more cogent than Moeletsi Mbeki, the President's brother. In 2003 he called for a complete rethink of BEE whose objective, he said, 'as conceived by conglomerates like Sanlam and Anglo-American was not to restructure the economy, but to create a black elite buffer entrusted with protecting the interests of big business and to ensure that the status quo under which conglomerates operate stays firmly in place. Now the state has internalized this model and is trying to implement it.'[90] Ever since Nail's inception, he argued, 'all the major empowerment transactions have involved the transfer of marginal assets to politically connected individuals' – and the market's true view of Nail was reflected in the fact that its valuation was less than its cash reserves, suggesting that Saki Macozoma was seen as subtracting value, whereas 'what we need are entrepreneurs, people who start new businesses, take risks and create new jobs. Under BEE people take no risks. It encourages people to live off the fat of the land. The only way to deracialize the economy is by black entrepreneurs creating their own companies . . . Show me an empowerment company that has produced any product.'[91]

This last was true enough: the only enduring new product pioneered by a BEE company was the e-tv channel, the work of a white (Johnny Copelyn) and a Coloured (Marcel Golding), who together ran Hosken Consolidated Investments. What enraged the new elite most, however, was Moeletsi's demand that BEE be stopped – because it enriched only a politically connected handful; because it gave assets to those with no idea how to manage them; and because South Africans should not still be 'talking race'.

The Black Business Council bitterly attacked Moeletsi, claiming that he himself had benefited from BEE – but his critique went unanswered. The Council's Dali Mpofu accused Moeletsi of providing ammunition for reactionary whites,[92] but this was simply the usual attempt to dispose of problems by racializing them, Mpofu being soon rewarded by President Mbeki with the post of Group Chief Executive of the SABC board. Kgalema Motlanthe bizarrely suggested that 'individual enrichment . . . is perhaps the inevitable outcome of the fact that black business is weak and disorganized. Organization was fundamental to Afrikaner empowerment. Because it was organized, emerging Afrikaner capital was able to link itself directly to the national movement of the Afrikaners. As a result, apartheid emerged as a plan not only to oppress and impoverish blacks but also to create rich whites.'[93] Although the notion that African nationalism should copy Afrikaner nationalism was undoubtedly in the minds of most ANC leaders, the comparison with apartheid was seldom so frankly and positively made. Moeletsi replied that BEE was merely the most concrete expression of the entitlement culture:

> We've created a powerful black elite that has its hands in many pies but, at the end of the day, doesn't have the technical know-how of running the companies they supposedly own. I am a living example of an entrepreneur. I do what I do because I know what I am doing. I haven't been given free assets, which I proceed to destroy like many black business people. If you get assets for which you haven't worked, there's another agenda, a political agenda. It's not a development agenda.[94]

Whenever business betrayed its true feelings about BEE there was a furore. In 2003 Sasol, South Africa's biggest industrial company, listing its shares on the New York Stock Exchange, was required to detail its risks. It listed BEE as one of them, unleashing a hail of criticism from a variety of ANC sources including Brian Molefe, head of the PIC, and

Reuel Khoza, the chairman of Eskom, who angrily claimed that Sasol was 'saying black people should be excluded from the economy', adding menacingly that 'they should consider the consequences of having the mass of black people excluded'. Yet, as the economist Pieter Haasbroek pointed out, 'Sasol was accurate in its report. Empowerment has a negative impact on productivity, on the cost of business and, therefore, on the competitiveness and profitability of companies. If the PIC is up in arms then it has no understanding of the dynamics of our business world.'[95]

In 2004 Tony Trahar, Anglo's CEO, told a US audience that political risk levels in South Africa, though still present, had declined. President Mbeki furiously denounced him. Trahar remained diplomatically silent. Sasol was also a favourite target. Thus Sandile Nogxina, Director-General of the Department of Minerals and Energy, reacted with fury when the oil giant appointed whites to its three top positions in 2005, claiming it was 'one of the least transformed' companies.[96] Similar attacks by the PIC's Brian Molefe led to the ousting of the conglomerate Barloworld's white chairman in 2007 and his replacement with Dumisa Ntsebeza, a former TRC commissioner. Even then, when Barloworld appointed a white deputy chairman to assist the inexperienced Ntsebeza, Molefe attacked the move as 'racist and patronizing'.[97] The deputy chairman resigned after three weeks.

The situation was beyond parody. Repeated public attacks on businessmen by leading public officials, including the President himself, were a dramatic demonstration of political risk. The fact that such attacks were both so vehement and so ignorant – for the President had clearly failed to understand the concept of business risk – added a further dimension to that risk. This was compounded when the chairman of the biggest public utility, Eskom, demonstrated that he too had not understood the concept of risk. Finally, these highly partisan attacks were made by Khoza, the head of a parastatal, Noxgina, a civil servant, and Molefe, the head of a public pension fund – an alarming demonstration of how politicized all such non-political posts had become. Molefe seemed to neither know nor care that he was in breach of his fiduciary duties by attempting to force changes which could well be inimical to the interests of the pensioners whose trustee he was.

Despite much public pretence about the benefits of BEE, real domestic business sentiment was negative and international business sentiment more so. Eighty-six per cent of businessmen saw BEE as doing little for the poor majority and 54 per cent saw it as a deterrent to investment and a handicap to growth.[98] Both the British and German Chambers of Commerce in South Africa expressed strong reservations about BEE.[99] Inevitably, the pressure to sell off 25 per cent of their equity at a discount as soon as they set up in South Africa scared away foreign investors: a survey by the American Chamber of Commerce in South Africa found that 74 per cent of US companies reported that BEE pressures 'negatively affected their investment decisions'.[100]

Under pressure, the government agreed that foreign multinationals who did not wish to do BEE deals could get a certificate of non-compliance instead. This was hardly a bargain for, as Mark Harris, IBM's general manager, pointed out, such a certificate 'has huge negative connotations'.[101] The IMF also expressed concern at the absence of safeguards to prevent BEE leading to extreme wealth concentration and a huge strain being put on the credit system by the need to fund these huge transfers of assets to just a few hands.[102] Indeed, the funds required to pay for BEE were estimated by *The Economist* at 10 per cent of the country's annual money supply for ten years: if the government footed the bill the effect would be to add ten points to inflation for a whole decade, simultaneously lowering growth by 2 per cent a year. In fact the costs were likely to be divided between the government, the banks, the companies selling their shares and their new buyers, but one way or another the costs were unavoidable unless the inexperienced new BEE owners could make their assets more productive than their previous, more experienced owners: an unlikely prospect.

One certainty was the disappointment of any hope that BEE would mean a better deal for black workers. Often quite the opposite occurred. Thus when, in 2003, Transnet sold off 51 per cent of Apron Services, its airport baggage-handling company, it specified that there had to be a BEE purchaser. This quickly emerged in the shape of Equity Alliance, a BEE consortium put together by the ANC MP, Mpho Scott. Within a year the workers were on strike after the new management had dictated new working conditions with longer working hours, pay cuts, reductions in sick leave and overtime payments, etc. The workers' placards read 'Mpho Scott, are you an ANC MP and South African? Why are you oppressing black people?'[103] (Scott's company was finally sacked by the Airports Authority at the end of 2007 because of the amount of baggage pilferage in transit – traceable, critics said, to the miserable wages the company paid.) A new trade union song made its appearance: 'Amabhulu amanyama asenzel'iwari!' (Black Boers are the cause of our worries).

This confusion of class and ethnicity allowed BEE to retain continued support in principle even from Cosatu and the SACP. Only slowly did reality break through. As Gwede Mantashe, leader of the National Union of Mineworkers, put it: 'Capital is capital, it has no colour. No black person buys into a company because he wants to do all sorts of things for blacks. People go into business because they want to make money. And that's it. Irrespective of their colour . . . the belief that BEE will be father Christmas is a big myth.'[104] An opinion survey at the end of 2004 found that 70 per cent of South Africans (including 65 per cent of blacks) thought that BEE had enriched only a select few, and 44 per cent thought BEE was stifling the country's growth.[105] As with affirmative action, the government and the media assumed that BEE was both inevitable and universally popular. Yet this was far from true: poorer blacks were quite smart enough to see that such policies could do them no good and might do them harm.

THE REAL PROBLEMS WITH BEE

The greatest worries about BEE concerned property rights and the lack of an educated middle class. What really happens to property rights, after all, when the government simply takes away someone's mine and suggests they apply instead for a lease, burdened with heavy conditions? But the question is broader. Where exactly are property rights when companies are put under overwhelming pressure to divest themselves of assets at a discounted price, thus lowering the value of shares held by all other shareholders? But it does not stop there. When the Khomani San had their land rights over six Kalahari farms restored they found they were in debt and so decided to sell one farm, but were told by government that this was impermissible because it would undermine the land reform process.[106] Does one really own an asset if one is not allowed to sell it?

There was also a tendency to assume that any assets (or even jobs) given to a black person must thereafter always remain in black hands. Thus if, for example, four jobs in a university department were held by blacks and they left for better-paid positions, the department is liable to be told by black academics that these are now 'black jobs' and that other races should not now be allowed to compete for them. Hence, too, the government's insistence that, in order to ensure that BEE deals were not undone, not even 1 per cent of assets in a mining or energy enterprise could be sold off without the minister's written permission.[107]

This raised the larger issue of racial classification. Although the apartheid Population Registration Act was repealed (by De Klerk), in practice the ANC government wanted to maintain racial classification and thus separate racial identities. The growing number of South Africans who did not want to be thus classified were told they must stay sorted into their segregated groups because racial criteria were used for everything from BEE and affirmative action, to determining university admissions and deciding whether banks were extending credit in the 'right' directions. In 2003 Telkom sold off discounted shares to 'historically disadvantaged', that is, black, people only, while in 2007 the state's National Empowerment Fund similarly sold off its MTN shares at a 20 per cent discount, the announcement reading, 'To be a participant in the scheme investors must be black. . .'[108] In practice, Africans were favoured over other previously disadvantaged groups. Zahid Parui-Dawood, president of the Congress of Business and Economics, reported that he was inundated with complaints from his Coloured and Indian members that whenever they approached white-owned companies with business propositions 'they are turned down and told that, to gain government business, the white company could only deal with Africans'.[109] The ANC Youth League openly called for the constitution of a 'black Broederbond', an elite black secret society which would advance African interests in the same way the Afrikaner Broederbond had looked after its own. Once the Broederbond would have been execrated as an apartheid institution; now apartheid institutions – with different personnel running them – were seen as the most appropriate for South Africa.[110]

Apartheid was an actively iniquitous policy but often it simply failed to leave things alone. It might have simply left alone the (often excellent) mission schools, and the English-speaking universities which, until the Separate Universities Act of 1957, a small but significant number of black students (including Nelson Mandela) attended. Had such institutions been allowed to continue they would have produced a well-educated black professional class whose children would have followed their parents in growing numbers, with huge and benign consequences for them and the country. Instead they were forced into inferior and racially distinct 'tribal colleges'.

This disaster was compounded by the ANC's refusal to accept how bad the damage was. Instead of accepting that there were few greater priorities than providing a good education for its citizens, the government proceeded largely as if education did not really count. The educational system deteriorated markedly in ANC hands and, effectively, the government insisted that expertise and good qualifications did not really matter. Anyone who argued that merit was the vital criterion in choosing future doctors or competent managers was accused of being racist *in principle*. Indeed, all talk of meritocratic criteria was regarded as intrinsically racist. This left the government free to appoint to positions throughout society people who lacked the skills or qualifications necessary to do their jobs properly: young black women with no technical background to run the railways, ambassadors who had, at best, spent a few weeks learning the skills serious foreign offices spend years inculcating, judges who, even as lawyers, had been inexperienced, incompetent and drunk, and senior policemen who had been thugs or crooks. All these are real examples.

In order for this to pass muster South Africa became a society of ubiquitous pretence, not only by the government but by politically correct whites. It was so nice to cheer the arrival of so-and-so to this or that leading position because he/she was young, black, a woman or a disabled person, and this said such nice things about the new society. To notice that such a person could not possibly do their job properly was the height of bad manners. ANC municipal office-holders, who needed no encouragement to treat their towns as merely part of a spoils system to be ransacked, happily took the lesson and would gaily get rid of trained planners, accountants, engineers and their ilk in order to be able to hand their jobs to unqualified cronies or relatives.

Only occasionally was reality allowed to break through. A young, well-trained and highly competent woman lawyer I knew returned home one day when I happened to be there. Though herself a politically correct young woman, she had had a hard day: 'I saw X go off to a pretend university where she got a pretend degree,' she said bitterly, 'after which she went into the sort of practice which was willing to have pretend lawyers. Now, because of her race and despite her ignorance of the law, she has been appointed a judge. Today I had to appear before her. Till now I have loyally pretended but today was terrible. I simply cannot pretend that she is a goddamn judge.' More typical was the reaction of Jimmy Manyi, chair of the Commission for Employment Equity, who, facing the rising anxiety of business and government over the desperate skills shortage, insisted that the shortage was merely 'an urban legend': white businesses were, he said, just dragging their feet about employing more blacks.[111]

Any attempt to repair the lack of a black middle class was always bound to be something of a botched, rushed job and there is no point being pedantic in one's requirements. But there was, too, a general failure to think clearly about what was happening. Take *Business Day*'s reaction to the MPRDA: 'the case for black empowerment in mining is so obvious it does not even need to be made here. Mining made the white middle class in SA and it must make the black middle class in SA. Until that black middle class is the dominant economic and political force in the country, we will never know tranquillity. It must happen quickly, and the minerals bill is a good vehicle for helping the process along.'[112] Yet the white middle class created by mining were not just a handful of tycoons at the top. They were a large class of surveyors, engineers, lawyers, geologists, accountants, doctors and experts in explosives or labour relations, served by large numbers of administrators, clerks, mine managers, policemen, electricians and foremen. BEE produces only the handful of tycoons.

Even that understates the problem. In many ways South Africa since 1994 resembles the United States after the Civil War, the period when Yankee businessmen, at last freed from the constraints imposed by the old South, happily exploited all their new opportunities, producing a period of dynamic growth and runaway corruption, the era of the Rockefellers, Morgans, Mellons and Carnegies, the so-called robber barons. The new BEE tycoons are clearly South Africa's robber barons but the difference is that their American counterparts were strikingly able financiers and businessmen who emerged meritocratically out of a furious competitive struggle. This is not true of South Africa's new tycoons, who are politically connected rentiers, utterly dependent on white business to continue to produce the goods.

The situation is best exemplified by the fact that in 2002, only 287 of the 18,802 chartered accountants in South Africa were Africans, alongside 961 Indians and 199 Coloureds.[113] This was so despite a great deal of effort and agonizing by the accountancy profession, including special tuition and scholarships, and the provision of computers, workbooks, stationery, transport and food for black students. Ultimately, said their spokesperson, the small numbers were simply 'a result of South Africa's education process'.[114] For the same reasons, there was only one black SAA flight captain in 2002, one black actuary and five black dentists in the whole of Cape Town.[115] Less than 3,000 African students left school each year with a pass in higher grade maths. By 2005, out of 21,092 accountants 543 were African, 341 Coloured and 1,482 Indian.[116] That is, the increase since 2002 was greater among Indians (of whom there were just a million in South Africa) than among Africans and Coloureds together (of whom there were some forty-three million). Yet the government continued to set targets as if oblivious of the educational facts: thus the financial and mining BEE charters alone set targets which could only be fulfilled if well over half of all black matriculants with higher maths grades were recruited by the banks and mines.[117]

The numbers are sobering. Less than a third of all pupils starting school make it through to the top class and of those less than 5 per cent pass higher grade maths, despite a deliberate dumbing down of matriculation standards by Kader Asmal when Education Minister. In 2003 of these 25,217 people only 35 per cent – less than 9,000 – were Africans. Similarly, there were less than 5,000 African graduates in engineering, commerce, business and management in 2004.[118] From this tiny pool of talent the government insisted, in effect, that the private sector must recruit many times that number of Africans every year, let alone the further large numbers required by the public sector. Worse, the whites, who made up 43 per cent of all higher grade maths passes in 2003 and well over half the university degrees in engineering, business, commerce and management,[119] were frequently told that they were not wanted because of their colour and ended up emigrating: a policy conceivable only in a madhouse. As so often, the government disliked this being pointed out. When in June 2007 the *Sunday Times* reported that, despite a chronic national scarcity of doctors, white medics were being turned down for jobs and emigrating as a result, President Mbeki furiously denied the truth of this report. The newspaper merely reprinted it, pointing out that every word was true.[120]

This education deficit meant that affirmative action was a greater threat to business than BEE. In the last analysis a company could afford to sell off 25 per cent of its shares at a discount and put up with a few BEE directors who might know little of the business. But given the paucity of qualified blacks the pressure to appoint staff at every level, including senior management, on demographic rather than business criteria was a major threat to company performance and even survival. Naturally, the tiny elite of black accountants and executives who were truly competent commanded a huge premium – and, as with all other South African institutions, businesses were happy to appoint competent Africans from elsewhere in Africa since it was quickly observed that appointing a black-skinned foreigner rather than a local white at least protected one from the charge of racism. But the government's affirmative action targets were not met: in 2004 the Labour Minister Membathisi Mdladlana reported angrily that there had been only a 1 per cent increase in the number of blacks in top management over the previous two years – due, he said, to 'resistance to workplace transformation'.[121] The truth was the opposite: companies desperate to appoint more black staff simply could not find them and, in the crunch, were not prepared to commit hara-kiri by appointing people clearly unable to do their jobs. Ultimately the whole country depended on that.

Naturally, it was no longer acceptable to have racially segregated business associations. The problem was that Nafcoc exemplified all the typical weaknesses of the African 'big man' culture: a tendency for the organization to be dominated by overweening egos; a correspondingly weak sense of corporate belonging and thus a permanently bad financial situation; and chronic factionalism as the big egos clashed. Nafcoc politics were a continuous pantomime of attempted coups, sackings and comebacks amidst allegations of manipulation, financial mismanagement and sexual harassment. Its white equivalent, the South African Chamber of Business, was never as entertaining. To the government's embarrassment many black businessmen wanted to retain segregation. Even when they merged in 2003 to form Business Unity SA (Busa), the Black Management Forum maintained its separate existence and, under Jimmy Manyi, ensured that black business remained in a state of semi-revolt inside Busa. There was constant sniping over the larger resources available to white business but, as so often, this was at bottom an educational divide with white-led corporations able to call on skilled analysts, lawyers and economists to make their point. 'When issues are raised,' said one participant, 'well-resourced white entities tend to produce well-researched positions, leaving little engagement space for their unprepared black partners.' Busa's head, Patrice Motsepe, was blunt about the lack of such expertise on the black business side.[122]

Government pressure for 'transformation' was insistent but, even by 2005, of 3,029 directors of listed companies only 307 were black – of whom only 60 were executive directors.[123] Most of these were directors for public affairs or human resources, almost never for finance. One result was that blacks who were reasonable – or even semi-reasonable – directors would get appointed to so many boards that they did little but move from one board meeting to the next, with little impact on any of them. So angry voices were raised, blaming white racism. But BEE had worked only because business itself had policed it. Companies had to report on 'equity employment' (affirmative action) to the Labour Ministry and its Commission for Employment Equity – and there lay the rub. In 2006 the Commission, as part of its 'name and shame' policy, listed 1,296 large companies that had not submitted employment equity reports and singled out thirteen companies for particular blame. This was, however, completely wrong. The companies named had not only complied but had documentary proof that they had been commended by government for their efforts.[124] The Labour Ministry and Commission for Employment Equity were revealed as completely incompetent, having failed even to keep proper records. The debacle let business off the hook. This was, indeed, the saving grace of the new South Africa: the government made crazy laws but in practice it was not competent to enforce or even monitor them. The situation resembled that under apartheid where one was bound to be breaking some crazy law or other most of the time, so people often ignored the law. The corollary was that when the police really wanted to pursue you, they could usually find you guilty of something.

ESCAPE ROUTES FOR BUSINESS

Business could not simply rely on government incompetence and attempted, manfully, to comply with the laws. But the business world had two other strategies too. First, it could take a company private.

Non-listed companies attracted far less attention; newspapers tended to ignore them since there were no newspaper-buying shareholders out there and anyway their annual reports and accounts were no longer public. And since there were no shares to be traded, there could be no compulsory BEE. (This applied particularly to agriculture: commercial farms were usually family businesses.) Occasionally voices were raised demanding that BEE be applied to family firms too,[125] but there was no obvious way to do this and since the family firm was the usual way up for black business, the government could hardly force such businesses to divest themselves of assets. Of course, even private companies might seek BEE points in order to qualify for government tenders, but they could protect themselves from official pressures far better than public companies. Not surprisingly, Brian Molefe, the head of the PIC, raged against the private equity deals which took a growing number of companies private.

The figures were striking. In 1998, 669 companies were listed on the Johannesburg Stock Exchange (JSE). By 2000 this had fallen to 616; by 2004 it was down to 410 and the number fell again in 2005 before stabilizing at last in 2006. The process saw a sharp down-rating of the JSE. In 1992 it had been the same size as the Australian exchange. Both had featured comfortably in the world's top dozen stock markets and were worth roughly 16 per cent of the London Stock Exchange. By 2003 the Australian market was worth 22 per cent of its London counterpart but the JSE, now twenty-third largest in the world, was worth only 6 per cent of the LSE.[126]

Small and medium-size businesses could go private but corporate giants could not. For them the main escape strategy was international diversification. Typically, the company would add a London listing to its listing on the JSE. Company headquarters would then move to London, its primary listing. The rapid internationalization of its shareholding would follow and soon a growing internationalization of its assets as it set about foreign acquisitions and mergers. All of which was easily defensible. South African companies had been forced into autarchy by years of sanctions and boycotts so now they could grow as they would always have preferred to do, especially since the cost of capital was cheaper abroad. Government could even trumpet the success of these national champions as, for example, when SA Breweries acquired Miller and became the world's largest brewer as SAB-Miller.

Such companies always made repeated declarations of how their heart would remain in South Africa, but in practice an ever-increasing proportion of their assets was located outside South Africa. BEE often played a useful part in such a strategy, enabling the company to sell off subsidiaries at home in order to finance investment abroad.

Anglo-American were, as usual, the flagship. They took over De Beers, moved to London and by 2004 had carried out twelve major BEE deals, simultaneously investing heavily in Australia, Latin America and elsewhere. In 1987 the company had controlled 60 per cent of the JSE. By 1994 this had fallen to 43 per cent and by 2004 to 19 per cent,[127] and its divestment of domestic assets continued pell-mell after that, with the AngloGold empire, Highveld Steel and Vanadium, Mondi paper and Anglo's share in the Tongaat-Hulett group (sugar, property, aluminium) also slated for sale. By 2004 only 26 per cent of the company's earnings were derived from South Africa, against 45 per cent from Latin America.[128] In 2006 an American, Cynthia Carroll, replaced Tony Trahar as CEO – and almost immediately confirmed an even more aggressive sell-off of South African assets. Even the Oppenheimer family sold a third of its Anglo stock to the Chinese billionaire Larry Yung.[129] In 2008 Nicky Oppenheimer featured at No. 18 in the *Sunday Times* (London) Rich List. 'He spends much of the year in Britain,' the paper added, 'on his home counties estate.'[130]

Far more was involved than a mere movement of funds. Anglo was not just South Africa's corporate flagship, it had carefully recruited Rhodes Scholars and always had the most sophisticated corporate ethos in the country, exemplifying what it saw as the best within the old Anglo–South African culture. It had been far more liberal-minded than other big companies, financing all manner of political and social initiatives, cultural institutions and academic research. It had believed strongly in South Africa through decades when it found itself at odds with those in power and through it all it retained its polish and its male Wasp intellectual culture. The choice of an American woman as its boss was just one sign of how far that culture was in retreat. The company had fallen behind BHP-Billiton and RTZ and was itself a potential takeover target and it was now unclear how much confidence it had in South Africa. Its decline was 'a corporate tragedy'.[131]

Anglo's shift was nothing less than a shift in the force-field itself. Others followed. Billiton (previously Gencor) had merged with the

Australian BHP and also moved off-shore. By 2004 less than a sixth of BHP-Billiton's income came from Southern Africa, and much of that from the Mozal aluminium smelter in Mozambique.[132] As Gencor it had been the flagship of Afrikaner capital; now again it mirrored what was happening with *die volk* – scattering to the four winds beyond South Africa. Old Mutual moved to London too and bought Skandia, making itself a major European player; Sasol, Investec, DiData and others followed.

Once a company's headquarters moved to London the ANC was unable to insist on affirmative appointments to the top staff. As more of the company's assets and staff moved abroad, less and less of it was subject to affirmative action, BEE and South African political risk. Hence the rationale for the refusal of men such as Tony Trahar to respond to Mbeki's ill-informed attacks, for Trahar was putting more and more of Anglo's assets beyond Mbeki's reach, reducing his risk all the time. In 1994 Anglo could probably not have survived the nationalization of its South African assets; by 2004 it clearly could. Thus at stage front there was a process going on with Cheryl Carolus dressed in Afro costume happily being anointed as a WaBenzi, while at the back stage door assets were being removed from the grasp of such WaBenzi as fast as possible.

How far the WaBenzi and Mbeki understood this strategy is debatable, for almost everything was obscured by the great commodity boom unleashed after 2003. By trebling prices on the JSE in only three years the boom made sure that the new WaBenzi prospered and the 5 per cent GDP growth rates it produced handily obscured the real costs of BEE. Better still, the boom attracted new FDI to South Africa so that by 2006 the investment ratio had risen to 19.2 per cent of GDP from its more normal 16–17 per cent – though still a far cry from the 27 per cent levels of the early 1960s.

Little of this new investment was productive: typically, it involved foreign investors buying out local companies; security companies like Chubb or ADT buying up a host of little local counterparts, Barclays buying Absa Bank or Vodafone buying more of its local subsidiary, Vodacom. This produced no new jobs but it helped to conceal the mining investment strike, and it helped fund the growing balance of payments deficit. Occasionally the mining companies were accused of lacking patriotism but this mistook the situation. They were, first and last, multinationals. They had warned strongly that the MPRDA would blight South Africa's chances of further investment in the sector on which it depended for over 60 per cent of its exports. Yet the government had decided to take on the mining companies head on, simply ignoring these warnings; a fateful choice. The only real parallel was the Mexican government's nationalization of foreign oil companies in 1938, after which Mexico found itself locked out of the international oil market for more than a generation.

BEE, THE UNEMPLOYMENT CRISIS AND EDUCATIONAL FAILURE

BEE was the government's over-riding economic policy: nothing else was given anything like the same priority. The only other objective strongly pursued was the reduction of public debt, massively assisted by the achievements of Pravin Gordhan, the South African Revenue Service commissioner who was allowed to ignore affirmative action and recruit a highly trained staff. He introduced sophisticated technology and year after year exceeded tax collection targets by huge margins. Otherwise economic policy was largely a matter of rhetoric. Thus while economic growth was hobbled by a skills shortage, the government was unwilling either to modify the affirmative action practices which were causing so many skilled South Africans to emigrate or even to liberalize the immigration restrictions which made the recruitment of skilled foreigners so difficult.

Similarly, despite a great deal of rhetoric about 'the developmental state' the state-owned infrastructure of ports, roads, railways, power stations and electricity distribution was allowed to run down to such a degree that by 2006 huge losses were being incurred through a failure of the railways and ports to handle increased demand for the country's mineral exports. Increasingly the mining houses begged to be allowed to take over parts of the rail network and run it themselves.[133] Indeed, by 2002 investment in infrastructure by the state and parastatals had sunk to its lowest level since 1946.[134] At the same time Johannesburg, the biggest city, was experiencing over a thousand power cuts a year and traffic on the Johannesburg–Pretoria highway, the country's most vital road artery, had tripled journey times. Clearly incompetent and slothful ministers were allowed to stay on indefinitely in economically vital ministries like Telecommunications, Transport, Public Enterprises and Public Works. ANC MPs, though loath to criticize any ANC minister, were finally goaded to fury by the failures of Stella Sigcau, the Minister of Public Works, when they discovered that her Ministry had done nothing to promote the government's much trumpeted Expanded Public Works Programme. The ministry showed a complete lack of concern that almost none of the Programme's deadlines had been met. In November 2004 several ANC MPs described Sigcau as out of her depth and not up to her job.[135] The response of the ANC chief whip, Mbulelo Goniwe, was to declare the party's 'unequivocal confidence' in the Minister and launch an investigation into the MPs concerned.[136]

Yet the Expanded Public Works Programme was intended to play a key role in fighting mass unemployment. The fact that the ANC was far more concerned to protect Sigcau from criticism than it was with her neglect of the Programme showed how unserious the government really was about dealing with unemployment. This was measured by two figures, both faulty. On the 'narrow' definition – which omitted those so discouraged by unemployment that they had ceased to look for work – the figure tended to oscillate around 25–27 per cent. On the 'broad' definition, including the latter group, the figure cited was usually 38–40 per cent, but even this latter statistic counted as employed those who had worked as little as one hour a week. When the Centre for Development and Enterprise surveyed unemployment among the 15–24 age group in July–November 2006 (that is, after several years of rapid economic growth) it found that in Johannesburg 56 per cent of young men and 65 per cent of young women were unemployed; in eThekwini (Durban) the figures were 66 per cent and 68 per cent; and in Polokwane (Pietersburg) the figures were 65 per cent and 88 per cent. Shocked by what she had found, the Centre's director, Ann Bernstein, commented that this horrific rate of unemployment 'is not receiving the attention it deserves'.[137] This is undoubtedly true, particularly when one takes into account the higher crime rates, higher prostitution levels and higher HIV incidence which such figures imply – let alone the fact that a young person of 24 who has never worked is unlikely to find employment thereafter. In May 2008 a Markinor survey found that only 42 per cent of work-eligible South Africans said they had jobs.

These mountainous levels of unemployment were the product of several factors. First, rural migrants were pouring into the cities partly because life in the rural areas had got harder, for rural employment had declined dramatically. The government had got rid of the bantustans – and the large subsidies to them which were a major source of rural jobs and income – and it put very little in their place. But farm employment also fell sharply not only because of the abolition of farm subsidies and a large body of counterproductive labour legislation which caused farmers to cut their workforces whenever possible, but also because of land reform and land restitution. The sad but almost invariable truth of such schemes was that commercial farmland transferred to black ownership saw a rapid collapse back into subsistence farming, with farmworkers' jobs the first to go.

The unemployment crisis was profoundly structural in two senses. South Africa has an extremely low savings rate, and thus a low rate of domestic investment. Household savings declined steadily as a percentage of GDP from 9.1 per cent in 1960–72 to 2.9 per cent in 1999. At the latter date gross domestic savings in South Africa were 15 per cent of GDP, compared to a world average of 25 per cent, an average 20 per cent in low-income countries and an average 26 per cent in other middle-income countries.[138] In part, of course, these low rates reflect the fact that white households, the most likely to save, were both declining as a proportion of the whole and, since the white group is heavily skewed towards the older age groups, also often dis-saving as a result of reaching retirement. This left the country heavily dependent on FDI but here it ranked low: in 2002 the World Investment Report of UNCTAD ranked it 113th out of 140 in its attractiveness to FDI.[139] This is hardly surprising when one considers that many BEE deals have actually involved foreign disinvestment from South Africa. The irony is that the ANC, during the anti-apartheid struggle years, campaigned actively for disinvestment. Finding itself in power it naturally wanted FDI, but in practice continued to encourage disinvestment. Of course this could easily be reversed. The government could make the country far more attractive to foreign investment if it really wanted to: it could sell off Telkom, SAA and the other parastatals, invite competition in telecommunications, make labour laws more flexible and skilled immigration easier, and allow jobs and tenders to be awarded on merit, but in practice it refused to do any of these things. Whenever faced with the choice between higher growth and more jobs on the one hand, and its own ideology and greater control over the economy on the other, the ANC unfailingly chose the latter.

Instead, it put its efforts into marketing the government's policies abroad, using its International Marketing Council, on which sat businessmen so tame that they publicly supported Mbeki on Aids and Zimbabwe. Inevitably, the Council found foreign opinion far less malleable than its own – a fact it put down to the bad-mouthing of the country by its émigrés and by some of its own businessmen who, having nobly kept their mouths shut at home, tended to vent their frustrations while travelling abroad. Thus the mix was exactly the same as under apartheid: a resolute refusal to change irrational and damaging domestic policies, opting instead to try to convince the world that these policies were not irrational and damaging and, when this inevitably failed, laying the blame on South African exiles and white liberals who spoke out of turn. Verwoerd would have felt as much at home with this as he did with the re-racialization of domestic policy.

The second structural cause of unemployment was the manufacturing gap. The primary sector – agriculture and mining – gradually shrank and until the 1980s manufacturing expanded to help fill the gap. Thereafter the economy's evolution was peculiar. The service sector, employing the better-educated section of the population, expanded rapidly to the point where, in 2000, it generated 65 per cent of national income, more than in a highly developed country like Germany. South Africa even began to generate its own hi-tech industries, buoyed in the 1970s and 1980s by military expenditure, a fear that US suppliers might adopt sanctions and a consequent urge to self-sufficiency. For a middle-income economy on the tip of Africa it was quite an achievement but the problem was that once they reached a certain size hi-tech companies got bought out; this is what happened to Mark Shuttleworth's Thawte, Idion, Prism, FrontRange and Softline. South Africa was hi-tech-friendly all right – it was a leader in the field with ATMs, cellphones and so on – but it was impossible to finance a world hi-tech company out of South Africa.

The ANC government, unconsciously though energetically, followed a policy of de-industrialization. Manufacturing, which had constituted around a quarter of the economy in 1990, fell back to 19 per cent by 2000 and to 16 per cent by 2005.[140] The ANC government slashed tariff protection on the one hand and agricultural subsidies on the other. The result was that, despite a boom in South African trade with the rest of Africa, employment in both manufacturing and agriculture nosedived. The situation was greatly worsened both by the rand's volatility and its relative strength after 2003, buoyed by high commodity prices. For many industries, notably textiles, the *coup de grâce* was administered by the growing wave of cheap Chinese imports. But for the large subsidies to car production, manufacturing would have shrunk even further. At the same time mining was mechanizing, employing more skilled labour and shedding many unskilled jobs. All of which spelt an unemployment disaster, alleviated only marginally by the buoyant growth of tourism.

What South Africa needed was a massive increase in manufacturing in order to absorb more of its super-abundant labour, but the only way to make manufacturing competitive would be devaluation on a heroic scale. Baulking at this, the government settled simply on the objective of faster growth. Conscious that unemployment was by far the top popular priority, it committed itself to halving the unemployment rate by 2014, some of which was to be achieved by faster growth and some by the Expanded Public Works Programme. This seemed unlikely to produce the goods. All that one could say with certainty was that no one genuinely concerned to cut unemployment and promote faster growth would have hobbled the economy with affirmative action, inflexible labour laws, BEE and the collapse of infrastructural investment, nor would they have provoked an investment slump in their main export sector.

A key consequence of the Mbeki years was to integrate South Africa ever more deeply into the global capitalist economy. As South Africa's big firms went international, so the country depended increasingly on globalization. With the sale of many big companies to foreigners the outward dividend flow grew enormously, requiring ever greater capital inflows to fund it. The dividend outflow, R8.1 billion in 1999, reached R44.5 billion in 2006 and was projected to top R60 billion by 2008.[141] And capital inflows accelerated enormously – between 2002 and 2005 alone they multiplied ten times. Most of this was 'hot' money, fuelling the surge in the stock market and the rand, but in practice the country had become increasingly dependent on it. As this integration galloped ahead so the left's hopes of more autarchic policies receded into the distance.

The other outstanding certainty was that much of the answer lay in producing a better-educated workforce. The mismatch was obvious: on the one hand a mass of unemployable unskilled workers, on the other hand a crippling skills shortage, with scores of thousands of jobs standing vacant. Yet South Africa had become a large net exporter of doctors, engineers and other skilled workers, placing its dominant services sector under threat. Indeed, both Botswana and Mauritius, whose enlightened economic management had enabled them to overtake South Africa in per capita income, were now taking aim at pulling financial service business away from South Africa too. But although Pretoria spent heavily on education, it was quite clearly not working; indeed most educationists concluded despairingly that the system had gone backwards even since the days of apartheid. In effect only a small number of private schools, formerly white high schools and formerly white universities worked at all well. Most of the rest of the educational system was simply dysfunctional.

The trouble was that fixing it would require a lot more than money. Many schoolteachers were semi-literate (and often truant) and no amount of retraining would change that. Purging the teaching profession of such irreformable elements was an indispensable first step, but this would mean a fight to the death with the powerful teachers' union, for which the government had no stomach. Secondly, huge numbers of the higher education students destined for the teaching profession were themselves all but ineducable. The decision to lower university entrance standards in order to admit them had been a mistake; in some cases university applicants were awarded extra marks simply for being black. Thirdly, the old tribal colleges were never going to be proper universities: it would be best to shut them down or turn them into community colleges. Finally, at every level of the education system administrators, headmasters, professors, deans, vice-chancellors and academics had been appointed essentially on grounds of politics and race. Competent whites had been retired early on a racially discriminatory basis and young white academics turned away by universities which frankly told them they were 'not hiring whites'. To achieve reform, all of these things had to be faced – and reversed.

But such changes would be met with furious resistance, often by groups that were a key part of the ANC's constituency. And the ANC would have to acknowledge that it had been wrong to insist that educational criteria should be simply overridden by racial politics. In this respect Mbeki bears a heavy responsibility. His deliberate encouragement of racial nationalism over the ANC's long tradition of non-racism created a climate which made these damaging moves inevitable, at huge cost to future generations of all races. Putting educational criteria first would have meant hanging on at all costs to good teachers, academics and administrators, trying to persuade as many as possible to return from abroad and to teach on after retirement in an effort to maintain and pass on the highest possible standards. It would have meant rejecting pressures to admit students, appoint academics or elect vice-chancellors and administrators solely on the grounds of their race, politics or gender. Such decisions resulted, inevitably, in the debasement of the entire educational system.

This would indeed be a battle for the soul of the ANC but if the Freedom Charter's promise to throw open 'the doors of education' was ever to be honoured it was a struggle that had to be fought and won. But even more was at stake. If there was ever to be true black empowerment, with the creation of a broad black middle class able to take its place in the world on an equal footing, the struggle for education was no whit less important than the struggle against apartheid had been.

12
Things Fall Apart

Following a well-known pronouncement of Kant's which couples the conscience within us with the starry heavens, a pious man might well be tempted to honour these two things as the masterpieces of creation. The stars are indeed magnificent, but as regards conscience God has done an uneven and careless piece of work.

Sigmund Freud

Time is a great teacher but unfortunately it kills all its pupils. Hector Berlioz

In March 2006 the finance minister of North West Province, Maureen Modiselle, announced that the province's department of agriculture, conservation and environment had ceased to exist. It was, to use her words, 'a non-functioning entity', unlikely to spend more than 2 per cent of its budget. It had collapsed due to corruption, with seven of the department's top officials suspended (four of them arrested, along with six businessmen). The finance minister said that 'simply speaking, there is no Department of Agriculture in the North West', pointing out that it had spent less than 1 per cent of its grant in the previous year.[1] This was merely a straw in the wind, for by this stage it had become clear that things were falling apart on a grand scale.

CRIME: THE BREAKDOWN OF THE SOCIAL CONTRACT

For most people the rot started with law and order. In 1995–6 the police reported some 27,000 murders; 74 a day (Britain, by contrast, averages around 700 murders a year). In the same year there were 123,000 robberies, 77,000 of them armed robberies. Eleven years later the murder figure had fallen to 19,200 but there were 198,000 robberies, 126,000 of them armed, that is, one armed robbery every five minutes.[2] The 54,000 rapes reported by the police in 1998 were estimated by the National Institute for Crime Prevention and Rehabilitation of Offenders to mean that in practice there were 934,960 rapes that year, though the South African Law Commission put the figure at 1,636,810. Either way, South Africa was, as Interpol put it, 'in undisputed first place as far as reported cases of rape are concerned'.[3] Crime was always cited in the first place as a reason for emigration and, equally, because the government's failure to uphold law and order broke a basic social contract, no other factor did more to undermine the government's authority and credibility.

The reasons for this deterioration were hotly debated. Mbeki and his first Safety and Security Minister, Steve Tshwete, argued that all that had happened was that township levels of criminality and violence had now generalized into the white suburbs, so whites were merely complaining about something blacks had long suffered. This was not a clever argument, for it conceded the fact of deterioration and also supported the stereotype of blacks as more prone to violence and criminality. So Tshwete attacked 'the mischief makers who bad-mouthed' the country, insisting it was 'the crime capital of the world'.[4] In order to stop the country becoming 'a victim of bad publicity' he ordered that information on crime statistics, police personnel shortages and related matters be released only annually – if that.

While no one conclusively explained why South Africans were so prone to commit violent crime, there was no doubting the deterioration in the whole criminal justice system, the police and the prisons, nor that a large part of the problem was, as usual, affirmative appointments. A good example was the Durban Metro police, for many years the most competent and popular police force in the country. By 2006 even the ANC city government was forced to admit that the 'transformed' force suffered from low morale and discipline as well as corruption. An inquiry showed a lack of daily inspections or any checking of dress code, absenteeism, ammunition, timekeeping or the distribution of vehicles. Moreover, misconduct, which was rife, was either poorly addressed or just ignored. The promotion of inexperienced and unskilled people had caused great bitterness, low morale and many resignations, and many critical positions remained vacant. The local media was rife with allegations that the weapons used in hijackings and against police officers had actually been sold to criminals by corrupt policemen.[5] The situation was hardly helped by the ANC's hostility to local police forces and its insistence on its own centralized control over a single national force.

Durban was just a microcosm of the whole. With many new and less-educated recruits being drafted into the force, it was, crazily, decided to cut the time spent in the police academy from six months to three. Young recruits now began as detectives without having served any time in uniform on the street.[6] Amnesty International expressed shock at the high rate of illiteracy in the South African police force as well as its reliance on torture and ill-treatment of prisoners, rather than detective work, to gain information.[7]

And torture was a problem. In 2002–3 the Independent Complaints Directorate reported that 'only' 528 prisoners had died in police custody, 10 per cent less than the previous year, but next year the figure soared to 767, of whom 363 died due to 'police action'. Amnesty was able to mention specific rooms used as torture chambers and to detail the various means used, usually electrodes and suffocation. The TRC found that 2,700 deaths had resulted from police action under apartheid from 1960 to 1994, an average of 77 deaths a year, but such deaths more than quadrupled in the post-apartheid period.[8] Perhaps not coincidentally, attacks on policemen multiplied. In 1994–2004 no fewer than 1,955 policemen were killed[9] and by 2005–6 there were 1,274 attacks on policemen in a single year.[10] Many of those killed were off duty, apparently slain in acts of revenge. Stress was inevitably high and was cited as a reason for the high police suicide rate, averaging 127 deaths a year.[11]

But the really key change in the police force was that the ANC viewed it just as it viewed the rest of the public service: as part of the spoils of office, providing jobs, salaries and status. Thus, as elsewhere in Africa, many of the new job-occupants were more preoccupied with the possession of a middle-class salary and 'big man' status than with performing any particular duty. This is why one found, in the Durban example above, a complete lack of interest in misconduct and the distribution of vehicles – indeed, vehicles were of 'big man' status and thus not a fit subject for monitoring. Senior policemen simply grabbed police cars and used them for their own commuting.[12]

A key indicator, found also in the armed services, was the number of senior officers (big men). By 2002 the police had four times as many sergeants as constables, an unparalleled situation. In Britain there are 5 constables per sergeant, in the United States 6.4. Remarkably, in South Africa there were also 5.5 times as many inspectors as constables. Indeed, constables made up only 7 per cent of the force. This had large cost implications, since the top ranks earned no less than ten times a constable's salary.[13] Thus the 'transformed' force was far more expensive and far less skilled; 60 per cent of policemen at police station level lacked even a driving licence. With resources so concentrated on high salaries for senior officers, the use of specialist equipment inevitably suffered. In 2002 none of the 98 local criminal-record centres had a properly equipped laboratory to conduct forensic tests, with the result that they were all legally prohibited from operating. Ignoring the law, forensic experts used toilets and kitchens for their tests. But this part of the force, being still predominantly white, was also understaffed, which helped explain why only 8 per cent of crimes committed resulted in convictions.[14]

In 2006, sentencing a farm labourer for having killed his mother, Judge Arrie Hattingh angrily pointed out that the accused would have walked free had he had not gone into the witness box and discredited himself. This was, he said, because eighteen months after the murder key DNA tests had not been processed due to chronic staff and equipment shortages at the National Forensic Laboratory in Pretoria. Hattingh furiously accused Captain Mthenjwa Kheswa, the police station commander, of 'throwing away evidence': various pieces of evidence, including the murder weapon, had simply disappeared from the police station. 'Captain Kheswa has no idea what happened to it. He can give no explanation as to why they disappeared. It is clear that there is no order in that police station.' As for the forensic laboratory's failure to do its job, Hattingh observed that 'This doesn't just make red lights flash. They are burning constantly. The structures have collapsed and someone must do something. Must we now close our courts, sit and count our fingers ... to accommodate a national police commissioner [Jackie Selebi] who is not doing his job?'[15]

Hattingh had put his finger on a national scandal. No less than 427,319 police cases (43 per cent of them involving murder, attempted murder, rape or assault) remained unsolved because the necessary forensic work was not done. In a further 780,000 cases the work was taking a year, so that many such cases were struck off the roll or endlessly postponed. Forensic specialists reported that the delays were due to chronic shortages of qualified staff and the appointment of staff inexperienced in processing data. R100 million worth of modern machinery for the fast testing of DNA samples was sitting unused. Commissioner Selebi furiously denied the report and a witch-hunt began to find the forensic specialists who had dared speak out.[16]

Police leadership was a further problem. Most controversial was the boss of the populous Ekurhuleni (East Rand) region, Robert McBride. As an MK guerrilla he had planted a bomb in a bar which had killed three white women and injured seventy-one others, all civilians. Caught, assaulted by both police and prisoners, McBride spent years on death row and, even when freed, was seldom out of the news. He was accused of involvement with one of Cape Town's top gangsters, was jailed in Mozambique for alleged gun-running and was accused by some of his own police of drunk driving. Yet it took years for him to be sacked.

A larger problem was Jackie Selebi, the Police Commissioner, appointed with no previous experience of police work. He tended to lash out publicly – once calling a black policewoman a 'chimpanzee' – and would frequently humiliate senior officers in front of their juniors. Elected the first African president of Interpol in 2004, he refused to apologize for his friendships with mobsters and boasted that he was unsackable. Conscious that Selebi had been on the ANC executive for decades and that he needed his support against Zuma, Mbeki treated him with kid gloves. When the businessman Brett Kebble was murdered in 2005, it emerged that he had been friendly with Selebi – and had enjoyed an extraordinary immunity. Kebble had misappropriated shares worth R1.5 billion, issued shares to fund bogus transactions and distributed bribes in all directions, all without any auditor, regulator or policeman making any attempt to stop him. 'Down here in the wild South,' the *Sunday Times* editorialized, 'there is no sheriff in town.'[17] It was a feeling the public had had for some time and not just where errant tycoons were concerned. Later, Selebi became the first Interpol boss to be suspended on corruption charges.

PRISONS: HURRY ON DOWN

The revelation before the Jali Commission of Inquiry in 2002 that prison inmates were being hired out as hitmen to murder political opponents[18] only received one headline before the commission was overwhelmed with evidence of sedition, kidnapping, gun-trafficking, drug dealing, prison escapes connived at by warders, sexual violence, assault and murder and corrupt allocation of contracts by the Prisons Minister and his Director-General. This led SABC's *Special Assignment* programme to approach the head of Grootvlei prison, Tatolo Setlai, to allow them to install video cameras at strategic points. Television viewers then watched as no fewer than twenty-two warders sold a stolen gun to a convicted double murderer, procured juvenile prisoners to be 'sold' and sodomized, sold stolen food and drugs to prisoners and smuggled in brandy for sale to the inmates. A week later Jackie Selebi could not explain why the police had taken no action against the transgressors. Police disinterest was the more striking since Aids has made prison rape into an effective murder offence. Whereas deaths in prison from unnatural causes stayed steady around 70 a year, due to Aids deaths from natural causes soared from 211 in 1996 to 1,689 in 2005.[19]

Tatolo Setlai, who had run Grootvlei prison in apartheid times, lamented the collapse in standards.

> Sadly, murderers, rapists, robbers and even right-wing militants are more trustworthy than some of the warders . . . During the apartheid era, if a prisoner was found with two grams of dagga it was like a terrorist action. It just never happened. Nowadays [prison] members are deeply involved in such activities. The warders take democracy as a laissez-faire government. They think they can do as they wish, and some of them, when they take prisoners' rations, say they are eating their taxes. It is as if some black members don't fear black management as much as they feared white management.[20]

Setlai said that 'for the apartheid government I did a very good job' but things were much worse now even though 'for this government I feel I have to go an extra mile'. He told the Jali Commission that his seniors in the prison service had wanted to destroy the incriminating videotape and, when he refused, asked that he hand the tape to the NIA – which he also refused, believing that they too would destroy the tape.

Such frankness about the deterioration in conditions since the apartheid period was unusual and unappreciated: the prison authorities, the police and Mbeki were all furious with Setlai. He was rapidly dismissed and arrested on twenty charges of corruption after Mbeki had personally commissioned an investigation into his activities. His trial collapsed two years later, however, when five prosecution witnesses admitted making false statements against him. He was cleared on all counts – but had lost his job. In 2006 the parliamentary committee on correctional services reported that the Minister had effectively lost all control of prisons in the Eastern Cape, especially Middledrift, and many were on the brink of collapse. This merely echoed the report of the department's own inspectorate in 2004, to which no one had paid any attention. Discipline and security regulations had broken down, the prisons were filthy and every sort of abuse – sexual, drugs, gangsterism – was rife.[21] The overall boss of the prisons, Linda Mti, brazened it out unscathed.

The state of the police and prisons has a special significance in South Africa, for a great anger runs through the history of the anti-apartheid struggle over sufferings at the hands of the police and prison-warders. Robben Island, where Mandela and the ANC leadership were held for so long, has become a virtual shrine, a major tourist attraction and a world heritage site. Few ideas burnt more brightly during the struggle than the determination that things should never be like this again. Few would have guessed in 1994 that the prisons would soon be worse than ever, that police torture would be worse than under apartheid and that far more prisoners would die in police custody. Yet the government treated such facts with complete unconcern, emphasizing how far the struggle had merely replaced one selfish elite by another.

NO HOME LIKE HOME AFFAIRS

For the first ten years after 1994 the Ministry of Home Affairs was held by the IFP leader, Chief Buthelezi. This was a problem, both because he gave much time to being a national party leader and to his base in KwaZulu-Natal, but also because Mbeki inflicted on him a series of directors-general all drawn from intelligence circles. Buthelezi objected strongly and was often at daggers drawn with his chief civil servants, whom, however, Mbeki forbade him to dismiss. Buthelezi tried to devolve key functions downwards to the provinces and municipalities but the centralist ANC and his directors-general refused to implement these reforms.

Meanwhile the department became legendary for hideous delays in the granting of passports, ID books and work permits, though these documents could be bought from corrupt officials in many local offices of the Ministry. From 2003 on the Auditor-General entered a qualified audit report on the department every year and in 2006 added a complete disclaimer due to the financial mismanagement and malpractice he found there; during the course of the audit alone twelve employees were suspended on suspicion of fraud.[22] The Auditor-General, Shauket Fakie, described how departmental officials had filibustered for seven months, dodged seven formal requests for specific information, falsely blamed auditors for losing records and ultimately just dumped huge volumes of unsorted documents at the auditors' feet.[23]

Alarmed, the government sent a series of high-powered directors-general to the department with a brief to turn things around. Each talked determinedly of what they intended to do but by 2006 five of them had come and gone in just seven years. In the 2006 audit disclaimer Fakie detailed multiple cases of chaotic documentation, malfunctioning accounting systems, ineffective debt collection, failure to provide any documentary proof of R572 million in expenditure and 144 vehicles which had gone missing. Moreover, 1.5 million people still lacked the bar-coded ID books required for voting.[24] The Home Affairs Minister, Nosiviwe Mapisa-Nqakula (wife of the Safety and Security Minister, Charles Nqakula), not wishing to be held responsible for the shambles, asked for a special task team to intervene, which it did in 2006. The Minister, to the Opposition's indignation, though remaining in the cabinet, took the attitude that her department's troubles were no longer her affair.

The team's interim report spoke of the 'sense of comfort and inertia' permeating the department. 'There's no sense of urgency and there's a lack of adherence to deadlines,' said the team leader, Odette Ramsingh. 'There's also a general crisis response to problems due to a lack of management plans.' Although over 20 per cent of posts in the Ministry were vacant, she found that appointment criteria were ignored and some posts filled without advertisement. Remarkably, expenses claimed for international trips by Ministry staff even exceeded those of the Foreign

Affairs Department.[25] Opinion surveys found that the public saw Home Affairs as more corrupt than any department save for the police: the sacking of 240 officials in 2004–6 was seen as barely scratching the surface.[26] After six months the task team left but the Minister herself said that the situation was still deteriorating, that there was 'a culture of looting' in the department and that some officials were there 'to steal'.[27]

THE PUBLIC SERVICE: TRANSFORMATION AND DEFORMATION

The public quickly became aware of the mess at the ministries of Safety and Security and Home Affairs because they could not obtain law and order, passports and ID books; only gradually was it realized that the situation in other departments was similar. The fundamental problem lay with the 'transformation' of the civil service – largely a process of ruination. Most of the senior, experienced whites were soon got rid of; and then those of middle and lower rank. Then the white and Indian radicals, appointed in the first flush of ANC victory, were also dispensed with. Since there were never enough qualified black candidates and the best got tempted away to the private sector, most departments not only made disastrous appointments but had vacancy rates of at least 20 per cent.

And, since many viewed their jobs as part of the spoils system, corruption grew while morale, discipline and the work ethic all suffered. In 2005 an extraordinary 10.8 per cent of all public servants took more than fifteen continuous days of sick leave. In provincial government 34 per cent of public servants had taken some sick leave in the year (almost invariably starting on a Monday or Friday in order to create a long weekend) while in national government the figure reached an astonishing 63 per cent: clearly national civil servants were twice as sick as their provincial counterparts. Early retirement was also frequently taken on (bogus) ill-health grounds. When the Public Service Minister, Geraldine Fraser-Moleketi, decided to study this process in detail in the police force, such retirements were immediately halved.[28]

The manufacture of false degrees and other qualifications was also widespread. When senior managers in the civil service were required to submit their qualifications for verification in 2001, 34 per cent failed to submit them. Even six months later 25 per cent were still refusing to submit them.[29] The Public Service Commission insisted that all senior managers must lodge performance agreements with it so as to build a 'performance management culture' – but only 20–30 per cent of managers actually signed such agreements, though almost all of them received performance bonuses, often without any actual performance appraisal.

When *Finance Week* investigated the matter in 2006 it found that in some departments the performance review for 2003/4 was still under way; that half of all government departments were headed by directors-general who had been in post less than eighteen months and many more by acting directors-general, although it took a director-general two years to really get to grips with his job. Moreover, when it asked what performance bonus the Police Commissioner, Jackie Selebi, had received it was flatly told that such bonuses – though taxpayers' money – were 'a private matter between employee and employer'.[30] The Minister of Labour, Membathisi Mdlalana, complained of being criticized for having failed to obtain a performance assessment of his Director-General, Rams Ramashia. 'I was told my leadership style was wrong and that the reason I insisted on performance assessments was . . . that I'm Xhosa and Ramashia is Sotho.'[31]

The standard excuse for poor performance of any kind was 'capacity problems', which broke down into skills shortages and the low capacity of many staff. In 2006, for example, there were vacancy rates of over 30 per cent across all government departments, with more than 40,000 jobs vacant. Even the presidency, with first pick of able candidates, had 161 jobs vacant out of a total complement of 582.[32] One result was the massive employment of consultants, often former white civil servants who, having taken severance packages, were now in demand to do their successors' jobs for them. The Auditor-General discovered that more than R2.6 billion had been spent on consultants in 1998–2000, commenting that departments seemed too quick to hire consultants when it would have been cheaper to train their own staff or pay for more overtime. In effect civil servants, faced with demanding work, simply dumped it on consultants.[33] In 2003 the parliamentary public accounts committee noted with dismay that in the Ministry of Public Enterprises one consultant, paid R10.9 million to advise on competitive tendering, had then been asked to make recommendations on issues including pension and medical funding, BEE, corporate governance and virtually the whole range of other issues facing the department. As the committee put it, 'This raises the question of both the competence and depth of the skills within the department.'[34] So much work was delegated to consultants that MPs called them 'the parallel civil service'. The situation in the provinces was similar with, as usual, the Eastern Cape providing the record of between R1.9 billion and R3.4 billion spent on consultants in 2002–4.[35]

But the commodity boom meant that the government, unlike almost any other government in Africa, was awash with money. Indeed, departments regularly failed to spend their capital budgets through chronic institutional incapacity, despite happily wolfing down huge salaries, taking huge performance bonuses and running up immense travel and entertainment bills. The fundamental reason for the chaos, malpractice and poor morale was affirmative action.

Few of the new black civil servants could be unaware that they had been appointed essentially because of the colour of their skin and their ANC affiliations. Thus from the outset the connection between holding a job and merit or performance was weak. The government seemed content to spend billions on paying the old guard to return as consultants. The reason one needed such people was that they were more competent than oneself. But if competence really mattered, after all, they would never have been kicked out in the first place. By entering the civil service and accepting its salaries, expenses and perks, the new civil servants were simply coming into their inheritance, earned by having suffered earlier discrimination and by being in the right place at the right time. Moreover, many, armed with a strong sense of entitlement and a belief in their own 'big man' destiny, saw their civil service jobs as platforms for further enrichment.

This made the tendering process critical, as civil servants strained to push departmental spending towards companies in which their families had an interest. Senior civil servants were best placed to do this but Parliament's public accounts committee expressed concern in 2004 about the way junior officials 'were allowed to commit their department to expenditures in violation of tender procedures and without the knowledge of their superiors'.[36]

The independent Public Service Commission reported in 2006 that the civil service was plagued by skills shortages, fraud and corruption, bad financial management, poor recruitment and inadequate performance evaluation. The Commission expressed alarm that those who exposed fraud or theft were likely to be victimized, not protected; that the number of senior managers submitting to performance evaluation was falling; that 30 per cent of senior managers (in the Eastern Cape 62 per cent) had failed to file the requisite reports on their outside business interests; that failures of government departments to file financial reports had doubled; that barely 10 per cent of requests under freedom of information law were answered within the legal deadline and that 63 per cent of requests were ignored altogether.[37] The following year the Commission reported that of 513 financial misconduct cases reported, 55 per cent were for fraud and theft, 29 per cent for misappropriation and abuse, 14 per cent for gross negligence and 2 per cent for bribery.[38]

The lack of responsiveness noted by the Public Services Commission was a major problem. It was not just that ministers increasingly failed to answer written parliamentary questions. Many were just unconcerned but they also simply could not get the information out of their department, for the government machine was now inert and unresponsive. In 2006, for example, the Finance Ministry enquired into aid distributed around Africa. It had become clear that there was a large, uncoordinated and unofficial South African aid programme, as ministers toured Africa acting as beneficent big men towards their hosts. The Finance Ministry wanted to know what had been given, when and to whom, for the issue had become an embarrassment, with the EU demanding to know whether South Africa's aid policy could not be co-ordinated with theirs. (The EU, indeed, funded the inquiry.) However, despite multiple requests and the weight of the Finance Ministry behind them, it was simply impossible to get many departments to respond. And if the machine could not respond to such a simple request, it meant that it would fail far worse when active policy implementation was required.

A glimpse into this mess is provided by the reports of the Auditor-General, Shauket Fakie. In 2003 Fakie warned that a large number of parastatals, public agencies and government departments had inadequate financial controls, frequently a sign of corruption. And the problem was getting worse. Of 163 national public entities audited, 77 had

had internal control problems in 2001–2 but this had increased to 133 in 2002–3. Almost invariably Fakie had had to qualify his audit report and in four cases he had had to give a complete disclaimer (signifying that he could not certify the accounts at all). Moreover, it was clear that many of the bodies audited were not trying to comply with audit rules. Although they were statutorily obliged to submit their accounts to Fakie's office, 31 per cent failed to do so. Unsurprisingly, when he did get to see their accounts they were in a worse mess than most.

In the cases of Home Affairs, Justice, Water Affairs and Public Works, audit reports were qualified for three successive years, ending with a complete disclaimer for Public Works. But, Fakie added, financial controls (and much else besides) were almost impossible in ministries like Social Development and Science and Technology, with vacancy rates at senior management level of, respectively, 47 per cent and 66 per cent.[39] Fakie found that senior civil servants would complain about him to Parliament's public accounts committee but that when he did the audit they seldom appeared, sending juniors along instead. They woke up only when they realized how bad their audit report was, a comment which caused the Treasury Director-General to speak of 'too many people hiding behind capacity problems to excuse non-delivery'.[40]

By 2006 the Auditor-General could give a clean bill of health to only three of the thirty-two entities examined, with twenty-nine national departments receiving qualifications or outright disclaimers. The situation was clearly deteriorating: all departments which had received qualifications or disclaimers the previous year did so again and four more joined them. Five departments (Health, Parliament, Home Affairs, Correctional Services and Defence) had had such black marks for three successive years.[41] Moreover, the audit process had broken down; when the audit was completed two-thirds of departments had still failed to submit their annual reports. Fakie, who was resigning, said gently that at least 'some' ministers now accepted there was a problem: 'In the past there was almost a state of denial.' The major problem, he said, was a severe skills shortage, a problem to which affirmative action had contributed. In this year alone he had found eighty-one people with financial interests in companies supplying goods to their departments, though doing something about it was 'someone else's responsibility'.[42] It was a responsibility no one else was keen to accept.

The Mbeki government's response was predictable: yet further centralization. The entire public service, national, provincial and municipal, should be unified into a single giant bureaucracy. Such a system was unknown outside the Communist bloc and was, indeed, unthinkable in any country where local democracy mattered. Helen Zille, the new DA leader elected in 2007, termed this proposal 'sinister'. Already, as mayor of Cape Town, she had had the experience of inheriting ANC-appointed municipal staff who tried their best to thwart the new non-ANC council majority. Given that the President insisted on appointing all the top civil servants, it was clear that in a unified civil service even the lowliest employees would be responsible upwards to the President rather than to the council which employed them. Zille warned that such a system would make local and provincial elections more or less irrelevant and would, indeed, probably presage the complete abolition of the provinces.[43] The larger point was that national government was not coping with the challenges it already faced. Accumulating ever more powers and responsibilities for that government would not only abolish local democracy but promised escalating chaos at the top.

In 2003 employers of domestic workers – in South Africa a substantial class – received blood-curdling warnings from the Unemployment Insurance Fund of the consequences of failure to make contributions to the Fund for domestic workers. Yet this was quickly negated by stories of corruption and mismanagement so that at one point the Fund (which receives R7 billion a year in contributions) was declared insolvent. The resulting cynicism among employers saw many attempt to evade contributions to the Fund. Moreover, some departments seemed hardly to care about corruption. When social grants were introduced it was soon discovered that R1.5 billion a year was being stolen and the Minister for Social Development, Zola Skweyiya, called in the police. 300,000 grants were cancelled, including 12,000 fraudulently received by government officials, though only 2,000 were asked to pay anything back and only 750 were prosecuted.[44] The other thefts were simply forgiven. At the Housing Ministry, when it was discovered that R323 million of housing subsidies had been wrongly paid to 50,000 recipients, including 7,000 civil servants who were ineligible to receive such grants, the Ministry did nothing, saying it would only consider action next year. It seemed quite nonchalant about the fact that it had paid out large sums to dead people, children and people who already owned houses.[45]

Failures within ministries were reflected by corresponding failures in their public role. The audits revealed that the Ministry of Justice was badly run but this also fed through into a cavalier attitude to the law, evidenced in 2006 when the Ministry, with the full knowledge and consent of the Minister, Brigette Mabandla, deliberately falsified its accounts in order to hide from Parliament the fact that it had underspent its budget.[46] Similarly, when John Hlophe, judge-president of the Western Cape, was discovered to have received large sums of money from a company in whose favour he then ruled in court, nothing was done. Similarly, when his KwaZulu-Natal counterpart, Vuka Tshabalala, received a large gift of shares from the presidential aspirant Tokyo Sexwale, there was no official reaction, although one of Tshabalala's tasks would be to appoint the judge to hear the case against Sexwale's presidential rival, Jacob Zuma; Tshabalala later claimed, however, that he had given the shares back. Or again, when the courts ruled that the government must make ARVs available to HIV-positive prisoners in jail, government simply ignored the court order. In the Eastern Cape judges repeatedly chastised the provincial government for its failure to obey the courts, but to no effect.[47]

RUNNING ON EMPTY

The chaotic state of the public service meant that virtually all ministries performed poorly but the public impact and thus the political fall-out varied. The dramatic collapse in the capabilities of the armed forces, despite the huge investment in new equipment, was a striking example of the shrinkage of state capacity but it excited little comment because South Africa faced no enemies and the public was unaffected. Similarly, when Stella Sigcau, the Minister of Public Works, died in 2006 her obituarist wrote that 'as a minister in three post-apartheid governments she seemed to be so inactive that it was easy to forget her existence. When she was remembered it was only to ask why she was still in the government. . . . Her entire period of high office was characterized by inactivity ("If you give a job to Stella Sigcau, nothing happens", sighed insiders, many of them in her own Department)'.[48] Sigcau was uninterested in the accusations levelled at her department of corruption, bribery, unauthorized spending and failure to follow tender procedures. The main sufferers from this situation were the poorest of the poor, rural, unemployed blacks who would have benefited from a proper public works programme. This group almost entirely lacks a public voice, so Sigcau received little public criticism.

On the other hand it had become obvious by 2006 that the Department of Trade and Industry (DTI) could no longer cope. Trouble began as the once thriving textile industry, now facing a flood of cheap Chinese imports, demanded more protection. The DTI negotiated with the employers, unions and the big garment retailers for two years – and then, without warning, suddenly capitulated to the unions and announced an immediate one-third cut in Chinese imports. The retailers, who signed import contracts months in advance, were thunderstruck – and startled to see the unions not only running a joint press conference with the DTI but answering detailed questions about the DTI's internal functioning, emphasizing how completely they were in control. When the retailers said they would be forced to buy other cheap imports to fill the gap, the DTI's deputy Director-General, Iqbal Sharma, denounced their 'white greed' while Deputy President Phumzile Mlambo-Ngcuka warned that such a recourse would be 'treason'.[49] Ultimately the DTI had to postpone the cut, but its behaviour had so undermined the confidence of employers and retailers that future negotiations became impossible. What particularly riled business was that, while they expected to have to negotiate with the unions in many other spheres, they had assumed the DTI was a pro-business organization trying to maximize growth and investment. Instead, quite clearly, many of the DTI's bureaucrats saw businessmen as the enemy.

Meanwhile the DTI had allowed the national lottery (on which many NGOs relied for their lifeblood) to become inoperable. Other programmes running years behind schedule included small business development, a national industrial policy framework and sector industrial policy frameworks. Several partners working with the DTI said, off the record, that it was suffering 'a systemic institutional failure'.[50]

Most dramatic, though, was the situation over the motor industry development programme, the subsidy scheme which had encouraged large-scale motor manufacture in South Africa. This programme, begun in 1995, was due to expire in 2012 but the manufacturers, with their seven-year cycle for new model lines, pressed – without result – for the DTI to clarify its future plans. In 2006, to their horror, the Minister, Mandisi Mpahlwa, told them the new deadline for a decision was the end of 2008. Ford immediately announced that it was moving production of its new model Fiesta to Australia, a loss of R2 billion in investment and thousands of jobs. The other manufacturers made similar noises, as did the components companies. Most motor jobs are in the ANC's heartland of the Eastern Cape and local politicians and trade unionists joined in the uproar. Only then did the DTI, which had simply ignored previous warnings, wake up to the urgency of the situation.[51]

South Africa, lacking membership of a major trading bloc and with a chronic industrial disadvantage due to higher unit costs, desperately needed a competent DTI. But the DTI's problem, apart from 'normal' civil service incapacity, was that it was a heavily loaded technical department. By 2007 it faced eleven separate trade negotiations with partners ranging from the WTO, the EU, the United States and South Africa's major regional groupings, SADC and the South African Customs Union, to China, EFTA, Mercosur, South Korea and Singapore. It was woefully lacking in capacity in this key and intricate area, with the result that negotiations flagged, the opposition took the initiative and business complained bitterly of lack of consultation.[52] Moreover, the government, with its massively interventionist ambitions, had saddled the DTI with the motor industry development programme, the textiles mess, the lottery, small business matters, a new credit Act, a competition authority, gambling, black empowerment and the framing of new industrial policies. As usual, the government's ambition to control so far outran its bureaucratic capacity that the result was pure shambles. Each crisis was met with frantic restructuring and the turnover of key personnel, resulting in the complete loss of institutional memory – almost everyone dealing with key subjects was a novice.[53] This resulted in humiliating and shambolic outcomes and further personnel turnover.

OPENING THE DOORS OF LEARNING AND HEALTH

The saddest department was Education. 'The Doors of Learning and Culture shall be Opened!', the Freedom Charter had proudly proclaimed. If only it had been that simple. It was easy enough to integrate the old white, Coloured and Indian schools and to act as if the problems all lay in racist resistance to such changes (although such resistance was extremely rare), but the real problem lay in the other 80 per cent of (effectively all-black) schools. Poorly educated and poorly motivated teachers, obstructive teaching unions, gross abuse and indiscipline of every kind and all the normal kinds of corruption and maladministration made these latter schools a nightmare problem. Only a tough-minded emphasis on higher standards would turn things around. Such a policy would have many immediate casualties – irredeemably bad teachers, weak students and the institutions that produced them – and would have to rate merit over affirmative action. No ANC minister had the stomach for that.

A snapshot of what was wrong may be seen by taking the results for higher grade maths in the school system, for entry to a large variety of courses in science, computing, engineering and accountancy requires an A, B or C pass in that subject. Of 467,985 pupils writing the Senior Certificate school-leaving exam in 2004, only 39,939 sat higher grade maths and only 24,143 passed it. Of these only 7,236 – just under 30 per cent – were Africans and of these only 2,406 achieved a C pass or better.[54] Thus well into the twenty-first century the majority of engineers, accountants and scientists would still be mainly white – or Africans would have to fill those jobs without being qualified for them. Moreover, 80 per cent of secondary schools averaged only one higher grade maths pass each and over half got none at all.[55] That is, most black achievers came from the middle-class minority now enrolled in ex-white schools. In 2005–6 higher grade maths passes actually declined.

The Freedom Charter had made equally extravagant promises about public health but even apart from the Aids tragedy, health was a major disaster area. Initially the government announced that it would reduce the resources spent on the upper end of the health system, including the teaching hospitals, while increasing expenditure on primary and community health care. There would be greater use of health auxiliaries and of Cuban doctors who were recruited to fill gaps in the rural areas, while all young doctors would have to perform a period of compulsory community service in a poor area. All of which sounded reasonable but, it transpired, the Ministry had initiated changes which soon ran out of its control.

The Cuban doctors were popular enough but they were expected to pay 57 per cent of their salaries to their government and to send back to Cuba any of their children who reached 15. Soon they began to apply to remain in South Africa, thus infuriating both Havana and Pretoria, for such behaviour was not in the ideological script. Some of those who applied were sacked, some forcibly repatriated. Faced with this many began to abscond.[56] By 2003, 107 Cuban doctors – almost a quarter of the total – had applied to stay in South Africa[57] and the programme effectively collapsed.

If the Cubans wanted to stay in South Africa, far too many local doctors and nurses did not. The institution of enforced community service for doctors (and then for other health professionals, including nurses) was a disaster. The Ministry clearly saw doctors as overprivileged whites and enjoyed the notion of making them spend a year on very low pay in some remote rural clinic. The government's attitude to Aids on the one hand and to South Africa's elite medical culture on the other quickly convinced many doctors that it had little regard either for rationality or for the things which had made South African medicine so distinguished. In the country which had carried out the first heart transplant such operations were forbidden in many public hospitals as catering only for the rich.

So doctors began to pour abroad, followed by increasing numbers of nurses and other medical personnel. Foolishly, the government closed down its specialist nursing colleges and, as nurses fled, it also refused to pay either doctors or nurses the sort of salaries necessary to retain them. By 2002, 29,000 posts in the public health system were vacant, a number which increased to 45,978 by 2005 – over 27 per cent of all such posts.[58] The Health Minister then doubled the period of obligatory community service to two years and simultaneously cut the salaries paid to such interns. Surveys of fifth-year medical students found that the number saying they would in that case prefer to emigrate was 70–75 per cent in Cape Town, 80–90 per cent at Free State University and, at the University of Natal, where virtually all medical students were African or Indian, 92 per cent.[59] Even among those who had opted to stay in the country and were performing their community service, 43 per cent said they planned to emigrate.[60]

By 2002, 5,000 South African doctors and another 18,000 health professionals were working abroad and the *South African Health Review* warned that 'the government can forget about a functioning health system' if current policies were maintained. The catastrophic effect of such policies on the public health system caused a stampede towards private health care. In the 1980s only a third of all doctors worked privately.[61] By 1998, 52.7 per cent of all general practitioners (and 76 per cent of all specialists) worked in the private system. A year later the figure for general practitioners was 73 per cent.[62] In some disciplines the effects were dramatic: only 91 psychiatrists were left in the public system by August 2003, one-third of the required number. The private health sector, catering for just 15 per cent of the population, had 234.[63]

Inevitably, these large personnel losses demoralized those who remained and increased their workload. By 2005 the Health Minister was forced to reopen some of the nursing colleges she had closed. By 2004 the government had proudly built 1,345 new clinics but 60 per cent of them had no properly trained nurses.[64] In 2006 the DA surveyed 220 nurses in six Gauteng hospitals; 72 per cent said they had considered employment overseas, 62 per cent said they did not expect to be working in health care in five years' time, 83 per cent said they did not feel safe at work, 25 per cent had suffered physical abuse, 20 per cent sexual harassment and only 13 per cent said they would encourage young people to join the profession.[65]

The government, typically, saw the reason for this situation not in its own policies but in the predatory recruitment policies of other countries. They got the British government to bar the further recruitment of South African health professionals and sought similar agreements with others – a pointless exercise given the international shortage of such professionals and the strong 'push' factors now built into the South African system.

The disaster over Aids had many malign indirect results, not least the demoralization of health staff throughout the system, the further incentive it gave to medical emigration and the undermining of such key institutions as the Medical Research Council, the Health Professions Council and the Medicines Control Council. In 1997 the MCC registrar, Professor Peter Folb, was forced out for refusing to allow trials for Virodene. Ultimately the government forced the appointment of Professor Anthony Mbewu to head the MRC and Professor Nicky Padayachee to head the HPC, both government 'yes-men'.[66]

It was partly in order to counter the hostility of the medical profession to the government's Aids policies that the government allowed the country's over 300,000 so-called 'traditional healers' (sangomas or witch-doctors) to be registered in the same way as orthodox doctors, thus boosting their status and enabling them to make claims on medical insurance schemes. As we have seen, this enabled Mbeki to win over the sangomas to his views on Aids. The Minister insisted there were great benefits in integrating the sangomas into the health system and warned the large pharmaceutical companies against stealing the sangomas' secrets. Nobody in this extraordinary charade attempted to explain why the most medically advanced countries saw no benefit in bringing witch-doctors into their systems. Employers were appalled that henceforth a sangoma's sick-note would have to be accepted as valid, for many sangomas had no 'training' – one might become a sangoma at the age of 10 if one's ancestors' spirits deemed it a good idea.

Africanist intellectuals, keen to believe that the roots of modern science were African, echoed the government's praise for 'traditional healing' and some, like the poet and former ANC MP, Wally Serote, actually became sangomas. Few ever mentioned the organic link between the world of sangomas and the dread practice of human muti, the use of human body parts in various forms of 'traditional healing' and magic. Yet the fact was that muti traffic remained a terrifying concern and traffickers attempted to penetrate the modern medical world. In 2001 a baby's body parts were found in a taxi in Eshowe after a nurse had smuggled them out of a hospital, and two Durban mortuary employees were caught trying to sell a man's tongue and testicles.[67] Many sangomas condemned this trade. Modern doctors maintained a diplomatic silence. Yet everyone knew that the 'integration of traditional and modern medicine' was pregnant with unfortunate possibilities. Mandrax, for example, had come to South Africa originally as a sleeping pill but the townships soon discovered that it had other narcotic possibilities, so that 70–80 per cent of the world's consumption of Mandrax now occurs in South Africa – which is also the world's second biggest user of marijuana (dagga).[68]

The Health Minister, Tshabalala-Msimang, was a particular problem. An alcoholic, a kleptomaniac and an Aids denialist, her energetic promotion of beetroot and the African potato to counter Aids earned her the sobriquet 'Dr Beetroot' and demoralized her staff, who left in droves.[69] Inevitably, the Auditor-General found her Department to be a shambles, with flaws in over 90 per cent of its spending. More than R100 million had been illegally spent on NGOs like NAPWA (National Association of People Living With Aids)[70] which was created essentially to combat the TAC (Treatment Action Campaign). Using taxpayers' money to set HIV sufferers to fight one another required a morality akin to cock-fighting – for sick human beings.

With public health in such hands, there was a rush to subscribe to private health care. Ideologically this was a red rag to a bull so in 2003 the Minister passed a law whereby every private practitioner had to acquire a (Ministry-provided) 'certificate of need' before they could practise. The Act included the need to correct 'inequities based on racial or gender factors' in the presence of doctors in any area. The Minister declared the private system to be rotten and corrupt (though she used it herself) and said that it was in need of 'total transformation' into a 'single unified health system'.[72] In seeking to restrict where individuals might live and work, the Act was of doubtful constitutionality. It merely increased medical emigration. By 2006 the public health budget, catering for 85 per cent of the population, accounted for only 44 per cent of health spending – the other 56 per cent being for private care of the top 15 per cent.[71]

In 2005 the Minister brought forward her health care charter. Private health companies must sell at least 51 per cent of their assets to black investors by 2014. Little time was given for consultation and there was no explanation of why this percentage was more than double that in the mining and financial charters. By 2010, 60 per cent and by 2014, 80 per cent of all procurement spending must be from black-owned companies – though in the medical field these hardly existed. The charter was short on crucial detail in many key directions and had clearly been drawn up very abruptly. It required private health care companies to discover or create (currently non-existent) black-owned health care companies to which they would hand over majority ownership and control in short order, an obviously impossible target. By this time, however, the ANC elite were all enrolled in private health schemes so that, most unusually, the Minister's draft bill was termed 'unrealistic' by the parliamentary health committee. The targets were amended to 26 per cent black ownership in ten years and 31 per cent by 2014. Although this was greeted with a sigh of relief, the targets were tough enough to send the major private health groups into a frenzy of diversification abroad: the more assets they could get out of the country by these due dates, the less they would lose. The link between BEE and capital flight could hardly have been clearer.

HEALTH ON THE GROUND

The effects of such maladministration and poor leadership were quickly felt in the public hospitals. By 2001 an audit of Chris Hani-Baragwanath Hospital in Soweto, the world's largest hospital, reported acute linen shortages, inadequate and outdated equipment, poor safety levels and communication, misconduct, low morale and violations of patients' rights, all problems exacerbated by staff shortages.[73] Simultaneously the Gauteng Public Works Department reported that 94 per cent of the province's hospitals were in dire need of repair, maintenance and upgrading and that the situation was deteriorating rapidly.[74]

Gauteng was the most favoured province in health care terms: the Eastern Cape was at the opposite extreme. There the provincial health minister, Dr Trudy Thomas, an ANC stalwart and winner of the 1996 Mandela Award for Health and Human Rights, resigned from her post, her seat in the provincial legislature and the ANC in 2001, declaring that the ANC promise of 'A Better Life for All' had in practice meant creating 'Worse Services for All'. She spoke of 'a steady, visible and measurable deterioration ... it is mindless, rudderless, decaying and a ridiculous scenario'.[75] Dr Thomas's successor as provincial health minister was suspended after a brief period of office to face over 1,000 charges of fraud. A glance at Mthatha General, one of the province's major hospitals, meant to offer specialist care to patients referred to it by more than fifteen district hospitals, bore Dr Thomas out. In the maternity ward anything up to 120 mothers shared 48 beds. The hospital had run out of disinfectant, antiseptic cream, antitetanus injections, gauze and the reagent necessary for HIV tests and there were periodic shortages of basic drugs like antibiotics. Even food was in short supply. Rubbish bins overflowed, there were used needles, blood and urine on the floors. The doctors joked that the health service was 'like Hollywood – everyone has an acting position'; this included managers, superintendents and the new provincial minister for health. Everyone agreed that things had deteriorated sharply since 1994.[76] I had visited many Johannesburg hospitals and been distressed by the obvious neglect, but nothing prepared me for a visit to Mount Frere hospital in the Eastern Cape in 2002. It lacked everything – staff, blankets, drugs – and the toilets were blocked solid with excrement. Everywhere there was stench and filth, a potent danger to health. A two-hour wait failed to produce a nurse, let alone a doctor.

As so often in post-1994 South Africa the reversal of old hierarchies was not accompanied by any working alternative (not just doctors but nurses or clerks could now become the boss of the hospital) and there was a grave loss of management skills. There were frequent complaints, hitherto unprecedented, about rude and undisciplined nurses. Often records were poorly kept and there were no clear lines of accountability. In 2005 it emerged that public hospitals had failed to recoup R1.2 billion in patient fees, a situation which the Minister sought to remedy by huge fee increases, until forced to back down by the threat of legal action. In eight of the nine provinces, auditors qualified health department accounts because of unpaid bills, poor staff management and inadequate stock records. Sometimes there had been no stocktaking for years on end and the ordering of new supplies was at best haphazard. When medicines did arrive they were frequently not securely stored.[77]

Such problems were repeatedly pointed out by hospital staff, politicians, trade unions and journalists, each time producing promises of amelioration though in practice nothing happened: the authorities had either ceased to care or had simply lost the means to respond. In 2005 Tshabalala-Msimang visited Chris Hani-Baragwanath and, as if perceiving the problems for the first time, said, 'I always tell people to use public hospitals, but from what I saw today I would hesitate to come here.'[78] A poll carried out in 2005 found that only 10 per cent of the population trusted public hospitals; 50 per cent said they gave poor service and nearly 40 per cent thought the staff rude and unprofessional.[79]

Predictably, the situation was worst in mental hospitals. In 1996 shocking allegations surfaced about the remote Umzimkulu Hospital but by 2005 it emerged that things were just as bad at one of South Africa's oldest and most famous psychiatric hospitals, Town Hill in Pietermaritzburg, with allegations of assault, sexual abuse, dirt, theft, bad food, drunken staff and improper administration of drugs: what *The Witness* described as 'a 17th century bedlam'.[80] An official inquiry confirmed all these allegations and found that there was constant staff theft of patients' food and belongings[81] – an irony given that the Minister herself had been guilty of similar behaviour. Nothing was done and the abuses continued.[82]

Some hospitals became positive health hazards. In 1999 the Auditor-General reported that up to 70 per cent of operations at Chris Hani-Baragwanath did not comply 'with the minimum mandatory requirements laid down by the South African Society of Anaesthesiologists'. Similar mismanagement at other Gauteng hospitals, pointed out in the 1997 audit but not acted upon, had led to a situation where over half the equipment used was older than the lifespan recommended by the manufacturers and some cases where the equipment was actually condemned. The problem was not a shortage of money but pure mismanagement, since the maintenance costs on such old equipment were often more than the cost of replacement.[83]

In 2005 the high rate of HIV infection of young children in the Free State was found to be due to the breakdown of infection-control procedures in hospitals there. Children were catching the virus simply because instruments were not sterilized and milk not pasteurized – indeed one-third of the milk in public hospitals there was found to contain the virus.[84] Remedial action was not taken and two years later further enquiry showed that the infection of child patients with HIV through inadequate infection control had become a major problem in public hospitals countrywide.[85] In 2005 the death of twenty-two babies in Mahatma Gandhi Hospital, Durban, was traced to bacterial infections picked up in the hospital as a result of their being fed with infected glucose. Over the previous eighteen months forty-nine babies had died from the same cause. The Health Minister insisted that no one could be blamed for this, an odd response given that 10 per cent of the hospital's nurses were carrying the infection as a result of failing to wash their hands.[86]

The challenges of Aids on the one hand and the emigration of medical personnel on the other threatened to overwhelm the public health system. But South Africa is also a country where the combination of poverty, shanty towns and climate produces continuous health challenges. By 2001 rabies deaths in Zululand had increased to one a month,[87] at a time when KwaZulu-Natal was facing a major cholera epidemic which by February 2002 had resulted in more than 114,000 confirmed cases and 259 deaths,[88] with other cases reported in neighbouring provinces.

The new government's culpability for this was obvious: there had been no comparable epidemic under apartheid. After watching the situation worsen for five months it panicked and appealed to the World Health Organization for help,[89] something which had also never occurred under apartheid. Health experts professed outrage that the government had done nothing to prevent the original outbreak (in Mandeni) from spreading, despite the obvious risk that migrant workers would carry the disease with them as they left for their Christmas holidays. But the basic failure was one of clean water supplies and the blame fell squarely on the Department of Water Affairs,[90] despite its public relations campaign about the water miracles performed by Kader Asmal. In 2005 there were serious outbreaks of typhoid at Delmas in Mpumalanga with four deaths officially reported, though the TAC claimed that the real death toll was forty-nine. There was serious rioting in Delmas's Botleng township (suppressed by the now customary firing of rubber bullets into a crowd of 7,000) where angry residents blamed the authorities for their second such outbreak in twelve years.[91] The problem was that the Department had passed over much of the local responsibility for water affairs to local municipalities which were entirely failing to cope. Indeed, only 58 per cent of them even monitored the quality of their water supplies. Professor Eugene Cloete, a former vice-president of the International Water Association, was blunt about the need to boil the water anywhere outside the metropolitan areas (hitherto an unnecessary precaution). 'Any small town is a sitting time bomb,' said Cloete.[92]

A new menace emerged in 2006: extremely drug-resistant tuberculosis (XDR-TB), a deadly threat to HIV sufferers. WHO experts were adamant that the cause was inadequate infection control in hospitals while treating normal TB – 'infection control in many public hospitals is either inadequate or non-existent', said the Medical Research Council's Dr Karin Weyer.[93] Emergency meetings involving not just local medics but the surrounding SADC countries and the WHO were held, for the possibility of XDR-TB spreading was a major international threat. The 78 cases reported from Tugela Ferry (KwaZulu-Natal) resulted in 74 deaths and the area was quarantined, though XDR-TB cases were later found in all nine provinces.[94]

It was remarkable that the ANC, whose primary constituency was the mass of poor Africans, should, despite fervent promises to the contrary, do so much so quickly to damage the public health system on which that constituency depended. Surveying the situation, Professor Solly Benatar, South Africa's greatest expert on health services, wrote of 'dysfunctional primary services and attrition of tertiary services in the public sector with greater losses than gains in healthcare in the short term and adverse implications for the future'.[95] He pointed out that Groote Schuur, South Africa's flagship teaching and research hospital where the world's first heart transplant took place, had been a major national resource in 1994 with more than 200 specialists. A decade later the number was 100 and by 2010 that would fall to 50. What the hospital once was had been destroyed. One result was that the number of cardiac operations at the hospital had fallen from 900 in 1994 to 300 in 2004, with a consequent loss in the ability to train new surgeons. The same degradation of key hospitals had occurred countrywide. Thus whereas in 1990 South Africa had the potential from which to develop a really strong public health system, that was now entirely lost. Moreover, medical education had been seriously degraded. As a result of affirmative action, black students, who made up 28.9 per cent of all first-year medical students in 1994, made up 64 per cent in 2004. By definition such students required stronger support and reinforcement in their medical education to compensate for their school education, usually inferior to that of the white students they were displacing. Yet simultaneously the medical curriculum was cut from six years to five and more of the teaching was done by nurses and social scientists.[96]

Inevitably, this calamitous mismanagement of the public health system began to have measurable results, quite apart from the Aids disaster. According to the 2003–4 South African Health Review, the standards of ante-natal care had 'steadily deteriorated' in the previous decade.[97] In metropolitan areas, where treatment was best, 63 per cent of stillbirths were avoidable. Even in Gauteng the chances of women dying in childbirth had doubled between 1998 and 2002, and this was by no means solely attributable to HIV/Aids, for while 'avoidable factors, missed opportunities and substandard care' were involved in 56.8 per cent of maternal deaths in 1998, by 2002 the figure had risen to 73.3 per cent.[98] Moreover, more children were dying under the age of 5 than had been the case at the height of apartheid.[99] This was only partly due to Aids; many children were dying of diarrhoea and malnutrition, a scandal in a middle-income country. Similarly, a UN report in 2006 found that 'There has been virtually no progress in reducing South Africa's newborn death rate in the past ten years', the co-editor of the report commenting that 'I think in a country . . . with such resources . . . there should be progress, but it doesn't seem to be on the agenda'.[100]

As with the cavalier treatment of Aids, one is forced to the conclusion that the ANC leadership did not much care about the deterioration of the public health system, or at least not enough to stop it. Hence the dismissal of the deputy Health Minister, Nozizwe Madlala-Routledge, after her visit to East London's Frere Hospital in July 2007. The *Daily Dispatch* had carried a series of damning articles about the situation in the hospital where 2,000 babies had been stillborn in the previous fourteen years, most of the deaths avoidable. The newspaper pointed out that the situation was clearly worsening, with at least 199 dead babies in 2006. Reporters even saw one baby delivered by a hospital cleaner. Madlala-Routledge, on a surprise visit to the hospital, was visibly distressed, terming the 'shocking situation' a 'national emergency'. Dr Nokuzola Ntshona, the superintendent of the neighbouring Cecilia Makiwane Hospital, wrote to Mbeki saying that the situation was even worse than the deputy Minister realized. Both she and Madlala-Routledge were dismissed. Mbeki sought to justify these actions by arguing that the death rate of babies at Frere Hospital was perfectly normal, introducing this justification with a discussion of 1960s mini-skirts and how 'one had to use one's head to visualize what lay beyond the hem of the mini-skirt to arrive at the reality suggested by the mini-skirt', and ended his peroration with 'We salute and thank the staff of Frere Hospital for its commitment to service delivery'.[101] The sight of an African President juxtaposing an almost lustful description of mini-skirts with a justification for dead black babies staggered most observers.

One result was to focus attention on how far South Africa was falling short of its commitment to the UN's Millennium Development Goals to reduce the infant mortality rate by two-thirds, from 60 deaths per 1,000 live births to 20. Health experts said there was no hope of maintaining the rate at 60; a rise to 65 was the best outcome imaginable. Seventy thousand children under 5 were dying every year, the highest number of deaths for any age group, and the number was increasing. The UNICEF representative to South Africa, Macharia Kamau, expressed her 'sadness and dismay' at the figures[102] but, given that the President saw such phenomena as perfectly normal, improvement seemed unlikely. As the medical professors Louis Reynolds and David Sanders commented, 'The denial that the situation at Frere Hospital reflects a more widespread crisis at all levels of the health sector [and] betrays a serious lack of leadership.'[103]

DISASTER AT MINERALS AND ENERGY (AGAIN)

One of the ANC's pleasantest inheritances from its apartheid predecessor was an abundant supply of the world's cheapest electricity. This situation derived not just from the large supplies of easily mined coal but because the governments of the 1970s and 1980s, overestimating the economic growth rate, built more power stations than were needed so that several of them had to be shut down and mothballed. The ANC government treated cheap electricity as a God-given right and it was one of the country's main selling points in attempting to attract investment. In 2004, for example, whereas a kilowatt/hour cost 10.97 US cents in Italy, 7.56 cents in the United States and 6.7 cents in the UK, in South Africa it cost 3.17 cents, 24 per cent less than the second cheapest country, Canada.[104] Despite that, in 1995 there was spare capacity of well over 40 per cent.[105]

This encouraged the government and the state-owned power supplier, Eskom, in some fairly grandiose thoughts. First, there was a drive to provide electricity to poor communities that lacked it: by the end of 2002 power had been provided to 3.75 million such households.[106] By 2007, 80 per cent of all households had an electricity connection[107] but South Africa's stratospheric rate of unemployment meant that many people were too poor to pay for electricity. Just as with telephone connections, the ANC made the provision of service connection a key political objective, implying that the apartheid government had failed to provide such services out of simple racism. In both cases they rebounded; the millions of new telephone connections were soon equalled by the number of disconnections through failure to pay, and something rather similar occurred with electricity: by 2001 new connections were running at 30,000 a month but disconnections (through failure to pay) were running at nearly 100,000 a month.[108] In addition, illegal connections proliferated in townships and squatter camps and many consumers ran up enormous unpaid bills. The government then compounded its difficulties by promising, during the 2000 local elections, 'free basic electricity' (and water) for the poor.

The bill duly came in. In 2003 Eskom wrote off R1.4 billion in electricity arrears owed by residents of Soweto and other Gauteng townships. Not unreasonably, the DA demanded to know why it had been decided to reward non-payers rather than payers and why those in relatively better off Reef townships had been favoured over poorer people elsewhere. There were bitter accusations from the Coloured township of Eldorado Park that only Africans had benefited. By 2005 the 'free electricity' scheme was also in bad trouble. The benefits had been so poorly targeted that while 1.7 million consumers had enjoyed free power, most were not poor and only 12 per cent of the really poor had received them, with the result that the programme had cost 2.4 times the budgeted amount.[109] In both cases the losses to Eskom were substantial.

But as its CEO, Thulani Gcabashe, put it, Eskom was 'not content with operating in a pocket of relative affluence in South Africa while it was surrounded by a sea of poverty on the rest of the continent'. Buoyed by the knowledge that they had inherited the world's seventh-biggest power utility, the new bosses of Eskom, which produced half of all Africa's electricity, accordingly set up the Southern African Power Pool, connecting national power systems all the way to Kenya and the DRC. Eskom also sought to move strongly into other African markets, securing contracts to supply Billiton's Mozal aluminium smelter in Mozambique and to operate and maintain a power station in Mali. It also built a 500 MW line connecting up the South African and Zimbabwean grids, enabling it to export power to Zimbabwe and, potentially, to Zambia, with other possible connections to Malawi, Tanzania, the DRC and Angola. Eskom also expressed interest in buying up privatized power utilities in Zambia and Uganda and set up a joint venture company with its Moroccan counterpart to carry out joint projects throughout Africa. Eskom spoke, indeed, of its ambition to become 'the leading energy and related services business throughout emerging markets world-wide.'[110] In 2003 Eskom forged links with a Russian power company, Factor, and decided to carry out a joint transmission project in Tunisia, plus other joint projects in Africa, eastern Europe and Russia.[111] Simultaneously, Eskom planned to spend $1 billion on connecting up with the giant Inga hydroelectric project in the DRC, which involved the building of a 2,000 kilometre transmission line. Great hopes were placed on the Inga project, for the Congo is the world's second most powerful river and if fully exploited Inga might yield 40,000 MW. The first stage of Inga alone was to cost $4 billion.[112] Eskom was thinking big. Enos Banda, CEO of Eskom Enterprises proudly told how 'On a recent visit to Saudi Arabia I was asked when Africa would be in a position to start exporting its surplus power to the Middle East. And Europe would be another natural market for Africa's power.'[113]

Reuel Khoza, the Eskom chairman who led this push, might have reflected on why Western power companies had neglected these projects. Even as the new transmission line to Zimbabwe was built it was already obvious that Zimbabwe could not pay for the electricity it received, and so it proved. Equally unsurprisingly, Eskom encountered large-scale corruption in its Nigerian office, resentment of 'big brother South Africa', poor infrastructure and near impassable terrain elsewhere.[114] Worse, Eskom was meanwhile savagely reducing its own organizational capacity by thoroughgoing affirmative action. Numerous white engineers, managers and technocrats were forced into early retirement, to be replaced by far less qualified Africans.

Meanwhile Reuel Khoza spent large amounts of public money on his African leadership project, taking frequent full-page advertisements to boast about it, and when a fraud of R129 million involving Eskom executives was reported to Gcabashe in 2003, he apparently did nothing. By May 2006 he was sitting on an audit report showing the collapse of financial controls, kickbacks and corruption, and five months later had still done nothing.[115] The newly established National Electricity Regulator (NERSA) was wracked by continuous corruption scandals and a rapid succession of CEOs.[116] Eskom's new executives awarded themselves record salaries and bonuses. Gcabashe was the highest paid executive in South African business in 2006, his salary increasing more than tenfold in five years, and yet, astonishingly, he also held a home loan from Eskom for R929,000. Eskom's finance director, Bongani Nqwababa, had a loan of R2.9 million.[117] Yet as this leadership enjoyed its perks and expounded on the nature of African leadership, it was presiding over an unparalleled process of de-skilling and the loss of institutional memory, gravely undermining the institution it headed.

Every year saw electricity consumption mount, and no new power stations were built. Given that it takes around seven years to build a power station – or, if one counts in the planning and design stages too, about ten years – the government had to start paying sharp attention to the need to build new power stations no later than 1996. It did not do so. Then in 1998 the Minister for Minerals and Energy, Penuell Maduna, proposed that in order to bring competition into the sector, 30 per cent of electricity should be provided by new private entrants to the market. The government accepted this and forbade Eskom to build any more power stations, in order to make room for the new entrants.

The government dawdled until 2000 and then produced a policy which, absurdly, did not allow private partners access to Eskom's electricity grid, insisted that electricity be kept dirt cheap and made all manner of stipulations about BEE partners. Not surprisingly, no private companies showed any interest in tendering. Eskom warned the Minister (from 1999 Phumzile Mlambo-Ngcuka) about the urgency of commissioning fresh capacity but she blithely maintained the power station building ban until 2004.

By then a power crisis was inevitable. Eskom's own projections showed that peak consumption would hit the capacity ceiling by 2006–7 and that by 2010 even baseload consumption would do so. Moreover, from 2010 on the old coal-fired stations would conclude their natural life and Eskom would need to commission an extra 1,000 MW a year just to stay steady. There was now no way in which large-scale new power stations could be brought on stream before 2012 at the earliest, so the country faced at least five years of worsening power cuts.[118]

For a sophisticated modern economy this was a catastrophe. The immediate concern was the football World Cup in 2010. Trying to deflect blame, the government said that economic growth had been faster than expected. The reverse was true: growth had actually been far slower than the 6 per cent Gear had predicted in 1996. What was worrying was that the main driver of economic growth was the commodity boom and the mining, processing and construction industries were extremely power-hungry.

As the first wave of serious power cuts hit in 2006, investors pulled back: 'We're not currently looking at South Africa,' said Brian Gilbertson, head of the Russian aluminium giant, Sual. 'We did eighteen months ago, but energy is an issue.' Other potential investors made similar noises.[119] Although Alec Erwin insisted, absurdly, that there was no threat to growth and no need to panic, Eskom desperately tried to rehire the skilled white experts previously laid off and made rather hollow promises to bring back online the power stations mothballed fifteen years before: such plants used technology that was now obsolete and the only way to obtain spares was to cannibalize other parts of the plant. In addition, those with the expertise to operate these plants had long since departed. Gcabashe himself quietly left in 2007.

The situation was further worsened by the government's decade-long hesitation over electricity distribution. In most of South Africa, Eskom distributes power via the municipalities, for whom their electricity accounts are an enormous cash cow. Typically they charge extra for their role in distribution and also earn large sums in interest on the cash flow through the account. The government decided, however, that they would instead set up a series of Regional Electricity Distributors to take over this role from the municipalities. This was met with great resistance from the municipalities, which would lose one of their chief sources of income and also have to pay for a whole further expensive layer of administration. So the government dithered, guaranteeing the worst of both worlds. The municipalities, faced with a large imminent revenue loss, saved by failing to carry out the repair and replacement of ageing distribution networks, but no new body actually took responsibility. The result was increasing power failures due to poorly maintained local distribution networks.

By 2005 the situation in Johannesburg, the country's main economic motor, had become critical. Traffic flows, already clogging due to the authorities' failure to plan for increased vehicle ownership, were slowed further by the continuous failure of traffic lights while the municipality's City Power company was merely trying (unsuccessfully) to keep power cuts down to 1,500 a year.[120] City Power reported that it could not account for no less than 13 per cent of electricity consumption – due to illegal connections and chaos over electricity billing – and urged customers to buy their own generators.

An audit showed that most of City Power's equipment was very old: 70 per cent of it was from twenty to forty years old and 7 per cent more than forty years old. In the city's central and southern regions some equipment was seventy years old – and running flat out.[121] Johannesburg city council had stopped investing in new equipment in 1990 when the dawn of democracy made it inevitable that the old council majority would cease to hold power, and the ANC council had maintained a zero-investment policy. The audit warned that maintenance was carried out simply in reaction to power failures; there was no proper maintenance programme. Auditors had found trees growing inside substations, which have to be kept clean, safe and free of water. There were 'massive and unacceptable' oil leaks from transformers which would cause substation fires, while water was leaking into tunnels where already antique underground cables lay. The audit warned that City Power lacked the necessary skilled personnel to prevent 'continuous and sustained blackouts'. In addition, there were unsafe working conditions, a failure to test protection systems, poor quality maintenance and chaotic record-keeping.[122]

Johannesburg residents were not mollified by hearing that the head of City Power, Mogwailane Mohlala, professed himself unworried: 'In my four years at City Power I've never been stressed.'[123] NERSA warned that such problems applied in varying measure to all 187 municipalities distributing their own electricity. There was, above all, a lack of skilled personnel; in some municipalities 60 per cent of skilled posts were vacant.[124] A 2002 study showed that 49 per cent of municipalities had no maintenance strategies for their electricity distribution networks and, indeed, lacked any understanding of power quality and performance.[125]

The Western Cape, lacking coal, relied heavily on the country's only nuclear power station at Koeberg and it was here that crisis struck in 2005–6 when a fault at Koeberg caused massive and repeated blackouts throughout the Cape, costing many billions of rand. On the eve of municipal elections Alec Erwin created a sensation by announcing that the NIA was investigating how a 15-centimetre bolt had been left inside one of the power units. Clearly with the aim of deflecting blame from the government, Erwin declared that 'the bolt that caused the generator's destruction did not get there by accident' – a clear imputation of sabotage.[126] 'The police have identified the suspects and they are investigating,' he added.[127] 'It was an act of human instrumentality. It was not an accident.'[128]

A NERSA investigation reported that the blackouts had been 'unnecessary' and were due to 'general indiscipline' among the Koeberg staff, including the breaching of licence conditions, inadequate maintenance, a failure – for years on end – to test equipment and to implement corrective measures recommended years before, an alarming situation at a nuclear plant. NERSA said that negligence was the cause of three out of four cuts. Alec Erwin admitted that no amount of investigation by NERSA, Eskom, the police or NIA had turned up evidence of the sabotage he had hinted at on election eve but now, staggeringly, he denied that he had ever suggested sabotage.[129] For many Eskom staff Erwin's imputation of sabotage had been the last straw. Morale was extremely low, as it invariably is in institutions where meritocratic criteria are discarded. A survey of 1,000 white employees – including many of the skilled staff Eskom was desperate to keep – found that 75 per cent were considering leaving and that 43 per cent wanted to do so right away.[130]

The power crisis torpedoed all plans for 'alternative' fuels and all reservations about nuclear power: there would be lots more coal-fired stations, whatever the environmental cost, although South Africa was, proportional to GDP, already one of the world's worst polluters. At the same time the government was belatedly realizing that it had neglected the rest of the infrastructure in much the same way as electricity. In 2006 the SA Institute of Civil Engineers delivered its own audit, rating Water at D+/E; Roads at D–/E+; Ports at C–/D+, Rail at E+; Airports at B– and Telecoms at E+. Everywhere the same gross dereliction was apparent.

Accordingly the government announced a R400 billion programme of infrastructural upgrading[131] with a simultaneous R100 billion electricity upgrade. Mbeki termed this the phenomenon of 'the developmental state', a phrase eagerly taken up by left activists. All it really meant was that the government had done nothing for so long that now it had to do everything and all at once, with the inevitable result of supply bottlenecks and increased costs. In any manual on governance this would be a textbook example of how not to do it. As the energy expert Andrew Kenny put it, the electricity problem had 'been looming for the past 10 years. It's been absolutely predictable and is in fact an exceptionally unsurprising crisis.'[132]

But Eskom still knew its priorities. It needed to recruit at least two new skilled staff, particularly engineers, every day for five years ahead. Of these at least half had to be black women so as to achieve the targets of 65 per cent black management and 40 per cent female representation by 2010 – despite the virtual non-existence of black women engineers.

How, Eskom was asked, could such targets be reconciled with producing a reliable and sufficient supply of electricity? 'For us employment equity is business as usual,' replied Mpho Letlape, Eskom's human resources director.[133]

The crisis really struck home in January 2008 with a series of major nationwide power cuts culminating in a complete shut-down of the mines. For the first time since 1886 the industry on which the country was built was silent. So too was much of manufacturing. Panic ensued. Economists immediately cut the predicted growth rate from 5 to 2 per cent or even predicted a recession. Eskom announced that it was pointless to seek new foreign investment projects before 2013 because there would be no power for them. Foreign capital fled, domestic capital flight and white emigration soared, while the rand fell by 15 per cent.

Eskom had contributed heavily to the crisis by its bizarre coal procurement policies. It had sold off its once enormous coal stockpile and was giving preference to small black coal producers, many of them situated far from the mines. The result was chaos, with huge transport costs in trucking the coal in, poor quality coal, unreliable delivery and in some cases coal which was merely coal dust that in rain became incombustible mud. Thus Eskom was operating at only 75 per cent of capacity. Symbolically, a crowd of foreign tourists were left stranded and freezing on the top of Table Mountain after the cable cars lost power. When finally rescued, they all swore they would never return to South Africa.

Infrastructural neglect was general. In a water-short country the government had also hopelessly mismanaged its inheritance of dams, pipelines, pumps and treatment facilities. No less than 43 per cent of dams managed by the Water Ministry were unsafe and required urgent repair. R130 billion was needed to replace ageing plant. Moreover, poor management had allowed waste water from the mines to seep into the groundwater system, an alarming fact given that many mines treat their ore with cyanide. Vegetables and fish sampled west of Johannesburg were found to be contaminated with radioactive uranium. Water and local milk in the same area was found to be similarly contaminated. 'Immediate intervention' was needed at 30 per cent of all municipal waste-water treatment works to prevent further outbreaks of water-borne diseases such as typhoid. Within the Water Ministry and the municipalities there had been a crippling loss of skills for the usual reasons and, as the researcher Jeff Rudin put it, the breakdown of water monitoring and treatment services was 'a national disaster waiting to happen'.[134] If one ventured into the Water Ministry you discovered two things. First, officials there were gloomily aware of these problems and were mainly just waiting for the time bomb to explode, for they had no plan to stop it. Secondly, one realized that white males were now quite out of place and, indeed, unwelcome there.

TRAINS AND BOATS AND PLANES

The nineteenth century saw South Africa bound together by a remarkably elaborate and sophisticated railway system and the next century saw the construction of a magnificent road network. The ports grew to the point where today Durban is the world's ninth-busiest port, though in actual tonnage handled Richards Bay is now bigger. South Africans are proud of this transport infrastructure which, for many, typifies the country's modernity. When the ANC inherited all this in 1994 things were actually a little less good than they looked, for once the NP leadership realized that the transfer of power could not be long delayed, there was a sharp decline in investment in an infrastructure which was soon to be someone else's prize – and problem.

The first ANC Minister of Transport, Mac Maharaj, carried out many sensible reforms. He was, however, no admirer of Mbeki and had been singled out by Mandela as a man of presidential timbre – a lethal mix. He left government as soon as Mbeki became President. His successors were notably less able and so were the heads of the state transport holding company, Transnet. Mbeki's follower, Saki Macozoma, faced up to none of the mounting problems at Portnet (ports) or Spoornet (rail) but instead chose to deal with South African Airways (SAA) along lines familiar in ex-colonial Africa. First, appoint a politically correct but unqualified black. Then, when he/she is fired, avoid picking a local white with relevant managerial and technical experience. Instead pick a foreigner who knows far less and costs far more but can be easily got rid of. The result was an American, Coleman Andrews, who duly spent a fortune, incurred record losses and departed with a king-size golden handshake.

The next head of Transnet was a politically correct local, Louise Tager, who achieved little. She was followed by Bongani Khumalo, who, prior to his appointment, had been Mbeki's advisor on Aids and rural development, both of them exercises in denial. Through all these regimes the one constant was huge underinvestment. Finally in 2004 Maria Ramos, a tough white manager, was drafted in as Transnet's CEO to conduct an emergency salvage operation.

By this time business complaints about the failure of the ports and railways had become overwhelming. Transnet's treasury department had decided to speculate against the rand and run up hedging losses of R6.1 billion, which came on top of SAA's debt burden of R32.6 billion by 2003.[135] SAA had steadily declined for ten years and, in contravention of both IATA rules and its operating licence, had been trading in insolvent circumstances for two years.[136] The head of the Civil Aviation Authority, Trevor Abrahams, had to be sacked amid a welter of corruption allegations, including that he had faked his own pilot's licence. Thereafter the organization was kept without a permanent head for three years, during which time Polokwane International Airport was allowed to continue operating with defective navigation systems, a source of considerable scandal in aviation circles.[137] The Civil Aviation Authority's next head, Zakes Myeza, had previously run a lottery and had no experience of aviation.

Meanwhile, the head of the South African Maritime Authority, Sipho Msikinya, was accused of financial mismanagement and massive wasteful expenditure. Even its chairman, Chris Nissen, was drawing two salaries, one as chairman, one as acting CEO – despite his having been dismissed as CEO after allegations of mismanagement. The Road Accident Fund (a state insurance fund for road accident victims) was racked by losses and fraud and a number of its officials had been suspended on corruption charges.[138] In 2003 Transnet had to pay R57 million in damages to a contract bidder it knew to be better qualified but whom it discarded on the intervention of the Minister.[139]

THE PORTS: A TAX ON TRADE

In 1996 Transnet predicted trouble due to lack of investment in the country's ports. Nothing was done and the backlog mounted. In 2001 the major shipping lines protested at the low productivity in container handling. In Durban, the biggest container port, cranes were handling only 8 containers an hour. In Cape Town the figure was 15 but both figures had to be set against a worldwide average of 35 and a Japanese average of 47.[140] This situation was often causing ships to wait at anchor 100 hours or more, an extremely costly situation for the owners. Dire warnings about the effect on the country's trade saw some improvement with crane movements at Durban doubling but this still left an unacceptable situation.

In 2002 the shippers lost patience. Emphasizing that they had suffered losses for five years past which could never be recouped, they announced the imposition of a $75 surcharge on every container moved through Durban in order to compensate themselves for the losses – R500 million in the second half of 2001 – incurred through delays.[141] The surcharge amounted to a large tax on South African trade and a considerable stain on its reputation as an international trader. Only this moved the government to action, but the problem persisted and in 2003 the shipping companies imposed a surcharge of $100 a container, to the fury of the responsible minister, Alec Erwin. Thereafter, although increased investment led to a gradual improvement, the shipping companies continually threatened the reimposition of the surcharge.

ROADS TO DISASTER

In 1988 some 75 per cent of South Africa's national and provincial roads were graded as being in good or very good condition. In 1999 the Automobile Association pointed out that this figure had dropped to 33 per cent while the roads in poor or very poor condition had leapt from 5 per cent to 33 per cent.[142] Nothing was done despite strong warnings that neglect of maintenance would result in far bigger bills down the line. In 2001 the SA Bitumen Association warned that 'a point of no return' could be reached when repairs became prohibitively expensive; just to prevent further deterioration road spending needed to be doubled and the government should realize that 'the state could find itself as a potentially unsuccessful defendant' in over 100,000 accident cases a year if the situation was left unattended.[143] Despite this, chronic underfunding continued. By 2006 the SA National Roads Agency estimated that it was getting funds sufficient to maintain only 40 per cent of the road network and warned that if roads were not repaired within the next five years costs would become eighteen times more expensive.[144] Dr Malcolm Mitchell, CEO of the SA Road Federation, pointed out that of the R43 billion the government collected by taxing motorists only R13 billion was being spent on roads. In the United States, he said, potholes on major freeways were repaired within seventy-two hours whereas in South Africa the norm was now six to nine months.[145]

Concerns over the 2010 football World Cup led to a sharp increase in infrastructural spending, though by this time road congestion in some urban areas had become acute. As elsewhere in Africa, luxury prestige projects had a fatal lure for the new elite, the most obvious being the Gautrain, costing in excess of R20 billion, that was to link O. R. Tambo (Johannesburg) Airport to Johannesburg and Pretoria. It was obvious that only the well-heeled would be able to afford the Gautrain yet it was allowed to consume three times Gauteng's budget for road construction and maintenance.[146]

Historically, the country's transport backbone had been the railways and tough measures were used to maintain the supremacy of rail. When I was a keen young rugby and cricket player in Durban, my school could only hire a coach to send a school team to tour neighbouring districts if the railways agreed – otherwise we had to go by rail. To my father's indignation, the same applied to his business of shipping oil from the coast to Johannesburg. When these protectionist measures were removed, passengers and freight shifted massively to the roads.

This came at considerable cost in human lives. No sociological study has been done to explain why road behaviour in Africa is so lethal but lethal it is. Whereas the road traffic mortality rate in the Americas in 2003 was 16.2 deaths per 100,000 population, in South East Asia it was 18.6 and in Africa 28.3, with South Africa at 26.9.[147] A perk enjoyed by Transport Ministry officials was their endless (though fruitless) trips to Australia to study conditions there, as that country has road volumes, weather and traffic conditions comparable to South Africa. Yet whereas the death toll on Australia's roads in December 2002, for example, was 96, South Africa's was 1,111.[148] By 2006 there were more than 14,000 road deaths a year in South Africa, with an additional 40,000 injured (of whom 7,000 were permanently disabled).[149]

These figures were probably large underestimates. In 2003 the MRC studied thirty-seven mortuaries across the country and claimed that road deaths were nearly three times higher than the figures released by the

Transport Department. There is reason to believe this is correct. The basic data come from the police, who are understaffed and under great pressure, but those with time to study the facts under less pressure come up with far larger numbers. For example, in 2000 the police reported 21,683 murders; Home Affairs counted 30,068 while the MRC, using mortuary data, counted 32,482.[150]

This would make sense. In a global study of road rage in 2004, South Africa came top.[151] The almost complete absence of breathalyser tests made it easy to drink and drive: six out of ten accidents involved alcohol abuse.[152] Moreover, surveys show that 97 per cent of back-seat and 36 per cent of front-seat passengers did not wear seat belts; that over 10 per cent of all heavy trucks were unroadworthy; that buses and trucks were on average twelve years and minibus taxis thirteen years old.[153] Moreover, not only were the police highly bribable but so were vehicle licensing and driver-testing centres. It was relatively easy to buy a driving licence and, indeed, the Speaker of Parliament, Baleke Mbete, did just that. In many countries that would have ended her career: in South Africa she brazened it out. In 2005 the Transport Department estimated that half the driving population had fake licences,[154] causing both Britain and Botswana to express reservations about accepting these licences, to the government's embarrassment.[155] The Road Accident Fund, which provides compensation to road accident victims, was permanently on the edge of bankruptcy. The Fund's chairman, Dr Saths Cooper, called it 'probably the biggest fraud story in South Africa's history' and in 2004 admitted that the previous figure of R500 million lost to fraud should be revised to R1 billion.[156]

THE RUNAWAY TRAIN

The railways were the heart of the matter. Just as Mbeki was dreaming of how he would become the de facto president of a united Africa and Eskom was dreaming of binding the rest of Africa into South Africa's electricity grid, so the transport bosses were dreaming afresh the Cape-to-Cairo dreams of Cecil Rhodes. Jeff Radebe, the Minister of Public Enterprises, wanted to use South Africa's parastatals as a lever for infrastructural development throughout Africa and encouraged Eskom, Portnet, SAA and Spoornet (the railways) to invest elsewhere in Africa as far afield as Uganda, Ghana and Cameroon. Radebe even authored a booklet, *Africa First*, in which he spoke happily of how South Africa would, throughout the continent, 'revive and rebuild infrastructure that has fallen into disuse or been marginalized'.[157]

This was pure vainglory. SAA bought 49 per cent of the bankrupt Air Tanzania Corporation for R20 million, despite having previously described it as a 'worthless' investment,[158] while Spoornet happily signed contracts in eighteen other African countries to rehabilitate run-down rail networks, often agreeing to supply rolling stock and locomotives although it needed all it had at home. Absurdly, when Spoornet itself was running at a R2 billion loss in 1999, it paid out large sums to these foreign ventures; it paid $77.7 million in 2002 for the concession to rehabilitate and run a major rail line inside Mozambique, for example. Bongani Khumalo, the Transnet chairman, explained that Transnet aimed at becoming 'the leading transport and logistics company in Africa'.[159]

Yet Radebe already admitted that all was not well with Spoornet at home: passenger numbers had collapsed from 45 million in 1982 to 4.2 million in 2001. Under 50 per cent of freight trains were leaving on time and only 22 per cent were arriving on time.[160] On average, Spoornet trains were already twenty-five years old and some had seen forty years of service. Radebe, absurdly, underestimated the fresh investment needed in the infrastructure at R450 million.[161] More realistically, Karl Von Holdt put the figure at R30 billion, adding that 'Human resource management is hopeless now. We have thousands of supervisors but no supervision.'[162]

Despite this, in 2003 Spoornet landed a $5 billion contract to rehabilitate the entire Zambian railway system. By end 2004 the giant project had ground to a standstill with little done and Zambia's railways continued to deteriorate. Two top Spoornet officials, Ravi Nair and Harry Mashele, were suspended to face charges over alleged mismanagement and reckless conduct relating to the Zambian project. Spoornet had contracted not only to upgrade the entire Zambian network – lines, rolling stock and all – but to operate it for twenty years ahead. As one Spoornet official admitted, this was preposterous: 'Spoornet does not have the capacity to fulfil its obligations in the Zambia concession. Spoornet has a big task here at home. It just won't be able to do the job in Zambia.'[163] In fact by then the government had become rattled by

Spoornet's continual losses and a plan to privatize the system, with huge job losses, was narrowly headed off by union pressure.

Bongani Khumalo, appointed chairman of Transnet in 2001, had clearly been influenced by his experience in the Presidential office. His first step was to set up an Office of Protocol to organize his trips around the Transnet empire, with advance teams sent out to decide such questions as where his car would be parked, which restaurants he would eat at, which hotels he would stay at, which lifts he would use and whose hands he would shake. When Transnet lost R6.3 billion in 2003–4, and the shaken government appointed Maria Ramos to clean house, she was horrified to find that Khumalo's office alone absorbed R30 million a year and that Transnet – a mere holding company which ran nothing itself – cost R600 million a year. Every Transnet employee, including each cleaner and receptionist, cost R800,000 a year.[164]

Zandile Javakula, appointed as Spoornet's CEO in 2000, was a former president of the Methodist Church, who opened meetings with prayers and frequently quoted the Bible. He had some experience of rail management but his consuming passion was 'the transformation of the workforce', a strange priority for an organization in such trouble. However in 2002 Javakula was suspended when it emerged that he had acquired a railway house on the upmarket Port Alfred waterfront overlooking the Kowie River for a pittance and then spent large sums of Spoornet money on renovating it.

The case followed the suspension of two executive directors of Spoornet on charges of misconduct and it emerged that Spoornet's head of asset protection, Chain Vilakazi, had assisted Javakula in his irregular house purchase. Javakula refused to admit that he had done anything wrong and tremendous pressure was brought to bear on the board. Javakula, a leading ANC member, lobbied presidential spokesman Smuts Ngonyama while representatives of the Black Management Forum, assisted by leading politicians, lobbied the Transnet board, claiming that the 'loss' of Javakula would threaten the transformation programme. Methodist Bishop Mvume Dandala also lobbied for Javakula, vouching for his integrity, an act which, according to *City Press*, 'raised eyebrows in professional circles'.[165] Ultimately both Javakula and Vilakazi had to go.

Javakula was succeeded by two youngish women, first Tshidi Nyama as acting CEO (later fired for corruption) and then, in 2003, by Dolly

Mokgatle. It is doubtful if any other major rail system would have hired Mokgatle as its boss. A human rights lawyer, she had worked for an NGO, been active in the Black Lawyers' Association, and then headed Eskom's Transmission Group. The PR handouts trumpeted the fact that she was not only the first woman but the first person with no technical background to hold her post. Similarly, she had no experience of transport or rail management before taking on the Spoornet job. She announced that her priority would be to recruit more young black women with technical and engineering qualifications (an almost non-existent category) and that her philosophy was 'Cast away the shackles of self-doubt and charge on ahead'.[166] She estimated that it would take her five years to put Spoornet 'well on the track to global stature'.[167] Mokgatle clashed bitterly with the company's (often white) engineers and technocrats and had to walk the plank after just eighteen months, swept away by Ramos. She went on to become a BEE millionaire with De Beers, just as Javakula also had a prosperous BEE rebirth, making much of his money through supply contracts to Spoornet.

As the commodity boom began the mining companies complained that Spoornet's lack of capacity meant they were unable to fulfil many foreign orders: the railways' dilapidated state was costing the country dear in lost exports. Even more serious was the drought of 2002 which led Grain SA to seek an emergency meeting with President Mbeki. Facing a situation comparable to that of the early 1980s when the El Niño droughts led South Africa to import more than 4 million tonnes of maize a year, supplying the food by train all over central and southern Africa, Grain SA's chairman, Bully Bothma, said the difference now was that 'we are very concerned about the infrastructure of Spoornet. You could have ships in [Durban] harbour with food and people in Johannesburg starving.'[168] Everything depended on rain in the next few weeks, for the rail network had nothing like the capacity in 2002 that it had had in 1982. Luckily, it rained.

In 2004 Highveld Steel, a major exporter, announced that it had lost all confidence in Spoornet's ability to get its products from Johannesburg to Durban and would henceforth truck its goods to Maputo and export through Mozambique. This came after repeated promises of improvement by Spoornet and President Mbeki's announcement of a R100 billion upgrade of the transport infrastructure. Already Columbus Steel had taken the Maputo route and Fiat, Ford and BMW were all considering switching to it. This meant a major loss of revenues not only for Spoornet but the ports. The cement manufacturers and the SA Grains Council also complained bitterly about Spoornet's service.[169]

Highveld's announcement triggered a fresh avalanche of complaints about the inability to cope of both the railways and ports. Moreover, although it was already cheaper to export through Maputo, Spoornet had just announced 40 per cent tariff increases. Con Fauconnier, the CEO of Kumba Resources and president of the Chamber of Mines, warned that South Africa was losing out in iron ore exports to China because its rivals in Australia, Brazil and elsewhere were able to export their ore and Kumba was not.[170] Kumba was missing out on R3 billion of exports a year due to Spoornet's incapacity. The Chamber of Mines listed 'substantial capital deficits in both ports and railways which, combined with poor services and excessive price increases, are severely undermining the ability of the mining sector to grow trade and exports', while Fauconnier said the Chinese had made it clear to him that they would like to double their iron ore imports from South Africa, but, due to the rail and port situation, they could not. As a result, South Africa was suffering a massive loss of exports and foreign exchange earnings.[171] Coal exports in 2004 were actually less than in 2002, despite booming demand and record coal prices: the coal terminals in Richard's Bay handled 3.7 million tonnes less than the year before.[172] Kumba, in desperation, ultimately agreed that it would itself help purchase sixty-nine new trains, fund improvements in infrastructure and upgrade railway yards.

Freight followed passengers in deserting rail for the roads. Whereas in 1990 63 per cent of freight went by road, by 2003 75 per cent did and by 2004 82 per cent. Meanwhile a third of Spoornet's 28,000 kilometres of lines lay unused.[173] The mining companies shipping coal to Richard's Bay continued to complain of cancelled trains and shortages of wagons – indeed in 2006 the amount of coal transported there fell by 7.8 per cent from the previous year.[174] 'We have a lot of locomotives that are sick at the moment,' admitted Spoornet's new CEO, Siyabonga Gama.[175] Mittal Steel aimed to increase its production from 7 to 9 million tonnes a year – but found Spoornet could not cope if it did. An official report on National Freight Logistics spoke of a complete lack of integrated planning, big information gaps, large skills shortages and the 'total absence' of the maintenance of railway track and embankments, many of which were eroding. Minister Radebe, quoting from the report, spoke of the 'disturbing' number of rail freight accidents: in 2002–4 alone there had been 418 leaking tankers, 117 derailed tankers, 661 incidents of 'decanting' and 53 spillages.[176]

Spoornet's deterioration created a spirit of desperation among its remaining passengers – mainly Africans who had no other choice of transport. Besides trains that did not come, there were trains that stopped and disgorged their passengers in the middle of nowhere and trains packed too tightly for people to breathe. Commuters in big cities dependent on Metrorail (as it was known) risked losing their jobs because the trains did not come, and bitterly complained how, under apartheid, replacement buses were provided in such circumstances. Station loudspeakers played jingles boasting of Metrorail's merits while the trains got fewer, shorter and dirtier. In February 2001, 6,000 commuters, maddened by the non-arrival of trains, burnt down Pretoria's main station.[177] Jackie Selebi, the Police Commissioner, chose this moment to slash the number of railway police, sending rail crime soaring. Inevitably, people avoided trains. Those assaulted and robbed often sued Metrorail.[178] Nothing was done.

On 14 September 2005 black commuters boarded a train in Daveyton, near Johannesburg, waiting patiently as the train stayed rooted in the station while engineers tried to fix an overhead power line to allow the train to move. After ninety minutes, the furious commuters burnt down the train. In the next fortnight angry Gauteng commuters burnt another five trains.[179] Despite promises of safe and efficient commuter transport for the 2010 football World Cup, nothing changed. In 2006 Metrorail's managers admitted that the system was on a 'knife-edge', that on average trains were thirty years old, that they were always breaking down, that passenger levels were still falling steeply and that of 4,600 Metrorail coaches only 3,200 were serviceable.[180]

Spoornet had divided its passenger services into three: Metrorail, Shosholoza Meyl (long-distance) and the five-star luxury Blue Train. But passenger trains were becoming increasingly overloaded and unsafe. And as 'unroadworthy' trains were withdrawn from service staff were 'forced by supervisors to certify train sets which they were not prepared to declare roadworthy'.[181] The (independent) Railway Safety Regulator reported 1,583 derailments and collisions in 2002–3 and 1,897 in the following year.[182] In 2003–4 there were 171 accidents at level crossings and 455 incidents of people struck by trains.[183]

In October 2005 Louis Kriel, the driver of a Shosholoza Meyl train, saw a Blue Train parked right across his line. Knowing that a collision was inevitable, he fought desperately to bring his train's speed down from 80 to 50 k.p.h. before grasping his deputy and diving for the back of the engine with the words 'Hier kom kak!' ('Here comes shit!'). Thanks to Kriel's prompt action, no one died: he fully deserved his hero's reception. But his words went echoing down the line. When one asked experienced railwaymen of the prospects ahead one often received the reply, 'Hier kom kak!'

Despite the hated symbolism of having to revert to white management, the government brought in Maria Ramos to sort out this mess. She was horrified by what she found and informed Mbeki that either Transnet and its management had to be completely overhauled or the whole organization would die. 'This is an organization that for many years had learnt to sweep all of the problems under every mat that was available. Nobody ever spoke about the problems until they became a crisis,' she said, adding that 'there were very many executives that would not last a year'. Asked, after three years, how many she had had to sack she said, 'I've lost count. It's quite a few people.'[184] Some of those sacked tried to play the race card and suggest that she had some sort of animus against black managers but, crucially, Ramos was an ANC activist and the partner of Trevor Manuel, the Finance Minister.

Ramos's appointment spelt the end of the imperial hopes of South Africa's railways binding the continent together, but grandiloquence was not easily quelled. Its next incarnation was the Gautrain and a proposed new high-speed link between Durban and Johannesburg. The government also spent billions on building a new port complex at Coega, based entirely on a political demand for jobs rather than any economic rationale for a new port in the Eastern Cape, and agreed, at enormous cost, to replace Durban's perfectly good airport with the new King Shaka International. As the Gautrain's cost estimate escalated from R7 billion to over R20 billion, Jeremy Cronin, who chaired Parliament's transport committee, pointed out that these were all 'vanity projects – nice-to-haves but do we need them?' Cronin argued that the same sums could be more profitably spent improving rail commuter services so that people did not burn down trains and so that Spoornet could attract custom back from the roads.[185]

But Cronin's was a lonely voice. Despite further cost escalation the

Gautrain sailed through cabinet. Its (secret) shareholders included two cabinet ministers, Naledi Pandor and Noziviwe Mapisa-Nqakula, as well as the Speaker, Baleka Mbete, and Nozizwe Madlala-Routledge (then deputy Health Minister). Other beneficiaries included Tokyo Sexwale, Mavivi Myakayaka-Manzini (ANC head of international affairs), Wiseman Nkhulu (Mbeki's former economic adviser), the prominent businesswoman, Danisa Baloyi, Bheki Sibiya, head of Business Unity SA, and other glitterati.[186]

It was far from clear that Ramos could succeed when such consortia could write their own transport policy and railroad it through cabinet. Nor could she undo the damage done by affirmative action: the demoralization of skilled staff and the loss of experience, expertise and institutional memory. The Railway Safety Regulator reported that in 2006 there had been 2,847 incidents of theft, murder, mugging, vandalism and assault on trains and also 2,950 train collisions or derailments, due mainly to human error as skilled staff were replaced by the less skilled.[187] If one reflects on a rail system having, every day of the year, eight derailments or collisions and the same number of major security incidents, one grasps something of the task Ramos faced.

Agrarian African states have experienced infrastructural decay, power cuts and the decline of public health facilities but it is an awesome sight to see what African nationalism can do to a developed modern economy; at times it feels like watching the *Titanic* go down. Yet it is a different experience. The usual reasons for such decay – lack of money and expertise – did not apply in South Africa. All this occurred while the economy was growing steadily and fast, when there was low debt and budget surpluses; when there was lots of money. And in 1994 the country had far more skills and expertise available than most developing countries can dream of. The new regime needed to hang on tight to its skilled manpower, use it to help train and expand the skills pool, while exploiting the worldwide goodwill towards the new South Africa to acquire whatever fresh help it could. This would have represented no threat to the black elite, whose predominance is guaranteed in perpetuity simply by demography. The saddest words are always 'it might have been'.

LOCAL GOVERNMENT: POWER TO THE PEOPLE

During the constitutional negotiations of the early 1990s I talked with Peter Mansfield, who had for many years effectively run Durban. 'Everyone's too fixated on the question of national power,' he said. 'But that's a foregone conclusion. They're paying no attention to local government, yet what actually determines the quality of life is whether people have adequate water, electricity, sewerage, garbage collection, hospitals, roads and schools – all local competences. And development projects only work if you can get local government to participate in them.'[188] He pointed out that the reshaping of local government to overcome old apartheid divisions would present many difficult problems, requiring much thought and finesse if things were going to work.

Yet local government boundaries were recast in a bold, almost cavalier way. The ten bantustans were reintegrated into South Africa, their capitals and administrations dismantled. The four provinces were divided into nine and 843 municipalities were reduced to 284. The promise now was 'power to the people' but this reorganization meant that most people experienced the process as one in which power went away from them, in which, indeed, they had been abandoned. In 1999 the Helen Suzman Foundation carried out a study on the growing crisis over the non-payment of rents, rates and service charges.[189] It was obvious that everything worked best where well-run old white municipalities, with competent staff and working systems, had incorporated surrounding black areas, stretching their staff and systems to cope. The next year all these were abolished in the cause of reform.

THE EASTERN CAPE AND THE XHOSA NOSTRA

The new boundaries took little account of practicality. The new province of Eastern Cape, for example, was formed by separating off the eastern fraction of the Cape, adding the two 'independent' homelands of Ciskei and Transkei, but leaving one piece of KwaZulu-Natal marooned inside

Eastern Cape as well as a piece of Eastern Cape marooned inside KwaZulu-Natal. The capital of the new province was neither the biggest city (Port Elizabeth) nor the biggest African town (Mthatha) but Bisho, an artificial bantustan town. Bisho boasted a well-staffed international airport at which no planes ever landed. Its bantustan rulers had, madly, bought Elvis Presley's old Boeing 707 when the singer died, proclaiming it to be the foundation plane of Ciskei Airways. Presley, growing fat and depressed, had used the plane most evenings to fly around America watching *Monty Python* videos. His old plane flew into Bisho on one engine and sat morosely on the tarmac for over a year, dreaming of rock concerts and orgies past while the strife and drama of the new South Africa flowed past it, before flying off, still on one engine, to be scrapped.

The ruling ANC elite was essentially Xhosa with its roots in the Eastern Province, and it was the ANC heartland. At ANC conferences the number of Eastern Cape delegates outnumbered those from any other province. Mandela had a holiday home back in his native village, Qunu, and many other ANC leaders, including Mbeki, streamed back to the province at election time to campaign among the home folks. It was no accident that the motor industry development programme, the great protectionist exception to South Africa's trade liberalization, benefited Eastern Cape's car factories, nor that the vast Coega port complex was there too. But all such development was at the coast. This was no answer to the unthinking abolition of decentralization incentives in 1994 which had killed off tens of thousands of jobs in the Transkei and Ciskei. Towns like Butterworth (which alone lost 30,000 jobs as factories closed down) virtually fell to pieces, with pavements crumbling, sewerage and electricity breakdowns and rubbish uncollected.

The Eastern Cape was, indeed, a complete mess. Its politics were faction-driven, with the old fault lines between the two bantustans and the rest never forgotten. Any provincial premier was invariably opposed by other factions in a continuous running battle. The first premier, Raymond Mhlaba, was clearly way past the age when he could have managed such a difficult province. As the foul-ups proliferated, Mandela was persuaded to pension Mhlaba off as ambassador to Uganda, a post he mainly slept through. His replacement, the Revd Makhenkesi Stofile, was known as Bra Stoff ('brother Stoff'). The local press continued to reveal that the foul-ups had in no way lessened under his rule, leading him to engage in tirades against the media of such violence as to belie his status as a man of the cloth. This in turn caused him to be universally known as Brassed Off.

The government watched nervously, aware that this was a province *pas comme les autres*. Despite the province's desperate poverty some departments routinely underspent through sheer lack of capacity and huge amounts vanished in corruption. There were thousands of 'ghost' employees in the public service, with salaries and pensions paid to fictional people. The Eastern Cape was also notoriously deficient at paying pensions, a matter of great import. One of the most beneficial social reforms the ANC carried out was to equalize all state pensions up to the old white level – for pensions, like everything else, had been disgracefully discriminatory – which meant a large increase in African pensions. Typically, the resulting income stream fed into households where it sustained many people other than the pensioner. A failure to pay pensions on time caused real distress, even starvation.

The national departments of Health and Education simultaneously signalled that the Eastern Cape's hospitals and schools were on the point of collapse. The government repeatedly dispatched high-power teams to help prevent the worst but as soon as they left the situation would deteriorate again, sometimes to an even lower level. In 1998 the government invoked Section 100 of the Constitution, enabling it to assume direct control, and the Finance Department ordered the Eastern Cape treasury to take control of the finances of all provincial departments. This provided temporary relief but the Auditor-General later reported that 79 per cent of all the province's budgets between 1996 and 2004 could not be accounted for. Not a single resolution passed by the province's financial oversight authority, the standing committee on public accounts, had been implemented during the entire period 1995–2002.[190]

Controversy surrounded the education department and the provincial health minister, Bevan Goqwana. Goqwana, contrary to the law, continued to run a private medical practice and a private ambulance service while serving as a provincial minister, but Stofile, who was determined to protect him, insisted all this had been known when he was appointed. When Goqwana was accused of defrauding a medical aid scheme, Stofile responded by giving him special leave on full pay until the charges were dropped.[191]

In October 2000 Modidima Mannya was appointed superintendent-general of education with a mandate to clean up the department's chaotic corruption. Finding a 'free for all', with scams in every direction, he suspended ten senior managers who immediately sought help from politicians (and in one case from Stofile's wife). 'Almost everyone you touch is connected,' he lamented. 'People are afraid to talk.'[192] He quickly received multiple death threats and sought police protection. When, mysteriously, this protection was withdrawn, he resigned in fear of his life – after just three months in post. Stofile then publicly attacked Mannya for mismanagement and lack of qualifications. When Mannya sued, Stofile settled out of court.

Stofile's acquiescence in his administration's chaotic state was clear, to the despair of the Auditor-General, who repeatedly singled out the province's housing, health and education departments as being out of control. Any progress at all was largely the result of hiring outside consultants: the Eastern Cape spent R3 billion on consultants in 2002–4, fifteen times what it spent on training its own staff.[193] At the same time the auditors reported that only two out of more than forty municipalities in the province had received unqualified audit reports while a significant number had simply not had their accounts audited at all for eight years and more.[194] The situation was clearly teetering on the edge of chaos.

This raised the question of a wholesale takeover of the Eastern Cape administration, but the Public Service Minister, Geraldine Fraser-Moleketi, insisted that 'We don't want to reach that state'.[195] Yet the administration was weak at every point. Nceba Faku, mayor of the province's biggest city, Port Elizabeth (aka Nelson Mandela Metropole), was chosen by the DA in 2002 – in the face of hot competition – as 'the worst mayor in South Africa'.[196] Stofile, for his part, announced years in advance that he was resigning as premier in 2004.

Stofile's announcement was followed by the resignation for 'personal reasons' of the provincial minister for education, Stone Sizani, who was the deputy chair of the provincial ANC and the chair of Nelson Mandela Metropole. The local press had been full of corruption allegations against Sizani, after a leak of the Auditor-General's (highly critical) report.[197] Education was indeed a disaster area. When Anthony Sampson's authorized biography of Mandela appeared one of its more embarrassing asides was that all the educational institutions which had nourished Mandela had since collapsed. A Mandela could be produced in colonial times, but no longer.

Normally party oligarchs like Stofile and Sizani did not give up their positions while they still breathed: it was a sign of trouble to come. Sure enough, the national ANC then pounced, annulling the provincial ANC's conference and elections on grounds of fraud. Partly this was because Mbeki, now locked in a struggle with Jacob Zuma, was alarmed at the left's growth in the province, clear Zuma fodder, but also because, for the sixth consecutive year, the provincial administration had failed to account for a majority of its budget. So an Interim Management Team (IMT) was sent to take over the province and probe corruption. Its work soon led to 286 cases of theft and fraud, over half of them involving the dismissal of corrupt officials.[198]

Reporting five months later, Fraser-Moleketi spoke of how the IMT had found the province 'in a shambles'.[199] The IMT's own report detailed a long list: corruption, inefficiency of every kind, a high vacancy rate in key posts, the failure to pay salaries and pensions and an education department which did not even know how many employees it had. Stofile, annoyed, termed Fraser-Moleketi's observations 'unscientific' – but insisted that he had known all the report's findings well before the IMT had been commissioned.[200] Stofile then quit the premiership and joined the cabinet, Mbeki unexpectedly replacing him as premier with Nosimo Balindlela, a previous provincial education minister sacked by Stofile. Stofile became Minister of Sport – almost all sports were run by figures from the Eastern Cape: Stofile's brother Mike was deputy head of the South African Rugby Union.

Balindlela immediately asked for another IMT. This would mean accepting that the province was incapable of self-government so instead a government team was sent merely to sort out the notorious education department. The department had just overspent by R600 million, had 60 per cent of its management posts vacant and still could not say how many staff it employed. This last problem had maddened central government but two previous teams set up to ascertain the correct number of personnel had both failed.

Ms Balindlela started off as a vigorous new broom, sacking high officials and bringing in two 'old regime' whites to run finance, economics and tourism. But she was up against a deeply ingrained culture of corruption; one survey showed that over half the province's civil servants believed that the acceptance of gifts in return for their services should not be punishable.[201] Balindlela's sacking of the finance minister, Enoch Godongwana, a powerful ANC and trade union figure, led to accusations that she was trying to purge the province of followers of Stofile (who remained the province's ANC chairman). So bitter were party divisions that the ANC secretary-general, Kgalema Motlanthe – and Stofile – came running to the province, concerned by this political instability in the party's heartland.

Balindlela soon found herself aligned with the minority faction around Mluleki George, ranged against Stofile's dominant faction. Balindlela was, in these terms, a lightweight and was regarded as part of Mbeki's plan to de-fang the province's pro-Zuma left; indeed, her opponents saw her as being remote-controlled by Mbeki and ANC headquarters in Luthuli House.

Stofile, a natural representative of the dominant interests within the local ANC coalition – chiefs, peasants, civil servants and trade unionists – had been content to let sleeping dogs lie, accepting corruption and mismanagement as the norm. Godongwana, while at finance, had taken a similar hands-off attitude, for he and Stofile both understood that to attack these things meant attacking the whole structure and culture of government in the province. When Balindlela began to attack this – firing Bevan Goqwana in April 2006 – it was easy enough for her opponents to surface corruption allegations against her supporters such as the provincial agriculture minister, Max Mamase, and his wife, Neo Moerane, the provincial social development minister. The premier was soon reduced to making bold speeches and doing nothing. She had effectively been defeated by the system – which went on much as before.

THE SPOLIATION OF LOCAL POWER

The reorganization of local government into 284 councils set the scene for the explosion to come. It was a fatal error, with the new boundaries drawn by an ANC ideologue, Mike Sutcliffe, with little regard for practicality and institutional continuity. Only in the larger cities were the new councils built around the skeleton of the more efficient white-run municipalities of old. Everywhere there was a mounting problem of unpaid rents, rates and service charges. By 2003 R36 billion was owed in arrears, an amount rising at 13 per cent a year. The ANC's response to this situation was agitprop – a mass mobilization campaign of astonishing naivety called 'Masakhane', attempting to encourage people to pay rates when in fact they could get away with not doing so. Inevitably, this failed. The instinctive assumption at grass roots was that (central) government must provide. Any shortfall in local rates or service charges should be picked up by the central Treasury with the money found out of general taxation. Local people, habituated by years of anti-apartheid rent boycotts, felt they could not and would not pay – indeed, they frequently made illegal connections to obtain free water, electricity and telephone services and huge amounts of copper wire and piping were stolen as fair game.

Inside the new councils a not dissimilar kind of pillage was going on. The new councillors awarded themselves large allowances, while the new managers and executives took unheard-of salaries. White engineers, surveyors and other specialists were 'transformed' out of their jobs, some of which went to the new rulers' friends and relatives, while others just stood vacant. The result was a dramatic loss of municipal capacity, soaring personnel costs and shrunken capital budgets. Thus the new councils became part of the spoils system, a set of enviably paid positions with little ability to deliver services of any kind to the voters. This was facilitated by the ANC decision to allow rule by their own one-party mayoral committees. Opposition councillors found themselves excluded as the mayoral committees met in secret, publishing no agendas or minutes, and often reporting decisions only months later. Inevitably this led to massive corruption in tenders and procurement. When the ANC took over Cape Town and ran the city thus, scandals of every kind proliferated.

It was a dramatic case. The Cape Town ANC had its base in a population of recent peasant migrants from the Eastern Cape and its style of governance, now applied to South Africa's mother city, was much the same as that which looted Eastern Cape country towns like Idutywa and Butterworth. The spectacle was staggering. Engineers, planners and municipal experts of every kind were dispatched in droves; the mayor's brother was made deputy head of police; tenders often went to the third- or fourth-highest bidder; procurement contracts went to clearly incompetent firms linked to ANC councillors; and the fire service suffered such cuts that it came close to mutiny. Collection of the city's traffic fines was handed to a BEE company which simply left hundreds of thousands of warrants and fines to pile up till they became invalid, costing the city millions.[202] Such abuses gained little publicity when applied to country towns in the Eastern Cape but in Cape Town they occurred in a glare of publicity, with many residents regarding the council in much the same light as Romans watching the Vandals sack Rome. They were spared the worst largely because the mayor, Nomaindia Mfeketo, refused to restrain her spokesman, Blackman Ngoro, who repeatedly hurled racist insults at Coloureds. Many previously ANC-aligned Coloureds helped vote out the ANC council in 2006.

Warning signs were seen first in 2002 in the Free State, with Bethlehem municipality reportedly on the verge of breakdown as a result of corruption.[203] But the real impact of municipal collapse was felt only from 2004 on as protests began to flare in numerous Free State towns against the non-delivery of services of every kind. Black people who had voted repeatedly for 'A Better Life For All', the recurrent ANC slogan, found their services as bad as ever and their schools and hospitals worse. Protests took the classic form of 1980s township unrest with burning tyres, toyi-toying youth and skirmishes with police who were as rough as ever; one protestor in Ntabazwe, near Harrismith, was killed. Unsurprisingly, there were problems over audit reports in all twenty-five Free State municipalities.[204]

In Mangaung, the biggest municipality (including Bloemfontein), the mayor, his wife, his political adviser, the chief operating officer and the city manager were all arrested in July 2005, accused of massive peculation, fraud and corruption.[205] Within a few months they were back in the saddle, ready for the elections, after which they again fell foul of the law. Thereafter the nearby municipality of Matjhabeng (including Welkom and Odendaalrus) suffered major riots over corruption, mismanagement and poor delivery. Several top officials were under police investigation.[206] The protests spread: within a year there had been protests in fifty towns or cities. Of the 284 municipalities 203 were unable to provide sanitation for 40 per cent or more of their residents. A quarter of all towns had no refuse removal and in 201 towns most people did not have flushable toilets. Residents in over half the municipalities lacked piped water.[207] Such people, who were often jobless, could hear every day of the country's headlong economic growth and the luxury expenditure of the new BEE millionaires. Meanwhile, the mayoral committee system ensured that neither voters nor opposition parties could restrain the new municipal elites, who treated local power as a simple means of self-enrichment.

This situation not only killed off the Masakhane campaign but caused non-payment levels to rise, bankrupting many municipalities. Even in the previously best run cities like Durban, debt soared into the billions, at which point it became politically uncollectable. To the Auditor-General's indignation, there was a widespread timidity over trying to collect debts, with many towns leaving debts uncollected for two to three hundred days.[208] One area which experienced no economy was the salaries of municipal managers, many of whom had higher salaries than the President, plus lavish 'performance bonuses' which, in a situation of chronic underperformance, were simply inflammatory. The highest paid manager of all, with a basic salary of more than R1.2 million in 2004–5 (Mbeki got R1.05 million), was in Ehlanzeni, Mpumalanga, where 73 per cent of residents had no refuse removal, nearly 60 per cent no sanitation and a third no access to water.[209]

The government said municipalities should aim at personnel costs not exceeding 30 per cent of their budgets but sometimes these costs escalated to 50–60 per cent. In Port St John's, one of the country's poorest municipalities, 46 per cent of the budget was spent on salaries, 0.2 per cent on capital expenditure. In Ntambanana (KwaZulu-Natal), 62 per cent was spent on salaries and just 20 cents a head on delivery.[210] Many of the municipal managers lacked any formal qualifications or expertise.[211] Seventy-four of the biggest municipalities lacked a single qualified civil engineer, while 36 per cent of all municipal managers had no tertiary qualifications.[212]

Ten years into liberation the ANC government thus found itself putting down township protest in much the same way as its apartheid predecessors. So in 2004 it launched Project Consolidate, deploying teams to 136 municipalities to assist with governance, service delivery, infrastructure development – in a word, everything. The situation was worst in the forty-seven rural district councils, of which forty-three qualified for the Project. Taking all provincial and local government together, 61 per cent of senior management positions were vacant.[213] Yet in all the towns assisted by the Project – which were, by definition, not coping – 67 per cent of municipal managers received large performance bonuses.[214] The Project sought to remedy some of the shortfalls by employing 'retired, skilled professionals who were lost during the downsizing of government'.[215] That is to say, the Project was in good part a matter of bringing back the expertise of senior white staff who should never have been got rid of in the first place. But the same process had happened throughout the civil service: overall, the Auditor-General found that only 8 per cent of government workers were highly skilled and 90 per cent were unskilled or low-skilled.[216]

No government reform went more catastrophically wrong than the reshaping of local government: within three years it had caused municipal collapse and rioting in the streets. Mike Sutcliffe, the man most responsible for the disaster, became city manager of Durban where his administration of what had been the country's best run city soon produced a decaying municipal infrastructure amidst growing local rancour. Sadly, the fears Peter Mansfield had earlier expressed to me had been entirely borne out. Problems requiring great finesse and a concern for institutional continuity had been subjected instead to a cutting-the-Gordian-knot approach. The result was complete disaster.

It had been an object lesson in retaining institutions that worked and insisting on democratic accountability. Predictably, Mbeki drew the opposite conclusion and sought even more radical centralization. The SA Local Government Association (Salga) was asked to play a stronger role. Salga was, like Sanco and Sangoco,[217] an ANC front organization of dubious *raison d'être*, but it was in any case plagued by the same problems as the municipalities themselves: corruption, sky-high salaries, audit problems and 'absolute anarchy' within its management and administration.[218] With Salga ineffective, Mbeki took direct action. Henceforth the President would appoint the executive mayors of the major cities and also choose their entire management team. Most remarkable, the President would only name the new mayors *after* the 2006 municipal elections. Voters were thus asked to vote a blank cheque, not knowing who their mayor would be if they voted ANC.

Unsurprisingly, the President's nominated mayors were much disputed, particularly in the Eastern Cape. Mbeki threatened that even individual councillors who did not toe the line might be struck down by central fiat. It was the old Leninist logic. The masses were there to be 'mobilized' and led by the vanguard. Mayors, managers and councillors were responsible upwards to the President, not downwards to the voters. Naturally, these further changes solved nothing: the uncollectable municipal debt got larger and Project Consolidate produced no permanent improvement in service delivery. It had been intended to last two years but at the end of that time not one of the 139 municipalities thus assisted had graduated to self-sufficiency, so, perforce, the government had to extend the programme indefinitely.[219] Protests against the failure of service delivery continued to proliferate across the country.

A STRANGE FORM OF LIBERATION

The co-existence of a crippled state with a private sector driving the country along at growth rates around 5 per cent is pregnant with social and political significance. Government ministers repeatedly insisted that 'business must help', for it was obvious that business could get things done while government could not. Not that this prevented government from adopting extremely ambitious programmes, but typically such legislation gave government large though passive powers – to supervise, monitor, license or control, though even such functions easily strained government's very limited abilities. All actual doing was left to others. 'For every action', the saying went, 'there is an equal and opposite government programme.'

At the same time that these failures of infrastructural management were emerging Mbeki convinced the whole ANC, including the Zuma-ite left, that the way ahead lay through 'the developmental state', that is, that the state would lead development via vast infrastructural investment. Yet the state had completely neglected the magnificent infrastructure it had inherited; it had caused a prodigious loss of skills by its affirmative action policies; and it was in no position either to manage a large investment programme or maintain whatever was built. The state's back had been broken. It consisted of large, incapable, sullen and de-skilled bureaucracies, full of empty promise, racial grievance and a sharp eye for commercial advantage. In effect, the ANC had re-created on a national scale the nightmarish bureaucracies of the old bantustans. Anyone who believed they might become the backbone of a developmental state had simply not been paying attention.

The asymmetrical relationship between the (overwhelmingly black) broken-backed state and the reasonably efficient (and mainly white-led) private sector was also a metaphor of South Africa's disabled sense of nationhood. Mbeki clearly did not think in terms of a single South African nation at all; his speech was littered with references to 'our people', just as Afrikaner nationalists had spoken of '*ons volk*'. This is partly why such moments as Mandela's donning the captain's No. 5 rugby shirt for the 1995 rugby World Cup are still so treasured: they are the rare glimpses of what might have been and what might be, a single South African nation.

But the problem goes deeper. Mbeki and the ANC have encouraged African dependence on the state. The state is not only there to provide blacks with welfare benefits and public sector jobs but to make up any shortfall in local government, to abolish poverty, to carry out land reform, to redistribute wealth and income – and to bully white companies into giving blacks affirmative action jobs, more jobs in general and BEE deals to the fortunate. And ANC ministers insist that affirmative action is not a temporary remedy but a permanent fixture.

As John Kane-Berman, director of the South African Institute of Race Relations, has pointed out, this 'means that the current generation of white school goers is in effect being told to prepare for a life of entrepreneurship – or emigration – while their black counterparts are being told to prepare for a life in which the government can be relied on to make whites do things for them, a life in which failure can always be blamed on someone else'.[220] The fixation with granting blacks a share in existing white-built companies or in taking over successful commercial farms run by whites, rather than in developing black entrepreneurs or peasant farmers, says the same thing: the whites are there to achieve, to build successful enterprises and the best that can be done for blacks is to force whites to share what they have built or even hand it over completely. The assumption is, at bottom, that whites will always be there; that they can do things that blacks cannot; but that blacks are nonetheless entitled to a share in the results. Perversely, in all public debate it is assumed that there is no white achievement which is not wholly explicable by unfair privilege. Even if one instances what a Jan Smuts, Christiaan Barnard or J. M. Coetzee achieved, one is told that they owed it all to racial privilege, as if what they achieved was simply normal for any white.

Everywhere one sees the results: young whites, determined to stay in the country, battling to build careers against the tide, are forced to re-learn the Protestant ethic. There are plenty of white beggars, but they are a minority. Mainly, though, one sees white schoolteachers forced to take early retirement from public schools become market-savvy entrepreneurs; white ex-policemen run private security companies; and large numbers of ex-public servants become consultants. Some even make a good living by setting up or manning rating agencies devoted to measuring how far white companies have succeeded in making jobs and BEE deals available to blacks, how far they have outsourced their supplies to BEE companies and so on. All of this applies in only slightly lesser degree to Coloureds and Indians.

In a fashion which would astonish early American colonists, these minorities have long since given up imagining that their interests will receive much consideration but still take it for granted that they will, in corporate and personal taxes, pay the lion's share of the fiscus. That is, they have morosely accepted taxation without (much) representation. Indeed, there are many minorities-only taxes. In practice the state makes no serious attempt to collect rates, taxes, traffic fines or television licence fees from those who live in townships, remote rural areas or squatter camps: indeed, it turns a blind eye to the fact that enormous sums of money are being leeched out of the system by inhabitants of those areas who make illegal connections to the telephone, water and electricity networks. Their bad debts are allowed to mount into the multi-billions before being ultimately written off, that is, paid by those who pay the rest of the rates, charges and taxes anyway. Such exemptions do not apply to those of any race who live in regularly constituted urban and suburban areas.

For English-speaking whites this merely means the prolongation of the effective political impotence they suffered under Afrikaner nationalist rule. They are a key pilot group. They were accustomed by long experience under apartheid to a situation in which madmen were in charge of government, in which things were desperate but not serious and in which the clock always stood at five minutes to midnight. They paid this price with a grimace for living in a superb climate and relative comfort in one of the world's most beautiful countries. Now, against all expectations, this recessive group of internal exiles has become the model to which other whites (and some Indians and Coloureds) are fast assimilating, a role strikingly expressed through the opposition DA, in which numerically superior Afrikaans-speakers have accepted English-speaking (and even Jewish) leadership as the norm.

Thus, despite their diminishing numbers, the three racial minorities, and especially the whites, remain, to use the ANC's language, South Africa's 'motive force'. Without them not only commerce and industry but the fiscus, black employment and virtually all modern institutions would collapse. In effect the government assumes this will remain the position for ever and, to use an older turn of phrase, seeks merely to increase the white man's burden. Yet this cannot remain a viable strategy for long: the white population is ageing, emigration continues and the white proportion of the total population is shrinking rapidly: down to 9.6 per cent by 2007. But there is absolutely no sign of an alternative view: the government seems trapped by its racial blinkers, with whites still at the centre of its imagination.

There is no sense of assertive, independent-minded citizenship for blacks. There are black entrepreneurs of note, but most of the entrepreneurial success stories are still about whites. As Kane-Berman puts it: 'We are building an economy in which whites have to become more and more self-reliant, while blacks become ever more dependent on what government forces whites to do for them. That is a strange form of liberation.'[221] Indeed it is; it is a society in which not only will blacks always be able to fall back on the support of affirmative action but where they will always need to.

13
A Bridge Too Far: The Struggle with Zuma

In absolute monarchies the king often has great virtues, but the courtiers are invariably servile. Alexis de Tocqueville

States decree the most illustrious rewards, not to him who catches a thief, but to him who kills a tyrant. Aristotle

Jacob Zuma was not left in much doubt that the better educated among the ANC elite, particularly the predominant Xhosas, with Mbeki their crown prince, never had much regard for an uneducated Zulu like himself. Mandela's biographer, Anthony Sampson, who spent a great deal of time in the company of the former group, once surprised me by declaring, apropos his hostility to the IFP, that 'Zulus are so bloody stupid'. The stereotype is widespread.

Zuma was the son of a domestic servant and a policeman, his father dying when he was 3. Cast into utter penury, he tried to learn to read and write by questioning those children around him lucky enough to be in school. His mother moved from his native Nkandla, deep in northern Zululand, to Durban and Zuma himself became a kitchen boy, a polisher of floors and windows and later a factory worker. It was only in jail on Robben Island that he was taught by his fellow-prisoner, Harry Gwala, to read and write in English. Despite this, the irrepressible Zuma, always cheerful and quick to learn, and displaying the sort of physical courage he had been taught befitted a Zulu man, rose in exile to become chief of ANC intelligence. But, returning to South Africa, he was quickly stripped of his intelligence job and saw Terror Lekota – a southern Sotho – preferred over him to head the ANC in KwaZulu-Natal.

Yet within KwaZulu-Natal the ANC–IFP struggle was a Zulu civil war. The ANC's leader, the fearsome Harry Gwala, now the ANC warlord of the Midlands area, openly described himself as a Stalinist. Gwala, whose right arm was paralysed, was widely known as 'the one arm bandit'. A ruthless killer, he scythed down opponents not only within the IFP but, quite frequently, within the ANC. Gwala was determined to capture the ANC leadership in KwaZulu-Natal and even aimed for the national deputy leadership behind Mandela. The prospect alarmed ANC headquarters, which determined to head Gwala off.

Thus in the run-up to the 1994 election, Zuma was asked by the party leadership in Johannesburg to go and take over the ANC's northern region in KwaZulu-Natal, then run by a Gwala-ite. This was achieved thanks to a coup mounted by the local Cosatu unions – but not without a fight. I arrived in Empangeni shortly afterwards to find a local union leader's house riddled with AK-47 bullets, the work of Zuma's losing opponents within the ANC. (Later, the probable culprit was bought off with a lucrative job.) Thereafter Zuma gradually edged out Gwala and took over the whole of the KwaZulu-Natal ANC, though this inevitably meant that he had to survive Gwala's assassination attempts: hence the remarkable sight of Gwala being suspended from the SACP for attempted assassination although the police were not brave enough to tackle him on the subject. Luckily for Zuma, Gwala died of old age shortly thereafter. The IFP won the elections and formed a coalition government in the province, Zuma becoming a provincial minister for tourism and economic affairs.

Zuma, showing himself a moderate and conciliatory man, won Buthelezi's confidence and the two men successfully ended the bloody civil war which had waged for over a decade. Unusually for an ANC leader, Zuma was comfortable within the traditional Zulu world, joining with Buthelezi to celebrate Shaka Day, dressed in loincloth and leopard skins. For Nkandla is part of the same 'deep Zulu' world as Mhlabathini, Buthelezi's home. As boys, both men had listened to the same stirring stories of the Anglo-Zulu war related round the campfire by the descendants of Cetewayo's warriors. Zuma, a warm and charming man, also had considerable 'people skills' and despite the social gulf between Buthelezi, an educated Zulu prince, and Zuma, the barely literate poor boy, the two men got on well. This peace negotiation in KwaZulu-Natal was actually more difficult than the white–black constitutional negotiations (where success had been preordained) and brought Zuma back into national contention, for Mandela was deeply conscious of tribal tensions and the need to have a Zulu at or near the top.

Zuma discovered, however, that a secret report was circulating, detailing his dismal administrative record as provincial ANC chairman and the utter shambles of his provincial ministry. In addition the report, doubtless commissioned from intelligence sources by Mbeki, carried an analysis of Zuma's relationship with the Indian businessman Schabir Shaik.[1] Zuma fought hard and won the ANC deputy presidency, universally assumed to imply that he would become state Deputy President, only to see this post offered to Buthelezi in 1999, an offer the latter regretfully refused. Thus Zuma became Deputy President almost by default and with every indication of the disdain in which he was held by Mbeki and other educated ANC leaders. This humiliating impression was confirmed by the way that the Deputy President's office, which, under Mbeki, had really run the government, was now dismantled and transferred wholesale to the presidency. Zuma was left with fewer staff and less power than any cabinet minister. Mbeki had used the deputy presidency to establish himself as the likely President, but Zuma was to be given no such opportunity.

A seldom-voiced though crucial objection to Zuma among the ANC elite was that he was openly polygamous. All told, Zuma was credited with twenty children by nine different women. Feminist and conventional Christian opinion was affronted by such mores while educated black opinion was embarrassed by this open display of traditional African social behaviour which had become publicly unfashionable once the white missionaries hit their stride in the 1820s.

The problem was that polygamy never really ceased. Indeed, the continuation of polygamy – part of the fabric and even the definition of patriarchal, chiefly society – was a key stumbling block for Christianity and probably the most important reason for the foundation of independent African churches which, *inter alia*, tolerated polygamy. Informally polygamy continued even within orthodox Christian sects, while the Zulu King Zwelethini and the Swazi King Mswati III continued to display their ever-expanding harems. Thus the notion retained considerable cultural currency, so that Zuma (himself ordained as a priest in one of the independent churches) was actually much closer to the African norm than, for example, the monogamous Archbishop Desmond Tutu, one of Zuma's strongest critics. It was perfectly normal for African men to keep one wife in the countryside, another in town and quite possibly several other girlfriends as well. Typically, such men defaulted on child support but the dream was doubtless to emulate just what Zuma was doing.

The subject is clouded by hypocrisy. President Mbeki was often accused of being, in the words of one of his trade union critics, 'a legendary womanizer', and many of the black elite had complicated sexual and marital lives. When I talked to Zuma, he confirmed this picture. 'Many of them have wives, girlfriends and children that they try to hide. I think that's terrible. I love all my wives and children and I'm proud of them, so I'm completely open about it, that's the only difference.' This certainly seemed to be true: one often saw Zuma's children clustered around him, regarding him with great affection. But for polite society, both black and white, polygamy was Zuma's Achilles heel, at least in his role as a modern politician.

ENTER THE SHAIKS

The Shaiks, a prosperous Muslim merchant family, had been close to Jacob Zuma for many years. The Shaiks were one of Durban's leading 'struggle' clans, with all five of the sons (Schabir, Yunus, Chippy, Faizel and Mo) ANC members. Mo had become an MK intelligence agent, working under Zuma when, in 1985, Zuma asked him to hide an MK agent, Ebrahim Ebrahim. Ebrahim was smuggled out, with the Shaik family used as decoys, which brought the wrath of the security police down on the family. Yunus and Chippy were both detained and tortured and their father, Lambie Rasool, was arrested. Mo, detained in a Durban jail, managed to turn one of his Security Police inquisitors to become an MK informant, with great consequent advantage for the ANC. Ultimately Lambie died under the strain and the whole period was one of complete trauma for the family. Zuma was deeply sympathetic, bonding even more closely with them as a result.

When the ANC returned from exile it was, as Mo Shaik put it to me, a situation no one had planned for. 'What were our guys to do? No one was paying them. They could hardly go to De Klerk and say "You'll have to support us while we negotiate to take power away from you."

So everyone had to do the best they could. Jacob was an intimate family friend and we supported him because it was the natural thing to do. It never occurred to us that one day we would be reviled for our generosity.'[2] It doubtless seemed equally natural to the Shaiks to cash in when they could – and there is no doubt that Chippy did well out of being the Defence Ministry's chief of acquisitions on the arms deal.

But there was little prospect that Zuma could pay back the Shaiks, for the aftermath of the 1994 election found him right at the bottom of the heap: a provincial minister in an IFP-led government, marooned in Durban while all real power lay in Pretoria. When Zuma was fired as Deputy President in 2005 he said bitterly that 'I have been treated extremely unfairly throughout the entire debacle, for about half a decade',[3] and, as he made clear when I talked to him about it, he took particular umbrage at being tarred with the arms deal, for while Joe Modise, with Mbeki's help, had been tying up that deal in Pretoria, Zuma had actually been down in Durban discussing provincial tourism.

Politically, the key Shaik was Mo. An able man, he managed to combine his career in MK intelligence with becoming a university lecturer in optometry. After 1994 he also served in the Ministry of Foreign Affairs and as ambassador to Algeria before returning to Durban to run the family business. He was to become Zuma's key adviser, but more attention fastened on his flamboyant brother, Schabir. Schabir claimed to have played his part in the struggle by being the ANC's banker, bringing large sums of clandestine money into the country to assist the struggle – by the end more than R100 million a year.[4] When the ANC returned from exile Schabir nourished the relationship in every way, paying the provincial ANC's office rent, bankrolling payments to IFP defectors and paying for the provincial leaders' transport.[5]

Zuma's own finances were chaotic and Schabir was, from the outset, his 'godfather', in return getting Zuma to introduce him to the ANC treasurer-general, Tom Nkobi. Nkobi wanted to develop the ANC in classic African nationalist style, turning it into a sleeping partner of various commercial enterprises and making it a holding company with resources of its own. Schabir worked closely with Nkobi, doubtless aware that the Asian families who had helped run Zanu-PF's holding for Mugabe in Zimbabwe had become wealthy and politically influential.

What Schabir Shaik was attempting was nothing new. Throughout central, southern and eastern Africa one can find entrepreneurial Asian families who threw in their lot with anti-colonial movements and ended up as their bankers, managers and fixers – a role not unlike that once played on the European stage by the Rothschilds. There is no reason to doubt their genuine commitment to the parties they supported but they are merchants at heart who inevitably seek to turn their networks to commercial advantage. It was, indeed, part of the scene in KwaZulu-Natal where 90 per cent of South Africa's Indians live. ANC partisanship is positively correlated with wealth – richer Indians and whites are more prone to support the ANC than their poorer brethren – so the (richer) Muslim minority plays an inordinate role in ANC affairs there, though some prosperous Hindus play a role too.

The role has a long history. If, twenty years ago, you managed to talk to older Africans they would tell you resentfully of how when Chief Luthuli, the ANC leader in the 1950s, came to Durban, he would immediately be surrounded by J. N. Singh, Ismael Meer, Monty Naicker and a host of other Indians – doctors, lawyers and other professional men – all offering him help and hospitality, which, of course, he accepted, as did Mandela on his somewhat rarer trips. For they could offer pleasant houses, telephones, copying machines, legal advice, transport, loans and offshore banking facilities, things which no African could offer. And while their sympathy was entirely genuine – they truly hated apartheid – they needed no instruction in the thought that attachment to a powerful black political leader might one day bring tangible benefits in its wake.

Within South Africa, Durban is a separate and different world. The old 'white' city of Durban actually contained more than twice as many Indians as whites and yet this was also the natural urban hub for South Africa's biggest ethnic bloc, the Zulus. Under apartheid, the Natal Indian Congress was part of the Congress Alliance with the ANC, bringing an ANC Zulu leadership into a symbiotic relationship with an Indian elite which, though it was often communist, was rooted in a merchant and professional class. Over time the Indian community became steadily wealthier and more cosmopolitan. This was particularly true of the Muslim merchants at whose tables one would meet business contacts from the Gulf, Malaysia and elsewhere in the Muslim world. This meant that they had ever more to offer in their relationships with Zulu political leaders, including sophisticated money management through offshore accounts in Mauritius, the Channel Islands and elsewhere.

Schabir Shaik stood in the tradition of Indians who had worked with and helped Luthuli. Now Zuma was the leading Zulu figure in the ANC so naturally the same applied to him. It was by no means a dishonourable tradition: many Indians who had decided to back the Congress side had been banned, harried and persecuted under apartheid and, as we have seen, the Shaik family had its full share of suffering too. But Schabir was luckier than his forebears of the 1950s and 1960s, for he lived in an era where at last some of those chips could be cashed in.

Tom Nkobi, the ANC treasurer-general with whom Shaik teamed up, fitted well into this model. An Ndebele, born in Southern Rhodesia (today's Zimbabwe), Nkobi, like all Ndebeles, easily passed as a Zulu in South Africa. His father, a taxi boss, had sent his son to school in Natal, including to Adams Mission where Luthuli was the headmaster.[6] Within the ANC, Nkobi had been part of the Alexandra Township group with Joe Modise and had been party to all manner of crooked activities in exile. On his return to South Africa in 1990, Nkobi faced far greater financial opportunities – but the ANC was also enormously money-hungry. Despite the large sums of international money that Mandela raised the party soon found that setting up and running a national organization, maintaining its leadership and preparing for elections took more money than it had. Indeed, the 1994 elections left the party with a R40 million overdraft. Schabir Shaik quickly came up with a scheme to liquidate this, using his connections with Malaysian investors, particularly the Renong Group which had made a fortune out of privatizations in Kuala Lumpur.

The Malaysians wanted to invest in numerous businesses and, to oil the wheels, would secretly liquidate the ANC's overdraft.[7] Nkobi was enthusiastic but he died in September 1994. Mbeki did not like the Renong scheme – over which he had no control – and told Shaik that the ANC did not wish to compromise its image with other investors by giving deals to such crony capitalist insiders.[8] He persuaded the rest of the ANC leadership of this and Mandela told Shaik to 'place everything on hold'.[9] Makhenkesi Stofile, another member of the 'Xhosa nostra', replaced Nkobi as treasurer-general and in May 1995 he told Shaik that the Malaysian scheme was dead. Stofile also told Shaik that all his proposals and programmes were now discontinued, that he had no status within the party and was to be completely frozen out. Mbeki informed the French company Thomson-CSF that Shaik's Nkobi Group was not a legitimate BEE concern – effectively an instruction not to deal with it.[10]

Despite this setback Shaik pressed ahead on his own, still trying to use his ANC connections. He founded Nkobi Holdings with, it was alleged, Zuma as a secret shareholder, and then sought to exploit Zuma's position as provincial minister for economic affairs and tourism to make a deal with the Renong Group over Durban's Point Waterfront development, but this too collapsed.[11] Shaik made regular financial transfers to Zuma whose chaotic financial affairs were in permanent need of being bailed out. But he got nothing for his money. As he later bitterly pointed out, his companies tendered for many contracts while Zuma was a provincial minister but his only success was with a housing contract for a white IFP minister, Peter Miller, over whom Zuma had no influence.[12]

Schabir, aware from his brother Chippy of the rich pickings in defence procurement, realized that he was wasting his time in Durban when the bonanza of the century, Joe Modise's R60 billion arms deal, was going through in Pretoria. Despite Mbeki's efforts to freeze him out, Shaik quickly established a relationship with Thomson-CSF, which changed its name to Thales and spawned Thint Holdings and African Defence Systems, both of which were to benefit from the R6 billion navy corvettes contract – and of both of which Schabir was a director. In 1997 Zuma was made leader of government business in Cape Town. Thereafter Schabir got Zuma to attend many of his business meetings, including with Thint/African Defence Systems, trying to impress them all with his high-level political backing.

PUSHING THE ARMS DEAL MODISE'S WAY

Mbeki was well aware of the links between Zuma and Schabir Shaik long before Zuma became ANC deputy president but kept this knowledge in reserve for possible later use. Mbeki himself was heavily occupied at this time in helping push the arms deal in the directions Joe Modise wanted – and in trying to suppress the rising clamour excited by the deal. One of the documents unearthed, ironically, by Schabir Shaik's trial was a fax from Pierre Moynot, chief negotiator for Thomson-CSF/Thales dated 28 November 1997, in which Mbeki is recorded as having told the company that they 'would be awarded the combat system and the sensors' – although this was seven months before the short list of bidders was drawn up and a year before the cabinet decided on its preferred suppliers.[13] Though Mbeki was continuously and intimately involved with the arms deal, his office later claimed the President had 'forgotten' about such things.

The correspondence makes it clear that Thales (and, doubtless, the other arms companies bidding for the deal) were very actively seeking out whichever figures they thought might be able to nudge the deal in their direction. There is a lot of comment about Mandela's tailor, Yusuf Surtee, often referred to only as 'the tailor', and his legendary influence with Mandela. At one point Moynot mentions that 'Surtee does in fact appear to be closer to Mandela than my first fax could suggest. It is through him that Bouygues obtained the motorway contract.'[14] Yet the same correspondence makes it clear that Mbeki was greatly opposed to Surtee, 'who has no political and/or historical legitimacy'.[15] Mainly, Mbeki wanted to freeze out those whose aim was to push the arms deal away from the directions ordained by Modise. But Mbeki was also a Leninist, indignant during the 1980s when the UDF leaders, Tutu and Boesak, took initiatives – they were not under party discipline, had 'no mandate' – and similarly disliked entrepreneurial Asians, who, in his eyes, represented an illegitimate interest group which had infiltrated the movement.

The attempted investigation of the arms deal was a farce. Parliament's Standing Committee on Public Accounts (Scopa) tried hard to probe the deal but was headed off at every point by the executive. As Andrew Feinstein, the ANC MP who eventually resigned over the matter, showed,[16] Mbeki achieved this by subverting the independence of every institution supposed to uphold such inquiries. The Speaker of Parliament, Frene Ginwala, to her everlasting shame, lent herself to this and ultimately used her office, not to protect the rights of Parliament, but to undermine its ability to hold the executive accountable. All the 'independent' bodies asked to examine the deal – the Auditor-General, the Public Protector and the National Director for Public Prosecutions – behaved in similar fashion, under Mbeki's pressure.

Scopa's only real hope lay with Judge Willem Heath's Special Investigating Unit. Mbeki used Zuma to help quash this inquiry, getting him to sign a tough letter to Scopa, written by Mbeki. The Scopa chairman, Gavin Woods, was shaken by this because he knew that

'Zuma had not been involved in the arms deal'.[17] In fact there was quite enough evidence to justify the investigation and prosecution of Joe Modise but this the National Director for Public Prosecutions, Bulelani Ngcuka, declined to do. The Heath unit was the sole wild card and Heath later claimed that the decision to bar the unit from investigating the deal had been illegal and that the Justice Minister, Penuell Maduna, had invented extra-legal grounds for refusing to issue a proclamation authorizing the inquiry.[18]

Mbeki was so determined to keep Heath away from the arms deal that he made a special national television broadcast on 19 January 2001 in which he quoted legal advice he had received that, since there was no reason to believe that anyone had committed any offence in relation to the deal, there was no basis for a Heath investigation. In fact it emerged that the lawyers concerned had said exactly the opposite, that it was 'imperative' that Heath be involved.[19] With wonderful convenience the Constitutional Court shortly afterwards declared that Heath's unit was unconstitutional and must be dissolved.

NGCUKA PLAYS HIS HAND

As early as 2000 Jacob Zuma became aware that he was under investigation. By 2001 the specialist police unit, the Scorpions, were hot on the trail of Shaik and Thales, raiding their offices in South Africa, Mauritius and France.[20] In a pattern which was to become all too familiar, a steady stream of leaks to the press from the Scorpions and the National Prosecuting Authority (NPA) built the pressure on Shaik and Zuma. Then on the day before the 2002 ANC conference news was leaked to the press that Zuma was now under investigation by the Scorpions, the aim being to pressure Zuma into resigning. This he declined to do. So in August 2003 Ngcuka called an informal meeting of black journalists, informing them that there was a 'prima facie' case against Zuma but not enough evidence to guarantee a conviction. Ngcuka then repeated this charge on television while sitting alongside his boss, Penuell Maduna, in the latter's house.[21]

Zuma realized early on that there was a deliberate and politically inspired campaign to force him out of the deputy presidency of both the ANC and the state. He took the fundamental decision that he would not give in to these pressures and that he would, indeed, stake his claim to the presidency after Mbeki. This was to prove a huge turning point in South Africa's post-liberation history. Until then whenever Mbeki mounted an assault against his rivals they had either dropped out of politics (Sexwale, Ramaphosa, Phosa) or had put themselves on the wrong side of ANC discipline (Holomisa). But Mbeki had not challenged a Zulu before. Zuma, behaving as a Zulu man must, stood his ground within the ANC and fought, always observing the ANC's mores and insisting that he was at the movement's disposal.

The ANC had been Zuma's life just as much as it had been Mbeki's. Indeed, as an uneducated man he had far fewer options than Mbeki. Mbeki's response was to increase the pressure on Zuma. There were more and more damaging leaks to the press about him and more and more money and manpower was devoted to pursuing the case against him. In a country where police time and personnel were under enormous strain only the strongest political imperative could explain the huge resources devoted to trying to ensnare Zuma, which in turn meant the orders had to come from the top. Zuma not only refused to budge but took his case to the ANC grass roots, claiming that state institutions were being abused in a partisan manner against him.

Zuma's decision to stand and fight was doubtless an unexpected development for Mbeki. Outwardly he adopted a lofty attitude as if above the battle but the longer the battle went on the more obvious his manipulation became, validating Zuma's complaints. It emerged that Mbeki had learnt of a move to interdict Ngcuka from announcing a decision to prosecute Shaik and Zuma, and that Ngcuka had been hurriedly persuaded to convene the meeting of black journalists (the racial exclusivity another telltale Mbeki touch) in order to get the charge of Zuma's prima facie corruption onto the public record. Similarly, Gerda Ferreira, the head of the NPA team investigating the allegations of arms deal corruption, recommended that the allegations against Joe Modise be pursued. This was quashed by Mbeki. Ferreira and another NPA investigator resigned.[22]

Popular sympathy for Zuma was based on an assumption even more dangerous to Mbeki, that Zuma was probably guilty but that it did not matter. As Sam Sole put it, Zuma's real defence was that 'his financial indiscretions are relatively minor and almost no Cabinet minister would survive with their reputation intact under similar scrutiny'.[23]

Increasingly, the press carried damaging material about the relationship between Zuma and Schabir Shaik, fed by leaks from the Scorpions and the NPA. In July 2003 the NPA put thirty-five questions to Zuma. A few weeks later the questions were all leaked to the press, causing Zuma to lodge a complaint against Ngcuka to the Public Protector's office about 'the constant leaks of information to the media . . . clearly designed to cast aspersions on my integrity'.[24] The Public Protector upheld Zuma's complaint though the media, fed with a constant stream of anti-Zuma titbits, was in feeding frenzy and never stopped to consider how it was being used.

Another target was the former cabinet minister Mac Maharaj, who after leaving the government in 1999 made no secret of his distrust of Mbeki. Maharaj was a struggle hero, a man who had resisted torture, long imprisonment on Robben Island and exile. Such men tended to judge the Mbeki government against the criterion of whether its performance justified all the sacrifices they had made. While Mandela was President the question could hardly be asked, since Mandela had sacrificed more than anyone, but Mbeki had lived the high life in exile. At one public dinner Maharaj was heard to speak of Mbeki in particularly choice terms.[25] Such sentiments quickly got back – Mbeki's spies were everywhere. When Ngcuka had attacked Zuma before the black journalists one of his charges had been that Zuma surrounded himself with Indians and was largely in their hands. From that angle Maharaj was just another Indian from KwaZulu-Natal, one of the nest around Zuma.

From 2003 on press leaks against Maharaj began, one detailing how he and his wife, Zarina, had had a trip to Disneyland paid for by Schabir Shaik, another how nearly R500,000 had been paid by Shaik to Maharaj for Zarina's 'consultancy', at a time when Shaik was benefiting from government deals connected with the N3 toll road, while Maharaj was Minister of Transport. Shaik had also paid for a computer installed at Maharaj's home and for the import duties on a marble table imported from India by Zarina.[26] Maharaj protested bitterly and to no avail that the NPA and Scorpions were systematically blackening his name without ever laying charges against him but the damage was done. First Rand Bank, of which Maharaj was a highly paid director, carried out its own inquiry which, while clearing him of charges of corruption, nonetheless left him no option but to resign, thus leaving him jobless.[27]

Maharaj was one of Mandela's closest friends, picked by Mandela as well worthy of being President of South Africa. To bring low a man of such stature was a major political act and it was universally assumed that Ngcuka would hardly have dared do it unless supported to the hilt by Mbeki. Given that Ngcuka's wife, Phumzile, was also a cabinet minister close to Mbeki the whole situation was, as one journalist put it, 'incestuous'.[28] Maharaj and Schabir Shaik's brother Mo now publicized their dark suspicions that Ngcuka had been an apartheid spy. As part of his MK intelligence duties Mo Shaik had had to investigate Ngcuka's case and had found it suspicious. Ngcuka had been detained on suspicion of high treason in 1981 when, remarkably, he was granted a passport – which he later used to leave the country.[29] The Security Police had never allowed political detainees to leave the country legally. Ngcuka could only explain this as an 'administrative error' by the police.

The real sting in the tail here was that Ngcuka had been a clerk in the Durban law firm of the ANC activist Griffiths Mxenge. Griffiths and his wife Victoria had both been brutally murdered by the Security Police. In Durban, where the tragedy remained a cause célèbre, rumour had it that Ngcuka might have passed information to the Security Police enabling them to waylay the Mxenges. That is, lurking not far behind the accusation that Ngcuka had been a police spy was the lethal accusation that he had been an accomplice to the murder of two major struggle martyrs.

Ngcuka now found himself not just under attack but virtually fighting for his life. And he had many other enemies. The publication of his full remarks to the black journalists showed that he had accused Maharaj of lying, sacrificing his wife to his own ends and of really controlling Schabir Shaik; that Zuma was in trouble because 'he had surrounded himself with Indians'; that the soccer boss Irvin Khoza, though admitting he had been 'naughty in the past', had pleaded with him not to send him to jail where he feared being raped; that the mining magnates Brett and Roger Kebble were bankrolling the ANC Youth League and then getting them to try to intercede with him, Ngcuka, not to prosecute the Kebbles; and that the Police Commissioner, Jackie Selebi, was spreading rumours against him.[30]

Naturally, all those fingered objected violently. The Kebbles (who were indeed financing the Youth League and many other ANC politicians, and who were outspokenly favourable to Jacob Zuma) angrily alleged that Ngcuka was a friend of their business enemy, Mzi Khumalo, and that his 'vendetta' against them was financially inspired. Indeed, Brett Kebble, who had launched court proceedings against Mzi Khumalo for R50 million, said that Khumalo had threatened him. 'He came into my office,' asserted Kebble, 'and said Ngcuka wants to fry a big white fish, and that it will be me if I am not careful.'[31] Various Indian cultural bodies angrily reported Ngcuka to the Human Rights Commission for his 'racist' slurs against Indians.

There was now a growing list of ANC worthies with a grievance against the Scorpions and the NPA. Mathews Phosa had been the first target. In March 2001 a torrent of information had been leaked to the media by the Scorpions implicating Phosa in corruption while he was premier, though no charges ever followed and the Scorpions never published their findings. Similar tactics were employed against two of the most prominent UDF leaders, Terror Lekota and Popo Molefe, whom Mbeki saw as a threat. Police raided Molefe, then premier of the North West, claiming that he had molested his own daughter. No evidence was found but the Scorpions leaked the police docket to the media and suggested that new evidence had been found; none was ever produced and no charges laid but Molefe's name was blackened. Meanwhile a Scorpions investigation of Lekota had found that he had various business interests he had not disclosed to Parliament. This was leaked to the media. Lekota had to apologize to Parliament, his reputation permanently damaged. Tony Yengeni, an early Mbeki favourite, had the same experience. Having lost Mbeki's favour, he found that the Scorpions had leaked to the media details of his bank accounts and the deal whereby he had purchased a Mercedes SUV at a large discount while head of the defence committee. Disgrace followed, with a conviction for perjury for failing to disclose his interests to Parliament.[32]

Ngcuka, as head of the Scorpions and the NPA, was a well-hated man but everyone knew that he could only do what he did because Mbeki backed him. Ngcuka was quite open about this. He related how, when Mbeki had recruited him for the job, 'I cannot do this without your support,' he told the President, 'and I cannot do this job without the support of the ANC. That's a fact. The day that I feel I don't have that support I will walk out of this job.'[33] Mbeki was at pains to deny that he had any control over Ngcuka, the NPA or the Scorpions but Ngcuka himself was quite open about the political nature of his job. 'A politically independent director of public prosecutions,' he averred, 'is wishful thinking.'[34] When Ngcuka finally decided to resign he said that one of the reasons for leaving was that his wife 'is a member of the ANC's national working committee and national executive committee and of cabinet. She sat through all those meetings where I was discussed day in and day out.'[35]

Sometimes, in their pursuit of Mbeki's opponents, the Scorpions (or in some instances the NIA) found real paydirt (few ANC politicians had entirely clean records) and released that. In other cases they just leaked all manner of rumours to the press, which happily published it all without reflection. Occasionally – as when the press published details of Mac Maharaj's (alleged) secret Swiss bank account – the whole game was entirely visible, for the the only way the press could know such data was if they were spoon-fed with it by the intelligence agencies. But such reflections were not popular. When the columnist David Gleason insisted on commenting on such things, the editor of *Business Day*, Peter Bruce, sacked him. In general the press was scared and deferential. It was quite normal for South African journalists to write about Mbeki as if he were a major philosophical talent and to suggest that he was likely to follow Kofi Annan as UN Secretary-General, sycophantic absurdities which no one outside South Africa took seriously.

THE HEFER COMMISSION

The accusations Mo Shaik and Maharaj made against Bulelani Ngcuka were thus a threat to an entire system of manipulation, a key element in the way Mbeki exercised power. Mbeki responded by setting out to crush Mo Shaik, Maharaj and Vusi Mona, the *City Press* editor who had dared to print their allegations. The commission, under Justice Joos Hefer, set up to investigate the allegations was a farce.[36] Its terms of reference were repeatedly changed and narrowed by Mbeki so that in the end it was charged specifically to find whether Ngcuka had been Security Police agent code number RS452 – although his accusers had never actually made such a designation. At the outset Mbeki, in his online *ANC Today*, denounced the allegations as untrue and promised that 'the wrath of the people' would be visited upon those who made them, thus prejudging the whole affair and making it clear that the commission would face a major conflict with the President if its conclusions did not follow the script. He then forbade the commission access to any of the police or intelligence records which could have settled the question of Ngcuka's career history. Even the normally placid Hefer protested at this fantastic exclusion. The director-general of the Office of the President, Frank Chikane, then wrote saying that, since Mbeki had access to all such intelligence and had seen nothing bearing on the allegations, the commission need not concern itself with such evidence – a self-serving piece of casuistry doubtless drafted by Mbeki himself.

Other, almost surreal nonsense followed. The evidence leader, advocate Kessie Naidu, earned great press admiration by the way he hectored and harassed Mona, Shaik and Maharaj. Less attention was paid to the fact that Naidu was not only a close friend of the Justice Minister, Penuell Maduna, but shared all manner of business interests with Maduna's wife. And Maduna was, after all, Bulelani Ngcuka's boss. Naidu had, moreover, business connections with the late Joe Modise, connections which were now the focus of the Scorpions' attention as they probed the arms deal. Maduna had replaced Steve Tshwete as Mbeki's fixer and was inevitably implicated in the misuse of the NPA and Scorpions to harass Mbeki's enemies. Under any normal set of rules Naidu would have had to recuse himself.[37] The other advocate grilling Maharaj and Shaik was Marumo Moerane, a cousin and confidant of Mbeki who had appeared before the Constitutional Court to argue that HIV-positive babies should not be given the ARV drugs which could save their lives. Moerane's presence was another indication of how closely the hatchet job on Maharaj and Shaik had been organized by Mbeki's team.[38]

Most of the media missed this. Instead it treated with breathless credulity the appearance of Security Police Lieut.-Col. Karl Edwards who had run agent RS452 and averred that this was not Ngcuka. Then, the pièce de résistance, Vanessa Brereton, now living in Britain, emerged to admit that she, as a lawyer then working in the Eastern Cape, had been agent RS452 and had systematically informed upon and betrayed her left-wing friends there. Astonishingly, no one in the press asked why Ms Brereton, having emigrated and carefully kept her shameful secret, should now be willing to publicize her singularly nasty role for the apartheid regime. Given that this would be bound to have unpleasant consequences for her in Britain, let alone South Africa, one might have expected the question to be raised of whether Ms Brereton had been given any incentives to testify thus. But no one asked.

The rest followed the script. Vusi Mona was duly humiliated and lost his job as editor, to be replaced by the loyal Mbeki-ite, Mthatha Tsedu. The Hefer Commission showed a strange reluctance to interview intelligence agents who could shed light on Ngcuka's past. Then, astonishingly, an ANC spokesman announced that the party forbade Jacob Zuma to testify before the commission. Zuma, as chief of ANC intelligence, had been in charge of the Ngcuka investigation and Mo Shaik had reported to him. Zuma made it clear that he knew more about the subject than anybody else and was willing to tell the Commission all he knew, but loyally said he would observe the party instruction. Hefer angrily noted that in effect the ANC was telling Zuma to ignore a subpoena. Commentators noted that a decision to bar the Deputy President's testimony could only be taken by the party's senior officials but that these had not met, so the instruction could only have come from Mbeki.[39] Hefer decided not to challenge the instruction by issuing a subpoena.

Mo Shaik attempted to call on the notorious former Security Police killer Gideon Nieuwoudt for testimony that Ngcuka had been working for the Security Police. Nieuwoudt was a classic apartheid monster, expert in all forms of torture and with an admitted role in the murder of Steve Biko and such notorious killings as the Pebco Three and the Motherwell Four. He had hunted down activists by gaining admission to their houses disguised as a dog-collared clergyman, earning himself the sobriquet 'the Priest from Hell' though, ironically enough, now serving a twenty-year sentence, he had become a born-again Christian. Nieuwoudt certainly knew many dark secrets and in filmed testimony agreed that Bulelani Ngcuka had indeed worked for the Security Police. However, Hefer then learnt that Mo Shaik had paid Nieuwoudt R40,000 in 'expenses' for his film appearance and, simultaneously, the state refused to pay Nieuwoudt's legal fees, without which he could not afford to testify – unless subpoenaed. Hefer decided not to subpoena him.

This was a remarkable decision, especially when set next to the failure to subpoena Zuma. Nieuwoudt was clearly the best-informed source available to the commission from the apartheid side, just as Zuma was the best-informed source on the ANC side. Moreover, Nieuwoudt was dying of lung cancer (he died in 2005) and knew it. His religious conversion was almost certainly real and he had no reason not to tell the truth. Yet Hefer decided not to hear what he or Zuma had to say; he said of Nieuwoudt that it would be 'a waste of time to hear a witness like this'.[40]

But Hefer did listen to the Home Affairs official Willem Vorster, who averred there was nothing suspicious about the decision to grant Ngcuka a passport. Hefer commended Vorster as a wholly reliable witness, somewhat surprisingly given that Vorster, it emerged, had just been convicted of an offence relating to 'negligence and misconduct', with his career hanging by a thread, making him intensely vulnerable to pressure of any kind.[41] Had he given evidence embarrassing to the state he would doubtless have lost his job.

Maharaj and Mo Shaik were humiliated in cross-examination; they were wholly unable to support their accusations, which had had a rhetorical edge – Maharaj had likened Ngcuka to the FBI director J. Edgar Hoover, who had abused his powers to persecute political opponents. Brett Kebble claimed that Ngcuka, Maduna and the Scorpions were controlled by the CIA.[42] In the end Hefer concluded that Ngcuka 'probably never at any time before 1994 acted as an agent for a state security service'.[43] Shaik and Maharaj had made 'ill-conceived and entirely unsubstantiated'[44] allegations. This was an open invitation to Ngcuka to sue Shaik and Maharaj for defamation but this, interestingly, he declined to do. Mbeki wanted to punish the two men further: his spokesman said they would now face ANC disciplinary proceedings[45] – but this never occurred.

Many senior ANC members were shocked to see a man of Maharaj's stature subjected to such public humiliation. The whole business had been hugely bruising and both Penuell Maduna and Ngcuka himself were keen to get out of a situation in which they were being used as a battering ram against Mbeki's opponents, attracting utter hatred in return. Maduna simply found the heat in the kitchen too great and, flouting the normal ANC convention that cabinet ministers were simple deployees (see p. 61), he resigned even before the Hefer Commission's proceedings began. Ngcuka was equally keen to go. Mbeki insisted desperately that he should stay but Ngcuka finally left in July 2004, setting up in business with several members of the old apartheid security forces.[46] Ngcuka set up his Amambubesi company as a conglomerate and was quickly seen as a desirable partner by white business. He boldly declared that he was giving himself '18 months to become a major player in the economy'.[47] Both men rapidly prospered but their role in the persecution of Zuma and his friends was never forgotten or forgiven. Nor were the Scorpions and the NPA.

The Hefer Commission was another blow in Mbeki's struggle against Zuma. Ngcuka had publicly thrown dirt on Zuma; Zuma's supporters had retaliated against Ngcuka – and had been publicly crushed. Ahead lay the long-anticipated trial of Zuma's associate, Schabir Shaik. Durban's Indian community were left in no doubt that Mbeki saw them as the last remaining island of pluralism in the ANC; their money gave them an independent power which the Leninist Mbeki could never accept. Mo Shaik had been humiliated and silenced; now his brother Schabir would be hunted down (their third brother, Chippy, was reported as having fled to Australia). Other Indian associates of Zuma were now clearly at risk. The hatches were battened down. Zuma's position was under greater threat than ever – but still he refused to resign. So, ironically, Mbeki had to allow Zuma to occupy the deputy president's position once again on the ANC's 2004 election list.

THE ELECTION OF APRIL 2004

The 2004 elections were fought under the triumphalist banner of 'ten years of liberation'. All manner of national and provincial government departments used the occasion for voluminous pamphlets and advertisements to celebrate the achievements of the period. These were undisguised ANC propaganda, paid for by the taxpayers. Naturally, Mbeki's face was on the front of all such propaganda and was ubiquitous elsewhere; Mandela's was nowhere to be seen. Zuma campaigned loyally and outwardly, at least, the party was united. It romped home with 69.7 per cent of the vote, well past the two-thirds required for constitutional amendment.

The DA leader, Tony Leon, repeatedly asked the key question: would Mbeki be content with the two presidential terms the constitution allowed? In fact he had really been in power ever since 1994 and was thus, in a practical sense, already entering upon his third term. Mbeki himself refused to answer the question – a silence pregnant with meaning – but Leon was showered with abuse for making the 'racist' assumption that the President's appetite for power might be unlimited. Mandela ended the controversy by announcing firmly that there was no question of an ANC president exceeding the constitutional limit. Leon saw the DA take 12.4 per cent of the vote and 50 seats, consolidating the party's leadership of the Opposition.

Mbeki faced a last turning point in his war with Zuma. Both he and Zuma would be 67 by the time the next President had to be installed in 2009 and now was the moment when Mbeki might have begun to prepare the succession. The best way to head off Zuma would have been to bring forward able younger men such as Tito Mboweni and Cyril Ramaphosa. But, of course, this was wholly foreign to Mbeki's closed and watchful personality. Even in the case of his clear favourite, Joel Netshitenzhe, there was no question of allowing him to assume the role of crown prince, for Mbeki would automatically see such a person as a rival and Netshitenzhe, knowing Mbeki all too well, was hardly eager to assume such a role. All Mbeki did was to try to drop Zuma from his cabinet but Kgalema Motlanthe intervened, saying that to do this to the party's and country's Deputy President would threaten party stability.[48]

The political elite knew that anyone who showed an interest in the succession would be quickly marked down as a threat and disposed of. No one was willing to lift their head above the parapet; indeed, there was a growing climate of fear which commentators began, nervously, to remark upon. Politicians and journalists were unwilling to talk frankly on the telephone and many ANC politicians began to keep two mobile phones, one for normal use, one for confidential conversations only. It became normal practice, even when talking not on the telephone, to remove the batteries of one's mobile phone when one had confidential things to say since it was known that with modern technology any mobile phone could be turned into a passive listening device.

Mbeki tried, in his usual manner, to throw a smokescreen around his intentions. In an interview with the *Financial Times* in 2005 he disclaimed any notion of seeking a third presidential term, suggesting disingenuously that this happened elsewhere in Africa only because of a shortage of suitable successors but that 'I don't think we would have a problem like that here'.[49] This was already ominous. The right reply was that a third term would be unconstitutional and therefore unthinkable. Mbeki was carefully ignoring this central fact and pretending that presidential unwillingness to give up power was not one of the major curses of Africa. Instead, the key criterion was simply that of finding a 'suitable' successor. No one imagined that Mbeki saw Zuma as suitable . . .

Mbeki clients, like the KwaZulu-Natal premier, S'bu Ndebele, began to tout the possibility of another term for Mbeki as ANC president. Mbeki carefully said this depended on his 'availability'. Presidential spokesmen repeatedly leaked the notion that Mbeki would like the Foreign Minister, Nkosasana Dlamini-Zuma, to be the next state President. This was ludicrous: the ANC would certainly not elect a woman. This was, of course, the point: since she was an impossible candidate, in practice it kept the slot free. No black journalist was stupid enough to believe in a Dlamini-Zuma candidacy though several white journalists swallowed it.

Other Mbeki clients floated the notion that the President would be in great demand for some major international job, as head of the UN or one of its major agencies. Mbeki's own lofty hint about 'availability' was an intentional encouragement for such fantasies. When I raised the question with Western ambassadors they raised their eyes to heaven and said that had all been ruled out long ago. Washington had put its foot down, and Mbeki's Aids denialism anyway disqualified him. The door was shut, Mbeki was locked in. The only alternative was the headship of the African Union but, as Mbeki knew, both it and Nepad depended entirely on Pretoria's subsidies so accepting either position meant being at the mercy of the next South African President. Which ruled that out.

For Mbeki, like Mugabe, was scared to give up power for fear of being at the mercy of his enemies. Only Mbeki's grandiosity prevented him from understanding how thoroughly his behaviour over Aids and Zimbabwe had ruled him out of consideration for any international job. When he realized he was not being considered for such posts he rushed desperately to ingratiate himself with the new men of power. When President Nicolas Sarkozy of France gave a speech about Africa which enraged many Africans, Mbeki rushed to praise him for it. Similarly, he greeted the advent of Gordon Brown as Britain's Prime Minister with extravagant praise, as if fawning could undo Aids denialism.

In January 2006 Mlungisi Hlongwane, president of Sanco, suggested that Mbeki should serve a third term as state President. Term limits were, he said, a foreign concept and it was important to keep the 'best minds' in power.[50] The idea, as the *Business Day* columnist Karima

Brown suggested, was clearly that this would test the water so that other organizations could make 'spontaneous' and 'popular' appeals which would 'force' Mbeki reluctantly to accept a third term.[51] Within forty-eight hours Hlongwane was the recipient of a R439 million deal whereby he and the ubiquitous Bridgette Radebe secured 25 per cent of the Vukile Property Fund.[52] Ironically, Bridgette's husband, Jeff Radebe, aware as any Zulu politician had to be of Zuma's massive Zulu following, was quietly assuring Zuma of his support, while remaining in Mbeki's cabinet. Ultimately Radebe was to be elected high on the Zuma list which routed Mbeki.

The SACP, Cosatu and the ANC Youth League all declared their hostility to the idea of a third term. Mbeki himself said nothing. For Mbeki had clearly decided not just to prevent a Zuma presidency but to retain power himself. The first step would be to remain ANC president. Then he could either put in a puppet as state President and rule through them or, more likely, allow himself to be coaxed towards a third term. Either way, it was game on. Given Mbeki's paranoia and grandiosity it is probably a mistake to assume that he merely wanted to stop Zuma. More likely, he was always determined to extend his term, with the war on Zuma a mere consequence.

SCHABIR SHAIK GOES TO COURT

Zuma had refused to fall on his sword, so the fateful decision was taken to bring Schabir Shaik, Zuma's principal 'godfather', to trial.

The prosecution case against Shaik showed that Zuma regularly received financial support from Shaik, from another Durban Indian businessman, Vivian Reddy, a white businessman, Jurgen Kogl, and an Mpumalanga businesswoman, Nora Fakude-Nkuna. The Scorpions used Zuma's and Shaik's bank records to show that Zuma was a child in financial matters, repeatedly running up bank overdrafts he could not pay. Shaik had frequently bailed him out of bad debt and had even set up arrangements to pay Zuma's children their pocket money. Once he was even recorded as having paid R10 for Zuma's car to be washed. Zuma's behaviour made him look bad but he was more typical of the new black elite than was generally allowed for. Many had no experience of managing a middle-class lifestyle, with its need for careful budgeting, and they often ran up bad debts, sometimes hoping that suppliers or banks would forgive their debts in order to win political favour.

In several respects the prosecution case was remarkable. It was leaked to the press before it went to court, although this was not lawful; information gained by warrant, such as an individual's bank records, was not supposed to be treated thus. The leak was clearly intended to place information before the public in a way that was highly prejudicial to both Shaik and Zuma.[53] The *Sunday Times* got a copy of the charge sheet before the judge – and published it. Meanwhile the auditors' report of payments made by Shaik to Zuma had been 'floating about for months' before the trial,[54] although the bank records it revealed had only been accessed under warrant. The law said such material had to be handled on a presumption of innocence. It was not.

Thus while Shaik was on trial, the objective was to do maximum political damage to Zuma, whatever might happen in court. The prosecution showed that Zuma had received R1.2 million from Shaik over a six-year period, that is, R200,000 a year. This was a small sum for anyone wanting to buy the country's Deputy President and was more suggestive of the Shaiks' regular family support for Zuma. And while Zuma had allegedly asked Thales for R500,000 p.a. for his help – a tiny sum in relation to a multi-billion arms contract – there was no proof that Zuma personally had received anything from Thales.

Moreover Ncguka had said there was a prima facie case against Zuma but there might not be enough evidence to convict him. In that case it was odd to put Shaik, and only Shaik, on trial, for clearly the case against him and Zuma was the same. And if Shaik's contributions had been made with the thought of future corrupt gains, why was the same case not brought against Reddy, Fakude-Nkuna and Kogl? One reason, doubtless, was that Kogl had spread his largesse around, providing Mbeki and his wife with a penthouse flat for two years in the early 1990s.[55] One could not investigate Kogl without turning up evidence about Mbeki's affluent godfathers as well.

This was further proof of the case's political nature. The 'godfather' phenomenon had applied to most top ANC leaders; indeed, Zuma may have received more modest help than many. It was common knowledge in Durban that Zuma's backers had contributed generously to several other leading ANC politicians but their affairs were left in secrecy. The decision to go for Shaik was clearly meant to force Zuma out of the battle for the presidential succession. If he pulled out, the charges against him might not be pursued; if he persisted, he clearly faced a furious legal battle. And the state was visibly willing to throw huge resources at the matter – the charge sheet against Shaik listed 105 witnesses, including twenty members of the Scorpions.[56]

Schabir Shaik was, however, a prosecutor's dream – boastful, flashy and easily punctured. He maintained a posture of exaggerated cockiness which would occasionally collapse into outbursts against policemen, the media or the prosecutors. Once he shouted at Anton Steynberg, the deputy state prosecutor, 'I'm not scared of you. I'll sort you out after the trial. You're a racist; get that into your thick skull. You will be running from me like Bulelani.'[57] This followed the laying of a *crimen injuria* case against Shaik by a white policeman outside the court after Shaik had allegedly subjected him to a racially abusive attack.[58] Shaik later apologized for such incidents but he also frequently got the court to adjourn early because he claimed to be suffering from stress-related illness, creating an impression of mercurial instability. There was no denying that he had frequently boasted of his friendship with Zuma and tried to browbeat associates into deals with claims of his political influence. He also had to admit that he had faked the engineering qualifications he had claimed and the three degrees credited to him in the Nkobi Holdings brochure. He also conceded having tried to deceive Mandela about his financial assistance to Zuma. Mandela did not approve of Schabir Shaik and, had he learnt of his involvement with Zuma, he might not have helped Zuma. As it was, Mandela had given Zuma R2 million to help with his debts, a large portion of which was immediately appropriated by Shaik to pay off some of the debts he himself had incurred in helping Zuma.[59]

This was bad enough. But the court also heard a great deal from Shaik's former assistant, Bianca Singh, who had a grievance against him: there had been a 'personal incident' between the two. She had brought a charge of sexual harassment against him and left the country the next day, apparently to escape his wrath. She had, moreover, unearthed one of his old appointments diaries, full of meetings between Shaik, Zuma and Thales. Singh also detailed many of Shaik's payments to Zuma for his children's school and university fees and recounted how Zuma was so dependent on such help that she had sometimes handed him amounts as small as R700 from Shaik's petty cash box. Singh also recounted how Shaik had complained of his relationship with various government ministers: 'He said he has to carry a jar of Vaseline because he gets fucked all the time, but that's OK because he gets what he wants and they get what they want.'[60]

Singh had other embarrassing recollections. Once, she said, in relation to the arms deal she had heard Shaik say that 'if a certain ANC member opened his mouth' they were in 'real trouble'.[61] She also claimed that Nkobi was a BEE front, with merely token black directors. Shaik had traded heavily on his connection to Zuma and other ministers as well as on Nkobi's BEE credentials but would privately sometimes say that he was 'just tired of these black people'.[62] Even the tribute of another businessman that the Shaik family 'had the balls of elephants',[63] did not do much to alleviate this disastrous impression, especially since Ms Singh – who had been talking to the Scorpions for more than three years – told them that she was scared and 'had reason to fear' Shaik, who had told her that 'he will not let anyone break down his empire and he would just eliminate or just get rid of them'.[64]

One of Shaik's former accountants, Celia Bester, also testified that he had paid bribes to ministers and then used 'creative accounting' to disguise such sums as 'development costs'. She said that Shaik had said that Nkobi had got one deal because of its 'political connectivity' and that he had to pay Zuma because he 'could not handle his finances because he had all those wives'.[65]

Although Bester testified that 'we were paying ministers money while Nkobi barely survived',[66] the prosecution showed no interest in these ministers. But every reference to Zuma was pursued: he was clearly the main target. The trial also further damaged Mac Maharaj. The court was shown five payments with 'MM' written next to them and a note saying 'Inv. MM invoices Flisane Inv.' – Flisane being a travel company run by Maharaj's wife. Maharaj had been Minister of Transport when an Nkobi subsidiary, Pro Con Africa, won a tender for the N3 toll road.[67] Moreover, the Nkobi group had a one-third share in the R650 million contract awarded by Maharaj in 1996 to supply credit-card-style driving licences, another consortium partner being Idmatics, a Thomson CSF/Thales subsidiary. The contract was a fiasco since the necessary scanning devices to read the cards arrived five years late.[68] Maharaj suffered a continuing series of press leaks against him and found that even old friends were now scared to help him. Even when they offered him money, it had to be in cash as cheques were traceable. Ultimately Maharaj had to go into exile again, teaching at Bennington College in the United States.[69]

So far, so bad. But the prosecution also produced two more secretaries – this time they had worked for the Thint boss, Alain Thetard, with whom Zuma and Schabir had had dealings. Susan Delique testified that she had feared for her safety with Thetard and had fled the company after three months. Marion Marais confirmed this impression, saying Thetard had been arrogant and volatile and had thrown things at her. Delique had lasted three months, Marais thirteen. Delique, happily for the prosecution, had 'found' various damaging bits of evidence against Zuma, Shaik and Thetard, having earlier lost them.[70] The Scorpions even managed to find a former employee of Schabir's, Sabeer Sheik-Ibrahim, who claimed that Schabir Shaik had bought the sexual services of a young Coloured woman known only as Robin, both for himself and Zuma. This item of irrelevant dirt – dug up and distributed to the press – demonstrated the state's utter determination to discredit Zuma, for Sabeer was by then living in Indonesia.[71]

Despite these embarrassing revelations the prosecution case was surprisingly thin. Although Shaik, claiming great political influence, had lobbied for a share of the arms deal and had gained a small slice of the corvettes contract via his association with Thint, there was no suggestion either that Zuma had helped him win this, or that Shaik's was anything but a tiny sliver of a larger contract which had benefited others far more. Shaik's most valuable investment was actually his holding in Kobitech with its 3 per cent holding in the mobile phone company, Cell C. His business interests totalled no more than $7–$8 million.[72]

What remained was the allegation that in March 2000 Shaik and Thint, alarmed by the row over the arms deal, had met with Zuma and asked for his 'protection' during the arms deal investigation in return for the promise of a R500,000 p.a. payment. This was difficult terrain in several ways. First, the alleged offer of R500,000 was written in shorthand on an encrypted fax from Thetard who denied it meant that and refused to come to South Africa to testify. Secondly, the key element of Zuma's 'protection' was his furious letter to Gavin Woods, the chair of the Public Accounts Committee (Scopa) – what the judge referred to as 'a hatchet job on your committee from somewhere on high in government' – and Woods agreed that the effect had been intimidatory.

Yet Zuma said that Mbeki himself had written this letter and demanded that he, Zuma, sign it, delivering it on the same day (19 January 2001) that Mbeki went on national television to attack Scopa and prevent it from allowing Judge Willem Heath's Special Investigation Unit to join the arms deal investigation. That is, Zuma's major act of 'protection' had actually been an Mbeki initiative. Given that Mbeki had launched the hostile investigation against Zuma a year earlier, the possibility obviously existed that Mbeki had set Zuma up.

Finally, on 16 February 2001, shortly after Zuma's (i.e. Mbeki's) letter to Woods, Thint paid R250,000 to the Development Africa Trust controlled by another Zuma ally, Vivian Reddy. Thereafter Thint took fright and payments ceased (though Shaik pursued Thint, demanding a further R250,000 for the Jacob Zuma Education Trust). In fact, the money was part of an ANC slush fund aimed at penetrating KwaZulu-Natal's IFP establishment, with money slipped to chiefs, the Zulu royal family and the key IFP defector, Walter Felgate.[73] There was no reason to doubt Zuma's claims that he had never benefited. The whole transaction was muddied by getting tangled up with Mandela's R2 million contribution to Zuma. Nobody asked what godfather arrangements had enabled Mandela to dispense such sums, for it was impossible for him to afford such largesse out of his presidential salary.

Woods had long suspected that Zuma's letter to him had actually been written by Mbeki. Zuma's lawyer put it to him that well after that letter Zuma had actually tried to support Scopa's attempts to investigate the arms deal and had protected Woods's Scopa colleague, Andrew Feinstein, who was under great ANC pressure. Woods conceded that this might well have been the case.[74] This left the question of Shaik's decade-long financial support to Zuma, which he described as 'a revolving loan agreement'. The judge, Hilary Squires, thought little of this. Deciding that Shaik's 'never-ending series of payments' to Zuma had been motivated by the hope of ultimate commercial gain and that the payments had allowed Zuma to 'maintain a lifestyle beyond what he could afford', Squires described their relationship as 'a mutually beneficial symbiosis'.[75]

Squires concluded that the prosecution case that there had been 'a generally corrupt relationship' between the two was overwhelming, though he did not himself use the same phrase, mindful of the fact that it had no status in law.[76] All he would say was that Shaik and Zuma had a 'symbiotic relationship' which, he inferred, must be corrupt because 'no rational businessman would conduct his business in this way without expecting anything in return'.[77]

Shaik's behaviour had alienated the old-school, straitlaced Squires – perhaps particularly the revelation that in 2005 he was, more than ten years on, still paying the Deputy President's way. He also disliked Shaik's boasting of his friendship with Zuma to boost his business affairs: 'Genuine friendship would not have resorted to such blatant advertising,'[78] said Squires, thus revealing his ignorance of the fact that this sort of blarney was by no means unique in the Durban Indian business community.

Analysing Shaik's demeanour as 'on the whole not impressive', Squires described Shaik as 'a man untroubled by a resort to duplicity or falsehood to gain one's end' whose testimony had been largely irrelevant despite 'surprising flashes of candour', and suggested he existed 'in a bubble of his own preoccupations and belief system'.[79] This was all fair comment but his sentence of fifteen years' jail for Shaik was astonishing – far worse than a convicted rapist or murderer might suffer. While Zuma might have wanted to help Shaik's interests and while Shaik's payments to Zuma might well have been predicated on such a hope, there was, after all, no evidence that such benefits had actually occurred. Zuma angrily pointed out that he himself had been blackened by the verdict without ever having had his day in court. Zuma, in no doubt that he had been the real target in the trial, had tried to get Shaik to change his lawyer and to behave more respectfully in court. 'But it was no good. In a sense Schabir sent himself to jail. He just wouldn't listen.'[80]

In the world of the arms dealers it must have seemed fantastical. The arms trade was notoriously corrupt and both the French and British governments had taken action to prevent revealing just how rotten some of the bigger deals were. Thales, Europe's biggest supplier of defence electronics, had been caught paying some $500 million in commissions to Taiwanese officials in 1993 for selling frigates at 50 per cent over cost to them for some $3.2 billion. Nobody went to jail for that deal any more than they did in the bigger (£40 billion) British–Saudi Al Yamamah deal arranged by Mrs Thatcher and her son Mark. Yet here was Shaik jailed for fifteen years for having given Zuma R1.2 million ($150,000) over fourteen years – for favours merely presumed. And here was the country's Deputy President having his career ruined for the sake of

$70,000, of which only half had been paid to a trust he did not control – and with even that in dispute.

There were other comic opera elements. Shaik appealed but meanwhile rushed off on pilgrimage to Mecca, returning to announce that he intended to give some of his wealth away. 'You begin to realize your nothingness. And it's beautiful.' He said the pilgrimage had renewed his faith in mankind. 'The judicial system and the political system obviously failed me. I felt failed. I felt let down.'[81] Meanwhile the uxorious Zuma appeared to lose the Swazi bride he had been courting. In his exile years Zuma had frequented Swaziland and, like any Zulu boy, saw the Zulu and Swazi kings as the apex of the old patriarchal structure and harboured ambitions to emulate them. His eye had fallen upon Princess Sebentile Dlamini, then working as a humble border official. Again Shaik had played the key role, introducing Zuma to the girl because of her striking resemblance to a younger version of Zuma's ex-wife, Nkosasana. But Sebentile's royal status implied a lobola of 100 cows. In the wake of Shaik's trial the Swazi queen mother called Sebentile to the palace to discuss the fall-out from the trial. With Zuma's declining image and fortunes the wedding was quietly put off.[82]

ZUMA'S SACKING AND THE NATIONAL GENERAL COUNCIL

Zuma too had been found guilty in the Shaik trial. Mbeki and most of the press expected that he would now resign. Instead Zuma went to see Mandela, begging for help. Mandela responded with a statement that the ANC should leave Zuma alone.[83] The old man wanted ANC unity before all else and by now had considerable reservations about Mbeki's behaviour. But the conclusive issue for him was, as usual, ethnic. Though mocked by the young for this preoccupation, his deep conviction was that if a Zulu deputy president was sacked and humiliated by a Xhosa president there would be trouble. His instinct was sound.

Zuma had been greeted as a hero at the 2005 Cosatu conference and the Cosatu leader, Zwelinzima Vavi, predicted that efforts to prevent Zuma becoming the next President would be like 'trying to fight against the big wave of a tsunami'.[84] This effectively meant that Zuma could also count on SACP support and he was already backed by the ANC Youth League. Meanwhile a poll in late 2004 found that 47 per cent of ANC voters thought the corruption charges against Zuma were a political ploy by his enemies; 80 per cent thought he was doing a good job and only 10 per cent thought he was guilty of corruption. Moreover, while Mbeki's popularity in office had subsided considerably, Zuma's popularity had almost doubled in office. His Zulu support was massive: even 63 per cent of IFP voters said he was doing a good job.[85]

All of which made it hard to sack him, especially since Zuma, the ex-head of ANC intelligence, knew where a lot of bodies were buried and openly admitted that 'there are no saints in the party leadership'.[86] Mbeki tried to persuade Zuma to resign but he adamantly refused.[87] The NPA's new boss, Vusi Pikoli, stepped up the pressure by letting it be known that he was considering charging Zuma with corruption. Zuma and his supporters indignantly declared that he had been tried and convicted by the media without ever having his day in court himself. This was truer than most realized, for it was the media that endlessly repeated that Judge Squires had found there to be a 'generally corrupt relationship' between Shaik and Zuma when in fact he had said no such thing. Indeed, when the Court of Appeal turned down Shaik's appeal it claimed to confirm Squires' verdict of a 'generally corrupt relationship' – thereby revealing that it too had not read the court documents properly, relying on media reports instead. (In a later Appeal Court judgment against Zuma news of the (negative) judgment was leaked to the media before the court had actually pronounced, revealing again that Zuma hardly had a level playing field there.)

Finally Mbeki sacked Zuma on 13 June, a decision greeted by enormous media applause and by exactly the opposite reaction in the townships. At ANC rallies on 16 June (the anniversary of the Soweto uprising) crowds chanted 'Phansi ngo Mbeki! Phambili ngo Zuma!' ('Down with Mbeki! Up with Zuma!'), much to the embarrassment of the SABC, which was not just an ANC mouthpiece but Mbeki's mouthpiece against Zuma. Mbeki then appointed Phumzile Mlambo-Ngcuka as Deputy President in Zuma's place. This was extraordinarily provocative, for she was Bulelani Ngcuka's wife. Worse, the President's office began to hint that she would make a good President in time although as Minister for Minerals and Energy she had been responsible both for the Minerals Act and the ban on building more power stations, the two greatest governmental blunders of the epoch. She was frequently booed and abused at ANC rallies. ANC activists explained that Mlambo-Ngcuka was part of Mbeki's conspiracy against Zuma. True, she was a Zulu, but she was married to a Xhosa and 'everyone knows the husband decides everything'.

The NPA then led corruption charges against Zuma, who attended the court hearings cheered by crowds of supporters, some of whom burnt T-shirts bearing Mbeki's image. Mbeki was anxious to evict Zuma from his deputy presidency of the ANC and got the National Working Committee (NWC) to agree that Zuma should withdraw from all party activities while his court case continued. Zuma resigned as an MP, thus forestalling embarrassing confrontations with Parliament's ethics committee over his so-called loans from Schabir Shaik. The NWC announced that Zuma had 'requested' to be relieved of the deputy presidency, though this was clearly untrue.

A key calculation for Mbeki had concerned the ANC National General Council (NGC) to be held at the end of June 2005 – in effect almost a full-scale conference, with 1,500 delegates plus representatives from Cosatu and the SACP. He had decided it was best to face the NGC with a fait accompli, including a new Deputy President, and use it instead to force through a series of far-reaching 'reforms', including a sweeping centralization of power within the ANC. National government would be given greater powers over provincial and local government; party branches would have to be closely aligned with state structures, with the elimination of leadership positions and decision-making powers which did not correspond to an equivalent government authority. Luthuli House would be given increased powers over branches and a central electoral commission would take over the election process throughout the party, abolishing factionalism, preventing 'personal agendas' and helping the centre impose its candidates everywhere. Mbeki's economic proposals included, notably, provision for a dual labour market, relaxing labour laws for younger workers and giving greater regulatory freedom to small businesses.

Mbeki's spin doctors persuaded much of the media that Zuma's support was confined to ethnic Zulus, that Zuma himself would be too busy in court to attend the NGC and that Zuma's sacking would sail through undiscussed. This was myopic. It hardly helped that 26 June was the fiftieth anniversary of the Freedom Charter, an event celebrated with great fervour. In the mass meeting in Soweto Zuma was given a hero's welcome. Moreover, the event coincided with the full flood of municipal protests at the failure of service delivery, that is to say, with a complete failure to fulfil the Charter's promises. This was bitter enough. Zwelinzima Vavi added a lecture on how much better a leader Chris Hani had been than those now in government, praising Hani for his 'intimate relationship with the poor and the working class' – something the genial Zuma was said to share – implicitly contrasting this with Mbeki's aloofness and arrogance.[88]

The NGC met amidst raucous scenes. Many delegates wore Zuma T-shirts and Mbeki was greeted with loud chanting of Zuma's name and even 'Msholozi [Zuma's clan name], my President'. Zuma's 'request' to resign the deputy presidency was rejected and he was triumphantly reinstalled, supported by seven of the nine provinces. Delegates chanted in Zulu, 'We don't want a capitalist agenda. It killed Zuma.'[89] All of Mbeki's 'reforms' were contemptuously thrown out. Mbeki's power to appoint mayors and provincial premiers was challenged. Mbeki himself looked shattered, playing with documents and looking at the ceiling, though nothing could disguise his public humiliation. He had not only underestimated Zuma's support but had failed to understand the populist wave sweeping through the organization. He had treated the NGC as if it were a conclave of exile activists but it much more resembled the hurly-burly of the UDF. Effectively it had voted no confidence in Mbeki and the NWC.

Mbeki refused to take the point. The NGC voted emphatically that it did not want to separate the offices of ANC president and state President, but Mbeki walked straight down the hall to a waiting television camera and stated that he was 'available' for the party presidency. 'It's as if he's Joan of Arc, listening to strange voices. He's certainly not listening to ours,' said one bewildered cadre. Once the NGC was over Mbeki's supporters suggested that it had all been a mistake: according to the ANC deputy secretary-general, Sankie Mthembi-Makhanyele, delegates had 'relied on hearsay and did not have full information on hand' when they supported Zuma.[90] This was, of course, a reflection of Mbeki's views. The NGC was a warning. If he persisted, he was headed for disaster. But he was angry, petulant and in denial.

THE VINDICTIVE AFTERMATH

Mbeki and Zuma were now clearly engaged in a fight to the death. Senior ANC leaders, starting with Kgalema Motlanthe, were appalled at the way the party was tearing itself to pieces and there were vain attempts to make truces. The ferocity of the struggle also meant that no one else dared enter the race. Mbeki still had the power of the state behind him (though many institutions, including the NIA, were now split down the middle) and would clearly use it against anyone who poked their head above the parapet. The ANC elite, well aware that Zuma had originally been picked as Deputy President because his lack of education and administrative ability made him an 'unthinkable' President, now watched horrified as Mbeki made certain that Zuma would be the only possible alternative to himself.

As with all those who suffer from paranoia, for Mbeki the possibility of losing morphed into nightmares of physical elimination. He had stepped back from the Aids debate only because he believed that otherwise the large pharmaceutical companies might arrange his assassination, and he now lived in a mental world where such things were possible. Those who criticized him were accused of wanting to 'destroy' the ANC (i.e. himself) and achieve the complete destabilization and overthrow of the regime, a fantasy often accompanied by imagined alliances with old apartheid counter-revolutionary forces. This was absurd. Such elements who remained were usually farming, running small businesses or serving as privateers in Iraq.

Insistent rumour had it that the President was increasingly reliant on alcohol and other 'little helpers' and that he was consulting an ever-narrower circle of advisers, often merely Essop Pahad and Mojanku Gumbi. He saw plots and conspiracies in all directions. When he took the visiting Indian President to celebrate Gandhi's anniversary at a stadium in Durban only to find it virtually empty, he railed against the sinister forces who had contrived such a result. This was ludicrous. It would normally have been easy to fill the stadium with Durban's Indian community for such an occasion but Mbeki had entrusted the rally's organization to Mewa Ramgobin, a veteran ANC MP locally regarded as a figure of fun, and Essop Pahad, a Johannesburg Indian strongly disliked by most Durban Indians. A better way of alienating the local Indian community would have been hard to devise.

The general atmosphere of *fin de règne* lacked only a Rasputin – and infallibly on cue there appeared just such a character, Ronald Suresh Roberts, who became Mbeki's principal propagandist and official biographer. He was a West Indian interloper whose behaviour earned him a newspaper profile headed 'The Unlikeable Mr Roberts'; the ever-litigious Roberts sued the paper and lost comprehensively. The judge described him as 'obsessive', 'vindictive and venomous', constantly guilty of threatening behaviour, 'excessive conduct', an 'evasive, argumentative and opportunistic witness', and judging that he had given 'untruthful' evidence in court, that his version of events was 'completely discredited', that his conduct was frequently 'improper' and his behaviour while working in a law practice so seriously improper as to cause him to be 'censured by the Law Society'.[91]

In any other country such a judgment would have caused Roberts to be considered an inappropriate spokesman or biographer for a President, but Mbeki continued to patronize him. Roberts's book was edited by Essop Pahad and Mbeki treated the book as his own, appearing at book launches at Roberts's side and actually signing copies of the book, *Fit to Govern: The Native Intelligence of Thabo Mbeki*. The book itself was a hagiography of schoolboy standard, purporting to show that Mbeki had never been an Aids denialist, that he had always been a multi-party democrat and had not simply supported Mugabe but had criticized him. It was easy for critics to punch holes in this. And Mbeki was even then ringing up another biographer, Mark Gevisser, to volunteer a document he had written in which Aids scientists were compared to Nazi concentration camp doctors, and black people who accepted their medicines as displaying a slave mentality. Mbeki's intent was clear, though, given the nugatory value of Roberts's book, pathetic. The book was supposed both to bolster his campaign against Zuma and make a final desperate bid to clean up his image in the hope of gaining a prestigious international job. The book received derisory reviews and achieved neither purpose.

After the NGC the gloves came off. The activities of the NIA and other privately contracted intelligence operatives increased exponentially. By the end of 2007 veterans of the apartheid intelligence services claimed to the author that even at the height of apartheid phone-tapping and letter-opening had never reached such epidemic proportions. Expensive (usually Chinese) equipment was bought which not only enabled the security services to intercept all cellphone calls, faxes and e-mails but to enter others' computers at will, turning them into listening devices, sabotaging their data or inserting false entries into their bank accounts. In the last four months of 2007 Zuma's security guards removed twenty-six electronic bugs from his sitting room, and reckoned there had been four separate assassination attempts on Zuma that year.[92]

The first sign of this tougher approach was the cutting off of funds to the ANC Youth League.[93] The wild, over-the-top Youth League tended to be much mocked in the media but no one had forgotten that Mandela, Tambo and Sisulu had taken over the ANC leadership in the 1940s thanks to its backing, so its support for Zuma now was symbolic. It was unprecedented for the ANC to cut off funds to the League – and the League also saw its fund-raising among ANC-aligned businessmen suddenly dry up, for word had gone out from the President's office that the League had to be brought to heel. This left the League dangerously dependent on Brett Kebble, who had fallen on hard times, with his JCI mining house suspended from the stock exchange. Naturally, the President's office encouraged a revolt within the League against its leader, Fikile Mbalula, but Mbalula fended off his challengers.

Mbeki was well aware that far-left groups such as the Landless People's Movement, the Soweto Electricity Crisis Committee and the Durban Shack Dwellers Movement had helped mobilize township protests against service delivery failure and that these in turn had fed into the general leftward movement seen at the NGC, so a much tougher attitude was adopted towards them. The ANC threatened to take strong action against members who supported violent protests,[94] while police action against protesters became noticeably rougher, with the use of rubber bullets, tear gas and baton charges even producing the occasional fatality and the Landless People's Movement complaining that some of its members had suffered police torture.

But Zuma, inevitably, was the principal target. No sooner had Zuma moved into a new Johannesburg luxury house provided by another Asian businessman, Mohamed Sayed Hoorzook,[95] than it was raided at dawn by the Scorpions, who simultaneously raided Zuma's homestead in Nkandla, Schabir Shaik's house in Durban, the Thint office and the home of Thint's managing director, Pierre Moynot, the offices of Shaik's

Nkobi Holdings, the homes of Zuma backers, Nora Fakude-Nkuna and the KwaZulu-Natal finance minister, Zweli Mkhize. Remarkably, the Scorpions also raided Zuma's attorney in Durban, Michael Hulley, and his former attorney in Johannesburg, Julie Mahomed, confiscating large quantities of documents.[96]

These raids, described by Cosatu as 'a systematic brutal persecution of Zuma', were a serious error. They produced a confrontation between the Scorpions and the Presidential Protection Unit guarding Zuma's house, created a huge furore within the ANC and also led to a legal row which Julie Mahomed won, for the Scorpions had seriously offended against the convention of attorney-client privilege. Not only did they have to return the confiscated papers to Ms Mohamed but the wrongful seizure of such papers was now prejudicial to the state's case against Zuma, especially since another judge ruled that Zuma's documents too had been unlawfully seized.[97] Tax evasion charges were launched against Zuma. But the state had overstepped the law in a manner reminiscent of apartheid police actions of yore, greatly strengthening the impression of a politically inspired witch-hunt. All notions of a political truce between Mbeki and Zuma vanished.

THE 'ASSASSINATION OF KEBBLE'

Brett Kebble was considerably larger than life: jovial, clever, culture-loving and a large patron of BEE ventures. His allegation that Bulelani Ngcuka was backing his erstwhile friend, Mzi Nkumalo, against him had put him in the same corner as Zuma. Kebble then gave large support to the (Zuma-supporting) ANC Youth League, with generous BEE schemes for its leaders, and large contributions and loans to several ANC politicians. But Kebble's enterprises were in difficulty and he was facing a sea of legal troubles, including cases of fraud. Later it emerged that he had stolen R2 billion from his various companies. But before this could break surface he was murdered, on 27 September 2005. Driving home in Johannesburg, Kebble had stopped his car on a quiet stretch of road and wound down his car window. He was struck viciously in the face with a gun muzzle and seven bullets were pumped into him at point-blank range.

Although given a solemn funeral, wrapped in an ANC flag, with passionate rhetorical tributes, Kebble had been a rogue: the money he gave away had been accumulated by fraud, theft and larceny. No one could explain how he had managed to file no tax returns since 1993, with more than R100 million owing in back taxes.[98] The taxman seized two of his homes, a luxury yacht and much else besides.[99]

Kebble's murder triggered various theories,[100] including that it was an assisted suicide (he had insured his life for R30 million days before the hit).[101] It greatly alarmed the Johannesburg business community; if such a high-profile businessman – and such a high-profile opponent of President Mbeki – could be thus struck down, who was safe? Jacob Zuma felt he had lost a friend: thereafter he referred to 'the assassination of Kebble'. The killer had used 'full copper jacket' 9 mm low-velocity bullets of an unusual type, used by bodyguards and crack security operatives, to ensure that the bullets did not pass through the body and hit bystanders.[102] Such a gun and its bullets were found only in the police or security forces. It was reminiscent of the murder of Hazel Crane, 'the queen of diamonds', in November 2003. Hazel, a bosom friend of Winnie Mandela, had made her way up from the slums of Belfast to being a multi-millionaire illicit diamond dealer. She had died, close to the site of Brett Kebble's murder, on a quiet road when she too had rolled down her car window and stopped six bullets at point-blank range.[103] At the time the Israeli diamond mafia were generally held responsible, but the similarity with Kebble's case raised notions of a contract killing carried out, perhaps, by the same professional outfit.

There were other oddities. The day after the murder Kebble's car was released by the police to a panel-beating firm. For the next eight days crowds of people flocked to the vehicle, went over it minutely, removed the bloodstains and generally rendered the car useless for forensic purposes. The police also failed to rope off the murder site which was, as a result, heavily trampled.[104] Even the Police Commissioner, Jackie Selebi, described the way in which the police allowed all evidence to be destroyed or slip through their fingers as 'strange' and 'incredible'.[105]

But why had Kebble stopped his car on a quiet road at 9.30 p.m and wound down his window? Kebble was security conscious: had he wanted to pick up a girl he would doubtless have opted for a safer, upmarket version. There was only one serious possibility: a real or fake police car had stopped him with its flashing blue light. Kebble had stopped, rolling down his front window as he saw a police officer approach. The 'policeman' had then murdered him with a police weapon, and associates within the police had obliterated the evidence. The notion of state agency in Kebble's killing occurred to one and all and certainly added to the general jumpiness of the Zuma camp.

But Zuma, who had looked like a winner ever since the NGC, was still riding high. The legal process against him was long and uncertain and hard evidence was difficult to come by. If he was to be brought down, it had to be done quickly and in a way which would make him an unthinkable President. The Mbeki camp was well aware of Zuma's weaknesses but none was more alluring than his apparently unlimited uxoriousness. You simply had to set a honeytrap, baited with a young woman, and Zuma, like Winnie-the-Pooh's Heffalump, would inevitably fall into it.

ZUMA'S RAPE TRIAL

In early November 2005 the police leaked to the press a report that Zuma had been accused of rape. South African law forbids the publication of the names of either the alleged victim or perpetrator of a rape, but the media immediately published Zuma's name and, in some cases, the victim's too. Worse, the SABC staged endless dial-in programmes where, with the sub judice rule thrown to the four winds, listeners poured a torrent of abuse against Zuma. For feminists, it seemed that any man accused of rape was guilty. A man was either a rapist or an alleged rapist and it was much the same. On their side was a long and disgraceful history of sexual abuse in South Africa generally and particularly within the ANC. There had been 'comfort women' in the guerrilla camps; women activists were pressured to provide sexual favours and even ANC women MPs spoke of constant sexual harassment by their male colleagues.

Once rape charges were laid the NWC immediately barred Zuma from all party activities, thus depriving him of a public platform. Mbeki meanwhile made speeches about women's rights, the liberation of women and the horror of violence against women.[106] Zuma's staunchest supporters, his fellow-villagers in Nkandla, were certain that the accusation was a set-up and an insult. 'We believe that this rape charge is a further attempt by Mbeki and his group to ensure that Zuma does not become President of the ANC. Mbeki is a dirty man,' said a local notable, Zitha Gcaba. 'They used Zuma to win the Zulu vote. They used Zuma to end violence between the IFP and ANC. They used Zuma to keep the alliance intact. Now they want to throw him like a piece of shit. We won't allow that. I wish I was young again.'[107] It was in this period that Zuma supporters began to wear 'Zuma, my President' T-shirts and Zuma began to rally his supporters with his 'Lethu Mshini wami' song ('Give me my machine gun', an old MK song). The government discouraged both practices: indeed, when a popular band, Izingane Zoma, had a hit with their pro-Zuma song, 'Msholozi', it was banned by the SABC even though the disc had gone gold.[108]

The state invested large resources into the case, which was jumped to the head of the queue of many other rape cases awaiting trial. Usually the main witnesses in rape cases are simply the complainant and the accused, but the State presented a list of twenty-eight witnesses including a cabinet minister, a provincial minister, medical experts and senior policemen, as well as Zuma's bodyguards. The judge, Bernard Ngoepe, nervously recused himself (he had granted permission for the illegal searches of Zuma's houses), as did Judge Jeremiah Shongwe (Zuma had sired an illegitimate child with Shongwe's sister) and Judge Phineas Mojapelo (Zuma had been a struggle comrade). Ultimately a white judge presided, Willem van der Merwe.

The alleged victim – nicknamed Khwezi – was given redoubled protection (her flat had been broken into and trashed) and more than 100 extra police were detailed to provide security around the court. The scenes there were pure circus. While a number of women's organizations held prayers and a public vigil in Khwezi's support, their partisanship was more than matched by the Zuma side. Large numbers of Zuma supporters arrived, some in traditional Zulu dress all the way from Zululand. A sangoma dressed as a Zulu warrior prated about God's messages to Shaka, founder of the Zulu nation. Opposite stood a similarly protesting group from Powa (People Opposed to Women Abuse), there to support Khwezi, who was a 31-year-old HIV-positive Aids activist and previously a close family friend of Zuma's. Prejudging the case just as much as the Zuma side, Powa's activists wore T-shirts with the message 'Against Her Will, Against the Law'. This enraged the Zuma-ites not only into hurling abuse and objects at Powa's (inferior) forces but burning photos of the complainant to shouts of 'Burn the bitch!'

Many Zuma supporters wore T-shirts reading '100 per cent Zuluboy'

– deliberately picking up the insulting township term used to denote Zulus as rural hicks, while on the back read the slogan: 'Conspiracy: Count 1: Corruption. Count 2: Corruption. Count 3: Rape. What Next???' Some brandished slogans: 'Zuma Was Raped' and 'SANDF/SAPS Be Ready For Civil War if Cde Zuma . . .' Zuma's supporters shouted abuse and 'bitch' at Khwezi as she entered court, while Zuma did little to calm the atmosphere by leading his followers in 'Lethu Mshini Wami' and performing Zulu war dances. When a loaded army-issue R-4 assault rifle was found in a vehicle with false number plates near the court this was immediately interpreted by the Zuma camp as evidence of a possible assassination attempt.[109]

Zuma, former head of ANC intelligence and a man who was no stranger to the darker side of ANC activities, was taking the threat of assassination quite seriously. The state also worried that Khwezi might be an assassination target. She was given a heavy security guard and removed to a safe house. Members of the Presidential Protection Unit were also assigned to guard her – though several of the Unit's members declined to do so either because 'they didn't want to take sides' or because they feared being suspected of being 'on the other side' if something happened to her.[110]

Every state organization was now split between the pro-Zuma and pro-Mbeki sides. This was dramatically visible in the NIA, whose boss, Billy Masethla, was fired after it was discovered that he had placed Saki Macozoma (a strong Mbeki supporter) under surveillance. But the ANC had placed its cadres in all state and parastatal organizations, so these were all politicized and, now, factionalized – and consequently paralysed. Feeling ran most strongly about the Scorpions. The Zuma-ites, angered by Zuma's long harassment, the repeated leaks and the illegal raids, demanded the abolition of the Scorpions and their absorption into the ordinary police, a move which Mbeki, as strongly, resisted.

In late February four armed men overpowered the guard on Khwezi's house, which was ransacked a second time, with the attackers boxing up and carrying away most of its contents,[111] although hers was a humble township abode, hardly worth such attention for the value of its contents. It also emerged that Zuma's right-hand man, the KwaZulu-Natal provincial minister, Zweli Mkhize, had spent much time talking to Khwezi and her mother, allegedly offering them 'compensation' if the rape charge were withdrawn.[112]

Like most rape trials the case consisted of two conflicting narratives, with no independent witness. While both parties agreed that sexual intercourse had taken place, Zuma's version was that Khwezi had surprised him by apparently inviting his attentions, explaining that in Zulu tradition nothing could be worse than refusing her gratification. He did himself lasting harm, however, by dwelling on the shortness of her skirt, as if any woman wearing such a garment was inviting sex; by his admission that he had had unprotected sex with someone he knew to be HIV positive; by his laughable admission that he had showered after sex as an anti-Aids precaution; and by the fact that he had had sex with a woman more than thirty years his junior who was an old family friend. The general impression was that Zuma was a man of innumerable sexual liaisons who drew no fine distinctions. When I asked Zuma about this later on, he admitted that it had been absurd to talk of taking a shower against Aids, 'but I'd never imagined I'd have to give detailed explanations about my activities in the bedroom and bathroom. I was flustered and said what came into my head.'[113]

But the damage done to Khwezi's credibility was far greater. Somehow Zuma's lawyers had procured the rough draft of her autobiography (this fact alone considerably disturbed her), quoting it to show that she had recorded being raped three times as a child; that she often slept next to other people through fear of sleeping alone; that she considered herself a lesbian but had sex with men; that an ANC tribunal had cleared two men she had accused of rape; that there had been a further two incidents of rape or near-rape and one further rape accusation, none of which had been properly established. The further it went, the more tangled it got. Khwezi denied several of her earlier statements, some of which were on record. She admitted that she had not cried out when approached by Zuma, though a security guard was less than ten metres away. Her mother agreed that Khwezi had been in a mental institution in Zimbabwe, that she had suffered frequent hallucinations and nightmares, and that her anti-HIV medication had turned her into 'a zombie'.[114]

Khwezi also reacted badly to cross-examination: by the end of the week she was a sobbing wreck. The final devastating blow was a procession of six witnesses, four of them priests, all of whom had been accused of rape by Khwezi. Naturally, this had had severe repercussions for their careers in several cases. One of the men, African Methodist Episcopal pastor Jeffery Matlhabe, said, 'I feel sorry for her, she is sick.

She must get help otherwise many families will be destroyed.'[115] Khwezi said she did not remember any of them.

Zuma told me that the minute he heard of the rape complaint he knew he was being set up.[116] His defence suggested that the whole incident – and the trial itself – had been set up by people in high places who had, effectively, used Khwezi as part of a honeytrap. The Zuma camp suspected that either the NIA or the Scorpions had set the trap, with fingers pointed at Ronnie Kasrils (the Minister for Intelligence) or Bulelani Ngcuka (the Scorpions' boss). The defence accordingly looked for links to either man, attempting to ascertain whether Khwezi had been taken on holiday to Dubai by the Deputy President, Phumzile Mlambo-Ngcuka, and her husband in 2005 when they had used the presidential jet for a controversial shopping trip. (Khwezi would only admit that she had been to Dubai 'some years ago'.[117]) It also focused on the fact that Khwezi had telephoned Ronnie Kasrils before she had reported the rape incident to the police and had also called Kasrils when the press told her it was about to publish details of the rape charge.

Khwezi was a friend of Kasrils ('Uncle Ronnie'), and her sister (whom she had also telephoned) worked in the Intelligence Ministry. Although the defence carefully talked of how 'an exterior force with an ulterior motive' had persuaded the complainant to take the line she did, Kasrils was clearly intended. Indeed, when Zuma testified he spoke of a plot to prevent him from becoming President and mentioned Bulelani Ngcuka and Ronnie Kasrils specifically as conspirators in that plot.[118]

The defence also repeatedly asked Khwezi's mother when she had last spoken to Kasrils: her insistence that she 'did not remember' hardly allayed their suspicions. For while Zuma and Kasrils were old comrades, Kasrils had thrown in his lot completely with Mbeki and, as Zuma knew, was at that moment purging the NIA of anyone suspected of Zuma sympathies – and given Zuma's previous position as chief of ANC intelligence there were inevitably many NIA operatives linked to Zuma. The director-general, Billy Masethla, was humiliatingly disposed of; Masethla fought his dismissal long and hard in the courts and ended up like a 1930s show-trial victim, weeping in court and saying how frightened he was. Also purged was Bob Mhlanga, the head of counter-intelligence, the head of operations, Gibson Njenje, and Funi Madlala, head of the agency's cyber unit.

Mbeki saw himself as threatened by shadowy conspiracies everywhere, so no half measures were taken with the NIA. The agency launched a qualifications audit, requiring all agents to resubmit their CVs, in order to facilitate their redeployment from the NIA to some less sensitive part of the public service. One agent, Nkosinathi Mazibuko, lost his job, allegedly on medical grounds – though he was fit to work, because, he explained, 'I once said that if I leave NIA I will go and work with Zuma. That's why I am persecuted.'[119] Naturally, the sight of his old comrades being purged was painful to Zuma and considerable hostility was directed at Kasrils. Kasrils protested vehemently against his depiction by the Zuma-ites. As well he might: there are few more dangerous situations than that of a divided intelligence agency – or of a white politician caught up in the midst of African factionalist intrigue. He was not helped by revelations that he had been writing on government headed paper trying to fund-raise for Khwezi to study in the UK.[120]

Long before the trial's end the case against Zuma had effectively collapsed. Zuma revealed that Khwezi had sent him a series of flirtatious text messages in the period before their tryst, and that he had had extensive conversations about paying lobola for her.[121] In mid-trial the state was already arranging for Khwezi and her mother to go and live abroad, for they could hardly be safe again at their Durban home. On the evening before the verdict the Durban ANC and local charismatic churchmen got together to pray for Zuma's acquittal and there was great rejoicing when he was duly acquitted. Zuma's support group, the Friends of Jacob Zuma, spoke of a flood of contributions to his defence fund and also announced several large gospel concerts to raise funds for Zuma's forthcoming trial for corruption.

Even the IFP hostels of Thokoza rejoiced ('As a Zulu I admire Zuma for his courage', said Thokozani Ndlela, a local IFP leader[122]) and Zuma was greeted by large, adoring crowds in Durban. The KwaZulu-Natal premier, S'bu Ndebele, an Mbeki supporter, tried to rally round Zuma but was booed for his pains. Zuma supporters expressed contempt for Mbeki and even compared Zuma's tribulations with Christ's crucifixion.[123] All this was capped by the tumultuous reception awaiting Zuma in Nkandla. Zuma was now a Zulu hero, one who could fill a stadium in Soweto with enthusiastic followers and admiring *maskandi* musicians. The rape trial had rebounded spectacularly, with Mbeki and Kasrils now cast by the ANC Youth League as the 'evil hand' behind it. Zuma's ANC functions were hurriedly restored.

THE FALL-OUT FROM THE RAPE TRIAL

The rape trial had two very different sequels. First, the NIA leaked the juicy fact that to raise the R12 million needed for his trial defence Zuma had flown to Tripoli and sought help from President Qaddafi. Qaddafi, whose aspirations to lead Africa had been checkmated by Mbeki, was believed to have given Zuma $2 million. Further embarrassing revelations followed that Zuma's trip had been preceded by visits to Libya by both the SACP's Blade Nzimande and Cosatu.[124]

The second and larger result was that in the eyes of South Africa's progressive intelligentsia, the trial did Zuma irreparable damage. Thereafter Zapiro, the *Mail and Guardian*'s cartoonist, always depicted Zuma as a Zulu nitwit with a shower fixed to the back of his head, an image which stuck. Even before the trial was decided it drew a furious response from forty-eight leading women, including the ANC's Cheryl Carolus and Gill Marcus and businesswomen like Wendy Appelbaum, attacking 'the signal the trial sends', a reference to Zuma's open polygamy and the fact that he thus had the 'right to infect' multiple women with HIV.[125] The fact that the leading signatories were all politically correct multi-millionaires did not lessen its significance for the feminist movement at large, which regarded Zuma with horror. *Business Day*, equally appalled, editorialized that neither the ANC Women's League, nor its Youth League, nor Mandela, nor 'the Motlanthes, the Ngonyamas, the Ramaphosas, the Sexwales and the Motsepes' had said a critical word about Zuma's sexual mores.[126]

But Zuma rebounded powerfully from the trial. By now the SACP, Cosatu and the ANC Youth League were all loud in his defence and their almost routine denunciations of Mbeki. On the streets Mbeki was openly vilified as the evil genius behind all moves against Zuma; T-shirts bearing his face were burnt; those who supported him, like S'bu Ndebele and Phumzile Mlambo-Ngcuka, received a rough ride including, sometimes, actual missiles thrown at them. The chants outside the courtroom of 'Siphi isifebe si kuMbeki?' (Where is Mbeki's slut?) summed it up, though when asked whether he saw Mbeki's hand in all his mishaps, Zuma carefully replied that he personally had 'not seen' this.

The rape trial considerably increased the tension between the Zuma and Mbeki camps, for most Zuma supporters now assumed that Mbeki would stop at nothing to prevent Zuma's forward march. In February 2006, when George Nene, the Gauteng regional chairman of Zuma's principal support group, the Friends of Jacob Zuma, was killed in a car accident, officials of this group were extremely suspicious and asked for a police investigation. No sooner, they argued, had Zuma paid tribute at a rally to Nene's sterling work for his cause than Nene had met his death.[127] When, seven months later, Nene's replacement, Zobaphi Sithole, was shot dead, Zuma met with the police and wrote to the NIA and Military Intelligence, asking that his own security be beefed up and saying that he feared assassination. His own security detachment was already on high alert and his key allies, Blade Nzimande and the Youth League leader, Fikile Mbalula, had also strengthened their security arrangements.[128] Moreover, it was increasingly assumed by Zuma's grass-roots supporters that Mbeki had been somehow involved in the Hani assassination. At the 2007 SACP Congress the party's chairman, Gwede Mantashe, led delegates in the song 'Thabo Mbeki siyabuza ubani owabulala uChris Hani' ('Thabo Mbeki, tell us who killed Chris Hani').[129]

In a sense it was poetic justice. Mbeki had always operated from behind the scenes, pushing others forward to do his bidding, preserving deniability and declaiming noble motives even as he sent opponents through the trapdoor. This style was predicated on the assumption that Mbeki was cleverer than his opponents so that his indirect agency would never be spotted. But now the man in the street had the idea that Mbeki's hidden hand was everywhere. Increasingly it seemed that while Mbeki commanded the state, Zuma had more mass support.

The press, until then carefully deferential towards Mbeki, could now see – every day – the SACP, Cosatu and the man in the street get away with denunciations of Mbeki. The open ANC split had given the press a choice and, clearly, neither Mbeki nor Zuma were angels. So, at long last, the press woke up and became increasingly bold. Such a spirit was catching. To the fury of the President's office (Essop Pahad raged impotently against it), the press had escaped from its kennel and it would be extremely difficult to get that dog back in again. Not that Zuma was a friend of the press: he kept threatening to sue over its often contemptuous coverage of him. But it became obvious that he had put himself in harmony with all the forces of opposition within the ANC – and that they were strong. In which case there was less reason to defer to government.

Increasingly Mbeki played the 'women's card', suggesting that the next President should be a woman, and that there must be complete gender equality in delegate selection in all ANC and governmental organizations. This was seen as a way of packing the ANC conference with women who were likely both to disapprove of Zuma's marital and sexual behaviour and to be grateful to Mbeki for their preferment. The more gullible in the press took this seriously, and ran features about a future woman President. For those who remembered that Mbeki had previously intervened personally to disqualify a woman (Winnie Mandela) from even running for Deputy President, it was obvious that the function of women delegates was merely to vote Mbeki back for an extra term.

Meanwhile, a constant stream of dirty tricks was played against Zuma, for example the manufacturing of hoax e-mails and then the circulation of the 'Browse Mole' report, in which Zuma was accused of having secured funding from Libya and the Angolans for a coup he was preparing against Mbeki, using ex-MK soldiers. Mbeki tried to dismiss this report as the work of rogue elements but it had actually been put together by the state.[130] A member of the Scorpions was ultimately found to have fabricated it.[131]

Zuma still had to face fresh corruption charges over his alleged payment from Thint for having exerted pressure to stop inquiries into the arms deal. His defence threatened to call Mbeki to testify that Zuma's key letter to Scopa had actually been written by him. But Mbeki declined, arguing that it would damage the image of the presidency were he to appear in court. But the prosecution was also in difficulty over the question of the admissibility of documents it had seized, so when the court met it immediately applied for an adjournment. Zuma argued that this case had been hanging over him for far too long, that he was unemployed and that it had already cost him the deputy presidency: it was high time for the state to put up or shut up. But even six weeks later the prosecution was far from ready and Judge Herbert Msimang impatiently struck the case from the roll. So on 20 September 2006 Zuma walked free amidst scenes of public jubilation. In an emotional speech to the crowd Zuma thanked the Zulu king, various Zulu chiefs and priests for their prayers of support, for he was more than ever the

Zulu champion now. A princess of the Zulu royal family was outside the court to greet him and ANC activists danced in celebration alongside Zulu warriors in traditional garb, an unthinkable sight during the days of IFP–ANC strife not so long ago.[132]

Zuma's supporters demanded that the state's long 'persecution' of Zuma must now end, but within days the Scorpions raided Zuma's accountants and intimated that fresh charges would be laid. Time, however, was now on Zuma's side. The state needed further time to lay charges. More time would elapse before they would get to court. Even if they won, there would be a lengthy appeal process. The ANC conference at Polokwane, where the leadership issue would be settled, loomed ever nearer. The NWC tried to prevent Zuma from speaking at the congress of the SA Democratic Teachers Union, mandating ANC chairman Terror Lekota instead, but as soon as Zuma stepped into the hall, flanked by Blade Nzimande and Zwelinzima Vavi, delegates burst into a bitterly anti-Mbeki song – 'Sihamba no-Zuma. Thina nalo Zuma sobulala igovu lenja' ('We'll go with Zuma and we'll kill this big ugly dog'). Lekota stood embarrassed while the Education Minister, Naledi Pandor, who had intimated that she did not want to share a platform with Zuma, was given an icy reception. For the first time Zuma then echoed Cosatu/SACP critiques of government, assailing it over its policies on Aids and the over-centralization of power in the presidency.[133]

With the case against Zuma thrown out, the NWC could not deny him other platforms – though he was heavily accident-prone. Having had to apologize humbly for having had unsafe sex and his remarks about showering to prevent Aids, he soon blundered again, happily telling a crowd that 'Same-sex marriage is a disgrace to the nation and to God. When I was growing up, a pansy boy would not have stood in front of me. I would knock him out.'[134] For this too he had to issue a grovelling apology though, as he told me later, he was just harking back to his boyhood when stick-fighting was the norm and those regarded as 'sissies' got short shrift. But Zuma had a distinct knack for putting his foot in his mouth. Such sentiments did him no harm at grass-roots level but they horrified 'respectable society'. Desmond Tutu, for example, declared that Zuma should stand down because he was simply 'not fit' to be President.[135]

THE ROAD TO POLOKWANE

As the ANC's Polokwane conference (December 2007) neared there was increasing desperation both within and outside the ANC at the coming clash. There was strong feeling that someone like Cyril Ramaphosa would be preferable to either Mbeki or Zuma, but Mbeki's clear hostility to such candidates was enough to keep others out. In the end, Tokyo Sexwale, now a billionaire, thrust himself forward. Immediately, the press carried damaging accounts of Sexwale's lavish gifts to politicians, judges and journalists, data which could only have come from the NIA. But it was far too late: activist opinion had long since polarized between Zuma and Mbeki.

Mbeki was in a strange and petulant state of mind in these final months. His writings for *ANC Today* became increasingly peculiar; his justification for his dismissal of the deputy Minister for Health, Nozizwe Madlala-Routledge, with its almost prurient juxtaposition of mini-skirts and dead black babies, has already been noted. Public opinion was shocked, too, by his decision to suspend Vusi Pikoli, the National Director for Public Prosecutions, after the latter had attempted to serve a writ on the Police Commissioner, Jackie Selebi, for corruption and involvement in gangsterism. Mbeki claimed that he had acted thus because of a breakdown in relations between Pikoli and the Minister of Justice but few believed him. Mbeki had long tried to shield Selebi. As clamour mounted over his association with gangsters, Mbeki had gone on television to defend Selebi, telling the public simply to 'Trust me'. When the uproar over Pikoli's suspension continued Mbeki appointed Frene Ginwala to investigate the case – and maintained that Pikoli had never briefed him about any case against Selebi. But already alternative lists of candidates for election to the NEC at Polokwane were appearing in the press and Ginwala's name featured on the Mbeki list, thus making it clear where her loyalties lay. Worse, Pikoli showed that he had briefed Mbeki and the Justice Minister on more than twenty occasions about the case against Selebi. In truth, having imposed his own man, Selebi, as head of the police, Mbeki did not want to lose him, let alone alienate him before Polokwane.

Equally unwise was Mbeki's passionate defence of Manto Tshabalala-Msimang, the Health Minister, when the *Sunday Times* exposed her as both a drunk who had insisted on alcohol in hospital while having a liver transplant, and a kleptomaniac who had stolen from patients when she had been in charge of a hospital in Botswana. Mbeki had long known all this, but his response was to have the editor of the *Sunday Times*, Mondli Makhanya, threatened with arrest. When this in turn was exposed Mbeki furiously denied that such a threat had been made. Indeed, by now he was in denial on almost every front – on Aids, on Zimbabwe, on the strength of Zuma's challenge and much else besides. Everyone who criticized him was accused of attempting to overthrow the government and destabilize the ANC, and of mounting a campaign, sometimes in liaison with counter-revolutionaries and mercenaries.

Mbeki was now losing ground on every front and, rather than face this reality, he retreated from it. He had always spent solitary hours surfing the net or writing *ANC Today*. Fidel Castro was amazed, on one of Mbeki's visits to Cuba, to find Mbeki creeping off to his room to write these weekly lectures, protesting, reasonably enough, that he could get other people to perform such work. But Mbeki believed in his own indispensability and 'preferred to consult his own genius'. Those who would warn him of unpleasant realities were cut out. He saw fewer and fewer people, almost invariably sycophants.

Nonetheless, few imagined that Mbeki would be beaten at Polokwane. Sitting African presidents, with all the power of patronage and incumbency, did not suffer such humiliations. To some extent this was wishful thinking: among the chattering classes the prospect of a Zuma presidency was simply too awful to contemplate. This mood was well captured by Mark Gevisser, whose large biography of Mbeki[136] appeared in the run-up to Polokwane. Gevisser was the epitome of the *Mail and Guardian* progressive journalist and had originally set out to write what might almost have been a hagiography of Mbeki. But Gevisser was also a gay activist, and Mbeki's attitude to Aids made everything a great deal more complicated. In the end, Gevisser pulled his punches by having little to say about Mbeki in power.

In the Polokwane run-up, Gevisser, enjoying enormous media coverage, acted as Mbeki's quasi-spokesman. In Mbeki's view, he said, a Zuma presidency would reduce South Africa to 'a neo-colonial basket case' or 'just another African kleptocracy'. He also reported that Mbeki now admitted that he had indeed written the Castro Hlongwane document on Aids allegedly authored by the late Peter Mokaba; that Mbeki saw Aids doctors as akin to Nazi concentration camp scientists, and blacks who accepted the orthodox view of Aids as guilty of a slave mentality; that he had withdrawn from the debate over Aids because he and his aides believed that otherwise he ran a serious risk of assassination by the big pharmaceutical companies; and that he had taken the attitude he had on Aids because of the dangers in its presentation – that it would allow people to say that Aids rather than racism or colonialism or imperialism was Africa's greatest problem. That is, people had to die for lack of ARVs because the real battle was about presentational questions. One might have thought this would have disqualified Mbeki from further consideration – yet Gevisser was sure he was still preferable to Zuma.

ZUMA'S INCOMING TIDE

Later it was said that Zuma had formed a 'coalition of the wounded' – all those who had been hurt or marginalized by Mbeki. There were indeed many of these, not a few of them obvious scoundrels, though for once Winnie Mandela was not amongst them: she had been caught out in yet another scam and only Mbeki's goodwill stood between her and the possibility of a substantial jail sentence. More significantly, Zuma found himself in natural sympathy with all the forces of opposition and discontent within the ANC, notably the SACP and Cosatu.

To these were added the out-group in every province, generally the faction fighting the imposition of an Mbeki client as provincial premier. For Zuma's emergence as a credible alternative within the ANC suddenly valorized the simmering discontent over Mbeki's extreme centralization of power. As my old MK friend Sibusiso Madlala explained to me,

> In exile the ethnic and factional factor was kept under control provided there was democratic election. It's true that some Xhosas and Zulus thought they were a cut above, say, a Venda or Tsonga, but if the comrades elected someone who was a Venda over them they'd accept it as OK because there's no quarrelling with a free vote. The real problem arose when people were just selected from on high – for example, the way that Xhosas always seemed to get picked for many of the scholarships to study abroad. Once you have appointment from above

people immediately start disputing it because they suspect ethnic or factional favouritism.[137]

The situation was worsened because many of those selected as premiers by Mbeki had few popular roots while truly popular leaders (Ace Magashule in the Free State, for example) were passed over. Such premiers inevitably felt responsibility upwards to Mbeki rather than downwards to their local grass roots.

In addition, few non-Xhosas missed the fact that the cabinet had become more and more heavily Xhosa in composition and that many of the departmental directors-general were Xhosas too. In fact, Mbeki was a Xhosa without any popular roots: he always appeared as an aloof black Englishman, an anomaly even in his own Eastern Cape. He was, though, playing with fire by disregarding the question of ethnic balance in a way Mandela would never have done. As in much else, he seemed genuinely to believe his own propaganda about the ANC being loftily above such considerations.

Zuma's coalition was far more formidable than either Mbeki or the media allowed for. In general the media despised Zuma; he was usually depicted as a corrupt, spendthrift, sexually misbehaving and illiterate oaf, a depiction which the Mbeki camp happily encouraged. Anyone could see that Zuma had a way with people and that he was in great demand as a man to sing and dance at weddings, but his followers were seen as the lowest of the low. The better educated, black and white, simply expressed incredulity at the idea that he might be taken seriously as the man to lead the ANC and the country.

This was to miss entirely the potential of Zuma's coalition. Zulus were, after all, the largest ethnic group, one which generally felt that it had been politically passed over. Buthelezi might have been rejected by the voters but his charge that Zulus had never before had to take second place to Xhosas, having never been defeated by them, had echoed a genuine popular sentiment. Zulus, whether IFP or ANC, were proud of the late Chief Albert Luthuli and after a succession of Xhosas leading the ANC for more than forty years – Mandela, Tambo, Mbeki – were quick to rally behind Zuma's bid. The phrase heard in the streets, insistently, was: 'It's our time.'

Cosatu and the SACP, seeing Zuma as their way back to equal status within the tripartite alliance, also rallied to him, with few exceptions.

And at every election the ANC relied heavily on Cosatu, with its 1.8 million members and large number of skilled organizers, to mobilize the ANC vote. Thus Zuma represented a coalition which began with a fairly solid bloc-vote from the country's biggest ethnic group, the support of the country's most powerful pressure group and two of the three members of the alliance. From there it reached into every province, attracting malcontents of every kind. It should have been apparent from the outset that this made Zuma a difficult man to beat.

ENVY, INEQUALITY AND THE REVOLUTIONARY TRADITION

Zuma had two further powerful dynamics working for him. First, the BEE policy and the growth of a black middle class produced great envy and resentment among the far larger number of Africans who did not benefit. Since those with political influence were the most pursued by companies wanting BEE deals, the NEC was now largely peopled by those with substantial business interests. Bheki Cele, a provincial minister in KwaZulu-Natal and hardline Zuma-ite, referred to the NEC contemptuously as 'a stock exchange', a view fairly representative of SACP and Cosatu opinion. Given Mbeki's reliance on the NEC as his principal political support, this was a dangerous development for him.

Even among ordinary ANC MPs acquisitive instincts were sharply to the fore: when the 'Travelgate' scandal (as it was known) broke in 2005 it emerged that almost all ANC MPs had stolen large amounts of money by falsifying their travel expenses. A forensic report identified 330 MPs (out of a total of 400) who had received improper benefits.[138] Only one DA MP, Craig Morkel, was among these.[139] Since the DA had 50 seats, this meant that the other 329 guilty individuals had to be found from among just 350 MPs. Virtually the entire ANC parliamentary elite – including many ministers – were guilty, though fewer than 30 ANC MPs were actually called to face the music and the high-ups were allowed to reach quiet settlements. The ANC chief whip, Mbulelo Goniwe, who crafted these quiet deals, was himself the beneficiary of such a deal,[140] though he lost his job soon after, having been found guilty of repeated sexual harassment.

Harry Charlton, Parliament's chief financial officer, had just begun unearthing a further Travelgate scam, bringing the total stolen to more than R55 million, when he was summarily sacked on trumped-up charges, manifestly in order to prevent him further embarrassing the elite.[141] For the ANC elite was transparently bent on self-enrichment in any way it could find. The results were perfectly visible from their cars, clothes, houses and their use of private health and private schools. None of this was missed by those further down the social scale.

The situation was not eased by evidence that both social inequality and even poverty had increased under ANC rule. When, in late 2007, the South African Institute of Race Relations reported that those living on less than $1 a day had increased from 1,899,874 in 1996 (4.5 per cent of the population) to 4,228,787 (8.8 per cent) in 2005, Mbeki's response was one of furious denial. But the huge increase in unemployment which had occurred between 1996 and 2002 alone explained the Institute's figures. In 2002 poverty had peaked with 4,451,843 (9.7 per cent) below $1 a day, whereafter the figure slowly improved as unemployment gently declined.[142] In the feel-good atmosphere generated by the commodity boom Mbeki's response was perfectly representative of the callousness of the new black bourgeoisie but politically it was asking for trouble.

What gave such grievances their popular resonance was the dynamic of the revolutionary tradition. Mbeki liked to speak grandly of 'the revolution' in his online blog and to quote Toussaint l'Ouverture, Fanon or Marx, but this was far too literary a way to capture and channel the revolutionary tradition in an ill-educated country. Mbeki was trying to impress the wrong audience. Suspicion lingered that he had returned to South Africa only to find himself appalled by the populist crudity of an African population with whom he had little in common. And yet the long and bitter anti-apartheid struggle had left an undeniable revolutionary tradition. With Winnie Mandela's eclipse, the field was wide open for a real grass-roots populist, happy to lead the revolutionary chants and sing the revolutionary songs, reviving brave memories of a militant past. Zuma was that man.

Any remaining doubts were dispelled by the voting by ANC branches just prior to the conference, which gave Zuma 2,236 votes to Mbeki's 1,394. Zuma scored almost a clean sweep in KwaZulu-Natal and even in Mbeki's home province, the Eastern Cape, he took 44 per cent of the vote. Most striking of all, the ANC Women's League, having waited to see which way the wind was blowing, came out for Zuma, spelling the failure of Mbeki's play for the women's vote. But Mbeki still ignored those who advised him to stand down and back someone who might be able to stop Zuma. Instead, Mbeki relied on the traditional advantages of incumbency. Delegates would be swayed with offers of jobs and contracts; the NIA would keep a running tab on delegate preferences and the SABC (now a packed, pro-Mbeki organization) would have sole broadcasting rights from Polokwane. It was nothing like enough.

POLOKWANE

Pietersburg (as the locals still call Polokwane) is not a nice place in December: sweltering heat, occasional hard rain, traffic jams and the general mess which overtakes a small Afrikaner town fast becoming a hub for black taxis and African street commerce. But nothing could dampen the spirits of Zuma's supporters. Zuma himself was in high spirits and someone – no one knew who – was clearly funding his campaign lavishly. On the radio phone-in programmes many black callers, doubtless SACP activists, celebrated the arrival of 'working class leadership' and the coming socialist revolution, though such calls were frequently punctuated by whites ringing in to say that a Zuma victory would be the last straw and that they were considering emigration.

As soon as the conference began the anti-Mbeki mood was clear. There was a great deal of singing of pro-Zuma songs. The chairman, Terror Lekota, who had been outspokenly anti-Zuma, found himself contested from the floor and only Kgalema Motlanthe was able to maintain order. The SABC had erected a large screen in the conference hall and began to pan through the dignitaries and ministers one by one, clearly hoping to awe delegates by emphasizing what VIPs were in their midst. As the camera got to Essop Pahad there were loud boos, whereafter every subsequent minister was booed. The exercise was hurriedly terminated. Mbeki's floor managers had wholly miscalculated. Most ministers had stood with Mbeki against Zuma and were already viewed with hostility by Zuma's supporters.

Moreover the ministers and other dignitaries at Polokwane parked their SUVs, Mercs and BMWs where Zuma's rank-and-file supporters could not but see them – though the leaders of the Zuma camp had equally flashy cars. At the end of each day the leadership of both sides would roar off to luxurious guest houses and hotels while ordinary delegates plodded back to their spartan rooms in the down-at-heel university residences, bearing the names of such revolutionary heroes as Amilcar Cabral and Friedrich Engels. The obvious class distinction ran flatly against ANC tradition and did more damage to the Mbeki side. Joel Netshitenzhe, acting as a spokesmen for the Mbeki list, was reduced to pleading that 'the well-off must be convinced that they have a responsibility towards the less advantaged' and that they should avoid 'conspicuous consumption and ostentation'. It was far too late for that.

The SABC's pro-Mbeki bias merely angered Zuma supporters, while cries of indignation greeted the news of the various material inducements being offered to Zuma delegates to switch sides. Zwelinzima Vavi said that it was just like the old apartheid days and that Cosatu had told its members to behave now as then, accepting any bribes offered and then voting the way they had always intended. But within the Mbeki camp great store was set by this battle for delegates. Each day brought fresh estimates of how many Zuma delegates had now been won over, estimates fed by increasingly optimistic NIA surveys. Then on conference eve the National Prosecuting Authority announced that it had further evidence with which to put Zuma on trial for corruption, fraud and tax evasion. Once again, full details were leaked to the press. As Zuma's associate, Mathews Phosa, pointed out, this was a clear abuse of power. How could the media have such intimate knowledge of the charges when the accused himself knew nothing of them? Cosatu declared that any further charges brought against Zuma must be regarded as 'trumped up' and even threatened a general strike in that event.

As the vote neared key members of the Mbeki camp such as Alec Erwin, Ronnie Kasrils, Frene Ginwala and presumably Mbeki himself, were convinced that just enough had been done to deliver a narrow Mbeki victory. But, not for the first time, the NIA had simply been telling its masters what they wanted to hear. There had been almost no slippage from the original vote in the branches – but the completeness of the Zuma victory shook many. Zuma not only defeated Mbeki by a better than 60 : 40 margin but all six executive positions in the ANC went to Zuma's team by similar margins and the same occurred again in elections to the party's eighty-strong NEC. Anyone who had spoken against Zuma was flung out, as was anyone associated with Mbeki. In all, fifteen cabinet ministers, ten deputy ministers, ten MPs and all but one of the provincial premiers lost their NEC positions. The lone survivor, S'bu Ndebele, hurriedly announced that he would not stand again for the premiership of KwaZulu-Natal.

The party had delivered a massive vote of no confidence not only in Mbeki but in executive authority throughout the country. Some of the turnarounds were dramatic. Mbeki's Deputy President, Phumzile Mlambo-Ngcuka, whom he had boosted as a possible future President, could not get elected at all in the top eighty-six and nor could the party chairman, Terror Lekota. Billy Masethla, the pro-Zuma intelligence chief sacked by Mbeki, was easily elected, while his former boss, Ronnie Kasrils, was thrown out. Both Pahads were out, as was Frank Chikane (head of the President's office) and Smuts Ngonyama (the President's spokesman).

Some ministers survived onto the new NEC because, like Jeff Radebe and Lindiwe Sisulu, they had quietly joined the Zuma camp; others, like Trevor Manuel, Zola Skweyiya, or Naledi Pandor, because they were seen as competent and not particularly partisan. The sacked Nozizwe Madlala-Routledge was elected in style, but Joel Netshitenzhe only just scraped back in. Around 30 per cent of the new NEC either were or had been in trouble with the law for one reason or another and there was a heavy SACP representation. Some speculated that Zuma could yet go to jail and that the new party deputy president, Kgalema Motlanthe, or treasurer-general, Mathews Phosa, might end up as the ANC's presidential candidate in 2009. Others concluded that the SACP had successfully used Zuma as a battering ram in order to mount a sort of disguised takeover itself; some were more impressed by the crooks and miscreants of every kind who had ridden in on Zuma's coat-tails. For the dominating emotion had been anti-Mbeki more than pro-Zuma. One delegate from the Northern Cape was seen packing up to leave Polokwane even before Zuma's closing speech. It was a long bus-ride back to Kimberley and he must needs be on his way. But how could he miss his new leader's speech? 'We came here to vote Mbeki out, not to vote Zuma in,' he said wearily.

THE ECLIPSE OF MBEKI

Mbeki seemed determined not to understand what had happened. He had never run in a contested election within the ANC before, so defeat was unimaginable. Now, he deplored the delegates' behaviour. The way he had been heckled on the first day of the conference had sent the wrong image to the world. 'I wasn't that highly surprised, but it was disturbing . . . It demonstrated that among some of the members . . . the level of understanding of what the ANC is, how it works, what it stands for – was rather low.' He was then asked whether he felt the result showed that people thought he had been inaccessible. Not at all. Ordinary people 'feel a very great ease of access'. Was the vote a rejection of him personally and his style of leadership? Not at all. 'It can't be because there is a rejection of members of the ANC on the basis that I failed to implement the ANC's policies.'[143] But there were many other reports and rumours. Some spoke of Mbeki raging against members of his own entourage who had begged him to withdraw, of copious amounts of Johnny Walker Blue Label being consumed all round, and of Mbeki in tears.

Zuma, who could have used his new power to force Mbeki out of the presidency and call fresh elections, took the fateful decision not to do so. Instead Mbeki would serve out his term while Zuma sat in Luthuli House, chairing the NEC and NWC, as he waited his turn in power. Thus was created the 'two centres of power' scenario which everyone had wanted to avoid. Six weeks before Polokwane ex-President De Klerk went to see Mbeki to plead that at all costs he must not allow such a thing. P. W. Botha, De Klerk pointed out, had created exactly this situation in 1989 by resigning his party's leadership but retaining the state presidency. De Klerk, the new party leader, realized this was intolerable and forced Botha out. Once again, Mbeki refused to listen.

Zuma's triumph was greeted with dismay by the media and most whites. When the full gravity of the government's failure over electricity became apparent in a series of national power blackouts in January 2008, a mood of deep depression descended and emigration soared. For those who left, Zuma's election was 'the beginning of the end', a slide down the slope to Zimbabwe.

In fact Polokwane was an earthquake, with many meanings, by no means all of them negative. The first was that South Africa had avoided the fate of so many African states which succumbed to prolonged rule by would-be philosopher-kings: Tanzania under Nyerere, Zambia under Kaunda, Senegal under Senghor, Guinea under Sekou Toure. All these rulers theorized their rule in grand terms, while hugely damaging their countries. Nyerere, who ruled for twenty-four years, preached a gospel of African socialism, ruined the Tanzanian economy and carried out forcible removals of people.[144] Kaunda ruled for twenty-seven years under the banner of 'Zambian humanism' while steadily immiserating his people. Sekou Toure, who ruled for twenty-six years, reduced one of the most mineral-rich states in the world to complete penury with his 'scientific socialism'. Leopold Senghor's twenty-year rule had less nightmarish results, although per capita incomes fell and his opponents were imprisoned while he preached 'negritude' and 'lyrical socialism'.

Mbeki similarly theorized about the 'African Renaissance' and 'the national democratic revolution' while centralizing all power in an imperial presidency. He effectively ran the country for five years under Mandela and at Polokwane was attempting to stay in power for at least another five years (which would have taken him to twenty years). His rule was almost equally ruinous: the collapse in life expectancy, the neglect of the infrastructure, the plight of Zimbabwe and the undermining of the state and parastatal institutions must all be laid at his door.

Mbeki undoubtedly belongs with this past generation – both his and the ANC's ideological development was arrested in the 1960s – but the circumstances of his coming to power were sharply different. Whereas these earlier African philosopher-kings ran one-party states, backed up by arbitrary rule and often by terror, the end of the Cold War had brought a sea change throughout Africa. At Namibian independence in 1990 the donor states were emphatic that there would be no aid of any kind for a one-party state whose leaders voluntarily ruined its economy by adopting policies which had failed everywhere else in Africa. Even the hidebound and authoritarian Sam Nujoma took the hint, as did a host of others elsewhere. There was never any doubt that Mandela and Mbeki – far more flexible men – would do the same.

Mbeki's failure was in part due to this contradiction. He wanted to run a hegemonic Leninist party – but in a society which allowed multi-partyism and had a liberal constitution, and in which locking up or shooting your opponents, let alone the full-blown use of terror, was simply not in the script. True, he tried to move towards a de facto one-partyism, wooing the IFP, bringing in the fragments of the PAC and Azapo and absorbing the NNP – but this strategy broke on the rock of the DA. Other parties could be pulled within the ANC's field of force because its leaders were negotiable or because its electorate overlapped enough with the ANC's for it to be won over. But the DA electorate was not biddable, nor were its leaders. Hence the ANC's furious attempts to so demonize and marginalize it that it would cease to be counted as part of the political community. This nearly worked: many journalists and commentators were so scared that they felt bound to attack the DA merely to establish their 'progressive' credentials. But the DA's marginalization was never fully achieved. The party had, after all, endured exactly the same treatment under apartheid. It survived, grew to be the official Opposition and fed a continuous liberal critique of ANC rule into the bloodstream of society. No other hegemonic African nationalist party had had to live with that and over time the effect on the political culture was considerable. Indeed, the continuous example of contestation and contradiction provided by the DA helped legitimate this spirit more widely. The party's critique grew in cogency as the government's failures multiplied, and its spirit of contradiction fed into the growing contestation within the ANC.

As with other Africa's philosopher-kings, much of Mbeki's 'philosophy' seemed unlikely to outlast the man. Just as 'negritude', 'African socialism', 'Zambian humanism' and 'ujamaa' are now merely quaint relics, so it is doubtful if, after Mbeki, we shall hear much more of the 'African Renaissance' or Nepad. But the scale of his failure was greater than that. If there was one thing Mbeki wished to disprove it was that 'Africans can't govern', yet by the end his administration had confirmed this negative stereotype in many eyes. Yet the stereotype is false. In next-door Botswana an entirely competent government, taking over one of the poorest countries in the world in 1966, had by 2000 made it the fasting growing economy in the world and was confidently aiming to reach a European standard of living by 2016.[145] Botswana happily retained skilled expatriates to train its own people and worked modestly but with determination to better its lot. In a coal-rich country, it insisted on the near-universal use of solar energy and by 2008 was offering to sell power to South Africa. There were no power cuts in Botswana. No one who visited the place could possibly believe that 'Africans can't govern'.

The besetting sins of Mbeki's administration had been grandiosity, denial and racism. Whereas Botswana opted for the most modest possible approach – in the Republic's early years the President often travelled economy class on planes – and had been so conscious of the need for skills that some former colonial administrators were invited back to help, Mbeki's administration had reached for the stars, dispensed with the whites and re-racialized much of South African society. This not only betrayed the ANC's heritage; it poisoned the atmosphere and pushed desperately needed skills abroad. It was the hole in the heart of the new South Africa and it was unnecessary. Had Mbeki, like Mandela, celebrated a common South Africanism, ANC rule would have been no whit less secure. But Mbeki, imagining enemies plotting against him in every corner, felt more secure by playing the race card.

Mbeki's paranoia and denial did great damage, but so did his grandiosity. He insisted on his own presidential jet, something even Brown and Sarkozy do not enjoy. Soon even the lowliest public servant assumed that they would only travel business class. Botswana's rulers had set out merely to make their own country as good as it could be. 'Zero tolerance for corruption' read the signs as you enter Botswana, with a list of the heavy penalties facing anyone who bribes a public official. Mbeki had no time for such parochialism. He wanted to lead Africa, to revolutionize it with Nepad, to lead its renaissance, to lead the Third World, to speak for the South – and to be regarded as a major intellectual. These were absurdly ambitious goals, driven by arrogance, based on little that was real. It was the reflection in the political realm of the same grandiosity one saw among the parastatals: Spoornet wanted to run Africa's railways, Eskom wanted to be its power hub, even to export power to Europe – absurd dreams of arrogance. One could see trouble was looming when Eskom spent so much and so loudly on its 'African leadership' project. It was mere bombast. There was no leadership because there was no humility and no realism.

This should have been obvious far sooner than it was. For too long the local and even the international media accepted Mbeki at the level of his own pretensions. The truth is that South Africa is a difficult country to govern. Its multiple fissures, its different histories, its ever-expanding pluralism guarantee that. Even a Smuts, with his great strategic grasp, came quite unstuck when he failed to concentrate sufficiently on the home front and was defeated in the 1948 election. And Smuts was a true giant. A key member of Churchill's Imperial War Cabinet, he helped draw up the UN Charter and was actually designated to succeed Churchill as Britain's wartime Prime Minister, should any mishap befall.

The comparison of Mbeki's defeat with Smuts' defeat in 1948 is poignant, nonetheless, for it illustrates again how ridiculous was the notion that South African history had somehow stopped in 1994 and then begun a new and incomparable era. In fact the transition was seamless and the comparisons between the two epochs were often exact to the point of embarrassment. Invariably, the best way of understanding why the ANC behaved as it did was to compare it with the analogous behaviour of the Afrikaner nationalists. At a time when the press spoke in awed tones of Mbeki as an intellectual giant, the only man I met who saw him in the more pragmatic light of that history was Bobby Godsell, the head of AngloGold. 'Looking at him purely as a chief executive,' Godsell said, 'I'd say he wasn't up to it. Running South Africa is a tough job. He'll struggle to see out two full terms.'

THE CHANGING ANC

Mbeki's defeat also said much about the evolution of the ANC. The exiled ANC had set itself to be a Leninist vanguard party, with complete discipline in the deployment of cadres to any walk of life. Returning to South Africa in 1990, the notion was that although South Africa was a capitalist society, the party would thus be able to remain above and aloof from society, able to guide a transition to the 'national democratic revolution' and then perhaps, beyond that, to a socialist society. The ANC could set itself so ambitious a task because it was unlike other African nationalist parties which, as a natural result of 'big man' patriarchalism, were prone to factionalism. This the ANC avoided through all the years of struggle because of the central role of the SACP, acting as the party's brain and instilling its organizational discipline throughout the wider Congress movement.

There was a clear contradiction between this image of the party and the ANC as a mass movement which Luthuli, Mandela and Sisulu had helped to build in the 1950s. Mandela referred to the party then as 'the parliament of the African people' because all tendencies coexisted within it – the chiefly Christianity and non-violence of Luthuli, the intellectual liberalism of Z. K. Matthews, social democracy, straightforward nationalism and Communism. Equally important for Mandela was the way the party appealed to all tribal groups and the fact that Indians, Coloureds and whites all played significant roles within the Congress movement. In the 1980s the UDF built on this tradition of the mass movement and added to it, with the churches, local civic associations, student groups and NGOs all playing significant roles. The overwhelming ethic of the movement was one of consultation. Care was taken so that even the humblest local community felt that its sensitivities were being taken into account.

Mbeki's exile group paid no heed to either of these two latter versions of the movement they led. They simply tried to affix an exile head onto the movement and enforce that vision of the party right through the organization, with few concessions made to the fact that the ANC, once it had been re-legalized in 1990, was once again a mass party. It was naive to imagine that this exile model could be so easily transplanted, but at each new critical point Mbeki reacted towards a tighter centralization of power, his answer to everything. This not only ran against the other traditions within the party and the fact of South Africa's strong provincialism, a force felt in all parties, but it also made insufficient allowance for the new circumstances brought about by the advent of democracy – and then of power. Almost immediately the new phenomenon of 'godfathers' began to exert a strong gravitational pull, and this was as nothing compared to the effects of BEE and of high office with all its perks.

Long before the end of the Mbeki period a clear majority of the NEC were businessmen and those who were not, wanted to be. Meanwhile the SACP declined in influence as it lost the advantages of exile and its sole charismatic leader, Hani, so that soon it became simply one faction among others. The Mbeki–Zuma split completed this evolution, with the whole party split into warring factions. Instead of the party remaining above and apart from society, society had conquered the party. Instead of being the highly disciplined organization it had been in exile the ANC became a much larger people's party, mirroring the interests of that larger society: labour and big business, a huge array of municipal and provincial interests, small black business, the SACP, a new black white-collar and middle class, and sections, at least, of both Indian and Coloured society.

This growing diversity was masked for some time by Mbeki's extreme centralization of power but by 2005 it was clear that both he and that centralization had been rejected. Zuma, as ANC president, would clearly never enjoy the unchallenged leadership that Mandela and the early Mbeki had enjoyed. Factionalism had come to stay and the ANC, no longer 'a party unlike the others', increasingly resembled other African nationalist parties.

Mbeki's eclipse suggested that South Africa was developing in a far more hopeful way than many African states. South Africa's national political culture contains a far stronger democratic element with a far longer history than is found elsewhere in Africa. Representative institutions involving the whites and a smattering of others have existed for well over 150 years and the black population watched the interplay of parliamentary forces like spectators at a tennis match. From its earliest days the ANC's demand was for the full incorporation of the black population into those institutions, and as mass black organizations arose within the country – particularly the trade unions and the UDF – there was a real concern to observe at least a semblance of democracy, to consult widely, to leave no one out. It was unsurprising that the population took to universal suffrage so easily and painlessly in 1994, for strong elements of a democratic national culture existed in a mature form among a considerable section of the population and in a semi-mature form among the rest.

The main threat to the growth of this democratic political culture came from Mbeki himself. He not only tried to subordinate it to Leninist notions and attempt a wholesale re-racialization of society, but he also politicized every corner of society. ANC cadres were deployed as judges, civil servants and in NGOs, the media, the universities and every provincial and municipal council in the land. He then demanded that those he had placed in such positions obeyed the party line, which in the last analysis meant obeying him. One by one he subverted the institutions on whose independence the constitutional order was based: the standing committees of Parliament, the Speaker, the Auditor-General, the Judicial Services Council, the Public Protector, the National Prosecutions Authority and so on. He suborned the SABC and exerted strong pressure on the rest of the media.

This generated an intimidatory atmosphere in which most people were frightened to put their heads above the parapet. Inevitably, many businesses, individuals and institutions, including the Constitutional Court, voluntarily toed the line. The same logic had applied under apartheid: some of the most despicable behaviour had resulted from voluntary collaborationism. And the old apartheid atmosphere was exactly re-created – sources willing to speak only on condition of anonymity, no one willing to trust the telephones, and so on.

THE NEW DAWN OF POLOKWANE

It was clear that if South Africa's fragile new democracy was to be saved, Mbeki had to go. It was a measure of Mbeki's aberrant behaviour that this sentiment was shared by actors as far apart as the DA's Tony Leon and the SACP's deputy secretary-general, Jeremy Cronin, who in the run-up to Polokwane repeatedly warned, 'We just can't go on like this.' The leading Africanist commentator Xolela Mangcu had come to the same conclusion: 'The man [Mbeki] has been a colossal failure' and 'a danger to our constitutional democracy', he wrote, two months before Polokwane. 'I am embarrassed for myself and my country that we surrendered our judgement to the faulty judgement of one man.'[146]

Hence the hopeful nature of Polokwane. Since 1990 South Africa has seen one President, De Klerk, voluntarily concede complete democracy when he had the military might to stay in power longer had he wished; the next President (Mandela) voluntarily surrender power when he could have had a second term by popular acclaim; and the next President (Mbeki) turfed out by a democratic vote of his own party when he tried to extend his reign. Every political culture has to be built through the lived history of its society. In this respect South Africa's history since 1990 is not only sharply different from that of any other African state but distinctly promising for the long-term construction of a political culture of stable democracy.

That Polokwane was met with public gloom was due to fears that Jacob Zuma might prove an even worse President than Mbeki. He was popularly reproached as a crook, a semi-literate peasant, a typically polygamous Zulu patriarch, a man who could not manage his own financial affairs and who had never managed a Ministry successfully. Moreover, Zuma was a true believer in ANC hegemony. On several occasions Zuma had told his followers that 'the ANC is more important than even the Constitution of the country',[147] and he had also boasted that 'the ANC will rule South Africa until Jesus comes'.[148]

Zuma's own life had after all been transformed by the ANC; he had been a country boy come to the big city who in his late teens had attended ANC political lectures in downtown Durban and been entranced. From then on his life had been lived in and for the ANC and here he was, just one step away from becoming President of South Africa and now able to have as many wives as a Zulu king. No wonder Zuma regarded the ANC with such reverence. 'Once you begin to think you are above the ANC, you're in trouble,'[149] he told another crowd. Asked about his views on policy he would always simply insist that the ANC would decide all that, his views were simply those of the ANC. 'There is no Premier who is a Premier out of nowhere. They are all coming from the ruling party. They are answerable and accountable to the party, including the President and everyone else. The President of this country is the president of the ANC. No one person can be above the ANC. He can't be.'[150]

At the time of writing no one can be sure what sort of President Zuma will be or even whether he will be President at all. The interregnum began well with ANC MPs, now keen to show loyalty to Zuma, hauling the head of the SABC, Dali Mpofu, over the coals for the corporation's shocking history of bias, reprimanding the Health Minister, and denouncing the Scorpions for having deliberately leaked false information aimed at undermining Zuma.[151] Of course, a Zuma presidency might see the independence of the same institutions abused for political purposes all over again and the same attempt to spread the influence of the hegemonic party into every nook and cranny of society. But such fears may also be exaggerated: one may hope that Zuma and his followers have learnt the hard way that it is better for everybody if constitutional guarantees mean what they say.

It is, however, difficult to imagine Zuma being able to exercise the same degree of party or personal hegemony over South African society that Mbeki did. The Mbeki state, after all, spent more than seven years trying to ruin Zuma's reputation and it did quite a thorough job. It is hard to envisage Zuma ever quite overcoming this handicap and it is certainly unlikely that sycophantic journalists will hail him as one of the world's great intellects in the way they fawned upon Mbeki. In any case, the ANC has factionalized and it is unlikely that it will again achieve the monolithic unity it had in the Mandela–Mbeki years. Not just Mbeki but the party itself has lost enormous moral credit both domestically and internationally. It is difficult to imagine that it will again be able to make convincing claims to occupy the 'moral high ground'. The spell has been broken. Mandela was idolized and so, for many years, was Mbeki. Both sat on pedestals far above that occupied by any president in older republics. Now South Africans have seen just such a president dragged off his pedestal, reduced to an object of contempt and then ejected by his own party. Early on, Americans idolized Washington, Adams and Jefferson but as time goes by republics learn that men like Chester Arthur and Richard Nixon can also be President. Idolatry is never so easy again. South Africa may be lucky in learning this lesson so early.

The larger problem, amazing in a country where political power has been so long and fiercely contested, is that with Mbeki struck down the country appeared virtually leaderless. Mbeki was now a humiliated lame duck, unable to lead, while Zuma seemed in no hurry to lead. The ANC elite, ridiculously, had always been too thin to be able to run a major country from its resources alone. Now that elite had split in two and there seemed scant prospect that Zuma could put together a competent ruling team. The presence on Zuma's NEC list of a number of people with criminal records led many to fear a further advance in the criminalization of the state, a phenomenon observed in many African countries. But really it was more an indication of how Zuma's team included the remnants and sweepings from the bottom of the barrel.

The crisis of leadership went wider. For hundreds of years white Afrikaners had supplied a long stream of determined and sometimes very capable leaders, but that stream had now dried up entirely. And the DA leader, Helen Zille, had bizarrely opted to remain mayor of Cape Town, a full-time job which not only kept her out of Parliament but which effectively absented the main Opposition from most of the great political dramas of 2007. The result was an eerie vacuum at the Republic's political summit. In a space where there had hitherto always been a plenitude of would-be leaders, jostling, arguing, offering alternatives, there was now a strange lack of all such actors. No one had predicted such a thing. As the young Republic moved on from Polokwane, its economy still clipping along despite a world downturn, it resembled nothing so much as a runaway train.

14
Democratic Renewal or Failed Colonization?

Historic continuity with the past is not a duty, it is only a necessity.
G. W. Holmes jun.

Two things we ought to learn from history: one, that we are not in ourselves superior to our fathers; another, that we are shamefully and monstrously inferior to them if we do not advance beyond them. Thomas Arnold

President Mbeki often spoke of the need 'to eradicate the 350-year-long legacy of colonialism and apartheid'.[1] Other ANC spokesmen spoke of having to 'overcome' 350 years of colonialism and apartheid or, as one Minister put it, of having to 'reverse 400 years'. What is meant is that the black man has found himself in a state of inferiority and subjection ever since whites arrived at the Cape. Now that is over they want to build a new era based on other values. So far so good.

GETTING THE HISTORY RIGHT

But no one can really 'reverse 400 years of history'. And other ex-colonials, be they Malaysians, Americans or Nigerians, do not talk about reversing or eradicating their history. In any case, in South Africa no one has to go back that far. In most of the country white rule lasted less than 200 years and in some places only 150 years, and it is less than a century since South Africa became one country. In 1800 there were only some 26,000 whites in the whole of what now comprises South Africa[2] – simply not enough to form a country-wide oppressor class. In 1875 there were still only 342,000 whites in the whole of South Africa and of these 236,800 were in the Cape.[3] Even in 1891 there were only 255,000 whites outside the Cape. Moreover, almost all the whites were concentrated in a few towns while most Africans were rural. What such figures mean is that white rule, outside the Cape, lasted barely a century in many parts of South Africa. The oppression and exploitation of blacks by whites was real enough not to need embroidering with wild claims that it lasted 350 or even 400 years.

The rhetoric of black emancipation was oblivious to such historical facts. It also tended to speak as if all whites were oppressors, forgetting that there was always a white minority which took the African side. This was not an innocent mistake: in the Museum of Apartheid in Johannesburg the significant contribution made by white liberals to the struggle against apartheid is almost wholly omitted. Similarly, one quite commonly hears that whites still own 80 per cent of the land, though it is easy to see that once you add up the old bantustans and the vast tracts of government land, let alone the urban areas and the game reserves, this cannot possibly be true. Nor, indeed, could it have been true for quite some time. The system of colonial oppression was an indubitable fact but it was odd to hear all whites depicted, quite timelessly, as wealthy and privileged; colonizers or the children of colonizers. For the white population has been in constant flux, the subject of large migratory flows, and many have been in the country for a generation or less. No allowance is made for the fact that before 1945 many whites were desperately poor, indeed, that Afrikaner nationalism was largely a response to the 'poor white' problem, and that white poverty, which never wholly disappeared, is today a large phenomenon again.

In the end, the more you interrogate the African nationalist version of history, the more you realize it has little to do with actual history and a great deal more to do with what Frantz Fanon described as the psychology of the colonial personality. In addition, of course, it serves the lower political purposes of founding myth, of keeping blacks polarized against whites, and keeping whites on the defensive. In large measure it is a throwback: yet another wave of nineteenth-century nationalism finally reaching the southern tip of Africa in the twenty-first century. And like all those previous nineteenth-century nationalisms, it is in large part a distorting and destructive force, just as Afrikaner nationalism and British jingo nationalism were.

And, of course, history cannot be eradicated. Just as with every other country, the South Africa of today is organically built on what went before. What was built was very impressive – by far the most developed industry and infrastructure in Africa. To use the SACP's famous formulation, white rule was colonialism of a special type. And, as Marx was the first to admit, colonialism was in many ways a progressive, modernizing force. The facts of oppression of Africans, Indians and Coloureds by whites, everywhere patent, often cruel and under apartheid indubitably so, cannot negate this larger fact any more than the terrible slavery which built the pyramids negates the achievements of Egyptian civilization. Successful ex-colonies like India and Malaysia have no difficulty in accepting that colonial rule, for all its cruelties and injustices, had its great achievements, starting with the unification of their countries, just as it also unified South Africa. Moreover, colonial rule to some extent contained its own emancipatory possibilities within itself. It created mission schools, colleges and universities and helped produce the educated indigenous elites who were ultimately to inherit power. Moeletsi Mbeki, the President's brother, makes the same point – albeit in a somewhat rose-tinted manner:

> democracy in South Africa pre-dates 1994 because we had democratic traditions in the middle of the 19th century, what is generally referred to as Cape Liberalism. But those were the beginnings of democracy, of modern democracy in South Africa. The whites had a vote and the blacks had a vote. And the blacks from the middle of the 19th century had their own newspapers, because they were participating in the electoral process and they had their own political parties.[4]

This was true, to some extent, even under apartheid. The imposition of Bantu Education was an unmitigated disaster – but record numbers of black schools were built. The pass laws prevented a rational or humane urbanization policy – but under Verwoerd a record number of township houses were built. In the end it was apartheid governments that conceded full trade union rights, the abolition of the pass laws and the abolition of the noxious Immorality Act. Indeed, in the end it was a white minority government which abolished apartheid outright and helped usher in the era of universal suffrage democracy. This is not to defend apartheid; it was indefensible and the fact that apartheid administrators belatedly repealed their own unjust laws is hardly a cause for congratulation. The point is simply to acknowledge that change in South Africa, as elsewhere, has been organic. The new is built upon the old.

African nationalists often find it hard to admit this in the way that, say, Indians or Vietnamese admit that they have built upon their colonial inheritance. The crucial difference, one realizes, is that Indians or Vietnamese can look back to ancient literate civilizations in a way that black Africans, in the main, cannot. The fact that sub-Saharan Africa never developed its own literate civilization is the original sin here. This was not because of any innate lack of ability – Africans were quick to learn, speak many languages, have produced Nobel literature laureates – but largely because of demography, disease and a desperate Hobbesian state of nature which militated against all forms of cultural accretion.[5] To this has to be added the failure to develop states other than a few ancient empires based on slave-trading.

Africanist intellectuals often assert that they want to resurrect a more African past and do away with all that is Eurocentric. Unfortunately this is quite impossible. There is simply no African past to which either such ideologues or the man in the street wishes to return; no one wants to resurrect traditional chieftaincy, for example, or return to a non-literate state or a slave-trading empire. If one lists European innovations and asks which of these innovations Africanist intellectuals would wish to reject, the problem is immediately apparent: ideology, constitutions, Marxism, political parties, nationalism, human rights, gender equality, newspapers, radio, television, modern medicine, football, socialism, motor cars, aeroplanes, electricity, railways, factories, ocean-going ships, telephones, schools, universities, libraries, museums, trade unions . . . well, why go on?

The politically correct stance is that all cultures are equal and equally valuable. The reality on the ground is that black South Africans have eagerly embraced these elements of modernity in much the same way that ancient Gauls and Britons embraced a clearly superior Roman civilization. There is no shame in this. Such inequalities have happened often before in human history. There is no racial element to them. Quite transparently, African nationalist assertion in this area is built precisely on a sense of shame, on the dread of an inferiority which the colonial personality feels is all too genuine, and thus wishes to reject. But once one understands there need be no shame in this, one can dispense with the rest. Britons and Frenchmen feel no shame in admitting that their ancestors were culturally backward compared to the Romans, Egyptians or Chinese. No amount of psychological posturing can change that.

Getting the history right is difficult but vital, for the alternative, a sort of imaginary history, is politically toxic. Thus, for example, in order to justify affirmative action, not just as a short-term expedient but as a permanent recourse, Mbeki divided the population into the 'historic beneficiaries' and the 'historic victims' of colonialism and apartheid.[6] He then called for South Africa to advance towards (i) the African Renaissance; (ii) the national democratic revolution and (iii) a non-racist, non-sexist South Africa.

This might sound reasonable enough but in fact it is highly problematic. The largest white group, Afrikaners, were victims of colonialism too. And how does one combine a Marxist construct like the national democratic revolution with the African Renaissance? Marxism and traditional African values are hardly compatible. Or again, gender equality is a product of the Western liberal tradition, resisted at every turn by traditional African patriarchalism. Moreover, the real purpose of all this rhetoric is to justify the use of affirmative action to achieve the Africanization of that prime colonial artefact, the civil service.

History is omnipresent in every issue. Mbeki and the ANC grew up in a victim culture, a blaming culture. The result was that no one, not the President, nor his ministers, ever took responsibility for failures; it was always the fault of apartheid. On taking office Mbeki declared that if the ANC government were to fail it would be the fault of the whites, thus absolving himself in advance. This was both self-defeating and dangerous, for it compromised the future, and encouraged the same attitude in others. I have often discussed with black students whether we should not want the best students accepted for medical and dental schools so that we can all get the best medical care in the future. Often, they say no, it is more important to remedy past injustices by admitting black students, even with poor marks. The past against the future; worse, the past crippling the future. Sadly, past injustices cannot really be remedied by such measures.

During the periodic and furious controversies over the renaming of towns, the objection that there was no preceding African town in that place was usually dismissed either as racist or as neglecting the fact that such towns were 'built on black labour'. And yet the objections were literally true. In the arguments thus engendered one often heard of entirely imaginary African towns predating later colonial cities. Rather than face the 'shame' of admitting that cities were a colonial invention,

African nationalism would thus invent an entire alternative history. But there is no shame in admitting to history as it was.

This was of a piece with the strange sort of history Thabo Mbeki peddled. When he visited, say, the Sudan, he would issue forth with a potted – and wildly inaccurate – version of Sudanese history, carefully tailored to serve the anti-colonial cause. It was, in a strict sense, imaginary history. Similarly, when the ANC came to power it spoke of Mugabe's Zanu-PF as its close ally in the liberation struggle. In fact the two movements had been opponents, the ANC backing Zapu against Zanu, and Zanu backing the PAC against the ANC.[7]

This willingness to recast even the recent past owes much to the non-literate nature of traditional African society and the corresponding reliance on purely oral sources. Such oral sources, unchecked against documentary evidence, are by definition malleable. Thus history can be constantly revised in the light of community pressure or political convenience. But this is a cul-de-sac – and imaginary history is a dangerous thing.[8] It always has its political purposes, typically purposes that cannot be supported by reason. Often it is a prolegomenon to large-scale social engineering to make the imaginary take flesh.

THE COSTS AND BENEFITS OF COLONIALISM

If we put imaginary history aside and instead look at the undeniable facts of social progress in the colonial period, common sense suggests that all South Africans were beneficiaries of colonialism, though very unequally so. Oddly, the ANC elite was able to accept such a judgement about the Soviet Union but not about South Africa, although the facts of Soviet empire were even more undeniable and the scale of suffering (at least 25 million dead under Stalin) was prodigiously greater than in South Africa, where it is difficult to put the apartheid casualty list as high as 30,000.

The justification for Soviet empire was that, for all its casualties, the benefits for the survivors were clear enough. Yet the same argument applied far more clearly to South Africa, where the casualties were so much fewer. All South Africans were better off in almost every way as a result of the construction under colonialism of a modern, industrialized and united country. Other Africans migrated happily into apartheid South Africa just as they do today and in most of Africa after 1994 the first thought was that South Africa could now come to their aid, for the country the colonialists had built was seen throughout the continent as uniquely successful. Indeed, most Africans accepted the equation that the larger the white population an African country had, the richer and more developed it was likely to be and that South Africa was thus uniquely lucky in having the largest white population of all.

This is not to say that Africans everywhere did not resent apartheid, but the motivations behind economic migrancy always overwhelmed the political objections to white rule. Today the bluntest comments on ANC rule often come from black immigrants. Frequently they express exasperation that local blacks do not appreciate their good fortune in inheriting a modern economy and infrastructure unique in the continent – and their fear that they will squander these advantages. 'My real fear is that South Africa could go like Zimbabwe,' a Zimbabwean refugee told me. 'There will be nowhere for us to run then. The whites will all leave but the blacks will all die.'

This should be a sharp reminder: the discussion of whether South Africa can eradicate its colonial past is not just rhetorical. It is potentially a matter of life or death. Symbolically the colonial inheritance may be repudiated – with new flags, new uniforms and new anthems providing the helpful (though inevitably false) notion that the independent state is a 'new nation', that the country concerned has gained what all human beings want, a fresh start – the truth is that what the French term *le fait colonial* cannot be reversed or eradicated and that even attempts to do so have terrible consequences. Those post-colonial regimes which have attempted to destroy their colonial legacy (none of them actually achieving it) – the Myanmar/Burma of the colonels, Pol Pot's Cambodia, Idi Amin's Uganda, Mobutu's Zaire/Congo, Mugabe's Zimbabwe, Barre's Somalia – have been utterly catastrophic for their own people. The lesson is simple. If you accept the colonial legacy and build on it, you can go beyond it. If you attempt to destroy or reverse it, you end with a failed state. History is unforgiving to those who wish to 'eradicate' it.

What clouds the discussion is that South Africa experienced not just colonialism but apartheid. This was rightly condemned – and, somewhat oddly, still is by the ANC, even as it seeks to re-racialize South African society along apartheid lines. A key moment, which still colours the debate, was the UN's condemnation of apartheid as a 'crime against humanity' in 1973. Despite the protestations of Western countries that the notion of crimes against humanity had to be strictly constructed so as to be justiciable and also should only include truly serious crimes such as genocide, the initial motion was sponsored by the Soviet Union and Guinea, ratified by mainly Soviet-bloc states and ultimately by seventy-six others. No Western country ever ratified the resulting International Convention on the Suppression and Punishment of the Crime of Apartheid.

This was ironic. The Soviet Union, the author of some of the worst human rights atrocities of the twentieth century, was a peculiar leader of the cause while Sekou Toure's Guinea was one of the bloodiest dictatorships in Africa: the former OAU secretary-general, Diallo Telli, was just one of many thousands to die in Toure's jails and torture chambers. Even at apartheid's height, South Africa's prisons were far better. The political hard core, the Robben Island prisoners, emerged relatively fit, many of them with degrees acquired in jail and often living long and fruitful post-prison lives, an outcome unimaginable in the Soviet Union or Guinea. Despite this, the International Convention remains a key document for the ANC, the scriptural basis for the victims-and-beneficiaries view of history. The irony is that South Africa had to wait for the liberation era to experience a crime against humanity in the classic sense: the denial of life-saving drugs to millions of HIV-positive sufferers. This policy has already killed many times the number that apartheid did.

This loss of life and the accompanying fall in life expectancy were very different from what went before. The first census of what now comprises South Africa, in 1904 enumerated 1,117,000 whites, 122,000 Asians, 445,000 Coloureds and 3,490,000 Africans. By 1988, as the apartheid period neared its end, there were 4,949,000 whites, 928,000 Asians, 3,127,000 Coloureds and 26,113,000 Africans.[9] Thus in this high period of white rule the white population increased 4.43 times; Asians 7.61 times, Coloureds 7.03 times and Africans 7.48 times. The fact that the oppressed multiplied so much more quickly than the oppressors certainly undermined white rule but such figures sit rather oddly with the contention that a 'crime against humanity' was being committed against the majority, particularly since the oppressing minority simply allowed itself to be overtaken. Moreover, as the table shows, all the oppressed groups shared in the general improvement in mortality rates in this period, which effectively coincides with that of the apartheid government (1948–90). The table is eloquent about the shocking inequalities of apartheid but also about the fact that all groups benefited from white rule. This is not a justification for apartheid: as Fukuyama says, this was true of most colonial regimes in Africa. Nor, even, is it a justification of colonialism – how can one justify taking over other people's countries? But the figures do not lie. It is clear that, at the least, the incidental effects of white rule were highly positive.

South African mortality and infant mortality rates, 1950–1987, by racial group (per 1,000 population and per 1,000 births)

	Mortality Rate				Infant Mortality Rate			
	Whites	Asians	Coloureds	Africans	Whites	Asians	Coloureds	Africans
1950	8.7	11.5	20.3	22.7	35.7	68.5	134.3	200
1987	8.1	6.2	9.2	12.0	11.9	19.0	46.3	80

Source: South Africa 1989–90, Official Yearbook of the Republic of South Africa (1990), p. 81. The infant mortality rate for Africans in 1950 is actually the average rate for 1935–40; no 1950 rate is given.

The data on GDP per capita are more uneven. In constant 2000 prices the figure (for all races) was R12,736 in 1948 when the apartheid government took power. This figure almost doubled by 1981 to R23,972 (in constant terms), despite the rapidly increasing population. To be sure, this income was extremely unequally divided, though black wages increased far more quickly than those for whites from the 1960s on.[10] Thereafter, in the traumatic 1980s, the figure drifted down to R22,241 in 1989. It was not until 2004 (R22,729) that the 1989 figure was finally surpassed and only in 2006 (R24,418) was the 1981 figure surpassed.[11] In fact this may be illusory, for by that date South Africa had attracted millions of illegal immigrants (some three million from Zimbabwe alone) uncounted in the population figures, so the real population was much higher than the official estimate. What is clear is that per capita income almost doubled in real terms under white rule to 1981 and that a dozen years of ANC rule merely recaptured that old landmark.

Thus while the demographic growth and diminishing mortality figures under white rule are quite unarguable and contrast strongly with the public health catastrophes of the post-1994 period, pointing strongly in the 'failed colonization' direction, the per capita income data certainly show strong growth under white rule but by 1990 some of that had been undone and the figures since then do not support the 'failed colonization' model. In some respects this has been just a matter of luck: the ANC's economic policies have clearly retarded economic growth in many respects. The ANC government enjoyed a one-off post-apartheid bonanza due to the abolition of sanctions, normalized trade relations, the removal of apartheid restrictions and the receipt of foreign aid. Above all, it has been a lucky winner from the commodity boom, despite a collapse in mining investment. But, in C. W. De Kiewet's famous adage, South Africa has frequently advanced by means of political catastrophe and economic windfall, so this has merely been more of the same.

What is clear is that by preaching the need to eradicate colonialism the ANC is operating within the wrong problematic. The attempt to divide the nation into beneficiaries and victims of history is equally unfortunate. For it is obvious that no attempt at nation-building can succeed if it encourages the vast majority to cling to a sense of victimhood, with all the debilitating effects that self-ascribed status brings, while simultaneously berating as guilty beneficiaries the group on which the country still heavily depends. What is entirely lacking from this depiction is any sense of confident, assertive and equal citizenship, without which the formation of a democratic national community is hardly imaginable. One can hardly build a sense of shared national community by trying to inculcate a burning sense of grievance and entitlement in a majority and a corresponding sense of fear and guilt among the rest.

SUSTAINING THE GAINS?

Fukuyama's question was whether the post-apartheid regime could sustain the gains made under white rule and then whether it can go beyond them. Economically, we have seen, the question is moot. But in many other respects it has failed to sustain that inheritance. Public health is certainly far worse than it was under apartheid and, as we have seen, there has been a steep fall in life expectancy. Mbeki's Aids denialism had a disastrous impact but the virtual collapse of much of the public health system suggests that even had HIV/Aids not existed there would still have been a major deterioration in the health of the poor. The group the ANC said it most wanted to help is precisely the group which has suffered most under ANC rule.

A similar deterioration was evident in the public education system. Despite repeated government promises, thirteen years of ANC rule had still left many black children without even proper classrooms, let alone schools with electricity, sanitation, library resources or decent teachers. Vast areas of township schooling stagnated at best and, at the top end, there was a clear decline in standards at many tertiary education institutions. The old education system was geared to produce a small, mainly white elite with reasonable education and skills. In general – as with the social system overall – all that has happened is that the racial composition of that elite has been altered to allow the entrance of a larger black component but the privileged group at the top has not expanded and the structural inequalities between the top and bottom are at least as great as before.

In some areas there were definite improvements. The old constraints on civil liberties – the bannings, censorship and detention without trial – have all gone. The ANC has turned the SABC into the same pliant propaganda tool that it was under apartheid but the rise of private broadcasting, satellite television and the internet have abolished the government monopoly on information. There are also some definite material improvements. By 2006 the proportion of households using electricity had risen to 81.4 per cent and 71.3 per cent of households had piped water.[12] And, thanks to mobile phones, far more were able to communicate. Everywhere one saw large numbers of little matchbox-like RDP houses dotting the veld; well over a million had been built by 2006. There were complaints about poor quality but they nonetheless represented a large improvement in housing standards for many. There was free basic education and even a free allowance of water and electricity for the poor. In practice the redistribution towards the poorest was larger simply because large amounts of water and electricity were stolen through illegal connections and because the government repeatedly wrote off the bad debts incurred by the refusal of so many to pay rent, rates and taxes. Ninety per cent of school-age children were in school and far more was spent on education though, sadly, so ill-spent that standards continued to fall.

At the top end, large numbers of the black middle and white-collar classes moved into (and often owned) what used to be white (and thus decent-quality) housing. Effectively the housing boom of 2002–7 saw private developers construct large numbers of middle- and upmarket houses, allowing many blacks to buy into them and, even more, for whites to move in, vacating their old houses and flats which were taken over en masse by first-time black buyers.

Another large success lay in the welfare payments, child allowances, disability allowances and higher pensions. Urban legend had it that teenage girls often had babies simply in order to qualify for child allowances, although evidence for this was lacking. In many African families the new or enhanced revenue streams represented by the welfare payments were appropriated by the wider family for a host of different purposes. But what mattered was that scores of billions of extra rand were pouring annually into many of the poorest households in the country. This reduced absolute levels of poverty and it also had a large, diffuse impact on poor rural areas. (South Africa has no poverty datum line but the proportion of households in which one or more members went to bed hungry declined from 6.9 per cent in 2002 to 2.5 per cent in 2006.[13]) In the Transkei, one of the poorest areas in the country, one could not but be struck by the sharp improvement in (often self-built) housing, the greater bustle of commerce in such towns as Dutywa, Butterworth and Mthatha, the larger number of cars and, thanks to the ban on plastic bags, the sharp reduction in roadside litter. The same was true in many other poor rural areas.

Many regretted that the same sums could not have been distributed through some form of workfare, helping the chronically unemployed into the world of work. But the state lacked the management resources even to run a large-scale public works programme, let alone a vast workfare system beyond that. Even giving the money away was problematic for a state so lacking in management capacity: there were innumerable scandals of benefits improperly claimed or improperly held back and stolen. But the pressure of the African poor was pervasive and insistent. In the end most of the money got through. The longer-term cost was a prolongation of the culture of victimhood and dependency. Meanwhile the immigrants from the rest of Africa who swarmed in and had no access to such grants showed a determination to work which often earned them jobs ahead of the locals, breeding inevitable resentment.

The welfare culture sat oddly with the glitz of the lottery, the multiplying casinos and the hype about the 2010 football World Cup, universally seen as a potential bonanza. Amidst the endless invocations of the national democratic revolution, the first stage of the advance towards socialism, the 'deepening of democracy' and the advance towards 'a non-sexist, non-racial South Africa' it was sobering to realize that the ANC's promised 'better life for all' really came down to something as old as the hills: a free water allowance and more casinos; a public works programme which had rural women building roads and Oprah on television talking about psychological self-fulfilment; higher pensions and the lottery; welfare payments and the World Cup. In a word, bread and circuses.

The ANC government was often congratulated on its good economic management but this is an uncertain judgement. True, there was positive growth throughout the post-1994 period. The public debt has shrunk, reserves are higher and inflation is lower than before, and the budget was, by 2007, in its second year of surplus thanks to vastly better tax collection. Belatedly, there is now in place a trade treaty with the country's biggest customer, the EU, and there has been some liberalization of tariffs. The country has opened up to the world. This has seen a large expansion of South African trade and investment into the rest of Africa and beyond. On the other hand much of the improvement had little to do with the government. The economy was artificially constrained by sanctions and boycotts before 1994: these fell away naturally. The greatest component of growth was the commodity boom; the government was simply a passive beneficiary of this happy trend. South Africa has also benefited from large amounts of aid from the United States, EU and elsewhere, quite remarkably for a country at its stage of development, though the government was often so bad and slow at spending this fruitfully that the donors had to take their money back again.

Government failures over the economy are many and striking. Affirmative action and BEE undoubtedly held back growth and investment and the incapacity of the government in such key areas as law and order and the granting of visas and work permits also hampered growth. Government attempts at land reform have seen many heart-warming cases of land restored to communities from which it had, effectively, been stolen, but almost invariably this saw a return to subsistence agriculture and a consequent decline in the country's food security, with higher food prices hitting the poor hardest. Government policies were also heavily responsible for the skills shortage which so hampers growth. The government machine itself and the parastatals all work less well than before. The management of the currency was poor, with chronic currency instability and the retention of exchange controls, both significant inhibitors of foreign investment. Moreover, government repeatedly intervened in the economy in the teeth of advice that its intervention was likely to be harmful; refused to listen; and then did enormous harm. Mining legislation was an outstanding case in point.

Although the government wished to achieve exactly the opposite, under ANC rule South Africa has partially de-industrialized and the economy has moved sharply backwards into greater dependence on the primary extractive sector. Huge numbers of jobs were lost in mining, agriculture and manufacturing. The boom in tourism helped, though many of the jobs created there were low skilled and dead-end. The government has no real idea what to do about this. Its industrial policy is merely a list of vague suggestions. For all the brave talk about the national democratic revolution, the government is rudderless, disorganized and, despite the boom, barely coping. Above all, while its objectives require more from the government machine than ever before, it has simultaneously so disabled that machine that its real capacity is at an all-time low.

Such objectives also sit oddly with the noticeable de-skilling and 'dumbing down' of society since 1994 as large numbers of the best educated leave the country and are replaced by far larger numbers of unskilled or semi-skilled immigrants from the rest of Africa. One sees the results quite clearly in almost any high-culture institution: in orchestras battling for their survival, art galleries and museums suffering shocking rates of pilferage, in the steady decline of university research output and in the universities themselves, many of which have suffered badly from affirmative action, erratic management and a large influx of students who are often less than fully literate and, sometimes, virtually ineducable.

Typically, the response to this situation is sought in marketing hoopla and a great deal of rhetoric about 'excellence' and the building of 'world-class' institutions, as if the mere invocation of such phrases does the work. The result is often unconsciously ironic. At the University of Cape Town, Mamphela Ramphele, when vice-chancellor, told an audience of medical alumni that the university was determined to build a world-class medical school, apparently without realizing that that was exactly what it had once been and that its subsequent deterioration had happened largely on her watch. At the University of KwaZulu-Natal, the vice-chancellor, William Makgoba, compared the white males who made up the largest proportion of his academics to superannuated apes without, apparently, considering how that reflected upon the university's slogan, 'The Premier University of African Research', which is to be seen on every campus lamp-post and palm tree.

This process of de-skilling seems likely to continue. On the one hand the government's initiatives in the realm of training and skills have been largely ineffective and the education system in general has been weakening, not strengthening. On the other hand, the white population – still the main repository of skills and qualifications – has been shrinking due to emigration and because it is heavily biased towards the older age groups. This continued shrinkage will have powerful effects. In institution after institution one notes that key roles are played by skilled people of middle age and older and that there are no replacements of equal calibre. If you go to any of the formerly white English-speaking universities and ask when the university reached its peak the usual answer is the 1980s, although that was a decade marred by huge unrest and the academic boycott. One gets a similar answer from many other cultural institutions, from theatres to newspapers.

This de-skilling and 'dumbing down' does not augur well for a society whose main hope lies precisely in a rising curve of educational participation and achievement. It was, however, inevitable once the regime decided to privilege race over merit as a principle of selection and once the argument from merit was deemed intrinsically racist. As in every other field, the fundamental mistake was the failure to live up to the promise of the ANC's multi-racialism. This was essential if it was to retain the maximum number of skilled South Africans, irrespective of colour, and ensure that they were given every incentive to impart their skills and experience to new generations. The full social and economic price for this folly has yet to be paid.

Thus even in the economic sphere one cannot say that the ANC government has achieved success. The rapid growth rate of recent years looks far less impressive if one realizes that it has actually been much slower, not only than emerging stars such as China and India, but than such Asian countries as Indonesia, Pakistan and Malaysia or many of the former Soviet-bloc states. When one considers that South Africa's unique mineral wealth meant that it stood to benefit from the commodity boom more than any other country, one realizes that the quality of its economic management has been, at best, modest.

THE PROBLEM OF GOVERNANCE

The greatest failure of the ANC government is, however, itself. Public criticism has fastened mainly on the government's failure to provide tolerable levels of law and order. This is, as social contract theorists from Hobbes on have emphasized, the most critical responsibility of government towards its citizens. And just as Hobbes would have predicted, the government's failure in this regard has undermined the whole sense of a social contract. The fact that Mbeki's response to this failure was too often mere sophistical argument, that the government has withheld the crime statistics to avoid embarrassment and that the Minister of Safety and Security felt so little sense of accountability that he suggested that those who nagged him about crime should simply emigrate, have vitiated any sense of public responsibility.

Worse, the new state has gravely attenuated the meaning of citizenship. To be fair, apartheid South Africa long denied citizenship to most of its people and there was only a minority civic tradition on which to build. But for the same reason there was also an opportunity to emphasize the expansion of that minority tradition to encompass a common citizenship. This chance was not taken. There is, as a result, very little sense of civic responsibility or even of a duty to obey the law. Again, apartheid created a situation where it was almost a moral obligation to break the law and in that period South Africans of all races learnt to get away with what they could: to break the pass laws, break the Group Areas Act, have affairs across the colour line and evade taxes.

In the new South Africa the failure of government to provide basic law and order on the one hand and, on the other hand, its attempt to legislate in many areas it is incapable of policing, has merely expanded the sense of a Wild West environment. So now the man in the street bribes policemen and Home Office officials, buys forged driving licences, makes illegal telephone, water and electricity supply connections, refuses to pay for television licences or rates and generally gets away with whatever he can. Since even the government does not uphold the law, why should anyone else? It is quite obvious that some of the new judges and senior police officers are drunks and lie like troopers when caught driving drunk, and that corruption in the public service has run amok. The fact, revealed by Travelgate, that a clear majority of ANC MPs were happy to steal from the public purse was no aberration: it expressed the general situation quite accurately. The corrosive public cynicism produced by the failure over law and order on the one hand and widespread corruption in government on the other is experienced across all race groups and has undermined the whole sense of national belonging.

The paralysis of government and the dysfunctionality of the public sector set strict limits on what could be achieved. By 2006–7 large numbers of ANC-ruled municipalities were in an almost permanent state of unrest over the complete failure of service delivery. In typical South African fashion one would hear nothing about this on the main SABC radio news until you tuned in to the traffic news, where you would be advised to avoid various highways because angry local residents, protesting at the lack of service delivery, were burning piles of tyres on the road. It was the same under apartheid, when the news would lead with some anodyne headline (often about rugby) and then there would be a warning that you should, for example, avoid the road to the airport because angry youths were stoning vehicles on the highway. It took only a dozen years for the old apartheid realities to reappear, as police shot rubber bullets and tear gas at strikers and township dissidents.

The virtual collapse of much local government has in turn doomed many centrally driven development objectives. The striking thing, however, is that while local government has collapsed over large swathes of independent Africa (only the large municipalities generally work at all), in South Africa, having repeatedly heard ANC promises of 'a better life for all', township residents are genuinely angry at the lack of better housing, sewerage, schooling and roads. Such things would be accepted as inevitable facts of life in much of Africa.

In practice, if not in theory, the ANC elite is merely waiting for expectations to adjust downwards so that the African poor expect no more of their leaders in South Africa than they do elsewhere in Africa. The new elite is utterly determined about its own continued tenancy of power, something it equates with liberation and even with democracy. It sees democracy not as a process or a set of procedures but as the glorious event which brought it to power. It follows that any change of government would be a reversal of liberation and democracy. The alternation of different governments in power, interpreted by the ANC to mean 'the return of apartheid', is thus off the menu. Accordingly, the only right outcome is, according to Jacob Zuma, for the ANC to rule 'until Jesus comes back'.[14] This sentiment is common to all the Southern African liberation movements – they believe that they should, effectively, rule for ever. Simon Muzenda, Mugabe's Vice-President, put it nicely in Shona: 'Tichatonga kusvika dhongi ramera nyanga!' ('We shall rule until a donkey grows horns!') So, if the elite is irremovable, the rest of society will simply have to adjust to whatever the elite is willing to deliver. Zimbabwe is a living example of what that can mean.

After thirteen years of ANC government it was clear that this meant that society would have to adjust to a very uncertain degree of law and order, indeed, to crime rates which bespeak a society at war with itself, with more than 275,000 murders in that period; and in which some areas of the country are without the rule of law. This situation has already been reached in many townships and squatter camps where vigilantism and lynch mobs are the only effective form of justice. It has also been reached in parts of the countryside, where murderous attacks on farmers are common, where game reserves have begun to suffer regular crime 'hits', and where locals are willing to drive extremely circuitous routes rather than risk travelling on certain roads on which highway robbery and car-jacking are endemic. In such areas a descent into full-scale banditry clearly looms.

Such factors helped explain the emigration of more than a million whites – nearly 20 per cent of the white population – since 1994. Within a larger context of pell-mell urbanization, there was a drift of whites (and many blacks) back to the Western Cape – a reversal of the Great Trek – and to the coasts. The result was mushrooming development and rapidly rising property prices all around the maritime fringe, with a large increase in the white population in many coastal areas. In this, age was the key demographic variable. As Christopher Hope rightly observed in *My Mother's Lovers* (2006), the whites were not really evicted from their role as rulers: they simply decided to retire from power. The same psychology was apparent in many coastal developments where whites at or nearing retirement retreated to beautiful and relatively secure settlements. In effect the metropolitan areas had become heavily contested space and those who took their chances there were, in the main, younger cohorts on their way up, willing to take risks.

The collapse of the social contract over law and order was felt by all communities. As the evidence of elite corruption mounted on the one hand and government incapacity on the other, South Africa increasingly became a broken-backed state, a country in which the private sector, civil society and private life all have their vitality and rewards but in which public authority lacks capacity, credibility and respect. So while the ANC, alone or in coalition, seemed to be the only possible government for some time to come, the ANC itself seemed increasingly less able to govern.

Thus the government often passed laws which it lacked the capacity to administer. There was in general a failure to understand that building effective institutions is a difficult process which takes time and effort, so old institutions were abolished in cavalier fashion and new ones created to replace them, with all the birth- and teething-pains new institutions suffer. There was, too, a general failure to make forward plans, so government was continually surprised by entirely predictable crises. This was obvious in the way the government failed to maintain the transport infrastructure and was then surprised by the bottlenecks at the ports, the traffic jams on the roads, the virtual collapse of the railways and the ever-worsening situation of the national airline. The most glaring case of all was electricity generation, where the government inherited massive over-capacity and watched this diminish year after year until finally it faced a full-blown crisis.[*] Yet there was plenty of warning of this wholly unnecessary disaster and no shortage of money with which to build new power stations: the crisis was simply the product of misgovernance.

In the early 1990s I attended a conference where I was part of a working group on the post-apartheid economy, which also included Thabo Mbeki. The discussion was dominated by clergymen keen to draw up an investment code forcing all foreign investors to subscribe to a long list of politically correct objectives. Finding this unrewarding, I suggested that we focus rather on the fact that the ANC, which through no fault of its own had no experience in running anything, would soon find itself running the most developed economy in Africa. Experience elsewhere suggested one concentrate on such basic questions as whether the government would manage to provide an adequate electricity supply. Mbeki got up and left, whereupon the clergymen berated me for my remarks which they thought Mbeki might have construed as racist. Perhaps this was so but the conversation often came back to haunt me as, increasingly, the electricity flickered out under Mbeki's presidency.

It was often politically incorrect to raise the right questions, let alone attempt to give truthful answers. I remember meeting a foreign development planner attempting to administer an aid project in the Eastern Cape. He told me how he had been at a meeting where the committee overseeing the disaster the project had become had pronounced that the project was 'inoperative' and accordingly needed to 'be adjusted'. Knowing full well that there was no hope while the same local ANC notable remained in charge, he had said, 'No, this is a *mistake* which needs to be *rectified* and we need to *change the personnel* making the mistakes.' He was ignored.

Mbeki's own style of government was also clearly at fault. On the one hand he centralized more power around himself than any preceding South African leader. Yet he spent a great deal of time abroad and even when at home devoted much of his time to foreign affairs, to purely symbolic matters, to writing articles for *ANC Today* and to intra-ANC politicking and intrigues. Having accumulated unprecedented power to govern, he seemed uninterested in governance, as if bored by South Africa's problems. It was a lethal mix. When problems got out of hand he always argued that what was wrong was merely popular perceptions of the problem. It was necessity to change these rather than solve the problem itself. He also kept clearly incompetent and inactive ministers in power more or less permanently. Given the shortage of management skills at every level of government, the government could hardly afford a President who seemed intellectually absent, as if still in exile.

These were largely unspeakable truths, for Mbeki's hyper-sensitivity about the old racist refrain that 'Africans can't govern' was notorious. It was a fear of a refrain from a bygone age. Admittedly, South Africa had more than its share of dinosaurs who continued to believe in nineteenth-century racial stereotypes far into the twentieth century but it is difficult to conceive of any modern man believing in inherent racial weaknesses or strengths. We belong to an age which has seen the Communist Chinese emerge as our most successful capitalists, in which the world record for sustained economic growth is held by Botswana, and in which South Korean children have the best maths scores. The whole notion of race as something denoted by skin colour or other physical attributes has anyway been exploded by modern genetic research. So the lamentable performance of the ANC government had nothing to do with racially inherent abilities or the lack of them. The damage was almost entirely done by ideology and the narrow nature of the ANC elite.

THE NATURE OF THE ANC ELITE

The French Third Republic was haunted by complaint of rule by 'the 200 families', but it is doubtful if the ANC elite is even that big. Its intelligentsia is so tiny that it has been unable to sustain even a single party magazine or newspaper. Even at the top it is often poorly educated. Moreover, it is not open to the broad mass of the South African population. The whites, Indians or Coloureds able to play a role in the movement are those who joined at least twenty years ago, and even many of those have been squeezed out. In practice, any member of these minorities joining the party today would have no hope of preferment, so there is no new generation of such people coming up. Even among Africans this elite is fairly closed to new entrants, consisting in the main of people who have spent decades in the movement. There is a sort of freemasonry, and anyone who cannot point to time spent in jail, detention or exile, or at least in the UDF before 1990, lacks status. It is the closed nature of this elite as well as its modest educational attainments which enable the archaic vocabulary of Marxism-Leninism to continue without challenge. There are few bright young men or women coming up with the education or ideas to make the movement adjust to the late twentieth century, let alone the twenty-first.

This elite is also grossly self-referential. South Africa, existing on its own at the far end of a continent from which it does not take its cue, has always been parochial. Just as Afrikaner society at last began to take note of modern developments in Europe and America, it lost power – to an even more parochial group. Mixing recently with young black journalists, I asked them what they read. They volunteered a series of other South African newspapers. No one read any foreign publication and few read any books. And these were newspaper people. The political class is no less parochial and it is also self-referential. When it talks about the masses what it really means is the few hundred thousand activists who make up the ANC membership. This is the group that attends conferences and to whom the leadership feels it must respond. But the people who really count come from a far narrower group. The ANC elite is highly interconnected both with itself and with the BEE world and it is the same small group that one can find on the boards of banks, parastatals, foundations and universities. Indeed, because the group is so small its members have so many directorships and trusteeships that they merely move from one meeting to another, networking all the time with the same tiny world.

Although this elite claims to represent the masses it is, to all intents and purposes, unaccountable. The proportional representation list system used in parliamentary elections means that there are no constituencies and the party bosses rule supreme. Moreover, MPs can be swapped into and out of Parliament at will by the parties so that very few voters could even name many MPs, let alone the MP 'allocated' to their area. All real power has moved upwards to the executive and ministers are fixed and immutable. Underperformance or corruption is seen as no reason to sack a minister. Several have died in office after long periods of illness when they were clearly incapable of doing their jobs. Ministers, well aware that they are immune from parliamentary or popular accountability, frequently ignore parliamentary questions or give insultingly cursory replies.

The President is elected by Parliament but Mbeki seldom appeared there. When he did, he seemed almost to make a virtue of non-accountability: he seldom replied properly to parliamentary questions, merely giving short prepared speeches of his own. He was never subjected to the sort of rigorous interview which is normal for British or American leaders. In this respect he compared very poorly with his Afrikaner predecessors. A Verwoerd or a Vorster treated Parliament with respect, were formidable in their replies to questions and always knew that they were in a competitive electoral struggle and answerable to a demanding *volk* and the caucus which had elected them. And they sought very seriously to persuade both domestic and international audiences far beyond that.

Hence the irony of South Africa's transition. Under apartheid it was ruled not just by a racial oligarchy but, within that, by a narrow

Afrikaner elite. Now that democracy has arrived it is ruled by an even narrower elite which is even more unaccountable than the group it displaced, and which also controls significant power in the private sector. Moreover, the role of minorities in government steadily declined. By the time the 2004 cabinet was formed only one Indian, two Coloureds and three whites (two of whom were communists and thus wholly unrepresentative) were left in a cabinet of thirty members. By some way the biggest group were Xhosas (twelve) and of the nineteen deputy ministers a further six were Xhosas. Among the departmental directors-general Xhosas were equally prominent. The ANC liked to set itself the target of demographic representivity in all spheres except this one – but this was a taboo subject. Even to notice that Xhosas specifically and Ngunis in general were way overrepresented at the top was regarded as reprehensible.

The real ruling elite was narrower still, for the preponderance of exiles within it meant the dominance of a tiny fraction even within these confines. And, just as the Résistance generation dominated French politics for decades after 1945 (Mitterrand, its last representative, was President until 1995), so the exiles will clearly dominate ANC, and thus South African politics, while they live. The contest for the ANC presidency in 2007 was between two exiles, Zuma and Mbeki, while Mbeki's putative successor, Netshitenzhe, was another exile.

The continuing dominance of this group is hardly popular – far less than 1 per cent of South Africans are former exiles, after all – but there is little to stop it. The ANC's electoral majority seems secure not only because of its patronage power but because the black majority will, judging by the example of nationalist movements elsewhere in Africa, continue for a generation to vote for the party associated with liberation. Moreover, in densely settled African communities many would be afraid to vote against the dominant party. In the South African case these factors are strengthened by a racial cleavage and the ANC's enjoyment of a steadily lengthening demographic advantage and by the system of welfare payments. At election time voters are reminded that the ANC gave them these payments – and told that a contrary vote might mean losing them.

THE ANC EXILES AND THE POLITICAL LOGJAM

There is continuous speculation that the ANC might split, with the SACP and Cosatu forming a left opposition. This seems unlikely: it would never be to the ANC's advantage and the left enjoys far greater patronage and opportunities within the alliance than it could hope for outside. One should remember that in the preceding case of the Afrikaner nationalists such a split only occurred thirty-five years after the NP took power. If the ANC follows suit, the split would happen in 2029.

Strong tensions certainly exist within the ANC bloc but they are merely a reflection of the diminished role of the SACP and thus the rebirth of the factionalism natural to such a large party, particularly given the 'big man' nature of African politics. They are also just the inheritance of any would-be revolutionary party which comes to power. Inevitably, utopian dreams are disappointed and these disappointments are phrased, equally inevitably, in terms of the revolutionary tradition which, in part or in whole, will always be unfulfilled. And so a contest develops for the inheritance of this revolutionary tradition. It was this revolutionary tradition which made first Hani and then Winnie Mandela such potent figures and was also what was at stake between Mbeki and Zuma. Naturally, the power of such a tradition is greatly amplified when its leader dies young, his promise still untarnished. In that sense those who murdered Hani failed, for in death he still looms, larger than life, over the political battleground.

The continued dominance of the ANC exile elite is highly problematic, for this group is not only the most ideologically hidebound but its exile experience practically disabled it from living in a democracy. Not only did it take its lead from the Soviet Union, East Germany and Cuba but the very condition of exile was disabling: the clinging together in tightly knit groups in foreign environments, the paranoid fear of spies and informers, living in a small bubble of one's own, isolated both from the currents of South African society and the societies around them. Security lay in knowing the party line and keeping to it. All discussion took place within narrow and ideologically determined parameters. Everything about Mbeki's political behaviour – his avoidance of Parliament, his unwillingness to engage with the Opposition, his refusal to answer questions, his determined search for enemies, his discomfort with the notion of the real give-and-take of public debate or rigorous interviews – bespoke a complete unease with democratic norms.

The other great disability of this exile group is that it was almost pathologically unwilling or unable to be inclusive. This meant, first, that it refused to use the talents at its disposal because, no matter how willing they were to help, they were, as Mrs Thatcher used to say, not 'one of us'. Even old UDF activists were frozen out. From cabinet level down, this meant recruiting second-, third- or fourth-best, with the result that the government failed even to maintain the (low) standards of the preceding white oligarchy and had no hope at all of transcending them. This was, for the ANC and the country, a huge self-inflicted wound. It was, moreover, a denial of the multi-racial genius of the country itself. What distinguishes South Africa from all other countries, even in Africa, what makes it itself, is its peculiar combination of Zulu and Afrikaner, English-speakers, Xhosas, Sothos, Vendas, Swazis and Shangaans, Coloureds and Indians, Christians and Hindus, Muslims and Jews. It is no easy job to govern this wonderfully diverse and dynamic society. To do so in a way that harnesses the talents of all its people remains merely the fleeting promise of the early Mandela years. Although it is what the vast majority wants, it has never yet been seriously attempted.

This political logjam seems unlikely to dissipate quickly. The same narrow ANC elite is likely to remain in power, overseeing a ruthless process of primitive accumulation of which it is itself a major beneficiary. Although this process is likely to be cloaked under a continuing barrage of left-wing rhetoric, its outcome will be the creation of a tiny elite of black super-rich, a larger supporting black middle class and deepening social inequalities. The emergence of Tokyo Sexwale as a presidential contender may well be a precursor of things to come, particularly if one looks at the fate of national liberation movements elsewhere in southern Africa. Mozambique's President Armando Guebuza is the country's richest man while President José Eduardo Dos Santos is not only the richest man in Angola but the second richest in Brazil (which is offshore Angola). Elsewhere data is harder to come by but Robert Mugabe is certainly one of Zimbabwe's richest men and Nelson Mandela, with his fine houses in Mozambique, Johannesburg, Cape Town and the Eastern Cape, would doubtless feature high up any South African rich list.

Simultaneously, we are likely to see a continuing decline in the standards of welfare, education, law and order and governance simply because the cumulative effects of broken-backed government have not yet all been felt. After 1994 the ANC discovered the UNDP Human Development Index and gave it great prominence. Because it ranked highly countries with good health services and long life expectancy, it rated countries like Cuba more highly than did GDP per capita tables. Before long, however, South Africa began to fall down the Index at an alarming rate and government interest evaporated. Mbeki began to question the basis on which the Index was compiled, just as he had questioned the basis of the unemployment data when joblessness soared. The country is likely to escape the worst, however, simply because of the wondrous luck bestowed by geology. South Africa is so blessed with mineral wealth that despite the handicap of a legislative environment which will slow growth and keep unemployment high, the economy should continue to grow, though more slowly than it could.

SOUTH AFRICA ADRIFT IN A WORLD OF GLOBALIZATION

The likely result of these processes is a continuing slide down the international league tables. When I wrote *How Long Will South Africa Survive?* in 1976 South Africa was the world's 18th largest economy and the world's 15th biggest trading nation.[15] In 2006 it was the world's 28th largest economy and the 37th biggest trading nation.[16] As one looks at those figures – and particularly at the countries which have overtaken South Africa in the last thirty years – one realizes how poorly South Africa's parochial politics equip the country to live in a competitive world. The countries which have overtaken South Africa are either smaller European states with highly educated populations producing high value-added services, or they are Asian states with burgeoning exports of manufactures.

South Africa is ill-equipped on both these fronts. It has been pushing its best educated citizens into emigration. Even when it produced a genuine IT wunderkind, Mark Shuttleworth, South Africa's foreign exchange laws quickly forced him abroad. Just before he sold his start-up business for $450 million I talked to him at length. He said there was nowhere in the world he wanted to live as much as Cape Town, whose quality of life he compared favourably with Silicon Valley. But go he did, as did thousands of top-class doctors and engineers. The government showed scant concern, as if oblivious to the crucial role of knowledge workers in a modern service economy. On the other hand, South Africa can hardly develop its manufacturing base if it hobbles investors with all manner of affirmative action and BEE requirements (at which its competitors simply laugh), when its labour laws are inflexible and its unit labour costs far higher than those of its competitors.

On top of that, Cosatu, the largest trade union federation, is willing to fight to the death for inflexible labour practices and insists that wages are nothing like high enough. Inevitably, it is in favour of sweeping protectionism. The SACP goes along with much of this and 'progressives' in general criticize the government, bizarrely, for its 'neo-liberal' policies. Thus South Africa, which has to compete with the likes of Ireland, India and Taiwan, is led by a government whose ideal model is Cuba, under pressure from a left Opposition which would like to go further still in the direction of autarchy. Many of the ANC elite admire Hugo Chavez and think he is charting a viable new path for states like South Africa.

It is difficult to know how seriously one should take this left critique. One is clearly looking at much the same sort of extreme African nationalism seen in Mugabe's Zimbabwe, whose own favoured model was North Korea. And yet while South Africa has fallen ten places in the GDP stakes, it has fallen twenty-two places among the trading nations, a tremendous warning signal that its failure to develop competitive industries is costing it dear. Since the ANC took power South Africa's share of world exports has fallen by no less than 30 per cent.[17] Yet at the same time South Africa is more and more integrated into the world market economy. Foreign investors may be leery of setting up production plants in South Africa, but they have a well-developed appetite for South African equities, bonds and high-yielding cash accounts. The economy has become completely dependent on these inflows of 'hot' money, for this is the only way the high trade deficit (9.5 per cent of GDP by 2008) can be financed. And given the weakness of South Africa's export performance any growth rate in excess of 4 per cent p.a. will result in a large current account deficit. A sharp move to the left would thus lead to a more or less instantaneous flight of hot money, a hideous slump in the rand, the rapid exhaustion of reserves and a major economic contraction. A move to the left would thus be immediately checkmated by a major economic crisis and a steep rise in unemployment. The left talks vaguely of the need to 'confront' globalization but is, as yet, far from understanding that South Africa's growing integration into the international economy has already rendered its programme obsolete.

The government's avowed aim is to build 'the national democratic revolution' and it has set targets of halving poverty and unemployment within a decade. It will clearly miss these targets, as also the targets it has set in housing, land reform and most other areas. (Mbeki also conceded that Africa as a whole would fail to meet its various Millennium Goals, though – inevitably – he blamed the developed world for this.) The idea behind the national democratic revolution is that once sufficient economic power has been transferred to a patriotic (i.e. black) bourgeoisie, the country will be ripe for a full-blown advance to socialism. This is, of course, utter fantasy though one cannot rule out the possibility that the left might one day gain sufficient power to attempt something of the sort. The result would be an investment and production collapse, a large panic emigration of whites, Indians and middle-class blacks, a collapse in the value of all assets and the currency, and a thunderous economic recession. Such an experiment would, inevitably, be short-lived but the damage it inflicted would not be so. Under such strains civil society would quickly break down, crime would soar, government would virtually cease and South Africa would become a failed state. The road back from that might be very difficult indeed.

Nobody, of course, would start down this path because they desired such an outcome. The danger is more that by keeping the national democratic revolution dream alive the government has encouraged the notion that it is possible, that all that is required to move on to this happy higher level is more pressure for more BEE, more affirmative action and more land reform, as if these were all one-way streets without a downside. In fact they are all extremely risky. BEE and affirmative action drive away investment, while the latter, having already crippled the public sector, could easily do the same to the private sector if pressed too hard. Land reform may sound a laudable objective but the driving of thousands of commercial farmers off the land since 1994 is a process pregnant with risk. Already by 2007 many of the strikes racking urban

South Africa were driven by rising food prices. It was clear that the collapse of Zimbabwean agricultural production was producing shortages and rising prices all along the line. To prevent a dramatic deterioration in the living standards of the black poor, South Africa needed to boost its own agricultural production, not reduce it by handing productive farms over to subsistence agriculture, which was what land reform almost invariably amounted to.[18]

Luckily, this 'land reform' was way behind schedule; by 2007 only 4 per cent of commercial farmland had been handed over (and its production lost, that is), though with South Africa's population increasing fast thanks to the immigration of millions of Zimbabwean and other refugees even a 4 per cent drop, when added to the Zimbabwean agricultural collapse, was significant. Government plans call for the redistribution of 30 per cent of commercial farmland by 2014. Dr Chris Jordaan, of the Transvaal Agricultural Union, estimates that of the 400 land redistribution projects he had looked at nearly 90 per cent were not viable and were clearly doomed. A Pretoria University study of such projects found that 68 per cent had resulted either in steep falls in production or its complete cessation.[19] So if the government reaches its target for 2014 there will be a hideous collapse in food production, soaring food price increases and strikes galore. One can only pray devoutly for the failure, if not of land reform, at least of what the government calls 'land reform'.[20]

The avowed government policy, after taking over 30 per cent of commercial farms, is to achieve a 'demographically representative' farming community. This target – which is also held out as the objective in many other areas – is absurd. There is no precedent for such a thing in Africa or, quite possibly, the world. Just as Jews are overrepresented in the medical, dental and cinematic professions of many countries, so farmers typically overrepresent other groups. And no other country bothers about the ethnic background of its farmers. Britons and Americans, for example, are unconcerned that very few Jews, Catholics or Muslims feature among their farmers, or even bother to enumerate them that way. They simply want farmers to do a good job of growing food. Moreover, although whites often effectively stole African land, the land has been sold and resold many times since then. In effect the initial injustice is as impossible to remedy as the Norman seizure of Saxon land in England. And modern farming is a difficult and highly skilled business which few wish to attempt. In practice the real demand is for housing land around cities. Few people actually want to be farmers.[21]

The expulsion of white farmers in Zimbabwe led to economic collapse and mass starvation. Should the same fate ever befall South Africa the results would be cataclysmic. One frequently saw other African leaders visit Harare to express support for Mugabe's 'land reform' while their governments simultaneously placed advertisements in the Zimbabwean press trying to entice white farmers to settle in their countries. The presumption was that white commercial farmers were a precious and non-renewable resource that any sensible country did its best to poach. Given that South Africa has the largest reservoir of such farmers, this should have been taken as a warning that whatever the country did about training a new generation of black farmers, it should hang on to the successful farmers it had.

Yet ANC ministers of Agriculture generally spoke about white farmers as if they were the enemy, frequently accusing them of maltreating their farmworkers, threatening them with expropriation, and insisting that even if farmers gave in to their pressure and offered to sell their farms, they were asking too much for their land. They also refused to take seriously the frantic demands by farmers for better security against the attacks which had cost over a thousand farmers their lives since 1994. In 2007 the deputy Minister of Agriculture suggested that the remedy for disputed farmworker redundancies should be land invasions, while the Minister himself suggested expropriation.[22]

What was striking was the cavalier attitude to an economically crucial group, though the same was true in many other areas. In general, the demands of economic rationality came very low in the order of priorities. How else to explain that thousands of key jobs in government were left unfilled rather than appoint non-Africans to them? Or that clearly disastrous appointments at the top of major institutions were left uncorrected if the incumbents were black? The moment the parochial dream of 'transformation' outweighs the demands of globalization, there is a situation which cannot last without creating a growing economic disjuncture. At some point South Africa is going to be forced to waken from this dream.

In this sense sport is a crucial metaphor. South Africans care passionately about sport but the ANC cares even more passionately about 'transforming' every sport to be demographically representative. This leads to racial quotas, to refusing to pick teams strictly on merit and to the emigration of many leading sportsmen. The problem is that the political criteria for 'transformation' are parochially racial, while the whole point of international sport is that it is fiercely competitive and thus meritocratic. Which is to say, if South Africa insists on its parochial criteria rather than merit, its teams are likely to get beaten by foreign teams who not only care about nothing but merit but are quite happy to incorporate in their ranks white South African refugees fleeing from racial quotas. In the 2007 cricket and rugby world cups one could find émigré South Africans playing for a host of foreign teams – against South Africa. This is an exact metaphor of what South Africa faces as a country within the international political economy. If it insists on appointing ministers, civil servants, ambassadors, company directors and chief executives on grounds other than merit, it will continue to lose ground rapidly to countries who do not thus handicap themselves, and will even find émigré South Africans working for competitors.

BUILDING DOWN THE STATE

South Africa's post-1994 government may live in a dream world but this is not as unusual as one might think. Samuel Huntington was prone to point out that if you looked at new regimes which had emerged as a result of a transition from authoritarianism to democracy, these successor regimes frequently exhibited a strong sense of unreality. Often they had been exile or revolutionary movements, had lived for years in a world of slogans, ideology and resolutions – but had no experience of government and little sense of how things actually worked. The first government of such a successor regime was always a failure. So, usually, was the second government. It was only with the third government that one saw a real differentiation. Some continued to blunder on in their own fantasy land, but others learnt their lessons and became more realistic and effective governments.

If one applies this formula to South Africa the result is unfortunate. Although Mandela was never much in charge, his government was clearly the most successful. It was the most inclusive and did much to engender a sense of common citizenship and national pride. The adoption of Gear in 1996 (for which Mbeki should be given most of the credit) was a brave and crucial step towards economic stabilization. And Mandela's strong stand against the Abacha regime in Nigeria gave a powerful moral lead, one soon vindicated by events. The first Mbeki government suffers by comparison: it was soon bogged down in the twin disasters of Aids denialism and Zimbabwe. The abuse of state institutions for partisan ends soon became routine, corruption accelerated and South Africa lost friends abroad.

The second Mbeki government was worse in every respect; no sign of third government improvement here. Despite the huge boost it received from the commodity boom, it met failure in every direction. The African Renaissance and Nepad projects effectively collapsed; by 2005 Mbeki found himself publicly disavowed by an ANC conference; and although the presidency continued to confer a degree of authority, his credibility was in ruins. His retreat on Aids bought some goodwill but a year later his maintenance in office of Manto Tshabalala-Msimang cost him domestic and international ridicule. His early Zimbabwe policy had been justified by the assertion that South Africa could not afford a Zimbabwean collapse. Zimbabwe was, after all, Pretoria's largest African trade partner and if it collapsed refugees would stream south. By 2007 it had collapsed and had been far overtaken as a trade partner, and Mbeki was reduced to observing that South Africans 'must learn to live with' millions of Zimbabwean refugees. Thus each government was less successful than the last. With standards of governance still falling it is not yet possible to know where things will 'bottom out'. The xenophobic riots of May 2008 in which more than sixty people died showed how toxic bad governance is. In any country suffering South African levels of unemployment failure to control immigration would inevitably cause trouble. Despite that, Mbeki deliberately blocked Buthelezi's attempts to devise such a policy and, ridiculously, even signed an agreement allowing free movement of people within the SADC area. In effect the rioters in the streets took the issue of immigration control into their own hands because their government had failed them.

There is a familiar ring to all this. A government increasingly racked by corruption and incompetence. Illogical policies blindly pursued with predictable and dire results. All power concentrated in the hands of an over-mighty President who attempts to prolong his rule. The decay of infrastructure through poor maintenance alongside a pronounced taste for prestige expenditures. Power cuts for the people, the arrogance of power for the elite and an ever-growing chasm of inequality between. A President with wacky ideas which are translated into national policy, his philosophical musings treated as a major contribution to knowledge. An absurd foreign policy based on opposition to a chimerical imperialism. Parliament robbed of power and significance, state institutions abused for partisan ends, patronage, spoils and clientelism overwhelming constitutional government, conspiracies everywhere. For we have seen all this before elsewhere in Africa. After the high hopes that South Africa would somehow be different, it is not. Mandela allowed the country the dream of exceptionalism but ultimately Mbeki brought it down with a thump to a wearily familiar African reality.

For decades pro-apartheid whites angrily resisted all the arguments advanced by those of us determined to push for African advancement precisely because they predicted that majority rule would have many of the features described above. Many whites who supported apartheid were ignorant and virtually all of them were racists. Those of us who fought them thought we were cleverer and more sophisticated than the apartheid-supporters – and we abhorred racism. It is painful to have to acknowledge that the racists often predicted the future better than we did, essentially because we accepted the ANC's non-racialism at face value whereas they insisted that the Old Adam would out.

This does not mean that apartheid was right. Indeed, the worst aspects of ANC rule are derived precisely from its imitation of apartheid. And whatever the ANC does now, there could never be the slightest justification for the exclusion of African, Indian and Coloured South Africans from a common society. Morally there was no real choice. I know of no one, black or white, who fought against apartheid who now regrets that for an instant. Ironically, it is the old Afrikaner nationalists who were the most passionate in their anti-black racism who became Mbeki's closest allies and praise-singers in government. And Mbeki insisted on white Afrikaner bodyguards. The liberals who were reviled by Afrikaner nationalists because they fought racism on principle are now reviled all over again by the new ruling group of nationalists. Theirs is a proud calling, speaking the truth to power then and now, men and women for all seasons.

The oddity is, however, that while the prejudiced views of white racists as to what majority rule might mean kept apartheid in power for more than forty years, ultimately De Klerk was able to conjure up a sufficient mood of optimism among the country's whites to win a referendum on constitutional change by a two-thirds majority in 1992. The result enabled De Klerk to say next day that 'The book has now been closed on apartheid'. Looking back, this was an extraordinary political achievement – but also a brief window of opportunity. White pessimism about what majority rule would mean did not long survive the experience of actual ANC government. But crucially, peaceful change had been achieved and, in De Gaulle's famous phrase, South Africa was able, at long last, 'to marry its century'.

South Africans of all stripes took – and still take – great pleasure from this peaceful and necessary transition. But the terrible anxiety which gnaws at their hearts still relates to what we have called the phenomenon of failed colonization. The blunt truth is that having done the morally right and humanly sensible thing of extending equal rights to all South Africans they have been rewarded by seeing an ANC elite entrench itself in power, an elite which not only runs the country very badly but which looks decreasingly able to run the country at all. Yet it seems likely that the ANC will be in power for years to come. The result is a continuing slide in standards backwards from the levels set in the days of white rule, posing the worrying question of where the slide will stop. It is galling to admit that this is just what white racists predicted and what white radicals like myself scorned.

No answer is to be found by looking elsewhere in Africa, for nowhere else has African nationalism come to power in a large modern state. In much of Africa, provided the cash crops thrive and the prices paid for them or the one or two minerals a state produces are reasonable, the country will get by. South Africa is emphatically different, its economy incomparably more sophisticated, various and developed. It is a country of six-lane highways, computers and jet planes. This is a great advantage – but there is a lot more to go wrong. Crucially, it needs far more managerial and technical skills simply to maintain what it has in place. In the same way, for example, power cuts are a normal part of life in many African states and, in that sense, are tolerated and tolerable. This is not the case in South Africa, where they are an immediate threat to the whole economy, let alone the prospects of staging a successful football World Cup in 2010.

One could sum up the ANC's performance by saying that it has managed South Africa as if it were an African state to the north in which lower standards were tolerable and the loss of skilled personnel a pity but not a catastrophe. The results are already extremely severe. The public health system has been almost destroyed and the government has allowed the transport infrastructure and power-generation system to run down. Moreover, it has undermined one institution after another; the police, army and civil service, municipal and provincial administration are all far weaker than they were and even many national departments are in a state of virtual collapse. Its policy interventions have greatly lessened the country's food security, have caused a major investment slump in mining and have erected considerable barriers to inward investment. African nationalist governments have led a number of countries into 'failed state' status and in general African nationalism has been an enormously destructive force right across the continent. Despite progress achieved in some areas, South Africa is no exception. There is no reason to believe that this destructive process has stabilized yet or stopped.

Indeed, to a considerable extent, failure is now built in, thanks to affirmative action. It is now standard practice for South African universities to practise 'affirmative' (that is, discriminatory) admissions and appointments policies which are bound to lower standards more and more over time. For example, the University of Cape Town medical school – once the best in the country – admits black and Coloured students who gain three Bs and three Cs in their school-leaving exam, against five As and a B required to admit a white or Indian student.[23] All this does is to encourage emigration by talented whites and Indians and ultimately produce black and Coloured doctors with sub-standard reputations.

Similarly, by 2006 there were 40,000 vacant posts at administrative level alone in national government departments – let alone scores of thousands more at other levels – essentially due to an insistence on appointing 'affirmatively' from a non-existent pool of qualified candidates. Or again, the Public Service Report for 2006 said that the public service was short of around a million people, of whom 780,000 needed to be highly skilled. One whole third of professional health posts in the public health sector were also vacant and over a third of all municipalities lacked a single civil engineer, technologist or technician.[24] This gives only a partial picture of the broken-backed state, produced by driving skills abroad and refusing to appoint skilled people of the 'wrong' colour. The real picture is far worse, for one also needs to take account of the fact that many of the posts that are filled are held by political cronies or affirmative appointees unable to do their jobs.

African nationalism – South Africa's third and last nationalist wave – is thus very different from its predecessors. English jingoistic nationalism after the Anglo-Boer War attempted to make English-speaking whites the masters while Afrikaner nationalism asserted at least a full equality for white Afrikaners. But African nationalism has attempted to integrate the whole society, including the whole 85–90 per cent of the previously excluded. To understand what a huge undertaking this was one only has to think of how the franchise and full citizenship was extended in Britain, in careful steps in 1832, 1867, 1884, 1918 and 1930, gradually including all adults in a process stretching over a century. The sheer ambition of what was attempted in 1994 commands respect. It would hardly be surprising if the new system took some while to 'bed down'.

That said, African nationalism generally suffers by comparison with its predecessors. Afrikaner nationalism, like the Anglo-nationalism before it, built up the state machine, not just the civil service but the police, the armed forces and a large parastatal sector. This was phenomenally successful – the state built huge highways, ports and dams, the army became the tenth strongest in the world, SAA became a major international airline and one parastatal, Sasol, became, when privatized, South Africa's largest industrial company. African nationalism has, by contrast, very rapidly run the state down, yet at the same time it has attempted to extend the state's functions and interventions in society. The result is a grotesque over-reach and, increasingly, public sector chaos. The fear is of a cascading series of malfunctions, each one causing further dysfunctions lower down, leading progressively to wholesale system failure. At that point one would face not just a failed colonization but a failed state. Yet at the same time the economy is clipping along at a growth rate of 3–4 per cent p.a. and, provided the 'commodity super-cycle' lasts – and many think it could last for another generation – this seems set to continue. Many countries would find that an enviable prospect.

In the first flush of victory in the Anglo-Boer War, Alfred Lord Milner planned for a lasting Jingo ascendancy. Such hopes soon evaporated, though Anglo-nationalism fought a long rearguard action over the flag and anthem before being finally vanquished in the battle over the republican form of government. The Nats thought they were in power for ever but they too have now disappeared. The ANC believe the same – that they will be in power 'until Jesus comes' – and they too will, in the end, be disappointed. So how long will ANC dominance last? Experience elsewhere in Africa suggests that a liberation movement that wins freedom/independence is often able to remain in power for a whole generation. Frequently, the movement's leader attempted to stay in personal power for that long too – as did Sekou Toure, Kenneth Kaunda and Robert Mugabe, though usually that means their going coincides with the complete collapse and disappearance of their party. But the ANC is different – it was not founded by Mandela, Mbeki or Zuma and will doubtless outlast them, in some form or another.

'FOLLOWING ZIMBABWE'S DOWNWARD SPIRAL'

One of the most frequently expressed fears among both blacks and whites is that South Africa could follow the dire example of Zimbabwe. This unconsciously echoes Mbeki's own domino theory anxieties. The power of the analogy rests upon the fact that Mugabe's long and self-destructive struggle against electoral nemesis was more than just another case of dictatorial megalomania in Africa. Quite clearly it represented the death agony of a whole liberation movement. Mugabe could still call upon a shrinking bevy of true believers and, extraordinary though it may seem, he and they exhibited the sense of utter self-righteousness which is the mark of all such movements. For Zanu-PF – or ANC – ideologues, maintaining their party in power indefinitely is not just opportunism but a duty. And Mbeki's theory is valid to this extent: the sight of any of southern Africa's national liberation movements losing power would undoubtedly alter the political climate throughout the region, just as the collapse of the Portuguese empire did in 1974. Africans had tended to view white rule as an immutable reality but the sudden exit of the white regimes from Angola and Mozambique gave a new sense of what was possible. The fall of any of the region's governing national liberation movements would have the same effect.

Some interesting indicators of how things may develop emerged from survey work I conducted for the Helen Suzman Foundation. In 1996 we carried out a survey of South Africa halfway through its first democratic Parliament and then in the first half of 1997 we replicated the survey in Botswana, Swaziland, Lesotho, Zimbabwe, Zambia and Namibia, providing us with an unparallelled view of political development across the region.[25] Among the plethora of data one could discern three distinct political cultures, a traditional one centred around support for the chieftaincy; a radical liberation culture which looked to the abolition of the chieftaincy, favoured socialism and strong state intervention, and did not wish to see an Opposition or critical press get in the way of such objectives; and a more liberal, post-liberation culture.

It was striking to see how thoroughly the liberation culture had already worn itself out in Zambia and urban Zimbabwe, with almost unanimous majorities wanting a free press and a critical Opposition, and flatly opposing the one-party system, detention without trial and other authoritarian accoutrements of the liberation state. (Indeed, the Zimbabwean data was so dramatic that we signalled that serious political trouble lay ahead.) Invariably, electorates were far ahead of their leaders in wanting a more liberal dispensation. Everywhere people tended to believe that the fruits of independence had been appropriated by small elites of politically connected educated people; even after just two years of democracy this was the dominant perception in South Africa. Quite clearly the liberation culture was under pressure. Already in South Africa that culture was weaker than it was in Namibia, despite South Africa's later liberation. The special circumstances of the anti-colonial (and anti-apartheid) struggle had brought to power radical regimes whose basic presupposition had been that they would be able to rely on Soviet-bloc support. That bloc's disintegration has left them in a state of suspended animation. All of them have had to stage ideological retreats but the continuing erosion of the liberation culture will ask awkward questions of them all.

Of the five southern African states where liberation movements came to power after armed struggle, only Mozambique has unambiguously embraced an alternative future. The ruling movement, Frelimo, has given up single-party rule, holds regular elections, has privatized more than 1,200 enterprises and turned the country into a magnet for foreign investment with a high (7–10 per cent) growth rate. Frelimo may well continue in power but if so, it will be as a capitalist party. Angola has never democratized. Dos Santos has been President since 1979 and in thirty-three years of independence there has been only one (crooked) election. Angola is ruled by a corrupt oligarchy buoyed up by oil and diamonds. None of the promises of a better life for its people have been kept, despite abundant mineral wealth. Namibia has not opted for socialism but its heart is clearly not in capitalism either. It attracts little foreign investment and has experienced slow growth. It has regular free elections with a solid, ethnically based one-party dominance. Zimbabwe alone refused the logic of capitalist development and has lurched back towards the radical nostrums of the liberation struggle. Mugabe has been President since 1980 and elections are always rigged. The result is complete implosion and a dire warning to all the rest.

South Africa's final option is still unclear, with the ANC still hedging on whether the national democratic revolution is merely the prelude to full-blown socialism. But such an adventure seems increasingly unlikely. With every passing year a capitalist future for South Africa seems more probable simply because of the country's increasing black capitalist class and its ever-growing integration into the international market economy. Elections to date have been reasonably free but how the ANC would react to the threat of defeat is an open question.

That is the likely nub of the matter: the paroxysm which has destroyed the Zimbabwean economy and crippled its society was, after all, Mugabe's reaction to the fear of losing power. The ANC might react with similar fury against the racial minorities if it faced the prospect of defeat. Such a prospect is, as yet, not in sight, however, and it is quite possible that the ANC will mellow over time. Moreover, Zimbabwe has been a dread lesson to every section of South African society. No one wants to go that route. The fear that 'we could go the same way as Zimbabwe' is thus misplaced at present. Really the fear is of something else, what we have referred to as the danger of a 'failed colonization'.

By 2008 Zimbabwe really had tried in practice what Mbeki only spoke about, the eradication of history. As a result all the gains of the colonial period had been reversed: the health and education systems had collapsed and the standard of living and life expectancy had fallen all the way back to what they were at the time of the colonial conquest. And whereas the colonial period had seen Zimbabwe's population climb from around 250,000 to nearly 8 million, the population was now contracting rapidly with the whole of the population increase (to around

14 million) seen in the independence period wiped out by death and emigration. By 2008 many estimates saw the population as back down to 8 million and headed lower.

Fears about 'another Zimbabwe' are often related, erroneously, to the land question. Even in Zimbabwe land was never really the main issue. In the repeated polls carried out by the Helen Suzman Foundation in Zimbabwe from 2000 on we never found more than 9 per cent of voters (and sometimes as few as 4 per cent) saying that land was the most important issue: it trailed miles behind unemployment, the standard of living and various other issues. In South Africa it is even less salient. Overwhelmingly voters say jobs, housing, education and many other issues are far more important, although the housing issue makes access to urban land of great importance. Nonetheless land is a symbolic issue for many ANC activists who have no interest at all in farming. Accordingly government has continued to threaten white farmers with expropriation and, to date, has adopted a cavalier attitude to diminishing food security. Despite this, Zimbabwe-style land invasions are unlikely, and not just because government knows that they would have a catastrophic effect on the investment climate. Even many land claimants make it clear that they would prefer to take cash in place of land. Very few people are actually keen to embark upon the tough business of farming in South Africa.

It is better to return to the question of why Zimbabwe evolved as it did. After a brief burst of growth in the early 1980s and a longer period of strong public spending on health and education, trouble emerged increasingly in the 1990s because Mugabe's avowed Marxism-Leninism and enthusiasm for the one-party state strongly discouraged foreign investment. The result was a huge public debt, slow growth and increasing unemployment, producing an increasingly sour public mood, ultimately eventuating in Mugabe's referendum defeat in 2000. The clear prospect of looming electoral defeat led Mugabe to unleash the attack on white farmers which in turn produced the country's economic and social collapse. Thus it was Mugabe's ill-advised economic policies which undermined his black support, which led him to try to scapegoat the whites, at the same time striking back hard at the black voters who had deserted him.

SOUTH AFRICA'S STRONGER DEMOCRACY

There is at present little sign of this scenario repeating itself in South Africa. True, Mbeki shared Mugabe's paranoid style and his whole strategy of racial nationalism and the re-racialization of politics tends towards scapegoating the whites whenever things go wrong, and many others within the ANC followed Mbeki's lead. But the situation was significantly different. It was of critical importance that the Mugabe regime had always been far more ruthless and authoritarian in style than the ANC government. Mugabe had used the army and secret police to kill and torture at least 15,000 of his opponents in the 1980s and had operated an effective one-party state until 2000. Thus when the MDC threatened to evict Mugabe from power, the full armature of anti-democratic rule was already in place in Zimbabwe. This is not the case in South Africa and no slide towards 'a Zimbabwe situation' is imaginable without it. In addition South Africa's economic and social situation differs sharply from Zimbabwe's. The serendipitous commodity boom provides South Africa with a growth rate far beyond Zimbabwe's hopes even in the 1980s. This growth generated some extra jobs and meanwhile the public debt was small and shrinking. The scapegoating of the whites did not work well as a strategy because Mbeki was strongly opposed by his own left wing (in a way which Mugabe never was). This left opposition was black and even Mbeki could not pretend it owed anything to the whites.

Moreover, South Africa has a far stronger culture of critical public comment than existed in Mugabe's Zimbabwe. The Democratic Party, founded in order to oppose apartheid, was able to renew and reinvigorate itself in the new context of liberated South Africa. Whereas opposition to Mugabe in the 1980s was monopolized by the old white right – Ian Smith's Rhodesian Front held all the parliamentary seats reserved for whites – in South Africa the white right was toppled and displaced by Tony Leon's outspoken liberals. Habituated to opposition under apartheid, the DP (and then DA) boxed far beyond its weight, providing a liberal critique of ANC rule which seeped into the domestic and international press. The English-speaking press mirrored this experience.

Almost – though never quite – brought low by apartheid, it collapsed into slavish deference to ANC rule, losing both journalists and readers in the process, but recovered its nerve as it realized that the ANC split had made criticism of the government far easier. Similarly, by 2008 the NGO world had sharply contracted but it too often contributed to the liberal critique of government.

Collectively the Opposition, press and civil society constituted a significant counterweight to government, particularly since its concerns – Aids, Zimbabwe and the political abuse of state institutions – were shared and relayed by Cosatu and the SACP.

The significance of this became clear as the ANC succession struggle mounted and Mbeki used the full force of the state against his opponents. More and more voices were raised against his 'vindictive and paranoid' style[26] and his increasingly intolerant attitude to criticism. Black journalists – especially Mondli Makhanya, courageous editor of the *Sunday Times*, and Barney Mthombothi, editor of the *Financial Mail* – earned Mbeki's particular hostility for daring to suggest that the President's behaviour had engendered a national mood of trepidation where no one dared to trust the mail or speak freely on their telephones, habits which recalled the darkest apartheid years. Mbeki's response was revealing:

> Wisely or otherwise ... our national democratic revolution has deliberately avoided any resort to the 'Jacobin option'. It has therefore not used revolutionary force to suppress and destroy its historical opponents, as did the English, French, Russian, Chinese and many other revolutions. In the aftermath of the 1994 victory the democratic revolution took no steps to suppress this [NP] and other formations ... it also did nothing to suppress the Democratic Party and the successor Democratic Alliance.

One result was that

> we did not succeed to uncover the army of thousands of intelligence agents, informers and their handlers, who constituted a critical part of the apartheid repressive machinery [and] we have former apartheid agents in the ranks of our political formations in our country, in the machinery of the democratic state, in business, the professions, including the universities and the media, and civil society in general, who will voluntarily act in a manner consistent with what they did in the past, or submit to blackmail by their former 'handlers' to advance a reactionary agenda.

In a subsequent instalment of this bizarre and rambling document ('The Enemy Manoeuvres but it Remains the Enemy') the list of enemies was further broadened to include 'the wolves in sheep skins who present themselves as members of the ANC'.[27]

Thus the President was seeing enemies under every bush and was musing aloud that it might have been wiser to suppress the Opposition altogether, as many other revolutions had done. Mbeki also repeatedly attacked the press which had, he said, launched a major ideological offensive aimed at dislodging the government – and he promised new laws aimed at 'media transformation', to make the press more susceptible to the ANC (i.e. his) view.

Mbeki was clearly feeling badly cornered and his judgement seemed increasingly irrational. He saw not opponents but 'enemies' everywhere. Still unable to agree that HIV caused Aids, the President seemed equally in denial on a whole range of subjects. Against all the evidence, he expressed his confidence that Zimbabwe would hold free and fair elections in 2008.[28] Asked about the widespread township protests, often amounting almost to insurrection, against the failure of service delivery, Mbeki asserted flatly that there was 'no service delivery crisis or for that matter a mass rebellion in the country'.[29] When the Health Minister was revealed as having a major drink problem, a criminal record and a continuing record of kleptomania, Mbeki nominated her as a national heroine.[30] Similarly, Mbeki became angry at press reports that there had been divisions at the SADC summit on Zimbabwe in August 2007, terming such reports as 'fictional', only for it to be revealed the next week that the deep divisions had effectively caused Mugabe to walk out.[31] Mbeki's writings in *ANC Today* became increasingly odd, including a long disquisition on 1960s miniskirts,[32] while his close association with Ronald Suresh Roberts raised numerous eyebrows. At the same time Dali Mpofu, the head of the SABC – now 'his master's voice' for Mbeki – attacked the rest of the media for criticizing the government, claiming it had 'converted to foreign, frigid and feelingless freedoms'.[33]

Mbeki also adopted a tone of virtual incitement against whites, speaking of

> the challenge to defeat the centuries-old attempt 'to dwarf the significance of our manhood', to treat us as children, to define us as sub-humans whom nature has condemned to be inferior to white people, an animal-like species characterized

by limited intellectual capacity, bestiality, lasciviousness and moral depravity, obliged, in our own interest, to accept that the white segment of humanity should, in perpetuity, serve as our lord and master . . . [are the majority of our people] truly aware that they too are people, and whether they do not, still, regard themselves as appendages of our self-appointed superiors.[34]

Yet not even Verwoerd in his prime had ever discussed black people in such terms: the images existed solely in Mbeki's own tormented imagination. This was the nadir and it was a dangerous moment. When one hears a president musing that his decision not to suppress the opposition was taken 'wisely or otherwise' one realizes that he is still weighing that option and that it has decided temptations for him. Similarly, Mpofu's attack on 'foreign, frigid freedoms' undoubtedly expressed Mbeki's attitude to press freedom. Mondli Makhanya was twice threatened with arrest in this period and it was obvious that such a threat against the editor of the country's biggest newspaper could only come from the top. It was all extremely ominous.

But by then, only three months before Polokwane, Mbeki had missed his chance. Authoritarian powers are usually taken when it is possible to point out a plausible crisis to the public. The resort to emergency rule under the Nats was justified by pointing not just to 'the total onslaught' in theory but to bombs going off in shops and bars, to huge and unruly demonstrations in the streets and to virtual insurrection in the townships. Had the ANC wanted to take emergency powers its best bet would have been to 'discover' an assassination plot against Mandela and the top ANC leadership just after Mandela's December 1997 Mafikeng speech, particularly if one could have got Mandela himself to justify the taking of such powers. Belief in a 'third force' was stronger then; the ANC was still united; the press more deferential, the Opposition weaker.

But the moment passed and Mbeki's later attempt to fabricate a 'presidential plot' against himself ended in farce. After that it would be difficult to 'discover' another such plot without attracting derision. And the only real unrest to point to was either violent strikes or township unrest over the lack of service delivery. Such events involved virtually no whites and no ANC leader would be keen to take emergency powers to put down black unrest. Moreover, the emergence of factionalism within the ANC meant that the 'out' faction would feel that emergency powers were aimed against it, so any such decision would split the movement – which had anyway stopped believing much in a 'third force'. (Indeed, some newspapers did not bother to report Mbeki's remarks above about blacks as 'an animal-like species' and none bothered to comment on them, treating them as a mere embarrassment.)

Nonetheless, Mbeki had raised the key question of whether South Africa might move towards a more authoritarian style of government. This would indeed constitute a big step towards the Mugabe model, but how credible was such a move? The answer has to be, not very. Any such move would be furiously contested not only by the Opposition and the press but by the SACP and Cosatu. The latter were not lacking in authoritarian instincts of their own but their renewed experience of opposition under Mbeki (and the increasingly rough tactics used by the police against strikers and township protesters) powerfully re-sensitized them to the need for democratic freedoms even under ANC rule. Moreover, civil society and the Mandela wing of the ANC would be severely discomfited by any move which brought back to mind the dark days of apartheid. Finally, a move towards authoritarianism would be strongly resisted by South Africa's major trading partners, by the Commonwealth and by the gallery of international opinion which supported the anti-apartheid struggle. South Africa is far more integrated into that international world than Zimbabwe ever was, and its leverage matters.

There are two other and perhaps larger reasons to hope that South Africa's young democracy cannot be extinguished in the same way that occurred in so many other African states. One factor of great weight is that whites-only democracy goes back to at least 1854 in South Africa. Ever since then blacks, with no right to vote, were like spectators at a tennis match, watching the ebb and flow of elections and parliamentary politics, understanding the game and wishing only to be included in it. In the end this is what happened. Despite its revolutionary rhetoric the ANC did not succeed in overthrowing the system. Instead they and all South Africans were incorporated into that polity, finally making it a full democracy. This history is a powerful force. It is no accident that Senegal, where a tiny elite of citizens in the largest communes also had a long history of democratic politics, is today one of the most successful African democracies: it has never experienced one-party or military rule and the government has allowed itself to be voted out of power.

The second reason is diffuse but equally powerful. Surveying what has happened to South Africa since 1994 it is easy to conclude that an exile elite has appropriated all power and increasing riches to itself; to understand that this elite was never democratic – it supported East Germany, Cuba, the Soviet invasion of Czechoslovakia – and that its purported attachment to human rights was often fraudulent; and to conclude that the freedom struggle was never really a struggle for freedom at all, merely a classic example of Pareto's theory of the circulation of elites, an endless and value-free game in which rhetoric and ideology are merely tools cynically used by upwardly mobile power-seekers, with the masses below remaining for ever inert, gullible and exploited.

But this would be a fundamental mistake. The overwhelming majority of the freedom movement did not consist of exiles but was always inside South Africa. It consisted of vast numbers of ordinary people who had no hope of ever becoming the new elite but who were thoroughly angry and fed up with being treated as less than equal beings. Anyone who played a part in that struggle, no matter how small or humble, knows this only too well and can tell stories of demonstrations in the face of power, of integrating beaches and buses by example, of police intimidation, interrogation and worse. It really was a people's struggle for freedom. The UDF, which embodied that struggle in the 1980s, was genuinely multi-racial, expressing a desire for a single national community and emphasizing the need for inclusive consultation at every level. It had many local leaders and eschewed a centralized national leadership. It was, moreover, a genuine popular manifestation of values held by South Africans of all races. Many of the exiles had such feelings too, felt at one with this huge popular assertion. This too is a powerful history, one that will not be easily set aside by a government tempted to cut democratic corners.

So, despite all the talk of overcoming or even 'eradicating' history, this cannot be done. And this applies to all of South African history. We cannot escape from the colonial past, from the sad history of slavery at the Cape, from the great battles of Isandhlwana, Rorke's Drift and the Anglo-Boer War, from the terrible, divisive history of apartheid. But nor can we eradicate the fact that the past bequeathed us a great deal that is positive: a single, united country, a modern, industrial state, a long record of parliamentary rule, a proud record in two world wars and a freedom struggle which was a truly popular phenomenon, a struggle which morally enlarged all who participated in it. South Africa – and the ANC – is a prisoner to this history, both good and bad. Whether the country will succeed in consolidating and building upon what was good in this history remains in doubt. The country's government is clearly not coping. But it is unlikely that the country will take the short cut to dictatorship that Ghana, Guinea and many others did. Our inability to escape from history can sometimes seem like a cruel fate but it can also be a saving grace.

FACING THE FUTURE

One might like to leave it there but South Africans never can. They feel their country has a peculiarly open-ended nature. Sometimes they quiz people who have only been in the country a week as to what they think the country's future will be. This has been a national pastime as long as I can remember. In the late 1950s I had English-teachers who set us essay topics such as 'South Africa: Five Minutes to Midnight?' There was always this sense that the country was doomed, would crack up very soon. Meanwhile it slumbered and developed and fought and grew. This makes one decreasingly able to believe in apocalyptic prediction. The situation reached after fifteen years of ANC rule is bad enough to make one ask whether this will be a failed colonization. But at the same time one is aware that this is no longer a young country and that it has come through many wars, trials and tribulations. And in history length is strength. One must refuse the immediacy of today's 'crisis'; remember the Italian saying that 'the situation is desperate but not serious'; and insist more on what Fernand Braudel (and the *Annales* school) called the 'longue durée'.

Mbeki's presidency, begun with such promise, ended in failure on every front. This was not just a personal tragedy, however, for what failed with Mbeki was an exile dream in which the main part was played by a romantic 1960s African nationalism, which had simply stayed frozen in exile. The ANC's Freedom Charter, the movement's seminal document, adopted in 1955, turned out to be not the frightening document the Nats long warned against but simply a chimera, making promises which the movement was quite incapable of fulfilling. To read back through its chapter headings now – 'The People Shall Govern!', 'There Shall Be Work and Security!', 'The Doors of Learning and Culture Shall Be Opened!', 'The Land Shall Be Shared Among Those Who

Work It!' – is simply to remind oneself of how far those (mainly white communists) who drafted it were from thinking about the realities of power. In practice a tiny and increasingly rich black elite governs, unemployment is off the chart, education is on a downward slope and the sad charade which passes for land reform has simply exacerbated the crisis over rising food prices.

The failure of this 1960s brand of African nationalism was hardly surprising; it had failed elsewhere in Africa and the ANC's claim that it had learnt from mistakes elsewhere turned out to be fairly empty. But the reason why the Freedom Charter turned out to be merely a romantic gesture was that in an industralized but racially segmented society, to give power to the representatives of a vast underclass largely lacking in education and skills is to reverse all the hierarchies which have accompanied successful social development elsewhere. One can, of course, lay great blame on the *ancien régime* for its criminal folly over black education and much else besides, and one could even argue that whites were getting a well-deserved comeuppance for such appalling insults as the Mixed Marriages Act, the Immorality Act, the 'Whites Only' park benches and all the rest of it. But this leads nowhere: the country is not just a morality play. The whites who framed those dreadful Acts are long since dead and in any case history's results are what they are. The question is how to make the country work with what there is to hand, for if it fails to work the main sufferers will be the black poor.

For the first decade of ANC rule the country was in effect running on the accumulated momentum of previous public sector investment in many areas, most notably in infrastructural provision of every kind. It was only towards the end of this period that the deleterious effects of this new type of governance began to be felt, particularly that of a public sector administration which lacks education and skills at every level. At the same time, both the new black elites and the black underclass, subjected for many years to policies of exclusion and discrimination, naturally had keen acquisitive instincts and were determined to use the opportunities presented by the new dispensation to make up for lost time. This led on the one hand to very low levels of competence in many areas of government and, simultaneously, the pillaging of the public sector. The combination threatens a sort of institutional implosion.

Logically, the combination of public sector failure and continued economic growth should see the privatization of hitherto public functions. Already private education, medicine and security companies have filled some of the gaps left by the undermining of their public sector alternatives. But the government has set its face firmly against further privatization and talks boldly about 'the developmental state', which means that public sector investment will be vastly increased, becoming a major motor of growth. Typically this is dressed up in left language and with allusions to what was achieved in the past by such policies in South Korea or Japan. The truth is a great deal less impressive. For no good reason the state failed for years to invest in transport, the infrastructure and electricity production, producing a crisis in many spheres. Having belatedly woken up to this, it now proposed a great spending splurge – which also coincided with large spending for the 2010 football World Cup. The resultant bunching was bound to produce huge capacity problems, delays and increased costs. At the end of it South Africa would be left with a number of white elephants such as football stadiums used to full capacity for just two games plus a great deal of expensive capital equipment in the hands of a public sector which has shown itself to be criminally inefficient at routine repair and maintenance. The fact that some 40 per cent of GDP is still in public sector hands – including abusive monopolies such as Telkom and the SABC as well as chronic loss-makers such as SAA – constitutes, indeed, a major restraint on growth.

The obvious failure of government on so many fronts, together with the continued prominence of the revolutionary tradition, has highlighted the left alternative within the ANC, namely the path favoured by Cosatu and the SACP. One cannot entirely rule out the possibility that such an alternative might be tried, though such an experiment would be a brief and disastrous cul-de-sac. Thus no serious and viable alternative exists within the ANC's alliance. So the question becomes, in part, how long the ANC's dominance can last. The general expectation is that the party can look forward to many more years in power. After all, other successful African nationalisms had a long run and South Africa's two preceding nationalist waves both lasted a long time – the Afrikaner nationalists held power for forty-six years. And the ANC will doubtless continue to exploit an African racial polarization against the other minorities, especially the whites, so that demography alone will guarantee continued ANC rule.

In fact none of these assumptions is very safe. The long dominance of African nationalist regimes to the north is not really comparable, partly because none of them faced so sharp a contradiction between the style of governance they could offer and the demands of a modern industrial economy, and also because many of them were artificially propped up by single-party rule and the absence of a true opposition. Secondly, the duration of the preceding Jingo and Afrikaner nationalist waves had no little to do with the fact that both provided highly effective governments which succeeded in building up the state and the economy, a sharp contrast with the ANC. And thirdly, it is not clear that polarization against a white minority that is already under 10 per cent of the population can continue indefinitely; the Zimbabwean example rather suggests that it cannot.

Moreover, African nationalism lacks most of the strengths which made Afrikaner nationalism so monolithic. Afrikaners were united by a single history, a single language, a single religion; they were all of one race and had one culture. They were also very consciously fighting to reverse 'a century of wrong' and the bitter memories of the Anglo-Boer War and its concentration camps deeply marked succeeding Afrikaner generations. The ANC is very different. It consists of many different groups with different histories, languages, cultures and religions. It tries to overcome this by emphasizing the anti-apartheid struggle which united all these groups but this is a wasting asset. If you ask young blacks what they think about apartheid their answers are vague and disparate. When told about pass laws, bantustans and all the rest of it they are inclined to associate these things with their grandparents. Often they are incredulous that such things could ever have existed.

One must remember, too, that most of the ruling African nationalist parties which won independence looked invulnerable for a while, but ultimately declined and collapsed, sometimes wholly disappearing. The decline of the 'liberation culture' appears to be a secular, indeed a routine phenomenon – and a one-way street. Finally, there are reasons to wonder if the 'normal' decline of African nationalist parties is not proceeding faster in the ANC's case. The eruption of factionalism within the party only six years after it gained power is one such pointer. Another is the bitter destructiveness of that factionalism. As one senior government official put it in the wake of Polokwane, 'Mbeki's people are pursuing a scorched-earth policy. They want to leave nothing for the new

[Zuma] government. They want to set them up to fail.'[35] Such deliberate sabotage of the next government would have been unthinkable for either of South Africa's earlier nationalisms. It is difficult, indeed, to see how Jacob Zuma can ever enjoy the same authority as either Mandela or Mbeki did.

Finally, it is worth noting how often the challenge to a ruling African nationalism has been trade-union based. Frederick Chiluba, the Zambian union leader, successfully evicted Kenneth Kaunda from power in 1991 and, had there been free elections, Morgan Tsvangirai would have evicted Mugabe in 2000. That is, in Zambia this occurred after Kaunda's UNIP party had ruled for twenty-seven years and in Zimbabwe the process would have taken twenty years since independence. Yet Zuma, Cosatu's candidate, achieved the same after only thirteen years of ANC rule. South Africa is clearly waiting for its MDC: a party with a broad African following which also enjoys the support of the white minority.

If, however, ANC rule continues – still the most likely outcome – what will be the consequences of its inevitable and accumulating failure? The fact that Mbeki could talk of a Zuma government reducing the country to 'a neo-colonial basket case' revealed that Mbeki, for all his 'African Renaissance' posturing, realized how close South Africa was to such a fate. The most positive result of the Mbeki period, paradoxically, is that while he undermined democratic institutions to a very dangerous degree, ultimately this produced a reaction which led to his defeat and disgrace. With him disappeared any serious risk that South Africa could decay into dictatorship. One may similarly rule out any possibility that accumulating misgovernance would lead the country to split up. To be sure, it seems likely that more and more areas will escape effective government control, leading to regional banditry in extreme cases. But one cannot imagine the emergence of regional baronies or of outright secession.

For the one consistent theme of all three nationalist waves has been national unity. The Jingo nationalists would not tolerate separate Boer republics and achieved the country's final unification. The Afrikaner nationalists may have created bantustan dependencies but they were fierce enemies of any real regional challenge: they cut back on federal powers, would not countenance Natal secessionism and even refused to have anything to do with the KwaZulu-Natal Indaba movement of the 1980s. The ANC has maintained this tradition, reintegrating the bantustans and cutting back even further on provincial powers. So secession will not take place. There will no South African Tshombe or Ojukwu.

What this leaves is the probability of an ineffectual central government, prey to populist currents of every kind, but increasingly unable to control the society it nominally heads. Such an environment will be hard on the poor, hard, too, on established high-culture institutions of any kind (universities, museums, art galleries, archives, etc.) but will probably leave enough loopholes for the rich, the opportunist and the criminal to prosper. It will be a very far cry from anything the Freedom Charter talked about.

The broken-backed state and the abysmal quality of governance are major handicaps but need not be fatal. The great hope has to be the emergence of a South African MDC – a liberal party led by Africans but with significant support from the minorities. All the constituent elements for such a party already exist but they have yet to cohere. This process took twenty years from independence in Zimbabwe, so it could now be quite close in South Africa.

Even without that there are two huge elements of hope. One is simply geology. Already it has been discovered that the platinum belt of the North West extends all the way into Limpopo province. There seems almost no limit to the country's natural riches. And, almost certainly, there is oil and gas in its coastal waters. Together with a continuing commodity boom this would spell ongoing economic prosperity. This would not be a substitute for good governance but greater wealth would dilute many woes.

A far greater improvement could be achieved if only the ANC would revert to its non-racist tradition and start employing all the human resources available on a meritocratic basis. This would mean placing properly qualified people in leading positions, regardless of race or ANC connections. Undoubtedly this would be fiercely resisted both for the loss of political patronage it represented and by the black elite, which has come to feel it has a natural monopoly on all leading positions in the public sector. But the ANC, with its huge majority, could easily face down such complaints. There is, after all, no doubt that South Africa will be governed by its black majority more or less for ever, so that dominance can hardly be threatened by having somewhat fewer blacks in leading positions now – until social and educational change mean that they win those posts on merit anyway. Meanwhile, the interests of the entire society, including the black middle class, would be far better served by having public institutions that worked.

In a sense such a policy would merely acknowledge the reality that South Africa can only work as a multi-racial country. What was painfully proved in the previous generation was that the country could not be ruled by excluding blacks, that is, ruled against the blacks. What just fourteen years of ANC rule have shown is that the country also cannot be ruled by excluding – and thus against – its minorities. The probable result of such a policy would be that South Africa would evolve, as Fukuyama suggested, in a Latin American, probably Brazilian direction, a mixed race, unequal, violent but dynamic, open and fast developing society. This is not the national democratic revolution of ANC dreams but then those are just dreams. The ANC's exiles may well be the last ruling group in the world which has to give up believing in the relevance of such old Marxist formulas but in the end even they will have to do so. Brazil may not be anybody's ideal but it is already the world's tenth-biggest economy (ninth if one uses a purchasing power parity basis) and is on the verge of great-power status. Most pertinently, Brazil is a case of a colonization which has decisively succeeded – and that is the criterion South Africa has to use.

There is an even greater imperative here, which is the nature of the country itself. Mbeki was easily bullied by African taunts that South Africa was not wholly African but this was exactly the wrong response. As Desmond Tutu and Nelson Mandela rightly saw, the country's glory and its essence was precisely that it was a rainbow nation and that there should be nothing but pride and pleasure in accepting that heritage – and that opportunity.

The early founders of the ANC's armed struggle were much influenced by the example of Algeria. This is now a history which could profitably be reviewed. The Nobel laureate Albert Camus, a native of Algeria, strongly supported its struggle for independence and was a bitter critic of colonialism. But he gradually fell out of sympathy with the National Liberation Front which led the independence struggle because it saw Algeria's future purely as an Arab, Muslim country. This was, he protested, a denial of the country's entire history. It had, for thousands of years, belonged to 'Mediterranean society'. And the whole point of that history was that it had seen the mixing of Phoenicians, Carthaginians and Egyptians with Jews, Arabs, Portuguese, Spaniards, Italians, French, Syrians and Maltese. The glory of Algeria was that it had been part of all of that, that it was at ease with it, that it shared that richness and understood it. To conceptualize its future purely through the lens of a narrow Muslim Arab nationalism was to do terrible violence not only to that history and society but also to diminish it in a way that could only be sad, cruel and horrible.[36] Camus lost but anyone who looks at modern Algeria is bound to regret that he did. Most Algerians do.

South Africa is the same. It has for centuries been the meeting place of different peoples and cultures. They have oppressed and discriminated against one another, they have fought, they have interbred and they have finally learnt to work and even to play together. It is, in its best aspect, a fine example for the whole of mankind. It is precisely because the world saw this and recognized this spirit in Mandela that it wished endlessly to celebrate him on his consecutive birthdays. This is a precious inheritance. It must not be squandered and it must not be ruined by another narrow nationalism which seeks to obliterate the nation's history and nature. Whether this spirit is carried on by a South African version of the MDC or by the ANC itself is not really the question: ideally it should be common ground for all parties, all South Africans. All Algerians are the poorer because Camus's message was ignored. There is no need or reason to immiserate South Africans in the same way.

15
Denouement

Life must be lived forwards, but can only be understood backwards.

Søren Kierkegaard

In the wake of the seismic eruption at the ANC's Polokwane conference tremors swiftly spread throughout the ANC, the state machine and the parastatal industries, for Mbeki had been pushing in his placemen for well over a decade and now everything was threatened by Zuma's victory. Many of those who had flourished under Mbeki not only made it plain that they would fight for their positions but there were insistent rumours of an Mbeki fight-back, fed by the fact that the National Prosecuting Authority and the Scorpions continued to try to land a knockout blow against Zuma in the courts and also by Mbeki's hasty appointment of a new SABC board only days after Polokwane. The SACP and Cosatu cried foul, for the board was full of Mbeki supporters and the corporation became the site of furious factional struggle, with each side trying to sack or suspend the other. By June 2008 a situation had been reached in which the SABC seemed to have two CEOs and a third waiting in the wings; two spokespersons; two people each attempting to be the chief operating officer; a board divided in three; and several competing sets of lawyers fighting a whole series of intra-SABC lawsuits.[1] The corporation was paralysed, suffered large numbers of resignations and became a sort of national pantomime – though a costly one: apart from licence fee and advertising income it demanded another R2 billion from government.[2] But the SABC was simply the most visible site of struggle. Throughout the public sector Mbeki clients tried to hang on or change sides, while Zuma supporters hoped that their faction's victory would eventuate in well-paid jobs, patronage and favours of every kind for themselves.

With so much at stake, ANC meetings in many provinces quickly degenerated into shambles, with physical violence not uncommon, including two stabbings, one of them fatal.[3] In the Western Cape opposing factions actually held two rival provincial ANC conferences. Feeling now that great advantages were nearly in their grasp, many Zuma-ites were seized with anxiety lest some way be found to deprive them of what they sought. Accordingly they demanded that the NPA be brought to heel, the Scorpions abolished and that Mbeki be dismissed right away, a cry taken up strongly by the SACP, which had been one of the biggest winners at Polokwane: Mbeki, it argued, had only been deployed as President and could therefore be 'recalled'. The SACP's dominance in the new situation was quite naked, with the SACP chairman, Gwede Mantashe, now also the ANC secretary-general and usually the party's principal spokesman. Old-timers shook their heads: in the past the SACP would never have so crudely advertised its influence over the ANC.

Mbeki himself retreated ever further – into his own office, consulting only with Mojanku Gumbi and (sometimes) Essop Pahad; into endless foreign trips; and into denial on every front. He gave up attending meetings of the ANC NEC and the NWC, now both dominated by his enemies. Without doubt he was undergoing a major psychological crisis: the ANC which, far more than family, had been his life, had publicly and humiliatingly rejected him. Mandela, now 90, was still lionized around the world while he, Mbeki, was loathed and rejected. Enoch Powell's famous dictum that 'all political lives end in failure' was seldom so true. Even a far more robust psyche would have been affected. In January 2008 Mbeki told the nation that he had had no clue that there was a corruption case against the police commissioner, Jackie Selebi, 'until just a few days ago'.[4] But Vusi Pikoli, the director of public prosecutions whom Mbeki had suspended, then showed that over the previous eighteen months there had been more than twenty-three meetings with the President or Minister of Justice in which the Selebi case had been exhaustively discussed. The oddity was not just that Mbeki had lied but that he had done so in a way that was bound to be exposed: it was as if the President inhabited his own reality which he felt he could fashion for himself.[5] Another clue to the strange mood inside the presidency was the report by President Bush's former chief speechwriter, Michael Gerson, that Mbeki had written an 'outrageous' letter, 'packed with exclamation points', to Bush in April 2008, denouncing the United

States for its hostility to Mugabe and telling Bush 'to butt out, that Africa belongs to him'.[6] A poll among South Africans living in the country's major cities found that Mbeki's approval ratings had fallen from 61 per cent in 2005 to only 37 per cent by May 2008, a low figure for the leader of a party steadily taking over 67 per cent of the vote. Moreover, a clear tribal cleavage was now visible, with only 39 per cent of Zulus approving of him, compared to 65 per cent of Xhosas.[7]

The nationwide power cuts which began in early 2008 were a crucial psychological moment. They were an unmistakable announcement to the world that the ANC government had failed, that despite all the promises made since 1994 the ANC could not even guarantee the minimum conditions for modernity. Power failures are hardly unusual in Africa. Power stations required forward planning and huge expenditure, and it was always easier to let tomorrow look after itself. The ANC had vowed that it would not be like that. Yet it was just the same. There was a fresh wave of white emigration – the power cuts, the end of the economic boom that they signalled and the approaching Zuma presidency convinced many that the country was going down the drain. But one could see African heads go down everywhere too. It was not just that jobs were threatened in all directions by the power cuts. Far more, it said that our side just cannot cope, reinforcing all sorts of inferiority complexes and confirming all sorts of apartheid stereotypes. No one said out loud that power cuts never happened under apartheid, but then, no one needed to: the thought was omnipresent.

Providentially, at just that moment it emerged that some young Afrikaners at the University of the Free State had made a video in which the black domestic staff had collaborated, humiliatingly yet enthusiastically, fulfilling various white stereotypes of black inferiority. It was a student prank in lamentable, indeed racist, taste, though that is all it was. For the government it was a godsend and it was given massive television coverage, with the most offensive video clips played over and over again in a clear attempt to refocus angry black feeling back onto the old white enemy.

But something far more sinister was brewing. In effect, immigration control had broken down completely. Official, legal immigration was strictly controlled so that bringing in expertise from abroad was devilishly difficult, particularly if the experts were white. But illegal immigrants flowed into the country from all over Africa as untold millions of Zimbabweans, Congolese, Somalis, Nigerians and others sought refuge or just a better life there. The government had withdrawn the army from border protection duty in 2004, replacing it with a woefully inadequate (and easily bribed) police detachment only a quarter of the required size. As Minister of Home Affairs, Mangosuthu Buthelezi had fought for ten years to construct a more sensible immigration policy, but the ANC had thwarted him at every turn. While the economy roared along at 5 per cent growth rates South Africans were remarkably tolerant of this vast foreign influx, despite the obvious pressure it exerted on housing, schools and hospitals, and despite the fact that the foreigners were competing in a labour market already marked by 40 per cent unemployment rates.

The power cuts changed all that. With mines closing and many construction projects cancelled through lack of power, it was clear that the boom – and job growth – was over. For the unemployed the boom had at least held out the hope that they might get jobs but the power cuts killed that hope. In the new, sourer atmosphere many focused angrily on the immigrants and the unwanted extra competition they provided. Moreover, protests against poor service delivery had become endemic in many townships, so unemployed youths were already in the habit of taking part in marches, burning tyres in protest and exercising mob rule. It was an easy progression to turn one's anger against the foreigners in one's midst. By early April 2008 I had become aware of regular nightly battles taking place on the outer fringes of Johannesburg between large gangs of locals and Zimbabweans, with several deaths a night. Eerily, however, there was no word of this in the South African media. It was only on 11 May, when the violence moved into Alexandra Township, in the heart of Johannesburg's plush northern suburbs, that the media began to report it. This in turn broadcast news of the xenophobic riots to the nation at large. Street opinion was extremely receptive to such news, so xenophobic violence rapidly spread throughout the country. More than sixty people were killed and tens of thousands displaced.

The government treated the outbreaks of township violence exactly as P. W. Botha had treated them in the 1980s, denouncing them as the work of outsiders and criminals. Then, when the fact of popular xenophobia became clear, ANC leaders behaved as if they were priests attempting an exorcism, by preaching and prayers to cast out the devil (xenophobia), as if the real problem was inside the heads of the rioters when, quite clearly, the root causes lay in high unemployment and the government's failure to control the country's borders. This gross failure of governance had simply handed the problem of immigration control to people on the street, who dealt with it by predictably brutal and direct means, several victims even being necklaced with burning tyres. Mbeki remained invisible as the violence escalated, only ordering the army into the townships after mounting criticism of his inaction, and then flew off to an AU summit in Tanzania to discuss the formation of a United States of Africa. He then flew back home and gave a television broadcast in which he deplored the damage done to South Africa's international image by the violence, pointing out that in 2001 the United Nations had chosen South Africa to host a conference on racism and xenophobia because of the country's achievement in overcoming racism.[8] He blamed the violence on 'a few criminals' and insisted that there would be no change in immigration policy[9] – indeed, shortly thereafter he signed a protocol allowing for the free movement of labour within the entire SADC region. He then flew immediately to Japan to attend a conference on African development, his fourteenth foreign trip in five months. It was a bizarre performance. He had visited no township or informal settlement, met no victims of the violence, and seemed only concerned at the diplomatic ramifications of the violence. Some thought he was bored with South Africa's problems, others that he was reacting with petulance after his public rejection at Polokwane.

The country was, indeed, leaderless. Much of government had ceased to function, not only because the civil service barely worked, but because ministers were almost wholly taken up with ANC factional politics. Mark Lamberti, chairman of Business Against Crime (BAC), a major organization in the world of law and order, complained publicly that while the relationship between government and the BAC was not entirely non-existent, 'it was absent. Because the government right now is out to lunch. It's in "wait and see" mode, and those who deal with the government know it's exceptionally difficult to get things done.'[10] The result was increasingly chaotic drift. The government's mid-term review of the Motor Industry Development Programme, though billions of rand and tens of thousands of jobs depended on it, missed its deadline.[11] It emerged that South Africa's trade deal with the EU, of which Alec Erwin had been so proud, had actually created major difficulties for the surrounding countries in the Southern African Customs Union (SACU) and had also resulted in an annual trade deficit for South Africa with the EU of 2 billion euros (and growing). The whole relationship of SACU with the EU hung in the balance. Yet it received scant attention. Amazon.com announced that it would no longer send goods to South Africa by post because of rampant theft by post office workers – the only country in Africa to receive such a humiliating ban.[12] South African Airways, which had taken R2.8 billion from the taxpayers in 2007, asked for a further R3 billion in 2008[13] – yet, like the SABC, it was facing competitors who got no such subsidy and still made a profit. Almost all the other state-owned industries were in a similar condition. The EU warned South Africa that it might have to ban its exports of ostrich meat – already worth R1 billion a year – not because of any problem with the meat but because the government was failing in its commitment to monitor health standards.[14] It emerged that, for the first time in living memory, South Africa had become a net food importer, largely as a result of the so-called land reform, which had seen many large and highly productive farms become barren, subsistence areas. Moreover, a sword of Damocles hung over every commercial farmer and many were unwilling to invest, so this once fabulously productive sector was steadily running down. South Africa could not afford this: large numbers of farm-worker jobs were being lost, food was becoming too expensive for the poor and the loss of agricultural exports was producing a current account deficit approaching 10 per cent of GDP. Perhaps the lowest point came at the end of June when the Johannesburg Metro Police went on strike and, some of them swilling from beer cans, used their official vehicles to block traffic on a major highway in protest. When the (national) South African Police arrived there was a shoot-out, with the stranded motorists cowering beneath the bullets. No one was disciplined and wage negotiations continued as if this was a routine boys-will-be-boys incident.[15]

There was disarray in every direction. So uninterested had the government become in governing that it was becoming hard to remember quite why the ANC had spoken with such passion about 'the conquest of power'. Many of the political elite seemed far more interested in the fruits of power than in policy and some just exhibited a 'big man' need to be in charge, though without taking responsibility for what happened on their watch. Meanwhile the judge-president of the Western Cape, John Hlophe, had been accused of trying to persuade two of the judges of the Constitutional Court to go easy on Zuma – and it was rumoured that he saw himself as a future Chief Justice in a Zuma-ruled South Africa. The Constitutional Court took action against Hlophe and he counter-sued them, presenting a picture of complete judicial disarray. Given Mbeki's attempts to trap Zuma in court actions, the judges in any case found themselves at the centre of the fray. Gwede Mantashe, the ANC secretary-general, spoke of the judges as being part of 'the counter-revolutionary forces' trying to topple Zuma.[16] Increasing concern was expressed as to how judicial independence could possibly survive in such a climate, though in fact a graver threat lay in the appalling quality of many of the new judicial appointees. Some senior judges were notorious drunkards and could sometimes be seen blind drunk on public occasions. I was given firm evidence of how another judge-president regularly received bribes in return for fixing judicial decisions. Many judges were so notoriously incompetent that if they were appointed to preside over an important commercial case the contending parties would immediately agree to arbitration rather than allow the case to continue in court.

But Mbeki paid more attention to Zimbabwe than South Africa. Following the first round of the presidential election in March, in which Tsvangirai had heavily outdistanced him, Mugabe, ignoring the constitutional requirement that the run-off be held within three weeks, delayed it for three months, during which he conducted a grotesque reign of terror and prevented Tsvangirai from campaigning. Tsvangirai withdrew from the election in protest and Mugabe accordingly 'won'. The Western powers put forward a UN resolution condemning Mugabe and calling for further sanctions but South Africa hotly opposed this and helped persuade Russia and China to veto the resolution, drawing a ringing denunciation from the US ambassador to the UN, Zalmay Khallizad, about South Africa's betrayal of its own past, when international sanctions had played so large a role in ending apartheid.[17] But Mbeki now played the key role at SADC, first in suggesting that he should lead the mediation between Mugabe and Tsvangirai, and meanwhile that Mugabe should be accepted as Zimbabwe's President at SADC meetings. Only Botswana refused to accept this de-facto recognition of Mugabe's legitimacy.

The MDC had to accept Mbeki's mediation, though it had every reason not to trust him. Indeed, it now emerged that Mbeki had deliberately suppressed the report submitted by the two leading judges, Sisi

Khmapepe and Dikgang Moseneke, to observe the 2002 presidential election in Zimbabwe when they had reported that the election had been stolen. When attempts had been made to force publication Mbeki 'threw his toys out of the cot'.[18] A court ruling also found that the Foreign Minister, Nkosasana Dlamini-Zuma, had repeatedly lied to Parliament over Zimbabwe.[19]

With great fanfare Mbeki concluded a power-sharing agreement between Mugabe and the two MDC factions, but the whole thing turned out to be a foul, the agreement the sides had actually reached being quietly replaced by another draft which gave Mugabe power to obviate the entire deal. In addition, no mention was made of which portfolios would be allocated to each party and Mugabe then insisted on retaining everything of any significance so that the whole deal broke down. Mbeki then attempted to persuade Tsvangirai to accept Mugabe's terms – a remarkable outcome when one considers that since the MDC had led the presidential election and won the parliamentary elections outright, there should have been no need for a power-sharing deal at all, let alone one which gave all power to the loser. Then, as Zimbabwe began to collapse, the Elders – as the team of Jimmy Carter, Kofi Annan and Graca Machel styled themselves – arrived to see for themselves. Mbeki, acting as Mugabe's messenger,[20] informed them they would not be given visas to enter Zimbabwe where the state media labelled them 'unemployed busybodies masquerading as Elders'.[21] With over half the Zimbabwean population now facing starvation and 1.4 million at risk of cholera, the nightmare continued to deepen. The MDC refused all further negotiation until Mbeki was removed from the role of mediator.

In April 2008 I met with Jacob Zuma again. I put it to him that it was reported on all sides that Mbeki was conducting a scorched earth policy and would leave Zuma with an impossibly difficult transition. The country was in a complete mess and things were rapidly slipping out of control. Zuma seemed fully aware of the situation. When I suggested that Mbeki would continue to lay obstacles in his path, he merely sighed and said, 'Every day and in every way.' He had learnt, he said, that Mbeki often said things which he neither meant nor believed, but the man was 'ruthless – and thorough'. I also pointed out that Polokwane had been an enormous psychological blow to Mbeki, for the ANC had been his whole life, and that many people believed he was psychologically disturbed. 'Indeed, yes. And for a long time now,' Zuma replied.

In which case I wondered whether there was not a strong case for deposing him quickly before more damage was done? 'You are forgetting what you've said,' Zuma replied. 'Mbeki is paranoid and he is cornered. The situation is potentially very dangerous. If one were to move against him, there is just no knowing what he might do. It might seem that the national interest means he should go quickly – and for my part, I can tell you that waiting as long as I have to, if, indeed, I am ever to be in charge, is no easy thing. Living under such pressures is not easy. But my feeling is that if we were to push Mbeki out early, the ANC would develop a big wobble. And if the ANC develops a wobble, so does the whole country. So I've decided that the best thing to do is to let him serve out his term.'[22]

It was not to be. Zuma's supporters had the scent of power in their nostrils and every fresh report of the continuing legal pursuit of Zuma put them on tenterhooks: even at this stage their hero and thus their victory might be torn from them. Hence their fury at the judges, the NPA and the Scorpions. First Mbeki was forced to disband the Scorpions and then in early July Zuma and Mantashe angrily confronted Mbeki about his continued resistance to their wishes: Kgalema Motlanthe must be appointed to the cabinet to represent them there and two of Mbeki's strongest supporters, Nosimo Balindlela, premier of the Eastern Cape, and Ebrahim Rasool, premier of the Western Cape, were both axed. Mbeki reluctantly complied. The pro-Mbeki Limpopo premier, Sello Moloto, was also sharply brought to heel, deprived of the provincial ANC chairmanship and warned that his survival as premier depended on strict obedience to the Zuma ANC.[23] That same day the Mbeki forces leaked to the press a report by Judge Ronnie Pillay suggesting that Balindlela's enemy and predecessor as Eastern Cape premier, Makhenesi Stofile, together with his brother Mike, the vice-president of SA Rugby, and other relatives, had benefited hugely and illegitimately from public funds during Stofile's premiership.[24]

But Mbeki was clearly on the skids. One sure sign was the sudden and ferocious attack on him by the vice-chancellor of the University of KwaZulu-Natal, Malegapuru Makgoba, who had previously gone to great lengths to woo Mbeki. Disregarding the notion that university heads should avoid partisan display, he described Zuma as one of the greatest African leaders while excoriating Mbeki as 'a classic dictator of our times',[25] comparable to Idi Amin. Mbeki ignored such sallies and infuriated the left by continuing to defend his economic policies, including his decision to launch a scenario-planning process, to 'help the country anticipate and plan better for 2015'[26] – the year after Zuma's first presidential term would finish.

The end came suddenly and unexpectedly when, early in September, Justice Chris Nicholson set aside the case against Zuma on the grounds of procedural unfairness, pointing to the constant political interference in the case. Zuma's supporters were jubilant, Mbeki's were livid and many lawyers questioned whether Nicholson had been right to let a judicial decision rely so heavily on political interference. But Zuma was off the hook and so was the judiciary; the country's new ruling group suddenly had nothing but praise for judges. And, by inference, Mbeki was in the dock, accused of having abused his position as President to pervert the ends of justice. Zuma's supporters were not men to look a gift-horse in the mouth and within a week – against Zuma's pleadings – the NEC had met and, in a tumultuous meeting, voted to 'recall' Mbeki as President. Among those most vocal in calling for this were Jeff Radebe, Cyril Ramaphosa, Blade Nzimande (the ANC Youth League leader), Julius Malema, Lindiwe Sisulu and Tokyo Sexwale, the latter telling the meeting: 'We can't live another day with this man.' Trevor Manuel sat silently through the meeting.[27] But Mbeki was barely in the country, flitting from his mediation efforts in Zimbabwe to the Sudan, with a trip to the UN in New York planned for the next few days. In the end, the ANC top six, led by Zuma, delivered the humiliating news to Mbeki. Zuma tried hard to sugar the pill, arguing that Mbeki should be allowed to fly to the UN and make his farewells as President, resigning only on his return, but the majority took the view that Mbeki was far too tricky a customer to be allowed any wriggle-room. Despite Zuma's fears, Mbeki meekly submitted. The UN trip was cancelled.

Few wept at Mbeki's departure: as *The Economist* concluded, he had been 'a rotten president'. But the manner of his going shocked many. A man twice elected President and confirmed by Parliament had been removed at the behest of an intra-party conclave of less than a hundred members. Since Zuma was not an MP and was still facing court charges, it was decided to make Kgalema Motlanthe President, a man whom polls showed was unknown to 52 per cent of the population.[28] It was a remarkable event. Only a minority of the NEC which made the decision were MPs and Motlanthe himself had never been popularly elected, having simply been appointed an MP by the ANC in May. A number of cabinet ministers tendered their resignations immediately, either because they knew they had no political future or simply because they had held their posts at Mbeki's pleasure. Mbeki released all the names of the resignees at once, which, since Trevor Manuel was one of them, caused both the markets and the rand to plummet. Since, in fact, Manuel was quite willing to continue to serve under Motlanthe it was difficult to argue with the SACP's view that Mbeki had acted out of spite.[29]

When the dust settled those who had gone included the Deputy President, Phumzile Mlambo-Ngcuka, Alec Erwin, Ronnie Kasrils and both Pahads, while Manto Tshabalala-Msimang was replaced as Health Minister by Barbara Hogan, who energetically set about repairing the immense damage done under her predecessor. It was the end of Aids denialism. A study by the Harvard School of Health concluded that Mbeki's decision to declare available anti-Aids drugs to be toxic and dangerous had cost 365,000 unnecessary extra deaths between 1999 and 2005, including 35,000 babies,[30] a judgement which led some to argue that he should be put on trial. It was a measure of how destructive the Mbeki regime had been that his ex-ministers were almost universally unpopular. Erwin, for example, had come up through the ranks of Cosatu and the SACP but was now loathed by both, as well as by the ANC and the Opposition. Essop Pahad announced that he was looking for a new job, but one of the businessmen whom he asked for a job told me: 'Essop doesn't seem to realize he's the most unemployable man in the country.'[31] Mbeki himself appealed against the Nicholson judgment, despite the fact that he had not been party to the original case. This was variously described by lawyers as 'breathtaking', 'unprecedented', 'extraordinary' and 'going off sideways'.[32] No one had a good word for him.

But Zuma had been right. Such a regicide was impossible without major repercussions within the ANC. Within weeks Terror Lekota and the now-resigned premier of Gauteng, Mbhazima Shilowa, had split from the ANC to form the Congress of the People (COPE), which immediately began to attract many more defectors from the ANC. By the time I interviewed Lekota on 16 October[33] he confidently predicted that the ANC could no longer win five of the eight provinces: the Eastern, Western and Northern Cape, the Free State and the North West. He claimed that the SACP and Cosatu had rigged and packed the election of delegates to the ANC's Polokwane conference, that they were now foisting an extreme and impossible Communist agenda on the ANC, that they had no respect for the constitution, the judiciary or the rule of law and that Zuma was 'not an appropriate person to be President'. Although, like many COPE supporters, he had been shocked by the manner of Mbeki's axing, he quickly distanced himself from Mbeki: 'I don't talk to him. Thabo's had his time and now it's over. I have never counted him as a friend.' He accused Zuma of naked tribalism, but denied that COPE's support was in any way tribal.

But while COPE clearly appealed to the black white-collar and middle classes, there was a tribal element. Xhosa-speakers had become used over four decades to the ANC being led by a Xhosa and thus to the notion that it was 'their' party. Moreover, as Sibusiso Mdalala noted with some asperity, 'When I go to Pretoria I can't help but notice that many of the ministers and most of the top civil servants are Xhosa. But what really upsets me is that so are 40 per cent of the receptionists, secretaries and security guards. Yet Pretoria is not a Xhosa area and many of the locals are unemployed. It's incredibly insensitive.'[34] For the same reasons, in the long slow burn after Polokwane, the opposition to Zuma had become increasingly ethnicized. Amongst the Xhosa of the Cape provinces, Mbeki's defeat at Polokwane and his humiliating recall nine months later spread a growing sense of unease and dispossession. The '100% Zuluboy' T-shirts worn by Zuma supporters were a clear declaration, in their eyes, that henceforth patronage would trickle down towards Zulus, not Xhosas. The sacking of Rasool and Balindlela spread anxiety that the Zuma-ites would purge everyone connected with the Mbeki regime.

In KwaZulu-Natal I found the same thing in reverse. In every bus and in every taxi queue the phrase you heard was that 'it's our time now'. Everyone seemed to believe that a deal had been reached at Codesa whereby Mandela and then Mbeki would succeed Tambo but that then it would be a Zulu's turn. The ANC was, after all, 'Luthuli's party' and Zulus were the biggest single ethnic group. Mbeki's attempt to prolong his rule was viewed as the typically treacherous action of a tricky Xhosa. The general feeling was that not only would Zulus not stand for that but that any attempt to push in a non-Zulu such as Ramaphosa would be an intolerable insult. Already the amakhosi (the Zulu chiefs) had met and warned that if the ANC attempted to prevent a Zulu succession they 'would send the buses in' – a deliberate evocation of the ANC–IFP strife of the early 1990s. Those buses, it was understood, would be full of men with guns and assegais and little would be left of ANC headquarters once they got there. I found the local ANC traumatized by the threat, which they took extremely seriously. The grass roots of KwaZulu-Natal were all singing for Zuma, including previously IFP areas, and Mandla Gcaba, biggest of the taxi bosses, was paying tens of millions towards Zuma's legal costs.

As Zuma's campaign began it was clear that a very different rhetoric had replaced Mbeki's 1960s exile style. Where Mbeki's oratory had touched base in semi-educated fashion with a host of fashionable left icons, and had striven to mix literary quotation and Marxist concepts, Zuma's style was quickly classified as 'village fundamentalist'. It was not only more earthy and fundamentally less educated but Zuma was flanked by the intemperate Julius Malema, who repeatedly announced his willingness to die or kill for Zuma. Indeed, at the ANC Youth League conference at the end of June 2008 the main slogan chanted was 'Shoot to Kill for Zuma!'[35] Malema's enemies circulated his (lamentable) matriculation results from school and Malema became a bogeyman for many, the very picture of feral youth. He was one of the so-called 'lost generation', whose childhood had been dominated by township violence and all that went with the 1980s ANC slogan of 'Liberation Now, Education Later'. He was only 9 when he was first enrolled as an ANC activist, learning ANC slogans and songs, how to use a handgun and how to use burning tyres as an instrument of struggle. He had been a full-time activist all his life, first for the Young Pioneers, then for the ANC-aligned Congress of South African Students (which he headed). Now 27, he was a Marxist-Leninist, a well-paid ANC full-timer living in a middle-class suburb and he was extremely rough and ready.[36]

Malema's prominence was merely one more sign of the dumbing down of public life in line with the general de-skilling of society. It was noticeable that whereas in the past if one visited the SACP or Cosatu websites one could read long and extremely tedious policy papers, when you visited the same websites in 2008 all you got was more or less off-the-cuff speeches by Comrade Zwelinzima Vavi or Comrade Blade Nzimande. The closer the left got to power the more its policy was being made on the hoof and the less it resembled proper policy at all. Even when Jeremy Cronin stepped up to the plate the style was essentially literary: one could not say X because then it might be thought that one was implying Y and that was ideologically impermissible, so instead one should opt for Z. Not that Z was tested, feasible or possible but just on general principle. Although Trevor Manuel remained loyal to the ANC he made the central point that South Africa's current account deficit meant that it needed a steady R200 billion a year from foreign investors to stay afloat. It did not much matter whether these investors were individuals, companies, the IMF or the World Bank: they would all demand much the same things and South Africa was now far too integrated into the world political economy to ignore their wishes. Which included: no expropriation or nationalization; a known and stable policy stance which meant no making of policy on the hoof; and predictable, reasonable returns on their money. If they did not get what they wanted they would withdraw their funds, without which South Africa simply could not manage.

Zuma's rhetoric was innocent of all such sophistication. Just as he had once said that his faction should not attack Mbeki because that was merely 'beating a dead snake', so now his and Malema's speeches were full of farmyard similes. The new breakaway movement, COPE, was referred to by Zuma-ites as snakes, dogs or, most alarmingly, cockroaches – for that was how Hutu extremists had justified their genocide in Rwanda. Zuma himself often seemed to say whatever he felt the audience in front of him wanted to hear. He deplored 'the erosion of morality' in modern society and called for the restoration of traditional values so that orphans and old people were cared for in the community, not in orphanages and old people's homes. He also favoured a return to the good old days when traditional leaders were blessed by medicine men and women 'to make them strong'.[37] He hinted at the return of the death penalty; said that unmarried teenage mothers should have their babies taken from them and placed in institutional care while the mothers were sent to special colleges; that children found on the streets during school hours should be taken away and forced to learn; that criminal suspects should be denied the right to remain silent and should be 'made' to speak to the police; that school prayers should be compulsory and children made 'to fear God'; that all South Africans should be made to fear their ancestors; that there was too much sex and nudity on television; and that the long-passed deadline for land restitution should be reopened.[38] He seemed unaware that many of these demands were unconstitutional. The bizarre aspect of this performance was not lessened by the fact that Zuma raced around the country in motorcades of up to thirty-three cars on occasion, at speeds in excess of 100 mph – the classic 'big man' style, aped by many ANC leaders. In one celebrated case, a car travelling in the fast lane failed to move over for the car of a provincial minister and his bodyguards shot at the vehicle, which crashed, injuring eight people. The bodyguard did not stop.[39]

Not long before, Zuma had been ordained as a preacher, a fact he used to some effect. Addressing a crowd in Polokwane he likened those who had split from the ANC to the donkey which had borne Jesus into Jerusalem. 'The people were waiting for the Son of Man who was on the donkey. The donkey didn't understand and thought the songs of praise were for him.' Then, freely inventing from non-biblical sources, Zuma added that later the donkey returned to Jerusalem on its own so as to enjoy another such glorious welcome, only to be driven away. Zuma also compared the COPE leaders to a snakeskin left behind after winter while the real snake (the ANC) went its own way. 'The old skin may look like the snake but it isn't the snake,' said Zuma, adding that the ANC should not fight for a two-thirds majority but for 'a three-thirds majority'.[40] Such rhetoric was not just light years away from Mbeki's Marxist scholasticism but was itself a clear sign of the disintegration of the old ANC culture. For Zuma's views were not party policy; they were just individual opinions, a style more suited to the rough and tumble of 'big man' African populism than to the old, highly disciplined ANC. And if Zuma felt free to invent policy on the hoof, so, increasingly, did others. Thus Butana Komphela, the ANC chairman of the parliamentary sports portfolio committee, announced that the Springbok rugby team might be denied travel visas if not enough black players were picked; demanded that the team give up the 'racist' Springbok symbol and name and even suggested that the government would expropriate all the country's rugby stadiums away from their owners.[41] None of this was party policy. As the election neared Gwede Mantashe announced that the ANC would deploy both Mandela and Mbeki to campaign for it. Both men said they had no intention of playing any role in the campaign. So much for 'deployment'.

Similarly, COPE spoke a wholly new political language: its leaders said that the leadership of the ANC was too unintelligent and too incompetent to run the country and that it had appointed notorious drunks to important positions simply because they were ANC cadres. 'If these guys take over, the country will be gone in three years,' said Mluleki George.[42] Similarly, Lekota was quite happy to talk of deracializing affirmative action: why should a privileged black child be given preference over a privileged white child?[43]

Even as the election campaign opened in late 2008 incidents multiplied in which ANC supporters tried to disrupt or prevent COPE meetings. It seemed all too likely that the campaign would become more violent. In the early 1990s the ANC had used its muscle against all-comers in black politics, though then it had been able to invoke the exigencies of the liberation struggle to justify such behaviour, something it could not do now. It also seemed likely that tribalism would become a growing force, although the ANC's whole rationale, when it was founded in 1912, was to reject tribalism. If, as seemed likely, Zuma emerged as President, he would begin his term aged 67, with a far lower popular standing than any previous ANC leader, reviled (wrongly) as a rapist by some, and still mocked by cartoonists for his shower-to-prevent-Aids. He would be easily the least-educated President in South African history, rather resembling the populist Zulu leader, Sixpens, whom Arthur Keppel-Jones had once imagined leading South Africa to ruin.[44] The only alternative outcome would be a coalition government in which COPE would share power with the DA and other smaller parties. No one doubted that if the ANC lost power and patronage it would also quickly lose even more ground. So the stakes would be higher in 2009 than in any election since 1994.

The key to comprehending this turbulence was to understand the ANC's evolution. The ANC of 1912 had been a body of African notables who wanted to put tribalism aside and command attention as the representatives of the whole African people. In reality, tribalism remained a potent force and the ANC of this period had no mass following. In the post-1945 period the party metamorphosed into Albert Luthuli's ANC, best understood as a classic African nationalist party of the 1960s era of African independence. In this period the ANC began to acquire a mass audience though it was by no means assured of it and quite often its attempts at mobilization failed. The ANC of this period was aptly summed up by Mandela's phrase 'the parliament of the African people', a broad church in which liberals, communists and nationalists all coexisted.

Joe Slovo and his wife, Ruth First, then staged a successful putsch in which their protégé, Mandela, a man of chiefly origin but also an SACP member, was groomed for leadership and launched Umkhonto (MK). In a sense this meant the takeover of the ANC by MK, for the armed struggle was to dominate all else for the next three decades. It was, in effect, a sort of double putsch. It catapulted Mandela to leadership, effectively displacing Luthuli, and it also meant that Slovo leapfrogged many senior Communists to become the most important Communist. Obeying party orders, other Communists stayed in South Africa, were detained, house-arrested and jailed. Slovo, ignoring orders, fled abroad and cynically capitalized on his freedom to become the SACP boss.

There followed a quarter of a century in which the ANC existed in exile, in jail and, in a shadowy way, on the ground, bursting forth with great mass support in the shape of the UDF after 1983. The trade unions became increasingly important and the SACP went to huge efforts to penetrate them and then rolled them together into Cosatu, the party thus gaining a majority within the tripartite alliance.

The ANC which came to power in 1994 was an amalgam of these currents. The ex-Robben Island group (Mandela, Sisulu) was the window dressing on the top but the exiles ruled. However, Mandela still visualized the ANC as he had done in the 1950s: the parliament of the African people. Thus for him the NEC was the party's authoritative voice and he submitted meekly to its will on the frequent occasions when it outvoted him. In practice, the NEC was controlled by the Mbeki-led exiles, so the reality was a party run in exile fashion.

This reality became fully apparent after Mbeki took over. The new model was Leninist, with the party leader the chief ideologist and philosopher-king. There was no more nonsense about the NEC outvoting the leader, around whom power was now completely centred. Mbeki's endless invocations of ANC history had the effect of marginalizing those from the UDF and other relative newcomers, for it was a language which meant little to them. To their fury, even the SACP and Cosatu found themselves marginalized under the new maximum leader, a fact symbolized by the adoption of Gear.

The Mandela-model ANC and the Mbeki-model ANC were very different but they had this in common: they were almost wholly abstracted from South African sociological reality, because for almost three decades Mandela and the Robben Islanders were in their own separate little world in jail, while Mbeki and his comrades were in their separate little exile world. In fact, of course, even in those two bubbles some elements of African reality still showed through – for example, the opposition in jail between Mandela and Gwala pitted the ANC against the SACP, but also a Xhosa against a Zulu. Similar ethnic strains were seen in the exile world, which also knew its full share of thuggishness and corruption. But, crucially, in both models there was no real interface with the realities of black South African life.

The assumption of both Mandela and Mbeki was that after liberation the ANC could remain detached from those realities, floating above the masses in a detached way, providing vanguard leadership. The party would thus retain the moral high ground and would be the source of a remoralized society. Indeed, Mbeki believed that the party would remodel society: through its endless mass campaigns it would change popular attitudes about gender, racism and other protean realities. It would even change and uplift the moral values of the whole society through its Moral Regeneration Campaign and it would create 'the new man'. Zuma's oft-repeated statement that no one could ever be 'above the ANC' expressed the same notion: the ANC was the supreme moral and political authority in society, above the law, the constitution and mere humanity.

The reality was the opposite. The ANC's mass campaigns had no discernible effect. Society stubbornly refused to be morally regenerated and no 'new man' appeared. For the ANC elite the social reality they interfaced with was one of perks, power, privilege and opportunities for enrichment. For those determined to get into that charmed world, the social reality became one of all-out struggle against their intra-party competitors. And Zuma, ejected in the power struggle and persecuted by the organs of state, had to gain financial and other support wherever he could – from highly questionable white and Indian businessmen, taxi bosses, the amakhosi and Zulu tribal culture.

The inevitable result was that the realities of South African society percolated upwards, for of course the ANC was part of that society and could not float above it. The NEC came to consist of businessmen. Cabinet ministers became rich, became farm-owners and soccer bosses. In the provincial parties all the talk was of tenders, contracts and diverting government spending into one's own pocket. Many state institutions saw straightforward nepotism and looting. The whole public sector was now seen as part of a gigantic spoils system. Factionalism, once kept in check by the iron hand of the SACP, now flourished and the SACP was just another faction. The collapse of the police and the criminal justice system meant that there was a desperate need for enforcers who could make things stick, so recourse to heavy-mob tactics became common. By early 2008 one ANC insider told me: 'The party of Mandela has gone, vanished. Today's ANC is a federation of warlords, sub-lords, of patrons and clients. And you'll find that the head of every state or police department has profitable arrangements with those he is supposed to be controlling. Those controlling the prisons will themselves be running corrupt rackets, the head of the drugs squad will have arrangements with the drug-dealers, and so on. There has been a huge criminalization of the state.'[45]

As the 2009 elections neared it was clear that the new government would face an unenviable situation. Thanks to the world recession, growth was falling off a cliff, and jobs were being shed even before the election date had been announced. Commodity prices had collapsed and with them house prices and the consumer boom. Jeff Gable, Absa Capital's head of research, suggested that South Africa would find it extremely hard to acquire the foreign capital necessary to fund its whole infrastructure-building programme. At worst it might, ironically, find itself building football stadiums for the World Cup but nothing else.[46]

Cosatu and SACP leaders, who displayed a naively unlimited faith in the state, spoke of the need for government to create 5 million jobs in short order, not noticing that America's President-elect Barack Obama was only promising to create 2.5 million jobs in a country which was six times more populous and more than twenty times richer than South Africa. Once again, we seemed to be back at the beginning, with another miracle expected. Too few people said out loud that miracles had not occurred in 1994, that they were not on offer now and that South Africa's size and diversity made it a tough country to govern. Inevitably, the drastic downward revision in national prospects led to a great deal of naming and blaming.

Mandela had celebrated his ninetieth birthday in June – in London, with yet another pop concert where, as usual, he was flanked by film and pop stars and other celebrities. The Mandela-cult, for that was what it had become, had now floated entirely free of South Africa. By the time of the concert South Africa was wallowing like a dismasted ship in a storm, but no one remarked on that. Later, his ex-wife Winnie spoke of how she wished she could stop him reading the newspapers or hearing the news, for the ANC split was 'deeply hurtful' to him. It was, she said, 'cruel' that everything he stood for was now crumbling before his eyes. Yet it was Mandela who had put both Mbeki and Zuma in place, refusing to allow a free election in either case. Mandela had been President when the government allowed Aids to get out of hand – and ignored it. And he had been President during the arms deal, which had poisoned the whole political system. There were many lessons here. Perhaps the first was that liberation was endlessly celebrated as if it meant that all the problems were over. But instead liberation meant simply that new problems began.

Notes

Chapter 1

1 *Business Day*, 6 Oct. 2004.
2 F. Fukuyama, 'The Next South Africa', *National Interest*, Summer 1991.
3 *ANC Today*, 7/28, 20 July 2007.
4 See K. Marx, 'The British Rule in India', *New York Daily Tribune*, 25 June 1853.

Chapter 2

1 See R. W. Johnson and L. Schlemmer (eds.), *Launching Democracy in South Africa: The First Open Election, April 1994* (1996).
2 C. Barron, *Collected South African Obituaries* (2005), p. 118.
3 I am grateful to the then secretary of the ANC's Mafikeng branch for information regarding this and related incidents. Disillusioned, he emigrated soon afterwards.
4 W. M. Gumede, *Thabo Mbeki and the Battle for the Soul of the ANC* (2005), p. 72.
5 See 'Kerzner and his American Dream', *YOU*, 28 Nov. 1996.
6 *Business Day*, 24 Jan. 2001.
7 See *Business Day*, 6 Oct. 2000; *Noseweek* 33 (2001); *Sunday Times*, 15 July 2001.
8 Reported in *Sunday Times*, 29 Dec. 2002.
9 *Business Day*, 26 Feb. 2003, and *Sunday Times*, 16 Nov. 2003.
10 *Financial Mail*, 9 Sept. 2005
11 The *Sunday Times* (London) Rich List, 2005.
12 See the (Johannesburg) *Financial Mail*'s special souvenir edition, 'Donald Gordon: His Life and Legacy', 1 July 2005. This publication was remarkable in that all fifteen contributors studiously avoided mention of Gordon's emigration, clearly a forbidden subject.
13 *Sunday Times*, 23 Jan. 2005.
14 Ahead of the 1994 elections I broached the godfather phenomenon with Anton Harber, editor of the *Weekly Mail* (later to become the *Mail and Guardian*), and asked him why his paper made no mention of this cardinal fact. His reply – that his paper's proud anti-apartheid history made him unwilling to focus on the corruption of the new black elite at such a delicate time – was candid, but sadly symptomatic of the way the press failed to do its job.
15 Interview, Durban, 10 Nov. 1991.
16 Interview, Maseru (Lesotho), Jan. 1994.
17 Interviews with Idasa–ANC Dakar participants, Cape Town, 23 July 1999.
18 Interview with Rian Malan, Johannesburg, May 2007.
19 Interview with Gen. Bantu Holomisa, Pretoria, July 2005.
20 *Mail and Guardian*, 22–8 April 1994.
21 Private source.

22 V. Shubin, *ANC: A View from Moscow* (1999), pp. 84–8.
23 This occurred during Mbeki's courtship of Buthelezi in 1997–9 when Mbeki was securing all bases in the run-up to his presidency.
24 Interview with Sibusiso Madlala, 5 May 2001. As so often with MK personnel, this was his *nom de guerre*.
25 C. Glaser, *Bo-Tstotsi: The Youth Gangs of Soweto, 1935–1976* (2000), p. 55.
26 Ibid., pp. 64, 56.
27 See the obituaries of Modise by Paul Trewhela (*The Independent*, London, 30 Nov. 2001); by his close friend, Ronnie Kasrils, in *ANC Today*, 1/45, 30 Nov. 2001; and in *The Guardian*, 29 Nov. 2001.
28 Interview with Sibusiso Madlala, Johannesburg, 20 Aug. 1999.
29 S. Sole, 'The Real Joe Modise', unpublished MS. Sam Sole is South Africa's premier investigative journalist and I am grateful to him for allowing me to see this account.
30 *Mail and Guardian*, 30 Nov. 2001.
31 Vladimir Shubin, the ANC's Moscow mentor, relates how he asked one member of the ANC executive who had killed Makiwane and was tersely told 'Narod' (the people); Shubin, *ANC*, p. 136.
32 Sole, 'The Real Joe Modise'.
33 Ibid.
34 Ibid. This was confirmed by Modise's batman in testimony to the TRC: he had been sent into South Africa to buy Modise expensive shoes and suits. See obituary by Trewhela, loc. cit.
35 Private sources. Allegations of drug dealing were to haunt another prominent ANC exile, Tokyo Sexwale, who always indignantly rejected them.
36 Sole, 'The Real Joe Modise'.
37 Ibid.
38 *The Star*, 6 Oct. 1997.
39 Sole, 'The Real Joe Modise'.
40 Interview with serving intelligence official, 30 Aug. 2005. The same man warned me that anyone else who pursued inquiries into the Hani affair 'can expect to have all manner of unpleasant things start happening in his life'.
41 TRC Report, vol. 2, ch. 7, paras. 311–12.
42 See e.g. *The Star*, 6 Oct. 1997.
43 Interview, Pretoria, 23 March 2008.
44 Interview, Pretoria, 22 March 2008.
45 *Mail and Guardian*, 31 Jan. 1997.
46 Private source.
47 *Mail and Guardian*, 31 Jan. 1997.
48 *Mail and Guardian*, 14 Feb. 1997
49 *Mail and Guardian*, 31 Jan. 1997.
50 *Mail and Guardian*, 24 April 1998.
51 *Mail and Guardian*, 14 Feb. 1997.
52 *Mail and Guardian*, 31 Jan. 1997.
53 *Mail and Guardian*, 14 Feb. 1997.
54 Ibid.
55 *Mail and Guardian*, 31 Jan. 1997.
56 Interview with Julie Wilken, 23 May 2007.
57 *Mail and Guardian*, 31 Jan. 1997.
58 *The Star*, 30 April 1997.
59 *The Sowetan*, 8 July 1997.
60 Sole, 'The Real Joe Modise'.
61 *Sunday Times*, 28 Aug. 2005.
62 *Sunday Times*, 7 Jan. 2007.
63 *Sunday Times*, 28 Jan. 2007.

64 *Mail and Guardian*, 2–8 Feb. 2007.
65 *Mail and Guardian*, 9–15 Feb. 2007. Georgiadis was the previous husband of Elita De Klerk.
66 *Southern Africa Report*, 25/6 (9 Feb. 2007).
67 *Mail and Guardian*, 30 Nov. 2001.
68 Ibid.
69 Ibid.
70 Gumede, *Thabo Mbeki*, p. 139.
71 *Business Day*, 20 Dec. 2005.
72 Gumede, *Thabo Mbeki*, p. 139.
73 This R8 billion deal for eight A400M military transport planes was rammed through in April 2005 without the deal ever going before Parliament. After the huge row over the earlier arms deal the cabinet had agreed to say as little as possible about the deal in public – so once again any proper public accountability was avoided. See *Financial Mail*, 14 Oct. 2005.
74 *Business Day*, 11 March 1997.
75 *Financial Mail*, 14 Oct. 2005.
76 Recounted to the author by Tony Leon, 21 May 2005.
77 *Mail and Guardian*, 30 Nov. 2001.
78 *Mail and Guardian*, 24–30 May 2002.
79 *Mail and Guardian*, 2–8 Feb. 2007.
80 Private source.
81 See Feinstein's own summary in *Mail and Guardian*, 9–15 Feb. 2007.
82 See A. Feinstein, *After the Party: A Personal and Political Journey Inside the ANC* (2007).
83 Sibusiso Madlala told me how, after he had returned to South Africa, he would sometimes see in the street members of ANC Intelligence who had been among those who beat and tortured him in Quatro. Well after 2000 they were still working for ANC intelligence (which was, of course, not supposed still to exist) and were keen to be friendly, as if to put the bad old days behind them. Madlala decided it was best to respond in friendly fashion but would never share food or drink with them for fear of poisoning.
84 *Business Day*, 17 Aug. 2005.
85 *Mail and Guardian*, 17 Aug. 2001.
86 Obituary by Trewhela, loc. cit.
87 *Cape Times*, 4 Dec. 2001.
88 Ibid.
89 *The Star*, 8 Nov. 2005.
90 *City Press*, 30 July 2006.
91 J. Lacouture, *De Gaulle: The Ruler, 1945–1970* (1991), p. 574.

Chapter 3

1 For the election campaign and the political sociology of South Africa in the crucial 1990–1994 period, see R. W. Johnson and L. Schlemmer (eds.), *Launching Democracy in South Africa: The First Open Election, April 1994* (1996).
2 *The Citizen*, 19 April 1994.
3 *The Sowetan*, 11 April 1994.
4 *Business Day*, 11 May 1994.
5 The newspaper was originally entitled the *Weekly Mail*, becoming the *Weekly Mail and Guardian* in 1992 and finally the *Mail and Guardian* in 1995.
6 Lekota's nickname came from the soccer field, not from bomb-throwing.
7 *The Star*, 25 April 1994.
8 *Business Day*, 20 May 1994.
9 *Mail and Guardian*, 12–18 May 1995.

10 See e.g. *The Citizen*, 3 July 1995.
11 *The Citizen*, 28 May 1994.
12 *Business Day*, 20 Oct. 1994.
13 *The Citizen*, 15 Sept. 1994.
14 *The Citizen*, 28 Oct. 1994.
15 *Financial Mail*, 16 Dec. 1994.
16 *Weekly Mail and Guardian*, 27 Jan. 1995.
17 *The Star*, 14 Feb. 1995.
18 Gavin Evans, Blog 12, 30 Dec. 2007.
19 *Business Day*, 14 Oct. 1994.
20 *Business Day*, 5 Oct. 1994.
21 *New Nation*, 7 Oct. 1994.
22 *The Sowetan*, 24 June 1994.
23 *The Star*, 10 June 1994.
24 *The Star*, 4 July 1994.
25 *Weekly Mail and Guardian*, 14 Oct. 1994.
26 Ibid.
27 *Business Day*, 11 Nov. 1994.
28 *Business Day*, 10 Feb. 1995.
29 *The Citizen*, 13 Feb. 1995.
30 *Business Day*, 10 Feb. 1995.
31 *The Sowetan*, 11 Jan. 1995.
32 *The Star*, 3 Nov. 1994.
33 *The Sowetan*, 4 Jan. 1995.
34 *Weekly Mail and Guardian*, 29 April 1994. Ramaphosa had been a provisional SACP member before 1990 but stood down once membership became a public affair. Nonetheless, he had chaired the SACP's homecoming rally and the party had strongly supported him for the secretary-generalship.
35 *The Star*, 2 Dec. 1994.
36 *Financial Mail and Guardian*, 16 Dec. 1994.
37 *The Sowetan*, 20 Dec. 1994.
38 *Business Day*, *The Citizen*, 19 Dec. 1994.
39 Private source, interview July 1988.
40 *The Star, The Citizen*, 15 Feb. 1995.
41 *The Star*, 23 Feb. 1995.
42 *The Citizen*, 30 May 1995.
43 *The Citizen*, 10 May and 14 June 1995.
44 *The Citizen*, 14 June 1995.
45 *The Citizen*, 29 June 1995.
46 *The Sowetan*, 28 Feb. 1995.
47 *The Star*, 1 May 1995.
48 *The Citizen*, 17 Feb. 1995.
49 *The Sowetan*, 4 May 1995.
50 *The Star*, 25 April 1995.
51 *The Sowetan*, 4 May 1995.
52 *The Sowetan*, *Business Day*, 24 April 1995.
53 *Business Day*, *The Citizen*, 25 April 1995.
54 *The Citizen*, 27 April 1995.
55 Most of Boesak's donors dropped the matter. A few months later, however, the Dutch government found itself involved in a similar row over the Radio Freedom Institute it had funded in Johannesburg to perpetuate the work of the exile ANC's Radio Freedom. The RFI was an immediate disaster, its director guilty of 'gross public misbehaviour', and its trustees were indebted for over R1 million of missing money. The Dutch moved swiftly to prevent a court case, paid off the debt and closed the RFI down. *The Sowetan*, 26 July 1996.

56 *The Star*, 14 Feb. 1995.
57 Ibid.; *The Sowetan*, 7 March 1995.
58 *The Star*, 14 Feb. 1995.
59 *Sunday Times*, 19 Feb. 1995.
60 *The Sowetan*, 16 Feb. 1995.
61 *The Citizen*, 24 Feb. 1995.
62 Ibid.
63 *Business Day*, 7 March 1995.
64 *The Star*, 17 Feb. 1995.
65 R. W. Johnson, 'The South African Electorate at Mid-Term', *Focus* (Helen Suzman Foundation), 6 (Feb. 1997), pp. 12–13.
66 *The Star*, 7 April 1995.
67 *The Citizen*, 21 Feb. 1995.
68 Points made by De Klerk's adviser, Japie Jacobs. *Sunday Times*, 26 Feb. 1995.
69 Interview with Bishop Magoba, Johannesburg, 13 Aug. 1998.
70 L. Page, *Conflict of the Heart* (2003), p. 209.
71 Ibid., p. 225.
72 Ibid., p. 195.
73 *Sunday Times*, 26 Feb. 1996.
74 *Business Day*, 26 April 1995.
75 *Weekly Mail and Guardian*, 3 Feb. 1995.
76 *Sunday Times*, 12 Nov. 2006.
77 A. Hirsch, *Season of Hope: Economic Reform under Mandela and Mbeki* (2005), p. 176.
78 Ibid., pp. 94–5.
79 Private source.
80 C. Simkins, 'The RDP', paper given at Queen Elizabeth House, Oxford, 21 Feb. 1995.
81 Hirsch, *Season of Hope*, p. 95.
82 This point recurs repeatedly in Hirsch, *Season of Hope*, doubtless echoing Mbeki's emphases.
83 *Sunday Times*, 28 March 1996.
84 *Sunday Independent*, 31 March 1996.
85 Hirsch, though greatly and lengthily concerned to justify Gear, somehow finds no room to mention these no doubt embarrassing projections.
86 For the orthodox left view, see H. Marais, *South Africa: Limits to Change. The Political Economy of Transition* (1998).
87 Hirsch, *Season of Hope*, p. 81.
88 *The Sowetan*, 3 May 1995.
89 *The Citizen*, 1 June 1995.
90 *Mail and Guardian*, 8 Sept. 1995.
91 *The Citizen*, 19 Oct. 1995.
92 *The Citizen*, 25 Nov. 1995.
93 *The Citizen*, 16 Aug. 1995.
94 *Business Day*, 4 Sept. 1995.
95 *The Citizen*, 8 Dec. 1995.
96 *The Star*, *The Citizen*, 3 July 1995.
97 *The Citizen*, 14 Oct. 1995.
98 For this discussion, see *New Nation*, 6 Dec. 1996.
99 The ANC shares the admirable left tradition of educational agitprop, and all such documents are available on its website.
100 *The Star*, 21 Nov. 1995.
101 *The Citizen*, 20 March 1996.
102 Holomisa's Transkei government had opened bribery charges against Kerzner but while

the Transkei remained an independent state Kerzner merely had to desist from going there in order to avoid the charge. With the Transkei's reincorporation into South Africa, the charges, laid by the Transkei Attorney General, Christo Nel, became effective against him within the united jurisdiction.

103 *The Star*, 7 June 1996.
104 *The Citizen*, 2 Aug. 1996.
105 *The Star*, 2 Aug. 1996; *Financial Mail*, 9 Aug. 1996.
106 *The Citizen*, 3 Aug. 1996.
107 *The Star*, 4 Aug. 1996.
108 *Financial Mail*, 9 Aug. 1996.
109 *Sunday Tribune*, 9 June 1996.
110 *Sunday Independent*, 9 June 1996.
111 *The Citizen*, 3 Aug. 1996.
112 Ibid.
113 *Financial Mail*, 9 Aug. 1996.
114 *Mail and Guardian*, 8–15 Aug. 1996.
115 *The Citizen*, 5 Aug. 1996.
116 *Mail and Guardian*, 8–15 Aug. 1996.
117 See R. Gibson, *Prisoner of Power: The Greg Blank Story* (1997). Blank, who had carried out one of South Africa's biggest stock market scams, worked for Leslie and Sidney Frankel; see C. Barron, *Collected South African Obituaries* (2005), pp. 117–18. Barron suggests that Leslie Frankel must have known what Blank was up to and certainly benefited heavily from Blank's activities.
118 *Mail and Guardian*, 8–15 Aug. 1996.
119 *The Star*, 4 Aug. 1996.
120 *The Sowetan*, 11 June 1996.
121 The money had gone missing during the period when Adelaide Tambo had been the League's treasurer and Baleka Kgotsisile (parliament's deputy Speaker) had been secretary-general. The ladies of what was often called the Wives League pointed an accusing finger at Winnie Mandela but the mess seems to have had several authors. *Mail and Guardian*, 21–7 June 1996.
122 *Mail and Guardian*, 2–8 Aug. 1996.
123 *The Star*, 13 Aug. 1996.
124 *Business Day*, 12 July 1996.
125 *The Citizen*, 31 Aug. 1996. Holomisa later produced another letter from Sun International attesting to the free hospitality given to Mbeki, Jay Naidoo and the Agriculture Minister, Derek Hanekom. *Sunday Times*, 1 Sept. 1996.
126 *Cape Times*, 5 Sept. 1996.
127 *The Citizen*, 13 Aug. 1996.
128 *The Sowetan*, *Business Day*, 26 Sept. 1997.
129 *The Citizen*, 18 April 1997. No explanation was ever offered as to why the case had been delayed so long that many of the key witnesses had died.
130 Ibid.
131 *Sunday Tribune*, 9 June 1996.
132 *The Citizen*, 27 Sept. 1996. Pro-Holomisa rallies were held not only in the Transkei but in such Reef townships as Thembisa and Kathlehong.
133 *The Citizen*, 13 Aug. 1996.
134 *Eastern Province Herald*, 27 Sept. 1996.
135 *The Star*, 16 Sept. 1996.
136 *The Sowetan*, 16 Sept. 1996.
137 *New Nation*, 1 Nov. 1996.
138 *The Citizen*, 11 Sept. 1996.
139 *The Sowetan*, 22 Oct. 1996.
140 When the Helen Suzman Foundation surveyed national opinion in October 1996 we

found that most provincial premiers had only 15–25 per cent of voters in their respective provinces saying they were doing a good job. Phosa was the sole exception, scoring 61 per cent, and was the only premier with a strong following in other provinces as well.

141 *The Star*, 25 Oct. 1996.
142 *Cape Argus*, 27 Nov. 1996.
143 *Mail and Guardian*, 4–10 Oct. 1996.
144 *The Sowetan*, 12 Nov. 1996.
145 *New Nation*, 1 Nov. 1996.
146 *The Citizen*, 1 Oct. 1996.
147 *The Star*, 18 Nov. 1996.
148 *The Sowetan*, 18 Nov. 1996.
149 *The Citizen*, 9 Dec. 1996.
150 *The Citizen*, 6 Dec. 1996.
151 *Sunday Times*, 8 Dec. 1996.
152 *Mail and Guardian*, 6–13 Dec. 1996; *Sunday Times*, 8 Dec. 1996.
153 *New Nation*, 22 Nov. 1996.
154 See C. Goodenough, 'Mystery that Surrounds the Armed Robberies', *KwaZulu-Natal Briefing* (Helen Suzman Foundation), 10 (Feb. 1998), and 'Who Killed Sifiso Nkabinde?', *KwaZulu-Natal Briefing*, 14 (March 1999).
155 *Cape Times*, 24 Oct. 1996.
156 *Daily Dispatch*, 11 Nov. 1996.
157 In March 1997, for example, he told the South East Asian Forum flatly that 'Thabo Mbeki is really in charge of South Africa'. *The Citizen*, 8 March 1997.

Chapter 4

1 *New Nation*, 10 Jan. 1997.
2 Ibid.
3 Interview with Sibusiso Madlala, 20 July 1997.
4 *The Star*, 15 April 1997.
5 *Sunday Independent*, 26 Jan. 1997.
6 *Business Day*, 19 Feb. 1997.
7 *New Nation*, 21 Feb. 1997.
8 *The Star*, 14 Feb. 1995.
9 *Business Day*, 13 Jan. 1997.
10 *New Nation*, 28 Feb. 1997.
11 *Business Day*, 20 Jan. 1997.
12 *Business Day*, 27 March 1997.
13 *The Sowetan*, 9 April 1997.
14 See *The Sowetan*, 18, 19 March 1997 and 9 April 1997.
15 *New Nation*, 9 May 1997.
16 *The Citizen*, 28 April 1997.
17 *Business Day*, 15 May 1997.
18 *Business Day*, 2 May 1997.
19 *The Citizen*, 15 May 1997.
20 Private source, interview 31 May 1996.
21 D. Hemson, 'Beyond BoTT? Policy Perspectives in Water Delivery' (preliminary report, cyclostyled, Jan. 1999).
22 *Mail and Guardian*, 22–7 March 2002.
23 *The Mercury*, 24 May 2002.
24 J. Nuttall, *The First Five Years: The Story of the Independent Development Trust* (1997), pp. 217–18.
25 Ibid., p. 212.
26 It is, perhaps, difficult for anyone who did not live through the period to grasp the

strange combination of political militancy, self-righteousness and determined rent-seeking which characterized this group. Many of its most egregious personnel gravitated to the South African National NGO Coalition (Sangoco). When Michel Camdessus, managing director of the IMF, visited South Africa they demanded that he meet with them. When he did he was asked to explain, in the first instance, how he thought they could morally justify sitting down with a self-evidently evil person such as himself. Sangoco also drew up a Code of Conduct for Northern NGOs (i.e. US and EU donors) which sought to bind them hand and foot to accountability to South African activists, attempted to regulate their internal pay-scales and how far they were allowed to employ non-South African staff, and to insist that they appoint South African activists to their governance structures. See Sangoco, 'A Code of Conduct for Northern NGOs' (draft, Oct. 1997). Sangoco itself was plagued by internal scandals and soon lost credibility.

27 *Mail and Guardian*, 20–28 Feb. 1998.
28 *The Star*, *Business Report*, 20 May 2003.
29 *Mail and Guardian*, 12–19 April 2001.
30 *Mail and Guardian*, 11–17 May 2001.
31 *Mail and Guardian*, 12–19 April 2001.
32 'DA to request Investigation of NDA: Statement by Mike Waters, MP', 3 Feb. 2002 (statement issued by the DA).
33 *Business Day*, 9 April 2002.
34 *Mail and Guardian*, 22–8 Aug. 2003.
35 *This Day*, 11 Nov. 2003.
36 *Mail and Guardian*, 19–25 March 2004.
37 *Business Day*, 9 March 2005.
38 *Mail and Guardian*, 9–15 Sept. 2005.
39 *Business Day*, 14 March 2005.
40 *Sunday Times*, 8 Oct. 2006.
41 *The Mercury*, *Business Report*, 2 Feb. 2007.
42 *Business Day*, 14 Dec. 2006.
43 *Beeld*, 1 Feb. 2007.
44 *Finance Week*, 26 June–2 July 1997.
45 *Business Day*, 25 March 2002.
46 *Sunday Independent*, *Business Report*, 20 May 2001.
47 *The Mercury*, 2 Feb. 2007.
48 R. W. Johnson, 'Who Needs Affirmative Action?', *Focus* (Helen Suzman Foundation), 19 (Sept. 2000).
49 Ibid.
50 *Focus* (Helen Suzman Foundation), 6 (Feb. 1997).
51 *Business Day*, 21 April 1997.
52 The Nguni language group comprises the Xhosa, Zulu, Swazi and Ndebele tongues.
53 *Mail and Guardian*, 27 June–3 July 1997.
54 *Sunday Times*, 22 and 29 June 1997.
55 *Sunday Independent*, 31 Aug. 1997.
56 *Mail and Guardian*, 11–17 April 1997.
57 *The Citizen*, 14 May 1997.
58 *The Sowetan*, 4 Aug. 1997.
59 *Sunday Tribune*, 25 May 1997.
60 See ANC 1997 conference documents, 'Nation Formation and Nation Building: The National Question in South Africa'.
61 *Financial Mail*, 13 June 1997.
62 Ms Ginwala had played a leading role in the exiled ANC and was an exceptional case. In an organization dominated by African males she rose to the top without marrying or even sleeping with any leaders and without joining the SACP. She was merely tough, able and clever. Unfortunately she could not contain her impatience with those less able than

herself and was thus widely regarded as bossy. She fought with most people, was thrown out of Tanzania by Julius Nyerere and even managed to wear Mandela's tolerance thin. But to have both her and Asmal in the cabinet would have meant that discussion was dominated by 'bossy Indians'. Naturally, the woman, though the more able of the two, was the one to be excluded.

63 *Sunday Independent*, 18 May 1997.
64 *The Sowetan*, 30 Sept. 1997.
65 *Sunday Independent*, 31 Aug. 1997.
66 *Sunday Tribune*, 31 Aug. 1997.
67 Ibid.
68 Ibid.
69 Ibid.
70 *Mail and Guardian*, 3–9 Oct. 1997. Palazzolo had fled to South Africa, where he had found various Ciskei and NP politicians willing to smooth his stay. He was expelled from South Africa as an illegal immigrant in 1991 but was soon back.
71 *Sunday Tribune*, 21 Sept. 1997.
72 Private source, interviewed in Durban, June 1997.
73 J. Myburgh, 'Some Notes on the Origins of the Trials of Jacob Zuma', <www.everfasternews.com>, 1 May 2006.
74 *Sunday Tribune*, 21 Sept. 1997.
75 *The Star*, 23 April 1997.
76 *Mail and Guardian*, 3–9 Oct. 1997.
77 *Sunday Tribune*, 26 Oct. 1997.
78 *Financial Mail*, 24 Oct. 1997.
79 *Sunday Tribune*, 26 Oct. 1997.
80 *The Citizen*, 8 Oct. 1997.
81 *Sunday Independent*, 12 Oct. 1997.
82 Ibid.
83 *Sunday Times*, 9 Nov. 1997.
84 *Sunday Independent*, 3 Nov. 1997.
85 *The Sowetan*, 17 Oct. 1997.
86 *The Citizen*, 18 Oct. 1997.
87 *The Star*, 21 Nov. 1997.
88 *The Citizen*, 12 Nov. 1997.
89 *The Star*, 21 Nov. 1997.
90 *Sunday Tribune*, 26 Oct. 1997.
91 *The Star*, 13 Nov. 1997.
92 *Financial Mail*, 5 Dec. 1997.
93 *Sunday Independent*, 30 Nov. 1997.
94 *The Citizen*, 3 Dec. 1997.
95 *The Sowetan*, 17 Dec. 1997.
96 *Sunday Times*, 21 Dec. 1997.
97 *The Citizen*, 18 Dec. 1997.
98 *The Citizen*, 19 Dec. 1997.
99 *The Citizen*, 22 Dec. 1997.
100 *The Citizen*, 27 Jan. 1998.
101 *Sunday Tribune*, 21 Dec. 1997.
102 *The Citizen*, 20 Dec. 1997.
103 *Business Day*, 18 Dec. 1997.
104 *The Citizen*, 20 Dec. 1997.
105 The SACP leader, Blade Nzimande, distributed an article he had authored in *Mayibuye* at the conference in which the key villains were named: the UDM, the Institute of Race Relations, the Helen Suzman Foundation and the historian, Hermann Giliomee. A year earlier the cabinet had identified these same institutions and people along with the country's

leading sociologist, Lawrence Schlemmer, as the greatest threat to 'transformation'. *Finance Week*, 8–14 Jan. 1998.

106 All quotes from South Africa Communications Services, 'Political Report of the President, Nelson Mandela'.

107 *City Press*, 21 May 2006.

108 *The Citizen*, 9 Dec. 1997.

Chapter 5

1 *The Star*, 2 April 1998.

2 Ibid.

3 P. Pillay, 'Reflections on Co-ordinating and Monitoring the Implementation of Policy', talk at the Human Sciences Research Council, Pretoria, 13 Jan. 2000.

4 *Financial Mail*, 3 July 1998.

5 *The Citizen*, 9 Feb. 1998.

6 Ibid.

7 *Business Day*, 29 Sept. 1998.

8 *The Citizen*, 18 April 1998.

9 *Financial Mail*, 7 Aug. 1998.

10 *Mail and Guardian*, 20–26 Feb. 1998.

11 See farewell speech, 7 Aug. 1999, on <www.polity.org.za/html/govdocs/speeches/1999/sp0807a.html>.

12 See e.g. *Sunday Times*, 7 May 1998.

13 *This Day*, 28 Oct. 2003.

14 *Sunday Independent*, 5 July 1998.

15 *Sunday Independent*, 11 Feb. 1998.

16 *Cape Times*, 13 Oct. 1998.

17 *Mail and Guardian*, 17–23 April 1998.

18 *Daily Dispatch*, 18 May 1998.

19 *Sunday Times*, 3 May 1998.

20 *Business Day*, 8 May 1998.

21 *The Citizen*, 3 Nov. 1998.

22 *The Star*, 13 Oct. 1998.

23 *The Citizen*, 18 Nov. 1998.

24 *Cape Times*, 27 Oct. 2005.

25 Desai was accused of raping a colleague, Salome Isaacs, while attending the anti-globalization World Social Forum in Mumbai, India. Initially he told the Indian police that he had not had sex with Ms Isaacs but later changed this to say the sex had been consensual. Desai, the chairman of the National Council of Correctional Services and vice-chair of the Foundation for Human Rights, came under enormous pressure from his legal and judicial colleagues to resign. Ms Isaacs, under great pressure, withdrew her accusation and Desai brazened it out. *Sunday Times*, 15 Feb. 2004.

26 South African Institute of Race Relations, *South Africa Survey 1997–98*, p. 471.

27 Ibid.

28 *The Citizen*, 3 Nov. 1998.

29 Cited in L. Luyt, *Walking Proud: The Louis Luyt Autobiography* (2003), p. 306, and see pp. 293–309.

30 *The Citizen*, 24 April 1998.

31 Private information. Pahad confided to some participants at the Chile meeting that if they had known the TRC would thus escape from ANC control, they would never have agreed to set it up.

32 *The Star*, 28 Oct. 1998.

33 *The Citizen*, 18 April 1998.

34 *Sunday Times*, 3 May 1998.

35 *The Citizen*, 25 Aug. 1998.
36 *The Star*, 11 Nov. 1998.
37 Private information, parliamentary interviews July 1999.
38 In 1997 Mohammed, as Chief Justice, was appointed as head of the Court of Appeal and replaced on the Constitutional Court by Zac Yacoob, a courageous blind lawyer and long-time ANC supporter. On Mohammed's death soon thereafter Chaskalson assumed the title of Chief Justice.
39 F. W. De Klerk, *The Last Trek: A New Beginning* (1998), p. 213.
40 Ibid., p. 260.
41 See H. Hamann, *Days of the Generals* (2001), pp. 177–93.
42 See A. Jeffery, *The Natal Story: Sixteen Years of Conflict* (1997), pp. 717–20, 775.
43 De Klerk, *Last Trek*, p. 259.
44 See A. Jeffery, *Natal Story*, pp. 481, 499, 504, 694–6.
45 Private information.
46 South African Institute of Race Relations, *South Africa Survey 1995–96*, p. 465.
47 Ibid. The Court also declared corporal punishment incompatible with the Constitution.
48 Private information.
49 Luyt, *Walking Proud*, pp. 307–9.
50 South African Institute of Race Relations, *South Africa Survey 1999–2000*, p. 325. 82 per cent of likely ANC voters had bar-coded IDs compared to only 71 per cent of NNP voters and 65 per cent of DP voters.
51 *Mail and Guardian*, 29 Jan.–4 Feb. 1999.
52 Ibid.
53 South African Institute of Race Relations, *South Africa Survey, 1999–2000*, p. 518. Judge Kriegler recused himself from the court's consideration of the issue.
54 Ibid., pp. 319, 334.
55 Quoted in A. Jeffery, 'Every Vote Counts', *Focus*, (Helen Suzman Foundation), 20 (Dec. 2000), p. 17.
56 Ibid.
57 *The Star*, *The Citizen*, 16 Feb. 1999.
58 *Mail and Guardian*, 25 June–1 July 1999.
59 Ibid.
60 Ibid.
61 *Mail and Guardian*, 12–18 Feb. 1999.
62 *Mail and Guardian*, 30 July–6 Aug. 1999.
63 *Mail and Guardian*, 29 Jan.–4 Feb. 1999.
64 *Mail and Guardian*, 23–9 April 1999.
65 It was not the end for the resourceful Motshekga, who remained a member of the Gauteng legislature and founded his Kara Heritage Institute with a government grant. Meanwhile his wife, Angie, became provincial minister of education and was soon in trouble for not declaring some of her many business interests and directorships, one of which was with her husband's Institute, which was simultaneously awarded contracts by the Gauteng and national governments. *Mail and Guardian*, 21–7 July 2006.
66 *Business Day*, 24 May 1999.
67 *Business Day*, 23 May 1999.
68 *Mail and Guardian*, 21–7 May 1999.
69 *The Citizen*, 21 April 1999.
70 *Sunday Times*, 25 April 1999.
71 Private source.
72 *Sunday Independent*, 18 May 1999.
73 *Business Day*, 17 May 1999.
74 *The Star*, 9 April 1999.
75 *Sunday Independent*, 24 Jan. 1999.
76 See e.g. Smuts Ngonyama in *City Press*, 8 Aug. 1999.

77 *The Citizen*, 10 June 1999.
78 Buthelezi, Zuma and Mbeki chaired two cabinet subcommittees each in acknowledgement of the former's special status. *Business Day*, 10 Oct. 2006.
79 Interview with Jacob Zuma, 6 Oct. 2006.
80 *The Star*, 12 Jan. 1999.
81 *Mail and Guardian*, 25 June–1 July 1999.
82 See C. Goodenough, 'Mystery that Surrounds the Armed Robberies', *KwaZulu-Natal Briefing*, 10 (Feb. 1998), and also her 'Who Killed Sifiso Nkabinde?', *KwaZulu-Natal Briefing*, 14 (March 1999). *KwaZulu-Natal Briefing* was published by the Helen Suzman Foundation.
83 *Mail and Guardian*, 29 Oct.–4 Nov. 1999.
84 Quoted in *Sunday Independent*, 24 Jan. 1999.
85 *Umrabulo*, 7/3 (1999).
86 The South African Institute of Race Relations, the Free Market Foundation and the Helen Suzman Foundation. In addition, the Centre for Development and Enterprise and the Institute for Security Studies carried out much valuable work in as politically neutral a fashion as they could manage.
87 The Yale political scientist Leonard Thompson, interviewing Mbeki before 1994, had asked him what the ANC would do with Cosatu, a large, unruly labour organization with a will of its own, something the ANC had never had to reckon with before. Mbeki was emphatic that it would have to be 'disciplined' and 'brought to heel'.
88 See *Business Day*, 23 Nov. 1999.
89 Ibid. All directors-general now had to sign contracts with the presidency, not their own ministers.
90 *Financial Mail*, 17 Dec. 1999.
91 *Sunday Independent*, 19 Dec. 1999.
92 *Business Day*, 1 March 2007.
93 Hanekom attempted, for example, to extend land rights to labour tenants, which resulted in farmers cutting their labour forces and evicting workers for fear of losing control of their farms. When the Helen Suzman Foundation brought out a report which forecast exactly this result, Hanekom said on air that he was proud to say he had not read the report and had no intention of reading it.
94 H. Dolny, *Banking on Change* (2001), p. 211.
95 Ibid., pp. 295–6.
96 *Business Day*, 29 March 2007.
97 *Business Day*, 18 July 2007.
98 *Sunday Times*, 11 and 18 Nov. 2007; *Business Day*, 8 Nov. 2007; *Mail and Guardian*, 16–22 Nov. 2007.
99 *Mail and Guardian*, 17–23 Feb. 2006.
100 'May the best bid win', *Focus* (Helen Suzman Foundation), 21 (March 2001).
101 Ibid.
102 *Business Day*, 28 Dec. 1999.

Chapter 6

1 F. Fanon, *The Wretched of the Earth* (1967), p. 28.
2 Ibid., p. 40.
3 J. McCulloch, *Black Soul, White Artefact, Fanon's Clinical Psychology and Social Theory* (1983), p. 66.
4 Fanon, *Wretched of the Earth*, p. 131.
5 South African Institute of Race Relations, *Frontiers of Freedom*, Jan. 1993, pp. 7–8.
6 Private source.
7 *Sunday Independent*, 9 July 2000.
8 *Sunday Times*, 21 Jan. 2001.

9 *Mail and Guardian*, 2–8 Feb. 2001.

10 V. Van der Vliet, 'South Africa Divided against AIDS: A Crisis of Leadership', in K. D. Kauffman and D. L. Lindauer (eds.), *Aids and South Africa: The Social Expression of a Pandemic* (2004), p. 48.

11 See e.g. S. Cross and A. Whiteside (eds.), *Facing Up to AIDS: The Socio-Economic Impact in Southern Africa* (1992).

12 Van der Vliet, 'South Africa Divided', p. 50.

13 Ibid., p. 52.

14 Ibid., n. 5, p. 89.

15 De Klerk later complained that his government had also bequeathed a detailed anti-AIDS action plan to the Mandela administration, which ignored it. *This Day*, 5 Oct. 2004.

16 I have followed the general habit of using data gathered from ante-natal clinics. There is inevitable controversy over the reliability of Aids statistics in the developing world. See R. Malan, 'AIDS in South Africa: In Search of the Truth', *Rolling Stone*, 22 Nov. 2001. But where one has a control group such as prisoners both the fact of Aids deaths and their rapid increase is beyond question. Between 1996 and 2004 the number of jail inmates in South African prisons dying of unnatural causes remained steady at about 70 a year but, thanks to Aids, the total number of deaths increased eightfold, from 211 to 1,689. *Business Day*, 12 Oct. 2005.

17 *The Star*, 17 Nov. 1998.

18 *The Citizen*, 16 Nov. 1998.

19 *Mail and Guardian*, 5–11 July 2002.

20 Van der Vliet, 'South Africa Divided', p. 56, and W. M. Gumede, *Thabo Mbeki and the Battle for the Soul of the ANC* (2005), p. 154.

21 *Mail and Guardian*, 5–11 July 2002.

22 *Sunday Times*, 25 Sept. 2005. One in four girls and one in six boys in South Africa are sexually abused before the age of puberty. *The Times*, 16 Oct. 2002.

23 See C. Campbell, *Letting Them Die: Why HIV/AIDS Prevention Programmes Fail* (2003).

24 I am grateful to Dr Brian Williams of the World Health Organization for this data.

25 *The Star*, 30 Nov. 2001.

26 Private source.

27 Van der Vliet, 'South Africa Divided', p. 58.

28 Ibid.

29 Interview, Johannesburg, 25 June 1998.

30 Van der Vliet, 'South Africa Divided', p. 60.

31 *Sunday Independent*, 25 June 2000.

32 *Sunday Independent*, 2 July 2000.

33 Van der Vliet, 'South Africa Divided', p. 60.

34 Ibid., p. 61.

35 Private source.

36 *Sunday Times*, 15 Oct. 2000.

37 Campbell, *Letting Them Die*, esp. pp. 83–99, 124–31, 144–6, 188, 192.

38 Ibid., p. 156.

39 *The Star*, 9 March 2001.

40 Campbell, *Letting Then Die*, p. 192.

41 *The Star*, 18 July 2001.

42 *Business Day*, 20 April 2001.

43 Van der Vliet, 'South Africa Divided', p. 63.

44 Ibid.

45 Ibid., p. 65.

46 See e.g. *Sunday Independent*, 8 April 2001.

47 *Mail and Guardian*, 19–25 March 1999.

48 *Mail and Guardian*, 7–13 Sept. 2001.

49 *Mail and Guardian*, 28 Sept.–4 Oct. 2001.
50 *The Star*, 2 Oct. 2001.
51 *Mail and Guardian*, 25–31 Oct. 2002.
52 *Mail and Guardian*, 27 Sept.–3 Oct. 2002.
53 V. Van der Vliet, in *AIDS Alert* (Omega Investment Research), 27 Sept. 2005.
54 *Mail and Guardian*, 5–11 July 2002.
55 Ibid. See also *Mail and Guardian*, 28 June–4 July 2002.
56 Ibid.
57 Ibid.
58 Ibid.
59 *Sunday Times*, 10 June 2001.
60 Van der Vliet, 'South Africa Divided', p. 66.
61 *Mail and Guardian*, 22–8 Sept. 2000.
62 Van der Vliet, 'South Africa Divided', p. 67.
63 *Sunday Times*, 14 Oct. 2001.
64 Ibid.
65 *The Star*, 8 April 2002.
66 Van der Vliet, 'South Africa Divided', p. 67.
67 *Business Day*, 10 Oct. 2001.
68 *The Star*, 17 Oct. 2001.
69 *Business Day*, 3 Oct. 2001.
70 *Mail and Guardian*, 8–14 Sept. 2000.
71 *Mail and Guardian*, 6–12 Oct. 2000. This sort of nonsense was encouraged by Aids dissidents such as David Rasnick, an American member of the Presidential Aids Advisory Panel who argued that Mbeki's stand made him a threat to 'the business interests, prestige and US global hegemony' and accused the FBI, CIA and National Security Agency of pouring millions of dollars into trying to neutralize Mbeki and 'orchestrating' the African media. *Business Day*, 9 May 2001.
72 *The Star*, 4 Oct. 2000.
73 Stuart Farrow, the DP member of the Parliamentary Medical Scheme Committee, learnt in October 2000 that there were already 68 such cases among the 400 MPs. I am grateful to David Maynier for this data.
74 Van der Vliet, 'South Africa Divided', p. 69.
75 Quoted ibid., p. 72.
76 Ibid.
77 *The Sowetan*, *The Star*, 28 March 2002.
78 *Business Day*, 26 March 2002.
79 *Sunday Tribune*, 7 April 2002.
80 Van der Vliet, 'South Africa Divided', p. 73.
81 *New York Times*, 31 March 2002.
82 *Mail and Guardian*, 22–7 March 2002.
83 *Sunday Tribune*, 7 April 2002.
84 *Mail and Guardian*, 19–25 April 2002.
85 *Business Day*, 9 Nov. 2000.
86 His wife and his mistress fought over his Sandton home, his BMW and the shares he held in several companies. The ANC secretary-general, Kgalema Motlanthe, was pulled in to referee the fight between the feuding women. *City Press*, 12 Feb. 2006.
87 *ANC Today*, 2/14, 5–11 April 2002.
88 *Sunday Independent*, 16 Dec. 2001.
89 *Mail and Guardian*, 30 Nov.–6 Dec. 2001.
90 *ANC Today*, 2/14, 5–11 April 2002.
91 *Business Day*, 19 April 2002.
92 *Sunday Tribune*, 21 April 2002.
93 Ibid.

94 *City Press*, 28 Sept. 2003.
95 *Mail and Guardian*, 11 Jan. 2002.
96 Gumede, *Thabo Mbeki*, p. 163.
97 Ibid., p. 168.
98 Ibid., p. 172.
99 *Mail and Guardian*, 15–21 Sept. 2001.
100 *The Citizen*, 29 June 2001.
101 DA, Press Statement by Sandy Kalyan MP, 21 May 2002.
102 *The Star*, 28 Nov. 2002.
103 *Sunday Tribune*, 29 July 2001.
104 *The Times*, 16 Oct. 2002.
105 Anita Kleinsmidt of the Aids Law Project, cited by Van der Vliet, 'South Africa Divided', p. 71.
106 *Business Day, The Star*, 25 Feb. 2002.
107 Van der Vliet, 'South Africa Divided', p. 75.
108 Ibid., p. 76.
109 Ibid.
110 *The Star*, 19 Dec. 2002.
111 As reported in *The Star*, 27 July 2002.
112 *Sunday Independent*, 23 Feb. 2003.
113 *Sunday Independent*, 13 April 2003.
114 *Cape Times*, 1 Aug. 2003.
115 *The Star*, 15 July 2003.
116 *Sunday Independent*, 30 Jan. 2005.
117 *Sunday Times*, 22 July 2001.
118 *The Star*, 14 July 2003.
119 *Cape Times*, 30 July 2003.
120 *Business Day*, 24 July 2003.
121 *Sunday Independent*, 13 June 2004.
122 R. Loewenson and A. Whiteside, *Report on HIV/AIDS in South Africa*, prepared for UN General Assembly, 2001, quoted in *Mail and Guardian*, 29 Nov.–5 Dec. 2002.
123 *City Press*, 10 Aug. 2003.
124 See e.g. *Business Day*, 20 Nov. 2003, and *Mail and Guardian*, 21–7 Nov. 2003.
125 *The Star*, 10 Oct. 2003.
126 *This Day*, 9 March 2004.
127 *This Day*, 13 Feb. 2004. This did not prevent Tshabalala-Msimang falling out with Ira Magaziner, chair of the Foundation's Aids Initiative.
128 See *Mail and Guardian*, 7–13 March 2003, and *Business Day*, 11 Nov. 2003.
129 *This Day*, 8 June 2004.
130 *This Day*, 7 June 2004.
131 *Business Day*, 15 July 2004, and *Sunday Times*, 18 July 2004.
132 *Cape Times*, 19 Oct. 2004.
133 *Business Day*, 3 Dec. 2004.
134 *Mail and Guardian*, 24–31 March 2005.
135 *Mail and Guardian*, 6–12 Jan. 2006.
136 *Sunday Independent*, 19 Dec. 2004.
137 See e.g. *Mail and Guardian*, 24 Dec. 2004–6 Jan. 2005.
138 *Mail and Guardian*, 18–23 and 24–31 March 2005.
139 *Business Day*, 13 April 2005.
140 *Sunday Independent*, 8 May 2005.
141 *Business Day*, 28 June 2005.
142 *Business Day*, 29 June 2005.
143 *The Star*, 30 June 2005.
144 *Sunday Independent*, 10 July 2005.

145 *Sunday Independent*, 24 May 2004.
146 *Business Day*, 5 Oct. 2005.
147 *Mail and Guardian*, 2–8 Sept. 2005.
148 *Business Day*, 12 July 2005.
149 *City Press*, 26 Feb. 2006.
150 *Sunday Times*, 25 Sept. 2005.
151 *Business Day*, 26 Sept. 2005.
152 Ibid.
153 *Business Day*, 27 Sept. 2005.
154 *Business Day*, 19 Oct. 2005.
155 *Mail and Guardian*, 28 Oct.–3 Nov. 2005.
156 *Business Day*, 30 June 2005.
157 *Sunday Times*, 30 Oct. 2005.
158 *Sunday Times*, 5 March 2006.
159 *Sunday Independent*, 12 March 2006.
160 *City Press*, 12 Feb. 2006.
161 *Sunday Independent*, 2 April 2006.
162 *Mail and Guardian Online*, 2 June 2006.
163 *Sunday Independent*, 20 Aug. 2006.
164 *Business Day*, 21 Aug. 2006.
165 *Sunday Independent*, 3 Sept. 2006.
166 *Mail and Guardian*, 1–7 Sept. 2006.
167 *Sunday Independent*, 30 April 2006.
168 *Business Day*, 7 Sept. 2006.
169 *Business Day*, 20 Sept. 2006.
170 *City Press*, 24 Sept. 2006.
171 *Business Day*, 8 Sept. 2005.
172 *Business Day*, 19 June 2001 and 25 Oct. 2005.
173 *Business Day*, 26 Oct. 2005.
174 *Sunday Independent*, 30 Oct. 2005.
175 Van der Vliet, 'South Africa Divided', p. 86.
176 *Washington Post*, 6 July 2000.
177 See Nujoma's address to the International Labour Organization meeting of 8 June 2000 in Geneva for a typical outburst: 'It is also a historical fact that HIV/AIDS is a man-made disease. It is not natural. States that produced chemical weapons . . . are represented here, they know themselves too . . . It is condemnable that those in positions of strength owing to their powerful use of the media show HIV/AIDS as emerging from Africa, produced by a green monkey. That is a lie. . . . Those who have engaged in chemical warfare against other nations must make resources available.' To prevent further scandal Nujoma was prevailed upon to sit down without finishing his speech which is, however, available as an annexe to the Provisional Record, 13/6.
178 Centre for Actuarial Research, 'HIV Risk Factors: A Review of the Demographic, Socio-economic, Biomedical and Behavioural Determinants of HIV Prevalence in South Africa', Jan. 2002 (cyclostyled report). See esp. pp. 23–6.
179 *Sunday Times*, 25 Sept. 2005.
180 *Le Monde diplomatique*, Oct. 2005.
181 *Mail and Guardian*, 21–7 May 1999. In 1987/8, 27.1 per cent of all reported rapes resulted in a conviction; by 1995–6 the figure was a mere 7.1 per cent.
182 Mbeki letter to Leon (MS), 17 July 2000, p. 11.
183 *Sunday Independent*, 24 Oct. 2004.
184 Quoted by Gumede, *Thabo Mbeki*, pp. 165–6.
185 *Le Monde diplomatique*, Oct. 2005.

Chapter 7

1 Interview with Jacob Zuma, 5 Oct. 2006.
2 See R. Hyam and P. Henshaw, *The Lion and the Springbok: Britain and South Africa Since the Boer War* (2003), pp. 267–8. Nkrumah suggested that the whole question of South Africa's Commonwealth membership could simply be deferred; Tafawa Balewa said Nigeria would leave the Commonwealth if South Africa remained a member.
3 *Africa Confidential*, July 1996. Nigerian sources said the sum was $50 million. *The News* (Lagos), 15 Jan. 2001.
4 *The Star*, 24 July 1995.
5 *The Citizen*, 24 Aug. 1995.
6 See Tokyo Sexwale's revealing comments on this, *The Citizen*, 25 March 1996.
7 *The Sowetan*, 9 Nov. 1995.
8 *The Star*, 2 Nov. 1995.
9 *The Citizen*, 10 Nov. 1995.
10 *The Citizen*, 15 Nov. 1995.
11 *Business Day*, 17 Nov. 1995.
12 *The Citizen*, 20 Nov. 1995.
13 *The Citizen*, 23 Nov. 1995.
14 *The Citizen*, 28 Nov. 1995.
15 *The Sowetan*, 14 Dec. 1995.
16 The *Star*'s reporter sent to canvass opinion in Abuja encountered unanimous support for Mandela and hatred of Abacha. *The Star*, 30 Nov. 1995.
17 *Business Day*, 5 June 1996.
18 *Mail and Guardian*, 2–8 March 2001.
19 R. W. Johnson, *The Condition of Democracy in Southern Africa* (1997).
20 R. W. Johnson, *Political Opinion in Zimbabwe 2000* (2000).
21 This was pointed out to me by Michael Hartnack, who had trawled through the newspaper archives of that event. Michael was an original and courageous journalist who continued to report on the realities of Zimbabwean life with a rare historical perspective until his death in 2006.
22 Interview with Morgan Tsvangirai, Harare, July 2003.
23 *City Press*, 13 Feb. 2000.
24 *The Star*, 16 Feb. 2000.
25 *Sunday Tribune*, *Business Report*, 12 Feb. 2000; *The Citizen*, 14 Feb. 2000.
26 Ibid.
27 *Business Day*, 18 Feb. 2000; *The Star*, 22 Feb. 2000.
28 Private source.
29 *Sunday Times*, 26 March 1995.
30 *Saturday Star*, 22 April 2000.
31 R. W. Johnson, *Zimbabwe's Hard Road to Democracy* (2000).
32 *Mail and Guardian*, 2–8 June 2000.
33 Ibid.
34 *Africa News*, 8 May 2000.
35 Ibid.
36 See e.g. Anthony Sampson's slavish interview (reprinted in the *Cape Argus*, 8 Feb. 2001). When Sampson asks, 'But what about the bombing of the *Daily News*?' Mbeki replies, 'Naturally we would condemn the bombing in principle, but we're trying to find out who might have done it.' No one in Harare had the slightest doubt that the blowing up of the independent newspaper's presses had been carried out by the state: it was only the latest in several such bombings and the explosives used were issued only to the Zimbabwean army. But in any case, the idea that condemnation would have to await South Africa's own detective efforts in a foreign country was fantastic. Sampson simply let this go and never raised the issue in print again. Mbeki never condemned the bombing.

37 *Sunday Times*, 9 July 2000.
38 Mondli Makhanya, in *Sunday Times*, 21 Sept. 2000.
39 Private source.
40 *Business Day*, 16 Feb. 2001.
41 Again, a credulous press flattered Mbeki by treating seriously the notion that he was a key mediator of the Middle East conflict. See e.g. the main headline story 'Mbeki tipped for Mideast peace bid' by John Battersby in the *Sunday Independent*, 2 Sept. 2001. Battersby was ultimately rewarded with the job of London representative of the International Marketing Council, the government's overseas propaganda arm.
42 *Sunday Times*, 24 Sept. 2000.
43 *Mail and Guardian*, 20–26 Oct. 2000.
44 Poll by Community Agency for Social Enquiry for the *Youth 2000* report. *Mail and Guardian*, 30 March–5 April 2001.
45 A *Sunday Independent*/Harris poll (4 Nov. 2001) found that 83 per cent of online readers and 66 per cent of offline readers (all drawn from black townships in Gauteng) believed these propositions. More than half of the entire sample knew of Aids-related deaths among their family or friends.
46 Interview with Jacob Zuma, Durban, 5 Oct. 2006.
47 See S. Uys and J. Myburgh, 'South Africa: Thabo Mbeki's Presidency: A Profile' (Occasional Paper, 2001). These figures were based on all respondents, i.e. including the 20 per cent don't knows/won't says normally excluded in reports of poll results.
48 *The Star*, 19 April 2001.
49 *Mail and Guardian*, 25 April 2001.
50 *Mail and Guardian*, 6–12 July 2001.
51 *Sunday Independent*, 3 June 2001.
52 Ibid.
53 *Cape Argus*, 8 Feb. 2001.
54 *Time*, 4 Sept. 2000.
55 *Mail and Guardian*, 26 Oct.–1 Nov. 2001.
56 *Business Day*, 9 May 2001.
57 *Sunday Times*, 29 April 2001.
58 *The Citizen*, 12 May 2001.
59 Ibid.
60 *Sunday Times*, 29 April 2001.
61 Ibid.
62 Ibid.
63 *The Citizen*, 1 May 2001.
64 Both Nkambule's report and affidavit are reprinted in full in the *Sunday Times*, 29 April 2001.
65 *Mail and Guardian*, 4–10 May 2001.
66 Ibid.
67 *Sunday Times*, 29 April 2001.
68 *The Economist*, 5 May 2001.
69 *The Star*, 4 May 2001.
70 *Financial Times*, 4 May 2001.
71 *The Citizen*, 11 May 2001.
72 *Sunday Times*, 29 April 2001.
73 *Saturday Star*, 5 May 2001.
74 *The Star*, 30 April 2001. Nkrumah had died peacefully in Guinea.
75 *The Star*, 24 May 2001.
76 *The Star*, 12 July 2001.
77 *The Guardian*, 29 May 2001.
78 Reprinted in the *Sunday Independent*, 3 June 2001.
79 *Sunday Times*, 19 Sept. 2004.

80 *Business Day*, 2 Oct. 2001.
81 *Mail and Guardian*, 5–11 Oct. 2001.
82 *Sunday Times*, 5 Aug. 2001.
83 *Business Day*, 26 Oct. 2001.
84 *Business Day*, 29 Oct. 2001.
85 Private source.
86 Floor-crossing was allowed only during specified time periods and only if one-tenth or more of a party's representatives wished to cross. For the small parties this would mean that one or two individuals would find it easy to cross the floor but that it was impossible for the ANC, with its iron discipline and vast numbers, ever to lose such a large group.
87 *Mail and Guardian*, 7–13 Dec. 2001.
88 *Sunday Times*, 26 May 2002.
89 Particularly since one of the operatives used, Stephan Whitehead, had led the 62-hour interrogation of the anti-apartheid activist, Neil Aggett, who committed suicide after seventy days in detention, torture and that appalling interrogation. *Mail and Guardian*, 24–30 May 2002.
90 *Cape Times*, 13 June 2002.
91 *Business Day*, 27 May 2002.
92 *Business Day*, 24 May 2002.
93 See Chapter 5, note 25.
94 Interview with Greg Krumbock MP, 6 June 2002.
95 Interview with James Selfe MP, 6 June 2002.
96 *Business Day*, 12 Sept. 2002.
97 *Mail and Guardian*, 26 April–2 May 2002.
98 Interviews with Lungwisa Gazi, Regina Lengisi, Mambele Makeleni and Helen Zille, Cape Town, 29–30 April 2002.
99 Interview with Mcebisi Skwatsha, Cape Town, 30 April 2002.
100 *Sunday Times*, 17 Oct. 2004.
101 Speech by Tony Leon, Royal Show, Pietermaritzburg, 26 May 2002.
102 *Cape Times*, 14 June 2002.

Chapter 8

1 A. Boraine, *A Country Unmasked: Inside South Africa's Truth and Reconciliation Commission* (2000).
2 The most outstanding case was that of Andre Du Toit, a political scientist of unquestioned integrity with all the requisite research experience. He was turned down for the posts of both Commissioner and Research Director. A similar omission was that of Archbishop Denis Hurley, by far the most balanced and intellectually able anti-apartheid churchman.
3 See A. Jeffery, *The Truth about the Truth Commission* (1999), pp. 68–9.
4 Boraine explicitly cites these four kinds of truth as the key to 'our wrestling with truth-seeking'. Boraine, *Country Unmasked*, pp. 1–2.
5 Jeffery, *Truth*, p. 28.
6 Ibid., p. 29.
7 Ibid., pp. 29–30.
8 Ibid., p. 67.
9 Ibid., pp. 41–3.
10 Quoted ibid., p. 45.
11 Ibid., p. 99.
12 Ibid., p. 114.
13 Quoted ibid., p. 124.
14 Quoted ibid., p. 121.
15 Quoted ibid.
16 Ibid., p. 123.

17 Quoted ibid., p. 17.
18 For Malan's own views of the trial and the TRC, see M. Malan, *My Life with the South African Defence Force* (2006).
19 This account rests on Jeffery, *Truth*, pp. 152–3.
20 Ibid., pp. 150–51.
21 Ibid., p. 153.
22 Ibid., p. 142.
23 Ibid., pp. 154–7.
24 R. Wilson, *The Politics of Truth and Reconciliation in South Africa: Legitimizing the Post-Apartheid State* (2001), p. 93.
25 J. Gibson, *Overcoming Apartheid: Can Truth Reconcile a Divided Nation?* (2004), p. 1.
26 Boraine, *Country Unmasked.*
27 T. Bell, with D. B. Ntsebeza, *Unfinished Business: South Africa, Apartheid and Truth* (2003).
28 J. Allen, *Rabble-Rouser for Peace: The Authorized Biography of Desmond Tutu* (2006).
29 The Azanian People's Liberation Army, the armed wing of the PAC.
30 Moreover, both the Ministry of Intelligence and the presidency illegally took part of the TRC Archives. See the critical remarks of Dr V. Harris, Director of the South African History Archive, <www.saha.org.za/research/publications/FOIP>, esp. the Harris and TRC Codicil pdfs.
31 This account relies heavily on Bell with Ntsebeza, *Unfinished Business*, pp. 319–43.
32 Boraine, *Country Unmasked*, pp. 149–50.
33 Wilson, *Politics of Truth*, p. 72.
34 Boraine, *Country Unmasked*, pp. 84–5.
35 Ibid., pp. 177–8.
36 As it swallowed other parties the original Progressive Party became the Progressive Reform Party, the Progressive Federal Party, the Democratic Party, then the Democratic Alliance.
37 Private sources.
38 Boraine, *Country Unmasked*, p. 9.
39 *Sunday Times*, 3 Sept. 2000.
40 *The Star*, 12 Dec. 2000.
41 *The Citizen*, 14 Dec. 2000.
42 *The Star*, 12 Dec. 2000.
43 *Mail and Guardian*, 5–11 Jan. 2001.
44 *Cape Times*, 28 Feb. 2008.
45 Quoted in D. Pinckney, 'Dreams from Obama', *New York Review of Books*, 6 March 2008, pp. 41–5, a review of Shelby Steele's *A Bound Man: Why We Are Excited About Obama and Why He Can't Win* (2008).
46 *Business Day*, 23 Feb. 2005.
47 *Business Day*, 13 March 2005.
48 *Business Day*, 8 Feb. 2005.
49 *Sunday Times*, 27 March 2005.
50 News24 website, 28 April 2005.
51 R. Tingle, 'What Role for the Churches in the New South Africa?', in R. W. Johnson and D. Welsh (eds.), *Ironic Victory: Liberalism in Post-Liberation South Africa* (1998), p. 209.
52 *Mail and Guardian*, 2–8 Nov. 2001.
53 Ibid.
54 South Africa's foreign debt was, by international standards, small and to have defaulted would have ruined the country's creditworthiness and closed capital markets to it for many years ahead. In addition, the whole notion of the 'apartheid debt' was difficult. Even under apartheid, spending on the security forces had always been a small part of government expenditure. Moreover, public debt had really exploded only in 1990–94 after the death of apartheid, with money thrown at teachers' salaries and the black homelands in particular.

55 R. Debray, *Praised Be Our Lords: The Autobiography* (2007), p. 19.
56 C. Hope, *White Boy Running* (1988), pp. 16–24.
57 Ibid., p. 99.
58 The oddity is that for Mbeki this was all a matter of empathy and imagination. He enjoyed an elite schooling and was then sent off on scholarships abroad, where he was always treated as the crown prince of the ANC. He was always a recipient of donations and allowances, almost invariably from white donors. His personal experience of racism has been less than for any other African of his generation.
59 See <www.anc.org.za/ancdocs/pubs/umrabulo/umrabulo22/strategic.htm>.
60 See <www.anc.org.za/ancdocs/pubs/umrabulo/umrabulo23/neoliberalism.htm>. Mufamadi is also an ANC NEC member.
61 *Cape Times*, 12 Feb. 2008.

Chapter 9

1 The German political foundations had helped fund the IFP and various liberal organizations but had helped the ANC too. Perhaps more importantly, many leading ANC cadres had trained in East Germany and absorbed a strong antipathy to West Germany.
2 *Mail and Guardian*, 26 Nov.–2 Dec. 1999.
3 *Mail and Guardian*, 7–13 Dec. 2001; *The Star*, 13 Dec. 2001; *Sunday Independent*, 16 Dec. 2001.
4 *City Press*, 1 Oct. 2006.
5 *Mail and Guardian*, 27 Oct.–2 Nov. 2006.
6 *Business Day*, 2 Sept. 2005; *Sunday Independent*, 3 Dec. 2006.
7 Private source.
8 *Business Day*, 12 July 2001.
9 P. Fabricius, in *The Star*, 13 July 2001.
10 *Business Day*, 21 Aug. 2001.
11 *Business Day*, 10 July 2002.
12 *Mail and Guardian*, 5–11 July 2002.
13 *Business Day*, 27 Nov. 2003.
14 *Mail and Guardian*, 17–22 Sept. 2004.
15 *Business Day*, 24 Nov. 2006.
16 *Business Day*, 16 Sept. 2004.
17 *The Citizen*, 27 Sept. 2001.
18 *Sunday Independent*, 13 Jan. 2002.
19 *Saturday Star*, 12 Jan. 2002.
20 *City Press*, 16 Feb. 2003.
21 *This Day*, 21 May 2004.
22 Quotes from the Iran News Agency, quoted by J. Kirchick, 'Going South', *Azure*, Summer 2007, Shalem Centre, Israel.
23 *Sunday Times*, 9 Sept. 2001.
24 *Sunday Independent*, 2 Dec. 2001.
25 *Sunday Tribune*, 6 Jan. 2002.
26 *Independent on Saturday*, 23 March 2002.
27 *Sunday Independent*, 15 April 2007.
28 Once Mbeki was safely back home his spokesmen denied the shootings had ever taken place and most of the other salient facts of the visit. See *Business Day*, *This Day*, 7 Jan. 2004.
29 Section 201 of the South African Constitution requires the President to inform Parliament of the dispatch of any military personnel abroad. A Boeing 707 laden with arms and South African military personnel had been dispatched to Haiti without this provision being observed. *Business Day*, 16 March 2004.
30 *This Day*, 5 March 2004.
31 *Mail and Guardian*, 8–14 Sept. 2000.

32 *The Star*, 27 Jan. 2001.
33 *Cape Times*, 10 April 2003.
34 *Business Day*, 18 Nov. 2003.
35 *Sunday Tribune*, 10 Nov. 2002; *The Citizen*, 10 July 2002.
36 *Business Day*, 6 Oct. 2004.
37 *Business Day*, 26 Sept. 2003.
38 *Sunday Times*, 23 June 2002.
39 *Business Day*, 6 Oct. 2006.
40 *The Mercury*, 2 Nov. 2006.
41 *The Star*, 14 Nov. 2006; *Business Day*, 26 Aug. 2006.
42 *The Star*, 10 July 2003.
43 *International Herald Tribune*, 26 June 2007.
44 *Mail and Guardian*, 18–24 Aug. 2000.
45 *The Mercury*, *Business Report*, 12 Oct. 2000.
46 *Daily News*, 9 Nov. 2000.
47 *Business Day*, 11 Jan. 2002.
48 *Sunday Tribune*, 7 Jan. 2001.
49 *The Mercury*, 24 Jan. 2001.
50 *Saturday Star*, 17 Feb. 2001.
51 *Mail and Guardian*, 2–8 March 2001.
52 *Business Day*, 30 March 2001.
53 *The Citizen*, 26 May 2001.
54 When Wits was choosing a new vice-chancellor in 1997 student activists and the campus unions bitterly and loudly opposed any white candidate daring to put their name forward, claiming that the job must go to a black. Then, following the unexpected death of the successful nominee, a white candidate acceptable to the ANC, Colin Bundy, had perforce to be put forward. The student and trade union activists, clearly under discipline, suddenly fell silent and accepted him without demur.
55 *Sunday Times*, 8 Sept. 2002.
56 He accused 'Jews in South Africa, working in cahoots with their colleagues here', of conspiring to shut down textile factories in Zimbabwe. In 1992 he had declared that white farmers were 'so hard-hearted you would think they were Jews'. *Sunday Independent*, 2 Sept. 2001.
57 Even when Mugabe didn't like South African press coverage of the murder of a white tourist in Zimbabwe, the press were denounced as 'insensitive, un-African and inhuman'. *The Star*, 26 June 2003.
58 *Sunday Times*, 4 Nov. 2001.
59 *Mail and Guardian*, 14–19 Dec. 2001.
60 *The Citizen*, 16 Feb. 2002.
61 *The Star*, 18 Feb. 2002.
62 *Sunday Times*, 24 Feb. 2002.
63 *The Citizen*, 8 March 2002.
64 *Business Day*, 4 March 2002.
65 *Sunday Independent*, 10 March 2002.
66 *The Star*, 14 March 2002. The SADC mission had been funded by Western donors who had warned them that they had to take the SADC electoral code seriously or face a withdrawal of funding.
67 *Sunday Times*, 24 March 2002.
68 Ibid.
69 Private source.
70 Private source.
71 *The Star*, 18 March 2002.
72 *The Star*, 19 March 2002.
73 *Mail and Guardian*, 22–7 March 2002.

74 *Sunday Independent*, 31 March 2002.
75 *Independent on Saturday*, 16 March 2002.
76 *Sunday Tribune*, 24 March 2002.
77 See R. W. Johnson, 'Tracking Terror through Africa: Mugabe, Qaddafi and al-Qaeda', *National Interest*, 75 (Spring 2004), pp. 161–72.
78 *Business Day*, 15 Jan. 2003.
79 *Mail and Guardian*, 14–20 Feb. 2002.
80 Ibid.
81 Ibid.
82 See 'Secretary-General's Report to the Commonwealth Chairpersons' Committee on Zimbabwe' (typescript), March 2003.
83 *Sunday Times*, 30 March 2003.
84 *Mail and Guardian*, 20–27 March 2003.
85 *Sunday Tribune*, 20 Dec. 2002.
86 *Sunday Independent*, 20 April 2003.
87 Private source.
88 *Mail and Guardian*, 9–15 May 2003.
89 Private source.
90 *The Star*, 17 Sept. 2003.
91 *Mail and Guardian*, 5–11 Dec. 2003.
92 *Business Day*, 8 Dec. 2003.
93 *This Day*, 12 Dec. 2003.
94 Ibid.
95 *Mail and Guardian*, 9 Jan. 2004.
96 *Mail and Guardian*, 12–18 Dec. 2003.
97 *Cape Times*, 16 Dec. 2003.
98 *Sunday Independent*, 21 Dec. 2003.
99 *Business Day*, 24 Dec. 2003.
100 *Sunday Times*, 11 July 2004.
101 *Business Day*, 11 Feb. 2005.
102 *Business Day*, 4 March 2005.
103 *Sunday Times*, 20 March 2005.
104 *Business Day*, 8 April 2005.
105 *Mail and Guardian*, 3–9 Dec. 1999.
106 A. Sparks, *Beyond the Miracle: Inside the New South Africa* (2003), pp. 268, 271.
107 *Sunday Times*, 11 July 2004; *This Day*, 12 July 2004.
108 *Sunday Times*, 17 July 2005.
109 *Business Day*, 15 Aug. 2005.
110 *City Press*, 30 Jan. 2005; *Business Day*, 5 July 2006.
111 *City Press*, 6 Feb. 2005.
112 *Financial Mail*, 1 June 2007.
113 *Sunday Times*, 13 May 2007.
114 *Business Day*, 14 June 2007.
115 Agence France Presse, 31 March 2007.
116 *Sunday Independent*, 15 April 2007.
117 *Financial Times*, 3 April 2007.
118 *Southern Africa Report*, 25/17 (27 April 2007).
119 *Sunday Independent*, 27 May 2007.
120 Interview with Willias Mudzimure MP, Harare, 2 April 2008.
121 Interview with Chris Mbanga, Harare, 3 April 2008.
122 This account relies on the testimony of MDC MPs and their contacts within the Zimbabwe Electoral Commission. They necessarily have to be nameless.
123 *Cape Times*, 17 March 2007.

Chapter 10

1 W. Makgoba, *Mokoko: The Makgoba Affair. A Reflection on Transformation* (1997), p. 46.
2 S. P. Huntington, *The Clash of Civilisations and the Remaking of World Order* (1997), pp. 59–64.
3 *Saturday Star*, 5 April 2008.

Chapter 11

1 *Business Day*, 10–11 May 2007.
2 *Cape Times*, *Business Report*, 30 Nov. 2006.
3 *Cape Times*, *Business Report*, 17 April 2007.
4 *The Mercury*, *Business Report*, 15 May 2007.
5 See *Business Day*, 24 April 2007.
6 *Creamer Media's Engineering News*, 7 May 2007.
7 *ANC Today*, 6/46 (24–30 Nov. 2006).
8 *Business Day*, 24 April 2007.
9 See J. Kane-Berman, *South Africa's Silent Revolution* (1990).
10 *City Press*, 11 June 2006.
11 *Sunday Times*, 11 June 2006.
12 *Business Day*, 24 March 2004.
13 For example, Mandla Mchunu, formerly chief electoral officer of the Independent Electoral Commission, Vincent Mntambo, chairman of the Council for Conciliation, Mediation and Arbitration, and Gordon Sibiya, chairman of the South African Bureau of Standards. By definition holders of such posts were ANC members.
14 *Business Day*, 16 Jan. 2006.
15 *City Press*, 4 and 11 Aug. 2002.
16 *Business Day*, 11 Jan. 2002.
17 Anne Crotty, in *The Star*, *Business Report*, 1 Aug. 2001.
18 *Business Day*, 13 Aug. 2001.
19 *Business Day*, 22 May 2002.
20 *Mail and Guardian*, 24–30 May 2002.
21 *The Star*, *Business Report*, 22 May 2002.
22 *Sunday Times*, *Business Times*, 26 Jan. 2003.
23 See *Business Day*, 16 June 2003; *Mail and Guardian*, 18–24 July 2003 and 18–24 Nov. 2005.
24 *The Mercury*, *Business Report*, 22 March 2002.
25 *Cape Times*, 19 Oct. 2003.
26 *Sunday Tribune*, 23 Oct. 2001.
27 *Sunday Times*, 22 Dec. 2002.
28 *Mail and Guardian*, 8–14 Aug. 2003.
29 *Sunday Times*, *Business Times*, 25 Jan. 2004.
30 *Sunday Times*, 20 July 2003.
31 Ibid.
32 *Sunday Times*, 13 July 2003.
33 *Business Day*, 17 June 2003.
34 *Mail and Guardian*, 31 March–6 April 2000.
35 *Mail and Guardian*, 10–16 Nov. 2006.
36 *Mail and Guardian*, 2–8 July 2004.
37 *Sunday Independent*, 12 May 2002.
38 See *Business Day*, 30 Aug. 2002.
39 *Business Day*, 25 June 2002.
40 *Business Day*, 21 June 2002.

41 *City Press*, 23 June 2002.
42 *Business Day*, 31 July 2001.
43 *The Star*, *Business Report*, 1 Aug. 2001.
44 Ibid.
45 *Business Day*, 3 May 2005.
46 *Sunday Tribune*, 11 Aug. 2002.
47 *SA Times*, 28 Jan. 2005.
48 *Business Day*, 23 June 2004.
49 *Business Day*, 9 Sept. 2004.
50 *Business Day*, 12 Aug. 2004.
51 *Business Day*, 9 Sept. 2004.
52 *The Mercury*, *Business Report*, 23 Nov. 2005.
53 *Business Day*, 30 Jan. 2006.
54 *Business Day*, 20 Feb. 2006.
55 Ibid.
56 *Business Day*, 20 April 2006.
57 Private source.
58 *Business Day*, 13 Oct. 2006.
59 *The Mercury*, *Business Report*, 31 Oct. 2006.
60 Ibid.
61 *Business Day*, 8 Nov. 2006.
62 *Mail and Guardian*, 15–21 June 2007.
63 *Business Day*, 12 June 2007.
64 *Cape Times*, *Business Report*, 3 Oct. 2007.
65 *Financial Mail*, 21 March 2008.
66 Ibid.
67 Ibid.
68 *Business Day*, 11 March 2008.
69 *Business Day*, 4 May 2004.
70 *Cape Times*, 17 Aug. 2004.
71 *Business Day*, 8 Dec. 2003.
72 *Business Day*, 18 Nov. 2005.
73 *Business Day*, 11 Nov. 2005.
74 *Business Day*, 7 Feb. 2007.
75 *Business Day*, 25 May 2007.
76 *Sunday Times*, 17 June 2007.
77 *Weekend Argus*, 13 Nov. 2004.
78 *Business Day*, 10 Nov. 2004.
79 Ibid.
80 *Weekend Argus*, 13 Nov. 2004.
81 *Sunday Times*, *Business Times*, 14 Nov. 2004.
82 *Mail and Guardian*, 16–22 Sept. 2005.
83 Ibid.
84 *Business Day*, 17 May 2004.
85 *Business Day*, 2 Sept. 2005.
86 *Mail and Guardian*, 2–8 Dec. 2005.
87 *City Press*, 23 April 2006.
88 *Sunday Times*, 10 Sept. 2006.
89 *The Weekender*, 9–10 Sept. 2006.
90 *City Press*, 8 June 2003.
91 *Sunday Times*, 6 April 2003.
92 *Sunday Times*, 17 Aug. 2003.
93 *Business Day*, 4 Oct. 2004.
94 *This Day*, 30 April 2004.

95 *Business Day*, 1 Dec. 2003.
96 *Business Day*, 17 March 2005.
97 *Business Day*, 8 June 2007.
98 *Sunday Times*, *Business Times*, 27 June 2003.
99 *The Star*, 22 Aug. 2003.
100 *Business Day*, 14 Dec. 2004.
101 *Business Day*, 31 March 2005.
102 *Business Day*, 23 Jan. 2004.
103 *This Day*, 9 Feb. 2004.
104 *Sunday Times*, *Business Times*, 9 May 2004.
105 *Transformation and BEE in South Africa*, Report of the F. W. De Klerk Foundation (April 2006), p. 31.
106 *The Star*, 3 Dec. 2002.
107 *Business Day*, 23 May 2007.
108 *The Mercury*, *Business Report*, 26 June 2007.
109 *Business Day*, 3 Oct. 2003.
110 *The Mercury*, *Business Report*, 28 June 2007.
111 *Business Day*, 23 May 2007.
112 *Business Day*, 25 June 2002.
113 *Sunday Independent*, *Business Report*, 31 July 2005.
114 *Business Day*, 25 March 2002.
115 *Sunday Independent*, 19 May 2002.
116 *Sunday Independent*, *Business Report*, 31 July 2005.
117 *Business Day*, 4 Nov. 2003.
118 *Business Day*, 28 May 2007.
119 Ibid.
120 See *Sunday Times*, 3 and 17 June 2007.
121 *Business Day*, 25 Feb. 2004.
122 *Financial Mail*, 1 June 2007.
123 *Business Day*, 4 March 2005.
124 *Business Day*, 14 Sept. 2006.
125 See *Cape Times*, *Business Report*, 1 March 2005.
126 *Business Day*, 23 Dec. 2003.
127 *Business Day*, 20 Oct. 2005.
128 *Business Day*, 24 Feb. 2005.
129 *Sunday Independent*, 12 Nov. 2006.
130 *Sunday Times* (London), 27 April 2008.
131 See *Business Day*, 28 Aug. 2006.
132 *Mail and Guardian*, 25 Feb.–3 March 2005.
133 *Business Day*, 16 Sept. 2004.
134 *Business Day*, 27 Aug. 2004.
135 *Sunday Times*, 7 Nov. 2004.
136 *Sunday Times*, 14 Nov. 2004.
137 *Business Day*, 5 July 2007.
138 *The Mercury*, *Business Report*, 18 July 2002.
139 *Business Day*, 18 Sept. 2002.
140 *Business Day*, 3 Feb. 2005.
141 *The Mercury*, *Business Report*, 5 July 2007.

Chapter 12

1 *Mail and Guardian*, 24–30 March 2006.
2 A. Altbeker, *A Country at War with Itself: South Africa's Crisis of Crime* (2007), p. 50.
3 C. Smith, *Proud of Me: Speaking out against Sexual Violence and HIV* (2001), p. 74.

4 *The Star*, 12 Feb. 2002.
5 *The Mercury*, 26 July 2006.
6 *Business Day*, 17 April 2003.
7 *Mail and Guardian*, 12–18 July 2002.
8 See *Mail and Guardian*, 19–25 May 2000; 10–16 Nov. 2000; and 12–18 July 2002. Also *Business Day*, *This Day*, 3 June 2004.
9 *City Press*, 1 Feb. 2004.
10 *Sunday Independent*, 12 Nov. 2006.
11 Ibid.
12 *Business Day*, 17 April 2003.
13 *Sunday Independent*, 21 July 2002.
14 Figures for 2000. *The Star*, 4 July 2002.
15 *Sunday Times*, 3 Sept. 2006.
16 *Sunday Times*, 1 Oct. 2006.
17 *Sunday Times*, 16 July 2006.
18 *Mail and Guardian*, 10–16 and 17–23 May 2002.
19 *Business Day*, 12 Oct. 2005.
20 *Sunday Independent*, 23 June 2002.
21 *City Press*, 10 Sept. 2006.
22 *Mail and Guardian*, 14–20 July 2006.
23 *Sunday Times*, 15 Oct. 2006.
24 Ibid.
25 *Cape Times*, 24 Aug. 2006.
26 *Sunday Times*, 15 Oct. 2006.
27 *Sunday Independent*, 11 June 2006.
28 *Sunday Times*, 31 July 2005.
29 *The Citizen*, 8 Nov. 2001.
30 *Finance Week*, 21 Sept. 2006.
31 Ibid.
32 *Sunday Times*, 29 Oct. 2006.
33 *Business Day*, 16 Oct. 2002.
34 *Business Day*, 12 Feb. 2004.
35 *Business Day*, 19 Dec. 2005.
36 *Business Day*, 12 Feb. 2004.
37 *Sunday Times*, 28 May 2006.
38 *Cape Times*, 4 Aug. 2006.
39 *This Day*, 12 Nov. 2003.
40 *Mail and Guardian*, 28 March–3 April 2003.
41 *The Star*, *Business Report*, 6 Oct. 2006.
42 *Sunday Times*, 5 Feb. 2006.
43 *Business Day*, 18 June 2007.
44 *Business Day*, 19 June 2006.
45 Ibid.
46 *Sunday Times*, 23 April 2006.
47 *The Weekender*, 2–3 Sept. 2006.
48 *Sunday Times*, 15 June 2006.
49 *Financial Mail*, 27 July 2007.
50 Ibid.
51 *Financial Mail*, 31 Aug. 2007.
52 *Financial Mail*, 12 Oct. 2007.
53 *Business Day*, 23 July 2007.
54 Centre for Development and Enterprise, *Doubling for Growth. Addressing the Maths and Science Challenge in South Africa's Schools* (2007).
55 *Cape Times*, 5 Oct. 2007.

56 *Sunday Independent*, 22 Sept. 2002.
57 *This Day*, 31 Oct. 2003.
58 *The Star*, 24 Oct. 2002; *Business Day*, 8 Sept. 2005.
59 *Cape Times*, 11 March 2003.
60 *Mail and Guardian*, 28 March–3 April 2003.
61 *Cape Times*, 14 Jan. 2005.
62 *The Star*, 29 July 2004.
63 *Sunday Times*, 24 Aug. 2003.
64 *Business Day*, 8 Sept. 2005.
65 *City Press*, 14 May 2006.
66 *Sunday Times*, 7 May 2006.
67 *City Press*, 25 Nov. 2001.
68 *Business Day*, 27 June 2002.
69 *Sunday Times*, 30 May 2004.
70 *Cape Times*, 8 Oct. 2004.
71 *Cape Argus*, 18 June 2005; *Business Day*, 15 June 2006.
72 *Business Day*, 27 Aug. 2003; 24 Feb. 2004.
73 *The Citizen*, 8 Nov. 2001.
74 *The Citizen*, 18 July 2001.
75 *Mail and Guardian*, 4–10 May 2001.
76 *Sunday Times*, 17 March 2002.
77 *Business Day*, 7 Dec. 2005.
78 *City Press*, 25 Sept. 2005.
79 *Sunday Times*, 15 Jan. 2006.
80 *The Witness*, 9 Feb. 2005.
81 *City Press*, 10 July 2005.
82 *The Witness*, 1 Aug. 2005.
83 *The Citizen*, 27 July 2001.
84 *Business Day*, 13 July 2005.
85 *Cape Times*, 17 Sept. 2007.
86 *Sunday Independent*, 10 July 2005; *Business Day*, 13 July 2005.
87 *The Citizen*, 24 Oct. 2001.
88 *Business Day*, 11 Jan. 2002; *The Sowetan*, 28 March 2002.
89 *Business Day*, 3 Jan. 2001.
90 See *Sunday Tribune*, 31 March 2002.
91 *Mail and Guardian*, 23–9 Sept. 2005.
92 *Business Day*, 26 Sept. 2005.
93 *Business Day*, 18 Oct. 2006.
94 Ibid.
95 *Cape Times*, 14 Jan. 2005.
96 Ibid.
97 *Business Day*, 29 July 2004.
98 *The Star*, 29 July 2004.
99 Ibid.
100 *Cape Times*, 23 Nov. 2006.
101 *ANC Today*, 7/29 (27 July–2 Aug. 2007).
102 *News* 24, 21 June 2007.
103 *Cape Times*, 22 Aug. 2007.
104 *Business Day*, 20 May 2004.
105 *Finance Week*, 23 March 2006.
106 *Business Day*, 14 May 2002.
107 *ANC Today*, 7/42 (26 Oct.–1 Nov. 2007).
108 *The Star*, 22 Aug. 2002.
109 *Business Day*, 19 Jan. 2005.

110 *The Mercury*, *Business Report*, 28 June 2002.
111 *The Star*, *Business Report*, 21 Oct. 2003.
112 *The Star*, *Business Report*, 27 Aug. 2002.
113 *This Day*, 20 Oct. 2003.
114 *Cape Times*, 29 March 2006.
115 *City Press*, 15 Oct. 2006.
116 *Business Day*, 25 Feb. 2003.
117 *Finance Week*, 23 March 2006.
118 *Finance Week*, 2 and 23 March 2006; *Cape Times*, 29 March 2006; *Business Day*, 7 June 2006.
119 *Sunday Times*, 12 March 2006.
120 *Business Day*, 1 July 2005.
121 *Business Day*, 3 Aug. 2004.
122 *The Star*, *Business Day*, 31 Aug. 2005.
123 *Sunday Times*, *Business Times*, 11 Sept. 2005.
124 *Business Day*, 1 Sept. 2005.
125 *Business Day*, 4 Aug. 2004.
126 *Business Day*, 2 March 2006.
127 *The Star*, *Business Report*, 1 March 2006.
128 *Sunday Independent*, 5 March 2006.
129 *City Press*, 13 Aug. 2006; *Business Day*, 14 Aug. 2006; *Cape Times*, 16 Aug. 2006; *Cape Times*, *Business Report*, 18 Aug. 2006.
130 *Business Day*, 9 March 2006.
131 *Sunday Times*, 26 Nov. 2006.
132 *Finance Week*, 2 March 2006.
133 *Financial Mail*, 3 Feb. 2006, special supplement: 'Eskom Power Play'.
134 *Sunday Times*, *Business Times*, 3 Feb. 2008.
135 *Business Day*, 1 April 2004.
136 *This Day*, 10 Sept. 2004.
137 *Sunday Times*, 5 March 2006.
138 *Mail and Guardian*, 24–30 Jan. 2003.
139 *Mail and Guardian*, 1–6 Feb. 2003.
140 *Business Day*, 20 Sept., 3 Oct. 2001; *The Mercury*, *Business Report*, 4 Nov. 2001.
141 *Business Day*, 13 Feb. 2002.
142 Automobile Association of South Africa, 'Road Conditions and Funding 1988–1999' (cyclostyle), p. 1.
143 *Business Day*, 11 June 2001.
144 *Sunday Independent*, 7 May 2006.
145 *Business Day*, 29 May 2006.
146 *Business Day*, 7 June 2006.
147 *This Day*, 26 April 2004.
148 *Financial Times*, 7 Jan. 2003.
149 *Business Day*, 13 Oct. 2006.
150 *Sunday Independent*, 25 May 2003.
151 *Business Day*, 18 Aug. 2005.
152 *Business Day*, 21 July 2005.
153 *Business Day*, 19 Oct. 2006.
154 *Business Day*, 10 May 2005.
155 *The Mercury*, 30 May 2005.
156 *Sunday Independent*, 18 July 2004.
157 *Mail and Guardian*, 3–9 Dec. 2004.
158 *This Day*, 26 May 2004.
159 *Business Day*, 10 Dec. 2002.
160 *Mail and Guardian*, 16–22 Feb. 2001.

161 *Business Day*, 11 June 2001.
162 *Mail and Guardian*, 16–22 Feb. 2001.
163 *Mail and Guardian*, 3–9 Dec. 2004.
164 *City Press*, 29 Aug. 2004.
165 *City Press*, 18 Aug. 2002.
166 *City Press*, 10 Aug. 2003.
167 *Sunday Times*, *Business Times*, 14 Sept. 2003.
168 *The Mercury*, *Business Report*, 5 Dec. 2002.
169 *Business Day*, 12 Feb. 2004.
170 *Business Day*, 13 Feb. 2004.
171 *Business Day*, 3 Nov. 2004.
172 *Business Day*, 8 Feb. 2005.
173 *Business Day*, 8 Feb. and 19 May 2005.
174 *Cape Times*, *Business Report*, 10 Aug. 2006.
175 *Business Day*, 27 March 2006.
176 *Cape Times*, 11 Oct. 2005.
177 *Mail and Guardian*, 23 Feb.–1 March 2001.
178 *Mail and Guardian*, 8–14 March 2002.
179 *City Press*, 13 Nov. 2005.
180 *Business Day*, 23 Oct. 2006.
181 *Sunday Times*, 30 Oct. 2005.
182 Ibid.
183 Ibid.
184 *Business Day*, 10 Oct. 2006.
185 *Mail and Guardian*, 29 Sept.–5 Oct. 2006.
186 *Sunday Times*, 6 Nov. 2006.
187 *Cape Times*, 22 Aug. 2007.
188 Interview with Peter Mansfield, Durban, 25 Jan. 1994.
189 R. W. Johnson, *Not So Close to Their Hearts: An Investigation into the Non-payment of Rents, Rates and Service Charges in South Africa's Towns and Cities* (1999).
190 *Mail and Guardian*, 26 Aug.–1 Sept. 2005.
191 *Business Day*, 12 April 2006.
192 *Mail and Guardian*, 1–7 Nov. 2002.
193 *Mail and Guardian*, 21–7 Oct. 2005.
194 *Business Day*, 14 Sept. 2005.
195 *City Press*, 18 Aug. 2002.
196 *Mail and Guardian*, 27 Sept.–3 Oct. 2002.
197 *The Star*, 21 Nov. 2002.
198 *Business Day*, 4 Aug. 2004.
199 *City Press*, 6 April 2003.
200 *Mail and Guardian*, 11–16 April 2003.
201 *Mail and Guardian*, 27 Aug.–2 Sept. 2004.
202 *Cape Times*, 17 May 2005.
203 *City Press*, 8 Sept. 2002.
204 *Business Day*, 7 Sept. 2005.
205 *Sunday Times*, *City Press*, 31 July 2005.
206 *Mail and Guardian*, 9–15 Sept. 2005.
207 *Business Day*, 14 July 2005.
208 *Business Day*, 18 Nov. 2005.
209 *Business Day*, 14 Sept. 2005.
210 *Mail and Guardian*, 18–24 Nov. 2005.
211 *The Star*, 3 Aug. 2005.
212 *Business Day*, 27 June 2006.
213 *Business Day*, 15 Aug. 2005.

214 *Sunday Times*, 8 Jan. 2006.
215 *Business Day*, 17 Aug. 2005.
216 Ibid.
217 The South African National Civic Organization and the South African National NGO Coalition. Both were attempts to centralize control over independent local constituencies and both were plagued by corruption and maladministration.
218 *Business Day*, 11 July and 16 Aug. 2006.
219 *City Press*, 8 Oct. 2006.
220 *Business Day*, 27 Sept. 2007.
221 Ibid.

Chapter 13

1 *Sunday Times*, 6 Nov. 2005.
2 Interview with Mo Shaik, Durban, 24 June 2006.
3 *Sunday Times*, 6 Nov. 2005.
4 *Sunday Times*, 3 Oct. 2004.
5 *Sunday Times*, 13 March 2005.
6 See S. Gastrow (ed.), *Who's Who in South African Politics*, vol. 2 (1987), pp. 245–6. One of Nkobi's fellow-Ndebele schoolmates at Adams was Joshua Nkomo.
7 *Sunday Times*, 14 Nov. 2004.
8 *Cape Times*, 22 Feb. 2005.
9 Ibid.
10 *Sunday Times*, 14 Nov. 2004.
11 *Sunday Times*, 21 Aug. 2005.
12 *Business Day*, 14 Oct. 2004.
13 *Business Day*, 26 Oct. 2004.
14 Ibid.
15 *Mail and Guardian*, 29 Oct.–4 Nov. 2004.
16 A. Feinstein, *After the Party: A Personal and Political Journey Inside the ANC* (2007), pp. 154–207.
17 *Cape Times*, 1 Dec. 2004.
18 *Business Day*, 3 Dec. 2004.
19 *Mail and Guardian*, 3–9 Dec. 2004.
20 *Sunday Times*, 3 Oct. 2004.
21 *Sunday Independent*, 11 Dec. 2005.
22 *Mail and Guardian*, 24 Dec. 2004–6 Jan. 2005.
23 Ibid.
24 *Business Day*, 15 June 2005.
25 Private source.
26 *Sunday Times*, 3, 17 Aug. 2003; *Business Day*, 1 Aug. 2003.
27 *Mail and Guardian*, 15–21 Aug. 2003.
28 D. Gleason, in *Business Day*, 8 Sept. 2003.
29 *The Star*, 15 Sept. 2003.
30 *City Press*, 28 Sept. 2003.
31 *Business Day*, 10 Oct. 2003.
32 *City Press*, 14 Sept. 2003.
33 *Business Day*, 12 Nov. 2003.
34 *Mail and Guardian*, 30 July 2004.
35 *Sunday Independent*, 14 Dec. 2003.
36 See *Mail and Guardian*, 5–11 Dec. 2003.
37 *Mail and Guardian*, 8–14 Aug. 2003.
38 *Business Day*, 26 Nov. 2003.
39 *This Day*, 24 Oct. 2003.

40 *This Day*, 21 Jan. 2004.
41 *Mail and Guardian*, 19 Dec. 2003.
42 *Mail and Guardian*, 17 Oct. 2003.
43 *This Day*, 21 Jan. 2004.
44 Ibid.
45 *Business Day*, 23 Jan. 2004.
46 *Mail and Guardian*, 13–19 May 2005.
47 *Sunday Times*, *Business Times*, 26 Feb. 2006.
48 *City Press*, 14 June 2006.
49 Quoted in *Business Day*, 31 Jan. 2006.
50 Ibid.
51 Ibid.
52 *Business Day*, 1 Feb. 2006.
53 See *Sunday Times*, 3 Oct. 2004.
54 *Business Day*, 4 Oct. 2004.
55 *Business Day*, 31 Oct. 2003.
56 *Mail and Guardian*, 1–7 Oct. 2004.
57 *Business Day*, 14 March 2005.
58 Ibid.
59 *Business Day*, 1 March 2005.
60 *Mail and Guardian*, 22–8 Oct. 2004.
61 *Business Day*, 19 Oct. 2004.
62 Ibid.
63 *Mail and Guardian*, 8–14 Oct. 2004.
64 *Mail and Guardian*, 22–8 Oct. 2004.
65 Ibid.
66 *Cape Times*, 18 Nov. 2004.
67 Ibid.
68 *Mail and Guardian*, 5–11 Nov. 2004.
69 See P. O'Malley, *Shades of Difference: Mac Maharaj and the Struggle for South Africa* (2007).
70 *Mail and Guardian*, 22–8 Oct. 2004.
71 *City Press*, 4 Dec. 2005.
72 *Business Day*, 22 Oct. 2004.
73 *Mail and Guardian*, 3–9 Dec. 2004; *Cape Times*, 28 Oct. 2004.
74 Ibid.
75 *Business Day*, 2 June 2005.
76 Ibid.
77 *Mail and Guardian*, 3–9 June 2005.
78 Ibid.
79 Ibid.
80 Interview with Jacob Zuma, Cape Town, 15 April 2008.
81 *Cape Times*, 8 Nov. 2005.
82 *Weekend Argus*, 18 June 2005.
83 *Business Day*, 9 June 2005.
84 *Business Day*, 8 March 2005.
85 *Sunday Independent*, 10 Oct. 2004.
86 *City Press*, 14 Nov. 2004.
87 Some of Zuma's advisers also urged resignation but he was adamant that this would be an admission of guilt. *City Press*, 14 June 2006.
88 *The Star*, 29 June 2005.
89 *Business Day*, 1 July 2005.
90 *Sunday Times*, 10 July 2005.
91 High Court of South Africa (Cape of Good Hope Provincial Division), Case No.8677/04:

Judgment in the Matter between Ronald Suresh Roberts and Johncom Media Investments Limited, 8 Jan. 2007.

92 Private source.
93 *Sunday Times*, 14 Aug. 2005.
94 *Business Day*, 19 Aug. 2005.
95 *City Press*, 14 Aug. 2005.
96 *Mail and Guardian*, 19–25 Aug. 2005.
97 A judgment overruled, remarkably, by the Supreme Court of Appeal (which tended to have an anti-Zuma stance), so Zuma appealed again, to the Constitutional Court.
98 *Business Day*, 6 Oct. 2005.
99 *Sunday Times*, 5 Feb. 2006.
100 See e.g. B. Sergeant, *Brett Kebble: The Inside Story* (2006).
101 *Sunday Times*, 30 Oct. 2005.
102 *Sunday Times*, 6 Nov. 2005.
103 D. Kray, *Hazel Crane: Queen of Diamonds. Testimony from Beyond the Grave* (2004).
104 *Saturday Star*, 22 Oct. 2005.
105 Ibid.
106 *City Press*, 11 Dec. 2005.
107 Ibid.
108 *Sunday Times*, 5 Feb. 2006.
109 *City Press*, 19 Feb. 2006.
110 *City Press*, 12 Feb. 2006.
111 *City Press*, 6 March 2006.
112 *Business Day*, 7 March 2006.
113 Interview with Jacob Zuma, Durban, 29 Nov. 2007.
114 *Cape Times*, 10 March 2006; *Weekend Argus*, 11 March 2006; *Mail and Guardian*, 10–16 March 2006.
115 *Business Day*, 12 April 2006.
116 Interview with Jacob Zuma, Durban, 29 Nov. 2007.
117 *Sunday Independent*, 12 March 2006.
118 *Business Day*, 4 April 2006.
119 *City Press*, 30 April 2006.
120 *City Press*, 25 June 2006.
121 *Cape Times*, 10 April 2006.
122 *Sunday Times*, 14 May 2006.
123 Ibid.
124 *Sunday Times*, 16 April; 23 April 2006; *Mail and Guardian*, 5–11 May 2006.
125 *Sunday Times*, 12 March 2006.
126 *Business Day*, 12 April 2006.
127 *The Mercury*, 9 Feb. 2006; *Sunday Times*, 12 Feb. 2006.
128 *City Press*, 10 Sept. 2006.
129 *Mail and Guardian*, 20–26 July 2007.
130 See N. Daes, S. Sole and S. Brummer, 'Inside the Browse "Mole" Row', *Mail and Guardian Online*, 3 Aug. 2007.
131 *Cape Times*, 27 Feb. 2008.
132 *Cape Times*, 21 Sept. 2006.
133 *Sunday Times*, 3 Sept. 2006.
134 *Mail and Guardian*, 29 Sept.–5 Oct. 2006.
135 *Cape Argus*, 24 Aug. 2006.
136 M. Gevisser, *Thabo Mbeki: The Dream Deferred* (2007).
137 Interview with Sibusiso Madlala, Johannesburg, 7 July 2006.
138 *Mail and Guardian*, 6–12 Oct. 2006.
139 He left the DA in order to avoid expulsion and ultimately joined the ANC.
140 *Mail and Guardian*, 6–12 Oct. 2006.

141 *Mail and Guardian*, 27 Jan.–2 Feb. 2006; *Sunday Independent*, 19 Nov. 2006.
142 See South African Institute of Race Relations, *South Africa Survey 2006–2007*, pp. 202–5.
143 News.24.com, 23 Dec. 2007: 'Delegates "disappointed" Mbeki'.
144 See R. W. Johnson, 'Nyerere: A Flawed Hero', *National Interest*, Jan. 2000.
145 Between 1966 and 1999 Botswana averaged 7 per cent growth p.a., ahead of Singapore (6.2 per cent) and South Korea (6.1 per cent). Source: World Bank.
146 *Business Day*, 11 Oct. 2007.
147 Quoted by H. Zille in 'SA Today: A Weekly Letter from the Leader of the DA' (weekly blog), 15 Feb. 2008.
148 Ibid.
149 Ibid.
150 Ibid.
151 *Cape Times*, 27 Feb. 2008.

Chapter 14

1 *ANC Today*, 7/28, 20 July 2007.
2 *South Africa 1988–89*, Official Yearbook of the Republic of South Africa (1990), p. 80.
3 C. Feinstein, *An Economic History of South Africa: Conquest, Discrimination and Development* (2005), p. 257.
4 *This Day*, 30 April 2004.
5 On the significance of the development of a script, see F. Mansur, *The Process of Independence* (1962); on Africa's continuous demographic disasters see, above all, J. Iliffe, *Africans: History of a Continent* (1995). Others have argued with some success that African states today succeed best where they stand in line of descent from an ancient state: Ethiopia, Mali, Ghana, etc. Such ancient states often had access to a borrowed Koranic script, but South Africa had neither ancient state nor script.
6 *ANC Today*, 7/28, 20 July 2007.
7 J. Todd, *Through the Darkness: A Life in Zimbabwe* (2007), pp. 438–9.
8 For the imaginary history of the Aryan races, see H. Pringle, *The Master Plan: Himmler's Scholars and the Holocaust* (2006). For Afrikaner nationalism's own imaginary history, see A. du Toit and H. Giliomee, *Afrikaner Political Thought: Analysis and Documents*, vol. 1: 1780–1850 (1985).
9 *South Africa 1989–90*, p. 83. This gives the African population as 20,613,000 but excludes the 'independent' bantustans which collectively accounted for a further 5.5 million Africans.
10 C. Feinstein, *Economic History of South Africa*, p. 232.
11 All figures from Reserve Bank.
12 *Business Day*, 25 July 2007.
13 Ibid.
14 South African Press Association press release, 14 March 2004. Zuma frequently expresses the true spirit of the ANC, e.g. 'the ANC is more important than even the Constitution' and 'How can a person live, if not for the ANC?'
15 R. W. Johnson, *How Long Will South Africa Survive?* (1977), p. 28.
16 Figures from WTO.
17 *Business Day*, 5 Sept. 2007.
18 See P. du Toit, *The Great South African Land Scandal* (2004).
19 D. de Jager, 'Land Redistribution: The Value of Commercial Agriculture in South Africa', *Solidarity Magazine*, 4 (31 July 2007).
20 For a sensible discussion of the problem, see Centre for Development and Enterprise, 'Land Reform in South Africa: A 21st Century Perspective' (June 2005).
21 Ibid., pp. 42–6.
22 *Business Day*, *Cape Times*, 14 Sept. 2007.

23 Statistics taken from T. Leon, 'A Truth That's Told With Bad Intent', August 2007. Available on the DA blog, *Inside Politics*.
24 Ibid.
25 R. W. Johnson, *The Condition of Democracy in Southern Africa* (1997). Lawrence Schlemmer acted as an invaluable special adviser to this project. A summary of the survey may be found in *Focus*, 9 (Jan. 1998).
26 *Southern Africa Report*, 25/35 (31 Aug. 2007).
27 *ANC Today*, 7/33–4 (Aug.–Sept. 2007).
28 *Business Day*, 31 Aug. 2007.
29 *Cape Times*, 31 Aug. 2007.
30 *ANC Today*, 7/34 (31 Aug.–6 Sept. 2007).
31 *Business Day*, 7 Sept. 2007.
32 *ANC Today*, 7/29 (27 July–2 Aug. 2007).
33 *Sunday Independent*, 2 Sept. 2007.
34 T. Mbeki, 'Address on the 30th anniversary of the Death of Steve Biko', *Cape Times*, 14 Sept. 2007.
35 *Mail and Guardian*, 18–24 April 2008.
36 See O. Todd, *Albert Camus: Une Vie* (2000).

Chapter 15

1 *Mail and Guardian*, 6–12 June 2008.
2 *Business Day*, 9 June 2008.
3 *Sunday Independent*, 7 July 2008.
4 *Sunday Times*, 11 May 2008.
5 See also *Mail and Guardian*, 9–15 May 2008.
6 *Business Day*, 6 June 2008.
7 *Sunday Times*, 8 June 2008.
8 *Business Day*, 12 June 2008.
9 *Business Day*, 26 May 2008.
10 *Business Day*, 6 June 2008.
11 *Business Report*. *Cape Times*, 1 Sept. 2008.
12 *Business Day*, 18 June 2008.
13 *Business Report*. *Cape Times*, 17 July 2008.
14 *Business Day*, 16 July 2008.
15 *Sunday Times*, 29 June 2008.
16 *Business Day*, 7 July 2008.
17 *Sunday Independent*, 13 July 2008.
18 *Business Day*, 14 May 2008.
19 *Business Day*, 18 Aug. 2008.
20 www.swradioafrica.com/pages/hotseat261108.htm
21 *The Herald* (Harare), 21 Nov. 2008.
22 Interview with Jacob Zuma, Cape Town, 15 April 2008.
23 *City Press*, 20 July 2008.
24 *Sunday Independent*, 13 July 2008.
25 Ibid.
26 *Business Day*, 27 July 2008.
27 *City Press*, 21 Sept. 2008.
28 *Cape Times*, 26 Sept. 2008.
29 *Business Day*, 25 Sept. 2008.
30 http://news.bbc.co.uk/2/hi/africa/7716128.stm
31 Private source.
32 *Mail and Guardian*. 26 Sept.–2 Oct. 2008.
33 Interview with Terror Lekota, Pretoria, 16 Oct. 2008.

34 Interview with Sibusiso Mdlalala, Johannesburg, 23 June 2008.
35 *Sunday Times*, 6 July 2008.
36 *Sunday Independent*, 22 June 2008.
37 *Cape Times*, 21 Nov. 2008.
38 *Sunday Times*, 23 Nov. 2008.
39 *SA Today. DA News*, 21 Nov. 2008.
40 *Beeld*, 19 Nov. 2008.
41 *Cape Times*, 21 Nov. 2008.
42 *Business Day*, 24 Nov. 2008.
43 Ibid.
44 A. Keppel-Jones, *When Smuts Goes. A History of South Africa from 1952–2010, First Published in 2015* (1947)
45 Private source.
46 *Financial Mail*, 21 Nov. 2008, p.35.

Index

The italicized suffix '*n*' denotes note number on the relevant page